HARVESTING PA CHAY'S WHEAT

ALSO BY KEITH QUINCY

SAMUEL

HMONG: HISTORY OF A PEOPLE

HARVESTING PA CHAY'S WHEAT
THE HMONG AND AMERICA'S SECRET WAR IN LAOS

Keith Quincy

 Eastern Washington University Press, Spokane, Washington 2000

Library of Congress Cataloging-in-Publication Data

Quincy, Keith

Harvesting pa chay's wheat: The Hmong and America's Secret War in Laos
/ Keith Quincy

p. cm.

Includes bibliographical references and indices.

ISBN 0910055602-(pbk.)--ISBN 0910055610 (hbk.)

     1. Vietnamese Conflict, 1961-1975--Laos. 2. Vietnamese Conflict, 1961-1975--
Secret Service--United States. 3. Vietnamese Conflict, 1961-1975--participation,
Hmong. 4. Hmong (Asian people)--History--20th century. 5. Laos--Politics and
government. I. Title.

DS559.73.L28 Q56 2000

959.704'38--dc21

                                                     99-059813

*This book is dedicated to Tou Hmong Zong Qdj,
and the new generation of American Hmong*

CONTENTS

Note on Hmong Words

Throughout the book I employ English equivalents for Hmong names and places. Hmong names are also made to follow western conventions, with the surname (clan affiliation) appearing last, the exceptions being names of historically famous Hmong known to the west in their normal, and sometimes contracted, form. Thus, Vang Pao remains Vang Pao and is not rendered as Pao Vang, and Touby LyFoung does not appear in the text as Touby Foung Ly. Occasionally, I add the original Hmong, in parenthesis, using the popular Smalley-Bertrais Roman Phonetic Alphabet (RPA) to avoid confusion when my transliteration differs from others, or when none has been previously provided.

PREFACE

In the broad sweep of Laotian history, the Hmong appear only as a footnote. They arrived late on the scene, settled in the mountain wilds, and for nearly a hundred years remained in the shadows of national life. Only after the arrival of the French in the late 1800s were they reluctantly thrust into the mainstream of Laotian history: first as troublesome insurgents, and later as opium farmers and skilled mountain guerrillas.

Between 1898 and 1922 Hmong rebelled against colonial rule; however, relations improved in the 1940s once the French used Hmong opium to supply state-run opium dens throughout Indochina and, later, employed Hmong guerrillas to resist Viet Minh (Vietnamese communist) efforts to establish a beachhead in northern Laos. The French sponsored schools for Hmong children and political reforms to enhance the power of Hmong politicians. This patronage ended with France's defeat in Indochina. Yet in less than a decade the Hmong had a new patron—America. Standing in for France, the U.S. assembled, trained, and equipped a Hmong army to deny the Vietnamese communists complete mastery of Laos.

The Vietnamese communists coveted Laos not for its enormous mineral deposits nor its vast tracks of virgin timber, but for its strategic value in war. In the war against France (1946-1954), Vietnamese guerrilla units sought sanctuary in Laos' rugged northeastern territories to avoid annihilation by the French Expeditionary Corps and its legionnaires. Laos became even more important in the U.S. war because of the Ho Chi Minh Trail.

Used by the Vietnamese communists to infiltrate troops into South Vietnam, the trail's main route eventually stretched 625 miles, feeding 12,500 miles of arterial roads. By the late 1960s,

3,000 miles of pipeline had been laid along the trail to keep trucks and tanks supplied with fuel. Fifteen thousand transport trucks delivered troops and supplies to the south. By war's end two million people had used the trail and forty-five million tons of material had been transported along its length.[1] The Ho Chi Minh Trail was the heart of the communists' logistics and nearly all of it was on Laotian soil running straight down the Laotian panhandle—which is why the communists sought to control Laos, politically and by force.

Laos was a land unknown to most Americans until the late 1950s, when a young physician named Tom Dooley appealed to fellow Americans in interviews and public appearances to lend their support to stop the spread of communism in Laos. Dooley's message reached a large audience, for he was one of the most admired men in America. The source of his fame was his widely publicized humanitarian work in Southeast Asia. In 1954 Dooley established aid stations and refugee camps in South Vietnam for the tens of thousands of Vietnamese fleeing the communist regime in the north. Dooley chronicled his relief effort in *Deliver Us From Evil*, a best-seller that helped to popularize the 1950s image of Ho Chi Minh's communism as repressive and hostile to Christian values. Conservative anticommunists and fundamentalist Christians took up Dooley's cause and raised funds to support his medical work in Vietnam and, later, in Laos.

Dooley arrived in Laos in 1956. After a brief stay in Vientiane, the nation's capital, he set up a crude hospital fifty miles to the north at Vang Vieng. Later he moved further north to the jungle wilderness of Nam Tha Province to work in isolated villages close to the Chinese border. In two books, *The Edge of Tomorrow* and *The Night They Burned the Mountain*, Dooley gave American readers their first glimpse of life in the primitive jungles and mountains of Laos: "The people of Laos are not a happy, carefree people. They laugh and smile, but they suffer. Their existence is eked out of this life with great effort, just as their villages are hacked from their savage jungles with great difficulty."

Dooley told of Laotian peasants living in constant fear of assaults by communist guerrillas. It was this danger, more than tropical disease and malnutrition, that primarily concerned Dooley. He was convinced that Laotian communists, known as the Pathet

Lao, were puppets of the North Vietnamese, who in turn were controlled by the Chinese and Soviets. Dooley urged Americans to help stem the communist tide in Laos, to lend "our hands, our hearts, our economic support, and our diplomatic prestige."[2]

Actually, the U.S. was already deeply involved in turning back communism in Laos. It was a very clandestine operation. Even president-elect John Kennedy was unaware of its existence until Eisenhower briefed him on the matter the day before his inauguration. Eisenhower warned Kennedy that "Laos is the key to the entire area of southeast Asia . . . if we permit Laos to fall, then we will have to write off all the area."[3]

Once in office, Kennedy learned that U.S. military personnel had been operating covertly in Laos since 1957, training and leading troops against communist insurgents. Kennedy pondered whether to continue the operation. His advisors convinced him not only to stay the course but to increase American involvement. Lyndon Johnson would do the same, as would Richard Nixon (at least in his first term).

To conceal the scope of America's involvement, most of the money for U.S. operations in Laos was funneled through the CIA, with smaller amounts laundered through more visible agencies ostensibly involved in humanitarian aid. Over a ten-year period perhaps as much as twenty billion dollars were spent on the secret war—equal to about 15 percent of total expenditures on the more visible war in Vietnam.

The secret war was fought in the air and on the ground. Between 1968 and 1973, Laos was the focus of one of the largest bombing campaigns in military history. The targets were units of the Pathet Lao and several divisions of invading North Vietnamese (NVA). On average, American aircraft dropped a bomb every eight minutes, twenty-four hours a day, eventually delivering more than two million tons of explosives—fifteen hundred pounds for every man, woman, and child in the country, making Laos the most heavily bombed nation in history.

Despite the massive scope of the bombing, hardly a hint of the massive air war was to be found in the American press, and certainly nothing to indicate its scope. It was as if the American aircraft did not exist. In a sense they didn't. Many had been laundered by the CIA, with duplicates bearing the same markings and engine numbers showing up at various military airfields across the globe to be duly logged in while their twins were over Laos on combat missions. If the planes were shot down, the CIA possessed documentation proving they were still flying and nowhere near Laos. Some Air Force planes were completely sanitized after delivery to the CIA, with all military insignia and engine numbers removed, essentially having no documented existence. Other planes were removed from USAF records by being sold as military surplus to the pilots who flew them. The buyers, identified in the bills of sale as civilian aviators, were all U.S. Air Force personnel dropped from the military rolls and listed as forest rangers with the United States Agency for International Development (USAID). The planes carried a price tag of a dollar each.

To keep the secret air war secret, the U.S. Air Force banned the news media from air bases like Nakhon Phanom in Thailand, from which squads of aircraft were sent into Laos daily. On the few occasions when reporters pressured the U.S. government for information about the large number of American aircraft in Thailand, official sources spoke in generalities or plain lied, listing southeast Asia or Vietnam as the actual area of operation, or describing flights into Laos as nothing more than reconnaissance missions.

The press seldom complained. Reporters were preoccupied with Vietnam, where the fighting was official and the military obligingly provided daily briefings. Only a handful of reporters were in Laos (there were six hundred in Vietnam), and nearly all of them stayed put in the main towns. Journalists sipping drinks at the Ratry, a bar in Savannakhet, or eating Khaophoun, a popular noodle dish, at the Constellation Hotel in Vientiane, were hardly well positioned to provide a detailed account of air raids hundreds of miles away.

The ground war was shrouded in just as much secrecy as the air war. One Associated Press reporter who had covered the Vietnam War for three years encountered nothing but frustration after reassignment to Laos. He would hear rumors about a battle over a provincial capital, of civilians scattering for the hills, and receive reports of artillery captured by the enemy and then retaken. The so-called battle would rage for days, and yet no casualties were ever reported. His growing cynicism was inevitable: "That kind of thing led you to believe there was no war going on really . . . And then [there was] the endless war for the Plain of Jars, which none of us ever saw, but every year would change hands."[4]

Though out of sight of journalists, the fighting was real—and furious. In terms of battle casualties, it was every bit as devastating as the air war. Between 1968 and 1971, when the fighting was at its heaviest, the death toll for the noncommunist side was staggering, comparable to the U.S.'s suffering one thousand battle deaths daily for three years. Losses on the communist side were likely even higher. Even America's Civil War, the nation's bloodiest, did not come close to this level of carnage.

As far as the outside world was concerned, the ground war against the communists was fought by the Royal Laotian Army (RLA). In reality, units of the RLA seldom engaged the enemy, and when they did they were invariably defeated. The major battles were actually fought by a clandestine guerrilla army entirely equipped and financed by the CIA at an estimated cost of $1 billion (close to $4 billion in current dollars). Spawned from an original paramilitary organization of only a few hundred, the secret army grew into an air mobile force of nearly forty thousand. Supporting this secret army became the single largest enterprise in CIA history.[5]

Most of the soldiers in the CIA's clandestine army were Hmong hill tribesmen, descendants of the Hmong montagnards (called *Miao* by the Chinese) of southwest China, where most Hmong still live today. Between 1962 and 1973 they held back an ever-expanding North Vietnamese military force that swelled from seven thousand to seventy thousand. It was a considerable achievement, recently acknowledged by former CIA director William Colby in testimony before a congressional committee: "The Hmong forces for ten years held the growing North Vietnamese forces to approximately the same battle lines they occupied in 1962."[6]

The effort cost the Hmong dearly. Thirty-five thousand Hmong fell in battle, which would be comparable to America losing 16.5 million men in Vietnam (rather than the actual 57,000). Almost one-third of the Hmong, most noncombatants, perished during the war from disease and starvation when entire villages were forced to flee into the highland wilderness to evade advancing enemy forces.

It was a war the Hmong could not win. Though superb guerrilla fighters, they lacked the manpower to hold captured territory. By contrast, the North Vietnamese were willing and able to sacrifice thousands to regain lost ground or destroy key targets. By 1973 communist forces occupied most of the strategic areas in Laos. Already in the process of disengaging from Vietnam, the U.S. informed the Laotian government that it could not count on continued American support. The flood of money and supplies to the Hmong army slowed to a trickle, then ceased altogether. In May 1975 Pathet Lao forces, backed by NVA troops, occupied Laos' major cities and assumed control of the country. Within a few months thousands of Hmong were herded into concentration camps—revenge for Hmong resistance that delayed the communist victory for nearly a decade. For those spared the camps, hard choices remained: make peace with the communists, take up arms and resist, or flee the country.

While most opted for an anxious accommodation with the new government, a substantial minority chose resistance. Gathering weapons hidden in caves or buried in the forest, they ambushed Pathet Lao patrols and blew up bridges used by Vietnamese truck convoys to deliver arms and soldiers to prop up the new regime. The communists struck back with a massive military campaign, forcing the rebels to retreat into the highlands of Phu Bia, the tallest mountain chain in Laos. The rugged mountain terrain served as an equalizer until the Vietnamese brought in artillery and tanks, jets and poison gas. The application of advanced military technology, including weapons that civilized nations had sworn never to use in war, broke the back of the resistance. Fifteen thousand Hmong (including rebels and their dependents) surrendered or were captured. The resistance would later resurface, but only as a shadow of what it once had been, a minor irritant rather than a real threat to the regime's hold on the nation.

Over a ten-year period nearly half of Laos' Hmong fled the country, a substantial number perishing en route. Fifty thousand escaped during the first few months of the new regime. Escapes then slowed to a trickle, until the government began to crack down on Hmong rebels, creating another flood of refugees. By 1988 more than 130,000 Hmong had crossed the border into Thailand. Most would eventually immigrate to the U.S. [7]

This book traces these events within the larger context of Laotian national politics under French, American, and Vietnamese domination, and explores the dynamics that led Hmong politicians to draw their people into drug trafficking and later recruit them for the CIA's secret army. The book also documents the plight of the Hmong after the communist victory in 1975: the privations they were forced to endure, the brutality of the concentration camps, their efforts to resist repression, the desperate flight of thousands to reach refugee camps in Thailand, and the attempt to transplant Hmong politics to American soil.

Plain of Jars, March 1970

Mekong River along border with Thailand.

1

SOWING PA CHAY'S WHEAT

Geographically, Laos is not unlike the state of Idaho. Both are about the same size and shape with a bulge and panhandle, though the two are flipped images, with Idaho's panhandle in the north and Laos' hanging south. Like Idaho, Laos is mostly mountainous and, in the north, heavily forested with conifers. Laos even has its own Palouse, a heart-shaped expanse of rolling grassland known as the Plain of Jars. There is a demographic affinity as well. Like Idaho, Laos is sparsely settled with a population density less than the average in the U.S.[1]

Here the similarity ends. Idaho is the gem state, whereas Laos is a fairy tale land, ancient and mysterious, a place at home in the pages of *National Geographic*, famous not for its precious stones or robust potatoes but for tropical jungles that spread over river valleys with kudzu-like exuberance, and for highland forests that once teemed with elephants, tigers, rhinoceros, and short-tempered gaur.

Deep in the Laotian jungles lie ancient tumbledown temples choked with Bombax roots and shrouded in lianas. Here and there flame trees line roads, and on river islands magical trees grow fruit that by legend turns monkeys into men. Strange lichen-encrusted limestone pots, some as tall as eight feet and weighing up to three tons, litter the sinuate hills of the Plain of Jars, memorials of an unknown race that used the pots to house their dead.

Everywhere there are waṭs (Buddhist temples) with rococo-tiered roofs that curl at the edges like lapping tongues, and legions of Bonzes (Buddhist monks) in saffron robes collecting alms from the faithful. The great Mekong River borders the nation, racing through its switchbacks in the north before unkinking into a gentle curve that cleaves Laos from Thailand, running narrow and swift, until it nears Cambodia, where it suddenly turns lazy and spreads out like a lake. Then there is the rain, monsoons that arrive in waves from May to November, drenching the lowlands and re-charging highland aquifers until they overflow in geysers that shoot straight out of the sides of sodden mountains.

A NATION OF MINORITIES

The people are as varied as the landscape. For much of its history, Laos has been a destination rather than a place of origin. Only the Khmu are native to the region. They occupied the river valleys before the T'ai began to arrive in waves from China, im-pelled southward by Kublai Khan's invading armies and the ethnic cleansing campaigns of the T'ang, Sung, and Ming dynasties. The T'ai migration began in the ninth century and continued in trick-les, spurts, and occasional torrents until the thirteenth century.

The press of newcomers forced the Khmu into the highlands, where they became montagnards. The T'ai seized the Khmu's aban-doned paddy fields and evolved into the lowland Lao, though a portion with lingering wanderlust pushed on into Laos' north-eastern wilderness to live as montagnards and become the highland T'ai. Hmong, Akha, Lolo, Lahu, Yao, Yi, and a dozen or so other ethnic groups, with populations so small they attract the attention only of anthropologists, were latecomers arriving in drops and dribbles from the 1750s onward to settle in the uninhabited moun-tains of Laos' northern provinces. The last bit of seasoning added to this ethnic stew was the Vietnamese, brought to Laos by the French.

No group in this mix is large enough to make a majority, not even the ethnic Lao. At the start of America's secret war, Laos had a population of three million. Of this number only 1.4 million were ethnic Lao. The rest, a slight majority, were highlanders or montagnards. This included 750,000 Khmu and about 350,000 highland T'ai. The Hmong added another 250,000, and the Akha, Lolo, Lahu, and Yao montagnards another 250,000.[2] Though a minority themselves, the ethnic Lao have nevertheless dominated politics and long ago placed their stamp on the national culture.[3]

This is not a testimony to their political skill. It was power by default.

Despite their common lot as hill farmers and victims of Lao prejudice and oppression, the montagnards have proved incapable of cooperation. United, they would have had a voice, perhaps even the deciding one, but they disliked each other as much as they despised the Lao. Highland T'ai warlords and bandits periodically savaged the Hmong and Khmu who, in turn, slaughtered each other. The worst conflict between Khmu and Hmong occurred at the turn of the century in a dispute over land rights: the Khmu claimed title to land occupied by Hmong, demanded tribute, and tried to intimidate the Hmong by killing scores of them in a raid. The Hmong responded with fury and butchered several thousand Khmu. The Khmu fled the area in great numbers, many resettling in northwestern Laos.

Even within particular montagnard groups there has been little real solidarity.[4] Rivalries between clans, tribal prejudice, and ancient blood feuds between notables and their kin have made it difficult for Yao to unite with Yao, Khmu to join hands with Khmu, or Hmong to close ranks with fellow Hmong. On the rare occasion when a particular mountain minority has united as one people, it has been a fragile solidarity dependent on the leadership of a single charismatic individual, falling apart with his death.[5]

Even among the Lao, spontaneous stirrings of ethnic nationalism have been rare. Laos existed as three separate kingdoms for two hundred years before the French assumed control. During these centuries, three royal families spawned twenty or so aristocratic clans, each jealous of its privileges and dedicated to denying them to rival clans. After the French forcibly reunified Laos, Lao politicians paid lip service to the larger goals of the nation only because French bureaucrats were looking over their shoulders. Backstage they continued to work to advance the narrow interests of a particular family line, such as the Champassaks, Voravongs, or Sananikones.

Nationalism did eventually take root, but only because it was nurtured by outside forces. The first groundswell of Lao nationalism occurred during the Second World War when the French promoted Lao cultural pride to counter Thailand's ambition to absorb all of the Lao, and the land on which they lived, into Thailand. What the French did not count on was a flurry of agitation for political independence following this exercise in consciousness-raising.

Nationalism received another shot in the arm when unrepentant Lao nationalists forced into exile by the French linked up with the American Office of Strategic Services (OSS) in Thailand. American instructors in the guerrilla training camps played on ethnic pride and nationalist sentiment to raise morale and fan hatred for the invading Japanese. The alumni of these camps formed the core of the Lao nationalist movement after the war.

Twenty years later North Vietnamese agents were in Laos' hinterlands, championing ethnic nationalism for the montagnards. The communists carried credentials. For over a decade the hill tribes of North Vietnam had enjoyed cultural autonomy: Hanoi did not interfere with traditional lifestyles or religion, and provided schools for montagnard children with courses taught in their native language. This idea appealed to Laos' montagnards, especially when the North Vietnamese preached hatred for Lao lowlanders to drum up support for Laos' own communist movement, the Pathet Lao. Within a decade highland T'ai, Khmu, Yao, and Hmong filled the lower echelons of the Pathet Lao's party bureaucracy and made up the bulk of the Pathet Lao's army.[6]

FROM KINGDOM TO DIVIDED NATION

As the dominant group in Laos, the ethnic Lao wrote the nation's history, portraying it as a pageant of their own race. The story begins with the ascension of Fa Ngum, the nation's first king. Fa Ngum's father was a politically ambitious Lao nobleman who came up the loser in a power struggle and fled with his family to Cambodia to enter the service of the Cambodian monarch Jayavarman Paramesvara. Jayavarman took an interest in the nobleman's precocious son, instructing him in Buddhism to make him civilized and drilling him in matters of war as preparation for the future command of an army which would invade the northern territories that would become historical Laos.

The military campaign began in 1340. It took Fa Ngum thirteen years to completely pacify Laos, a territory he called Lan Xang (the land of a million elephants). An army of Bonzes from Angkor streamed into the new kingdom to convert its people to Buddhism and instruct them in the ways of karma, the cosmic force that repays meritorious deeds with a better life in the next reincarnation. The mass conversions served a political purpose. Buddhism sustained an Asian version of the divine right of kings. Individuals born to nobility, or seated on royal thrones, were presumably put there as reward for moral virtue in past lives, transforming de facto privilege and power into moral entitlement.[7]

Fa Ngum enjoyed unchallenged power for two decades, then suddenly lost all interest in politics. While his ministers happily pocketed tax collections and abused power, Fa Ngum frittered away his time in wild debaucheries that scandalized the royal court packed with straitlaced Buddhist converts. Forced into exile in 1373, Fa Ngum died within two years, a broken man.[8]

By a combination of well-managed matrimony and good luck, the kingdom survived its founder's death and enjoyed relative peace for over three hundred years. The integrity of the western border was preserved by diplomatically inspired marriages with members of Thai royalty, while the good luck came in the form of the expansionist Chinese who kept the bellicose Vietnamese busy with repeated invasions of Tonkin (northern Vietnam).

In 1694, after centuries of holding powerful neighbors at bay, Lan Xang collapsed from within. Suligna Vongsa had ruled the kingdom for nearly sixty years. A stickler for law and order, he allowed his only son to be executed for adultery. This left two grandsons as heirs to the throne, but neither had reached maturity before Suligna's death. As the boys did their lessons and put on height, various nobles vied for control of the kingdom, plunging Laos into civil war. When the fighting was over, Laos had divided into three realms: Champassak in the south, Vieng Chan (Vientiane) in the center, and Luang Prabang in the north.[9]

For two centuries the separate principalities survived by practicing the diplomacy of the impotent: they paid tributes to Vietnam, Cambodia, and Thailand as bribes against invasion, and formed alliances with the ascendant power of the moment. It was a dangerous game with little margin for error. By the 1830s Vietnam had already annexed most of northeastern Laos, and Thailand occupied a large chunk of Laos' western provinces. France's decision in the late 1880s to add Laos to its Indochinese empire likely saved the tiny nation from being completely assimilated by its neighbors.

FRENCH COLONY

The French were not the first Europeans in Laos. The Dutch preceded them by nearly two hundred years, first sending missionaries as shock troops to accustom the natives to European ways, determine their susceptibility to exploitation and, if time permitted, save a few souls. The missionaries found the people to be carefree and charming but resolute Buddhists with absolutely no interest in Christianity.

The businessmen who followed hoped for better luck. One Dutch trader looking for a good deal on stick-lac (a lacquer-like substance exuded by insects) and benzoin found the trade moderately profitable but the people entirely too promiscuous for a good Calvinist. He gave up evening walks because he could scarcely travel twenty yards without encountering "horrible fornications" in the bushes beside the road.[10] Other merchants, more concerned with profit than morality, came away sadly disappointed. Except for a few odd items like stick-lac, there seemed very little in Laos worth exploiting, especially the native work force which would later be described in the *Atlas des Colonies Françaises* as "friendly . . . hospitable and *opposed to hard work*."[11]

This dismal assessment deterred everyone but the French. They obstinately sent explorers to poke around the country to measure its potential. For a time it was hoped that the Mekong River could be used as a back door into China, where the British were making fortunes in trade while using their navy to control China's eastern seaboard and keep everyone else out. The French desperately wanted a piece of the action. In 1868 they sent an expedition up the Mekong to determine the feasibility of using the river as a trade route into China. After two years of braving rapids and hacking through jungle, a report was submitted detailing the treacherous nature of the river, especially as it nears the Chinese border where waterfalls and rapids arise every few miles.

After decades of drawing maps, sending expeditions upriver, and collecting ore samples, the French finally established an official presence in Laos in 1886 with a small vice-consulate in Luang Prabang. In that same year Britain seized control of Burma, preparing its own back door into China. Nine more years passed before France officially absorbed Laos into its empire.[12] Territories lost to Thailand and Vietnam were restored and the three kingdoms joined into a unified state, with the city of Vientiane as its administrative capital.

Given the bleak economic forecast, it might appear something of a mystery why the French went to all the bother. In 1917 Albert Sarraut offered what would become a popular justification for French colonialism in Southeast Asia. Speaking before a predominately Vietnamese audience following his appointment to the post of Governor General of Indochina, Sarraut announced, "I want to give you the instrument of liberation which will gradually lead you toward those superior spheres to which you aspire."[13]

The instrument of liberation to which Sarraut referred was capitalist economics seasoned with French culture, a mixture that was supposed to transform the backward natives of Vietnam, Laos, and Cambodia into civilized beings. This lofty goal, immodestly referred to as *La Mission Civilisatrice*, rang nearly as false then as it does now.

A more forthright explanation for colonizing Laos is that professional soldiers garrisoned in the country saw an opportunity to advance their careers by holding onto the territory and lobbied hard for colonization. The French navy, anxious for deep water ports in the Orient, had earlier campaigned against the abandonment of Vietnam for much the same reason.

Such lobbying efforts were successful because at the time Europe was obsessed with colonization, for political as much as economic reasons. Class struggle had become a dominant feature of European politics. This was particularly true in France, where the government habitually served the interests of the owning classes, making it difficult for French politicians to claim with a straight face that they ruled in the name of all citizens of the nation. Only in a French colony could state officials make such a claim, for it was only in Indochina or Algeria that a French bureaucrat or soldier, surrounded on all sides by alien peoples, might without obvious self-deception consider himself first and foremost a Frenchman and view his activities as service to the French nation rather than to a particular economic class.[14] Through this contortion of reason, colonizing Laos became an unarticulated exercise in legitimizing the French state.

Still, the French felt obliged to find some way to make economic sense out of the enterprise, and desperately searched the country for hidden pockets of profit. Unlike Vietnam, with its tin and coal mines in the north, rubber in the central highlands, and rice in the Red River and Mekong deltas, there was almost nothing in Laos worth exploiting. Rice harvests were small, and mineral deposits of coal and tin were usually to be found only in inaccessible mountain regions.[15] There was opium, of course, grown in abundance by the montagnards, but the French had yet to fully comprehend the drug's enormous economic potential.

For a brief period the fantasy was revived that the Mekong could somehow turn a profit. French bankers were persuaded to invest 100,000 francs (about $600,000) to establish trading posts along the river all the way to the Chinese border. Instead of French goods penetrating China, Chinese traders used the posts as outlets for their own products. The venture went belly-up after only two years.[16]

The only lucrative enterprise in Laos of any significance was a small strip-mining operation for tin in the northern panhandle close to the town of Nam Pathene—and the mine did not yield substantial returns until the 1930s, when an international tin cartel forced up world prices. Even with inflated prices, the mine failed to generate enough revenue to pull the French administration in Laos out of the red.[17]

It did not take long for administrative policy to reflect resentment over low revenues. While the French would invest vast sums in Vietnam to develop the nation's economy, they spent next to nothing in Laos to upgrade its infrastructure or to encourage economic development.[18] While Vietnam had dams, bitumen highways, railways, vast irrigation systems, canals, dams, bridges, ports, and harbors, the only thing the French built in Laos was a crude road network (Routes 4, 5, 6, 7, 13, 42 and 72) of single-lane dirt roads that was generally unusable during the rainy season. Consistent with this bare-bones approach to governance, in the early years only seventy administrators were allocated to oversee the affairs of the entire nation. French bureaucrats unfortunate enough to find themselves assigned to this colonial backwater "generally spent most of their time chasing the local women, seeking or avoiding addiction to alcohol or opium, and dreaming of their return to Saigon or Hanoi" where promotions were possible and French cuisine available in the better hotels.[19] Even the most libertine administrator was careful to set aside enough time from pleasures to oversee the collection of taxes. However, once this duty was fulfilled French bureaucrats were content to leave most of the actual governing of the nation to the royal court at Luang Prabang, where the principal source of power was the distribution of offices to members of the old elite of the defunct kingdoms of Champassak, Vientiane, and Luang Prabang—sinecures that were the object of intense rivalry, between and within these royal families, and that continued well into the future.

This is not to say that the French gave up on Laos. Contrasting the sleepy kingdom to energetic Vietnam, the French concluded that one obvious cause of Laotian poverty was its people. They were inferior: not just to Europeans, which was the standard view toward all conquered Asians and Africans, but to the Vietnamese as well. Serious and industrious, the Vietnamese were the object of grudging admiration. By contrast, the ethnic Lao, fun-loving and lethargic, were considered absolutely useless. Even lower in estimation were the Laotian montagnards. As one colonial official noted, "This savage race, indolent and superstitious, non-progressive," cannot "be called upon to play an important role in Indochina."[20]

Race mixing seemed the logical remedy, so the French administration encouraged Vietnamese to immigrate to Laos. By French estimates, the population density of Laos was four people to the square mile. In Vietnam's Mekong delta the figure was close to fifteen hundred.[21] Whereas Vietnam was cramped, Laos had elbowroom to spare. The French hoped Vietnamese would fill up the river valleys and mountains of Laos, interbreed with the natives, and create two hybrid races: lowlanders with intelligence and drive, and hardy montagnards amenable to civilization. To hedge their bet on the beneficial effects of hybridization, the French also intended to bring in sufficient Vietnamese to alter the demographics in their favor.

If judged by the ambitious goal to bring in so many Vietnamese that they would "reduce the Lao to a minority in their own country,"[22] the immigration program was not a complete success. Acclimatized to Vietnam's sweltering heat and humidity that can curl paper while you look at it, few Vietnamese were eager to venture into the rugged Laotian mountains where ice sometimes forms on winter ponds. Still, the French were able to fill up the tropical lowland towns with Vietnamese, bringing in traders and merchants to the major cities and appointing Vietnamese to mid-level posts in the colonial bureaucracy.

So successful was this effort that just prior to the Second World War the nation's largest city, Vientiane, had become 53 percent Vietnamese; the next largest city, Thakhek, 85 percent; further south in Pakse, 62 percent.

What the French could not know was that the Vietnamization of Laos would lay the groundwork for a determined communist movement in the country and guarantee that it would be controlled from Hanoi.

PRIMED FOR REBELLION

As Laos' budget was perpetually in the red, the French tried to reduce administrative overhead by leaving the traditional Lao bureaucracy in place: the king and his ministers, and below them the provincial bureaucracies, vast and cumbersome, with villages (*bans*) arranged into cantons (*tassengs*), cantons clustered into provincial subdistricts (*kongs*), subdistricts into provincial districts (*muongs*), and provincial districts into a province (*khoueng*). Each province was ruled by a governor (*chao khoueng*), the first link in the provincial chain of command that coursed down through district superintendents (*chao muongs*), subdistrict heads (*nai kongs*), canton supervisors (*tassengs*), and came to ground with the village chiefs (*nai bans*).

Theoretically, provincial governors were directly answerable to the king's ministers, and the chain of command from the governors down to village chiefs unbroken. But governors often functioned as independent princes or warlords. More than a few chao muongs paid little or no attention to the rulings of provincial governors, and some tassengs ruled over their canton as if it were a personal fiefdom. Taken as a whole, it was an unwieldy and consistently ineffective bureaucracy, shot through with corruption.

On the back of this sprawling structure the French placed their own tiny capstone administration. The top French bureaucrat was the *Résident Supérieur* in Vientiane. Beneath him were the French commissioners, or *résidents*, one for each province, whose job was to loosely monitor the Lao provincial bureaucracy and use it to collect taxes and implement colonial policy. For muscle, each commissioner had at his disposal a full brigade of the *Garde Indigène*, a militia of mainly Vietnamese recruited from Vietnam.

It was a cheap and relatively nonintrusive form of colonialism, described by one scholar as a form of rule that "floated gently on top of the old native administration . . . with which it did not interfere."[23] Yet it had a drawback, and it would take decades for the French to realize clearly what it was. In 1921, following a four-year Hmong uprising, the commissioner of Xieng Khouang noted that "we indirectly set up an aristocracy over the rest of the population who effectively screened out all of the complaints of the less fortunate population below them, making it difficult for us to ascertain their real situation."[24] The commissioner obviously had the Hmong in mind when he wrote these words, for they did not take abuse lightly. His concerns were echoed a decade later by a German anthropologist, an avid outdoorsman who lived with the Hmong and often joined them on hunting trips for large game: "Their urge for independence, their fearlessness bordering on defiance of death, their glowing love for freedom, which had been strengthened through thousands of years of fighting against powerful oppressors and has given them the reputation of feared warriors, will perhaps make difficulties for the colonizer."[25]

For decades the French remained oblivious to this danger and believed this administrative system would actually enhance their standing with the nation's ethnic minorities. By interposing the Lao between the montagnards and the colonial administration, it was imagined that resentment for high taxes would be deflected away from French bureaucrats and onto the Lao who collected them. No one considered the possibility that the toleration of oppressive rule by native bureaucrats might ignite a general uprising and result in considerable bloodshed.

In 1896 colonial revenues in Laos were only 45 percent of budgeted expenditures.[26] To close the gap the French increased taxes and, with an eye towards getting their hands on Hmong opium, demanded that the Hmong pay a portion of their tax in the drug at an assessed value far below the market price. Unhappy with the new tax, the Hmong turned to their chieftains for relief.

From their days in China the Hmong had fallen in the habit of addressing their principal chieftains as *kaitongs* (little kings).[27] There were three kaitongs in Laos, drawn from the Lo, Ly, and Moua clans, ruling as a triumvirate with the Lo kaitong, Pa Sy Lo, serving as spokesman. Pa Sy Lo met with Kham Huang, the native governor of Xieng Khouang Province, to complain about the new tax. Huang shifted the blame from his own administration, which only collected the tax, to the French commissioner who set tax policy. Pa Sy Lo sought an audience with the commissioner, but the Frenchman refused to discuss fiscal policy with an upstart illiterate aborigine. After brusquely dismissing the kaitong, the commissioner sent units of the Garde Indigène into the mountains to intimidate Hmong villagers.

The saber-rattling was hardly necessary. The Hmong already feared the French, whom they called the "Fakis" (*fab kis*) after the Chinese expression *Fa Kouie* (French devils). Pa Sy Lo would have let the matter rest had he not been prodded into action by the governor. Huang's ancestors had ruled the province for generations as an independent principality. He was royalty, yet the French treated him as an inferior. He wanted them humbled. Knowing that the Hmong hated being ruled by anyone not of their own race, Huang entered into a secret agreement with Pa Sy Lo, promising greater autonomy for the Hmong if they ran the French out of the province.

The Hmong first attacked the French at Ban Khang Pha Nien, a small military post northwest of Nong Het. After a brief skirmish the French drove them off. The rebels regrouped, recruited additional warriors, and assaulted the provincial headquarters at Xieng Khouangville.[28] The Hmong carried crossbows and flintlock rifles, accurate only at close range. The native troops under the command of French officers had modern carbines, and cut the

Hmong down in droves before they got near enough to fire their primitive weapons.[29]

The French discovered Huang's role in the affair and forced him out of office. They were more lenient with the *Meos* (the name the French gave to the Hmong). The montagnards had rattled veteran officers with their ferocity, even in defeat. Harsh reprisals might put them back on the warpath.[30] There were also financial reasons for mending fences with the Hmong. Their poppy fields stretched for hundreds of miles across the mountain slopes of Guizhou and Yunnan in China and blanketed the limestone hills of northern Laos. The French had plans for a government monopoly in the drug that would control its purchase, distribution, and sale throughout all of Indochina.

The commissioner for Xieng Khouang convened peace talks at Ban Ban, a village far enough from the provincial capital to pass as neutral ground, on Route 6 and therefore accessible by automobile. This enabled the commissioner to return nightly to his official residence (palatial quarters that dwarfed the native governor's mansion next door) where he was guaranteed a decent meal and a good night's sleep in his own bed.

Pa Sy Lo played no part in the negotiations. Disgraced by his drubbing at the hands of the Garde Indigène, his place was taken by Tong Ger Moua, the kaitong of the Moua clan. The commissioner found the new Hmong leader a tough negotiator. By the end of the talks Tong Ger Moua had secured a pledge to lower taxes and to cut back on the use of Lao intermediaries.

The French kept their word. Taxes declined and a handful of Hmong were absorbed into the provincial bureaucracy. Tong Ger Moua became the tasseng of Nong Het, the first Hmong in the nation to hold such a position.[31] Other Hmong became nai bans. It was a noteworthy event. By Lao administrative tradition, nai bans were supposed to be chosen by village election and advised by a council of village elders; but this held only in the lowlands populated by Lao. In the hill country and in the mountain highlands the selection was invariably by appointment from above, with the position filled by an ethnic Lao, or by a T'ai in the far northeast where the highland T'ai were a political force. Now, at last, a sprinkling of Hmong villages had their own nai ban, chosen by Hmong.

Also the Hmong had their own tasseng, giving them political standing and a margin of official control over their own affairs.

Despite these concessions, within twenty years the Hmong were again on the warpath. Behind the backs of French bureaucrats, Lao officials had been illegally collecting their own taxes, confiscating opium, and requisitioning Hmong ponies without payment.[32] It was an attempt to reintroduce the old Lao tax system in effect prior to the French protectorate: arbitrary and open-ended taxes, levied mainly on montagnards, that included not only a household tax of two silver coins but occasional tributes in the form of elephant tusks, rhino horns, deer meat, and opium.[33]

Hmong chieftains lodged a protest with the French commissioner, but nothing was done to end the abuses. Frustration only deepened in 1916, when the French Administration increased the official tax on Hmong households from a single annual tax to two annual per capita taxes that covered teenagers as well as adults.[34]

From the perspective of the colonial administration the Hmong were undertaxed, at least compared to the Vietnamese and Cambodians. While no one imagined the Hmong were capable of bearing the crushing taxes imposed on Vietnamese peasant farmers, it was presumed they could manage the imposts borne by average Cambodians. For years Cambodian farmers had been paying a per capita tax levied on every member of the household as well as a property tax, duty on all livestock, and sales tax on alcohol and salt.[35] Cambodians also had to perform corvée labor.

It was this last reform, inaugurated in Laos in 1917, that caused the greatest resentment. The French needed forced labor to defray the costs of the construction of a road network linking Laos and Vietnam. The roads were yet another futile attempt to make Laos profitable. The theory behind the scheme, which the French dubbed the *débloquement* (opening up) of Laos, was that economic growth could be stimulated in Laos by a process of economic osmosis. By linking Laos to Vietnam, it was hoped the brisk economy of Vietnam would diffuse into Laos.

Many of the new roads crossed Hmong territory, and most of the corvée labor for the work gangs came from Hmong villages in Xieng Khouang and Sam Neua provinces, where workers were "driven hard by civil engineers eager to set new construction records."[36] Duty on the work crews usually lasted three weeks at a stretch. One of the weeks was unpaid labor; the other two weeks earned a worker twenty-eight kip (the basic Lao currency), enough to cover a Hmong family's tax liability for the year.[37]

For the freedom-loving Hmong, doing corvée labor was akin to slavery—an intolerable loss of face. Also, they could hardly fail to notice that the lowland Lao invariably possessed sufficient income to redeem their corvée through cash payments, stigmatizing Hmong participation in the work gangs as the labor of an underclass.[38] Some Hmong found the corvée work so mortifying that they migrated out of the region rather than submit to such humiliation, and did not return until the roads were completed in 1924.[39]

The Hmong were primed for rebellion. When it came it was with Hmong hearing voices from heaven and bearing magic totems into battle. It was a Hmong rebellion in the old style, new to Laos but familiar in China, where Hmong messianism had turned more than a few uprisings into holy wars.

HMONG MESSIANISM

Hmong jihads in China were inspired by legends of an ancient Hmong kingdom, once glorious but destroyed by the Chinese. It wasn't all myth. A Hmong kingdom of sorts did emerge in the fifth century A.D., rising out of the ashes of the collapsed Han empire. At the time, China's monetary system was in shambles. Coins were minted in copper but the metal had become scarce. Peasants and merchants fell back on barter. Markets contracted, commerce languished, and the general economy collapsed.

Politics mirrored the ruined economy. The central government was no more. Independent warlords competed for power, some enjoying momentary success, such as Sima Yan who crushed all opposition then crippled his army by melting down weapons to mint coins to pay for rebuilding the central government. The nation rendered defenseless, Mongolian nomads invaded China from the north; Tibetan warriors streamed in from the southwest; and Hmong tribes in the Five Lakes region of Hubei and Hunan provinces united in a loose confederation to drive off the Chinese and exercise self-rule.[40]

The Hmong had long bridled under the rule of the Chinese, who considered the Hmong inferior, not only because of their pale skin and Caucasian features[41]but for their refusal to assimilate Chinese culture, branding them forever as wild barbarians and earning them the name *Miao* (savage). Feeling no obligation to respect the rights of feral aborigines, the Chinese abused the Hmong at will, demanding their land and the right to rule over them as a subject people.

References to Hmong insurrections pepper the ancient annals of Chinese history. Most of these episodes were desperate backlashes against relentless oppression, but the forty Hmong uprisings recorded between 403 and 561 reflect a genuine attempt to capture political power and exercise self-rule.[42] By the middle of the sixth century, official Chinese records grudgingly conceded the existence of a Hmong kingdom in the Five Lakes region, hinting it had been functioning more or less uninterrupted since the beginning of the fifth century.[43]

China was back on its feet at the close of the seventh century and sent armies against the Hmong. In one terrible battle the Hmong king, along with his principal generals, perished in combat. Over the next two hundred years, Chinese peasants under military protection occupied Hmong farmland. Like the American Indians trying to turn back a flood of settlers, the Hmong retaliated by attacking Chinese garrisons. Not unlike the U.S. cavalry, Chinese soldiers hunted the Hmong down, slaughtering thousands and justifying the carnage as the protection of decent pioneers bringing civilization to the wild frontier. Hmong who survived these pogroms retreated into the rugged mountains of Guizhou, Yunnan, and southwestern Sichuan, where most Hmong in China still live today.

Kept alive in legend, the memory of the lost kingdom was passed down through generations and later carried across the border into Southeast Asia. A myth accompanied the legend. It was that a Hmong "king will rise again, . . . unite his people, gather them together, and lead them victoriously against the hated oppressors."[44] The myth's central figure is Chue Chao (*Tswb Tchoj*), a legendary Hmong wizard born of the union of a woman and a magical wild boar, who called up storms and earthquakes and destroyed China's armies. According to legend, the terrified Chinese proclaimed Chue Chao emperor, then used deceit and trickery to kill him. Like Christ, Chue Chao rose from the dead. Again he ruled China, only to be murdered a second time by the Chinese.

The myth attests that when the moment is right, Chue Chao will rise a third time and reestablish the Hmong kingdom. This last coming will be announced by a Hmong messiah, either Chue Chao himself or a Hmong acting as his agent, displaying feats of magic. The magic might appear in various forms, but in most versions of the myth there is a magic flag and a virgin who will sustain its power so long as she remains chaste.[45]

The messiah, or his messenger, will prove his authenticity by displaying knowledge of a Hmong script. It was a sore point with the Hmong that they had no writing of their own, leading them to concoct face-saving stories of Hmong books lost long ago, fat tomes containing their complete history, their legends, and glosses on their religion, all accidentally dumped into a river when fleeing the cursed Chinese.[46]

For consolation the Hmong took pride in their oral tradition, yet in their hearts they knew writing was power. With their indecipherable ideograms the Chinese were able to make contracts and manage a far-flung state bureaucracy. The illiterate Hmong were at their mercy in courts of law. They could not read a contract or verify the contents of a treaty. Literacy had enabled the Chinese to cheat the Hmong and rule them as inferiors. The Hmong imagined that with a script of their own they might be similarly empowered.[47]

The messiah legend has inspired Hmong insurrections down through the centuries, but none was as fierce, or as bloody, as the rebellion that flared up in 1854 in the Guizhou Province in southern China, a rebellion that dragged on for thirty years. The insurrection claimed millions of lives, nearly one half of the province's population if we are to believe one Chinese scholar's estimate. The government's losses were also high. Entire armies were decimated, both by the fighting and by rampant diseases that sometimes felled nine out of every ten Chinese soldiers during the sweltering insect-ridden summer months.

There were economic reasons for the revolt. Decades of high taxes and the seizure of Hmong farmland by state authorities had reduced the Hmong of Guizhou to utter destitution. Hmong dug up family graves to obtain the silver jewelry that adorned the corpses in order to purchase rice and pay taxes. When fighting broke out, thousands were already on the verge of starvation. But dire want alone cannot account for the intensity and duration of the conflict, or why leaders of the rebellion assumed titles like "King of Heavenly Light" or "Great King." One rebel chieftain, Tao Xinchun, was said to have a mother with "magical powers," another preached the coming of a new age—all signs that the Hmong were inspired by messianism.[48]

The Hmong were in strong defensive positions, either high ground enclosed by stone walls, or on a high mountain plateau surrounded on all sides by cliffs so steep that Chinese officials claimed only monkeys could reach the top. Venturing out from these strongholds, the rebels sacked major cities and occupied government offices, in some instances for more than a decade.

At the time Beijing was preoccupied with the even larger Taiping rebellion in the eastern provinces, giving the Hmong rebels some breathing space. Not until the late 1860s was the central government finally in a position to send the nation's armies against the Hmong. The imperial troops pouring into Guizhou carried modern European rifles recently purchased from William Mesny, a British arms merchant. Looking for future sales, Mesny accompanied the troops to Guizhou to train them in the use of the new firearms and to fight at their side to prove he had faith in his product.

The extra soldiers and modern weapons turned the tide. The Chinese scattered rebel forces and cut supply lines. Starving Hmong turned to cannibalism, which became so widespread that slabs of human flesh appeared on the butcher's block in the marketplaces of many towns. By 1873 most of the rebels were dead. Three decades of fighting had turned the province into a wasteland. Major cities were ruins enclosed by broken walls. Civilian survivors of the long war could be found on the outskirts of the wreckage huddled in crude straw huts.[49]

Guizhou had still not recovered from the war's devastation by the turn of the century when Methodist missionaries, led by Cornish minister Samuel Pollard, arrived to proselytize Hmong in the border region of Yunnan and Guizhou. Despite the miserable state of the Hmong in the region, messianism had still not lost its magnetism, as Pollard would soon discover.

Pollard's mission was at Zhaotong, a border town of mainly Lolo tribesmen who owned the surrounding land on which impoverished Hmong labored as tenant farmers. One of Pollard's goals was to make the Bible accessible to the Hmong. Using a modified version of a hieroglyphic script developed by Methodist missionaries for American Indians, Pollard developed a Hmong script and had Bibles in the new language printed in Japan and delivered to the mission.

As word of the Bible spread, Hmong began arriving in groups of ten and twenty to see what they presumed was one of their ancient books lost when their ancestors fled the Chinese.[50] Soon the numbers swelled into the hundreds. Pollard was amazed by the response, especially on the occasion when a thousand Hmong appeared in a single day. He considered the turnout a major achievement, given the miserable weather. "When they came the snow was on the ground, and terrible had been the snow on the hills they crossed over. What a great crowd it was."[51]

Pollard's delight turned to alarm when his new converts began to interpret the story of the resurrection of Christ as a prophecy of the return of the Hmong messiah. Hmong shamans arrived on the scene, wild-eyed with predictions of the imminent arrival of a Hmong savior who would deliver the Hmong from the hated Lolo and Chinese.

The messianic prophecies struck fear in the hearts of the Chinese and Lolo residents of Zhaotong. Hemmed in by swelling crowds of jubilant Hmong, and sensing a holy war in the making, they forced Pollard, nearly killing him in the process, to relocate his mission across the border in Guizhou at a place called "Stone Gateway," a desolate mountainside site donated to Pollard by a wealthy Lolo Christian convert.[52]

The same messianism that so agitated the Hmong at Pollard's mission flared up again in the region fourteen years later. Beginning in 1917, drought conditions prevailed in southwest China. Guizhou and Yunnan suffered the worst. The bad weather continued into the next year. Crops withered and floated away with the dust, and stomachs growled across the two provinces.

Hmong on the borderland of Yunnan and Guizhou were already digging up roots to survive on by the time Methodist missionaries established a Hmong relief fund. After collecting substantial donations in London and Shanghai to purchase a mountain of food, the missionaries distributed the provisions during daily sermons before large crowds of the grateful. Miraculously saved from starvation and told they owed it all to the Messiah, record numbers presented themselves for baptism. As with Pollard's earlier mass baptisms, Hmong began to talk of the imminent arrival of the messiah of their legends.[53]

One actually showed up: a Hmong shaman from the border region claiming to be the true Hmong Mahdi. Playing on the emotions stirred up by the missionaries, he assembled a small army of believers and went on the offensive. The provincial government sped military units to the area to crush the rebellion. When the two forces clashed, the Hmong discovered that their flintlocks were no match for carbines. The bodies of dead rebels littered the battleground. For the Chinese, the victory was made even sweeter by the capture of the shaman.

The trouncing did not end the rebellion. Survivors of the debacle tried to break their shaman out of jail in the dead of night. The jailers beat them back, wounded several rebels and sent the rest packing. Checked at every turn, humiliated and seething with frustration, the Hmong set upon a defenseless T'ai village. During their rampage they pillaged homes and shops, murdered a few villagers, and dragged local officials from their offices and executed them in the street. One of the spoils of their plunder was the discovery of a cache of modern rifles.

Having finally bloodied their hands, and now in possession of modern weapons, the rebels announced their intention to form an independent Hmong state. Almost as soon as the words passed their lips, Chinese troops fell upon them from all sides. T'ai vigilantes were also on the scene, armed to the teeth by sympathetic provincial bureaucrats. The rebels were allowed no quarter. According to French reports, the suppression was extremely cruel and violent.[54]

One surviving rebel, a Lolo clansman, fled to Laos and settled near Sam Thong. His account of the insurrection, heavily weighted with mythic themes, highlights the impact of messianism on Hmong perceptions.

The tale begins with a miraculous birth of a Hmong infant with the power of speech and a touch that healed wounds and livened aged flesh. Hmong gathered at the infant's feet to listen to his prophecy of a coming Hmong kingdom and to gaze at the vial containing his afterbirth, a magic elixir which they were told would one day make the Hmong invincible. Without explanation the infant disappeared, leaving behind only the vial of placental fluid. An itinerant Hmong named Pao Yoi discovered the vial hidden in the forest, drank its contents, and was transformed into a great athlete, mystic, and magician. He could leap as high as a house, speak to forest spirits and the souls of ancestors, and produce objects out of thin air. He wandered the countryside in the company of a talking pig named Chue Chao, who served as his counselor. Preaching liberation, Pao Yoi gathered a following and used magic to call up storms to decimate the armies the Chinese sent against him. At one town he split boulders open with the wave of his hand and rifles spilled out (a mythic rendering of the rebels' discovery of cases of carbines), enough weapons to provision an army. The Hmong went from victory to victory until the talking pig deserted them. Suddenly Pao Yoi lost his magic. At the Red River (known as the Yuan in China), he commanded the waters to part, but the river rolled on. Pao Yoi plunged into the water and drowned. Leaderless, the Hmong were at the mercy of the Chinese, who slaughtered them at will.[55]

PREPARING FOR THE MESSIAH

Survivors of the 1917 Yunnan-Guizhou rebellion scattered in all directions. Some wound up in the Sip Song region of northern Vietnam, ragged groups of refugees with mothers leading children in the company of stooped old men and frail old women, all nearly dead from the exertion of the trek and seeking sanctuary among Hmong clansmen. At night around cooking fires, the refugees told the Sip Song Hmong of the savagery of the T'ai who had ruthlessly hunted down and butchered the rebels. The Sip Song was T'ai country, a hundred-kilometer wedge of highlands a stone's throw from the Laotian border, ruled by T'ai autocrats with no love for the Hmong. Tales of T'ai savagery, circulating by word of mouth from one Hmong village to the next, their grisliness magnified with each retelling, found receptive audiences.

It was early June 1918 when the first Hmong raiding parties came down from the mountains to take hold of the tip and tail of the Sip Song, assaulting the town of Lai Chau at the northernmost edge of the T'ai domain and Son La on its southern rim. The fury of the raids had less to do with hatred for the T'ai than with a rumor that a Hmong king had arisen. The Hmong were preparing for liberation.

Hundreds had already left their villages to seek out this king and pay him homage. One remote Hmong village proclaimed a local Hmong woman queen of all the Hmong. Members of her clan flocked to the village to attend her as royalty. Curious, the French looked into the matter and came away convinced that the woman was simply given to hysterics.

A Catholic priest with sympathies for the Hmong tried to alert colonial officials that there was more afoot than mass hysteria. "An entire race does not turn fanatic overnight for no apparent reason, swept up by the voice of the first sorcerer who comes along." The priest warned that the real underlying cause of the sudden religious fervor was pent-up anger over long-standing abuses. T'ai despots required the Hmong to pay three times the taxes normally collected by the colonial administration: five piasters, or two hundred grams of opium, for each adult in a family. Hmong had to entertain T'ai tax collectors lavishly and allow them to bed the prettiest women in the village.[56]

The French ignored the priest's warning. For decades it had been unwritten policy to tolerate T'ai exploitation. Conceding its existence would be to acknowledge French duplicity. However, once reports began to trickle in from every corner of the Sip Song confirming that the Hmong were on the verge of a general uprising, colonial bureaucrats rushed to initiate talks with Hmong chieftains, promising to look into T'ai abuses. The Hmong wanted more than an official inquiry. They demanded that all T'ai intermediaries be replaced by Hmong empowered to deal directly with the colonial bureaucracy.

The overlord of the Sip Song was Deo Van Khang, a T'ai autocrat descended from a long line of Sip Song despots. Illegal taxes on the Hmong kept him in palaces and palanquins. If the peace talks were successful and Hmong allowed self-government, thousands of silver piasters would slip through his fingers. To shatter the uneasy peace, Deo Van sent raiding parties to ravage Hmong villages. Hmong chieftains appealed to the colonial government for protection. The French commiserated, shrugged their shoulders, and as usual did nothing.[57]

PA CHAY

At a mountain village near Dienbienphu, three hundred Hmong came together and formed an army. Their leader was Pa Chay,[58] an individual completely unknown to French authorities. He was not a documented troublemaker, not even a chieftain of note. His name appeared nowhere in the thick dossiers profiling tribal politicians and notorious brigands, stored in a back room at provincial headquarters.

Pa Chay was an unlikely candidate for messianic leadership. Born into the Vue clan in Yunnan near the Burmese border, he lost his parents at an early age. In his teens he left for northern Vietnam to seek out relatives at Na Ou, a mountain village near Dienbienphu. Song Tou Vue, the village chief, took Pa Chay in and loved him as a son.[59] Na Ou was a poor village, and in poor villages everyone, including the chief, labored in the fields. Pa Chay toiled with the rest, respected only for the sweat on his brow and the calluses on his hands. He knew no magic, received no visions, and could neither read nor write.[60]

This was before the rebellion in China and rumors of the impending arrival of a Hmong king. Suddenly, Pa Chay was transformed. In a dream he ascended to heaven and conversed with Chue Chao. The Messiah taught him to read and write the lost Hmong script and commanded him to raise an army and drive the hated T'ai from the Dienbienphu region and establish an independent Hmong state.

Though the Hmong at Na Ou longed for a savior, when Pa Chay presented himself all they could see was a peasant farmer like themselves, talking nonsense. To bring them around, Pa Chay leaped to the roof of a house in a single bound and jumped down with a basket full of magic eggs that held their shape after he crushed them in a rice grinder.[61] This may have been mere trickery, but when Pa Chay wrote unique characters on a piece of cloth, claiming they were letters from the lost Hmong script, the village was won over. Neighboring Hmong flocked to Na Ou to witness these miracles for themselves, some staying on to enlist in Pa Chay's liberation army.[62]

Pa Chay marched his tiny military force west and took command of a stretch of Colonial Route 41. Running from the top to the bottom of the Sip Song, the road was the main route for all commerce and for the movement of troops. The French could not allow it to fall into rebel hands. A French patrol ventured forth to reclaim the road. Pa Chay ambushed the soldiers and sent them packing for Lai Chau. Seventy miles east at Yen Bai, a larger detachment assembled and set out to engage the insurgents. The soldiers traveled over Route 31, registered on maps by a dashed line indicating a footpath. Even the dashed line was overgenerous; much of the trail was overgrown, necessitating some hard slogging. It would take a week for the troops to complete the journey.

Meanwhile, Pa Chay swooped down on the T'ai town of Muong Phang and put it to the torch. West of the burning village lay the river valley of Dienbienphu, a major T'ai stronghold surrounded by T'ai towns and hamlets. Pa Chay made straight for the citadel, scattering T'ai and burning crops and villages on his way.

When the troops from Yen Bai finally arrived, Pa Chay had already left the lowlands for the mountains, pillaging T'ai villages on his way. The soldiers set off in pursuit but Pa Chay set a furious pace. The Yen Bai troops tried to keep up, flagged, then finally gave up the chase.

French officials were soon at Dienbienphu, assessing the damage and pondering their options. They decided to seek a negotiated peace. Through Hmong intermediaries they made contact with Pa Chay and began talks. Pa Chay was unbending on every issue. The French tried to draw out the talks and wear Pa Chay down with diplomatic thrusts and parries. Tiring of the game, Pa Chay executed their negotiator. The act infuriated the French, who decided Pa Chay had to be eliminated.

The first major engagement between French-led troops and Pa Chay's rebel army was in the mountains near Na Ou. The French had mustered *tirailleurs* (colonial riflemen) from Son La and Yen

Bai, well-armed Vietnamese foot soldiers, and French noncoms brimming with confidence. Following two days of hard fighting, and with many dead and wounded, the tirailleurs withdrew, the wind gone from their sails. More clashes followed. Pa Chay's guerrillas rolled rocks down on colonial troops as they struggled to negotiate steep mountain trails. They ambushed them in narrow ravines, tearing apart bodies with the heavy slugs of their ancient flintlocks and turning hearts cold with terror by threading their crossbows with poisoned arrows, missiles that inflicted a hideously painful and lingering death.[63] The rebels suffered few casualties in these early engagements, all due, they believed, to Pa Chay's magic.

In these early skirmishes, a Hmong maiden led the rebels into battle. She was Ngao Nzoua, a young girl of seventeen, and a virgin as required by legend. During the fighting she positioned herself between the guerrillas and French forces, waving a large white flag to magically sweep away French bullets.[64] Pa Chay's soldiers carried smaller flags tucked into their blouses, a patch of white cloth inscribed with sacred Hmong script to protect them from harm. The rebels also drank sacred water before battles, an elixir that was supposed to make them invulnerable to French bullets.[65]

While Pa Chay was busy humiliating French forces, a second Hmong declared himself the Messiah of legend. Identified in colonial documents only as "Camxu," he raised an army and raided several T'ai settlements northwest of Dienbienphu before retreating back into the mountains to hole up at Long He. The French mustered additional troops and assaulted the mountain fortress. Once the fighting turned fierce, Camxu's soldiers deserted him and he was taken prisoner.[66]

The victory over Camxu was a turning point. After nearly two years of mountain fighting, the tirailleurs were finally getting the hang of it. After scouts tracked Pa Chay to his fortified camp at Ban Nam Nghan, the French gathered their forces, including artillery pieces that had to be hauled up steep mountain trails, and converged on the fortress. The cannons chewed away at Pa Chay's fortifications, exposing his men to withering fusillades from the tirailleurs' rifles. Pa Chay attempted a desperate breakout. French bullets ripped into his troops. To the left and right, Pa Chay saw his men fall around him, yet he miraculously escaped through the French lines without a scratch. Pa Chay fled south to the highlands above Son La where he recruited new volunteers, performed magic rites, and distributed new flags. Before he had a chance to test his new recruits in battle, the French discovered his location and came after him with everything they had.

THE REBELLION MOVES TO LAOS

It was now mid-1920. Pa Chay had been tramping up and down the Sip Song through sweltering summers and torrential monsoons. He had eluded the French and surprised them in ambushes by relying on intelligence supplied by Hmong villagers, who also donated food for his hungry soldiers and filled his army's ranks with fresh volunteers. Civilian support had been crucial, yet there was no getting around the fact that the Sip Song was T'ai country, and Hmong communities were but tiny islands in a sea of T'ai. Directly across the border in northeastern Laos the Hmong were in the majority and the French had only a token force of regular soldiers. With the enemy close on his heels, Pa Chay led his partisans in a dash across the border into Laos.

The Hmong of Phong Saly, Sam Neua, and Xieng Khouang were primed for his arrival. Weary of high taxes and still stinging from the ignominy of forced labor, many were already on the brink of insurrection, with or without Pa Chay. When he appeared he was received as king and savior. Hundreds of Hmong bearing crossbows and flintlocks left their homes to enlist in the holy war they knew would come.

The shift of the battleground from Vietnam to Laos was a strategic nightmare for the French. Only a few years earlier they had five thousand soldiers in place in northern Laos, assembled to crush a bandit force of nearly three thousand Chinese and T'ai who for years had been running cross-border raids into Vietnam. The French had flushed the bandits out of their fortifications with mountain artillery, then harassed them with relentless infantry assaults. Most of the brigands fled north into China, but some were taken prisoner and the French made a show of their executions, which was thought to have a very salutary effect on the native

The Village of Pak Pui

Hmong house with livestock

population. Only a skeleton force was left to police the region and serve as a reminder of the efficiency of French firing squads. New civil disorders were thought unlikely.[67]

Once in Laos, Pa Chay established his headquarters on the high mountain plateau of Phoi Loi, a location with several advantages. Situated thirty miles north of the Plain of Jars, it stood midway between Sam Neua and Xieng Khouang provinces, making it the approximate geographical center of the Hmong domain in Laos. The high plateau was also near Route 6, the road the French would have to use to move troops into the Hmong heartland. If Pa Chay commanded the road, he could cut French supply lines and block their troop movements while moving his own forces north or south unimpeded. Phoi Loi had one additional virtue. Approaches to the plateau were so heavily wooded that visibility was limited to only a few meters. Every trail, every footpath leading up to the plateau was ideal for ambush.[68]

The Hmong domain in Laos embraced twenty-five thousand square miles of rugged mountains. Only here and there, such as in Nong Het near the Vietnamese border, were there settlements of more than a thousand souls. Villages were isolated and small, usually composed of less than forty families. To provision an army and provide it soldiers, hundreds of Hmong villages would have to enlist in the war effort. Pa Chay left the safety of Phoi Loi and crisscrossed the mountains, sending messengers ahead to announce his arrival at this or that village. Hundreds, sometimes thousands, hurried from nearby settlements to gaze at the savior.

Pa Chay did not disappoint them. He offered up magic and distributed political tracts in the new Hmong script, jeremiads prophesying a Hmong state looming like a phoenix from the rubble of shattered French garrisons and the ashes of smoldering T'ai and Lao villages. Being illiterate, no one could read the tracts, but it was an exhilarating experience to run a finger over the lines of text and make physical contact with the Hmong language. Pa Chay addressed his flock from on high, standing on a rise or sometimes climbing high into a tree, always positioning himself closer to heaven than the multitude. From his aerie he preached cultural purity, warning that only if the Hmong hewed to the traditions of their ancestors would they be worthy of Chue Chao's blessing.

And he announced what everyone already believed: he was the Chao Fa (the king made by god).[69]

Pa Chay had not assumed this title during the Sip Song uprising, claiming only to be the messenger preparing the way for the Messiah. Perhaps a revelation had changed his mind, or possibly the reverence in which he was held finally convinced him that he was more than Chue Chao's messenger. Whatever the reason, Pa Chay now spoke with the confidence of a divine prophet. He whetted imaginations with glowing images of the Hmong nation to come, a great chunk of mountain terrain extending from Dienbienphu in the east to the Phu Bia Mountains in the south, and all the way north into Phong Saly Province.

Men shook with excitement. Tears spilled down the faces of women. Entire communities pledged their support on the spot for the great campaign that would deliver the Hmong from bondage to the Lao and French. Men volunteered for military service. Young and old, male and female, offered to become the eyes and ears of Pa Chay's liberation army and gather intelligence on the enemy's troop movements. Husbands plucked silver jewelry from the necks of their wives; aged patriarchs dug up silver bars and French piasters buried in the forest; villagers rummaged through storage sheds for bricks of cured opium. This treasure they delivered to Pa Chay, piling it at his feet.

Though the French had few regular troops in the area to engage Pa Chay's forces, they did have three brigades of the Garde Indigène on hand to contain the rebellion. One of them was attached to the commissioner of Xieng Khouang. The other two brigades were in the far north where Phong Saly and Sam Neua were administered as military districts. From the summer of 1920 through the fall of 1921, elements of all three brigades clashed with Pa Chay's partisans. Garde patrols stumbled into ambushes; rock slides rained down on them in narrow passes; shrapnel from Hmong cannons ripped through their formations.

The cannons were a surprise. The Vietnamese, T'ai, and Lao serving in the 2nd, 4th, and 5th Garde Indigène brigades had expected hard fighting but took consolation in the belief that they possessed modern rifles whereas the firepower of the Hmong consisted only of crossbows and flintlocks. While the ambushes and rock slides naturally took a psychological toll, the cannons completely demoralized the native brigades.

Homemade black powder charged the cannons. Pa Chay had stockpiled hundreds of pounds of the explosive, made by distilling nitrates from bat guano and mixing it with charcoal and sulfur. It was an old recipe taught to the Hmong of Guizhou in China three hundred years earlier by Hwang Ming, a renegade Chinese general on the run who had traded his knowledge of weapon-making for sanctuary.[70]

Pa Chay's cannons were crude devices made of hollowed tree trunks banded with iron, inaccurate beyond a few yards and hurling only a handful of grapeshot—laughable weapons when compared to a 4.5-inch howitzer with a range of several thousand yards and enough explosive power to tear apart stone fortifications. But Pa Chay was not firing from one mountain to another, nor did he need to punch holes in fortresses. He used his primitive artillery up close where it had enough killing power to spread terror among the enemy's troops.[71]

French officers attached to the brigades struggled to contain a full-scale mutiny. Their soldiers were just as superstitious as the Hmong. Once rumors of Pa Chay's magic reached them, they began to imagine that he practiced a form of witchcraft so powerful that they were all doomed to die in battle. The officers stopped sending patrols into the mountains and instead kept their troops busy policing their barracks and doing close order drills to remind them that they were still soldiers, even if they no longer had the heart to go into battle.

The pause in the fighting enabled Pa Chay to direct his attention to the political side of his crusade. So far only his army had bureaucratic substance. Pa Chay shared authority with an aide-de-camp, a Hmong from the village of Lao Vang who looked after the day-to-day chores of managing a war. Two Hmong notables, one of them a close relative from Hoei Thong and the other a chieftain from Phou Gni, functioned as field marshals with their own forces. There was a war council of Hmong from a cross-section of clans. Some commanded guerrilla units; others were simply clan patricians allowed to offer advice on military strategy. The council's principal function, however, was output rather than input. It was Pa Chay's link to the clan power structure, and through it to the village chieftains. It was through the council that requests for recruits, supplies, and money were transmitted to the villages.

Pa Chay now turned this military organization to political ends. The war council was made to double as a civil administration. All village chiefs were accountable to the council's members, who were accountable to Pa Chay. To confirm that territory wrested from the French was now a Hmong domain, Pa Chay ordered his field marshals to stop harassing the French and devote their full energies to pacifying Khmu tribesmen and purging the region of ethnic Lao. There is no record of Khmu resistance. Many simply fled the area. Those who remained behind became virtual slaves, working as coolies carrying supplies or toiling in work gangs on construction projects. The Lao fared worse. Those living near the Vietnamese border were decimated, their villages burned, and their crops and cattle confiscated. A much larger number of Lao occupied the right bank of the Nam Ou River, by now the de facto western border of Pa Chay's nascent Hmong state. Before Pa Chay's partisans could set torches to their homes the Lao fled across the river to safety, abandoning their prime rice paddies to the Hmong.[72]

Pa Chay then turned his attention to Hmong who had held back from his crusade. Thousands of Hmong peasants had been unwilling to squander the lives of their sons in a war against the French, or to part with precious silver laid away over the years for bride prices that would guarantee the continuation of the family tree. Grim-faced guerrillas arrived at the villages of known fence-sitters, arrows in their crossbows and flintlocks loaded and primed. It was a rare village that did not instantly embrace the revolution at the sight of these marauders and offer up donations of opium and silver to the cause, as well a brace or two of village lads dragged before the guerrillas and passed off as willing recruits for military service.

Pa Chay went after bigger fish as well. A handful of Hmong chieftains had seen his meteoric rise as a threat to their own power. A few had openly spoken out against him and tried to prevent Hmong under their authority from joining the rebellion. The worst offender was LoBliayao (Blia Yao Lo), the kaitong of the Lo clan and tasseng of the canton of Nong Het. LoBliayao owed his high office to Commissioner de Barthelemy, a wellborn Frenchman (a marquis) with a strong sense of *noblesse oblige*. Barthelemy stood alone as the only high ranking French bureaucrat in Laos to express concern in official communiqués for the lot of the average Hmong. Sensitive to the fact that the traditional Lao bureaucracy brazenly exploited and abused the Hmong, he had urged policy makers to grant the Hmong greater self-government. Because of Barthelemy, LoBliayao believed there could be progress working with the French rather than against them. It was also a consideration that should Pa Chay's revolution succeed, Barthelemy's head might wind up on a spike, and the enormous prestige and wealth that attached to LoBliayao's office pass to Pa Chay or one of his subalterns.

LoBliayao did his best to prevent the insurrection from taking hold in his canton. His aides kept close tabs on the villages. Hmong caught up in the messianic movement, or involved in recruiting soldiers for the resistance, were beaten and occasionally executed. Not everyone buckled under. LoBliayao's own nephew, Song Zeu Lo, who for years had served as the tasseng's personal assistant, joined the cause and recruited guerrillas from Nong Het right under LoBliayao's nose. LoBliayao wanted desperately to lay hands on his turncoat nephew, but Song Zeu had captured the imagination of the people. Even when offered threats and bribes they divulged nothing about the activities or itinerary of their local folk hero.

Given the hatred between uncle and nephew, it naturally fell to Song Zeu to orchestrate the tasseng's assassination. Song Zeu came down from the hills and went after his uncle at his Pak Lak residence. After surrounding the house, he called LoBliayao out. The tasseng emerged and faced his nephew with utter contempt. Song Zeu's guerrillas, all members of the Lo clan, edged back, eyes downcast in the presence of their clan's chieftain. Song Zeu ordered his men to shoot, but as no one wanted to take responsibility for the great man's murder not a single flintlock was raised. LoBliayao simply walked away "with everyone staring at him."[73]

FRENCH VICTORY

While Pa Chay consolidated his power, the demoralized battalions of the Garde Indigène continued to hold fast to the safety of their garrisons. Reports of the dispirited state of the brigades and of Pa Chay's dominion over the stretch of territory between the Nam Ou River and the Vietnam border (see map "Pa Chay Campaign") convinced bureaucrats in Hanoi that more seasoned troops were needed. Selecting from the best battalions at Hanoi and Saigon, they assembled an assault force of four elite rifle companies, invested with crack artillery units skilled in the use of mountain cannons.

The French gave a name to the campaign: *La Guerre du Fou* (the Madman's War). Launched toward the end of 1920, it would become the largest military operation in Indochina up to that time. The French positioned their troops in Xieng Khouang and Sam Neua to regain control of Route 6. Once they had command of the road they cut Pa Chay's supply lines, leaving rebel forces dispersed and without provisions. The French went after these isolated units one by one.

For a span of three months the fighting was intense, especially as the Hmong were now better armed. Chinese merchants had crossed into Laos in caravans laden with cast-off rifles from the Chinese army and sold everything they had to the rebels. Yet even with the additional firepower, the rebels were no match for the French cannons that blew apart their mountain redoubts, forcing them to fight in the open where the best rifle squads in Indochina cut them down. By March 1921, the French had broken the back of the insurrection. Town jails and garrison prisons throughout Sam Neua and Xieng Khouang provinces overflowed with captive rebels.

Still on the loose, Pa Chay retreated to the Phoi Loi plateau to make his last stand. For a time he was sustained by intermittent caravans over mountain trails organized by fellow clansmen in Vietnam. But after a month of desperate fighting he finally admitted defeat and fled north with his family (a wife and three children) to Phong Saly.

Despite Pa Chay's retirement from the war, thousands of Hmong continued to fight on, sustained by handouts from mountain villages still sympathetic to their cause. To nullify this local support, the French launched an operation that foreshadowed America's "Strategic Hamlet" program in Vietnam. After burning highland crops to deny them to the rebels, French soldiers relocated entire village populations to holding centers in protected areas where they could no longer be of any use to the insurgents. The pacification program was a great success. By late summer most of the region was under government control.[74]

One last detail remained. With Pa Chay still alive there might be new uprisings in the future, so the French put a price on his head, quite literally as they demanded his head be delivered before they would pay the bounty. In November 1921, some of Pa Chay's former disciples killed him in his forest hideaway near the Chinese border.[75]

Commissioner Barthelemy considered the event worthy of celebration. With LoBliayao's help, he organized a huge fête and invited all Hmong in the region to attend. Thousands arrived in full ceremonial costume to feast on sticky rice, boiled chicken, roast pig, and barbecued beef. At five in the afternoon, French soldiers marched twelve rebel prisoners out for the event that was to cap the day's festivities. The soldiers tied the rebels to posts, formed a firing squad, and executed them. While the executions dampened spirits, they left no doubt about who was in charge.[76]

There would be more executions as well as demands for reparations. Barthelemy personally conducted formal courts-martial for Hmong prisoners identified as key players in the rebellion. He sentenced three to death by firing squad and was on hand for the executions. On Hanoi's orders, Barthelemy exacted reparations from the Hmong for all of the damage done during the war, for the homes burned, crops destroyed, and all the murdered Lao, T'ai, and Vietnamese. Setting the worth of an Indochinese native to be about fifty piasters, and possessing a rough body count, Hanoi bureaucrats had a target figure in mind, later inflated to cover burnt buildings and stolen livestock. In all, the French collected close to a half ton of silver, though apparently the Hmong tried to have the last laugh by using inferior grades of silver ore to cast their reparation ingots.

POLITICAL REFORM

With rebel leaders dead and Hmong silver in their coffers, French bureaucrats finally turned to constructive measures to pacify the Hmong, commissioning an inquiry to explore Barthelemy's recommendations for increased Hmong self-governance. The

study's recommendation was to do away with Lao and T'ai intermediaries and grant the Hmong complete self-governance. In
remarkably short order the findings became administrative policy.
Following a census of Hmong communities, all district lines for
cantons were redrawn to reflect Hmong demographics. By edict,
Hmong villagers were to elect their own nai bans, and in the cantons the Hmong were to have their own tassengs.

Entrenched Lao interests, plus the dead weight of tradition,
insured that implementation of the mandate would be imperfect.
Lao officials continued to exercise considerable direct power over
the Hmong. Even so, the number of Hmong in positions of authority increased steadily. Within fifteen years there were seventeen
Hmong tassengs and scores of Hmong communities with a nai
ban of their own choosing.[77]

MESSIANISM LINGERS

Five years after the policy change, officials in the field reported
that Hmong communities throughout Laos were generally peaceful and well disposed toward the colonial government. Though
the report was accurate on the whole, what French officials could
not see was the steady undertow of messianism that still remained.
Eight years after Pa Chay's death, a shaman from the Lo clan
named Xay Vang led disciples to Nong Het to construct a tower to
function as a bridge to heaven. He planned to climb to the top and
appeal to God for help against the French. LoBliayao had the shaman murdered before construction on the tower could begin.

A year later, another shaman named Shi Yi Xiong began
preaching messianism to Hmong communities on Phu Bia
Mountain.[78] Claiming to possess the soul of the talking pig Chue
Chao, the now legendary boar of the 1917 messianic rebellion in
southern China, the shaman raised a guerrilla force and raided
French outposts at the base of the mountain. His younger sister
joined him on the raids, waving a magic flag to deflect the enemy's
bullets. Villagers on Phu Bia donated silver bars and silver jewelry
to the cause, which Shi Yi Xiong melted into slugs for his guerrillas' flintlocks, believing silver bullets would kill French souls as
well as French bodies. Shi Yi Xiong carried the rebellion all the
way to the provincial capital. The French finally captured the mes-

sianic leader while repulsing a rebel raid on Lat Boua, a village close to Xieng Khouangville. Native soldiers under French command brutally tortured the shaman, knocking out all of his teeth before executing him, along with his sister.

Still messianism lingered. Word spread of a new species of flower that had mysteriously sprouted in the mountain meadows, a tiny, fragile plant with bright blue flowers that blossomed at the end of the monsoon rains. Hmong began to refer to it as Pa Chay's wheat, a symbol of rebirth and perpetual hope.[79] There were also rumors that Pa Chay had bequeathed a legacy to the Hmong: copper plates engraved with the Hmong script which he had entrusted to his wife, with instructions to pass them on at some future date.[80]

This prophecy was seemingly confirmed forty-four years after Pa Chay's death when, in 1966, a Yang clansman from Vietnam arrived in Xieng Khouang Province claiming knowledge of a sacred Hmong script. He led a religious revival that attracted thousands and rekindled messianic yearnings. The revival threatened the power of established Hmong leaders. They clapped the prophet in jail. When he escaped they sent a squad of assassins to hunt him down. After the prophet's death, the movement went underground, resurfacing in 1975 to unleash a frenzied rebellion against Laos' new communist regime, demonstrating that the dead hand of Pa Chay had a very long reach.

CLAN CONFLICT

A principal beneficiary of the French victory over Pa Chay was LoBliayao. Earlier in 1917 he had replaced Tong Ger Moua as tasseng of the Nong Het canton, making him the titular head of all Xieng Khouang Hmong. It was an event that signaled a return to the traditional structure of Hmong authority in Laos. The first Hmong to settle in Laos were Lo clansmen. Moua and Ly clansmen arrived later, followed by smaller contingents from other clans. By right of first arrival, the Lo had dominated Hmong politics. This ended with the failed 1896 revolt that finished Pa Sy Lo's political career and thrust Tong Ger Moua into the limelight. But the Lo still had the weight of tradition on their side, so when Tong Ger Moua announced his retirement, LoBliayao was able to reclaim his clan's time-honored prerogatives.

LoBliayao was decidedly pro-French. As kaitong of the Lo clan he had worked diligently to establish good relations with the French commissioner, and continued to build on this goodwill as tasseng. It made him a wealthy man. When village leaders complained bitterly about corvée labor, LoBliayao used the discontent to persuade the commissioner to increase the wages for Hmong on work gangs by a generous 30 percent. But instead of passing the increase on to the workers, LoBliayao pocketed most of it for himself. While the French commissioner turned a blind eye to the swindle, Hmong on the work gangs deeply resented the exploitation. Once Pa Chay's revolt spread to Laos, many joined the insurrection simply to bring LoBliayao down.[81]

Now, with Pa Chay dead and the French firmly back in control, LoBliayao set out to even scores. The French helped by giving him more power. After lavishing LoBliayao with military decorations (seven medals that he wore proudly on his mandarin tunic at all official events), the commissioner expanded the old canton of Nong Het into a subdistrict and appointed LoBliayao its nai kong, making him the highest placed Hmong in the country's native bureaucracy. With a population of nearly three thousand, the town of Nong Het was already the largest Hmong settlement in the nation. The new subdistrict added several large outlying villages to this mix, giving LoBliayao direct legal authority over as many as six or seven thousand Hmong, and, because of his stature as the only Hmong nai kong, indirect authority over nearly all Hmong villages between Nong Het and Xieng Khouangville.

LoBliayao's first act as nai kong was to extort money for the release of captured rebels still in prison.[82] Families paid small fortunes to get sons, husbands, and brothers freed, money that built a huge European-style, two-story stone residence that housed LoBliayao's four wives, close relatives, and many children (about fifty people in all). He also purchased additional cattle for his already substantial herd (it would eventually exceed one thousand head) that grazed in the hills near his new home at Pak Lak.[83] One prisoner who was not freed was LoBliayao's nephew Song Zeu. Despite popular demand for the former rebel's release (he was still something of a folk hero), and money offered by Song

Zeu's family to purchase his freedom, LoBliayao could not forgive the assassination attempt. Song Zeu died in the Xieng Khouangville prison, rumored to have been poisoned by guards.[84]

While it seemed nothing could dim the glow of LoBliayao's rising star, a family tragedy in 1922 permanently altered the course of his political career. In that year his favorite daughter, May, committed suicide. Four years earlier she had married a Ly clansman named Foung. As far as LoBliayao was concerned, his daughter had died of a broken heart.

LoBliayao had been against the marriage from the start. Foung was in his late forties, already had two wives, and was a social climber. LoBliayao was certain Foung was interested in May only as a way to advance his fortunes. But May was smitten and conspired in her own abduction—in Hmong culture the only way star-crossed lovers can overrule hostile parents. To save face, LoBliayao demanded a large bride price, leaving the impecunious Foung with no option but to work it off as LoBliayao's employee, precisely what Foung had desired in the first place. Soon he was serving as LoBliayao's personal secretary, learning the ropes and cultivating friendships with French bureaucrats. LoBliayao might have given Foung even more responsibility, but relations between the two cooled when he learned Foung was beating May. When she committed suicide by swallowing a deadly bolus of opium, LoBliayao sacked Foung and severed all ties with the Ly clan.[85]

Tensions between the Lo and Ly still ran high six years later. Worried that the hostility might evolve into armed conflict, the French reorganized the Nong Het subdistrict into two large cantons (Keng Khoai and Phac Boun), trading a nai kong for two tassengs so authority could be evenly divided. Keng Khoai went to the Lo, Phac Boun to the Ly.[86]

LoBliayao was getting on in years and in poor health, so his eldest son Song Tou Lo stood in for him as the tasseng of Keng Khoai. Foung Ly also decided it was time to pass the torch. Three wives had given him many sons. One of May's two children, Touby, was the youngest and brightest. Foung planned big things for the boy, but for the moment his eldest son would have to fill his shoes as tasseng of Phac Boun. The conflict between Foung and LoBliayao had now officially crossed into the next generation.

Foung did not leave everything to his sons. In 1931 he acted on his own to bring LoBliayao down. LoBliayao was still holding back part of the pay earmarked for corvée workers. Foung took him to court over the matter. For LoBliayao it was a humiliating experience. In one last act of defiance, LoBliayao persuaded a number of Hmong chieftains to withhold their village's opium harvest from the colonial administration's purchasing agents.[87] The French did not bother to retaliate. It was common knowledge that LoBliayao was an opium addict and suffered from advanced alcoholism. Patience would solve everything.

Less than two years later LoBliayao was dead. Leadership of the Lo clan passed to his eldest son, Song Tou, who dedicated himself to running through his father's fortune in gold, a thousand bars of silver, two thousand French silver piasters, and more than a thousand head of cattle and buffalo (in total, worth at least several million in today's dollars).[88] Given the size of the patrimony, squandering it could not be accomplished overnight. Song Tou gambled, womanized, and spent weeks at a stretch in the highlands hunting elephants, tigers, and rhinos, leaving little time for administrative duties. As dereliction of duties was commonplace among native bureaucrats, the French were not unduly alarmed until Song Tou committed the unforgivable sin of failing to collect taxes. It was the opening Foung needed to eliminate the Lo from provincial politics. Pledging to make up the lost taxes out of his own personal fortune, Fong persuaded the French commissioner to remove Song Tou from office and place himself in charge of Keng Khoai. The Ly clan now controlled both cantons.[89]

Faydang Lo, Song Tou's younger brother, was outraged. He appealed to the French commissioner to reverse the decision, was turned away, and left for Luang Prabang to plead his case before Prince Phetsarath, the Inspector of Indigenous Affairs who administered the Lao spoils system and was empowered to appoint or remove administrators in the Lao bureaucracy. Faydang presented the prince with a massive rhinoceros horn, darkened with oil and buffed to an onyx shimmer. The gift had the desired effect. Phetsarath issued an edict stating that upon Foung's death Faydang would assume the vacated post of native administrator for Keng Khoai. But when Foung died in 1939, the French ignored

Phetsarath's edict and placed Foung's youngest son, Touby, in charge of the canton.

The French could not help preferring Touby over the rustic and untutored Faydang. Lingering doubts about the administrative capacity of the Lo no doubt played a part in the decision, but there was also the fact of Touby's education. He had studied at a French Lycée in the lowlands, taken courses in the School of Law and Administration in Vientiane, spoke flawless French, and was an unabashed Francophile. For the French it was an unbeatable combination.

Faydang vowed vengeance, not only against the French but against Touby, who in his mind had become his mortal enemy. He would later adopt a rule of life that he would follow relentlessly: whatever Touby did, he would do the opposite. For his part, Touby felt obliged to attempt a reconciliation with Faydang. After all, the man was his uncle, and among the Hmong family ties were not dismissed lightly. Touby opened negotiations with an exchange of letters through couriers. It all came to naught, for Faydang could not forgive what he believed to be Ly treachery against his family. Touby reluctantly faced the fact that Faydang would remain an implacable enemy, someone to be feared and, if possible, eliminated.[90]

In time the personal vendetta between the two chieftains metamorphosed into a simmering feud between their respective clans, with every imagined slight or conflict magnified into a justification for hostility between Lo and Ly. One particular incident became a cause célèbre. As told by the Lo, a Ly and a Lo had competed for the hand of a young maiden. She rejected the Ly and married the Lo. The jilted suitor led a raiding party of Ly clansmen and abducted the woman. The Lo demanded reparations to cover the bride price already paid for the woman and a fine for the abduction, but the Ly refused to pay anything. The whole incident only intensified the Lo's bitter feelings against the Ly and persuaded many Lo to side with Faydang against Touby.[91]

The Ly had their own version. In the early 1950s when French forces engaged Vietnamese communists (Viet Minh)[92] near Nong Het, hundreds of Hmong families fled the area. Lo clansmen headed east into Vietnam, while Ly clansmen fled west onto the Plain of Jars. During the confusion, the wife of a Ly clansman became separated from her husband. Faydang's half-brother, Sao Lo, found her in the forest and took her with him to Vietnam. Within a few months they were living as man and wife. After the Viet Minh defeated the French at Dienbienphu in mid-1954, the Lo drifted back to Nong Het. Sao Lo returned the Ly woman to her village with the understanding that, if her husband no longer wanted her, she could join his household as his wife. The reunion was not joyous. When the woman's husband learned the truth, he immediately called fellow clansmen to arms. They dragged Sao Lo back to the village and beat him nearly to death.[93]

The heated rivalry between the two clans was still full of steam by the time the Japanese occupied Indochina. When French commandos parachuted into Laos in early 1945 to begin guerrilla operations against the Japanese, Touby volunteered to help. He organized work teams to clear airstrips, arranged for couriers to carry messages, established an intelligence network to keep the commandos informed of Japanese activities, and raised Hmong guerrilla bands to ambush Japanese truck convoys.

Following the rule that whatever Touby did, he would do the opposite, Faydang created the Hmong Resistance League, a guerrilla force of Lo clansmen under his personal command, to help the Japanese hunt down French commandos. After Japan's defeat, Faydang continued his vendetta against the French by linking up with the Viet Minh. When America replaced France in Laos and Touby cast his lot with the Americans, Faydang turned anti-American and joined the Pathet Lao.

2

JAPANESE
OCCUPATION

Ho Chi Minh left Vietnam in 1912. His first two years as an expatriate he spent as a kitchen helper on the French liner Latouche-Tréville. He worked another two years in England as a pastry chef, followed by four more in Paris as a part-time photographer and full-time socialist. Ho was not temperamentally suited for French socialism. He grew impatient with the endless disputations of the salon intellectuals who dominated the French socialist movement. Already committed to change, Ho yearned for action. Arguments were for people who had yet to make up their minds.

In 1920 Ho began reading the works of Lenin, poring over the French translations in his tiny apartment, grunting approval as he read. He was amazed at Lenin's "clearsightedness" and "overjoyed to tears" when he realized that he was part of a great revolutionary movement. Inspired, he co-founded the French communist party and began his career as a communist revolutionary.[1]

To better learn the tools of his trade, Ho made plans to visit Moscow. He eventually left Paris for the Soviet Union at the end of 1924. He had waited too long. Lenin died just a few weeks before his arrival, denying Ho the chance to meet his hero. For a brief period Ho felt like a boat adrift without a rudder. "Lenin is dead, what are we going to do?" he wrote in *Pravda*. Ho needed something to focus his energies. He decided to honor Lenin's memory with tireless study. He enrolled in the University of the

Peoples of the East in Moscow, where he learned the nuts and bolts of revolutionary organization. Ho also found time to teach some courses at the school and write occasional articles for *Pravda*.

Pleased with his development as a revolutionary, the Soviets sent Ho to China to help organize the Chinese Communist Party. In Canton he made contact with other Vietnamese nationalists living in self-exile or hiding from the long arm of the Sûreté, the criminal investigation branch of the French national police. Years earlier Ho would have found the nationalists' fervor invigorating, but now with his Soviet training he found it utterly naive. The nationalists were big on ineffectual protests, but drew back from real revolution. The leader of the group was an old Vietnamese nationalist named Phan Boi Chau. Ho knew him from childhood. His father and Phan had been good friends. But Ho didn't allow sentimentality to cloud his judgment. With Phan out of the way Ho could recruit the aged nationalist's followers for the revolution. Also, Phan had a price on his head. Ho turned the old man in, using the 150,000 piasters in Judas money as a seed fund for his own communist organization.[2]

After two years in Thailand establishing communist cells in Bangkok's Vietnamese communities, Ho returned to China to build a communist party for Vietnam. In 1930 he founded the Indochinese Communist Party (ICP) in Hong Kong. Begun as an all-Vietnamese organization, Ho aspired to expand the ICP to encompass all of Indochina. Party documents pictured this larger organization as a federation composed of Vietnam, Laos, and Cambodia, with leadership provided by Vietnam. The object was a Vietnamese empire, a goal made official at the Lao Dong (a new name for the old ICP) conference of 1951.[3]

As a first step in this direction, the party organized a cell in Laos. The members were all Vietnamese residents of Vientiane. There had been a concerted effort to recruit ethnic Lao, but Marxist-Leninism simply did not appeal to them. Assuming the intellectual backwardness of the Laotians to be the problem, the ICP ordered its cadres to educate them.[4] Leaflets were distributed and lectures delivered on the evils of imperialist exploitation and the necessity of revolutionary organizations to return power to the downtrodden proletariat. Even with the intense propaganda campaign, only three more cells were organized in the towns around the tin mines in Khammouane Province, and all of the members were Vietnamese. By 1935 a grand total of three ethnic Lao had joined the movement, and two of them soon dropped out.[5]

It was a dismal showing. The ICP had fared only marginally better in Vietnam. As in Laos, the working class in Vietnam was small, numbering slightly more than two hundred thousand in a country of seventeen million. A third of these workers toiled on rubber plantations, where conditions were harsh and the mortality rate unconscionably high. The brutality of the plantations created militant workers. Spontaneous strikes, many of them violent, were frequent. Yet despite worker militancy, less than two thousand Vietnamese had joined the ICP and, by the mid-1930s, many of them were in jail.[6]

The communist movement in Vietnam was clearly in trouble and in need of attention, yet the ICP continued to spend scarce resources to create a viable communist party in Laos. A particular concern was to get ethnic Lao into the fledgling Lao communist party lest it be viewed as a Vietnamese-controlled organization. The Lao already resented Vietnamese dominance in government, business, and education. Vietnamese filled the government bureaucracy, monopolized trade in Laos' major cities, and were overrepresented in the nation's schools.

Education was a particular sore point. Laos had the highest illiteracy rate in Southeast Asia. The reading public was so small that a newspaper in the national language would not appear until 1941. Such statistics were not only embarrassing, they created hard feelings toward the Vietnamese who filled the few schools that existed. The Lycée Pavie was a case in point. It was the only bona fide secondary school in Vientiane, or in the entire nation for that matter. Most of the teachers were Vietnamese or French, and nearly all shared the prejudice that Vietnamese were inherently brighter than Lao. This prejudice was reflected in the favoritism shown Vietnamese students in classes and in graduation rates. Throughout the 1930s, Vietnamese made up 65 percent of all graduates at the Pavie school.[7] The Vietnamese did not bother to conceal their haughty contempt for the less upwardly mobile Lao. This contempt "was matched by the latter's impotent hatred" for the "industrious and formalistic" Vietnamese.[8]

Not only were resident Vietnamese the object of considerable resentment, the image of Vietnam as a militarily aggressive and imperialist nation was burned into the national consciousness.[9] Before the French arrived, Vietnam already occupied most of northeastern Laos and had absorbed nearly all of Cambodia. Vietnamese imperialism had been ruthless and brutal while it lasted, not in the least masked by a moralistic rationale like *La Mission Civilisatrice*; the object had been "simply and purely a process of colonial conquest for material gains."[10]

This rapacious imperialism created a legacy of hatred and suspicion of all Vietnamese. In the nineteenth century Cambodian leaders expressed this hatred directly with bloody pogroms against resident Vietnamese, declaring that butchering such hapless civilians brought Cambodians the greatest imaginable joy. Cambodian mothers portrayed the *Yuon* (a derogatory term used by the Cambodians for the Vietnamese) as bogeymen, warning children to stay away from the jungle lest they be gobbled up by one of these Vietnamese demons.[11] The pitch of anti-Vietnamese feeling in Laos was perhaps not quite so extreme; nevertheless it was widespread and deeply felt, and at times exploded into a savagery that put even the Cambodians to shame.

Given such rancor for their race, it was imperative for the Vietnamese communists to bring ethnic Lao into the Lao [sic] communist movement. Frustrated by the lack of progress, in 1936 Ho Chi Minh ordered his agents to adopt a new tactic. They were to play down their communism, abandon lectures on Marxist-Leninism, and link up with nationalist and anti-French movements in Laos—anything to get Laotians involved in the revolutionary struggle. Correct ideology and ultimate control of the revolution could be settled later.[12]

The difficulty with this strategy was the anemic state of Lao nationalism. Almost no one was agitating for political independence. Fortunately for the communists, the Japanese occupation of Indochina precipitated events that gave Lao nationalism an unexpected boost.

JAPANESE INVASION

The Japanese had good reason to be interested in Indochina. They had invaded China in 1937 with the expectation of speedily crushing the inept Chinese army and sweeping unopposed across the land from Manchuria to Guizhou. Despite the tank-led columns of Japanese soldiers that "darted almost at will across the yellow plains of northern China" and a Japanese air force that "ruled the skies," the Chinese stubbornly refused to give in. Chinese soldiers, nearly all of them ill-equipped, close to starvation, and poorly commanded, continued to fight in the face of casualties that mounted into the millions.[13] It occurred to the Japanese that the Chinese might give in more easily if the food and munitions that helped fuel the Chinese resistance would stop flowing from French Indochina. Also Japan had a need for such things, if only the price were right.

After Germany invaded France in May 1940, the French administration in Indochina could no longer count on the homeland for support. Georges Catroux, the governor-general, anxiously cabled the British and Americans, asking for help to hold off the Japanese. He received notice that he was on his own. It was hardly necessary for Catroux to check the wall map in his Hanoi office to realize the Japanese were at his doorstep. They already occupied Hainan, the huge island dominating the Gulf of Tonkin. On his own initiative Catroux suspended all trade with China to appease the Japanese. He acted too late.

Six thousand Japanese troops invaded northern Vietnam in September 1940. A few months later thousands more arrived in the south, entering Saigon on bicycles like schoolboys on vacation. Before they could work the kick stands down on their bikes, Catroux received an overseas communiqué informing him that he was to clean out his office for his replacement, Admiral Jean Decoux.[14]

The Japanese wanted to control Indochina cheaply, maintaining a skeleton crew of their own soldiers while letting the French do most of the hard administrative work. With this goal in mind, the Japanese presented the new governor-general with an offer he could not refuse: full autonomy for the French bureaucracy as long as Japan received favorable terms of trade for Indochinese rice, coffee, rubber, tin, coal, and zinc. The only bitter pill in the deal was the need to set aside a portion of the colony's revenue for the maintenance of Japanese troops in Indochina, which, like most expense accounts, ran over budget, averaging about 200 million piasters per year.

Desiring above all else to keep the colony intact throughout the war, Decoux agreed to the arrangement, marking time until French soldiers would arrive from Europe or North Africa to drive the Japanese out.[15] It was not all drumming fingers on a desk; there was the small matter of an invasion of Laos by Thai soldiers intent on annexing a portion of the Lao kingdom. Decoux still had thirteen thousand troops at his disposal, along with a small air force and navy, so he was able to do more than simply lodge a protest. What he couldn't pull off was a quick victory.

The fighting dragged on into the next year, until the Japanese tired of the spectacle and forced a truce. The enforced settlement ceded a slice of western Laos to Thailand, fifty-four thousand square kilometers that included parts of Sayaboury and Bassac provinces. Aiming at something even larger, Thailand flooded Laos with propaganda leaflets, reminding the Lao of their T'ai heritage linking them genetically and historically to the Thai people and of the great many ethnic Lao already living in Thailand—more than resided in Laos itself.

The propaganda prudently failed to mention the reason for this demographic oddity. In 1829, following years of armed conflict between the two nations, Thailand invaded Laos, leveled Vientiane, and burned to the ground all the major towns along the Mekong. To insure that Laos would no longer pose a military threat, Thailand transported the destitute population to the Thai side of the Mekong. The Thai built a new city, Nong Khai, directly across the river from the ashes of Vientiane, intended to take the place of Vientiane and keep the ethnic Lao on Thai soil. For decades after the event, more ethnic Lao resided in Thailand than in Laos, and their numbers continued to grow. By 1930 they equaled the number of Thai in Thailand. If Thailand absorbed Laos, the combined population of Lao in the fused state would outnumber the Thais.[16] For many Laotians it was something to ponder.

Reading the Thai propaganda as preparation for the full annexation of Laos after the war, Decoux set out to win the hearts of

Laotians by building new roads, constructing schools, and sending mobile medical teams into rural areas to care for peasants. To drive a wedge between Lao and Thai, he launched a National Renovation Movement, a cultural awareness program to generate greater respect for all things Laotian. Upper-class Lao were encouraged to leave their business suits at home and stroll the streets in native dress. The Laotian flag bearing the ancient emblem of a three-headed elephant was set flapping on every pole. Plays were presented in the Lao language, and playwrights encouraged to explore themes highlighting the traditional culture. Lao dancers strutted their stuff before appreciative audiences in Vientiane, Thakhek, Luang Prabang, and Savannakhet—anything and everything to elevate respect for the distinctive Lao culture and defuse the dangerous idea that the Lao and Thai were one people.[17]

As hoped, Lao chests swelled with national pride. Not part of the plan was a bumper crop of overly enthusiastic Lao patriots spreading dangerous ideas about an independent Laos. A number were unceremoniously jailed. The rest wisely sought sanctuary in Thailand, where they were happily recruited into the Lao Seri (Free Lao), a creation of the American OSS (Office of Strategic Services) dedicated to making life unpleasant for the Japanese by transforming gentle natives into fearsome commandos. To raise morale, the OSS preached anti-colonialism to its cadets, which, in the case of the Free Lao, only reinforced their resolve to form an independent Laos at the end of the war.

USING HMONG OPIUM

For some time the colony's revenues had been in decline. It started when the Japanese established undisputed mastery of the South China Sea, ending all sea traffic between Indochina and the West and bringing an end to the steady supply of opium from Turkey and Iran that sustained the colonial administration's extensive narcotics trade.

Opium had long been a lucrative source of revenue for the colonial administration. By 1902, taxes on opium sold in state-managed stores and opium dens added up to a whopping one-third of all government receipts.[18] For the next three decades revenue from opium sales helped mask the unprofitability of the colony, encouraging European investors to loan millions to de-velop Vietnam's physical infrastructure. Thousands of miles of railbeds were laid, harbors deepened, new ports created, and vast dike networks erected to encourage commerce in the colony. Wealthy Frenchmen invested in rice farms, rubber plantations, tex-tile factories, and mining. Rice exports more than doubled, rubber production jumped an incredible 3,000 percent, and coal exports nearly quadrupled, all to the benefit of the Douanes et Régies (Indochina Customs Office), which levied a tax on every export.[19]

While the administration no longer had to rely on opium rev-enues to pad its accounts, opium still remained a major cash cow. On the eve of the Second World War opium sales accounted for 15 percent of the Customs Office's revenues from all sources.[20] The war ended this easy profit. Japan's interdiction of shipping greatly reduced, then completely eliminated, the supply of sixty tons of opium imported annually from Turkey and Iran to main-tain the habits of an estimated 125,000 Indochinese addicts.[21]

For years the French had purchased opium from Hmong com-munities in northern Vietnam and Laos, but vacillated over encouraging more intensive cultivation because a great deal of Hmong opium entered the black market, robbing the government of a portion of its monopoly profits.[22] The war ended this indeci-siveness. Cut off from their overseas suppliers, the colonial administration had no choice but to turn to the Hmong to take up the slack. The only problem was that the Hmong had little incen-tive to grow more poppies.

The colonial administration procured domestic opium through the Opium Purchasing Board, which had purchasing agents in nearly every opium growing area in French Indochina. Few Hmong sold directly to the Board, however, for the amount offered by its agents varied with the opium's morphine content. This meant chemical tests had to be run, requiring a farmer to wait several weeks for a report on the chemical analysis of his opium before receiving payment. Hmong farmers were unwilling to wait, espe-cially as the Board did not advance even a token down payment to hold them over. Instead they sold their opium to private brokers, usually Vietnamese or Laotians who served as middlemen for the Board.

The private brokers drove hard bargains. Never sure of the morphine content of their purchases, they seldom paid farmers more than half of the Board's going rate. Hmong got a better deal by selling on the black market, but a vigorous campaign to crack down on illegal drug merchants, begun by the French in the early 1930s, had greatly constricted this outlet.

Cut off from the black market and faced with tightfisted private brokers, the average Hmong farmer could not count on opium to supply his family's economic needs. Most were subsistence farmers, planting corn and rice after the first spring rains, keeping a few pigs and chickens and maintaining a modest vegetable garden for needed herbs and spices. Opium planted with the spring corn was only a specialty crop for earning a little extra cash to pay taxes. To change this economic calculus, the Opium Purchasing Board would have to pay more for opium, raising its wholesale price.

This option was not agreeable to stinting colonial bureaucrats. Instead they appointed Touby LyFoung to a seat on the Opium Purchasing Board (a post he would hold for eight years), the first Hmong to ever occupy a position on this sanctum sanctorum of the French opium monopoly.[23] It was an event comparable to the appointment of Douglas Fraser, president of the United Auto Workers Union, to Chrysler's board of Directors in the early 1980s. Like Chrysler bleeding a river of red ink and hoping to co-opt Fraser and get wage concessions from the autoworkers, the Opium Purchasing Board urged Touby to devise a scheme that would have Hmong farmers growing more opium without receiving a higher price for their product.

Touby did not disappoint them. His strategy was to raise Hmong taxes from three to eight silver piasters, well beyond what most Hmong could pay, and allow payment in opium instead of silver.[24] To insure that Hmong farmers delivered their opium, Touby arranged for Hmong at the village and district level to be in charge of the tax collection and to be paid commissions on all opium delivered over minimum target figures.

It was a brilliant political move. In one stroke it created a spoils system for rewarding the political faithful and brought an end to the opium shortage that had played havoc with the Indochina Customs Office's balance sheet. Under the new tax, opium production expanded rapidly, and Hmong tax collectors, all loyal supporters of Touby's leadership, grew rich.[25]

The French administration rewarded Touby by establishing two public schools for Hmong children, one in Xieng Khouangville and the other at Nong Het. Symbolically, the schools meant that the Hmong had arrived. There were few schools of any kind in Laos, and none in the highlands, and those that did exist were attended by the children of wealthy Vietnamese merchants or the Lao political elite. The new schools were an unmistakable gesture by the French administration to accord the Hmong a significant role in the political future of Laos.

The increase in opium cultivation developed its own momentum. Hmong farmers began clearing new fields, not only to produce enough to meet their increased tax liability, but to make extra money. By 1943 the Opium Purchasing Board's annual collection, the lion's share from northeastern Laos, amounted to sixty tons, the exact amount needed to replace the lost opium imports from Turkey and Iran.[26]

Silver piasters from the Bank of Indochina flowed into Laos, some of it reaching Hmong farmers, but the greater part carried by private opium brokers into the general economy. The inflation rate, normally hovering at ground level, suddenly soared into the stratosphere. Necessary commodities were quickly priced beyond the reach of ordinary Lao, and many could no longer afford to feed themselves.[27]

Isolated from the commerce of the lowlands, the Hmong did not suffer such privations, though the influx of silver transformed their economy. With the Opium Purchasing Board buying up every kilogram of opium harvested, the Hmong ceased to view it as a specialty crop. By 1943 Hmong farmers were earning an average annual income of $470 from opium sales. If a farmer had a good harvest, he might become rich, at least by Hmong standards.[28] Thousands of Hmong farmers, helped by wives and children, began to devote several months each year to worrying legions of weeds from their opium fields, and another tedious month to tapping opium pods to collect precious sap.

A few enterprising Hmong looked beyond the drudgery of opium farming to glimpse the larger economic picture. Youa Tong Yang saw that the real profits from opium went to the middleman and not the farmer. He borrowed money from relatives and set himself up as an opium broker, competing with the Lao and Vietnamese who trudged up the mountain trails to collect the opium from the more accessible villages. Unlike his competition, Youa Tong knew the highlands. Back country villages offered a vast supply of the drug that the Lao and Vietnamese brokers never tapped. Even in head-to-head competition with his rivals, Youa Tong was at an advantage, for the farmers trusted him more than they did the lowlanders.

Youa Tong's business grew so rapidly that he was able to bring in his brother, Chou Teng, as a partner. Their collection route encompassed hundreds of Hmong communities from the Nam Ngum River all the way to the eastern edge of the Plain of Jars. There was so much opium in the mountains they had to use pack horses, two dozen at the peak of their business career, to haul it all out. By the end of each season Youa Tong's home was crammed from floor to rafters with burlap-wrapped bricks of raw opium.

Within a few years the Yang brothers were the wealthiest Hmong in Laos. They built lavish homes, at least for Hmong, and could afford the luxury of raising horses and cattle. They were the first Hmong to own an automobile, a hulking French army lorry. It was more a status symbol than useful transportation, for there were few serviceable roads in the highlands, and those that did exist were unusable during the rainy season. But the admiring crowds the lorry attracted while bouncing over a dusty trail in the dry season made it worth the price.[29]

Touby also grew rich from opium, primarily through kickbacks from tax collectors. He financed the construction of several western-style stone residences in the province and would eventually purchase two homes in Vientiane. In addition to amassing a personal fortune, Touby gained greater power and prestige over the Hmong, for he never ceased reminding Hmong farmers that they owed their rising affluence to his position on the Opium Purchasing Board. And because of his influence with the French, the Hmong had their own schools.

FRENCH COMMANDOS ARRIVE

In August of 1944, the Allies liberated Paris from the Germans and installed a new government with Charles de Gaulle as president.[30] There was much to do. The Germans had sucked the marrow from the economy. Industry languished for lack of raw materials, and the printing of money had so cheapened the nation's currency that people were forced to barter on the enormous black market begun during the German occupation, crowding out normal trade.[31] But instead of tackling these problems, which would plague France for another decade, de Gaulle concentrated on restoring the nation's self-confidence and sense of national greatness that had been shattered by the German occupation. His prescription called for French military victories in Europe and the reclamation of France's colonies. After raising an army to participate in the Allied invasion of Germany, de Gaulle turned his attention to Indochina.

De Gaulle had earlier sent Colonel Boucher de Crèvecoeur, a veteran commander of Indochinese forces, to work in India with the SOE (Special Operations Executive), Britain's special office for unconventional warfare. With SOE assistance, Crèvecoeur's job was to develop a master plan for the introduction of French troops into Indochina to reclaim the colony from the Japanese. The plan was this: with SOE providing the training and logistics, and Crèvecoeur supplying the manpower from volunteer French soldiers, SOE-trained French commandos were to be inserted into northeastern Laos on the Plain of Jars and into southern Laos on the panhandle. Once in place, they were to begin guerrilla operations against the Japanese.[32]

The commandos would have two additional responsibilities: to deploy the tons of weapons and supplies soon to be dropped onto the Plain of Jars to various storage spots in Laos, Vietnam, and Cambodia; and to organize labor gangs from the native population to construct airfields. On the drawing board was a plan to use a twelve-hundred-man force of Free French, to be assembled and trained in North Africa, for an airborne assault against the Japanese throughout Indochina.

In November 1944, de Gaulle gave his approval for Crèvecoeur to begin inserting commandos into Laos. Crèvecoeur was ready to move, but worried about native support. It was crucial to the success of the operation that the commandos receive help from the montagnards, especially from Khmu tribesmen in the panhandle and from Hmong living near the Plain of Jars. Since within recent memory colonial troops had brutally suppressed a Khmu rebellion, there was little hope of enthusiastic support from the Khmu. But it was imagined that at least the Hmong would be sympathetic to the French cause and rise up against the Japanese.

Actually the Hmong had mixed feelings about the Japanese. Shiowa, a Japanese trading company with offices in Luang Prabang and Thakhek, regularly sent agents to Xieng Khouang Province to purchase Hmong opium. The transactions drove up local prices, which greatly pleased Hmong farmers. Even Touby was making a handsome profit, using his brother Tougeu as a business partner to serve as a middleman between Hmong farmers and Shiowa's agents.

A second Japanese firm had a more permanent presence, though a less salutary effect on the population. It operated the Pa Heo silver mine at the base of the Phu Bia massif. Since the Pa Heo mine was unsafe, it was difficult to attract workers. Japanese soldiers impressed hundreds of Hmong from local villages and put them to work in the mine as slave labor. The Hmong worked in the shafts for twelve to thirteen hours a day, taking their meals inside the mine, and sleeping in the shafts to insure they would be around for the next shift. The Japanese failed to make needed structural repairs and a main shaft collapsed, killing two hundred. The Japanese rounded up more Hmong to replace the dead. There were more cave-ins and more casualties. This time Japanese patrols had difficulty finding replacements. Villagers for miles around had abandoned their homes to avoid impressment, and relocated to the highlands of the Phu Bia massif.[33]

Touby likely fumed at the callous treatment of the Hmong working in the mine, yet he was too shrewd to risk military action against so powerful an adversary as the Japanese, at least without the French military as a backup.[34] Things changed on December 22, 1944, when two American B-24 bombers, piloted by British officers, took off at dusk from an airfield in India to airdrop the first French commandos into Laos. The commandos made their jumps in the dead of night, one group descending onto the Plain of Jars, the other onto the Laotian panhandle. Over the next two months eight more groups of British-trained French commandos parachuted into Laos, again landing in the panhandle and on the Plain of Jars.

To this point the Japanese had maintained only a skeleton military presence in the country. Troop movements were of modest-size units delivering supplies and ammunition to outlying posts. With the arrival of the French commandos, the Japanese strengthened their military position in Laos, financing the buildup with the sale of a truckload of Hmong opium confiscated from Chinese drug merchants. A full garrison sprang up in the Laotian panhandle in January 1945. A month later a second Japanese garrison was in place on the outskirts of Xieng Khouangville. Traffic picked up on Route 72, the main road between Nong Het and Xieng Khouangville, as Japanese trucks delivered troops to comb the countryside for French commandos and keep watch on the activities of the Hmong.[35]

The commandos operating out of the Plain of Jars were not hard to find. They had moved into a vacant stone house just off Colonial Route 7 as it enters the plain. The vacation home was the property of General Philippe Leclerc, commander of an armored division of the Expeditionary Corps.[36] As the only European-style dwelling in the area, activity at the house naturally attracted attention. Within a few days, French officers with the local Garde Indigène arrived to welcome the commandos. Not wanting his next guests to be Japanese, Captain Serres, the leader of the commando team, decided it was time to abandon the comfort of the general's vacation home for the anonymity of the bush.

One of the visitors at Leclerc's house had been Doussineau, commander (sub-inspector) of the French military post at Nong Het. Having served at the post for ten years, Doussineau knew nearly everyone worth knowing in the area. He was also on good terms with the Hmong, which was of great interest to Maurice Gauthier, the commando team's intelligence officer. Gauthier asked Doussineau if they could count on support from the montagnards. Doussineau was confident the Hmong would help, and advised Gauthier to make contact with their leader, Touby LyFoung.

Toward the end of February, Gauthier left the bush to seek Touby out at Nong Het. Not knowing the way, he stopped off at Ban Ban to recruit a salty ex-legionnaire named Tisserand as a guide. Tisserand was not eager to volunteer. Gauthier produced a revolver to remind him of his patriotic duty. Tisserand delivered Gauthier to Nong Het and introduced him to Touby. Barely five feet tall, Touby was accustomed to Frenchmen towering over him, but Gauthier was as short as a Hmong. This put Touby at ease. He listened to Gauthier tell of additional French troops that would soon arrive to launch a major campaign against the Japanese. Touby considered this good news. With the French military back in the game, he was eager to offer his full support. He told Gauthier, "I'm with you."

Never once during the meeting did Touby mention money, for he was anxious to avoid the impression that he was a mercenary with an army for hire. The effort did not escape Gauthier's attention, though the intelligence officer did not delude himself that the Hmong chieftain was willing to risk the lives of his people simply out of love for France. He supposed Touby was maneuvering for political advantage, seeing "an opportunity of gaining better positions for his people, politically."[37] Gauthier was right. What Touby needed more than money was France's goodwill, which could be leveraged later for money and for land, but most of all for increased local self-governance, and eventually representation at the national level in Vientiane where the Lao totally dominated politics.

The political reforms following Pa Chay's rebellion had greatly increased Hmong representation in the provinces, greater than any other ethnic minority in Laos. Yet there were still places where Hmong did not have their own nai bans or tassengs. And all higher offices were denied the Hmong. Not since LoBliayao's brief stint as nai kong had a Hmong filled that post. There were no Hmong chao muongs, and it was almost beyond imagining to conceive of a Hmong in the position of chao khoueng.

Touby had sufficient confidence in his own political skills to imagine that if all of these offices were opened to Hmong, they would be filled by individuals loyal to him. Since many of these posts came with salaries, Vientiane would be helping to defray the costs of rewarding his supporters. Also, there was enormous profit to be made from taxes. The tassengs were the principal tax collectors, receiving a ten-percent commission on the gross. Most skimmed from the top, a practice so widespread that it was more expected than condemned. This plunder could become a lucrative source of funds with which to underwrite a robust political organization, all under Touby's control. Exercising control over so many posts would gain Touby more power than he could ever achieve through the informal—and highly volatile—channels of clan politics, for it would bear the imprimatur of the state, a source of legitimacy that transcended tribe and clan. Only with this kind of authority could a Hmong politician hope to rise above divisive tribal and clan loyalties and speak for the Hmong as a people.

Touby's larger ambition was for Hmong representation in national politics to shake loose state money to build and staff additional schools for Hmong children, so they could compete on an equal footing with the Lao for the better jobs and occupy positions of responsibility in the national civil service. Funds might also be available for hospitals and health care for hundreds of Hmong who died needlessly of maladies easily cured with modern medicine. Equally important would be the creation of roads and a communications infrastructure in the highlands, which would help in integrating the Hmong into the national economy.

National representation might even alter the balance of power. The montagnards outnumbered the ethnic Lao, yet lacked the political machinery to make their voices heard. If the montagnards were unified under one political banner, a party of the highlands, not only the Hmong but the Khmu, Yao, highland T'ai, and all the other montagnards would be in a better position to demand fair treatment and a role in the life of the nation. Touby knew the Lao elite would never tolerate any of this unless it was forced on them by the colonial administration, which was why getting into the good graces of the French was so critical.

During the meeting Touby asked what the commandos needed from the Hmong. Gauthier had a long list. His team possessed two B-2 radios, ponderous battery-powered contraptions that had to be disassembled and carried on the backs of two men to be moved even a short distance. The radios' only purpose was to receive and send Morse code over long distances. This enabled the commandos to receive orders and send information to Crèvecoeur and the British SOE in India, but the radios were useless for local communication. Lacking normal field radios, couriers were needed to deliver messages between commandos. The commandos also required guides, interpreters, porters to carry and stash tons of material airdropped onto the plain, and scores of men willing to serve as guerrilla fighters against the Japanese. As an intelligence officer, Gauthier was also keen on getting help to collect information on Japanese troop movements.

Touby promised to find volunteers for all of these chores. As for gathering information, this turned out to be relatively easy. With the rapid buildup of Japanese troops in the province, Japanese officers were busy requisitioning food and supplies to provision their soldiers. Touby simply made himself available to the Japanese to help facilitate the process. Soon he was working hand in glove with Japanese officers, making the rounds of Hmong villages to commandeer rice, corn, and livestock to feed Japanese soldiers and Hmong ponies to serve as mounts for Japanese officers. The work kept him informed of the enemy's troop strength and the location of Japanese forces.

While Touby gathered intelligence, the commandos organized Hmong volunteers into work gangs to clear drop sites for supplies being airlifted to the Plain of Jars from India. Serres assigned his second in command, Captain René Bichelot, the task of organizing Hmong into a guerrilla force to harass the Japanese. Bichelot headquartered the guerrilla operation in the highlands of the Phu San mountains north of Route 7. Touby had recommended the site; the Hmong who lived on Phu San's ridges were loyal to him.

With French commandos prowling the jungles of the panhandle, and Allied planes making regular drops of supplies on the Plain of Jars, the Japanese began to suspect something big was afoot. When American planes bombed rail yards in northern Vietnam, they were sure of it. Though the bombing was unrelated to France's planned "big push," the Japanese were convinced that an Allied invasion was imminent, and that Governor-General Decoux and his colonial forces were simply waiting for the Allies to arrive to rise up and stab them in the back. The formerly cordial relations between the Japanese and the French colonial administration quickly soured. In early March 1945 the Japanese made a preemptive strike and assumed complete control of the civil and military administration of Laos, as well as Vietnam and Cambodia.

The larger cities were the first to come under the Japanese heel. Scores of Frenchmen in the colonial bureaucracy, or serving as officers in the Garde Indigène at Vientiane, Luang Prabang, Thakhek, and Savannakhet, fled to the jungle to avoid imprisonment. After taking command of the major towns, the Japanese fanned out into the countryside to gather up these fugitives.

French commandos kept abreast of the unfolding events through their intelligence network. Serres rushed a Hmong courier to Nong Het to warn Doussineau that a Japanese patrol was on its way to place him under arrest. The Frenchman collected all of the post's arms and supplies and delivered them to Touby for safekeeping. He then departed on horseback with Touby's brother, Tougeu, to alert Hmong villages throughout the region to the Japanese coup de force and to prepare them for military action. A few days later a Hmong guerrilla unit blew up the Nam Hin dam, temporarily halting all traffic entering Laos along Route 7. It took the Japanese only a day to repair the damage, but Touby's Hmong had struck their first blow against the Japanese and there was no turning back.

Believing the blown dam to be the work of Doussineau, the Japanese sent patrols into the hills to ferret him out. He was actually nearby, hiding in a Hmong village only a few miles from Nong Het. Having decided it was too dangerous for the Frenchman to remain in the area, Touby led him into the mountains and hid him in a grotto. Touby should have remained with Doussineau in the grotto, for the Japanese were certain he was shielding the Frenchman and knew the location of the missing arms. Spies posing as mineralogists with the Japanese Mineralogical Mission and as business agents for the Shiowa trading company had been gathering information on Hmong notables in the region for some time. Touby's cooperation in requisitioning supplies for Japanese troops had fooled no one. His allegiance to the French was well-documented.

A heavily armed Japanese patrol found Touby at Na Kong and hauled him away to Nong Het. It was a fortunate coincidence for Touby that Jean-Henri Mazoyer, the Bishop of Vientiane, was on an inspection tour of the Church's Nong Het mission when the Japanese arrived looking for Doussineau. Finding only Mazoyer, the soldiers placed the bishop under house arrest and confined him to the mission. Three weeks later Mazoyer witnessed Touby's return to the town under heavy guard. The Bishop prudently held back as the Japanese methodically interrogated Touby. After several days of torture, Touby admitted to receiving weapons from the French. When Mazoyer learned Touby was to be executed, he could hold back no longer. The bishop had spent the better part of ten years proselytizing to the montagnards, and had a special interest in Touby because of his influence with the Hmong. Mazoyer warned the Japanese commander that if Touby were killed, the Japanese could expect a general Hmong uprising. "Your position would quickly become untenable," he advised. "Even the French would no longer be safe in the area."[38] Though it was all bluff, the Japanese let Touby go.

Lucky to be alive, Touby put space between himself and the Japanese and linked up with the French commandos. Serres welcomed him with open arms. With more Japanese troops crossing daily into Laos from Vietnam, Serres desperately needed a substantial force of native guerrillas to augment his own tiny commando unit. Touby rounded up more volunteers for an expanded Hmong maquis and Serres provisioned them with modern weapons and explosives drawn from a stockpile that had grown beyond anything Serres had expected. The overabundance of arms and munitions was the result of a logistics error.

Months earlier, French engineers in Laos' Public Works Department, along with officers in the colonial military, had organized a clandestine resistance force, the *Service d'Action*. Led by a French officer named Mayer, the group acquired a long-range radio and made contact with Crèvecoeur and the SOE in India. Mayer asked for weapons and supplies, enough to outfit scores of citizen militias in central and southern Vietnam. He already had volunteers to pack the stuff out and deliver it to Vietnam. The SOE agreed to the plan, and eventually airdropped more than ninety tons of equipment onto the Plain of Jars.[39]

The airdrops were ill-timed. The crates descended from the sky just as the Japanese were increasing their presence on the plain. With enemy patrols everywhere, Mayer's resistance group had no hope of moving more than a fraction of the equipment to Vietnam. By default, the lion's share of the supplies and munitions became the property of Serres' commandos, who passed it on to the Hmong.

Armed with the new weapons, though not yet having fired them, a party of Hmong guerrillas went after a Japanese truck convoy moving down Route 7. Gauthier and two other French commandos went along as advisers. When the twelve-truck convoy loomed into view, the Frenchmen opened up on the lead vehicle with their submachine guns on full automatic. The Hmong turned tail and ran. They had never experienced automatic weapons fire. The din and clatter totally unnerved them.

Shortly after this incident Serres received information that two Japanese regiments were on their way from Vietnam to occupy Xieng Khouang Province. No doubt with considerable misgivings, Serres sent the gun-shy Hmong to intercept the Japanese, with orders to inflict maximum damage. To their credit the Hmong offered stiff resistance, slowing the enemy's advance.

The two Japanese regiments were only the beginning of a flood of Japanese reinforcements. Almost daily, truck convoys appeared on Route 7, carrying troops and supplies to the Plain of Jars, Luang Prabang, Vientiane, Paksane, Thakhek, and Savannakhet. Hmong guerrillas repeatedly blew up the Ban Ban bridge to slow down the traffic, but Japanese engineers and construction crews were always on hand to repair the structure.[40]

Once the buildup of enemy troops reached a critical mass, resistance efforts became futile. Mayer's Service d'Action had been conducting operations in Vientiane and Luang Prabang Province, with occasional forays onto the Plain of Jars. The group now disbanded, the French officers and civil servants melting into the highland forest to wait out the rest of the war and hopefully avoid capture. A much larger and more loosely organized resistance group of several thousand Lao, led by former Garde Indigène French officers, had concentrated its efforts in the panhandle with even greater success. This group also disbanded. Most hid in the jungle, though nearly a thousand Lao volunteers headed north with one of their officers, J. Parisot, and eventually reached Yunnan in China. The French would later describe the march as heroic and reward the Lao who made the march with rapid advancement in the Laotian army, where they became the nucleus of the nation's officer corps.[41]

The commandos on the Plain of Jars were also out of business. Serres had already been recalled to India, leaving Bichelot in command. With the Plain of Jars crawling with Japanese, Bichelot received orders from India to shut down the entire operation. The commandos were to divide up with some moving south while others went to northern Vietnam to gather intelligence. Only Bichelot and Gauthier stayed behind in Xieng Khouang to maintain contact with the Hmong and monitor Japanese activity in the province.

Now that guerrilla action proper was at an end, Touby dedicated himself to helping Bichelot, Gauthier, and the rest of the Frenchmen in hiding to stay alive until the Allies liberated Indochina. Hmong took wounded French soldiers into their homes and cared for them. Touby's guerrillas relocated Frenchmen to mountain grottoes. This was a great morale booster, for the Japanese dealt brutally with prisoners, piercing their noses at the base and attaching lead strings so they could be dragged about like livestock. The Japanese hitched some to plows so they could be worked like water buffalo in rice paddies.[42] Because of Touby's relief network, scores of Frenchmen eluded capture and were spared this fate.[43]

3

THE FRENCH RETURN

BRIEF INDEPENDENCE

Giving the Indochinese national independence had long been on Tokyo's agenda. Of course, it was to be only a paper liberation, with Vietnam, Laos, and Cambodia integrated into the Japanese empire under the umbrella of the Greater East Asia Co-Prosperity Sphere, slipping from the grasp of French colonialism into the tight fist of Japanese imperialism. The Japanese even imagined there might be some cheering in the streets. Exploitation of Asians by Asians was presumed less demeaning than subjugation by racist Europeans. But now, with the Allies closing in on Japan's home islands, pushing for independence seemed pointless. The Japanese high command of Indochina decided to free the natives anyway, if only to give the French headaches once they returned in force to reclaim the colony. Matters proceeded smoothly in Vietnam and Cambodia, but in Laos King Sisavang Vong, a steadfast Francophile, balked at the idea of severing all links to France. However, once the Japanese abducted Savang, the king's thirty-eight year-old son (the next in line for the throne) and removed him to Saigon, King Sisavang gave in.

The Japanese canvassed the Lao elite for a man to serve as prime minister of the newly liberated state. The natural candidate was Prince Phetsarath. Next to the king, he was the most respected figure in Laos. Bright and able, he had studied in France, spent a year at Oxford, published a book, and was a skillful bureaucrat. Since 1941 Phetsarath had served as the viceroy of Laos, functioning as the king's direct representative to the people.[1]

The Japanese assured Phetsarath he would be given a free hand in governing an independent Laos. Taking them at their word, Phetsarath set out to reform the civil service. For decades the French had used Vietnamese to fill administrative posts, until Vietnamese dominated the public works, post office, customs, telegraph service, and even the national police.[2] Having long detested this situation, Phetsarath tried to sweep the Vietnamese out of office and replace them with ethnic Lao. The majority of the Vietnamese bureaucrats obstinately refused to vacate their posts, effectively bringing the entire civil service to a standstill. Phetsarath continued to press the issue. It was a dangerous move. The Vietnamese were the majority in the large towns. Riots broke out. Vietnamese mobs roamed city streets and, in Vientiane, occupied government buildings. The new government was paralyzed. Phetsarath appealed to the Japanese for relief. They declined to become involved. As the war was effectively over, their only thought was preparation for surrender.

The French moved quickly to fill this power vacuum. In August 1945, Hans Imfeld, a French artillery officer enjoying Hmong protection, emerged from his hiding place to lead a small force of Touby's guerrillas west to occupy the old royal capital of Luang Prabang. Most of the city's population had already been evacuated by the Japanese. Only the royal family, and a few stragglers shooting anxious glances at the Mekong as they built canoes, had remained behind. Imfeld found king Sisavang Vong in an agitated state. There was a rumor afloat that thousands of Chinese soldiers were about to close in to occupy the capital. Once before, in the 1880s, Chinese soldiers turned bandit had swarmed over the city, pillaging and plundering and otherwise thoroughly terrorizing the population. Imfeld now understood the sudden rush to make canoes.[3]

The cause of the rumor was the decision by the Allies to assign China the task of disarming all Japanese troops in Indochina north of the sixteenth parallel; the British were to be responsible for Japanese troops south of the sixteenth. As Japan had spent the better part of seven years devastating China and butchering its population, Japanese soldiers in upper Laos and northern Vietnam began a hurried march to territory below the sixteenth parallel so they could surrender to the British.

The Japanese need not have rushed. Since China was presently consumed by civil war, and the armies of Mao Zedong and Chiang Kai-shek entangled in a race to take "physical possession of the body of China," several more months would pass before the first Chinese troops would begin to straggle across the border to carry out the Allies' mandate.[4] Sisavang could know none of this, of course. Playing on the king's fear of pestilent Chinese storming the capital, Imfeld offered France's pledge to defend Luang Prabang from marauding Kuomintang, if Sisavang would renounce Laos' independence and accept France's authority over his kingdom. A much relieved Sisavang gratefully agreed.[5]

When word of Sisavang's renunciation of independence reached former members of the OSS-trained Lao Seri, they indignantly formed their own government in Savannakhet, the largest Laotian town close to their former OSS base camp across the Mekong in Thailand. They were joined shortly by Prince Souphanouvong, serving as an agent of the Indochinese Communist Party (ICP) and accompanied by fifty Vietnamese bodyguards.

It was a bit of a surprise he had shown up. Souphanouvong was something of a loner, and in the past had deliberately shunned politics. Though born into a royal family as the youngest son of Prince Boun Khong, Souphanouvong was politically handicapped by the fact that his mother was a minor wife, a concubine from peasant stock. Early on Souphanouvong realized that Phetsarath and Souvanna Phouma, his older and more legitimate half-brothers, would always be given preference over him in politics. So he lowered his sights and settled on a career in civil engineering. Souphanouvong left Laos for school in Hanoi and later enrolled in France's Ecole des Ponts et Chaussées to learn how to build dams and bridges, staying on for an extra year for postgraduate work on the port structures at Bordeaux and Le Havre.

Instead of returning to Laos, Souphanouvong found a civil engineering job with the colonial administration in Vietnam, working at the machine shop near Vinh for the Trans-Indochinese Railway. The experience embittered him toward the French. The railroad paid his French co-workers, some with an education far inferior to his own, a great deal more than they paid him. He socialized little with the French and spent most of his time with Vietnamese. In time he began to prefer Vietnamese not only to the French but to Laotians. He eventually married a Vietnamese woman, Le Thi Ky Nam, an ardent disciple of Ho Chi Minh's who had once served as Ho's secretary. Shortly after his marriage, Souphanouvong joined the Indochinese Communist Party (ICP).[6]

At Savannakhet, Souphanouvong played the role of communist agent superbly. Drawing on the prestige of his older brother Prince Phetsarath, he got himself appointed president of the new government. His first official act was to establish a liberation army. To supply it with troops, he signed an agreement with the Vietnamese communists allowing Viet Minh soldiers to operate in Laos. The Vietnamese communists now had a front legitimizing their military presence in the country.

Further north at Vientiane, Phetsarath formed a second government, the Lao Issara (Free Laos). He drew up a constitution, selected members for a provisional assembly, and formed a cabinet. Phetsarath selected Souphanouvong's older brother, Souvanna Phouma, as minister of public works. An engineer by education, Souvanna had risen through the bureaucracy of Laos' Public Works Service to become its chief administrator. He would eventually be a leading player in Laotian politics, but at this early date he was viewed more as a technocrat than a politician.[7]

Anxious to cover all bases, Souphanouvong dashed to Vientiane to secure a position in the second independent government. Unlike Souvanna Phouma, he would not settle for a mere technical post and demanded something with political clout. Phetsarath made him the Lao Issara's first foreign minister.

FRENCH REINFORCEMENTS

While the Lao elite spawned new governments, the Vietnamese in the larger cities took up arms. Unlike the earlier riots, this was not a spontaneous uprising. Ho Chi Minh's agents had been sent ahead to stir them up so they would offer armed resistance to the French once they returned in force. Communist agents also made contact with the Vietnamese in the valleys and border region of Xieng Khouang Province, urging them to agitate for secession as a prelude to a north Vietnamese anschluss of the entire province. To allay fears of French reprisals, the agents promised villagers support from Viet Minh battalions that would soon assemble on the border and be ready to move.

By now French armored units were already disembarking from ships in Saigon's harbor. Other units followed, until the French had assembled an army of forty thousand. The main force remained in Vietnam, where fighting was expected to be stiff. The rest, approximately three thousand, headed for Laos and Cambodia. The detachment destined for Laos reached the panhandle in early March 1946.

Boucher de Crèvecoeur was there to greet them. Three months earlier he had left his desk at the SOE planning offices in Calcutta to get in on the action. It meant a promotion. Leclerc, the general whose vacation home Crèvecoeur's commandos had appropriated after parachuting onto the Plain of Jars, elevated him to commander of all French forces in Laos. For this honor Crèvecoeur was to assemble all commandos and partisans and clear the way for the French reoccupation army. Crèvecoeur gathered up two thousand men, arranged into four light infantry battalions, and roamed the panhandle, sending the Lao resistance in the smaller towns scurrying for cover. By the time he linked up with the French detachment from Vietnam, only two pockets of southern resistance remained: Savannakhet and Thakhek.

Moving as one army, the two French forces swarmed over Savannakhet, defended by OSS-trained commandos fighting under the Free Lao flag and by Vietnamese civilians carrying antique weapons. It was a few hundred loosely organized insurgents facing thousands of well-armed professional troops. After the first volley of gunfire, the resisters broke and ran. The easy victory buoyed the confidence of the reoccupation army. It was on to Thakhek.

There waiting for them was Souphanouvong. With the help of Viet Minh agents, he had organized Thakhek's Vietnamese residents into a scrubby militia. Souphanouvong expected the conflict to be fierce, but what occurred was beyond his imagining. French pilots flying British Spitfires suddenly appeared. Their bombs ripped apart the crowded marketplace, killing scores of people and wounding hundreds. French troops broke through the militia's perimeter and raged through the town. Buildings burned and people lay dying on the street. Soon the whole city was in flames. When the Vietnamese tried to escape, Crèvecoeur's Laotian volunteers went after them. For several hours they massacred the Vietnamese, killing more than a thousand.[8] As one French officer on the scene would later remark, it was "a savage demonstration of Lao hatred for the Vietnamese."

Souphanouvong eluded the Lao volunteers and made it to the river, where he scrambled onto an overloaded pirogue just launching for the Thai side of the Mekong. A Spitfire swooped over the town toward the river. The plane skimmed the water, strafing everything afloat. Bullets ripped into the long canoe, killing seven of the twenty-five on board and wounding twelve others. Souphanouvong caught a round in the chest, "within only a finger's breadth of his heart." He was clinging half-conscious to the sinking pirogue, gasping from a punctured lung, when three survivors hauled him to shore. With the help of some friendly Thais, Souphanouvong reached a hospital in time to for doctors to save his life.[9]

With Thakhek reduced to smoldering rubble, the French pushed on for Luang Prabang. The Royal capital fell to them without a struggle. Vientiane was the next to fall. On April 24, 1946, a full battalion parachuted onto the outskirts of city. As the soldiers assembled to march on the nation's administrative capital, the leaders of the fledgling Lao Issara government blew up the radio station, set administration buildings on fire, and smashed machinery in the city's tiny electrical plant. In a final act of resistance before fleeing for Thailand, they lobbed mortar shells toward the French troops advancing on the city.

For all practical purposes the reoccupation of Laos was a fait accompli. All that remained was to clean up pockets of resistance.

RETAKING XIENG KHOUANG

Stirred by Ho's agents and galvanized by the news that Ho had proclaimed Vietnam an independent state, Xieng Khouang's Vietnamese residents formed militias, flew banners, and announced their intention to hive the province off from Laos and deliver it to Ho's new Democratic Republic of Vietnam. The French were confident their battalions could easily brush aside these poorly armed militias, as they had at Savannakhet and Thakhek. Their only worry was the Viet Minh massing on the border. To keep track of them, the French turned to Touby.

Touby used his residence at Nong Het as the center for the intelligence-gathering operation. Hmong delivered reports to the house and Touby relayed the information to Crèvecoeur's headquarters over a radio operated by a French volunteer. Gauthier was at the house as a liaison officer. He had remained with the Hmong since the breakup of his commando unit. So had Bichelot, who was at Xieng Khouangville.

Out of habit as an intelligence officer, Gauthier had made himself familiar with the comings and goings of Nong Het. He was particularly interested in the town's Chinese merchants. He was certain they were selling information to the communists and that by now the Viet Minh knew what was going on at Touby's residence. Gauthier expected an attack at any time. At his insistence, every evening the post's staff left to sleep on a hill overlooking the house.

Early one morning before dawn, the intelligence team was awakened by gunfire below. Hmong guerrillas nearby also heard the shooting and joined them. The guerrillas moved cautiously down the hill. At first light they spotted the Vietnamese in the shadows, nearly a hundred of them surrounding Touby's house, all well-armed, some with machine guns. The guerrillas encircled the ambushers and initiated their own ambush. The fighting lasted until noon, when the final machine gun was silenced. Among the dead were Japanese soldiers, some of the several hundred Japanese troops who had turned mercenary rather than surrender to the Allies.

The fighting wasn't over. Several other Viet Minh units had also moved on Xieng Khouangville. Bichelot was there with the ex-legionnaire Tisserand, facing the Vietnamese alone without the help of Hmong volunteers. The two Frenchmen climbed into an ancient car that ran on rice whiskey and fled north into the hills. After a few miles they ran into a Japanese patrol. Machine gun fire swept over the vehicle. A bullet struck Bichelot in the back. Tisserand took the wheel and sped away, squeezing everything that was left out of the old car. By the time Tisserand reached a Hmong village, Bichelot had passed out and was in shock.

Gauthier and Touby were soon at Bichelot's side. Gauthier was relieved to see that Bichelot would survive. The downside was that he would be laid up for weeks recovering. Hundreds of Viet Minh were pouring into the province. Xieng Khouangville was already an occupied city and the communists were busy setting up a field headquarters nearby at Lat Boua. Though Gauthier felt it was urgent to hit the communists soon or lose credibility with the Hmong, he was reticent to act on his own. When early December rolled around and Bichelot was still bedridden, Gauthier could hold off no longer. He authorized an assault on Lat Boua. He might have selected a less well-defended target. The communists had ringed the base with an extensive trench network. Once well into the attack, Touby realized his guerrillas had no chance of breaking through. He pulled them back and retreated into the hills. His only consolation was that the Viet Minh suffered heavy casualties defending the base.

Bichelot continued to heal slowly; it would be another month before he would be able to stand unaided. This left Gauthier still in charge. He was under pressure from Touby and Sai Kham, the provincial governor, to liberate Xieng Khouangville. Militarily, the city was of little importance, but because it was the provincial capital it had great symbolic significance. The odds that the Hmong could dislodge the communists were slim. Gauthier presumed Touby could assemble no more than a few hundred Hmong for the assault, barely equaling the number of communists at Xieng Khouangville. He doubted that a ragtag guerrilla force of unruly Hmong was a match for highly disciplined Viet Minh soldiers. His misgivings led him to temporize, using Bichelot's slow recovery as an excuse for inaction. Touby continued to pressure him for action. At the end of December, Gauthier finally gave in and told Touby to collect his Hmong.

Instead of the few hundred guerrillas Gauthier had expected, Touby mustered more than three thousand. The attack began in the dark just before dawn. Ten Hmong clad in black sneaked into the Buddhist temple atop a rise overlooking the city. Viet Minh soldiers were on the temple roof, manning two machine guns and a mortar. The Hmong caught the soldiers by surprise and killed them silently with knives. A few hours later, just after sunrise, Touby's three thousand Hmong, carrying mostly old war surplus

French carbines, assaulted the city from all sides. Enemy troops stirred and rushed to mount a defense, only to be cut down by the captured machine guns on the temple roof. Over the next two hours the Hmong tightened their circle around the city. Hmong finally closed and engaged the Viet Minh in hand-to-hand fighting, breaking the enemy's will.

A month after this stunning victory Touby was back in Xieng Khouangville to receive official recognition for his contribution to the operation. Gauthier was there to do the honors, recently returned from Saigon with a box full of medals. Dressed in a Western business suit, Touby stood proudly as Gauthier presented him the French Legion of Honor. Then it was the turn of the clan leaders who had participated in the battle. Attired in the traditional Hmong ceremonial dress of pantaloons, brightly embroidered blouses, and ornate silver necklaces covering the chest from neck to sternum, each stepped forward in turn to receive the *Croix de Guerre*.

It was also a proud day for Gauthier. He had lived and worked with the Hmong for more than a year. He could not help but admire them, despite their utter lack of military discipline. Gauthier had become sympathetic to their cause, for a professional soldier a sure sign that he had gone native. He began to make promises he had no authority to keep: schools for Hmong children, hospitals for the sick, increased self-rule at the local level and representation in the national administration.[10] This of course was everything Touby wanted and only reinforced his resolve to help the French reestablish their rule in Laos.

Touby's guerrillas continued to harass the Viet Minh until March 1946, when regular French forces arrived to take command of the province. The guerrilla action had significantly checked Viet Minh efforts to establish an entrenched presence that might have tied down French forces for months. Facing little opposition, French troops hounded Xieng Khouang's Vietnamese residents. They stormed Khang Khay, the largest all-Vietnamese town in the province, then swooped south and drove thousands of Vietnamese farmers off the Plain of Jars. From the plain French units moved east toward the border, razing Vietnamese villages and herding their residents across the border into Vietnam.

The Vietnamese had occupied a special niche in the province. Many were prosperous merchants and artisans, the backbone of what passed for the middle class at Xieng Khouangville, where Vietnamese were more than 70 percent of the population. Other Vietnamese were successful farmers, working some of the best farmland in the province: thousands of acres of prime wet rice paddies on the southeastern edge of the Plain of Jars and in the lush Moung Ngan valley southeast of the plain, farmland that put to shame the scruffy dry rice plots Hmong farmers scratched out of the tired soil of the mountain slopes. These farms were now vacant and up for grabs. Touby wanted the acreage as spoils for clan chieftains loyal to him and for Hmong who had volunteered to fight the Viet Minh. The French would give him not only the land but also a substantial cash grant.

The ethnic-cleansing campaign in Xieng Khouang was not an isolated phenomenon. In southern Laos, and in Vientiane and Luang Prabang provinces, French soldiers harried Vietnamese out of the country. Few Vietnamese were left in Laos after this massive pogrom. Those who did remain were branded as fifth columnists, harassed by the police, ostracized from polite society, and effectively barred from normal trade. Within a few years nearly all of them would abandon Laos for Thailand or Vietnam.[11]

The Vietnamese exodus dealt a fatal blow to the ICP-sponsored communist movement in the lowlands, whose members had nearly all been Vietnamese. With the Vietnamese gone, and the lowland Lao singularly indifferent to communist propaganda, the ICP had no choice but to move the entire operation into the highlands and preach communism to the montagnards. The decision set communism in Laos on an entirely new course that would have fateful consequences for the Hmong.

FAYDANG

Prior to the French reoccupation of Laos, and for more than a year, Faydang had been carrying on his own personal war against the French. Leading a guerrilla force of Lo clansmen, he had helped the Japanese locate Frenchmen in hiding. After Japan's surrender, Faydang threw his support behind Viet Minh efforts to occupy Xieng Khouang and turn back the French reoccupation army. On his own, Faydang had ambushed a French company, killing eight soldiers. It was a very minor victory amidst a general rout.[12]

Once French patrols were able to move across the province unopposed, Faydang scurried for the border. Hot on his heels, Touby pursued Faydang into Vietnam and nearly nabbed him at Muong Sen, missing the Lo chieftain by only a few hours. A few weeks later Touby captured Faydang's brother Nghia Vu Lo and beat him nearly to death trying to discover Faydang's whereabouts. Nghia Vu managed to escape while being transported to the jail at Xieng Khouangville. Asking permission to relieve himself, he had moved to the edge of the forest and broken away. Terrified of recapture and more torture, he ran nonstop through the dark forest for hours, his hands still tied behind his back. The whole incident only further embittered Faydang toward Touby and the Ly clan.[13]

Faydang remained in Vietnam, joined by hundreds of his clansmen from Nong Het, now totally dependent on the communists for his survival. The communists absorbed Faydang's tiny guerrilla force into their "Resistance Committee of Eastern Laos." By 1947 the Committee had become the "Lao-Resistance," a Viet Minh front organization of disaffected Lao and montagnards. Faydang reentered Laos as the new front's vice-chairman. Fancy title aside, his real job was to head up communist guerrilla operations along Route 7, the same road hewn from the mountain forests by Hmong work gangs three decades earlier.[14]

With Faydang back in Laos, Touby began gathering intelligence on villages with concentrations of Lo clansmen. His agents arrested suspected collaborators and tortured them for information. There were even a few executions. Faydang struck back by hunting down Touby's spies.[15] The feud would eventually transcend personal vendetta and clan conflict and encompass all of the Hmong, dividing them into two camps: those who sided with the communists and those allied with the French-backed, and later American-backed, Royal Laotian Government (RLG).

CREATION OF THE PATHET LAO

Laos was once again a French protectorate. The exiled leaders of the Lao Issara thumbed their noses at the French by sending agents across the Mekong to ambush French patrols. The incursions were only an annoyance. Still, the French thought it prudent to offer some concessions to assuage nationalist sentiment. In 1947,

France gave Laos a new constitution that provided for a national assembly and limited self-rule. Two years later the French accorded Laos even greater autonomy over its internal affairs and, for the first time, a modest degree of influence over its foreign relations. While not completely independent, the country was moving toward genuine self-rule and democracy. It was something to celebrate, along with the return of the territory lost to Thailand during the Japanese occupation, relinquished by Thailand in a treaty with France.

Though the French acquired a newfound degree of popularity through making these changes, they realized the regime would never achieve full legitimacy in the eyes of the Laotians until the old political elite returned to take their place in the national administration. Phetsarath, Souphanouvong, and Souvanna Phouma were still living in exile in Thailand, keeping up the pretense of governing a fully independent Laos through the Lao Issara. The French offered all three princes, as well as their fellow nationalists in exile, full amnesty if they returned.[16]

Only Souvanna Phouma accepted the offer, returning to Laos to enter politics under France's new rules. He was one of the few nationalists still on good terms with the French. With a French wife and property in France, he was the only one of the exiled nationalists disposed to give a benign interpretation to French intentions. This made him a favorite of French diplomats, who were keen on finding a place for him in the new government.

Phetsarath turned down the amnesty offer because he did not like the shape of Laos' new constitution. The old post of viceroy, which he considered his rightful station, had been eliminated. He would remain in Thailand for another eight years, waiting for the political winds to shift in his favor.

Souphanouvong rejected amnesty because his ties to the Viet Minh and international communism were now permanent, making cooperation with the French under any terms unacceptable. He would soon depart for China to spend a year receiving Marxist indoctrination, then return to Thailand in 1948 to continue the struggle to drive the French out of Laos, living in modest luxury while fellow nationalists toiled as weavers and dishwashers.

The financial aid Souphanouvong received from the Viet Minh, sums which occasionally topped a million piasters, not only spared him the drudgery of sudsing dishes in hotel kitchens, but enabled him to organize military activities without consulting the Lao Issara for approval. Nearly every month Souphanouvong crossed the border into Laos, hiking over hills and through jungle to make contact with his freedom fighters and their Viet Minh advisors. It was very unprincely activity, but then Souphanouvong was not the usual hothouse royalty. He found the confines of an office oppressive and needed regularly to stretch his legs and sleep under the stars. In this he was like his eldest brother Phetsarath, who was a passionate hunter and the author of a book on hunting techniques in the upper Mekong. Happily for Souphanouvong, his mental health needs dovetailed nicely with the rugged outdoor regimen of a third world revolutionary leader. He spent weeks in the jungle recruiting guerrilla fighters, organizing workshops for the fabrication of crude rifles from scrap metal, and constructing primitive paper factories to produce the sheets for propaganda leaflets.

The other Lao Issara leaders complained loudly of Souphanouvong's independent military operations carried out in their name. Seeing him as nothing more than a communist agent, they had no wish to trade French for Vietnamese imperialism. The leadership demanded that he relinquish his position as commander-in-chief of Lao Issara forces. When Souphanouvong obstinately refused, they accused him of being a dictator and acting like a little god and complained about the "nationality of origin and political attitude of his wife." Furious, Souphanouvong labeled fellow nationalists "retarded fossils," and "resigned irrevocably" from the Lao Issara just months prior to the French offer of amnesty. In the company of a handful of supporters, Souphanouvong set out on foot across Laos for the Viet Minh stronghold in Sam Neua.

The Vietnamese communists had plans for Souphanouvong. Concerned that "nationalist elements of Laos and Cambodia might have suspected Vietnam of wishing to control Cambodia and Laos," they ordered him to establish a separate, and ostensibly Laotian-run, resistance movement, the Pathet Lao.[17] For the next fifteen years Souphanouvong would serve as the nominal head of this ICP front organization. Behind the scenes the North Vietnamese pulled all the strings, and Souphanouvong was not even the lead puppet. That title went to Kaysone Phomvihane.

Kaysone more closely fit the Vietnamese communists' ideal of a proper revolutionary. Unlike the aristocrat Souphanouvong, he was a mere commoner from Savannakhet, a man of the people blessed with a Vietnamese father. Kaysone had also attended school in Vietnam. The ICP had recruited him while he was still a student. As a party member, Kaysone formed an important friendship with Vo Nguyen Giap, the man destined to become the commander-in-chief of the Viet Minh. Such a connection paid off. In 1955 Kaysone became general secretary of the secretive Lao Communist Party, a post he still occupied when the communists rose to power in Laos in 1975.[18]

TOUBY'S RISING STAR

Laos' new constitution, which allowed for a modest drift toward self-government, gave the Hmong their first taste of national power. Voters sent thirty-two delegates to the first national legislature. The French managed the elections in Xieng Khouang Province, to insure that at least one of the delegates would be a Hmong. The seat went to Touby's brother, Toulia. It would have been Touby's for the asking, but he preferred to remain in the province close to his constituency as the first Hmong chao muong (district supervisor)—another French concession to Touby and the Hmong of Xieng Khouang Province.

The French bestowed other favors. Most of the prime farm land abandoned by the Vietnamese went to Hmong who would remain the core of Touby's political support for years to come. The French also awarded the Hmong a quarter of a million French piasters as war reparations for the suffering and loss of life incurred in support of the reoccupation of the province.[19] Touby distributed half of the money to chieftains faithful to him and to Hmong who had played a leadership role in the guerrilla operations. The rest of the money, nearly 108,000 piasters, he kept for himself, instantly becoming not only the richest Hmong in Laos, but a bona fide member of the nation's tiny monied class of wealthy merchants, opium traders, and land proprietors.

Besides wealth, Touby had power. The boundary of his administrative district spanned the distance between Nong Het and Xieng Khouangville and pushed north onto the Plain of Jars, placing the largest concentration of Hmong in the nation under his direct political authority. As befitted his high status, Touby opened an office in Xieng Khouangville, close to the governor's mansion.

Thousands of Hmong, mostly Ly clansmen, followed Touby west to settle in the highlands north of the provincial capital, the largest number congregating in the town of Lat Houang on the edge of the Plain of Jars. The migration nearly emptied Nong Het of Ly clansmen, leaving the field open to Faydang and the Lo, in time permanently altering the geographical distribution of Hmong political power. Nong Het would become the organizational center of Hmong communist activity in the province. Touby's political base, later co-opted by other Hmong politicians, would shift west and south.

Touby's rising political fortune was perfectly timed, for his other source of power, opium, seemed about to vanish. During the war, the U.S. had pressured France to end its drug trafficking in Indochina. France began to make motions in this direction in 1946. To Touby's relief, the French dragged their feet on the issue for the next five years, until international public opinion could no longer be ignored. In 1951 the Opium Purchasing Board ceased operations. Two years later France signed a United Nations protocol agreeing to end all state-sponsored trade in the drug.

Though France was officially out of the opium business, unofficially it continued to trade in the drug. Two years before the Opium Purchasing Board officially closed its doors, the French Expeditionary Corps began buying opium from hill tribes throughout Indochina. Touby was the Corps' main contact in Laos. At first he worried that the changeover would constrict the market. For a time (between 1949 and 1951) the Expeditionary Corps purchased only a fraction of the opium harvested by the Hmong. But the trade picked up substantially in 1951, when France's intelligence community took over the operation and greatly expanded purchases of Hmong opium. The motive was not only to make money, but to deny the opium to the communists.

When first formed, Ho Chi Minh's communist army, the Viet Minh, had numbered only a few thousand men equipped with a motley assortment of weapons: rusty French carbines from the old colonial period, rifles donated by the Japanese and later by the American OSS, guns purchased from the Nationalist Chinese, old

British rifles, and cases of weapons dredged up by divers from the holds of sunken Japanese ships in the Gulf of Tonkin.[20] To modernize his army, Ho needed money. He got it by turning to Hmong opium, available not only in the highlands of northern Vietnam, but also in the border region between Vietnam and Laos. Raids on Hmong villages produced tons of the drug, which the communists sold to narcotics traffickers in Hanoi. The drug money purchased rifles and ammunition from warlords in southern China, stockpiles of weapons donated by the United States to help in the struggle against the Chinese communists.[21] The Viet Minh army quickly grew to over one hundred thousand men, a large number carrying modern weapons.

For the French this meant a troublesome insurrection had grown into a good-sized war, and the cost of fighting continually mounted. The French Expeditionary Corps was in desperate need of additional manpower and funds, but France was unwilling to provide them. An antiwar movement had gathered momentum back home. Urging further escalation of the war was not a way for French politicians to gain votes.

Chronically short of funds, the French High Command decided that if the Viet Minh could use drugs to finance their army, the Expeditionary Corps could do the same. It would, of course, have to be an undercover operation undertaken outside legal channels. There was already an organization to take on the job, the *Groupement de Commandos Mixtes Aéroportés* (GCMA), created in early 1950 to organize montagnard guerrilla units. On paper, the GCMA was officially part of the Expeditionary Corps. In reality it was run by the Service de Documentation Extérieure et du Contre-Espionage (SDEC), the French equivalent of America's CIA.

Cut loose from the restrictions of the regular military, the GCMA was unencumbered by the normal constraints of propriety or conscience. Under the leadership of Colonel Grall, the secret organization had already proved itself exceptionally creative in using Vietnamese gangsters, known as the Binh Xuyen, to track the movements of the Viet Cong in the Mekong delta. It was therefore hardly out of character for the GCMA to traffic in drugs, and it would help the war effort. According to SDEC intelligence estimates, the communists were confiscating enough Hmong opium annually to underwrite the outfitting of a full division.[22] If the Hmong sold their opium to the GCMA, it would put a dent in Viet Minh finances. As an added bonus, it would forge links between the Hmong and the GCMA, facilitating a project already on the drawing board to create Hmong guerrilla units in Laos under GCMA control, an operation to be headed up by Major Roger Trinquier, Grall's second in command. Trinquier had already received assurances from Touby that the Hmong were eager to cooperate, but it was Trinquier's experience that material incentives were more dependable than high resolve. Opium was the sole source of Hmong wealth. If the GCMA purchased nearly all of the opium grown by Hmong in Laos, Touby's cooperation would be guaranteed.

Trinquier met with Touby to iron out the details of what would be code-named "Operation X." The essence of the arrangement was this: whenever Touby had close to a ton of opium ready to market, the GCMA would transport it in a DC-3 to the French commando training school at Cap Saint-Jacques on the southern tip of Vietnam. GCMA agents would then deliver the opium to Le Van Vien, Saigon's chief of police, who would turn it over to the Binh Xuyen.

Evolved from a loose federation of Mekong River pirates into a full-blown criminal syndicate, the Binh Xuyen controlled nearly all of the illicit narcotics traffic in South Vietnam. The syndicate ran two opium boiling plants in Saigon and distributed the processed opium throughout southern Vietnam, the lion's share destined for the opium dens and retail shops of Saigon, and especially the Cholon district (Saigon's Chinatown) where addicts were concentrated. Whatever surplus remained the Binh Xuyen sold to representatives of international narcotics syndicates in Hong Kong or Marseilles.

The Binh Xuyen kept half of the revenues from GCMA opium sent through this network and delivered the rest to the GCMA. Trinquier used the money to finance the training and provisioning of various GCMA-sponsored guerrilla organizations, though he always set aside enough to honor the guarantee made to Touby that he would receive five thousand piasters for every kilogram of Hmong opium delivered to Cap Saint-Jacques.[23] Besides increasing Touby's already substantial wealth, Operation X further enhanced his power and influence over the Hmong, so much so that colonial bureaucrats fell into the habit of referring to him as the *roi de Méos*—king of the Hmong.[24]

By late 1952, the GCMA needed more from Touby than opium. Intelligence reports indicated that the Pathet Lao were busy establishing administrative control over all of Sam Neua Province. Just across the border in Vietnam the Viet Minh had overwhelmed the French border post at Moc Chao and occupied the river valley of Dienbienphu, a gateway into Laos. Other Viet Minh units were gathering at the border. It all had the earmarks of preparation for an invasion of Laos through Sam Neua. The French needed ongoing intelligence to keep abreast of changes, ideally from agents on the scene. Touby's Hmong were perfect candidates for the mission.

None other than General Raoul Salan, chief of staff of the French high command, approached Touby on the matter. A devout believer in the utility of montagnard guerrillas, it was Salan who had cast the deciding vote to create the GCMA. It did not take long for Salan to realize that Touby was an unabashed Francophile anxious to curry favor with the French in any way possible. After the meeting, Salan gave Trinquier the green light to use the Hmong to monitor communist activity in Sam Neua and on the border.

MALO AND SERVAN

Trinquier selected Captain Desfarges as the GCMA's liaison with Touby. An alumnus of the commando team that had parachuted onto the Plain of Jars in December 1944, Desfarges had survived the Japanese *coup de main* by placing himself under Touby's protection. Touby hid Desfarges in a limestone grotto until the end of the war. The experience created a bond between the two men. When Desfarges showed up at Xieng Khouangville, Touby embraced him like a long lost brother. Trinquier had picked the right man.

Desfarges established two training camps run by French noncoms, one north of the Plain of Jars, the other on its eastern rim. Touby recruited two hundred Hmong for the first class of trainees for the new maquis, designated *Le Groupe Malo* (the Malo Force).

As French sergeants put the Malo Hmong through their paces, Desfarges sent his aide, Lieutenant Brehier, north to Sam Neua with Hmong guides and several Vietnamese radiomen to form a second Hmong maquis, *Le Groupe Servan*.[25]

By February 1953, the Servan maquis was operational and reporting increased Viet Minh activity on the border. A few weeks later the Viet Minh launched their invasion. The commander of the three invading divisions was Vo Nguyen Giap, the Viet Minh general who would shortly mastermind the defeat of the French at Dienbienphu.

VIET MINH INVASION

It was Giap's philosophy to never engage the enemy in a large-scale battle unless he enjoyed an overwhelming advantage in troops and firepower.[26] Giap had assembled nearly forty thousand troops for the invasion, carrying heavy mortar and recoilless cannon, with thousands of coolies transporting ammunition and supplies. His army was larger than the Japanese force that had invaded Burma in 1942, and easily outgunned and outmanned the ten thousand troops the French had in place in Laos.

The invasion had a political aim. Giap wanted to demoralize politicians in Paris with an expansion of the war into Laos. To achieve this goal it was unnecessary to hold ground and withstand counterattack. After inflicting maximum damage, Giap intended to withdraw back to North Vietnam as quickly as possible. If by chance his divisions easily overwhelmed the French and left an opening for an assault on major cities, he would hardly pass up the opportunity before sounding the retreat.[27]

Giap had factored in weather and logistics. The invasion was timed to run into the rainy season so that the French would be bogged down in the mud and unable to effectively pursue his forces once they began their retreat. To maintain supply lines, Giap had stockpiled weapons and ammunition at the border town of Moc Chau, earlier wrested from the French. Inside Laos, communist agents were already commandeering rice from villagers and storing the food in depots along the three planned invasion routes.

The plan was for the 312th Division to follow the course of the Nam Ou River toward Luang Prabang (see map "North Vietnamese Invasion of Laos in 1953"). The 308th Division would pursue a parallel course that would bring it to the western edge of the Plain of Jars. The job of the 316th Division was to route the main French garrison in Sam Neua and then push on to the plain's eastern edge. Once the two divisions (308th and 316th) were in place, they were to proceed in a pincer movement and close on French forces encamped on the plain.

Though the campaign was well planned, Giap was unaware that Brehier's Servan maquis would be tracking his forces the moment they entered Laos. This intelligence provided the French with sufficient advance warning to organize an effective defense.

Early in the invasion Giap's 312th Division encountered un-expected stiff resistance from a forward French post at Muong Khoua, where a single French officer commanded three hundred Laotian soldiers. The post refused to give in. After three days of mass assaults the post still held. The division bypassed the garri-son and moved on, leaving behind a portion of its forces to finish off Muong Khoua's defenders. The task would take thirty-three more days. The post was finally destroyed by an artillery barrage that smashed Muong Khoua's fortifications to bits. Only three survivors crawled out of the rubble to be taken prisoner.[28]

The French garrison at Sam Neua appeared doomed to a similar fate. Steep hills surrounded the post on all sides. Colonel Maleplatte and his three Lao infantry battalions would be at the enemy's mercy if the Viet Minh ever occupied the high ground. Over the post's radio Maleplatte learned that twenty battalions from the Viet Minh 316th Division were already closing in. The French high com-mand ordered Maleplatte to destroy the garrison's heavy equipment and retreat in a forced march to the Plain of Jars. On the way, Maleplatte was to keep an eye out for elements of the GCMA's Servan maquis. They would help guide the column to the plain.

As Maleplatte marched south, a Viet Minh regiment, aug-mented by elements of the Pathet Lao, raced ahead to wait in ambush at Muong Peune. When Maleplatte reached the town, his column was assaulted throughout its length. The soldiers fought hand-to-hand. After losing half his forces, Maleplatte finally broke out.[29]

Maleplatte regrouped in the hills and began a slow march southward. Brehier and his Servan Hmong finally made contact with the column the following day. The Hmong were familiar with the terrain, giving them an advantage over the communists, but there were so many wounded it was impossible to move beyond a snail's pace. In just three days the Viet Minh caught up. There was more fierce fighting and heavy casualties. Survivors scattered in all directions. The Hmong were able to locate only two hundred, all that was left of the original force of twenty-four hundred that had fled Sam Neua only a few days earlier. The Hmong delivered the survivors safely to the Plain of Jars.[30]

In coordination with the 316th Division's southward push, Faydang led a force of mainly Lo clansmen across the border toward Xieng Khouangville. Only a few days earlier five French battalions had been garrisoned near the provincial capital. The troops were now gone. General Salan had moved them to the western edge of the Plain of Jars to serve as a blocking force against Giap's 308th Division, which Salan believed, incorrectly, to be heading straight for Vientiane. With the battalions gone, Faydang took command of Xieng Khouangville with only slight resistance.[31] The victory would prove short-lived.

The movement of the five battalions was just part of the frenzy of mobilization that had gripped the French. Salan and his staff shared Giap's belief that a successful invasion could turn French public opinion against the war. If the enemy was not soundly repulsed, it could very well make a continuation of the war impossible.[32] General Albert Sore supervised an around-the-clock airlift of French troops, tanks, artillery, and supplies from Hanoi and Saigon to the steel mat airfield laid out by French engineers on the Plain of Jars. Help arrived from an unexpected quarter. The Eisenhower administration donated six C-119 transport planes to the airlift, each flown by pilots on contract with the CIA.[33]

Within a week ten battalions encompassing twelve thousand troops were in place on the plain; artillery was in position and barbed wire barricades stretched around the perimeter of dug-in troops. While the French waited for the communist divisions to arrive, General Sore assembled four infantry columns and sent them, along with Touby's Malo maquis, to dislodge Faydang's guerrillas from Xieng Khouangville. Faydang and his men were soon scurrying toward the border.

Sore also sent legionnaires into the hills around the Plain of Jars to buy up Hmong opium before the Viet Minh got to it. He was convinced a secondary motivation for the invasion was to tap into the stores of opium in Hmong villages around the plain. Sore's suspicions were well-founded. The Viet Minh were still highly dependent on opium to finance their war and desperately wanted to get their hands on the annual opium harvest, the lion's share of which lay stored in Hmong villages around the Plain of Jars.[34]

On May 13, two of the Viet Minh divisions (the 308th and 316th) penetrated the plain and ran into a devastating artillery barrage. Though suffering heavy casualties, the Viet Minh pushed on to the legionnaires' trench lines. The French held their positions, repulsing each mass assault. After counting their dead and realizing that they were on the point of having their two divisions wiped out, the communists withdrew from the plain.

However, further west Giap's 312th Division was still intact and causing mischief. By the end of the month the 312th was within striking distance of the ancient city of Luang Prabang. Over the next two days the French flew in artillery and three battalions of legionnaires. Salan doubted the legionnaires could defend the city against a full Viet Minh division, and urged Sisavang Vong to leave under armed guard. The king refused. He had been informed that all would be well. Pho Satheu, a blind bonze renowned for his ability to predict the future, had prophesied that the Vietnamese communists would not enter the city.[35] As it turned out, the monk was right. It began to rain. The road to the capital turned to mud, slowing the enemy's advance. Giap lost his nerve and ordered the 312th to pull back and return to Vietnam.

VANG PAO

During the invasion one RLA infantry company, the 14th, stationed at Muong Hiem north of the Plain of Jars, stood directly in the path of the advancing Viet Minh 316th Division. Vientiane ordered the post's commander, Captain Cocosteguy, to hold on and delay the enemy's advance. Cocosteguy ordered trenches dug and waited for the Vietnamese to emerge from the hills. French soldiers from advanced positions who were retreating from the Viet Minh onslaught began to arrive at the post in small bedraggled

groups, exhausted from marching nonstop. A B-26 flew low overhead toward the advancing Viet Minh. Ten minutes later four
helicopters passed over the garrison in the same direction.

Cocosteguy ordered his men into position to defend against
attack. As they waited, he learned over his field radio that Nong
Het, Xieng Khouangville, and Muong Ngat had already fallen to
the communists. Helicopters appeared again, this time from the
direction of the fighting, carrying wounded soldiers. The helicopters landed, paused for the wounded to be unloaded, and were
again airborne, returning to the battle scene to pick up more casualties. An hour later a reconnaissance plane landed on the post's
small airstrip and deposited more wounded. Another helicopter
landed with five additional casualties, all of them officers.

Just before dark Cocosteguy received a radio communiqué from
RLA headquarters in Vientiane. The news was grim. Fifteen Viet
Minh battalions were marching straight for Muong Hiem.
Cocosteguy was ordered to abandon the garrison just as a handful
of Vietnamese soldiers, probably advanced patrols, were spotted
moving in the hills around the post. The evacuation began shortly
after dark. Before departing, Cocosteguy had torches lit and the
dinner bugle sounded to give the impression that the post was
settling in for the night. The Vietnamese did not discover the ruse
until early the next morning.

Attached to the 14th infantry company was the only Hmong
officer in the RLA, a young lieutenant named Vang Pao. As he
was the only soldier at the post familiar with the surrounding
mountain terrain, Cocostequy put him in charge of leading the
column. On the second day of the retreat Vang Pao left the valley
trail and guided the column into the mountains. He sent scouts
ahead to find Hmong settlements, gather information on Vietnamese positions, and bring back food.

The French officers were not used to climbing mountains like
goats. Within a few days they were nearly dead from fatigue.
Cocosteguy insisted they move down into the valleys where the
going would be easier. Against his better judgment, Vang Pao complied. They were soon ambushed. The Lao soldiers dropped their
rifles and ran.[36] The French officers stuck with Vang Pao and his
Hmong and followed them back into the hills. After another hard
day of hiking up steep trails, Cocosteguy announced that he was

too exhausted to go on. Vang Pao left the Frenchman at a Hmong village to recuperate and pushed on to the Plain of Jars. A few weeks later Cocosteguy joined them on the plain. It was not a joyful reunion. As there was nothing left of the 14th company, it was ordered disbanded.[36]

NEW LIFE FOR MALO AND SERVAN

Giap made the best of the failed offensive by leaving several thousand troops behind in Sam Neua to establish a permanent foothold for future operations. Working with Pathet Lao cadres, the Vietnamese impressed thousands of T'ai and Khmu into military service with the Pathet Lao. There had been an effort to recruit Hmong as well, but many Hmong avoided conscription by abandoning their villages. The communists simply recruited more T'ai and Khmu to make up the difference. Fat with new troops, the Pathet Lao moved from mountain to mountain, establishing in a piecemeal fashion complete administrative control of the province.[37]

To counter the communists, Desfarges ordered Brehier back to Sam Neua to rejuvenate the Servan maquis. Brehier parachuted into the province in October. With him were seven French sergeants and fifty Hmong who had received advanced commando and airborne training in Hanoi. Brehier established Servan's new headquarters on the summit of Phu Pha Thi, a flattop mountain rising five thousand feet above the valley floor. After settling in, he had the fifty Hmong separate into teams and beat the bushes to drum up recruits. Within two months they had nearly a thousand volunteers.

The rapid buildup necessitated constant airdrops of additional arms and tons of rice onto Pha Thi's high plateau. The arms went to the guerrillas. The rice went to their families and villages as payment for full-time military service in the maquis. Brehier selected ninety of the guerrillas, mostly team leaders and radiomen, and sent them to south Vietnam for advanced instruction and airborne training at the GCMA camp at Cap St. Jacques.

When the trainees returned, Brehier began operations in earnest. He divided the maquis into three groups positioned at separate sites. Operating from these bases, the Servan guerrillas fanned out, constantly on patrol. They eliminated scores of Pathet Lao and ran the rest out of the area. So intense was the pressure that the communists shifted their headquarters from Sam Neua City to the more easily defended limestone caves of Vieng Sai nearby.

Not to be outdone by Brehier, Desfarges stepped up his own efforts to expand Malo in Xieng Khouang. His deputy, Lieutenant Max Mesnier, set up six new training sites ringing the eastern portion of the Plain of Jars. In all, two thousand Hmong would graduate from the camps. Like Brehier, Desfarges used them to root out Pathet Lao attempting to gain a foothold in the province.

The sheer size of Malo enabled Desfarges to skim the cream of his troops for an elite force and establish an advanced training camp at Kang Khay on the Plain of Jars. Captain Jean Sassi, the camp commander, ran partisans through the training course in groups of one hundred. Each group had a team leader, selected by Sassi as the best soldier in the lot. One of them was Vang Pao, seeking a career change now that his old RLA unit no longer existed.[38]

Back at Cap St. Jacques, Trinquier surveyed the progress of Malo-Servan and judged the project an enormous success. The two maquis had assembled more than three thousand guerrillas. In the north, Servan exercised virtual control over six hundred square miles. Farther south around the Plain of Jars, Malo had the Pathet Lao in total retreat.

TOUBY IN VIENTIANE

For thousands of Sam Neua Hmong, Servan's rejuvenation had come too late. Living under the thumb of the Pathet Lao (many of them T'ai and Khmu tribesmen strutting about in commissar tunics) had been unbearable. Voting with their feet, the Hmong spilled into Xieng Khouang Province, telling of requisitioned livestock, confiscated opium, and impressment into work gangs. On every lip was the complaint that the communists had defiled their women. Commissars conscripted the prettiest girls for their indoctrination teams, groups that traveled from village to village to lecture the Hmong on political correctness. On the road trips, both commissars and soldiers ravished the girls at will.[39]

Touby was happy to offer the refugees his protection. Every Hmong turned anticommunist by Pathet Lao oppression enlarged his own political base. But to retain their loyalty, and that of the thousands of Hmong in his muong, he had continuously to deliver material proof that his leadership was deserved: more schools for Hmong children, hospitals for the sick, and choice land for Hmong farmers.

Things would be easier if he wielded influence at the national level. The 1947 constitutional reforms gave the country democratic institutions, but the nation's minorities were effectively excluded from sharing power. It was only because of French sponsorship that one Hmong held a seat in the new national assembly. Left to its own inertia, the political system would continue to give preference to lowland Lao, and especially to the royals—aristocrats who could trace their lineage directly to the royal families of the old principalities of Luang Prabang, Champassak, and Vieng Chan (Vientiane).

It was Touby's plan to use his influence with the French to pressure the Lao elite into accepting crucial reforms: equal treatment under law for all ethnic minorities, minority access to positions in the state bureaucracy, and electoral reforms that would place more minorities in the national assembly. It was a strategy not unlike that employed by Black leaders in the U.S. during the 1950s and 1960s. Effectively barred from electoral politics in the southern states where most Blacks resided, and therefore unable to use the ballot box to end discrimination or advance their own welfare, Black leaders sought sponsorship and support from northern liberals to end discrimination nationally and open the political system to Blacks in all regions of the nation.[40] The French were Touby's northern liberals.

Pressing for minority rights was only the first step. Once Hmong, T'ai, Khmu, Yao, and other ethnic minorities were included in the political process, their leaders could use their electoral strength to broker deals with Vientiane. The trade might be for a place in the national administration, or perhaps something less self-serving such as new roads, schools, and hospitals in the highlands. Eventually, leaders with a larger vision would look beyond brokered politics to coalition building with other minorities and the formation of a national party.

As a step in this direction, Touby's brother Toulia pushed hard in the national assembly for an official change in the nomenclature of the nation's citizens. Lowlanders would be called *Lao Loum*, montagnards who lived at high altitudes the *Lao Soung*, and those who lived at altitudes in between would be known as the *Lao Theung*. It was a simple yet clever way to create a sense of common identity for diverse ethnic groups who traditionally viewed each other as adversaries. Predictably, the ethnic Lao in the national assembly tried to block the change, but arm-twisting by the French pushed the measure through.

With the new classifications in place, Touby made tentative steps toward building relations with other minority politicians. Several Khmu chieftains had been jailed at Luang Prabang for protesting the corrupt state of politics in that province. Officials governing the Khmu were all absentee bureaucrats, successful businessmen in Luang Prabang who never set foot in a Khmu community. The Khmu chieftains had gone to Luang Prabang to lodge a complaint and to request that the businessmen be replaced by Khmu tribesmen. Outraged authorities clapped the Khmu in jail.

Touby persuaded French bureaucrats to intervene and get the men released. He also pressed for the reforms the Khmu had requested.[41] It was asking too much too soon. The absentee bureaucrats remained in office. But the Khmu were out of jail and grateful for it, which forged a tie between Touby and Khmu notables in the province.

Touby was not alone in viewing the mobilization of the nation's minorities as the key to altering the balance of power in the nation. The communists had the same idea. Having made little headway among the ethnic Lao, they redirected their energies to recruiting montagnards: the highland T'ai, Khmu, Yao, and Hmong. Excluded from the political life of the nation and the objects of considerable prejudice, the montagnards were ripe for politicization.

Touby planned to beat the communists to the punch by broadening his own Hmong power base to acquire a greater voice in national government, not merely as a representative of the Hmong, but of all of the nation's montagnards. This could happen, of course, only with the continued patronage of the French and their resolve to use military force to prevent the communists from taking over the country.

Touby's calculations were overturned when the North Vietnamese defeated the French at Dienbienphu, forcing him to turn to the Americans for help. He found the transition difficult. Touby's only real success was with American missionaries rather than with individuals whose opinion carried weight—the American diplomats, CIA agents, and military attachés who were now in charge of Laos' future.

Catholic missionaries had been in Laos since 1642, struggling decade after decade to find converts, but without success. A special group of fourteen priests arrived in northern Laos in 1878 to set things right. The pilgrimage was a disaster. All of the priests perished from disease or from assaults by bandits. Some small progress was finally made at the turn of the century with the innovation of purchasing Laotian slaves in Thailand (montagnards captured by Thai raiding parties) and repatriating them to Laos, where they were given their freedom.

The liberated slaves were the Church's first converts. But after that the well went dry. Lowland Lao were confirmed Buddhists with no interest in Catholicism. The priests turned their attention to the montagnards, but again failed miserably. In the end the only real growth in the number of Catholics came from the Vietnamese immigrants brought in by the French to fill up the nation's major towns, nearly all of whom were already long-time Catholics and therefore no credit to the priests' proselytizing skills.

To turn things around, in 1934 Pope Pius XI delivered all of northern Laos to the Oblates of the order of Mary Immaculate. If the Jesuits were the Catholic Church's Marines, the Oblates were the Church's SEALs. When all others failed, Rome ordered the Oblates into the field.

Jean-Henri Mazoyer (the bishop who interceded to stop the Japanese from executing Touby at Nong Het) was one of the first Oblates to arrive. Over the next decade Mazoyer worked with the fervor of the anointed to bring Christianity to the hill tribes. To make headway with the Hmong, he established a mission at Nong Het and later built a school for Hmong children.[42]

From the start, Mazoyer sought Touby as an ally in bringing Catholicism to his people. Touby was a willing accomplice, hoping to use the bishop to enhance his position with the colonial bureaucracy and to get new schools for the Hmong in the bargain. For in addition to being a dedicated priest, Mazoyer was an intensely chauvinistic Frenchman, a quality that placed him on good terms with the Résident Supérieur of Vientiane, the French bureaucrat who governed Laos. Aware that Mazoyer had the Résident's ear, Touby welcomed the Catholic mission at Nong Het, lobbied for a Catholic school,[43] and encouraged Hmong to convert to Catholicism.

Despite Touby's encouragement, only a handful of Hmong ever became Catholics.[44] Though Mazoyer's priests presented the Hmong with an easygoing Catholicism that indulged their traditional rites and icons, it nevertheless took ten years of study for a Hmong to qualify as a deacon and another eight to become a priest. Only a handful of Hmong, youngsters with a bent for learning, stayed in school long enough to become deacons. None reached the priesthood. For Catholicism to have caught on, the Hmong would have needed Hmong priests, preferably former shamans. Shamans were the central religious and cultural figures of Hmong

Shaman shaking, Laos, 1960s

society, the curators of Hmong tradition and mythology, and the historians of the travails of their race. Only they were able to fall into a trance and enter directly into the spirit world. It was the shaman who healed the sick and guided the souls of the dead on their journey to rebirth. The authority of the shaman had been a fixture of Hmong culture for thousands of years. It was not something the Hmong could easily discard or replace with Frenchmen in frocks.

With so few Hmong converts, Touby was able to coax only one Catholic school from Mazoyer. Yet because of Mazoyer's ties to the Résident Supérieur, Touby continued as a steadfast ally of the Oblates, at least until 1950 when Etienne Loosdregt replaced Mazoyer as bishop. Though a Frenchman like Mazoyer, Loosdregt's ultimate allegiance was to Rome, which did not endear him to the Résident Supérieur. Nor was Loosdregt interested in new schools in Xieng Khouang Province. Since Loosdregt had nothing Touby wanted, Touby turned his back on the Catholics and embraced Protestantism.

There had been American Protestant missionaries in Xieng Khouang since 1939, when the Whipples, a husband-and-wife team, started a small mission at Xieng Khouangville. Targeting the local ethnic Lao, the Whipples preached and prayed without much effect. Because of the Japanese occupation, the Whipples abandoned the mission in 1943 and returned to the U.S. But after the war, in 1949, another husband-and-wife team, Ted and Ruth Andrianoff, arrived at Xieng Khouangville to revive the mission, but this time with an emphasis on reaching out to the Hmong.

Within a year the Andrianoffs had their first real convert, a shaman from the Moua clan named Yao Thao. The shaman delivered his entire village to the Andrianoffs, then went on the road to preach the faith. A second shaman, a woman, also joined the movement and became an enthusiastic evangelist. By the end of the year the Andrianoffs counted more than a thousand converts. They telegraphed for help. Other missionaries arrived to establish a church school at Xieng Khouangville which would prepare lay preachers to go into the field to administer to the converted and save additional souls.[45]

The Andrianoffs had stumbled upon the secret of spreading Christianity to the Hmong: co-opt the icons of Hmong religion, the shamans, and employ them as the emissaries of Christ. Necessity also nudged them in the right direction. Because of their limited budget, the missionaries were compelled to use Hmong lay preachers (catechists) to tend the growing flock and to do most of the day-to-day evangelical work in the field. With shamans lending religious legitimacy to the movement, and Hmong functioning as Christian priests, the Andrianoffs had a better chance than Mazoyer had to win converts.[46]

The only drawback was quality control. The missionaries really had no idea what was being preached in their name in highland villages far from their headquarters in Xieng Khouangville. Heresies were inevitable. The idea of the Trinity received an odd twist when three Hmong, doubtless shamans caught up in a messianic fever, identified themselves as Hmong demigods (calling themselves respectively Father, Son, and Holy Spirit) and claimed supernatural powers, including the ability to fly. One of them leaped from a cliff to prove it could be done and fell to his death.[47]

Touby made a great show of supporting the Andrianoffs' missionary efforts. He selected Yao Thao Moua, the missionaries' first convert, as his own personal spiritual advisor, began Bible lessons with a missionary named Gustafson, joined the three hundred Hmong regularly in attendance at the mission's church services each Sunday, and encouraged Hmong throughout the province to become Christians. And many did. By 1957 the mission's records counted nearly five thousand Hmong as active converts. The missionaries considered winning Touby over one of their greatest triumphs.

Touby's support was not a matter of personal religious conviction. Once he realized how many Hmong were caught up in the movement, he did what was necessary to co-opt them, though he was careful never to admit publicly to being a Christian, so as not to alienate diehard Hmong purists disturbed by the evangelical movement's corrosive effects on traditional shamanism. Touby's enthusiasm for the Andrianoffs' evangelism was also pure expediency. The missionaries were committed to a program of village schools for every Christian Hmong community in the province. In a single year the movement established thirty-eight of them. Hmong students at the Xieng Khouangville Bible school were being taught to read and write Lao so they could teach in the villages.[48]

It was the first step toward universal education, something Touby had always wanted for the Hmong. If Paris was worth a Mass, then attending church services and sitting through Bible lessons was a small price to pay for schools for Hmong children. Of course, Touby took as much credit for the new schools as credulity would allow, trumpeting them as the result of his political savvy and his ability to influence foreigners for the benefit of the Hmong.

Unfortunately for Touby, his popularity with the American missionaries did not carry over to the American diplomats and military attachés in Vientiane. In time this would undermine his power and relegate him to a supporting role in Hmong politics.

After purchasing a home in Vientiane in 1947, Touby was a frequent visitor to the capital, conferring with his brother Toulia, a delegate to the assembly, on national politics, and cultivating friendships with capital politicians and high-placed French bureaucrats. Touby discovered he much preferred the lively atmosphere of capital life to the humdrum pace of Xieng Khouangville. As his visits grew longer, attention to local politics suffered. By the mid-1950s, several district officials, all Touby's appointees, began to abuse their offices. They collected unauthorized taxes, ordered people beaten, and coerced sexual favors from village women. Hmong grumbled and complained, but Touby ignored them. His attention was focused on the national scene. In 1958 Touby stood for a seat in the national assembly and won easily. In 1960 he became Minister of Social Welfare. After that he spent little time in Xieng Khouangville. Vientiane was his new home; and it was filling up with Americans.

Prior to 1954, the only official U.S. representative in Laos was a single foreign service officer in Vientiane. America's first ambassador to Laos, Charles Yost, arrived in late 1954. He was soon joined by American military officers, enlisted men, and civilian employees. The CIA set up a station in Vientiane, headed by Milton Clark and staffed by several agents. Clark immediately created an intelligence network to keep tabs on the various political factions and their leaders. The ambassador's staff grew. Military advisors arrived and their staffs grew. Within two years, more than a hundred U.S. officials were in the country, most of them residing in Vientiane. This number would soon double, then triple.

The Americans were now supposed to be in charge, yet the old Lao elite maintained close ties with French diplomats in Vientiane and to the large French community in the country, numbering in the thousands. There were even Frenchmen in high positions in the Royal Laotian Government bureaucracy (nearly two hundred were attached to cabinet ministries).[49]

As a cultural force, the French easily overshadowed the Americans who spoke no Lao and seemed ludicrously homespun compared to the cosmopolitan French. All of this naturally became a sore point with U.S. personnel, who had difficulty concealing their growing distaste for everything French. The CIA in particular had no patience for high-ranking Lao who turned to the French for counsel, becoming the "most vigorous opponent of Lao whom it considered under French influence or control."[50]

In this increasingly anti-French atmosphere, Touby imprudently wore his officer's rosette of the French Legion of Honor at all official functions and continued to socialize with French diplomats. Proud of his impeccable French and too old to acquire English with a similar polish, Touby simply did not bother to develop even a pidgin English. The Americans considered him far too French for their taste. Touby lost his position as vice-president of the national assembly and wound up in the King's Council, the Laotian equivalent of England's House of Lords, all pomp and of no real circumstance.

Over the years Touby had lobbied national politicians for new schools and hospitals. With his election to the national assembly he was able to transform the requests into law. But once he was relegated to the King's Council, he no longer had the political clout to see that the law was enforced. The head of the Department of Social Affairs charged with implementing the reforms stubbornly procrastinated. The new schools were never built and only two crude hospitals, best described as first aid stations, were established in his province. Lao officials in Xieng Khouang Province resumed the old habit of dealing with the Hmong as inferiors, treating them with contempt and paying Hmong employees half the wage paid to Lao doing the same work.[51]

Even if Touby had remained a force in national politics, government was not the place to win favor with American officials. Laotian politics seemed like something out of *Alice in Wonderland*.

The nation was supposed to be a democracy, but all of the principal politicians were titled royalty. Even the head of the communist faction insisted on being addressed as "Your Highness." Nothing could be accomplished without coalitions, and they took forever to build and unraveled almost overnight. It was a politics of endless drift that enabled the North Vietnamese to occupy territory and, bit by bit, gobble up the country.

It did not take long for policy makers in Washington to conclude that the salvation of Laos would come on the battlefield rather than in the squat National Assembly building in Vientiane. This state of affairs placed a premium on military prowess, a virtue in scarce supply in the RLA. Inevitably, the attention of the Americans shifted to Vang Pao, by then a colonel in the RLA doing extra duty organizing a ragtag force of Hmong guerrillas supported by American special forces officers and a CIA agent. Not only did Vang Pao's Hmong irregulars win battles, they were practically the only force in the field respected, and therefore feared, by the North Vietnamese.

Once the Americans diverted money and support to Vang Pao, Touby was forced to accept a subordinate role in Hmong affairs. But whatever the Americans may have thought of him, Vang Pao never underestimated Touby's political talents. He forged a family tie with Touby by having one of his sons marry one of Touby's daughters.[52] Touby became Vang Pao's link to Vientiane, keeping him abreast of the latest political machinations and insuring that American military aid reached his guerrillas in the field instead of being diverted into the corrupt network of Lao politics.

Touby performed a similar service for Hmong refugees. Hundreds of Hmong communities were devastated by the war, both through communist predation and later by American bombs. Over half of the Hmong in Laos would wind up in refugee camps south of the Plain of Jars. Touby monitored relief supplies and made sure they reached the camps instead of the black market where they were magically transformed into shiny new Cadillacs and riverside villas for the Lao elite.

Working quietly behind the scenes in Vientiane, Touby's efforts went unrecognized by most Hmong. Only a few Americans working in refugee relief knew of the contribution he made to the war effort. Obscured by Vang Pao's lengthening shadow, Touby was no longer referred to by diplomats and fellow politicians as the *roi de Méos*.

4

EXIT FRANCE, ENTER
AMERICA

ROOSEVELT

During World War II Franklin Roosevelt brooded over the consequences of imperialism. Japan's attempt to ape Europe and develop Asian colonies led inevitably to the attack on Pearl Harbor and the war in the Pacific. Germany was also caught up in imperialism, though by a more indirect route. Having suffered a near mortal blow to its national pride from its defeat in the First World War, and lacking significant colonies abroad where it might vent its pent-up nationalism, Germany set out to conquer its neighbors and colonize Europe.

Roosevelt was confident that the Allies would eventually defeat the Axis powers, yet feared that when peace came it could prove fragile. The greatest threat was from European imperialism in Asia and Africa, where a legacy of ruthless exploitation had created a bitter hatred among colonized populations for their colonial masters.

Roosevelt was especially concerned with French colonialism in Indochina. It was hardly a model of enlightened government. Roosevelt complained to Cordell Hull, his Secretary of State, that "France has milked Indochina for one hundred years. The people of Indochina are entitled to something better than that." Roosevelt anticipated that after the war there would be armed struggles for national liberation in French and British colonies, conflicts that would shatter the peace which at that very moment was being purchased with American lives in Europe and the Pacific.

In 1943, Roosevelt expressed these concerns to the Allies, causing leaders in Britain and France considerable distress, for they would not be able to stand in the way of America if she decided to free their colonies. They need not have worried. The war had yet to be won. Roosevelt was unlikely to compromise victory by antagonizing his country's allies. Thus, when France moved to retake Indochina from the Japanese and resurrect its colonial empire, Roosevelt demanded no more than a vague commitment from de Gaulle to grant the colonies some degree of independence at war's end.

Still, Roosevelt felt strongly enough about the issue to order American troops in China not to intercede on behalf of the French should the Vietnamese take up arms against them. Shortly before his death, he was working on a unified command of Allied forces in Asia to insure that neither the British nor the French could make a move into southeast Asia without America's consent.[1]

TRUMAN

Five months after Roosevelt's death, Charles de Gaulle was in Washington for talks with Truman to discover whether the new president shared Roosevelt's reservations about colonialism. Truman assured de Gaulle that "my government offers no opposition to the return of the French Army and authority in Indochina."[2] The sudden change in policy toward European colonialism was due to the growing perception that an expansionist Soviet Union was more of a threat to world peace than were restless natives in southeast Asia.

Over the next few years the Soviets did little to discount this fear. They occupied eastern Europe during the final Allied push to invade Germany and refused to withdraw their forces once the war was over, buying time so they could set up puppet regimes in Poland, Romania, Bulgaria, Albania, Hungary and Czechoslovakia. There was concern that western Europe might be the Soviets' next victim. The war had devastated the economies of France, Germany, and Italy. With the Soviets in control of eastern Europe, these nations were cut off from the food and raw materials traditionally supplied by the East: oil from Romania, coal from Silesia, pigs and potatoes from Poland and eastern Germany, and grain from Poland and Romania. Unemployment and poverty were widespread and politics was in turmoil, precisely the conditions to render communist doctrine palatable. There were already large communist parties in Italy and France; a Soviet invasion to tip the scales in their favor was by no means unthinkable.[3]

To blunt communism's appeal, Truman launched the Marshall Plan, a program of massive economic aid to invigorate the economies of Europe. The U.S. distributed nearly $13.2 billion to sixteen European nations to help rebuild their industrial bases. The economic aid helped to stem the tide of communism in Europe, but did nothing to prevent its spread in Asia. By 1947 a bloody civil war between communists and nationalists was already underway in China. Farther south, other communists were attempting to drive the French out of Vietnam. Truman wanted the U.S. to take major responsibility for turning back the tide. Before Congress in March of 1947, he announced what would come to be called the Truman Doctrine: that "it must be the policy of the United States to support free peoples who are resisting subjugation by armed minorities or by outside pressure."[4] It meant committing American money and even military advisors to nations anywhere in the world struggling with communist insurgents. It was the beginning of the Cold War, a struggle for which the United States was ill-prepared.

CONTAINMENT

For most of its history America had remained aloof from the power politics of Europe, concentrating instead on westward expansion, acquiring new territory by wresting it from Indians or purchasing it from foreign powers. Shielded by two great oceans and with weak neighbors to the north and south, the United States could afford the luxury of avoiding "entangling alliances" with European nations caught up in an endless game of shifting coalitions, a pursuit which Benjamin Franklin attributed more to the "pest of glory" than to an attempt to balance power to prevent war. As a result, America's foreign policy became both reactive and short-sighted. The nation mobilized with energy and moral fervor to meet perceived external threats, but resumed its preoccupation with internal affairs once the danger had passed. Long-term commitments and abiding alliances were seldom sought or maintained.

The policy had its critics, but it was not until the eve of World War Two that opinion began to shift in favor of increased involvement in world affairs. In 1940, in a commencement speech at the University of Virginia, President Roosevelt openly questioned the wisdom of America's isolationism. Trying to prepare Americans for entrance into the war, he warned that the United States could no longer remain an island of peace in a world of brute force: "Such an island represents to me and to the overwhelming majority of Americans today a helpless nightmare of a people without freedom—the nightmare of a people lodged in prison, handcuffed, hungry, and fed through the bars from day to day by the contemptuous, unpitying masters of other continents."

Once America entered the war, other voices were raised to prepare the country for world leadership after victory. The influential journalist Walter Lippmann touted America as the new center of Western civilization, charged with the responsibility of defending Europe from the jackboot Soviets. Congressmen from both sides of the aisle sought photo opportunities to affirm America's role as a world power and "a trustee for civilization." The idea appealed to the military. Jockeying to get a step up on the army, Frank Knox, Roosevelt's Secretary of the Navy, interpreted the charge as a sacred responsibility to "police the seven seas."[5]

The Second World War devastated the world's great powers. Only the United States emerged from the conflict unscathed. Not only had America escaped the bombs that obliterated the industrial base of nearly all of western Europe, the war had reinvigorated the nation's ailing economy. As John Maynard Keynes predicted, massive deficit spending cured America's depression. Midway through the war the federal deficit stood at an unprecedented 31 percent of GNP (in today's dollars, about $1.6 trillion). Borrowing to cover the imbalance, the government got its hands on, and promptly spent, the billions of dollars that had been squirreled away by cautious investors, prolonging the depression. Within four years the economy expanded by 64 percent. Unemployment, which stood at eighteen percent when the war started, was down to less than two percent at its end.

In military strength and economic might, America had become the most powerful nation on earth. A little muscle flexing was inevitable. Lacking both the international experience and habits of thought essential to successful diplomacy, the U.S. undertook the enormous task of containing communist expansion by mobilizing its military instead of upgrading its diplomatic corps.

As an idea, containment suited the American mindset. It did not require complicated or enduring alliances, for it was a task America would undertake alone. It was also essentially a concept of reaction. Only after the communists probed new regions would it be necessary to ponder the appropriate response to parry the thrust. No theoretical limits were placed on the countermeasures to be taken, no serious thought devoted to the possibility that such an open-ended commitment might seriously drain the nation's resources or create divisions among its citizens.[6]

This high resolve was in great part due to the religious-like zeal aroused by the contest of Marxist and liberal democratic principles. Communism had risen from the ashes of failed nationalism that preached racial and ethnic solidarity as an antidote for oppression. Nationalism fanned rebellions and revolutions, toppled governments, and gave people leaders who looked like themselves, spoke the same language or dialect, and harbored the same prejudices. But what nationalism could not do was cure the mass poverty that afflicted Europe throughout the adolescence of industrial capitalism. Capitalists everywhere, whatever their nationality, exploited workers, regardless of their nationality, suggesting true solidarity might be found in class rather than race or culture. For the Marxists the only real solution to mass poverty was an international movement of workers dedicated to replacing capitalism with communism, a great crusade by "the immense majority in the interest of the immense majority." The Bolshevik revolution gave this movement a home base, insuring its survival and a continuous flow of propaganda promoting communism as "the wave of the future."[7]

Being the wave of the future was a role America had reserved for itself. The Great Seal of the United States, designed in 1782, bears the motto *Novus Ordo Seclorum* (new order of the ages), reflecting the conviction that the American Revolution had forged an entirely new form of society, both politically free and without classes. These blessings were attributed to America's liberal democracy that combined limited government and respect for individual rights with a robust and open capitalism that rewarded hard work and talent. Such blessings made America a beacon to the world, in John Adams' words: "a grand scheme . . . for the illumination of the ignorant and the emancipation of the slavish part of mankind all over the world."[8]

Confidence in this judgment only deepened when decades of open immigration failed to generate the intense and bloody ethnic warfare that had plagued Europe following the abortive nationalist revolutions of 1848, uprisings that set the stage for fascism and the Second World War. The lesson in this seemed obvious. America had banished mass poverty and subdued ethnic passions. Founded on universal principles that transcend race, culture and religion, America's brand of liberal democracy could be adopted by any people anywhere on the earth.[9] Yet it was the French Revolution, and later the Russian Revolution, that drew all of the attention, "while the American Revolution, so triumphantly successful, . . . remained an event of little more than local importance."[10]

This dearth of attention helps explain the shrillness of America's anticommunist crusade of the 1950s and early 1960s. As Robert Heilbroner put it, it was "the fear of losing our place in the sun . . . that motivated a great deal of anti-Communism on which so much of our foreign policy" was founded.[11] Though drab and impoverished when compared to the United States, the Soviet Union had nevertheless become the inspiration for Third World revolutionaries, while America with all of its accomplishments and shining ideals was viewed by the same people as the enemy of freedom and progress. What went generally unnoticed by American policy makers was that what inspired these revolutionaries was not so much the supposed virtues of a communist society, but the Marxist hypothesis that colonialism was a natural outgrowth of the capitalist economic order and the most blatant expression of its capacity for exploitation.

Whether or not capitalism caused imperialism, it was certainly true that the workings of capitalism in the colonial territories of Asia and Africa had hardly been an uplifting experience for native populations. Long-standing bitterness for centuries of economic exploitation, coupled with resentment over cultural and political domination by the West, provided would-be revolutionaries with the tinder to ignite mass support for wars of independence. Marxism not only lent intellectual respectability to this collective rancor, it supplied readymade slogans to harness its energy and proven organizational techniques for capturing power. From the revolutionaries' perspective it was also an advantage that Marxism vindicated uncompromising autocratic rule. Having risked everything to capture power, few revolutionaries were disposed to gamble it away in democratic elections.

Lastly, Marxism gave revolutionaries a justification for imperialism. After relying on nationalist sentiment (and emphasizing the right of all people to ethnic and cultural self-determination) to topple colonial rule, revolutionaries could blithely undertake the military conquest of their neighbors, justifying the enterprise as an effort to expand communism, a doctrine that does not recognize nationality as a legitimate political ideal.

If resentment at being ignored brought passion to America's containment policy, the conviction that the Soviet Union posed as great a threat to world peace as had Nazi Germany lent it urgency. When members of Truman's cabinet "looked into Stalin's face they saw Hitler." Hitler's *Mein Kampf*, full of bluster and bizarre demonology, had not been taken seriously despite its blueprint for world conquest. The members of Truman's administration were hardly eager to repeat the same mistake with Stalin. Convinced that Stalin was a diehard Leninist, they faced the chilling fact that Lenin had proclaimed that war between communism and capitalism was inevitable.[12] Toward the end of the Second World War Stalin had boasted that Soviet industrial capacity and military technology would soon match America's own, a challenge that was interpreted by some as a declaration of World War Three.

The Truman administration had offered the Marshall Plan to Stalin in the hope that linking Russia's economy to the economies of the West might encourage moderation in his foreign policy. Stalin obviously needed the aid, having hamstrung his nation's recovery by squandering scarce resources to underwrite the occupation of the Balkans and eastern Europe. Yet Stalin flatly rejected the offer, which was proof to the Truman administration that he was more interested in spreading communism and totalitarian rule across the globe than in advancing the vital interests of his nation.[13]

GRADUALISM

It was a dispiriting assessment that ruled out moderation toward the Soviets. Communism had to be contained, regardless of the cost. And in these early years it was still possible to imagine that the costs of containment might be modest. Military strategists assured Truman that America's monopoly on atomic weapons was sufficient to counterbalance Russia's conventional military strength and serve as an effective deterrent to Soviet expansion.

The appraisal was faulty on both counts. Prior to the mid-1950s, America possessed only a handful of atomic bombs. In 1947, when Truman proclaimed America's commitment to contain communism, few of the atomic weapons in the nation's tiny nuclear arsenal were actually assembled and its new triggering device had yet to be tested with an actual explosion.[14] Even had the bombs been ready for use, there were too few of them to turn the tide in an all-out war with the Soviets.

Nor did America's nuclear threat curb Soviet expansionism. The atom bombs dropped on Hiroshima and Nagasaki were meant to terrorize the Russians as much as the Japanese, for at that moment Stalin was attempting to gain a foothold in Asia by invading Manchuria. Truman hoped the awesome power of the new weapons would encourage Stalin to have second thoughts. While "Stalin was frightened to the point of cowardice by news of the American atomic bomb," he did not call off the invasion, and Manchuria became a Soviet satellite. Stalin continued to suffer anxiety over America's nuclear monopoly and the superiority of America's air force, which he believed to be "the best in the world," yet he never allowed these fears to restrain Russia's imperialism.[15] Between 1947 and 1948, the Soviets sponsored a communist coup in Czechoslovakia, fomented revolution in Greece and Turkey, and cut Berlin off from the West.

Not only did the atom bomb fail to halt Soviet expansion, but within a few years the United States lost its monopoly on nuclear weapons. The Soviets had the bomb in 1949. Britain joined the nuclear club three years later, followed by France in 1960 and Communist China in 1964. Once the Soviet Union broke America's nuclear monopoly, it was a race between the two nations to outpace the other in total destructive force. By the late 1960s, MIRV technology (multiple, independently targetable re-entry vehicles) greatly magnified the number of warheads that could strike enemy targets. In the 1970s the U.S. expanded its stockpile of strategic warheads from four thousand to twelve thousand. By the mid-1980s, the U.S. possessed 27,000 nuclear weapons, compared to the Soviets' 21,000.[16]

Long before this point had been reached the two superpowers already possessed sufficient nuclear weapons to devastate each other's infrastructure and population, and in the process spread deadly radiation across the globe. This altered the concept of deterrence. America stockpiled nuclear weapons not to deter Soviet military adventurism, but to dissuade the Soviets from ever using their own bombs and missiles. Such weapons must never be used in war; to do so courted Armageddon.

This development changed the nature of conventional war. Total victory in an ordinary war was now considered perilous, for it might encourage the insane decision to retaliate with a nuclear attack. American strategists were slow to grasp these implications or to realize that containing communism could not be accomplished cheaply. Nor was it imagined that intelligent diplomacy might lighten the burden of policing the world. Instead, academic analysts developed a strategy of gradualism whereby military power was to be used sparingly and only slowly escalated, to permit the enemy time to negotiate a settlement before plunging into unlimited war.

Gradualism made sense on paper, for it was obviously dangerous to panic the Chinese or the Soviets into global thermonuclear warfare. But gradualism also hobbled America's military, making it impossible to conduct even limited war effectively. In testimony before congress during the Korean War, General Douglas MacArthur warned that if "you practice appeasement in the use of force, . . . you are doomed for disaster."[17] The strategy of gradualism ruled out aggressive countermeasures that might inflict sufficient damage to persuade an adversary to sue for peace.

This was certainly the effect of the strategy in Vietnam. "The signal Hanoi got was that the United States was not serious about fighting or ending the war in Vietnam."[18] By sending the wrong message, Washington unintentionally prolonged the war, which eventually destabilized domestic politics in the U.S. and strengthened the hand of the communists.

THE PROBLEM WITH ASIA

The original targets of the Truman Doctrine were the Soviet-sponsored civil wars in Turkey and Greece, but with the collapse of Chiang Kai-shek's anticommunist regime in China and North Korea's invasion of South Korea in July 1950, the focus of containment shifted to Asia.

America's experience in China should have made policy makers wary of involvement in Asian politics. During the Second World War, U.S. efforts to help China mount an effective defense against the Japanese proved daunting because China had no real national government. The country was a vast expanse of peasant villages, some ruled by warlords who exploited people mercilessly, others governed by nothing more than custom. To unify China militarily required unifying the Chinese politically. A true national government had to be created, one that could claim the allegiance of hundreds of millions and call upon them to fight, suffer, and die in defense of their country.

America threw its support behind Chiang Kai-shek. Stridently anticommunist and married to a Christian, Chiang was a figure with whom Americans could identify. Mao Zedong, who cared nothing for free markets or liberal democratic ideals, frightened them. Yet Mao knew how to mobilize the masses.

The Soviets had begun their revolution in Russia's great cities, then moved into the countryside to take control of the peasants. Defying the orders of his Soviet sponsors, Mao conducted his revolution in reverse order, starting in the countryside before moving on to China's industrial areas, major ports, and administrative centers.

Mao liberated peasant villages from corrupt warlords, enacted land reforms, absorbed villagers into his communist bureaucracy, created regional governments that ruled the peasants without corruption, and organized villagers into communist guerrilla units to further the conquest of new territories and the expansion of communist control. Mao had discovered the secret of rapid nation-building in peasant societies: establish local, then regional control of the population; then recruit the masses into communist liberation armies to maintain and expand control into new regions.

General Joseph Stilwell, the commander of U.S. and Chinese forces in Asia, tried unsuccessfully to have Chiang replaced with a more able leader, one who would sweep away corruption and reach out to the people by establishing a common front with communists and noncommunists alike, drawing upon nationalist sentiment to transcend the ideological conflicts ravaging Chinese politics. Stilwell's recommendations were ignored. Washington continued to give Chiang unquestioning support, and removed Stilwell from command.

Much of Asia, and especially French Indochina, was like China before 1949. True national governments did not exist and would have to be created before peasants could be expected to rally and turn back communism. But as the China experience demonstrated, America did not know how to create a government in an underdeveloped nation, or at least one capable of commanding the active loyalty and obedience of its subjects rather than mere sullen acquiescence.

Beneficent imperialism was an option, but only a theoretical one. America had successfully forced democracy on Japan and Germany at gunpoint after defeating them in war. This was not true nation-building; it only provided a new direction for existing governments. Still, it was a considerable achievement. Possibly even more could be accomplished with an American occupation army in Vietnam or Laos that not only engaged communist forces in the field but defended a democracy forced on the population, a democracy guided by American advisors and staffed by competent leaders recruited from the native population. Even if such an experiment could succeed, it would be blatantly imperialist and therefore morally unacceptable. The ideal of national self-determination, championed after the First World War by Woodrow Wilson,[19] had acquired the status of a reigning moral idea, making a well-intentioned imperialism politically unacceptable.[20]

Lacking the ability to spawn governments, and absent the will to force competent government on foreign populations, the U.S. vainly tried to strengthen weak regimes by increasing economic and military aid, essentially throwing money at the problem. Eisenhower's Secretary of State, John Foster Dulles, stated the position bluntly before the Senate Appropriations Committee in 1954. Characterizing Laos as a dike holding back the spread of communism into Southeast Asia, he said "the only thing we have to build that dike with is this money . . ."[21]

This approach only compounded the problem. The flood of money made it possible for native politicians to rule without the allegiance of citizens, for a subsidized budget made it unnecessary to gain voter approval for revenue to run the state. American aid also provided money for graft which insured the loyalty of bureaucrats, bought off potential opponents, and transformed the nation's military into a praetorian guard dedicated to protecting the regime from the people. Having backed and indirectly fostered ineffective leadership, the U.S. would inevitably be forced to use its own troops as proxies for patriotic peasants, who either did not exist or had already been co-opted by the communists.

The only other option, once things had gone this far, was to abandon the country in defeat and humiliation. But after 1949 it was unlikely that policy makers in Washington could easily abandon an Asian country once a commitment had been made to prevent it from going communist. Few could forget the enormous political backlash from the loss of China to the communists. Not only had conservative Democrats and Republicans vilified President Truman for having sharply reduced aid to Chiang Kai-shek's anticommunist nationalists, Senator Joseph McCarthy charged Truman with harboring communists in his administration. Under McCarthy's leadership, highly publicized congressional investigations of top personnel in the federal government ruined the careers of scores of professional bureaucrats. In the State Department alone, twenty foreign service officers lost their jobs. Truman never regained his popularity with the public or shook the lingering suspicion that he was soft on communism, despite his prompt response to communist aggression in Korea. In March 1952, with his popularity at an all-time low, Truman announced he would not seek a second term.[22]

Few politicians wanted to share Truman's fate, which is why they consistently ignored the pessimistic counsel of Asia scholars and listened instead to the less gloomy insights of political scientists and economists who imagined nation-building in Asia on a Western model to be entirely feasible. One of these economists, Walt Rostow, became an important advisor to the Kennedy administration. In a 1960 book, *The Process of Economic Growth*, he challenged the Marxist presumption that politics plays no significant role in economic development. Rostow argued, contrary to Marx, that the evolution from pre-capitalist society to industrial capitalism required a political commitment to pursue modernization in banking, capital investment, scientific research, and technology. Applied to the still undeveloped countries of Asia, Africa, and South America, this meant that prosperity lay with the rise to power of political leaders dedicated to modernization. Once these societies achieved "takeoff" into sustained economic growth they would, like the advanced capitalist societies of the West, raise average incomes and nullify the appeal of communism.[23]

Rostow's analysis has been confirmed by the economic success of South Korea, Taiwan, Hong Kong, Singapore, Malaysia, and Thailand. In each country semi-authoritarian regimes embraced modernization and purposely directed their economies to "export-led growth with great single-mindedness."[24] Within the span of fifteen to twenty years, each of these nations achieved a level of economic growth greatly exceeding that of the industrialized nations of the West and twice that of Japan.[25] As Rostow predicted, communism has had little appeal amidst such rising affluence.

But Rostow's theory offered little guidance for underdeveloped nations whose main problem was not a backward economy but the absence of a viable state. There must be real political leaders before there can be leaders who embrace modernization. Failing to grasp this distinction, Rostow imagined South Vietnam's salvation from communism would come from the Western educated elite commanding the nation's military, individuals who "knew the modern world."[26] Once they got into power (or once Washington pulled strings and put them into power), they would begin the process of modernization and set the country onto the path of sustained economic growth, saving it from communism. As it turned out, Rostow's elite neither had the will nor the capacity to command the allegiance of South Vietnam's peasant masses, and without the support of the peasants they could not defend the country from communist insurgents or turn back invading forces from North Vietnam. This task would fall by default to American soldiers.

The Korean war only helped to confuse matters. Unlike South Vietnam's fragile political regime, South Korea's government under Syngman Rhee enjoyed sufficient legitimacy to persuade South Koreans to fight with determination alongside American troops to turn back the North Koreans and Chinese, creating the false impression that other Asian nations could be expected to do the same. Also, the fact that the war was badly managed, and probably unnecessary, seemed to elude nearly everyone in Washington.

North Korea's invasion of South Korea posed no threat to the security interests of either Europe or America. Just prior to the invasion, Secretary of State Dean Acheson had officially proclaimed that South Korea was not a vital defense concern for the U.S. Yet once it was determined that the Soviet Union was behind the invasion, the U.S. felt obliged to employ military force to repulse the communists.

Not only was American involvement unnecessary, the predisposition to seek military solutions to political problems needlessly prolonged the war. After the counteroffensive at Inchon, America's military position in Korea was at its strongest, providing the communists an incentive to consider peace; but instead of entering negotiations, America further escalated the war, prompting the communists to respond in kind. The U.S. turned to diplomacy only after the enemy had marshaled its forces sufficiently to cause a stalemate. As peace talks commenced, the U.S. foolishly halted most military operations, losing all leverage to force the communists into a speedy settlement.[27] Over the next two years, the lives of thousands of American soldiers were squandered defending isolated firebases spread out over the 38th parallel. Only after the U.S. increased air attacks over North Korea did the communists finally sign a peace agreement.

Though badly managed, the Korean war announced America's willingness to commit ground troops in Asia, an ominous sign given Washington's growing interest in Indochina. Even before the Korean war, policy makers in Washington had expressed concern about containment in Southeast Asia. State Department analysts noted the large Chinese populations in the region, giving Communist China an obvious interest in expanding its influence into the area, which also happened to be the "greatest rice producing area in the world" and the source of "80 percent of the free world's supply of natural rubber and half of its tin."[28] In a memorandum that would play an important role in shaping thinking about Southeast Asia, the National Security Council announced what would come to be known as the domino theory, warning that Thailand and Burma "could be expected to fall under Communist domination if Indochina were controlled by a Communist-dominated government," leaving the rest of Southeast Asia "in grave hazard." The memorandum urged that "the Departments of State and Defense . . . prepare as a matter of priority a program of all practicable measures designed to protect U.S. interests in Indochina."[29]

Such thinking transformed France's desperate effort to retain its Indochinese empire into a holy war against world communism. France had already spent $11 billion on the war, and it was becoming more expensive by the day. The U.S. offered to subsidize the effort so France could stay in the game. By 1953 America was funding 78 percent of the costs of fighting the Viet Minh and would eventually contribute a total of $2.5 billion to the cause, more than France had received under the Marshall Plan to help rebuild its shattered economy.[30]

According to an early fact-finding mission, the military aid was not a wise investment. The study group submitted its report on Vietnam to American policy makers in late 1950. The report concluded that the French were so hated that the Vietnamese would support anyone, communist or otherwise, dedicated to expelling the French from Vietnam.[31]

Paul Mus had come to a similar conclusion two years earlier. A French scholar and expert on Indochina, Mus had represented France in negotiations with Ho Chi Minh in 1946 and 1947. Describing Ho as an "intransigent and incorruptible revolutionary, à la Saint-Just," he warned that Vietnamese peasants were not "a passive mass only interested in their daily bowl of rice, and terrorized into subversions by agents."[32] They were passionate nationalists, ripe for insurrection. As this was not the sort of advice French politicians wanted to hear, they ignored Mus' warning.

American policy makers were no more receptive to bad news than the French. Panicked by the spread of communism, they disregarded the recommendations of the fact-finding mission and gave the French full support. The futility of the enterprise would be confirmed at Dienbienphu.

DIENBIENPHU

On the morning of November 20th, 1953, two battalions of French paratroopers descended from the sky onto the western edge of an elongated foot-shaped basin known as Dienbienphu. The place was completely encircled by high mountains, a protective wall—or a trap, depending on your point of view. Rice grew in the basin, arranged in neat side-by-side paddies, a latticework of plots that covered the entire valley right up to the mountains. The only relief to this geometric regularity was the Namyoum River running a serpentine course down the middle of the basin, and Route 41 which ran parallel to the river and continued on to Laos only fifteen miles away.

It had been raining for more than a week when the legionnaires landed. The rainfall swelled the Namyoum to overflowing with coffee-colored runoff from the mountains, turning the valley into a sea of mud. The paratroopers slogged through the muck to take up defensive positions against incoming rifle fire and a mortar barrage. Dienbienphu was the headquarters of the elite Viet Minh 148th Independent Infantry Regiment. But as French intelligence had predicted, only a single battalion of the 148th was on hand to challenge the paratroopers. The battle raged for several hours until the French called in air strikes. After suffering heavy casualties, the Viet Minh battalion withdrew south and abandoned Dienbienphu.

By the end of the month nearly two thousand French troops were added to the original two battalions, and by early 1954 an additional thirteen thousand soldiers, including two hundred Hmong volunteers,[33] arrived to help with the building of fortifications and the construction of a kilometer-long airstrip. Work crews set up the garrison's headquarters at the west end of the valley and erected five defensive posts around its perimeter, with four more in forward positions. The code-names for the posts (Claudine,

Eliane, Dominique, Huguette, Francoise, Isabelle, Beatrice, Gabrielle, and Anne Marie) were drawn from a list of the base commander's past mistresses as a tribute to his overactive libido.

The garrisoning of Dienbienphu was important to the French for three reasons. First, the surrounding mountains were prime opium-growing country, and the Viet Minh had been extracting about a million dollars worth of the drug each year to help finance their army. The French intended to keep the opium out of enemy hands by taking command of Dienbienphu.

Second, the communists had been using Route 41 as an escape route to Laos, seeking sanctuary across the border after failed campaigns. More than once the French had surrounded Viet Minh divisions only to have the communists sacrifice small units to cover their retreat into Laos and safety. Also the French had become obsessed with keeping the Viet Minh out of Laos. Only a few months earlier the Viet Minh had moved the better part of three divisions over Route 41 and launched a full-scale invasion. Though driven back, the communists left troops behind in Laos' northeastern provinces with the clear intention of establishing a permanent presence for future operations. French military strategists in Hanoi had concluded that a powerful garrison at Dienbienphu would effectively block all movement into Laos, rendering a communist presence there useless.[34] To make the politicians happy, French strategists clothed the enterprise in high ideal. France had just signed a treaty of friendship with Laos, pledging to defend it against future invasions.[35] It was incumbent on the Expeditionary Corps to honor the nation's word.

Third and most important, the Corps' new commanding general, Henri Navarre, intended to lay a trap for the Viet Minh. By establishing a stronghold in their own territory, Navarre hoped to lure one of the Viet Minh's divisions into a major battle. With the garrison blocking its escape into Laos, Navarre meant to hold the division in place and decimate its troops.[36]

Navarre's plan was an act of desperation to achieve a major victory as quickly as possible. French public opinion had turned against the war. It was not a recent development. For some time French citizens had harbored doubts about the wisdom of maintaining a colony in Indochina. As early as 1947, a national opinion poll revealed that 42 percent of the French interviewed favored a negotiated settlement with the communists; 8 percent voiced the opinion that France should simply pull out of Indochina; only 36 percent were for staying the course no matter what the cost.[37] By 1953 the number in favor of abandoning the struggle had grown significantly.

In the minds of the French public, the war in Indochina had become *la sale guerre* (the dirty war), a struggle without honor, a conflict with too many defeats. University students staged mass demonstrations. Young men dodged the draft. New recruits deserted almost as soon as they were inducted into service, some literally jumping ship from troop transports steaming out of Marseilles harbor. Respect for servicemen was at an all-time low. It was not uncommon in Paris to witness French citizens spitting in the faces of returning soldiers, despising them for their brutality against the Vietnamese and for the fact that, even with their savagery, they were unable to defeat them.

Even more ominous was the furious clash of views in France's National Assembly only a month before Navarre began investing Dienbienphu with legionnaires. During the course of the debate it became clear that nearly all of the deputies to the assembly were in favor of a negotiated settlement, and disagreed only on how to go about it.[38] Navarre needed a major victory to turn things around.

For the Vietnamese communists Navarre's strategy was heaven-sent. As early as 1951 they had been testing French positions in the area, isolated posts "strewn in dribbles over roadless expanses at the end of precarious supply lines and far away from French airfields."[39] These earlier forays led the communists to the conclusion that the decisive battle of the war must be fought in this isolated region, where the French would face insurmountable difficulties maintaining supply lines and bringing in reinforcements. The communists had been biding their time, waiting for the right moment to begin what they hoped would be their last major offensive. With the French pouring men and supplies into Dienbienphu, that moment had arrived.

It did not cross Navarre's mind that Dienbienphu might be overwhelmed by the enemy. To accomplish this their commanding general, Giap, would have to field several divisions and bring in heavy artillery. Navarre found it inconceivable that the communists could supply such a force for any length of time, let alone lug dozens of pieces of artillery over hundreds of miles of jungle and mountain trails to reach Dienbienphu.

Yet this is precisely what happened. By employing more than a hundred thousand coolies for road construction and repair, one thousand trucks for transport (two hundred of them GM trucks captured by the Chinese from UN forces in Korea),[40] and 260,000 porters to carry rice, the communists were able to deliver 230 pieces of heavy artillery, thousands of tons of food, and hundreds of thousands of rounds of ammunition to the mountains overlooking the French garrison. Giap also mustered eighty thousand light infantry soldiers, enough to overwhelm the Expeditionary Corps' mere fifteen thousand troops. It would be a grossly uneven contest— precisely what Giap desired.

Far from the scene of the conflict, Ho Chi Minh was in his jungle headquarters talking to a British reporter. The journalist asked him about rumors of a great battle unfolding at a place called Dienbienphu. Before responding, Ho removed his white sun-helmet and set it upside down on the table before him. He slipped a hand into the bowl of the hat. "Dienbienphu is a valley," he said quietly. "And it's completely surrounded by mountains. The cream of the French expeditionary corps is down there." Ho ran his fingers along the rim of the hat. "And we are around the mountains. And they'll never get out."

Giap had his own words for what would happen. The French had guillotined his sister, hung his wife by her thumbs and beat her to death, and let his daughter die of neglect in one of their prisons. At his mountain headquarters overlooking Dienbienphu he confidently informed his staff: "We will take the French by the throat."[41]

It was the ideal moment for a devastating victory over the French. In just a month France, Great Britain, the Soviet Union, and China would meet at Geneva to discuss the future of Indochina. Defeating the French at Dienbienphu would give the communist side a decisive edge in the negotiations.

The French had intended to supply the garrison by air, but Viet Minh antiaircraft cannon reduced air supplies to a trickle. Low on food, medical supplies, and ammunition, the French faced withering attacks by enemy artillery hidden in dugouts in the hills surrounding the garrison. As many as three thousand shells fell on the garrison within the stretch of a single hour.[42] One soldier in the field hospital, his eyes still wide with terror, told the surgeon what he had experienced at Beatrice, one of the forward posts: "If you could have seen them, Major, thousands and thousands of them, jumping over each other, over the ones who were already dead, mowed down by our fire. Then the thousands of shells—when they had finished falling, half our shelters had collapsed."[43]

Viet Minh attacks followed a simple and unvarying pattern. Suicide squads of sappers, dragging bangalore torpedoes or carrying explosives strapped to their bodies, leaped onto the base's wire barricades and detonated the charges. Once there was a breach in the perimeter, massed troops streamed through. Behind them marched supporting units providing covering fire, poised to dash through the wire to join the storm troopers if the assault was going well, or cover them on their retreat if the legionnaires repulsed the charge.[44]

The mass assaults continued almost daily. The garrison's outposts fell, one by one. French losses mounted. The small forty-two bed hospital bunker, buried under four feet of earth, was unable to accommodate all of the wounded. Casualties were placed head-to-foot in roofed trenches waiting their turn on the operating table. The high number of battle deaths forced field surgeons to send all wounded, including amputees who could still fire a weapon, back to their posts to face the enemy.

Toward the end, one machine gun, a four-barrel weapon, was fired almost nonstop for several days, its spent shell casings carpeting the ground to a depth of three feet. By May 7, the French had lost thousands of men, hundreds of them piled up like cordwood on top of the morgue, a large square pit next to the hospital bunker.[45] With all forward posts overrun, the base's perimeter was reduced to the size of a baseball field. The French were out of food and medical supplies. There was no more ammunition. The communists simply walked in and took command.[46]

When the final count was in, French battle deaths numbered slightly under five thousand. The Vietnamese communists lost nearly five times that number.[47] These were horrific casualties to obtain victory, but the communists were willing to pay almost any price to win a battle that would end the war.

News of France's defeat reached Geneva, where negotiations were still in progress. It changed everything, and gave the communists the bargaining power they needed to bring an end to France's rule in Indochina. The timing of the communists had been perfect.

THE U.S. COMMITS TO SOUTHEAST ASIA

Defeat at Dienbienphu forced France to grant major concessions at Geneva: Vietnam was to be divided at the 17th parallel and North Vietnam would be recognized by the western powers as an independent state, momentarily segregating the communists in the north. The U.S. hoped it would be a permanent quarantine, though it did not seem likely. At the end of the Geneva Conference one of North Vietnam's delegates had boasted that if the war had gone on for another year the Viet Minh could have won all of Vietnam, Laos, and Cambodia. As they were arrogant and self-assured, it was unlikely the Viet Minh would tolerate being bottled up in the north for long.

The U.S. would not tolerate their breakout. Eisenhower was now president and as committed as Truman to turning back communism, portraying the struggle in cosmic dimensions as one of "freedom . . . pitted against slavery; lightness against the dark."[48] Eisenhower made it clear that the U.S. did not feel bound by the Geneva agreement and would not tolerate communist aggression in Southeast Asia. To demonstrate this resolve, only two months after the Geneva meetings the United States formed the Southeast Asia Treaty Organization (SEATO).

While fashioned on the model of NATO as a multilateral defense organization, the members of SEATO were not natural allies linked by contiguous boundaries and concerned with a potential invasion by the Soviet Union. Of SEATO's eight members (United States, Australia, Britain, France, New Zealand, Pakistan, Thailand, and the Philippines), only Thailand was a Southeast Asian nation. South Vietnam, Laos, and Cambodia were off the list because a mutual defense alliance between the three nations was explicitly prohibited by the 1954 Geneva Accords. SEATO was supposed to nullify this handicap through its pledge to confront military aggression in Southeast Asia. The difficulty was that, unlike NATO, the new treaty organization made no provision for a standing army. This was a serious defect and the tacit understanding was that the United States would assume this military responsibility, though the Eisenhower administration was eager to explore alternatives that would make doing so unnecessary.

A year before the fall of Dienbienphu, Eisenhower had urged the French to train, equip, and employ elements of the Vietnamese National Army to combat the Viet Minh.[49] The failure of the French to adopt this plan was later viewed by American military analysts as a factor contributing to their defeat. With the creation of SEATO, the idea of training native forces to turn back communist insurgents in Southeast Asia received renewed attention. The notion resonated with America's self-image as an enemy of colonialism. Also, if it proved successful, there would be no need to commit American forces to the region.

Beginning in 1955, the United States expanded its military and economic assistance programs in Thailand, South Vietnam, and Laos. Millions were spent in Thailand to double the size of the Thai army and beef up the nation's air force.[50] In South Vietnam, General John O'Daniel, head of the United States' Military Assistance Advisory Group (MAAG) for the country, set about organizing a seven-division South Vietnamese army.[51]

The United States was already supplying aid to Laos under a 1950 agreement,[52] but the amount was minuscule and haphazardly administered. When Ambassador Charles Yost arrived in Vientiane in 1954 there was only a single Foreign Service Officer in the country, who had no staff and did his own typing. To his dismay, Yost discovered that his official embassy headquarters was a rat-infested house with a leaky roof.

The following year Washington authorized a United States Operations Mission (USOM) for Laos. USOM's job was to take charge of administering aid to the country, which was about to increase dramatically. The organization's headquarters was a tent pitched in a Vientiane pasture. Secretary of State John Foster Dulles soon arrived to survey the progress. Appalled by the primitive conditions and the tiny skeleton crew assigned to handle matters, he immediately ordered increased funding and more personnel.

USOM's staff grew from twelve to eighty-two.[53] Millions in additional aid funds poured into the country, over $300 million by

1960, more U.S. aid per capita than for any other nation. It was the start of an eighteen-year military commitment that would cost billions and involve America in a secret war.

CREATING GRIEVANCES

Though Laos was a nation of peasant farmers, only a small fraction of the millions in American aid going to the country was earmarked for agricultural projects. Between 1955 and 1959 less than $1.4 million went for model farms, crop improvement, or soil conservation. The Royal Laotian Army, on the other hand, received almost $200 million in aid. By the end of the decade the RLA had grown from a motley ill-equipped force of seventeen thousand to a modern army of twenty-five thousand, with the dubious distinction of being the the only foreign military force in the world entirely financed by America.[54] The price tag for this growth was considerably larger than Washington was willing to admit. A good deal of the money was funneled through the CIA at the Defense Department's request, to conceal the total figure from Congress. Washington laundered even larger sums via a shell game called the Commodity Imports Program.[55]

This is how it worked. Instead of giving money directly to the Laotian government, Washington deposited millions in American banks under accounts in the name of the Laotian Treasury. This enabled the RLA to print bales of kip to meet expanding government and military payrolls without causing hyperinflation. For every thirty-five kip printed, the U.S. deposited an additional dollar into the secret Lao bank accounts, essentially backing the kip with the dollar at a ratio of thirty-five to one. The expanding bank accounts gave the RLA dollar denominated assets, which encouraged foreign firms to sell goods to Laos and accept payment in kip.

Only outsiders not privy to the scheme were utterly mystified by Laos' growing prosperity fueled by an ever-expanding money supply. Seigniorage (printing money to finance government debt) was not supposed to work. Germany had tried it in the early 1920s, with disastrous results. Within a two-year period the value of the German mark declined by 55,000 percent, essentially making it worthless. Not surprisingly, Germany's economy collapsed. The failed German experiment was supposed to be a demonstration of the foolishness of the policy to all nations for all time, yet it seemed the same policy was now mysteriously breathing life into the Laotian economy without significant ill effects.

There was actually an import side to the Commodity Imports money laundering scheme. Laotians with an import license could exchange kip for dollars at the ratio of thirty-five to one at the National Bank of Vientiane (created by the U.S. to make the Commodity Imports program possible), where the U.S. government had deposited millions to cover the transfers. The hope was that the dollars would be used to purchase foreign, preferably American, products. With goods flowing into Laos, and buffalo cartloads of kip circulating through the country to buy them, the standard of living in Laos was bound to rise, making communism less attractive.

Statistically, income per capita did rise rapidly, with nearly 86 percent of the increase due to American aid.[56] But the reality behind the statistics drew a different picture. Real income (income adjusted for inflation) of average Laotians living near major towns declined. Within two years the price of rice rose by 112 percent; the cost of chicken increased 300 percent.[57]

The inflation could be traced directly to the Laotian treasury flooding the country with new kip. Despite an informal agreement to harness the Laotian money supply to available American dollars, the number of kip put into circulation constantly overreached the ratio of thirty-five to one. Reflecting this imbalance, a black market in kip emerged with the exchange ratio hovering at about 120 kip per dollar.

Importers took full advantage of this disparity between the official and the black market exchange rates. A quick trip to the National Bank of Vientiane with 35,000 kip netted importers $1000 to buy foreign goods. These purchases were then sold on the open market at 120 kip to the dollar. Then it was back to the bank to exchange the 120,000 kip for $3,400, a neat profit of 240 percent. In the words of one journalist, "Laos' importers had found the secret of the philosopher's stone."[58]

Only a handful of Lao, those with the right connections, or the money to bribe officials, got import licenses and made fortunes. It had been hoped that the rapid increase in imports would help raise the standard of living, but ordinary Lao were too poor to buy the goods streaming into the country. Even the nation's wealthy elite could find little use for the "sleek Cadillacs, Buicks, and Fords" which the *Wall Street Journal* noted had suddenly appeared in sleepy Vientiane, for there were few paved roads in the country.[59] Radios and televisions were also a bad bargain, for Laos had almost no electricity. There was a small electric plant in Vientiane run with diesel furnaces, but almost the entire output of the plant went for illuminating the street lights along Lan Xang Avenue, the capital's main street. No power lines ran from the plant to homes or shops, which were lit by kerosene lamp.[60] Being of little use to the rich and beyond the means of the poor, most of the imported goods were ferried across the Mekong and marketed in Thailand, where a car owner could actually drive on a proper bitumen highway and television viewers could pick up a few channels, at least in Bangkok.

Even money set aside for ostensibly beneficial items like new roads somehow went astray. Washington had dedicated millions in aid for road construction, but much of the money wound up in the pockets of American businessmen who were better at fraud than at grading roads and laying asphalt. The main offender was Universal Construction, a company hastily organized in Bangkok by two American businessmen with a journeyman's understanding of the way business was conducted in the region. Using bribes, they landed millions in contracts, failed to build anything, and were awarded more contracts. Haynes Miller, an auditor on the scene, detected many of these irregularities and complained to Washington. His boss, Ambassador Parsons, ordered Miller back to the U.S., citing personality problems as the cause of the transfer.[61]

Designed to deliver money surreptitiously to the Laotian military, and defended as a way to raise the standard of living of average Laotians, the Commodity Imports Program wound up enriching the few at the expense of the many. Especially disastrous was the overnight wealth of the Lao elite, most highly visible as high-ranking officers in the military or ministers in the government.

Prior to American aid, the gap between rich and poor in Laos was one of the narrowest in Southeast Asia. Wealthy Laotians were not terribly rich and poverty was not grinding. This was a considerable achievement in a region of the world where, in the words of Gunnar Myrdal, officials were more or less expected to "exploit their position in order to make a gain for themselves, their family, or social group."[62]

The Commodity Imports Program brought an end to Laos' exceptionalism. Members of the Lao elite were soon building villas on the Mekong and being chauffeured through Vientiane in long black limousines. Domestic servants were in such demand that their average wage jumped by 130 percent. Meanwhile, rising inflation ate away at the standard of living of the average Laotian, widening the gap between rich and poor. In 1955 a Laotian farmer could take a pig to market and come home with "a shirt for himself, a shirt for his son, and a simple cotton skirt for his wife." By 1957, inflation had reduced his purchasing power to such an extent that if he took the same pig to market "he could return with only a shirt for himself."[63]

American aid was "creating grievances instead of eliminating them."[64] Charges of official corruption were so commonplace that the government ordered bureaucrats to attend more religious services to prove to the people that public servants were animated by something more than pecuniary interests. The communists could not have asked for better propaganda if they had arranged it themselves.

CORRUPTION IN THE MILITARY

The corruption set in motion by American economic aid spread to the military. Money simply did not reach soldiers. With few exceptions, prior to 1954 the officers in the RLA had all been French. Now they were all Laotian. Overnight, former sergeants had become colonels and generals. Lacking the tradition of an established officer corps to guide them, many allowed self-interest to dictate their conduct.

The army formed battalions and placed recruits on the payroll, but commanding officers often failed to call up flesh and blood soldiers for training or duty. The pay going to these phantom soldiers they pocketed for themselves. The worst offender was General Kot, commander of the 4th military region in the south. He built two mansions in Pakse, kept a harem in luxury, and bought tractors for his farm, all with money that was supposed to go to his troops, most of whom did not exist.[65]

Padding military rolls and pocketing the pay of nonexistent soldiers was a common practice in the declining years of the Roman empire. It had taken centuries for one of the best armies of the ancient world to slide into such corruption.[66] The modern Laotian Army, less than a decade old, inaugurated the practice as soon as American military aid made it feasible. It was not a good portent.

Even when soldiers actually reported for service, they received little training. In accordance with the Geneva treaty, the five thousands French soldiers attached to the Mission d'Organization de la Gendarmerie Royale were responsible for training the Laotian Army. Two training camps were planned, but only one of them ever became operational, and it was constantly understaffed. Having lost the colony, the French did not consider turning out crack Laotian infantrymen a priority. In any case, French soldiers attached to the Gendarmerie were preoccupied with quitting Laos for Algeria, where Arab freedom fighters faced a half-million French soldiers.[67] With Indochina lost, north Africa was now the place to advance a military career. Hours spent filling out requests for transfers left little time for drilling raw Laotian recruits.

The French would eventually acknowledge their complete indifference to the fate of the Laotian Army in 1961, when they finally closed the training camp and withdrew their forces from Laos. A small contingent of legionnaires remained behind, retiring from service to become mechanics and restaurateurs, soldiers of fortune, or narcotics traffickers.[68] A few would eventually return to military service as contract agents with the CIA.

PEO

From the start, Washington had no intention of granting the French military complete control over the training of Lao soldiers. To place the American military on the scene, in 1955 Washington created the Programs Evaluation Office (PEO). For appearance's sake, it was part of the United States Operations Mission (USOM), the organization overseeing the delivery of economic assistance to the country. In reality, PEO was a military assistance program headed by retired Brigadier General Rothwell H. Brown and served by a staff of professional soldiers, all dropped from the military rolls and posing as Foreign Service Officers for cover—though with so many ramrod backs and arms tattooed with mottoes such as "Third Infantry Forever," the masquerade was not entirely effective.[69]

PEO constantly grumbled over the Geneva mandated arrangement that put the French in charge of training RLA units. One complaint was that the French were not familiar with the American 50-caliber machine guns and 57-caliber recoilless rifles. It was hardly a valid objection, since the 50-caliber machine gun had been standard issue for French units since 1942 and the 57-mm rifle had been widely used by the French from the late 1940s.[70] The real, though unstated, objection was France's humiliating defeat in Vietnam, which was taken as proof that French soldiers were incompetent.

The French weren't doing much training in any case. PEO trips into the field confirmed this judgment. Laotian soldiers performed poorly against the Pathet Lao and were invariably routed by the North Vietnamese. Equally disconcerting, supplies and arms requisitioned for fighting units were not reaching soldiers; money simply disappeared.

After three years on the sidelines, watching the French sit on their hands, the PEO decided it was time to become directly involved. Brigadier General John Heintges, who had replaced Rothwell Brown as chief of the program in February 1959, convinced the Departments of State and Defense to authorize an additional five hundred military personnel to train RLA troops and join them on combat missions. Heintges recruited an elite unit of Filipino soldiers, all combat veterans of their own government's campaign against communist insurgents, to instruct RLA units in counterinsurgency techniques. He also brought in teams from the 7th Special Forces Group at Fort Bragg. Operating under the code-name White Star, they were organized into two groups: an elite combat battalion and a corps of twelve Field Training Teams (FTTs). The FTTs, eight to twelve men to a team, trained RLA units and irregular forces and led them into battle.[72]

The hands-on approach did not appreciably increase the RLA's battle readiness. The White Star teams found Laotian soldiers temperamentally unfit for war. They would do almost anything to avoid real combat, and used "tactical noise" (firing heavy weapons or stomping about in large groups) to warn the enemy of their presence in hopes of scaring the communists away. Lao troops from one White Star team fled the enemy with such regularity that someone in the PEO presented the team with fake patches for their troops that displayed crossed tennis shoes.[73] After months of frustration in the field, one American advisor assessed their progress: "Only a few months ago, the Laotians used to retreat without their weapons; now they take their weapons with them when they run away."[74]

It was an entirely different matter for White Star teams working with montagnards. The montagnards were eager to learn and impatient to engage the enemy. Colonel Arthur "Bull" Simons, the commander of White Star, began to shift more teams into the northeastern highlands to work with the Hmong and onto the Bolovens Plateau in the Laotian Panhandle to train Khmu tribesmen.

By 1961 the montagnards had proved themselves the only soldiers in Laos capable of defeating communists in the field. In the panhandle, five FTTs organized a Khmu force of six hundred men into light infantry companies. The Khmu recruits routed the Pathet Lao and drove them off the Bolovens Plateau.[75] Even more impressive were the accomplishments of Hmong montagnards in the north. In a fierce battle near the Plain of Jars, a single company of Hmong, facing a numerically superior force of well-armed North Vietnamese regulars, inflicted heavy casualties. These achievements, magnified by the dismal failures of the RLA, were difficult to ignore and would eventually force American military advisors to consign the RLA to minor operations and divert most of America's military support to the montagnards, primarily the Hmong.

5

BACKING THE WRONG MAN

Following his return from exile in 1949, Souvanna Phouma had quickly moved to the forefront of Laotian politics. Within two years he was prime minister; in two more he concluded negotiations with France that brought Laos full independence. Having tamed the French, he turned his energies to domesticating the Pathet Lao.

Souvanna assumed that the Pathet Lao were nationalists dressed up as communists, allied with the North Vietnamese out of convenience rather than conviction. National elections were scheduled for 1955. If Pathet Lao candidates won seats and shared power, it could legitimize the government for all Laotians and persuade the Pathet Lao to cut their ties to the North Vietnamese and perhaps spare Laos the agony of a civil war.

In mid-1954 Souvanna met with Souphanouvong at Kang Khay on the Plain of Jars. Souvanna urged his half-brother to put forward Pathet Lao candidates for the upcoming elections, and hinted that there would be a high place reserved for him in a coalition government. Though Souphanouvong had promised nothing, Souvanna left the meeting full of optimism. To his dismay, the Pathet Lao not only boycotted the elections but stepped up military action against the RLA.

In late 1957, Prince Phetsarath ended his self-imposed exile in Thailand and returned home. The old post of viceroy had been resurrected and held out to him as an enticement for repatriation. Once back in harness, he urged his two younger brothers to settle their differences. Following a series of meetings, Souvanna and Souphanouvong signed an accord to integrate the communists into the government. Souphanouvong assumed a ministerial post and Souvanna looked forward to the May 1958 elections with some confidence.

The Pathet Lao made government corruption the central issue of the campaign. Every year hundreds of millions in American aid dollars poured into the tiny country and nearly everyone high up in the government was skimming money. Even Souvanna Phouma, who now wore only expensive three-piece suits tailored in Paris, had a hand in the corruption. He had become one of the richest men in Laos, a considerable achievement for an individual who had once earned less than $2,500 a year as a civil servant. Souvanna was part owner in two banks and an airline, owned large tracts of land, was the proprietor of apartment buildings in Vientiane and Luang Prabang, and owned property in France. These holdings would mount over the years. By 1964 a listing of Souvanna's French assets alone filled a fat account book, their value amounting to about $2.25 million.[1]

Attempts by the government to refute America's corrupting influence were hampered by CIA efforts to rig the election. Agents were visiting villages in the countryside, purchasing votes for pro-American candidates. The agency also provided Rightist candidates with lines of credit so they could purchase gifts for voters or hand out money.[2] One element of the vote-buying effort was a program called Booster Shot. CIA operatives tried to convince villagers that the U.S. was all altruism and goodwill by digging wells, erecting flood control dams, and repairing roads.

The communists exposed the vote-buying as proof of America's wickedness. When the ballots were counted, the communists had garnered one-third of the popular vote and captured more than half of the contested seats in the national legislature. The Red Prince Souphanouvong emerged with the largest margin of victory of any candidate. In its first session, the national assembly elected him chairman of the legislature.

One place the communists made a poor showing was Xieng Khouang Province, where Touby stood for a seat in the assembly against a challenger put up by Faydang, a Hmong from his own clan named Foung Lo. Touby easily defeated his old nemesis' surrogate.[3]

The election returns stunned CIA and State Department officials assigned the task of steering Laos away from communism. Anti-communists still controlled the majority of the fifty-nine seats in the national assembly, but the unexpected strength of the Pathet Lao at the polls suggested the future of the Rightists was not bright.

The Eisenhower administration was unqualifiedly opposed to all coalitions that included communists. The spokesman for this position was Walter Robertson, Assistant Secretary of State for the Far East. Robertson held up the communist takeover of Czechoslovakia in 1948 as the definitive illustration of what happened when communists were allowed into a government.[4] In the Czech elections of 1946, communists received a third of the total votes cast, about the same percentage won by the Lao communists in the 1958 elections. It took only two years for the communists in Czechoslovakia to bring the government down and install Klement Gottwald, the head of the Czech communist party, as president.

The official line in Washington was that in the cold war one had to take sides. Neutralism was unacceptable. Eisenhower proclaimed it unimaginable that a reasonable person could stand "aloof from today's worldwide struggle between those who uphold government based upon human freedom and dignity, and those who consider man merely a pawn of the state."[5] Vice President Nixon tarred neutralism as equating freedom with tyranny.[6] John Foster Dulles, Eisenhower's stridently anticommunist secretary of state, saw it as simply immoral.[7]

Ambassador J. Graham Parson hewed the party line and was rewarded with a promotion to Assistant Secretary of State. Washington chose Horace Smith for his replacement. When Smith began his duties as ambassador in March 1958 it was presumed he would follow in Parson's footsteps as a staunch opponent of neutralism. This might have occurred if Smith had not had a falling out with Henry Hecksher, the new chief of the CIA station in Vientiane.

Hecksher was a replacement for Milton Clark, who had singlehandedly transformed the Vientiane station into a topnotch intelligence network, generating the only reliable information on military and political affairs in the country. Ambassador Parsons had relied on this intelligence to make policy, and even included Clark in policymaking sessions. When Hecksher took over for Clark, Ambassador Parsons continued to accord the CIA complete autonomy and worked with the new station chief as a partner rather than as a subordinate. This changed when Horace Smith took over the embassy. Smith demanded more control. He wanted only intelligence from the CIA, and excluded Hecksher from policymaking. Hecksher dug in his heels and the two began to feud.

Smith's battle with Hecksher led him to challenge the CIA's assumptions, including the necessity of defeating neutralism in any form. Less out of conviction than pique, Smith began to support Souvanna's efforts to maintain a coalition government. On this issue Smith stood alone. Behind his back the embassy staff supported the CIA's position, as did Washington. Over Smith's protests, Washington cut off all aid to the country. To get the money flowing again, the national assembly ousted Souvanna Phouma and replaced him with Phoui Sananikone, a diehard Rightist who proclaimed undying opposition to the coalition idea.

To insure Souvanna Phouma would not be around to stir up support for new experiments with neutralism, Sananikone sent him to Paris as ambassador to France.[8] Smith was also scheduled to leave, though a year would pass before Winthrop Brown would arrive in Vientiane to take over the reins of the embassy. Three different ambassadors within the space of a year might lead someone to imagine Washington did not have firm control of the situation.

Prodded by Washington, the new prime minister looked for a pretext to remove communist legislators from the national assembly. First Sananikone needed more power. In December 1958, NVA units invaded Laos and set up posts in Savannakhet Province. Sananikone milked the incursion for all it was worth. He demanded and received dictatorial powers for a year to rally the country to prepare for a possible full-scale invasion. The North Vietnamese had no intention of taking over Laos by force of arms— at least not yet. Their intentions were to occupy border territory to construct the Ho Chi Minh Trail.[9]

Part of the 1957 accord to integrate the Pathet Lao into the government was a provision to assimilate two Pathet Lao battalions into the RLA. Both battalions were still operating independently of the regular army. Sananikone had his pretext for cracking down on the communists. He set a twenty-four-hour deadline for the errant units to accept integration or surrender their arms. If they balked, Sananikone planned to use the disobedience as an excuse to purge the communists from the government.

RLA forces surrounded one of the two battalions billeted at Xieng Ngeun south of Luang Prabang. Hemmed in, the Pathet Lao commander complied with the ultimatum. The other battalion, encamped on the Plain of Jars in the old legionnaire post at Thong Hai Hin, had different plans.[10]

VANG PAO

After his company was dissolved in 1953, Vang Pao's new assignment was to work with Hmong volunteers. He formed a company of veterans from the old Malo maquis and engaged Pathet Lao and NVA troops trying to gain a foothold in the province. During one battle near Nong Het, Vang Pao was badly wounded in the leg. He healed just in time to lead a rescue team into North Vietnam to retrieve French survivors of Dienbienphu.

In early 1955, Vang Pao was again without a job. The French were withdrawing troops from Indochina and disbanding their various maquis operations to comply with the Geneva accords. Malo officially closed down in April. The French urged the Lao Army to absorb the maquis units (probably the best soldiers in the country) into the regular army, but the Laotians were reluctant to do so. Their only concession was to accept Vang Pao's volunteer unit as an irregular force, designated as the 21st Volunteer Battalion loosely attached to the regular army.

Vang Pao commanded the 21st for a year, then was pulled from the field to serve on the staff of the Chinaimo Military Camp. It was an opportunity to shake loose from special forces work with the Hmong and rise within the normal ranks of the RLA. After Chinaimo, Vang Pao returned to the Plain of Jars to direct the noncom school at Khang Khay. A year later he was promoted to major and given command of the RLA 10th Infantry Battalion, headquartered only a few miles from Thong Hai Hin, the billet of the Pathet Lao 2nd battalion under orders to integrate with the RLA.

Vang Pao visited the post to assess its intentions. He found the camp mobilized and prepared for military action. Guards in full combat dress confronted him at the gate. Machine guns were in place, bands of ammunition at the ready. Inside the camp he found NVA officers and an all-Hmong unit commanded by Saychou Tou Thao, the future commander of all Hmong forces in the Pathet Lao. Vang Pao knew the man by reputation only. Saychou had fought alongside Faydang against the French and was rumored to be a superior officer.[11] Colonel Chan Niem, a métis of T'ai-Vietnamese descent, commanded the post. Chan Niem was evasive when pressed about his plans. Vang Pao left the camp with the conviction that an operation would soon be underway, which he reported to his superiors.

Vang Pao set up camp on the summit overlooking Thong Hai Hin. Another RLA unit led by an ethnic Lao, Captain Vongsouvan Kettsana, was already on the move to guard the road to Ban Mone, the most likely avenue of the 2nd battalion's escape. Shortly after midnight, Vang Pao noticed flames rising below. He sent scouts to investigate and learned the communists had evacuated the camp and put it to the torch. Vang Pao set off in pursuit, hoping to drive Chan Niem right into Kettsana's lap.

Kettsana allowed the 2nd battalion to pass right under his nose without firing a shot. Vang Pao was dumbfounded, then livid. Kettsana blamed his failure to engage the enemy on his Buddhism, which prohibited the taking of human life. It was a common excuse for a timidity that guaranteed communist victories. Kettsana would later be assassinated in his home at Phong Savan by Pathet Lao soldiers, all fellow Lao and Buddhists.

Vang Pao quick-marched the 10th battalion through a pelting rainstorm to catch up with Chan Niem. On three occasions he closed briefly on the enemy, killing three Pathet Lao officers and wounding Chan Niem in the leg. Then the Pathet Lao battalion pulled away, making a sprint for the border. Vang Pao could not help but admire the brutal pace Chan Niem set for his fleeing battalion. Hmong could hardly march faster. This was high praise from a man renowned for his own incredible powers of endurance.

One of the traditions at the Dong Hene officer candidate school was a two-and-one-half-mile foot race in full uniform. Vang Pao had set the record, finishing in just fourteen minutes. He could still march nonstop at a quick pace for sixteen hours. Only Hmong troops could keep up with him. There were only a handful of Hmong in the 10th. The rest were ethnic Lao, and they were played out. Vang Pao paused to let them rest and to receive fresh airdropped supplies.

This delay enabled Chan Niem to widen the gap. The escaping battalion would have to cross the border mountains to enter Vietnam. Vang Pao took a detour, heading straight for Chant du Coq (Cock's Crow) mountain, where a narrow pass led directly into North Vietnam. He was certain that was where Chan Niem planned to cross. If he could get there first, it would be an ideal spot for an ambush. But the pause to rest his troops had allowed too much time to slip away. When Vang Pao arrived, Chan Niem was already in the pass, joined by a unit of Dac Cong commandos, the NVA's counterpart to America's Special Forces, suicide squads renowned for fighting to the last man. While the Pathet Lao 2nd battalion made its escape into Vietnam, Dac Cong moved into position to cover the battalion's withdrawal and pick off anyone foolish enough to follow.

Vang Pao was confident he could clear the NVA off the crests, but he couldn't do it alone. He asked for volunteers. None of the Lao in battalion stepped forward. They were terrified of the Dac Cong, much more so than they feared their own commander. They saw Vang Pao as their social inferior; from the moment he had assumed command of the 10th his authority over them had been tenuous. If Vang Pao ordered them into the pass, they would likely mutiny. To Vang Pao's relief, one of the Hmong in the battalion volunteered, an adjutant named Ndjouava Ly.

Vang Pao and Ndjouava Ly worked their way up the mountain, each providing cover for the other as they darted from one boulder to the next. They found the Dac Cong dug in, two men to a trench, the trenches spaced one behind the other at twenty-yard intervals. The two Vietnamese in the first trench spotted them and rose up to take aim, exposing their heads and shoulders. Before they could squeeze off a round, Vang Pao and Ndjouava cut them down. Vang Pao led his adjutant to the next trench, killed two more Dac Cong, and moved on, eliminating the enemy in one trench after another, as though it were a well-practiced drill. After they killed the twelfth Dac Cong, the remainder fled.

It took hours for Vang Pao to coax the rest of his battalion into the pass. By then Chan Niem was already well inside Vietnam, heading for the town of Muong Sen.[12]

COMMUNIST OFFENSIVE

Looking for a scapegoat, the RLA high command blamed Sang Kittirath, commander of MR II, for Chan Niem's escape. He was relieved of command and replaced by Colonel Khamkhong Bouddavong. On the political front, Sananikone blamed the communist deputies in the national assembly for the 2nd battalion's treachery, charging that they had conspired to prevent the 2nd from integrating into the regular army. He placed the communist deputies under house arrest. For the next eight months armed guards were on post round-the-clock at their Vientiane residences.

The Pathet Lao replied with bullets. The fighting first broke out in Sam Neua, where the communists maneuvered to crush every Royalist stronghold and isolate the province from the rest of the country. Led by NVA officers, the Pathet Lao committed only two thousand troops to the campaign,[13] making up for their lack of manpower with ingenuity and guile. The RLA's garrisons were mostly crude mud forts surrounded by trenchworks, and entirely dependent on local militias for the bulk of their troops. To unsettle these amateur soldiers, North Vietnamese agents circulated rumors in nearby towns of the overwhelming numerical superiority of the communist forces, lending an air of reality to the bluff by purchasing large stores of rice for phantom battalions. Panicked residents of towns and villages fled their homes and hid in the jungle. News of the empty towns reached the garrisons. Militiamen abandoned their posts in droves, some shooting their officers in the back before departing.

Even with the mass desertions, the Pathet Lao's offensive was mostly stillborn. Having launched the campaign in the rainy season, the communists moved at a snail's pace, making it difficult to rush in reinforcements where needed. Unexpectedly, the Royalist posts defending Sam Neua City put up a good fight. While undermanned Pathet Lao units fought heroically in miserable weather to dislodge the government forces, Royal Lao Air Force (RLAF) pilots kept the besieged posts alive, flying through monsoon rains between towering mountains in war surplus Beavers and C-47 transport planes to deliver fresh troops and supplies to the small grass airfield on the outskirts of the provincial capital.[14] Once the campaign fizzled, the Pathet Lao dispersed their forces and launched raids and harassing missions in nearly every province in the country, hoping to generate the perception that they controlled the countryside.

In the last phase of the offensive, running through August and September of 1959, the Pathet Lao returned to Sam Neua to try once again to route the Royalist garrisons.[15] Only two posts fell, those at Muong Het and Xieng Kho. Both were only a stone's throw from North Vietnam. NVA artillery set up just across the border pounded them for days. Ironically, when the cannons finished their work, it was Pathet Lao 2nd battalion, rested, replenished, and commanded by a Hmong, Colonel Saychou Tou Thao, that spearheaded the final assault.

Communication between the besieged posts and RLA headquarters in Vientiane was poor. Unable to determine the exact nature of the assault, imaginations in Vientiane played. There were rumors of an impending North Vietnamese onslaught comparable in scale to the 1953 Viet Minh invasion. A desperate Sananikone lashed out at the communist deputies who had been whiling away their days sipping tea in their living rooms under house arrest. After branding them all traitors, he had them rounded up and trucked to the Phone Kheng police camp just outside the capital so they could do hard time in cramped cells like common criminals.[16]

The staff at the American Embassy cheered the move. All along they had been lobbying Washington for increased military aid to support the Rightist cause. Sananikone's "get tough" posture was just the touch needed to loosen purse strings. Washington immediately authorized an additional $25 million to beef up the RLA.[17] As events would prove, it was a waste of money.

RIGHTIST COUP

Sananikone's year of dictatorship was scheduled to end in December of 1959. He asked the national assembly to extend his mandate through April of the next year, when new elections were to be held. He got what he asked for, but this time there was grumbling from the far right.

A clique of younger politicians and army officers, organized as the Committee for the Defense of the National Interest (CDNI), openly complained that the prime minister was dragging his feet in organizing a viable military response to the new Pathet Lao offensive. The CDNI's leader was Colonel Phoumi Nosavan, a CIA protégé. Station chief Hecksher had backed the CDNI since its inception, and pressured its members to present a united front and demand greater influence in the government.

Nettled by the clique's audacity, Sananikone purged all CDNI members from his cabinet, including Phoumi, who held the position of secretary of state for defense. Phoumi did not react well. With tacit CIA approval, he ordered his troops to take over all government buildings on December 25, 1959, staging what came to be known as the "Christmas Coup." Sananikone was at home at the time, peering through his windows at the troops in mottled battle fatigues surrounding his house and at the tanks and M-8 armored cars parked on his front lawn. He decided on an early retirement. Phoumi replaced Sananikone with the aged Vientiane politician Kou Abhay.

Phoumi had wanted to head the government himself. The CIA also thought it was a good idea. Ambassador Smith did not. It was one of the few times Washington supported Smith during his brief tenure as ambassador. The State Department worried about image. Laos was supposed to be a democracy. Allowing a military strongman to take over through a coup sent the wrong message. Phoumi would have to be satisfied dictating from behind the scenes.

Elections were scheduled for April 1960. To make sure communists won no seats, Phoumi raised the educational requirement for voters, increased the filing fee for candidacy, and redrew district lines in the northeastern provinces to dilute the electoral strength of the communists. Such tinkering reduced the total of eligible voters to a mere twenty thousand people, and eliminated nearly all opposition candidates. Out of the fifty-nine contested seats for the national assembly, the communists were able to put forward only nine challengers. Determined to leave no stone unturned, Phoumi took a page from the 1958 elections and, with full CIA support, sent teams of army officers into the countryside to buy votes with CIA money. CIA agents also got into the act. One U.S. Embassy official saw several agents "distribute bagfuls of money to village headmen."[18]

With communist politicians in jail, or hiding in northern provinces, they had difficulty campaigning—although it didn't matter, since the Rightists tampered rather freely with the ballots. One Pathet Lao candidate in the south received just four votes, even though five members of his immediate family had cast ballots.

Phoumi's American advisors were enormously satisfied with the election results. Less pleased, the Pathet Lao responded with a terrorist campaign that, in the end, amounted to little more than a few feeble assassination attempts on government officials and American diplomats. The communists did manage to kill one bureaucrat. The target had been an American official but the assassins bungled the job and inadvertently murdered a representative from the United Nations. The terrorists were thoughtful enough to post a letter to the victim's wife apologizing for the mistake.[19]

Phoumi judged the time right for a show trial for Souphanouvong and his fellow communist politicians languishing in cells at the Phone Kheng police camp. When the judges at the preliminary hearing found no legal grounds for initiating formal proceedings, Phoumi conspired to assassinate the prisoners under the ruse of an attempted escape. Souphanouvong learned of the plan from a sympathetic informant. Pathet Lao agents moved quickly to bribe the prison guards. Doors were left unlocked and warders looked the other way as Souphanouvong and the other communist deputies made their escape. A few months later the entire group was back at the Pathet Lao stronghold in Sam Neua Province.

The communists used the breakout for propaganda, claiming Souphanouvong had raised the revolutionary consciousness of the guards, "preaching in a simple way about the meaning of politics, about Laotian realities, and about the needs of the country," a "full course in political and civic thinking, based on national traditions and a social consciousness." Years later the fabrication was still in circulation, having become even more inflated with time: "The whole story of the escape, and the ideological preparatory work done by Souphanouvong in the seemingly impossible conditions of his imprisonment, is a worthy theme for a great novel of human adventure and courage, a thriller which no imagination could improve on. Once again it testified to the extraordinary qualities of this prince turned revolutionary."[20]

Though the escape of Souphanouvong and the other communist legislators was something of a setback, Phoumi was generally satisfied with the course of events. The communists were barred from politics and their leaders were in hiding. The Rightists were fully in charge. American policy makers congratulated themselves that real progress was being made at last.

KONG-LÊ

Just four months after the managed elections the Rightists were suddenly out of power and a diminutive twenty-six-year-old RLA colonel with a boyish face and toothy smile was in the driver's seat, declaring the Rightists and their American sponsors enemies of the state.

Colonel Kong-Lê commanded the RLA's 2nd Parachute Battalion. Widely viewed as the best unit in the army, the 2nd was known as the "fire brigade." The battalion repeatedly demonstrated its prowess in engagements against the communists, both in the rugged mountains of Sam Neua, where Kong-Lê was advised by two Filipino counterinsurgency veterans on contract with the CIA, and in the jungles of the Laotian Panhandle.[21]

The 2nd battalion was an American creation. Kong-Lê had received special training at the U.S. Army Ranger School in the Philippines to prepare him for command of the elite unit. He did not find the training an uplifting experience. He sensed that the instructors viewed Laotians as an inferior race. This set him to thinking. In the big picture Laos was merely a pawn in the Cold War. The Americans really didn't care about Laos or its people. It was then that Kong-Lê began pondering the feasibility of a coup. He was already an experienced coup-maker. Phoumi had used his "fire brigade" to occupy government buildings during the Christmas Coup, and later showed Kong-Lê contingency plans (likely worked up by the CIA) for a much larger military occupation of Vientiane. Everything was worked out to the last detail. It never occurred to Phoumi that Kong-Lê might use the plan to take over the government himself, for the young colonel had married his niece.

Kong-Lê was in Vientiane in early August 1960, recently returned from hard fighting in southern Laos. The army billeted his troops in shacks mired in the mud flats on the edge of the city. Kong-Lê complained of the miserable accommodations and that his troops hadn't been paid in two months. He was told building material would be delivered so his men could erect their own quarters. The construction supplies never arrived. Instead, the 2nd battalion was ordered back into the field to confront Pathet Lao forces operating northwest of the capital at Vang Vieng. Kong-Lê's battalion had been in the field for a year doing the only real fighting in the RLA. The new assignment was the last straw.

Except for the city's police force, Vientiane was defenseless. The government's top officials, as well as most of the army's leading generals, were away at Luang Prabang. King Sisavang Vong had died a year earlier after a fifty-four year reign. His eldest son, Savang Vatthana, had taken his place after a simple investiture ceremony at the Hotmam Sapha Wat in October 1959, with the crown prince seated on a rug in a modest white tunic, facing priests, Laotian Boy Scouts, and shoeless members of the diplomatic corps sitting uncomfortably cross-legged on the floor. Only one formality remained to make the transfer of the monarchy complete: the cremation of Sisavang Vong's remains. While Kong-Lê fumed on the mud flats, nearly every member of Laos' political and military elite were assembling at the royal palace at Luang Prabang to finalize arrangements for a state funeral for the deceased monarch.

On August 9, 1960, Kong-Lê's troops took over the radio station, all government offices, and Vientiane's power plant and airport. Taking command of the radio station was crucial to the coup. Kong-Lê had distributed transistor radios (purchased with American aid) to his men. Speaking over the radio station microphone, he guided individual platoons and squads to specified targets.[22] One unit occupied the army camp at Chinaimo outside Vientiane and commandeered the camp's armored cars and tanks.

A special detachment went to General Sounthone Patthammavong's new mansion to place the RLA's chief of staff under house arrest.[23] The only resistance was at the army camp. Two soldiers fired on Kong-Lê's troops and were killed.

The entire operation lasted only a few hours. Over the radio Kong-Lê addressed the nation, explaining his reasons for the coup: "Leaders of the government and armed forces have more than once announced that those engaged in bribery, those living off the labor of others and those advancing their interests at the people's expense would be punished. But these evils continue to appear."[24] As Kong-Lê spoke, jeeps and trucks circulated through the city, distributing leaflets denouncing those who had collaborated with the Americans as traitors "who would sell us to America."[25]

Two days later, in front of a packed audience seated on the weathered wooden bleachers of the soccer field that doubled as the Vientiane Sports Stadium, Kong-Lê defended neutralism as the only sure road to "peace in our nation," which he later interpreted to mean a virulent anti-Americanism. "It is the Americans," he proclaimed, "who have bought government officials and army commanders, and caused war and dissension in our country." Kong-Lê insisted it was imperative to "drive these sellers of the Fatherland out of the country as soon as possible." To stir up support he emptied Vientiane's jails and ordered the inmates, a few of them political prisoners but the majority petty criminals, to march through the streets toting placards bearing anti-American slogans.[26]

Fearing for their safety, Washington ordered the evacuation of seven hundred American civilian and military personnel and their families.[27] Some of the evacuees worried that the cars they left behind would be looted, so the automobiles were evacuated as well, taken across the Mekong to Thailand by ferry, six at a time, by employees of the United States Agency for International Development. As the Americans departed, Kong-Lê used the radio station as a personal forum to heap invective on former government ministers, attacking their corruption. In the charged atmosphere, most former bureaucrats stayed clear of the capital. The few who did show their faces were careful to leave their limousines in the garage and their chauffeurs at home and do their own driving in a borrowed Fiat or Morris Minor. The street agitation and radio broadcasts expressed the limits of Kong-Lê's political imagination. Having no idea how to implement neutralism, he turned the government over to Souvanna Phouma, who set about forming a cabinet.

Washington was understandably agitated by the anti-American demonstrations, and especially unhappy with Winthrop Brown, Smith's replacement as ambassador to Laos. Brown turned out to be no more of a team player than Smith. His sympathy for neutralism and personal friendship with Souvanna Phouma were viewed as partly responsible for the coup. He too would have to be replaced after a suitable interval. For the present, the only option available to Washington was to halt all economic aid to the country.

Sarit Thanarat, Thailand's ruler and Phoumi's cousin, had something more forceful in mind. He mobilized paratroops for an operation to take over the Laotian capital. American officials got wind of the plan and persuaded Sarit to call the operation off. However, Washington did allow Sarit to close the Nong Khai ferry that was Vientiane's economic lifeline. Ten thousand tons of U.S. aid material destined for Laos piled up in Bangkok warehouses. There were severe food shortages in Vientiane and in the nation's other major cities. The only exception was Savannakhet, the site of Phoumi's headquarters. Sarit insured that goods and military supplies continued to flow to his cousin.[28]

Souvanna turned to the Soviets for help. Russian transport planes crammed with crates of food began landing at Vientiane's Wat Tay Airport. Soon there was a Soviet embassy in the capital and, to the horror of the Americans, Souvanna opened talks with the Pathet Lao.

Since Ambassador Brown was not to be trusted, former ambassador Graham Parsons, an unbending foe of neutralism, was sent to Vientiane to speak with Souvanna. Parsons dogged the prime minister from home to office, urging him to break off talks with the communists and include Rightists in his government. Though Souvanna refused to end discussions with the communists, he agreed to allow Rightists in his cabinet. The concession was enough to persuade the State Department to back the new government.

PHOUMI IN CHARGE

Despite Washington's official endorsement, the CIA considered Laos' new government unacceptable. Desmond FitzGerald, head of the covert action branch of the agency, gave the green light to Gordon Jorgensen, the new Vientiane station chief, to bring the government down. Eager to prove his worth, Jorgensen canvassed the RLA's Rightist generals and settled on Phoumi Nosavan, already an experienced coup-maker, to mount a counter-coup and oust Souvanna Phouma and Kong-Lê from power.

Phoumi Nosavan was at Savannakhet in the panhandle, surrounded by his troops and advised by Jack Hasey, a former French legionnaire now working as an agent for the CIA. Four PEO officers soon arrived to offer their services to help plan the counter-coup.[29] They were joined by counterinsurgency specialists from the Thai military. The CIA flew in new uniforms, weapons, ammunition, armor, and artillery. Everything was in place. Phoumi even had the backing of most of the commanders in the RLA, working without pay since the cutoff of American aid. Phoumi came up with money owed them, courtesy of the CIA, delivered to Savannakhet in a Helio Courier carrying stacks of American dollars in C-ration boxes.[30]

In December 1960, just four months into Kong-Lê's coup, Phoumi led his troops toward Vientiane, accompanied by teams from the U.S. Army.[31] His column reached the outskirts of the city on the 13th. For thirty-six hours a Catholic church on the edge of Vientiane was the front line of the fighting. Kong-Lê's soldiers occupied the second floor of the church's school. Phoumi's troops were across the street in the cemetery, firing from behind tombstones.[32]

Driven from the church school, Kong-Lê's forces retreated into the capital. The fighting in the streets had a distinctive Lao flavor. Both armies were similarly clothed in American military fatigues. To tell friend from foe, it was agreed that Phoumi's men would wear white armbands and scarves and Kong-Lê's soldiers would wear red. Civilians quickly made armbands and scarves of white and red cloth, displaying the appropriate color depending on the ebb and flow of the battle.[33]

Phoumi possessed 104-mm howitzers, supplied by the Americans. Kong-Lê also had artillery, a gift from the Soviets and manned by crack North Vietnamese crews. Both sides began to unleash this firepower. The artillery duel killed six hundred civilians and reduced entire sections of the capital to rubble.[34] The devastation only delayed the inevitable. Hopelessly outnumbered and about to be overrun, Kong-Lê planted charges and blew up the city block that housed U.S. government offices. He then gathered his twelve hundred troops and Soviet artillery and fled north to Vang Vieng.

Phoumi was now in charge. As was so often the case in Asia, America had backed the wrong man. Phoumi's only strong point was his ambition. Though his family was one of the wealthiest in Savannakhet, it was not royalty, and this disbarred Phoumi from a career in national politics. This left him the military. Phoumi trained with the OSS and became a freedom fighter in the Lao Issara. Souphanouvong tried to recruit him into the Pathet Lao party organization, but Phoumi fancied himself a professional soldier and wanted nothing to do with politics, so Souphanouvong put him in contact with the Viet Minh. For two years Phoumi trained with Vietnamese guerrillas, preparing himself for life as a revolutionary soldier. It was a career move, having nothing to do with ideology. Then in 1949 Phoumi was confronted by a fateful choice. The Lao Issara were returning to Laos and former freedom fighters were welcome in the French-run national army. Phoumi pondered whether to stick with the communists or throw in with the French. A complete opportunist, his only concern was to back a winner, but at this early date it was difficult to see who would emerge victorious. Reportedly, Phoumi drew straws, got the long one and headed for Vientiane instead of Hanoi.[35]

The French took Phoumi on as a noncommissioned officer, promoted him to lieutenant in 1950, and four years later made him a major. When the Americans took over, Phoumi quickly advanced to the position of RLA chief of staff, a meteoric rise facilitated by family connections. The minister of defense, Kou Voravong, was Phoumi's cousin. Sarit Thanarat, a top general in the Thai army (and soon to be the ruler of Thailand) was also a cousin with a personal interest in Phoumi's career.

Enjoying such success in the military, Phoumi gave no serious thought to politics until Prince Boun Oum took him on as his personal protégé. The tall, rugged-looking prince was heir to the defunct Champassak throne and a favorite with American reporters, who described him as a "Lao version of John Wayne."[36] The view at the time was that Boun Oum was a rising star and that Phoumi had grabbed on to his coattails. But the relationship soon became a case of the tail wagging the dog. Phoumi learned how to posture as a rabid anticommunist to curry favor with the Americans, and it paid off handsomely. With American (and especially CIA) support, Phoumi soon had no need of Boun Oum's sponsorship to obtain power. Phoumi's final act of emancipation from Boun Oum's tutelage was to appoint the prince prime minister, using him as a puppet and mouthpiece for his military dictatorship.

Immediately following the coup, Phoumi's American advisors begged him to go after Kong-Lê and finish him off, but Phoumi refused. He wanted time to relish his victory with lavish celebrations. Also, he was reluctant to leave Vientiane in the hands of his deputy, Colonel Kouprasith Abhay. Abhay had played a key role in the coup, having committed his own troops to Vientiane before Phoumi's arrival. The man was an ally, but he was also ambitious. Fearing Abhay might attempt to liberate the city a second time in his absence, Phoumi wanted to consolidate his power before leaving Vientiane for the field.

The delay enabled the communists to contact Kong-Lê and bring him into their camp, not as a communist but as an ally against Phoumi and the Rightists of the CDNI. The Soviets initiated airlifts to deliver supplies to Kong-Lê's troops and his Pathet Lao supporters. By U.S. intelligence estimates, the Russians flew 184 supply missions. A Soviet official would later reveal that it was Moscow's largest supply operation since the Second World War.[37] The Russians delivered North Vietnamese commandos as well as weapons. Entire companies of these elite soldiers integrated into Kong-Lê's tiny army, headquartered on the southern edge of the Plain of Jars.

Though Phoumi had extensive military training, including a stint at France's École Supérieure de Guerre, he was not an adroit tactician. When he finally moved against the Neutralists it was at an extremely leisurely pace, covering a mere sixty-five miles in twenty-nine days. The glacial speed was due in part to Phoumi's insistence that his new armored vehicles (a gift from the Americans) lead the column. This tied him to the roads, more suitable to ox carts than armored cars, offering numerous opportunities for Kong-Lê to put his store of land mines to good use.[38]

The advance of Phoumi's columns was also slowed by a widespread unwillingness to engage the enemy. There were numerous and unverified reports of several North Vietnamese divisions, including the 316th, which had fought at Dienbienphu, rushing into Laos to join the conflict.[39] It was one thing to face a few North Vietnamese soldiers integrated into Kong-Lê's forces, but the prospect of going toe-to-toe with entire divisions of battle-hardened Vietnamese regulars had RLA soldiers and their officers looking nervously over their shoulders toward Vientiane and safety.

There were many desertions. One unit, led by an armored car and moving sluggishly along Route 13, ran into an ambush north of Hin Heup. The column sped up and emerged from the trap with slight damage. Five kilometers away, the column ran into another ambush. This time the enemy's aim was a little better and there were casualties. As the commander of the column would later report: "My intelligence officer soon decided he enjoyed life in Vientiane a little more than the excitement of Route 13 and he disappeared."[40] Once the fighting heated up, such disappearances became endemic, especially for units going into battle without their officers, who were still behind the lines "crawling out of the brothels around noon each day."[41] Things might have been different with more competent commanders, though American military advisors on the scene could not help but observe that "it is impossible to exaggerate the incompetence—and frequently the cowardice—of the Royal Lao Army."[42]

The sentiment reached the press. In the last week of January 1961, an article in *Time* magazine described the fighting as an American-backed army of nearly thirty thousand routinely routed by a three-hundred-man force led by a former captain in the RLA. Phoumi couldn't win battles, but he was able to have the issue of the magazine banned from Laos.

FIRST AMERICAN POW

The fighting slowed in February, presenting an opportunity for both sides to consolidate their forces. To get a better idea of the disposition of communist units, the U.S. employed a newly modified SC-47 reconnaissance plane to photograph the Plain of Jars. For nearly a month the SC-47 crisscrossed the plain, taking pictures with a state-of-the-art K-17 camera and searching with advanced radio direction-finding gear for the Soviet radio beacon guiding Ilyushin-14 transport planes, in good weather and bad, to the Xieng Khouangville airport. Knocking out the beacon was a high priority. The Ilyushins were delivering crates of AK-47s, Molotova trucks, armored cars, and 37-mm radar-directed antiaircraft guns, accompanied by teams of NVA technicians to operate them.[43]

Photos from the reconnaissance flights revealed that the communists were doing more than increasing their troops' strength. An army of bureaucrats had moved onto the plain. The Soviets had set up a small embassy at Kang Khay. The Chinese had a cultural and economic mission at Xieng Khouangville and another economic mission at Khang Khay headed (as later intelligence revealed) by an officer of the People's Liberation Army.[44] Less impressive, but in clear view, was North Vietnam's small information office located at the end of the single block business section of Phong Savan, close by the NVA's new field hospital.

On March 23, 1961, the SC-47 was again flying over the plain searching for the Soviet beacon. As the plane passed over Phong Savan, recently delivered antiaircraft guns opened up below. One of the shells ripped into the SC-47's right wing, bursting a fuel tank. Flames gushed from the gaping hole. Liquefied metal was spewed into the air. Realizing the plane's spar was melting, the crew rushed for the stowed parachutes. Only Colonel Lawrence Bailey Jr. made it through the open side door before the wing snapped off and the SC-47 nosed into a tight spiral to the ground.[45]

Bailey wasn't part of the SC-47's regular six-man crew. His job as an assistant army attaché was to pilot a twin-engine Beechcraft, flying Ambassador Brown and other embassy staff to meetings in Thailand and South Vietnam. Bailey had hitched a ride on the SC-47 to get to Saigon where his Beechcraft was waiting, refitted with a new engine. The flight was considered a milk run, a quick cruise over the Plain of Jars for some pictures and radio beacon hunting, then on to Saigon. Bailey was the only one on board wearing a parachute—the backpack variety, cumbersome to put on and uncomfortable to wear, and the only one on the plane. The crew preferred the chest-pack parachutes stored in the forward bulkhead; they were easy to slip on and were quickly secured with only a few snaps. Unfortunately for the crew, the SC-47's wing broke off before they could reach the stored parachutes.

When Bailey jumped from the doomed aircraft he was caught up in a vortex of burning metal. A chunk of the disintegrating plane slammed into his left side, breaking his arm. Unable to maneuver his chute, he floated with the wind. The currents carried him to a grassy field and deposited him next to a startled water buffalo. The huge animal lumbered off, leaving Bailey flat on his back trying desperately to get up. His legs were badly bruised and he was unable to stand. With only one free hand, he used the shroud lines of the parachute to immobilize his broken arm by tying it to his side.

An airplane appeared on the horizon, flying a search pattern. It was a DeHavilland L-20 Beaver sent to check on the downed SC-47. The Beaver disappeared without sighting Bailey. A few hours later Bailey heard soldiers shouting to each other. A dozen appeared over a ridge line. They were Neutralists, nearly all of them teenagers, more frightened of Bailey than he was of them. The soldiers approached cautiously and surrounded him.

After screwing up their courage by waving rifles and firing over Bailey's head, the soldiers searched him and took his wallet, pocket knife, cigarettes, and shoes. The teenagers giggled as they showed off their trophies to each other. Feeling in control now, they took Bailey to the new NVA field hospital at Phong Savan. English-speaking North Vietnamese doctors attended to Bailey's wounds and casted his arm.

Bailey was bedridden for a week. As he lay on his cot in a haze from pain-killing medication, an intelligence officer pumped him for information about the location of the U.S. Seventh Fleet and other matters which he knew absolutely nothing about. Bailey entertained himself by inventing answers, changing them from one day to the next. To his surprise, a Chinese reporter from the *New*

China News Agency arrived to conduct an interview and wound up lecturing Bailey about U.S imperialism.

Once the doctors decided he was well enough to be moved, Bailey was flown to Sam Neua City and confined to a tiny cell, fed starvation rations, and kept constantly under guard. For several weeks a Pathet Lao officer came to the cell to spend the day questioning Bailey about the war. Then the officer disappeared and Bailey was left alone, watched over by sullen guards, who Bailey decided were just peasants in uniforms. Bailey was the Pathet Lao's first American POW and they really didn't know what to do with him.[46] For the next year and half he would remain in his cramped cell, guarded but generally ignored.

The downing of the SC-47 crippled Washington's ability to maintain a steady flow of intelligence on communist activities on the plain, intelligence that was essential for assessing policy options. Washington quickly replaced the SC-47 with more advanced, and less vulnerable, RT-33 reconnaissance jets.[47] Photos from the new reconnaissance planes revealed the communists were continuing their buildup, apparently preparing for a major offensive.

NEW COMMUNIST OFFENSIVE

The offensive began in early April. Backed by Kong-Lê's troops and seven battalions of NVA,[48] the Pathet Lao easily overwhelmed Phoumi's forces in every engagement. Phoumi retreated in disarray toward the capital. Within a month the communists occupied nearly all of the Plain of Jars and were making inroads into five provinces.

The loss of the plain was a serious concern, for it was one of the few areas in northern Laos where the Vietnamese could make good use of their Russian tanks. It was also the hub of the nation's primitive road network, putting the enemy in position to command all land communication in northern Laos, and opening a direct link to North Vietnam (Routes 6 and 7 ran from North Vietnam's border to the Plain of Jars). There was another danger. West of the plain, Route 7 intersected Route 13, the highway linking Luang Prabang and Vientiane. Should the communists gain control of the intersection they could mount an assault against the nation's political capital, or move north to occupy the seat of the nation's ancient monarchy.

As if anticipating America's worst fears, during the second week of their offensive the Neutralists and Pathet Lao occupied Sala Phu Khun at the crucial crossroads of Routes 7 and 13. Phoumi was up against a wall. So were his American advisors. On the direct authorization of President Kennedy, the PEO cast aside its cover as a civilian aid mission and assumed the mantle of the United States Military Assistance Advisory Group for Laos (MAAG/ Laos). Special Forces soldiers exchanged sport shirts for military uniforms and took to the field to lead RLA troops into battle.

In an air cavalry operation, CIA helicopters delivered Special Forces advisors and two Lao battalions to Muong Kassy, north of Vientiane, to head off the enemy force, which by now had pushed beyond Sala Phu Khun and was pressing down Route 13. Two Lao regiments were scheduled to join the blocking force, but as the days passed and the communists closed their distance it was clear the regiments would not show. Isolated and undermanned, the Special Forces officers had no choice but to order a withdrawal.

Farther south other American military advisors did their best to get the two irresolute Lao regiments to advance to their preassigned blocking position. By April 22, the two regiments had advanced no further than Vang Vieng. There, an entire regiment of Pathet Lao with armor slammed into the RLA force and overran the town. American military advisors struggled to organize an orderly retreat but the Lao troops fled in a panic, abandoning the Americans to face the enemy alone.

Captain Walter Moon and his Special Forces team were in an armored car at the head of one of the regiments when the communists unleashed their assault. Artillery shells raked the column. There was small arms fire from both sides of the road. Moon watched the entire regiment bolt from the highway into the jungle, leaving his team to fend for itself. He turned the armored car around and sped south straight into an ambush of automatic weapons and grenades. The salvo killed two of his team members riding on the top of the armored car and disabled the vehicle. Moon and Sergeant Orville Ballenger leapt from the car into a ditch. Pathet Lao soldiers swarmed over them. Within a few days both Moon and Ballenger were at Lat Houang on the Plain of Jars, imprisoned in an abandoned USAID agricultural aid station. Because he kept trying to escape, the communists executed Moon. Ballenger became a prisoner of war.[49]

While the Pathet Lao at Vang Vieng were busy routing RLA troops and taking American prisoners, NVA units stormed RLA garrisons near the river town of Paksane. As at Vang Vieng, the Lao soldiers broke and ran, scurrying for the Mekong.[50] This second humiliation dashed any hope the Americans might have had of relying on the RLA to turn back the communists.

Earlier, in September 1959, the PEO had already begun to hedge its bets by training and arming Hmong guerrillas. PEO had established a training base near Khang Khay on the Plain of Jars, and PEO advisors worked with Hmong guerrilla units in the field. Vang Pao led one of these units, his new job since losing command of the 10th infantry battalion. By early 1960, PEO advisors had singled out Vang Pao as their choice to command a Hmong paramilitary army. To bolster Vang Pao's standing with his people, PEO delivered helicopter-loads of food and supplies to Vang Pao for distribution to Hmong communities.[51]

The PEO's investment in the Hmong was still minuscule when compared to the vast resources going to the RLA. And most of it dried up after Kong-Lê's coup. Attention shifted to Phoumi's forces at Savannakhet and the campaign to assault Vientiane and oust the Neutralists. It left Vang Pao with impression that the Americans were an unreliable source of support and that if there was ever to be a Hmong army, he would have to raise it on his own.

6

COLONEL BILLY
DISCOVERS VANG PAO

Kong-Lê's coup put the Neutralists in power for only four months. During this brief period the communists positioned troops to crush RLA forces in Sam Neua and Xieng Khouang provinces, an area designated on military maps as MR II (2nd Military Region).[1] Khong Vongnarath commanded three of the RLA battalions in Sam Neua targeted for elimination by the Pathet Lao. When the assault began, Vongnarath immediately retreated south to avoid annihilation. The communists gave chase and caught up. Vongnarath ordered his troops to dig in and fight for their lives. As the battle raged he radioed Vientiane to plead for relief. The RLA high command now took its orders from Souvanna Phouma, who relied on handouts from the Soviets to keep his government afloat. Vongnarath was informed he was on his own. Encircled by the enemy, and cut off from his supply lines and suffering heavy casualties, he surrendered.

Farther south on the Plain of Jars, another Royalist commander kept close to his field radio for updates on Vongnarath's situation. Colonel Khambou Boussarath was not unduly alarmed when he learned of Vongnarath's surrender. Unlike Vongnarath, Boussarath had cast his lot with the Neutralists. With Souvanna Phouma making overtures to the communists, Boussarath presumed the Pathet Lao and North Vietnamese would view him more as an ally than a threat. Boussarath began to re-examine this assumption when thousands of exhausted refugees from Sam Neua straggled onto the Plain of Jars. The refugees told of a concerted effort by the communists to establish complete administrative control over Sam Neua.

Shortly after the refugees arrived, NVA units appeared on the plain, clearly maneuvering to envelop Boussarath's forces. Boussarath appealed to Vang Pao to rally the Hmong and come to his aid. Since Boussarath had good reason to despise Vang Pao, the request was truly an act of desperation. Vang Pao refused to budge though not because of the bad blood between Boussarath and himself. Vang Pao desperately wanted to lead Hmong against the communists. Thousands of Hmong were ready to follow him, if only he would give the signal. He held back because all of the pieces were not yet in place.

VANG PAO'S PLAN TO REVIVE MALO

When Kong-Lê first seized power, Vang Pao had watched the Pathet Lao consolidate their forces in Sam Neua with foreboding. It was obvious they would take advantage of the political chaos to eventually seize control of the Plain of Jars. If Phoumi remained in the south, there would be nothing to prevent it. Vang Pao's plan was to organize a Hmong guerrilla army and harass the communists once they entered the plain, cut their supply lines, and bog them down. The manpower for the army would come from the Hmong villages surrounding the plain. At the right moment, thousands of villagers would relocate to strategic locations, organize guerrilla units, receive weapons and training, and begin operations.

It was not an original idea. Seven years earlier Vang Pao had served in the French-run Malo maquis, organized by a veteran French Special Services officer named Max Mesnier. Mesnier had established six base camps at strategic locations around the Plain of Jars: one west of Nong Het, another on the southeastern rim of the plain, and four additional camps at Phou Dou, Moung Hiem, Tha Lin Noi, and Muong Ngan. Running operations out of these sites, Mesnier and his Malo guerrillas easily checked the Pathet Lao and Viet Minh at every move and drove them across the border into Vietnam. Recalling the success of Malo, Vang Pao borrowed Mesnier's ideas with only slight modification. Instead of six bases Vang Pao chose seven, though five of his strategic locations were identical to, or just a few miles away from, Mesnier's original sites.

Unlike Mesnier, who was able to rely on the GCMA for arms and supplies, Vang Pao was on his own—support from PEO had mostly disappeared and he could expect nothing from the RLA. Reviving Malo was possible only if thousands of Hmong offered their support, especially those living on the eastern half of the Plain of Jars, for it would be from them that the guerrillas would be drawn, individuals who knew the area intimately and would be able to count on nearby villages for food, supplies, sanctuary, and intelligence on enemy activity. The problem was getting them to back the plan, for Vang Pao lacked the stature, as well as the raw power, to insure their collaboration. He was admired, of course, as the only Hmong officer in the RLA, but this was purely a matter of ethnic pride. Actually, he was not particularly popular, especially among those whose opinion carried weight, and changing those opinions was difficult.

Later, after assuming command of his own Hmong army, and with the full backing of the CIA, it would still be some time before Vang Pao could command the level of respect Touby had enjoyed at the height of his own political career. Vinton Lawrence, a CIA agent who worked at Vang Pao's side when the Hmong secret army was in its infancy, was amazed by the utter lack of respect shown to Vang Pao by ordinary Hmong. "There was absolutely no barrier of deference given to Vang Pao by the people." Hmong would march in and scream at him "for this, for that, and the other thing."[2] The day would eventually come when only a handful of Hmong, all close political associates, would ever dare to dress down Vang Pao in public. However, at this early date Vang Pao was painfully aware that he lacked serious standing. Many considered him something of an upstart. Also, his clan was tainted with sin. But most important, since he was from Nong Het and Touby's protégé, Hmong living on the Plain of Jars simply did not trust him.

Though born to a poor family Vang Pao found a sponsor, Chao Saykham (the future governor of Xieng Khouang),[3] to pay his tuition so he could attend the private primary school at Nong Het. As a teenager, Vang Pao persuaded Touby to give him a job as translator and messenger for French commandos, duty that earned him a position in the French-run Laotian Gendarmerie where French officers took him under their wing and got him into the officer candidate school at Dong Hene. Always Vang Pao was advancing, but never could he rise far enough. His was the sort of ambition that invited censure.

When Vang Pao broke custom by burying his father beside a major road (he had done so on the advice of a shaman), an elder of the Ly clan took it as a deliberate act of haughtiness; a normal burial site was not good enough for the father of the self-important Vang Pao. Standing before the gravesite, the Ly elder had grumbled, "Vang Pao is a fool if he thinks he has the makings of a great leader." This grousing led to a comedy of errors. Vang Pao's hard-of-hearing aunt reported back that the Ly clansman had prophesied that Vang Pao would one day become a great leader. When ants swarmed over the grave and worked it into a giant mound fourteen feet high, Vang Pao took it as a sign that the Ly clansman was indeed a prophet. Years later when Vang Pao was in his full power and the Ly elder had fallen on hard times, Vang Pao provided a pension to keep him in modest comfort and support his opium habit. Only on his deathbed did the Ly elder reveal the truth to Vang Pao, who considered the whole incident a great joke on himself.

In addition to his ambition, Vang Pao was tainted because he was a Vang. Rigidly exogamous, Hmong must marry outside of their clan. Any deviation, even between distant cousins, was considered incest and viewed with revulsion. Hmong who committed this sin were uniformly ostracized by both their clan and general Hmong society.[4] Of all the clans, only the Vang failed to religiously honor this taboo. The principal offenders were Vang clansmen at Sam Thong and Long Cheng, whose easy tolerance of clan incest scandalized the other clans and spread shame to all Vang.[5]

Then there was the fact that Vang Pao was from Nong Het. Hmong living at Phong Savan, Nong Pet, Pha Kha and other Hmong villages on the Plain of Jars referred to Nong Het Hmong as "pla law" (*plab laoj*), or greedy, because they welshed on debts. Living close to the Vietnam border, and with relatives on the other side, they sometimes migrated to Vietnam to avoid honoring their financial obligations. The moral was that Nong Het Hmong were not to be trusted.

But the worst black mark against Vang Pao, at least for Hmong on the plain, was his link to Touby LyFoung. In the late 1940s Touby had appointed Pa Ngcha Ly as tax collector for the eastern portion of the plain. Within a decade, Pa Ngcha had so alienated Hmong on the plain that they came to hold Touby in the same contempt once reserved for tyrannical Lao bureaucrats. Touby had recruited Pa Ngcha, a Ly aristocrat, to curry favor with the Ly aristocracy. Touby was powerful and rich, but he was lowborn. His grandfather had come to Laos not as a free man but as the servant of a Chinese merchant, the lowest level to which a Hmong could fall. Ly patriarchs would have nothing to do with him. Touby's father, Foung Ly, struggled throughout his life to raise his family's social status, pinning his hopes on Touby. Yet even after Touby's rise to political prominence, the Ly aristocracy continued to treat his family as outsiders.

Personally, Touby did not care that Ly bluebloods did not count him their social equal. He was unimpressed by pedigree. What he admired was political talent and intellectual polish, which is why he seldom attended his clan's New Year celebrations. Not only were they boring, Touby found the fawning of commoners before gentry distasteful. Each New Year he was usually away in Vientiane attending a party hosted by well-educated French or Laotians where the discussion was lively and usually about politics.

But as a politician, Touby could not ignore the fact that the social prejudices of the aristocracy had political ramifications. Discomfited by having to take orders from a social inferior, Ly patriarchs occasionally balked at his leadership, sending waves of resistance down the Ly social hierarchy. To co-opt the old Ly establishment, and to create a debt he could use as leverage for political support, Touby began to absorb a number of Ly aristocrats, including Pa Ngcha Ly, into his administration.

Of all of Touby's appointments, Pa Ngcha Ly was clearly the worst. During his tax collection tours Pa Ngcha required each village to butcher pigs and chickens and prepare a feast for him when he arrived. He violated young maidens with impunity and illegally requisitioned livestock to be used as sacrifices at the new year festival at Nong Het. It was customary for tax collectors to supply their own porters to convey taxes in silver or opium to the district headquarters. Pa Ngcha violated this custom by forcing villagers to perform the service, taking them away from their families for weeks at a time. The man was also plain unreasonable, insisting that the roads he traveled be cleared of all debris. The slightest infraction resulted in fines and beatings.[6]

The appointment of Pa Ngcha Ly was not Touby's only political blunder. After 1957, when he entered national politics, Touby lost interest in local affairs and allowed the corruption and oppression associated with Pa Ngcha to spread throughout his provincial district. Hmong officials began to impose unofficial taxes, expropriate property, and abuse villagers at will. The abuse eroded Touby's authority, which remained unchallenged only in the area between Xieng Khouangville and Nong Het.

Presumed dishonorable because he was from Nong Het, morally suspect because he was a Vang, and thought politically treacherous because of his association with Touby, Vang Pao had little hope of persuading Hmong on the Plain of Jars to back a guerrilla campaign on his own. Other Hmong with influence would have to do the persuading for him. For this Vang Pao turned to Youa Tong Yang.

We encountered Youa Tong earlier as the 1940s opium broker who became one of the richest Hmong in Laos, lived in a western-style home, and was the first Hmong to own an automobile. Now, nearly two decades later, Youa Tong was no longer fabulously wealthy. Back in 1950, a Frenchman, who for years had flown Youa Tong's annual opium cache to Saigon for a percentage of the profits, departed with the opium and never returned. Three years later, using a Vietnamese woman as his Saigon connection, Youa Tong attempted to make a killing on a good harvest. He risked his entire savings, thousands of dollars in silver, on a pack train and fifteen assistants to purchase all the opium he could lay his hands on. Like the Frenchman, after the Vietnamese woman received the opium she disappeared. Youa Tong got out of narcotics trafficking for good and became an ordinary merchant until Touby LyFoung appointed him head of a Hmong subdistrict on the Plain of Jars.

Vang Pao and Youa Tong were cousins and their fathers had been best friends—strong ties that persuaded Youa Tong to stand in as Vang Pao's spokesman. He was the ideal emissary. At one time or another Youa Tong had purchased opium from nearly every Hmong village in the area and had a reputation for fair dealing, not only as an opium broker but as a subdistrict chief. For Youa Tong it was like being back in the opium business, making the rounds of villages in the mountains surrounding the plain, renewing old friendships and swapping tall tales.[7] But instead of buying opium he was selling a plan: on Vang Pao's signal, nearly seventy thousand Hmong from two hundred villages would pack up and relocate near the old Malo training camps; these sites would become support and training centers for guerrilla operations to harass communist troops, interdict supplies, and cut communications.

In addition to the Hmong on the plain, Vang Pao had the support of Hmong on the plain's southern rim, nearly all of them recent transplants from Nong Het, Pak Lak, Keng Khoai, and Phac Boun. The migration occurred shortly after Kong-Lê's coup when Pathet Lao troops began gathering in strength just across the border in Vietnam, only a day's march from Nong Het.[8] Fearing the communists were preparing to cross the border and occupy Hmong villages, thousands of Hmong fled as a group to the southeastern edge of the Plain of Jars to camp out at the USAID station at Lat Houang, where there were food and supplies. Many of the transplants were Thao clansmen and their chief was Sao Chia Thao. An able politician, Sao Chia quickly established leadership over all of the Hmong on the plain's southern rim. It was a piece of luck for Vang Pao. A long-time friend and close cousin by marriage (Vang Pao's second wife was a Thao), Sao Chia pledged full support for Vang Pao's guerrilla army.

WINNING TOUBY OVER

When communist troops swarmed over the Plain of Jars and encircled Boussarath's battalions, the time for action had obviously arrived. Seventy thousand Hmong were ready to move, thanks to the politicking of Youa Tong Yang and Sao Chia Thao. Yet Vang Pao hesitated. He wanted Touby on board. Unfortunately, Touby was openly allied with Souvanna Phouma and the Neutralists, wearing two hats in Souvanna's cabinet as the Minister of Justice and Minister of Health and Welfare. With Vientiane exploring every avenue for reconciliation with the Pathet Lao, Touby could hardly support guerrilla action against the communists. The only solution was to get Touby to bolt from the Neutralist camp. As if by magic, within a few weeks Touby parted ways with Souvanna Phouma and left the government.

Years later, in a short memoir, Vang Pao explained how he pulled it off, a version of events that obscures a successful attempt to manipulate Hmong public opinion. In Vang Pao's account, the pressures of capital politics had kept Touby in Vientiane cut off from the Hmong in Xieng Khouang and oblivious to events unfolding on the Plain of Jars. Vang Pao used spirit magic to draw Touby back to Xieng Khouangville so he could see what was happening for himself: "[Touby] was in Vientiane, and we had no communications with the city. We called on the great shaman Ya Shao of Khang Kho to invoke the spirits of our ancestors to make Touby favor our cause. We had promised for this service the sacrifice of a white steer and a black steer."[9]

While Vang Pao was as superstitious as any Hmong, he was also fully capable of manipulating religion for political ends as easily as a Renaissance pope. The spirit ceremony was a ruse. He didn't need Ya Shao to send spirit messages to get Touby's attention. An RLA pilot flew a helicopter daily from Vientiane to Xieng Khouangville to deliver and pick up communiqués. For weeks prior to Touby's return to Xieng Khouangville there had been a steady stream of messages between himself and Vang Pao. Vang Pao kept Touby current on communist activities on the plain, while Touby briefed him on the increasing fragility of Souvanna Phouma's regime.

The prospect of a communist takeover of Xieng Khouang finally convinced Touby of the folly of neutralism and the need to organize a Hmong maquis. It was probably at this moment that Vang Pao revealed that Youa Tong and Sao Chia had already prepared the way and needed only a signal to start things rolling. What Vang Pao wanted from Touby was a pledge to rally those faithful to him to back the plan as well. Touby was not entirely confident that he could persuade his stalwarts to support a guerrilla campaign. Having ignored local politics for years, he feared his authority had eroded. Things would have to be carefully orchestrated to pull it off. Touby's plan was for Vang Pao to gather the village chiefs and clan notables at Xieng Khouangville for a general meeting to solicit their advice on what to do. Then Touby would arrive and address the gathering and try to convince those assembled of the need to take up arms.[10]

Vang Pao's contribution to the plan was to use Ya Shao Yang to sanction the mobilization. If ancestor spirits had whisked Touby to Xieng Khouangville to rally the Hmong for action, who would defy the edict of heaven? According to Hmong beliefs, willfully angering the spirits invites untold misfortune, pestilence, and disease.

Vang Pao greeted Touby at the Xieng Khouangville airfield with a public display of the sacrifice of the two steers promised to Touby's ancestors by Ya Shao. With the spirits appeased and their will confirmed, Touby and Vang Pao hurried to the meeting to confront the clan chieftains. By meeting's end, there was near-unanimous support for Vang Pao's plan to raise a guerrilla army and a pledge from several clan chieftains to provide intelligence, supplies, and recruits.

Sai Kham, the provincial governor, had also attended the meeting. He was enthusiastic about Vang Pao's plan, seeing it as a way to advance his own political agenda. With national politics in disarray and various factions seeking allies as they jockeyed for advantage, Sai Kham believed the time was ripe to bargain for the political autonomy of Xieng Khouang Province. In private, he exhorted Touby to form an alliance with Phoumi and to pledge Hmong troops in return for Xieng Khouang's political independence.

Touby did form an alliance with Phoumi, but it is unclear whether it involved a deal to grant Xieng Khouang increased political autonomy, though many Hmong came to believe that such a deal had been struck and that it was the first step toward an autonomous Hmong state,[11] a rumor that neither Touby nor Vang Pao challenged or sought to lay to rest. What is known is that on Touby's request Vang Pao sent a message to Phoumi Nosavan announcing his intention to form a Hmong maquis that would be even larger than the old Malo-Servan guerrilla organization.

Phoumi received the news with mixed feelings. To stop the communists was welcome, but an independent Hmong army could prove difficult to control. Phoumi viewed the Hmong as "untrustworthy and primitive."[12] His preference was for Vang Pao to rally RLA forces on the plain. After an exchange of communiqués,

Phoumi hit on a compromise. He authorized Vang Pao to assemble Hmong volunteers, but also ordered him to take command of the Royalist camp near Lat Houang on the southeastern edge of the Plain of Jars.

Vang Pao arrived at Lat Houang at the head of 350 Hmong. His guerrillas were poorly armed. Vang Pao had been able to scrounge up only thirty-four old rifles for his Hmong troops, some of them ancient cavalry muskets. The Lao soldiers at the camp offered no resistance to Vang Pao's taking command. Nevertheless, as a precaution, Vang Pao cracked open cases of new rifles and distributed them to his Hmong.

The troops at Lat Houang hadn't been paid in months. To win their loyalty, Vang Pao flew to Phoumi's headquarters at Savannakhet to get their back pay. Before Phoumi handed over the two hundred thousand kip (provided by the CIA), he offered Vang Pao command of MR II. An officer grade of colonel or higher was customary for commanders of military regions.[13] Vang Pao was only a major. Phoumi made it clear that a promotion would not come with the new job.[14]

VANG PAO'S STALLED CAREER

Vang Pao had enjoyed one promotion after another when the French were in charge, advancing to the rank of captain within a couple of years. French commanders had singled him out for special attention over the protests of Lao officers, who considered the socially inferior Hmong unsuitable officer material. Vang Pao received advanced training and rapid promotions, sometimes with French officers dictating answers to written exams so bad grammar wouldn't hinder a promising military career. But after the departure of the French, four years would pass before Vang Pao was promoted to major, and this was at a time when the RLA was restructuring, replacing French officers with Laotians. Overnight, mid-level Lao officers had become generals. Lowly lieutenants were catapulted to the rank of colonel. Sergeants became lieutenants and then captains. Meanwhile, Vang Pao remained frozen in rank.

Racial prejudice played a part. With ethnic Lao in charge of the army, few soldiers from tribal minorities were likely to advance very far through the ranks. This was especially true for Khmu and

Hmong montagnards, stigmatized in Lao culture as barbarians. Having risen to the rank of captain, Kong-Lê stood out as a singular exception among the thousands of Khmu tribesman serving in the RLA. While Vang Pao had advanced even further to major, he now seemed fixed in rank—though for other reasons than simple racial prejudice.

Vang Pao was called on the carpet in late 1959 for pocketing the pay of Hmong troops organized earlier in the year as a self-defense force under his command. The unit was part of the PEO's outreach to montagnards. American Special Forces soldiers trained the troops in the use of field radios and modern weapons. Members of the self-defense unit were to be paid a monthly salary, but for a stretch of several months Vang Pao held back the pay. One of the Hmong confronted him and demanded his salary. Vang Pao shot the soldier in the leg.

The event was the first in a long list of brutal incidents that checkered Vang Pao's otherwise distinguished military career. Later, as commander of his own Hmong army, he executed a number of his officers on the spot. He shot one between the eyes for selling CIA rice to the Pathet Lao and fired point blank into the chest of another for pilfering soldiers' pay without his permission. Vang Pao's treatment of prisoners was equally savage. He placed many of them in fifty-five gallon barrels buried in the ground, a psychological torture designed to loosen the tongues of captured North Vietnamese and Pathet Lao who refused to divulge information about their units. Vang Pao sent other prisoners to his interrogation center at Pha Khao, where they were brutally tortured before being executed.[15] In 1965, when a CIA operative "demanded" that Vang Pao allow his intelligence experts to interrogate six recently captured enemy soldiers, Vang Pao had the prisoners taken out and summarily executed. The CIA agent got the message and changed his tone. "What I meant to say, general, is that I would appreciate it if you would allow us to interrogate prisoners, please."[16]

But in 1959 Vang Pao had yet to rise far enough to do such things with impunity. At the time, Boussarath was the RLA's provincial commander. He brusquely ordered Vang Pao to produce the money owed to his Hmong irregulars. The dressing down left Vang Pao in a rage. Several days later, thirty of his Hmong ambushed Boussarath as he approached Lat Houang in a jeep.

Boussarath stomped on the accelerator when the first shots rang out and sped by the assassins, bullets plinking into his jeep. Miraculously, he reached Lat Houang unscathed.[17]

Boussarath radioed Vientiane to report the assassination attempt. Ouane Rattikone, the RLA chief of staff, flew to Xieng Khouang the next morning to confront Vang Pao. By one account, after charges were read, Vang Pao prostrated himself before the general, weeping profusely, and begged for forgiveness. To Vang Pao's relief, he was not cashiered. Perhaps it was his abject display of contrition, but more likely Rattikone was pressured into leniency by American Special Forces officers working behind the scenes training Hmong guerrillas. In any case, the affair tarnished Vang Pao's reputation with the RLA high command. The general feeling was that his career in the army was finished.[18]

Vang Pao refused to accept this judgment. He turned down Phoumi's offer of command of MR II without promotion. Competent RLA officers were a rare commodity. He believed that if he held out, the promotion would come. Vang Pao collected the camp's back pay and returned to Lat Houang to see if he could transform the Laotian troops under his command into an effective fighting unit and test them in battle. The opportunity never came.

VANG PAO AT NAM CHAT

Vang Pao had been tracking Kong-Lê's movements as he neared the Plain of Jars. It soon became clear to him that Kong-Lê's ultimate destination on the plain was the RLA post at Nam Chat. Vang Pao related the information to Vientiane and was ordered to take charge of the post and turn back the Neutralists. Vang Pao hesitated just long enough to extract the promotion he felt he deserved.

Though the chance to test the Lao troops at Lat Houang had slipped away, Lieutenant Colonel Vang Pao now faced an even greater challenge: to make the untried Lao soldiers at Nam Chat battle-ready for the coming assault. To Vang Pao's consternation, he found the camp in complete disarray. Colonel Don Sasorith Sourith, commander of MR II, was on the scene and in a panic. He had just learned over his field radio that three NVA paratroop battalions had linked up with Kong-Lê's forces. Sourith gave Nam

Chat up for lost and was ready to bolt. His defeatism was contagious. The Lao troops at Nam Chat were ready to cut and run with the first incoming round from the enemy's artillery.

There were two 105-mm howitzers on the post. Vang Pao ordered the artillery officer to move them into position on the airfield to prepare for an artillery duel. The officer suddenly forgot his years of training and announced that he had no idea how to operate a 105. Vang Pao cursed the man's cowardice and set about positioning the cannons himself.

The post needed more time to organize. Vang Pao loaded six cases of dynamite onto the side litters of a medevac helicopter and ordered the pilot to fly for Lat Ngone, a village six miles away. Kong-Lê's armor would have to use the village's bridge to get across the river. With the bridge blown, the vehicles could be held up for hours. The pilot landed a short distance from the town and helped unload the cargo. He waited by the helicopter while Vang Pao lugged the cases to the bridge. Each box of dynamite weighed over a hundred pounds and it took Vang Pao several trips to get all the explosives into position. He placed the charges, connected the detonating wires, lit the fuses, and ran. Advanced units of Kong-Lê's armor appeared just as the bridge was launched into the air.

When Vang Pao returned to Nam Chat he found that Colonel Sourith and most of the camp's soldiers had already deserted. Vang Pao could round up only five volunteers to help him harness the 105s to two Dodge 4-wheel drive trucks, load all available ammunition (two hundred rounds), and transport the cannons to the crossroads of Routes 7 and 4. There Vang Pao waited for Kong-Lê's column. There was a rumble in the distance accompanied by rising clouds of dust. Vang Pao loaded the howitzers and lobbed two shells toward the advancing troops. He kept the cannons busy, spacing out his shots, making the two hundred shells last four hours.

Out of ammunition, Vang Pao returned to Nam Chat. He found the post completely deserted. It seemed ironic to Vang Pao that on the day he received his promotion the troops under his command would run away, leaving him to celebrate his new stripes "by carrying cases of dynamite and firing cannons." Without troops to command, he had no choice but to join the mass retreat of soldiers, government officials (including Governor Sai Kham), and civilians, many of them Hmong, "trampling over one another in the confusion," heading south along Route 4, an unimproved dirt road deeply rutted by jeep and truck traffic.

Colonel Sourith had sufficiently regained his composure since abandoning his troops at Nam Chat to take charge of the mass retreat. When the column reached the village of Thavieng, he assembled the remnants of two battalions for a first line of defense, then led everyone else south, including most of the civilians, to set up a second defensive position at Tha Thom fifteen miles away.

RAISING HIS OWN ARMY

Vang Pao was one of the officers left behind at Thavieng. To help beef up his position, he sent couriers to nearby Hmong villages to gather volunteers. He soon had a thousand men and their families assembled and ready to fight. By now he was in radio contact with Phoumi, promising to hold the line and requesting a favor. Vang Pao's family was at Thavieng. He wanted them flown to Vientiane out of harm's way. Phoumi contacted the CIA to see what could be done. The next day an Air America helicopter arrived to gather up Vang Pao's wives and children.

Though Vang Pao's Hmong volunteers were officially an appendage of Sourith's makeshift front line of defense, Vang Pao began to toy with the idea of using them as the nucleus of an all-Hmong army. He had only to send word to Touby, Youa Tong Yang, and Sao Chia Thao to set things in motion. If he fought the communists in his own way with diehard Hmong guerrillas, he could defeat them. It would perhaps be his only chance to eclipse Phoumi and the other Lao generals who led armies from behind a desk.[19]

For years an unpleasant reality had scratched at Vang Pao's consciousness, a mental irritant that would not go away. It was that his only chance of making a mark in the military was by leading Hmong into battle. It had inspired his idea of reviving the old Malo maquis. Yet Vang Pao could not quite let go of his aspiration to achieve distinction leading Lao troops within the regular army. It was this lingering ambition that led him, against his own better judgment, to accept Phoumi's offer of command over Lao troops, first at Lat Houang and then at Nam Chat. It was easy to rationalize the decision. Lao soldiers could fight well if provided with adequate leadership. They had done so under French command and, in isolated instances, under the leadership of a handful of exceptional Lao officers. Yet in his heart Vang Pao knew Lao troops would not allow themselves to be commanded by a Hmong officer, however competent.

Before joining the regular army, Vang Pao had served for four years in Laos' French-run national Gendarmerie. Originally patterned after the French national police, in the late 1940s the organization was turned into a paramilitary force to fight communist insurgents. The Gendarmerie's new mission gave a boost to Vang Pao's military career. He was assigned to an isolated Gendarmerie post at Muong Ngan, close to the Vietnam border. Captain Fret, who ran the post, realized instantly that his new Hmong adjutant was a born commando. Fret gave Vang Pao a free hand to conduct guerrilla operations against Pathet Lao and Viet Minh. Leading an all-Hmong platoon, Vang Pao liquidated an entire Viet Minh unit and captured documents that revealed details of the Viet Minh organization and its operations in the area. As a reward, Fret secured Vang Pao a slot in the RLA's Officer Candidate School.

After graduation Vang Pao reported to the 14th infantry company at Muong Hiem. As the garrison was in Hmong country, his job was to develop an intelligence network in the villages and recruit Hmong for military service. Past abuses by government officials had poisoned the well, so it took some time to gain the trust of local villagers. Eventually the intelligence network was in place and seventy-three Hmong had signed on as soldiers. Mixing the Hmong recruits into the company caused racial tension. The Lao demanded transfer to a different post. The garrison's commander, Captain Cocosteguy, resolved the issue by segregating the Hmong into a special unit within the company, with Vang Pao in command.

This incident portended difficulties for Vang Pao's future career in the regular army. If Lao would not serve with Hmong, they certainly would balk at being led by one. Possibly this was his moment of epiphany, a grim realization that he would never achieve military greatness commanding Lao units. Or the realization may have come later: after the 14th infantry had been disbanded; after his career in the regular army was put on hold while he led Hmong volunteers; after special training in the Philippines and a return to the mainstream as commander of the NCO school at Khang Khay, followed at last by command of a predominantly Lao unit, the RLA 10th infantry battalion.

From the outset, the Lao troops in the 10th had bridled at taking orders from a Hmong. Vang Pao had pushed his authority to the limit during his dash after the renegade Pathet Lao 2nd battalion, and there were aftershocks. Following the operation, his troops turned truculent, then mutinous. Vang Pao began to fear for his life. Temporarily abandoning his post, he sought refuge with an American special forces unit stationed at Khang Khay.[20] Shortly after this incident he was reassigned to resume work with Hmong volunteers.

If Vang Pao was doomed to command only Hmong, at least they were natural guerrilla fighters, and guerrilla war was something for which Vang Pao believed himself uniquely qualified. In 1952, following his graduation from the officer training school at Dong Hene, the French sent Vang Pao to Hanoi for two weeks to observe the inner workings of the French High Command. What he saw troubled him. The French were fixated on traditional stratagems and set-piece battles, the sort of thing that would lead to their defeat at Dienbienphu. As a noncom with the Gendarmerie, Vang Pao had led Hmong into battle and defeated the Vietnamese by using guerrilla tactics that came naturally to a Hmong. He sought out the rough terrain and drew the numerically superior enemy into ambushes. Whenever the fighting turned against him, he retreated into the mountains, covering six to eight miles per hour, sometimes nonstop for two days. The enemy inevitably dropped from exhaustion and gave up the chase, or caught up at a location of Vang Pao's own choosing, too weary to realize they had fallen into a trap.

Military historians labeled this strategy the Fabian Tactic, a technique perfected two thousand years ago by the Roman general Quintus Fabius Maximus, also known as Cunctator (the delayer), who refused to engage Hannibal's superior army until he had the Carthaginians worn out from dogging his retreat. But Fabius was successful only because Hannibal could not count on reinforcements. North Vietnam was not Carthage, situated an ocean away; it was next door to Laos, and its ability to provide reinforcements would prove to be seemingly boundless. Against the NVA, a Fabian strategy might win battles, but never the war.

Finally committed to raising his own army, Vang Pao dispatched communiqués to Youa Tong Yang and Sao Chia, asking them to join him at Thavieng. He wanted one last chance to confer before giving the signal for Hmong on the Plain of Jars to relocate to the seven strategic locations ringing the plain. His plan was to use the Hmong troops under his command at Thavieng as the core of his future guerrilla army. After establishing a home base for these troops, he would begin organizing and training Hmong volunteers assembled at the resurrected Malo bases.

At the moment, however, his most pressing need was weapons. The valley at Thavieng was wide and flat, ideal for an airfield. Vang Pao rounded up three hundred Hmong from local villages to provide coolies to knock down the dikes in the rice fields and fill in the low places. As the coolies worked, Vang Pao got on the radio to Phoumi to request that he fly in weapons and supplies for his Hmong volunteers. He assured Phoumi that he was still loyal to the RLA, that his Hmong were still part of Sourith's fragmented corps, and that if weapons and supplies could be delivered to Thavieng, the Hmong would act as a blocking force to protect Sourith's main force at Tha Thom.

Vang Pao did not hold out much hope of getting what he asked for. Everything was going to Sourith at Tha Thom: supplies, artillery, and an infusion of fresh troops. He suspected that Phoumi and the other generals in Vientiane had already decided that the Hmong at Thavieng were expendable, and that sending them weapons would be a waste of resources. What Vang Pao did not know was that Phoumi was under pressure from both the American embassy and the CIA to divert more resources to paramilitary forces. Several days after Vang Pao's appeal for weapons and supplies, a Thai colonel and an American arrived at Thavieng in a helicopter. The American was an odd-looking fellow with a square-shaped head that seemed too big for his body; he spoke with a Texas drawl and called himself "Colonel Billy."

COLONEL "BILLY"

William "Bill" Lair began his life as a field operative in 1951 working in Thailand, attached to the Bangkok station. He was interested in counterinsurgency and persuaded the station chief to allow him to work with the Thai to develop an elite border patrol force. The outfit became the Police Aerial Reinforcement Unit (PARU), and by 1960 it had evolved into possibly the best paramilitary outfit in Southeast Asia.[21]

The operational headquarters for PARU was at Hua Hin, a seaport town in the far south of peninsular Thailand, a long distance from PARU's actual field operations in the border region of northern Thailand. There in the mountains, PARU teams trained hill tribesmen, many of them Thai Hmong, in the use of weapons and tactics for defense against border bandits and communist insurgents. The operation was so successful that in CIA circles PARU came to be known as an operation that worked. PARU received the hands-on blessings of Desmond FitzGerald, the CIA's chief of Far East operations, and CIA director Allen W. Dulles. Both officials took the time to tour the organization's headquarters.

By the end of the 1950s PARU had pretty much fulfilled its goal of pacifying Thailand's northern border region and Lair was looking for a new role for his elite paramilitary force, possibly training montagnards in Laos. The idea had already been advanced five years earlier by General Phao Siyanon, at that time the commanding officer of PARU (known then as the Royal Guards). The plan got nowhere. Considered too ambitious by generals in the regular Thai army, Phao lost out in a power struggle and was forced into exile.[22] Now it was Lair's turn to promote the idea.

Lair received an unexpected boost in this direction when the CIA asked him to contribute PARU teams as advisors for Phoumi's army during his December 1960 assault on Vientiane. With a foot in the door, Lair set about convincing the CIA's Vientiane station chief, Gordon Jorgensen, that PARU should begin working with Laotian montagnards. Lair knew that the PEO had been training Hmong since 1959. Lair argued that the CIA, using PARU, could do an even better job and for a lot less money. Also, PARU teams were Thai, and the Thai were physically indistinguishable from lowland Lao. They would blend in and provide the CIA great cover.

While Jorgensen mulled over the proposal, Lair established a PARU office in Vientiane and kept the PARU teams that had participated in Phoumi's counter-coup on hand in the capital, ready to move if Jorgensen gave him the nod to begin work with the Laotian Hmong. Lair was also eager to link up with prominent Hmong leaders to see if they were receptive. Earlier, in Thailand, he had learned from Thai Hmong about a remarkable Hmong officer in the RLA. His name was Vang Pao. Lair passed the word to CIA agents in Vientiane that he wanted to meet the man. On December 31, CIA officers working with Phoumi contacted Lair and told him that Vang Pao was at a place called Thavieng. Lair looked up Jorgensen and asked permission to fly out to meet Vang Pao. Jorgensen gave his assent but insisted that Lair be back that evening. He didn't want an American captured in the field.

Lair organized a five man PARU team and set out by helicopter. He had difficulty finding Thavieng. When they were close to where Lair thought Thavieng should be, he set down and left the PARU team with instructions to seek out Vang Pao and radio back if they found him. Lair returned to Vientiane and waited to hear back from Colonel Pranet Ritchenchai, the PARU team's commander. The next day Pranet radioed Lair that he had found Vang Pao. "He's the one we've been looking for," Pranet reported. Lair hopped a plane and joined Pranet at Thavieng.

Vang Pao greeted Lair wearing khaki, canvas jungle boots, and a floppy bush hat, the standard issue for a French commando. He was ebullient, exuding confidence. To Lair, Vang Pao seemed like a "miniature Genghis Khan." After taking a tour of the camp, Lair asked Vang Pao how many Hmong he could arm. Vang Pao was already in radio contact with a number of the key villages won over by Youa Tong Yang and Sao Chia Thao.[23] He told Lair that he could raise at least ten thousand men.

Lair took that in. He had seen the hundreds of Hmong working to build an airstrip, the scores of Hmong carrying ancient rifles, attentive to Vang Pao's every command. Everyone was working for this one man. Maybe Vang Pao *could* get ten thousand Hmong to follow him. Lair asked Vang Pao what he needed. Vang Pao ticked off a list: five thousand rifles, some machine guns, and supplies and uniforms for his men, with extras for the new recruits he expected to get. Lair wrote it all down and nodded, but promised nothing. He had worked with Colonel Pranet Ritchenchai for a decade in Thailand's northern highlands. Never had they encountered a montagnard leader like Vang Pao. For a paramilitary expert like Lair, Vang Pao was a dream come true.

Back in Vientiane, Lair went directly to the CIA station to talk about Vang Pao with Jorgensen. The station chief was there with Desmond FitzGerald, who had just arrived. FitzGerald was now the agency's chief of the Far East Division of Directorate for Plans, the agency's bureau in charge of covert actions in Asia. FitzGerald had come to Vientiane to talk with Jorgensen about the CIA's future role in Laos. FitzGerald asked Lair for his opinion. It was a fortuitous event.

Lair told FitzGerald about Vang Pao and expressed confidence that the Hmong colonel could organize a sizable guerrilla army, something the North Vietnamese hadn't faced so far. Using hit-and-run tactics, the guerrillas would give the communists a hard time. Even the North Vietnamese would find it difficult to completely eliminate them. Supporting this kind of guerrilla force would be cheap. The agency could supply the Hmong with surplus World War II arms. Lair's PARU, all Asians who looked like Lao, could train them. It would be a perfect clandestine operation. No Americans involved. Complete deniability.

FitzGerald was interested but guarded. It would mean a whole new direction for the CIA in Laos and a new policy for the U.S. government. The next day FitzGerald told Lair he liked his idea and asked him to submit a proposal. Lair sent an eighteen-page cable outlining his plan. Lair didn't expect an immediate reply. More than likely his ideas would be rejected. To Lair's surprise, within a few days he had his answer. The CIA had presented the idea to Eisenhower, now in the last days of his presidency, to solicit his reaction. Eisenhower had warmed to the idea.[24] This was enough to persuade Allen Dulles to personally approve the plan. The operation would be called "Momentum."

It was to start as a pilot program. Lair was authorized to train and provide weapons for a thousand men. He would be pretty much on his own, without close supervision or accountability. He would be under no obligation to report on a daily basis to either the CIA's Vientiane or Bangkok stations. And his funding would come from a special account under his control. If everything went smoothly, he had the authority to train and arm even more Hmong.[25]

Eager to get the pilot program off the ground, Lair returned to Thavieng for another meeting with Vang Pao. This time Youa Tong Yang and Sao Chia Thao were on hand, along with several clan chieftains, to pressure the CIA agent for a firm statement on how far America would go if the Hmong backed Vang Pao's plan for a guerrilla army. Lair pledged arms and supplies and training if the Hmong made a good accounting against the Pathet Lao and the North Vietnamese, and a new place to live if they were defeated.[26]

Lair had discussed this last item with FitzGerald just before he left for Washington. He had advised FitzGerald that if the CIA sponsored a Hmong guerrilla army, the agency should provide an out for the Hmong, some place to which they could retreat and survive if things got too tough. Off the top of his head Lair had suggested Sayaboury Province. It was the only portion of northern Laos situated on the western side of the Mekong. The river was a natural barrier, and Sayaboury was next to Thailand. Arrangements could be made with the Thai government to allow the Hmong sanctuary if the communists actually pursued the Hmong across the Mekong into Sayaboury.[27] The Sayaboury plan was only an idea. The CIA had not committed itself to the proposal, and Lair was not authorized to promise the Hmong sanctuary in case of defeat. But Lair promised it anyway.

The clan elders wanted something down on paper. Lair drew up an agreement that pledged the delivery within a few days of enough arms and ammunition to equip five hundred men. Vang Pao, Youa Tong Yang, Lair, and Colonel Pranet signed the document.[28] Though the agreement promised nothing more than the delivery of arms and ammunition, many Hmong construed it as an official treaty with the United States that guaranteed an independent Hmong state if the Hmong defeated the communists and sanctuary if they lost. In time, the belief that such a treaty existed became so widespread that most Hmong presumed it to be an indisputable fact. Long after the war, Hmong still believed the treaty existed. In a March 1997 letter to President Clinton, Hmong refugees in Thailand facing forced repatriation to Laos respectfully reminded the President of the contract signed by "American

Colonel Billy Lair" (incorrectly giving the date as November 1959) that "pledged that the U.S. government would take care of the Hmong people because of their cooperation with the U.S. government in fighting the war in Laos."[29]

The sanctuary idea was Lair's fault, for he had indeed made the verbal promise that the U.S. would find a safe haven for the Hmong, if needed. However, Vang Pao also shared part of the blame. For political reasons, he encouraged Hmong to believe that Lair's verbal pledge had official status, trumpeting it as a selling point for backing his guerrilla army, assuring those with reservations that if the Americans lost the war "and we get [into] trouble—cannot live in Laos—they are willing to find a place for us to live."[30] Later, once the sanctuary idea no longer served his political ends, Vang Pao played it down. But for Lair it remained a moral millstone that would nag at his conscience for years to come. On several occasions he attempted to make good on the pledge, but each time Vang Pao stood in the way, fearing that if a fallback area were created in Sayaboury, it would erode the Hmong commitment to continue fighting.

Unlike the sanctuary pledge, the promise of an independent Hmong state had not come from Lair's lips. One of the first questions Lair had asked Vang Pao on their initial meeting was whether he was seeking political autonomy. Washington wanted Laos intact and noncommunist, and would not have appreciated the CIA underwriting a Hmong separatist movement. To Lair's relief, Vang Pao had proclaimed his loyalty to the king and denied any interest in political autonomy. This was probably Vang Pao's true feelings at the time. But a short time later, when he saw it would rally Hmong support for his guerrilla army, he touted the idea and encouraged the belief that America would establish an autonomous Hmong state once the communists were defeated, creating the impression that this too was part of the imagined treaty with the U.S.

As Lair had promised, the CIA delivered several cases of weapons and four radios to Thavieng, along with an American instructor to explain their operation. It was only a fraction of what was needed, and it came too late. The enemy had already caught the scent and was closing in. On January 13, Kong-Lê's forces, joined by Pathet Lao units and elements of the NVA's 325th division, were finally near enough to Thavieng to set up heavy cannon. Artillery rounds chewed up the valley. Without air support and artillery, Vang Pao had no choice but to retreat. He momentarily considered moving south to Tha Thom to link up with Sourith's forces. This decision would have delayed, perhaps indefinitely, the creation of a Hmong guerrilla army.

It was the last time Vang Pao would vacillate on the issue. When he learned that Tha Thom was also under attack and barely holding on despite air support by T-6 fighter planes flown by Thai pilots, he stiffened his resolve and led his guerrillas west into the mountains. The die was cast.

A WAR THEY COULDN'T WIN

Once it became clear that the RLA was utterly worthless, turning to the Hmong was inevitable. It had been a standing policy with the Eisenhower administration to rely on indigenous forces to fight communist insurgents in Laos. The only other choice, save admitting defeat, was to commit American troops, which was unacceptable. Eisenhower was not opposed to foreign wars, only to wars that could not be won. He considered the logistics of fighting a war in a landlocked jungle daunting, the sort of thing that could leave the U.S. bogged down in a Korea-like conflict. Eisenhower had won the presidency on a promise to end the war in Korea. He did not want to leave office having committed the nation to a similar war in Southeast Asia.[31]

The Pentagon was equally unenthusiastic about committing troops to Laos, though for different reasons. Congress had made deep cuts in the military budget after the Korean War. Fixated on preparedness for conflict with the Soviets in Europe, the joint chiefs wanted to marshal the military's scarce resources for this purpose instead of squandering them on brushfire wars in Asia. The idea of having Laotians defend themselves was therefore appealing.

Even history seemed to justify the use of native forces. In the twentieth century, insurgents had fared well only against colonial armies. Uprisings against a native government defended by soldiers recruited from the general population, or a major ethnic group, had come off poorly (the only exceptions being China in 1949 and Cuba in 1959). Presumably, with an army staffed primarily with ethnic Lao, the Royal Laotian Government would confirm this historical trend.

Of course, the dismal performance of the RLA poked rather large holes in this logic. And turning to the Hmong as a substitute ignored history's lessons altogether. The Hmong hardly qualified as a major ethnic group. They were less than 15 percent of the population. In addition to being a tiny minority, they were a scorned minority, unlikely to enjoy genuine support from the larger population. Nevertheless, the imperative to establish an effective indigenous military force had gathered so much momentum that such esoteric considerations were ignored.

The one good idea was to keep Hmong units separate from the regular army, not only to insulate them from the corrupting influence of the RLA, but to insure that they would receive adequate support in the field, for Laotian officers did not hide their contempt for the Hmong, whom they considered both socially and racially inferior to Laotians.[32] Such feelings were not conducive to successful joint operations. But keeping the Hmong separate meant creating a fully independent Hmong army, a creature of the CIA responsible to it alone and cut loose from the lawful government of the nation. To the outside world this independence would foster the impression that the Hmong army was a purely mercenary force, fighting not out of patriotism but for profit. While there was some truth to the charge, it was also true that the Hmong paid a terrible price for their military chits.

Operation Momentum would evolve from a modest program to train and equip small Hmong guerrilla units into the largest paramilitary enterprise in the history of the CIA. In organization, the Hmong army would grow progressively more complex, shedding its chrysalis of company-sized units to become an army of battalions, and then of regiments. Air support would mature to match the evolution, going from World War II fighter bombers to fast-flying jets with laser guided bombs and B-52 Stratofortress bombers with such destructive power that in one pass a half dozen of them could make an entire army on the ground disappear without a trace. It would become a big war with high casualties. The Hmong would lose nearly a third of their population for a cause they never fully understood, in a war they could not have won.

The principal quality that distinguished Vang Pao's Hmong guerrillas from soldiers in the RLA was their willingness to fight. This would have been an enormous advantage had the enemy been as notoriously fainthearted as the government's troops. But the NVA's soldiers were every bit as tough and considerably more disciplined than the Hmong.

While there would be many occasions when the Hmong would display greater fortitude in combat than the Vietnamese, this only affected the outcome of particular battles, not the war. Only the wars of ancient history were won or lost in one major battle with a raucous head-on clash of massed forces in which victory went to the side that held its formation.[33] The war in Laos was altogether different. It was a modern war, not only in the sense that it employed the latest military technology, but distinctively modern in that it was a proxy war.

In the struggle between the United States and the Soviet Union, neither side dared face the other directly on the field of battle lest it invite a nuclear exchange. Only once, during the 1962 Cuban missile crisis, would the Soviet Union and United States come close to violating this principle, and this was because both sides took foolish risks.[34] To avoid repeating such mistakes, conflicts between the two superpowers had to be buffered by proxies, ideally between two proxy armies; less ideally, between one of the superpowers and the other's proxy. This doctrine of limited war, developed in the 1950s by academic theorists (mostly in the physical sciences) with little military experience, had become orthodoxy by the early 1960s, obliging the Army to revise its Field Service Manual to eliminate victory as an aim in war.[35] Central to the limited war doctrine was the notion of gradualism. In proxy conflicts, escalation must evolve slowly to permit the enemy time to reassess commitments and the opportunity to open negotiations for a settlement.[36]

There were two problems with gradualism. First, it sent the wrong message: a lack of resolve to engage and defeat the enemy. This was how the North Vietnamese read America's gradualism in Vietnam and Laos, which encouraged them to continue fighting and to reject a diplomatic solution.[37] The North Vietnamese were convinced they could win such a war and that their victory would be a model for defeating western armies throughout the third world. In the words of Vo Nguyen Giap, "If it proves possible to defeat the special war tested in South Vietnam by the American imperialists, this will mean that it can be defeated everywhere else as well."[38]

The second difficulty with gradualism was that it ignored political reality. Rulers of totalitarian regimes do not have to stand for election, which makes it difficult for discontent arising from dead sons and wasted resources to find expression. Leaders of democratic nations must face voters on a regular basis. As a rule of thumb, once a war lasts beyond five years, embarrassing questions are asked.[39] Continuing the war risks protests and political chaos. This was France's experience in Vietnam. French voters defeated the Expeditionary Corps, not the Viet Minh. French politicians were slow to take this lesson to heart. Only four years after Dienbienphu, France was close to revolution over another colonial war, this time in Algeria. It led to a coup that returned Charles de Gaulle to power.

Hanoi understood this dilemma better than policy makers in Washington. Believing North Vietnam to be only "a raggedy-ass little fourth rate country," President Johnson assured voters that America was destined to win the war. "Because we fight for values and we fight for principles rather than territory or colonies, our patience and our determination are unending."[40] Johnson was whistling in the wind, as was Henry Kissinger who asserted with confidence that "we are so powerful that Hanoi is simply unable to defeat us militarily."[41] North Vietnam's leaders did not challenge this claim, they simply considered it irrelevant.

Mao Zedong had taught that there were three phases to a "people's war." In the first phase resource-poor rebels use guerrilla warfare, fighting with hit-and-run tactics to avoid annihilation by their militarily superior adversary. To evolve beyond this stage the rebels must mobilize the population in the countryside to create their own resources and establish a vast pool of recruits for a larger army. In the second phase the rebels combine guerrilla warfare with limited conventional war, using larger units. To reach the third phase the resource base must expand even further and the military evolve into a modern conventional army. Only then can the rebels engage the enemy as an equal and obtain victory.

Mao's blueprint for victory made sense in China, where Chinese fought Chinese.[42] But Ho Chi Minh's guerrillas faced the army of a foreign power, not native Vietnamese, an added dimension Mao never had to confront. Ho Chi Minh believed it was this "additional dimension" that had ultimately defeated the French and would defeat the U.S. Speaking to a Polish diplomat in 1963, Ho predicted that the Americans would eventually pull out of Vietnam because "[w]eariness, disappointment, the knowledge that they cannot achieve the goal which the French pursued to their own discredit, will lead to a new sobriety, new feelings and emotions."[43] Giap put it more simply: democracies do "not possess . . . the psychological and political means to fight a long-drawn-out war."[44]

Ho's strategy was to exploit this weakness with military tactics tailored to "exploit contradictions in the enemy camp" and thereby strengthen antiwar feelings in America.[45] One tactic employed early by the Viet Cong was to fire on American troops on the outskirts of a village to provoke artillery fire. It turned the villagers against the Americans, and reports of the killing of civilians helped to turn segments of the American public against the war. The Soviets found Ho's strategy sufficiently convincing to assign the KGB the task for the duration of the war of delivering to Hanoi timely assessments of the political situation in America, enabling the North Vietnamese to shape military policy for maximum political effect.[46]

By waging a "political" war, the NVA did not need to defeat the U.S. militarily. The NVA simply had to endure. American voters would do the rest.

America's political vulnerability placed the Hmong at a fatal disadvantage. Time and demographics were on the side of the communists. If the North Vietnamese simply stayed the course in Laos, the Americans would eventually pull out and abandon the Hmong. By 1969, America was already moving toward disengagement. Nixon called it "peace with honor." That was for public consumption. The goal was what de Gaulle had achieved with Algeria, "to withdraw as an expression of policy and not as a collapse," to pull out by choice and by degrees, as if backing down slowly were not surrender.[47]

Even if America had not disengaged, the Hmong were too few to outlast the North Vietnamese. There were perhaps three hundred thousand Hmong in Laos, compared to eighteen to twenty million North Vietnamese. Vang Pao's army never exceeded forty thousand. By the early 1970s battle deaths had so shrunk the pool of able-bodied Hmong that half of the clandestine army was non-Hmong (mostly Thais). North Vietnam raised an army of a quarter million in the early 1960s; by the end of the decade it had grown to a half million. The majority of these troops were deployed in Vietnam, but a force in excess of sixty thousand was maintained in Laos, replenished and kept at full strength for over a decade.

North Vietnam's leaders were committed to fighting the war in Laos for another decade, if necessary. In 1969, Hanoi's military strategists studied the demographics of the villages and hamlets in the NVA's Northwest Military Region, an area adjacent to northern Laos, stretching from Moc Chau all the way to the Chinese border. Counting heads, Hanoi's military planners estimated there were sufficient infants, youngsters, and teenagers to guarantee a constant pool of recruits to replace up to ten thousand soldiers killed in action in northern Laos every year for another fourteen years.[48]

Pol Pot, the murderous leader of the Khmer Rouge, fantasized that Cambodian soldiers could easily kill fifty Vietnamese each, making it possible to defeat Vietnam in an all-out war.[49] Within the short span of two weeks in January 1979, a Vietnamese invasion of Cambodia brutally shattered that delusion. Vang Pao never entertained such fantasies, but he did hold out hope for decisive victories that would induce the North Vietnamese to retire from Laos. Hanoi did not think in such terms. The capacity to sustain enormous casualties in an open-ended war was the communists' ultimate strategy. As in Vietnam, the conflict in Laos was a war of attrition, but with a relatively short half-life for the Hmong. Vang Pao would turn to American air power to even the odds. It only delayed the inevitable. By 1969, he was already recruiting Hmong children to fill the decimated ranks of his guerrilla army.

There is a Hmong folk tale about a war between grasshoppers and monkeys. The grasshoppers sweep over the monkeys' kingdom like a plague. The monkeys go after them with sticks, but the grasshoppers jump onto the monkeys' heads and in their eagerness to kill the insects the monkeys crush in each others' skulls. When there is only one monkey left, he is so ravenous from all of the fighting that he begins to eat the grasshoppers, devouring thousands until his stomach finally bursts.[50]

There were simply too many Vietnamese for the Hmong to digest.

GETTING STARTED

After abandoning Thavieng, Vang Pao moved to Pha Khao, a mountain village on the southern edge of the Plain of Jars where there was a crude landing strip, making it possible to fly in arms and provisions. Lair had left a PARU team with Vang Pao. The team leader radioed to let Lair know their new location and to ask for more arms and ammunition. The hardware soon arrived, along with additional PARU to help with the training.

For years PARU had employed a three-day training course with Thailand's montagnards. It was quick and effective. The Thai team adapted the system for the Hmong at Pha Khao. On the first day of the training cycle they taught the Hmong how to use their M-1 rifles. The second day they taught them how to use mortars, bazoo-

Training soldiers to use a machine gun, in Touby Lyfoung militia, ca. 1954.

kas, and machine guns. The final day of training was a crash course on setting up ambushes.

Part of the ambush training was tying trip wires to grenades. Vang Pao had the first graduates use the technique to booby-trap the perimeter of the base. The next day a Pathet Lao patrol stumbled into the area and set off the grenades. Hmong trainees used their new rifles to catch the communists in a crossfire. The enemy fled, abandoning their dead and wounded. Lair was on hand to witness the ambush.[51] It looked like Operation Momentum might pay off.

With the enemy now aware of his location, Vang Pao moved his headquarters farther north a few mountaintops away to a place called Padong. The mountain village had once been a purchasing site for the French colonial administration's Opium Board. The French had constructed an airstrip so planes could transport the opium to government warehouses in Saigon. The airfield was still there, but badly overgrown. Vang Pao organized crews of mostly women and children from local villages and put them to work making the old airfield serviceable again. Within a few days, CIA transport planes began airdropping crates of weapons: WW II vintage carbines, M-1 Garands, Browning automatic rifles, mortars, and rocket launchers—enough to equip two full companies. PARU grouped two hundred Hmong volunteers into two companies, put them through the three-day accelerated training cycle, and handed the companies over to Vang Pao. He immediately sent them out on patrol south of Xieng Khouangville to see what they could do. Within a few days they ambushed a Pathet Lao column, killing fifteen.[52]

Vang Pao wanted more units in the field. Youa Tong Yang and Sao Chia Thao had already begun the mass mobilization that had thousands of Hmong from around the Plain of Jars heading for the seven preselected sites. Vang Pao got in radio contact with Youa Tong and Sao Chia and asked them to send some of these Hmong to Padong for training. Hundreds of new volunteers streamed out of the mountains to the base. Refugees also began to arrive, fleeing the war on the plain. Tents and huts were hastily set up to accommodate the swelling population. Two Dakotas crammed full of weapons and supplies landed daily at the camp to unload their cargo. Still it was not enough to keep up with the influx of refugees and volunteers, most arriving with their families.[53]

Two CIA agents, Joe Hudachek and William Young, arrived to give the PARU a hand. An airborne instructor during the Second World War, Hudachek was there to help with military training. Young was there because of his language skills. In addition to being fluent in Lao, he spoke several montagnard dialects. During the rest of January and through February, the two agents and five Thai trained an additional five companies.

By mid-March, five more CIA agents were on the scene. One was Anthony Alexander Poshepny, operating under the alias of "Tony Poe." A former Marine, Poe had already achieved an illustrious career as a CIA field agent. In 1957 Poe was part of a five-man team that worked with Sumatran rebels to topple Indonesia's Sukarno regime. After the rebellion fizzled he moved on to Tibet, where he organized the escape of the Dalai Lama. Poe continued to nettle Beijing's leaders by training Nationalist Chinese strike forces for incursions into Communist China.[54] With Poe came Tom Fosmire, Jack Shirley, Lloyd "Pat" Landry, and Thomas Ahern. Fosmire had worked with Poe in Tibet. Shirley was a PARU man, having been with the organization almost as long as Lair. Landry had been a field operative in Europe and Asia.[55] Only Ahern was new to field work. Unhappy with his desk job in Vientiane, he had finally wangled his first field assignment.[56]

Along with the five agents came four additional Thai PARU teams. Their collective task was to link up with Hmong who had arrived at Vang Pao's preselected sites and create six new training bases: one at Ban Na north of Padong, one at Phu Fa on the western edge of the Plain of Jars, plus three bases (San Tiau, Tha Lin Noi, Moung Ngat) on the eastern edge of the plain, and one at Houei Sa An, north of the plain (see map "Momentum Sites").

By the end of April, Operation Momentum had armed a total of five thousand Hmong and cycled them through the three-day training program. It was only a fraction of the Hmong Vang Pao wanted under arms, but it was enough for Bill Lair, who wanted to keep things manageable and low-profile. He felt there were already too many Americans in the field. Americans attracted attention, especially from the North Vietnamese. Lair preferred to have everything done by the Thai PARU.

Lair had failed to factor in the bureaucratic infighting that was inevitable once the program attained some size. The U.S. Army, originally organized as PEO and recently transformed into MAAG/Laos, wanted its White Star teams involved in the training of Hmong. A good deal of the money for the initial phase of Momentum had come out of the U.S. Army budget, giving the Department of Defense some leverage to pressure the CIA to cave in to the demand. However, the telling voice was that of the president himself. The Bay of Pigs disaster, organized and run by the CIA, was still front page news. Kennedy had become wary of the CIA and was unwilling to allow the agency complete control over paramilitary operations in Laos. He wanted the White Star teams involved to serve as counterweight to the CIA.

The first White Star team, commanded by Captain Bill Chance, arrived at Padong in late April. There were now a lot of white faces at the base. As Lair had feared, the North Vietnamese quickly developed an interest in Padong.

EDGAR BUELL

Almost daily Vang Pao flew out of Padong in an Air America Helio-Courier, an aircraft specially designed for short takeoffs and landings (STOL), to remote villages to supervise the organization of what he called "shock companies"—highly mobile guerrilla units capable of fast strikes and quick retreats. By the end of May, eighty-four units had been formed and positioned to encircle the Plain of Jars.[57] The units were mostly paper rosters. Few had any arms or training. CIA agents, PARU teams, and White Star advisors traveled to these remote locations to supervise the construction of landing sites where weapons and supplies might eventually be delivered.[58] It would be nearly a year before many of the shock companies had sufficient weapons to defend themselves, let alone undertake offensive operations.[59]

Though weapons were slow to arrive, food, clothing, and medical supplies fell from the sky with unceasing regularity. The object was not solely humanitarian. The eighty thousand or so Hmong who had mobilized to offer support, or become soldiers in Vang Pao's guerrilla army, had done so at the behest of Youa Tong Yang, Sao Chia Thao and, at the last moment, Touby LyFoung. Their

Edguar "Pop" Buell in front of hut at Nang Kai after he left LS20.

loyalty was to these men, not to Vang Pao. To transfer that loyalty to himself, Vang Pao needed to deliver tangible benefits. Bill Lair understood this and came up with the funding to mount the massive relief effort channeled through USAID and organized by Edgar Buell, a volunteer earning sixty-five dollars a month with the International Voluntary Service (IVS), a private aid organization.

Buell began his tour with IVS at Lat Houang, a town of a thousand on the southeast corner of the Plain of Jars. Buell was an Indiana farmer, scrawny, bowlegged, and nearly as short as a Hmong. He had retired from farming in his late forties after his wife's death. Chronically depressed by the loss, Buell had sought help from his family doctor, who recommended that he get into volunteer work of some kind, anything to fix his mind on something besides his own grief. What the physician had in mind was something local, not a tour with IVS in Laos. But Buell wanted to go where he was really needed, and IVS convinced him he could make a real difference in the Laotian highlands, where peasants were dirt-poor and worked the land with techniques evolved during the Stone Age.

Initially, Buell's job with IVS was to teach modern farming to Hmong peasants. A model farm, funded by USAID, was already in operation at Lat Houang. The farm had two tractors, disc harrows, mechanized corn planters, and power mowing machines. The soil at the site had been worked to exhaustion by Hmong and abandoned long ago. The IVS planted corn anyway, watched it struggle up to knee height, turn yellow, and die.

Buell was all for modern farming, but it had to be applied with some common sense. The model farm at Lat Houang was not only a waste of time, it gave Hmong the impression modern technology didn't work. Buell avoided the IVS offices and spent most of his time in the field with Hmong farmers, observing their ways and learning their language. He showed village blacksmiths how to fashion steel tips for wooden plows, a simple but practical innovation that earned him immediate respect. He appropriated a USAID bulldozer, hired Hmong for a construction crew, built earthen dams for irrigation, and later constructed a twenty-mile road.

During the road construction, Kong-Lê rose to power and the U.S. cut off all aid to Laos, leaving Buell no money to pay his workers. Buell paid them out of his own pocket and continued building the road. But once the fighting spilled onto the Plain of Jars, Buell immediately abandoned the road project to help Hmong displaced by the fighting. Working with refugees brought him into closer contact with USAID. Buell knew the organization was filled with CIA agents and it made him feel a little uncomfortable, but the agency seemed to have endless resources and was willing to share them with destitute Hmong.

By the end of January 1961, Buell was in Vientiane with other IVS volunteers setting up a special USAID-sponsored refugee relief program. The relief was intended for Vang Pao's Hmong, which was why Buell had been brought on board. Several months earlier, in a meeting with one of Vang Pao's partisans, Buell had been told of the plan to relocate two hundred villages and shown a map of the relocation sites. Buell was the only American aid worker who knew where the Hmong refugees were located.[60]

Daily for three months, Buell and the other volunteers loaded gunnysacks of rice (ninety-six pound bags), clothes, and medicine from their Vientiane warehouse into a C-47 and transported the supplies to the highlands surrounding the Plain of Jars. When they passed over a Hmong encampment, Buell strapped himself into a restraining harness and kicked out the lifesaving crates of supplies to waving Hmong below.[61]

The flights were dangerous. Hmong encampments were often located amidst craggy peaks, inviting head-on collisions with mountains. The C-47 took a lot of ground fire both coming and going. After one mission, Buell counted twenty-seven bullet holes in the C-47's wings. The danger only increased during the rainy season. Flying in near zero visibility, crashes into mountains were

Edgar "Pop" Buell, refugee relief, Laos, 1970-1971

a constant threat. Twenty-three American aid workers would eventually lose their lives in plane crashes.[62]

A few days into the flights Buell noticed isolated groups of Hmong moving south, people who were not part of Vang Pao's organized relocation, real refugees fleeing from the fighting that continued on the plain. After several weeks of counting heads he estimated there had to be about fifty thousand of them. Buell had heard rumors of a ceasefire.[63] He hoped they were true. If the fighting stopped he might have a chance to get supplies to the thousands of wandering Hmong before they starved to death or were killed by the communists.

7

WHILE SEEKING A POLITICAL SOLUTION

During the first few weeks of his presidency, reports of communist victories in Laos crossed Kennedy's desk nearly every day. Kennedy had promised in his inaugural address that America would "pay any price, bear any burden . . . to assure the survival and success of liberty."[1] Trapped by his own rhetoric, he pondered whether the United States should commit troops to Laos. Kennedy asked the Joint Chiefs of Staff for an assessment.

The generals did not tell Kennedy what he wanted to hear. U.S. military action was advised only if the president was willing to commit to an unlimited war in Asia. The North Vietnamese would probably become involved, and the Chinese. It would be a big war, with up to a quarter of a million American troops—every bit as large as the Korean conflict. Kennedy asked if that would be enough troops if the Chinese entered the conflict. The only contingency plan the generals had for dealing with the Chinese was nuclear weapons.[2]

While Kennedy did not shrink at the thought of a large war in Southeast Asia, Laos seemed the wrong place to stage it. The nation was politically unstable and its military notoriously ineffectual. The country was landlocked with no access to the sea, making logistics difficult—the same considerations that led Eisenhower to reject committing American troops to Laos. To Kennedy, Vietnam seemed a more reasonable choice, should such a war become necessary.[3]

These considerations enhanced the attractiveness of a political solution in Laos: establishing a coalition government that included the Pathet Lao and Neutralists, as well as the pro-American Lao right-wing. The problem was to get the communists and Neutralists to stop fighting and enter negotiations. Since they were winning on the battlefield, they had little incentive to talk. Kennedy's plan was to convince the communists, especially the Russians, that America was willing to commit its own troops to prevent a communist victory, using bluff to get them to the bargaining table.[4] The Soviet reaction was thought crucial because of the presumption (which was false) that the Soviets exercised complete control over the communist movements in China, Laos, and Vietnam. Also, the Soviets had equipped the Neutralists and Pathet Lao with Soviet-made weapons, making them dependent on parts and ammunition stored in the military arsenals at Kiev and Minsk. If the Soviets stopped their airlifts to the plain, the Neutralists and Pathet Lao armies would eventually sputter to a halt.[5]

In early March 1961, Kennedy initiated the bluff with a secret letter to Khrushchev declaring his resolve not to abandon Laos, even if this meant placing American troops on Laotian soil. He followed this message with a display of military might. While the Seventh Fleet steamed into the Gulf of Siam, five hundred U.S. troops arrived at Udorn Airfield in Thailand, joined by a fleet of helicopters to create the impression that the troops might be used as air cavalry and be airlifted at any moment across the border into Laos. To reinforce this image, military supplies were stockpiled at bases in Thailand, all near the Laotian border.[6]

There was one final touch to convince the Soviets of America's resolve. Kennedy authorized a special operation to be launched simultaneously with the CIA-sponsored invasion of Cuba scheduled for mid-April. Once the Cuban invasion was underway, a fleet of B-26s flying out of Tahkli Air Base in Thailand would drop bombs on the Plain of Jars and on Pathet Lao positions in Ban Ban Valley. Hmong units, joined by three hundred Marines airlifted from Okinawa, would then assault communist forces across the plain.[7]

The B-26s never dropped their bombs and the Marines never landed. When the Cuban invasion fell apart, Kennedy canceled the Laotian side of the operation.[8] But there were still the aircraft carriers off Thailand's coast, the five hundred American troops in Thailand, and the fleet of helicopters and stockpiles of military supplies near the Laotian border—enough to convince the Russians that America meant business. Kennedy went on television with maps and charts and "clichés about Laotian freedom being tied to American freedom," and warned that a threat to Laos was a threat to America's national security.[9]

The Russians fell for Kennedy's cozenage and pushed for a negotiated settlement. The North Vietnamese were against the idea. So was Phoumi Nosavan, who realized a coalition would mean an end to his rightist dictatorship. The Russians bypassed Hanoi and persuaded both the Neutralists and Pathet Lao to go to the bargaining table.[10] Following suit, Washington sidestepped Phoumi and put direct pressure on Prime Minister Boun Oum to begin the process of creating a coalition government

A ceasefire began on May 3, 1961. Two weeks later talks began at Geneva, involving representatives from fourteen nations, including the United States, the Soviet Union, China, North Vietnam, and delegates from the Rightists, Neutralists and Pathet Lao. To strengthen America's position at the talks, Kennedy ordered five thousand additional troops sent to Thailand.[11]

At Geneva the Soviets seemed as eager as the U.S. to establish a coalition government. But the Chinese, seconded by the North Vietnamese, dragged their feet. It was evidence of the growing rift between the Soviet Union and Communist China. While Khrushchev was moving toward détente with America and the West, Mao Zedong continued to endorse a never-ending struggle against capitalism with wars of national liberation throughout the third world. The Chinese were inflexible on this issue, and used international communist conferences as a forum to attack Khrushchev. In retaliation, Khrushchev cut off all military aid and economic assistance to China.

The tension between the two communist giants was observable at Geneva. After one particular tedious and unproductive meeting, the Soviet representative, Andrei Gromyko, observed sarcastically that "one cannot sit indefinitely on the shores of Lake Geneva, counting swans."[12] A census of Lake Geneva's waterfowl suited the Chinese just fine. Their delegation had signed a six-month lease for a villa, suggesting that from the very start they intended to draw out the talks as long as possible to permit the Pathet Lao, Neutralists, and North Vietnamese to mount military operations against strategic positions to gain a bargaining advantage.

PADONG UNDER SIEGE

While negotiations dragged on at Geneva, the communists moved against Padong, threatening to engulf and destroy Vang Pao's nascent Hmong army. The object was not just to improve their bargaining position at Geneva, but to eliminate the only force in the field that posed a threat to Pathet Lao and North Vietnamese military supremacy in Laos. This judgment was based on a single battle, the siege of Muong Ngat.

Earlier, prior to the ceasefire, the NVA had already begun testing the strength of the Momentum bases with an infantry assault on San Tiau. Three hundred Hmong were at the base, along with a PARU team and CIA agents Shirley and Ahern. They held on for three days. About to be overrun, Shirley ordered the base abandoned. The Hmong melted into the hills. Air America pilots airlifted the Thai and Americans to safety with helicopters.[13]

The NVA's next target was the Momentum base at Muong Ngat defended by a single company of Hmong, a six-man PARU team, and a handful of Khmu, all hunkered down in the ruins of a military post erected by the French nearly two decades earlier. The French had placed the post high on a bluff to monitor traffic on the heavily used byway running from the border to Route 4. It was still a strategic location and the NVA wanted it in communist hands.

The Hmong at Muong Ngat were led by Ndjouava Ly, the man who two years earlier had volunteered to enter Chant du Coq pass with Vang Pao to eliminate NVA sharpshooters. Remembering Ndjouava's earlier heroism, Vang Pao rewarded his former adjutant with a company command.

When the NVA struck Muong Ngat, Ndjouava was not caught by surprise. Two weeks earlier Vang Pao had contacted him over the company's field radio to let him know that a large NVA battalion, plus several companies of Pathet Lao, were heading his way.

Vang Pao had ordered Ndjouava to comb the hills for Hmong volunteers to serve as a harassing force to slow the enemy's advance. Poorly equipped with ancient carbines left over from the French era, the volunteer force of several hundred Hmong repeatedly ambushed the communists, detaining them long enough to give Ndjouava's company on the bluff an extra week to prepare the post's defenses. The PARU team showed the Hmong how to set up their heavy machine guns in an overlapping field of fire and how to lay out mines to impede enemy assaults.

The communists attacked Muong Ngat on May 12, 1961, with a combined force of nine hundred NVA and four hundred Pathet Lao, outnumbering the Hmong nearly fifteen to one. The attack commenced with a violent barrage from mortar and recoilless cannon. Within a few hours the enemy had completely encircled the post. At dawn the following day, waves of NVA charged the bluff. The post's defenders cut them down with machine gun fire. Exploding mines left yawning gaps in the attackers' formations. Hmong sharpshooters picked off NVA officers one by one. They were easy to spot, standing tall in plain view, close to the action with a radioman at their side, observing the battle scene through binoculars.[14]

The North Vietnamese continued the assault until dusk, the bodies of their dead piling up. The defenders had prepared for the worst. Days before the communists arrived, they had burrowed into the bluff, digging a tunnel that emerged close to a stream. When the North Vietnamese and Pathet Lao finally breached the post's defenses, defenders fired their weapons point-blank, then fought hand-to-hand. Only twenty-three made it out through the tunnel, leaving behind nearly sixty dead comrades.

Hmong partisans in the hills monitored the entire battle from start to finish, conveying the details by radio to Vang Pao. They reported the heaps of enemy dead strewn across the battlefield and the twenty-three survivors who had been whisked away by partisans into the hills. Ndjouava Ly was one of them. Vang Pao intended to give the man another promotion, but first he had to get him back to safety. Vang Pao maintained radio contact with Ndjouava to fix his position so he could airdrop supplies. It would take Ndjouava nearly a month, zigzagging his way across eighty miles of mountains avoiding enemy patrols, to reach Padong. He arrived just in time to witness the fall of the base to the communists.

By one account, reports of the battle at Muong Ngat undermined morale at Padong.[15] In reality, Vang Pao was elated with the outcome. A single Hmong company had eliminated twenty-seven NVA officers, including a colonel, and killed or wounded three hundred NVA soldiers. The defense of Muong Ngat confirmed what properly trained and equipped Hmong could accomplish against even battle-hardened NVA. In Vang Pao's words: "The Viets were now aware of our abilities, of our capacity to inflict heavy damage in combat."[16]

The battle of Muong Ngat was a shock to the communists. They had enjoyed easy victories against RLA forces, infamous for their penchant for retreating before the slightest resistance. The Hmong had fought nearly to the last man. By the communists' own reckoning the Pathet Lao and NVA had suffered nearly a thousand casualties in the early months of 1961, almost all of them attributable to Vang Pao's Hmong, making it imperative to eliminate the embryonic Hmong army forming at Padong before it had a chance to grow.[17]

In the early weeks of May, the North Vietnamese dug terraces to inch their artillery up steep slopes within striking distance of Padong. The first shells struck the Hmong encampment on May 15th. Eleven days later Padong was pounded with one hundred shells. Following a two-day pause, four hundred additional artillery rounds struck the base. The communists also shot down a CIA helicopter, killing two crew members and critically wounding an MAAG advisor.[18]

The Americans at Padong did not want to believe the attackers were NVA. Vang Pao sent out reconnaissance patrols. One unit returned with ears taken from ambushed enemy soldiers. Vang Pao showed the ears to White Star team leader Bill Chance, pointing out how the ears were slightly pointed. That meant they had to be Vietnamese. Chance doubted the ears of a Vietnamese were all that different from those of a Lao and remained unconvinced.[19]

The communist assault began in earnest in the first week of June 1961, led by elements of the NVA 148 Independent Regiment. At ten in the morning, twelve hundred communists soldiers, many of them NVA regulars, gained a foothold in the valley below the Hmong encampment. They walked mortar shells up the slope onto the first line of the camp's defenders, forcing the Hmong to pull back.

It was the onset of the rainy season and the Vietnamese made slow progress up the slope. For a week a heavy, dripping fog had shrouded Padong. There had yet to be a heavy rain, but the fog deposited enough moisture to transform the ground into slick mud. While the Vietnamese struggled to negotiate the slippery rise to the Hmong encampment, Vang Pao moved automatic weapons and mortars into position. Members of a White Star team helped the Hmong set the correct elevation. The shells found their targets and stalled the communist advance.

Two thousand Hmong civilians were at Padong, living in military tents donated by MAAG and the CIA.[20] Vang Pao's main concern was to hold off the Vietnamese long enough to get women and children out of the camp and down the other side of the mountain to safety. While his guerrillas dug in, the families left the tent city for the foothills, waiting for dusk. By late afternoon, the communists had closed the distance. Mortar shells tore the abandoned tents into tatters.

Edgar Buell had arrived at Padong earlier that morning, just before the battle began. He had come straight from Ban Na, a mountain village northwest of Padong that enjoyed the dubious distinction of being the first official Hmong refugee camp of the war. Buell had spotted Ban Na from a helicopter while searching for refugees, and discovered the mother lode. Five thousand Hmong were crowded onto the top of a narrow crest. He landed to assess their needs. There had been no food for three weeks. Small children with sunken faces sat listlessly in the ocher mud, the sores on their skin caked with dried pus. Buell saw a tiny infant nearly mummified from starvation tug futilely at its mother's- dried up breasts, hanging like leather pockets on her chest. Many other infants and children had already died.

Twice during his inspection tour of the encampment Buell heard the signal for a Hmong death, three shots fired into the air from a flintlock. He radioed USAID in Vientiane and, for the rest of the day, coordinated the delivery of food, salt, blankets, clothes and medicine. For some the help came too late. Flintlocks continued to sound throughout the night. More supplies arrived in the morning. Three more days would pass before the flintlocks stopped firing.[21]

As Buell sat at Padong, huddled with others on a hillside, cringing with each explosion of the artillery shells slamming into the empty tent city below, he suddenly wished he were back at Ban Na. A fourteen-year-old Hmong girl tugged on his shoulder. She carried an American M-1 rifle. A homemade cotton bandoleer weighted down with ammunition clips was slung over her thin shoulder. "Don't worry," she said. "I will protect you." She aimed the rifle down the hill toward the enemy and squeezed off a round. Buell suddenly found his courage. Vang Pao had asked him to collect the women and children and prepare them for evacuation. It was time to get to work.

The rain began at sunset, a driving, pelting storm that added a new sound to the cacophony of exploding mortars and artillery shells—the thunder-like rumble of water raging down gullies in flash floods. Vang Pao gave the signal for the civilians to move out. The evacuees formed a line that stretched a full mile as they snaked down the mountain, clutching at liana vines to maintain their balance in the watery mud. They marched eighteen hours before the sound of weapon fire at Padong finally died away.

The escape column pushed on for another full day before reaching Yat Mu, a mountain ridge already overflowing with Hmong refugees. They were fugitives from a communist push off the Plain of Jars into the mountains ringing the plain's southern rim, an operation dedicated to plundering Hmong rice and opium stores, impressing men into work gangs, and hauling away older teenagers for service in the Pathet Lao. Entire villages had fled before these army ants, making their way toward Yat Mu. Nine thousand Hmong eventually reached the narrow mountain ridge, crowding together for comfort, sharing what little food they carried, and slowly starving to death. When Edgar Buell arrived with the column from Padong, he circulated among the destitute Hmong to assess their needs. To his surprise he discovered that there were already aid volunteers on the ridge, led by Felix Romero, a physician with Operation Brotherhood, a private Filipino medical relief agency.

Romero's group was just a portion of the hundreds of Filipinos brought to Laos by the CIA, the majority of them military specialists, veterans of the early 1950s counterinsurgency campaign that crushed the communist "Huk" rebellion on the Filipino islands of Negros and Panay. Officially the Filipino soldiers were civilian employees of the Manila-based Eastern Construction Company building roads in Laos. Their real job was to train Lao soldiers and fight at their side. Some of them would soon be working with Hmong guerrillas.

Romero informed Buell that there had been nothing to eat for days. Bad weather had prevented airdrops from Vientiane. In addition, Romero was fighting an epidemic of dysentery and losing. The medicine was used up. He feared that if relief didn't arrive quickly the refugees would die in large numbers. Hundreds did die while Buell and Romero prayed for the weather to clear. Unwilling to wait for the inevitable, several dozen despairing Hmong committed suicide by swallowing raw opium. A thousand more, gaunt from starvation, struck out on their own rather than remain in the camp and starve to death. Given their physical condition, most of them probably died within a few days of their departure. On the eleventh day, Buell and Romero's prayers were answered at last. The clouds broke and transport planes from Vientiane airdropped rice, salt, blankets, and medicine.[22]

By this time Vang Pao was setting up his new headquarters at Pha Khao. He had fled Padong by helicopter shortly after the last civilians departed. Left behind to fend for themselves were several hundred Hmong guerrillas, PARU and White Star advisors, and CIA agent Jack Shirley. As the enemy closed in, some Thai and a White Star team formed a rear guard while the others attempted to break out. By late evening, the survivors of the assault were in a column moving quickly away from the base. They were still marching by first light. The Hmong in the retreating column soon vanished into the forest. Air America helicopters located and picked up the Americans and Thais and flew them to Pha Khao, which would function as Vang Pao's headquarters for the next sixteen months.

IMPATIENT TO FIGHT

The loss of Padong only intensified Vang Pao's commitment to get on with the task of equipping Hmong volunteers. But except for the troops at Pha Khao, and at the four remaining Momentum bases, few of his partisans had yet to receive weapons or training. Desperate for rifles, Hmong were roaming the countryside following rumors that weapons had been airdropped at one place or another.[23]

The fact that thousands of Hmong who were willing to fight lacked weapons or adequate training led Vang Pao to harangue Tony Poe and Vinton Lawrence, the two CIA agents assigned to him, about America's giving his people only food and holding back the weapons and supplies they needed to defend themselves. Buell was getting everything and he was getting nothing.[24] Lair flew to Pha Khao to get Vang Pao to lower his expectations, to work with what he had and become more self-sufficient. Lair knew negotia-

Hmong soldiers parading before diginitaries at Sam Thong

tions at Geneva might result in the U.S. abandoning Laos, or at least the withdrawal of support for the Hmong. He wanted to prepare Vang Pao for the possibility of continuing on alone.[25]

Lair's assessment only reinforced Vang Pao's desire to acquire more weapons and ammunition. If the Americans were going to leave, he needed to build stockpiles. His requests for more supplies went unheeded until repeated communist violations of the ceasefire and incessant lobbying by the head of the CIA's Far East Division, William Colby, goaded President Kennedy to reverse direction.[26] In August 1961, Kennedy approved plans for increasing the Hmong army to eleven thousand.[27]

Lair sent five new PARU teams to run additional training sites around the Plain of Jars. To train even more guerrillas, he began to use Hmong as instructors. After special training for the job at PARU headquarters at Hua Hin, a group of 120 Hmong formed ten Special Operations Teams (SOT) to take over for PARU at various Momentum sites, freeing up Thai instructors for training programs at new locations. In a few months Lair added another twelve SOT squads to the mix, and sent additional PARU, accompanied by SOT Hmong, to Sam Neua to expand the Momentum network north.

Even PEO contributed to the training effort. Several White Star teams settled in at Sam Thong on the southern edge of the Plain of Jars to begin the construction of a large logistics base, complete with a communications center and warehouses to channel supplies and arms to Hmong under training. The White Star teams also established their own training base to augment PARU's efforts.[28]

More Hmong than ever were enrolled in Momentum, yet Lair knew sheer numbers was not enough. As pessimistic as ever about the likely outcome at Geneva, he felt Vang Pao would be in a better position to fend for himself if he had an elite unit to fall back on in tough situations. At Lair's suggestion, Vang Pao sent five hundred of his best troops to Hua Hin for a month-long course of instruction as preparation for duty in his first Special Guerrilla Unit (SGU), a battalion-size guerrilla force.

Vang Pao now had more than seven thousand armed and trained guerrillas under his command. However, only a fraction of these troops were truly formidable: those in his single SGU and several dozen squads of elite Hmong SOTs with special training in commando raids. The remainder of his guerrillas were scattered around the periphery of the Plain of Jars, organized as *Auto Défense de Choc* (ADC) troops, a fancy label for local militias. The ADCs were capable of defending their homes, but lacked the organization or training for offensive operations.

From Washington's perspective this was fortunate, given the delicate negotiations at Geneva. The Kennedy administration did not want attacks by American-backed paramilitary forces to give the communists an excuse to delay a settlement. Vang Pao was told to limit military operations to intelligence gathering and to the defense of Hmong communities and refugee camps.[29] As an extra precaution, Air America delivered only small amounts of ammunition to Vang Pao's forces. Some of Vang Pao's commanders in the field, chomping at the bit to engage the enemy, found the order to avoid all contact with the communists difficult to obey.

Youa Pao Yang commanded an ADC company headquartered at Tha Lin Noi, one of the seven original Momentum sites. Despite his short stature (he was four feet, nine inches), Youa Pao was an intimidating figure. As broad as a tree trunk, and with a face frozen into a scowl, he was never without his pearl-handled revolver, strapped low on his right hip, gunslinger fashion. He drew the pistol often, waving it menacingly as he barked out orders, sometimes shooting a village dog to prove it was not all bluff. He was both fierce and fearless and his men offered him unquestioning obedience.

In April, Youa Pao received intelligence of communist troop movement nearby and requested permission to engage the enemy. Vang Pao ordered Youa Pao remain at Tha Lin Noi. A few weeks later, with more reports of enemy activity, Youa Pao again asked to go on the offensive. Again he was ordered to stay put. By early June, Youa Pao was no longer able to tolerate having his hands tied while the enemy roamed freely within striking distance. He led his entire company northwest to Phong Savan.

In the days of French rule Phong Savan was a center of commerce. Opium dealers converged on the town from across northern Laos to have their precious cargo flown to Vientiane or Saigon. The French pilots who flew the planes hung out at the local bars. Opium brokers patronized Phong Savan's shops and restaurants and purchased fresh produce at the town's open-air market. Hmong from across the Plain of Jars flocked to the town, for many a walk of several days, to sell a few goods and purchase items imported from France: toothbrushes, combs, jewelry, perfume, bolts of brightly colored cloth, factory-made tools, radios, and cameras. The town was a symbol of wealth and prosperity, a *coup d'oeil* of European technological civilization. Liberating the town from the communists would be a prize of major emotional importance to all Hmong in Xieng Khouang Province.

Youa Pao approached Phong Savan from the east, sneaking past Pathet Lao patrols until he reached the summit of the mountain overlooking the town's airport. Below, soldiers were unloading an Ilyushin transport plane. Youa Pao led his men down the mountain, through a bamboo forest and into the high elephant grass that grew right to the edge of the airfield. Three of his guerrillas remained behind on a rise to position their mortar tube, waiting for Youa Pao's signal. When he gave it, they lobbed shells onto the

Long Cheng U.S. /Hmong military base,
Northern Laos, ca.1963-1972

airfield. As the mortar shells exploded on the runway, Youa Pao and his men emerged from the tall grass, firing their weapons. Startled Russian technicians, Vietnamese troops, and Pathet Lao soldiers jumped into parked trucks and sped away to Phong Savan. Within a few minutes the entire installation was empty.

Youa Pao stationed his troops to repel a counterattack. They remained in position all day. By dusk the enemy still had not made an appearance. By now, Vang Pao had learned of the capture of the airport. He ordered Youa Pao to withdraw immediately. The stubby commander waited a few more hours, hoping the communists would mount a night attack. When the assault failed to materialize, he reluctantly pulled out.

After several weeks of inactivity at Tha Lin Noi, and considerable fuming, Youa Pao again set off with his guerrillas to engage the enemy, this time heading for Xieng Khouangville, only a day's march south of his headquarters. As at Phong Savan, the communists fled after the first shots were fired. Youa Pao had his troops hunker down and wait for the enemy to work up enough courage to return and put up a fight.

Vang Pao was livid. If the communists stormed back into Xieng Khouangville and there was a major battle, he would have to face the anger of his American advisors for upsetting the Geneva talks.[30] He ordered Youa Pao out of the city, and later dressed him down in front of his troops. Youa Pao quit the war, dropping out of sight, then resurfaced two years later with his anger finally spent, eager to take charge of another company. He would fight more battles and suffer many wounds. Toward the end of the war Vang Pao rewarded him with an administrative post in Xieng Khouang Province.

LONG CHENG

When the Geneva talks entered their final phase, Vang Pao moved his headquarters from Pha Khao to Long Cheng, a five-mile-long plateau south of the Plain of Jars. CIA agent Bill Young discovered the site. Young's new job after the fall of Padong was scouting out locations for potential Momentum bases. He explored the terrain south of the plain, moving in a westward arc all the way to Sayaboury Province where, at Lair's request, he searched for a fall-back position for the Hmong. During the trek, Young made contact with Hmong chieftains and found several promising locations for training sites. The most important by far was Long Cheng.

The place was a natural wonder. The limestone mountains girding the high plateau were towering sculptures of nature, their summits forming a linked network of serpentine ridges and razor-edged crests, shaped over the millennia by oceans of monsoon rains. White mist whirled around the higher peaks. A fur of dark green moss blanketed the hillsides. Gnarled trees with limbs twisted into fantastic shapes clung to the steep slopes. Years later when American pilots joined the mix of CIA agents, PARU teams, and U.S. military advisors already stationed at Long Cheng, nearly to a man they would stand slack-jawed the first day of their tour, taking in the incredible view. It was a Chinese scroll painting come to life, a Shangri-La, a place out of time and of indescribable beauty. [31]

Young had not selected Long Cheng for its breathtaking scenery. What attracted him was the plateau's protective barrier of mountains, making it a difficult place for the communists to attack. The vastness of the plateau also made it ideal for a large airstrip. It was this last feature that drew Edgar Buell to the place. He immediately moved six thousand refugees from Phao Khao to Long Cheng, staking a claim to the place for his refugee program. He then persuaded USAID and the CIA to begin construction a modern airfield to accommodate large transport planes.

The first cargo planes to land on the new airfield delivered more than food, clothing, and medical supplies. They disgorged tons of building material. Buell wanted to transform Long Cheng into a model refugee center. Since the CIA was willing to foot the bill, he had plans for modern living quarters for the refugees and aid workers, a well-supplied infirmary, school buildings, and sturdy warehouses to store food and supplies. Vang Pao arrived midway into the construction project, realized the potential of the place and took it over for himself, ordering Buell to move his operation to Sam Thong, a village six miles further north.

Within two years, the CIA would begin to expand Long Cheng's airstrip into a mile-long asphalt all-weather runway, suitable not only for large transport planes but also for the occasional jet fighter. The CIA constructed large storage facilities, new housing, a communications center, and a private residence for Vang Pao: a two-story structure in the style of an early Motel 6, with a small French balcony on the second floor to add a touch of elegance. The CIA's main office on the base was a bomb-proof building of thick reinforced concrete. The doors to the office were of heavy steel, like those used for bank vaults. The agency even established a hillside residence for King Savang Vatthana, should he ever visit the installation (he visited twice).[32]

Year after year, Long Cheng would continue to expand, becoming by the mid-1960s one of the largest American military installations on foreign soil, and the second largest CIA operations center on the globe, keeping Air America—and later another CIA airline, Continental Air Services—busy around the clock moving troops and flying in supplies. The main ramp where supplies were unloaded was larger than a city block. Toward the end of the war, air traffic at the CIA base was heavier than at Chicago's O'Hare International Airport.

To provide cover for this massive enterprise, humanitarian organizations like USAID and the International Volunteer Service (IVS) were used as fronts. In addition to providing food and medical services, USAID and IVS became conduits for CIA arms and munitions, contracting with Air America to deliver two types of rice to their clients: soft rice was real rice and hard rice was weapons and ammunition.[33]

The operation at Long Cheng would eventually become so large that the CIA attempted to disguise its importance by designating it as Alternate Landing Site 20, or 20A. Buell had moved to Sam Thong after Vang Pao elbowed him aside at Long Cheng. Designated as LS 20, Sam Thong soon became the principal refugee center in the nation. Congressmen, diplomats, and reporters who later toured LS 20 saw only humanitarian work. The CIA hoped that the visiting dignitaries would presume that whatever was going on at Alternate 20 was insignificant.

NEW COALITION GOVERNMENT

The negotiations at Geneva dragged on for nearly a year. By early 1962 even the Chinese were willing to accept a coalition government. The main obstacle to a settlement was Phoumi Nosavan, who entertained the delusion that Washington was not really serious about neutralism. To bring him back to reality, Washington cut all aid to Laos.[34] As the government was entirely dependent on the aid for its revenue, it soon went bankrupt.[35]

Phoumi ordered the national bank to print money to make up for the lost aid, causing rampant inflation. An equally silly but less damaging scheme was a gambling casino to generate revenue for the government. Phoumi housed the casino in a school building on the road to Wat Tay Airport and had posters printed to advertise the place. The casino attracted few gamblers and failed to turn a profit. Refusing to admit defeat, Phoumi used the national police to shake down citizens, demanding protection money from businessmen and forcing people to pay exorbitant bribes to get visas and passports.[36] It still was not enough to pay the bills. In desperation Phoumi opened a heroin lab on the outskirts of Luang Prabang, staffed by former members of Chiang Kai-shek's 84th regiment who had long ago become specialists in the narcotics trade in the tri-border area of Laos, Thailand, and Burma.[37] Though the lab turned a handsome profit, it still generated only a fraction of the revenue necessary to keep the government afloat.

With the nation's finances near collapse, Phoumi made the bold but foolhardy move of mounting a surprise April offensive against the Pathet Lao and NVA in the northwest province of Nam Tha. Phoumi thought he had all bases covered. If he defeated the communists, the Americans would embrace him as the country's savior. If his troops lost the battle, he would retreat into Thailand and the Americans would be forced to intervene to prevent Laos from falling to the communists. With North Vietnamese troops massing on its border, Thailand might even commit forces to the conflict.

American officials urged Phoumi to call off the offensive. He obstinately ignored their counsel, partly because his CIA case officer, Jack Hasey, encouraged his military adventurism. At the insistence of the State Department, the CIA transferred Hasey to a post outside of Laos. Even with Hasey gone, Phoumi stayed the course. Predictably, the offensive was a disaster. Phoumi's troops performed miserably and took a terrible drubbing. American military personnel attached to MAAG/Laos found it difficult to stand idly by while troops they had helped train were being annihilated. Six White Star teams flew to the battle site to advise and lead troops into battle.

Hanoi committed three infantry battalions to the conflict. The North Vietnamese caught one RLA paratroop battalion in an ambush and inflicted 50 percent casualties. Two weeks later enemy artillery opened up on the RLA's base camp. After several days of shelling, the White Star teams were unable to contain the growing panic. Suddenly, five thousand soldiers abandoned their artillery and weapons and ran. The communists moved onto the ridges overlooking the base and laid down withering machine gun fire, cutting down hundreds of fleeing infantrymen. The survivors made for the Thai border.[38]

Neither the U.S. nor Thailand were disposed to commit forces to save Phoumi who had lost all credibility as a military leader. As expressed in the *New York Times*: "The United States has written off the Right-wing Laotian Army as useless against the pro-Communist forces and is therefore losing interest in supporting the army's leaders politically."[39]

A month later, on June 11, 1962, Phoumi was demoted from military dictator to deputy prime minister in a coalition government with Souvanna Phouma as prime minister. American dollars once again flowed into the Laotian Treasury. At Geneva, representatives of fourteen nations signed the "Declaration on the Neutrality of Laos" that required all foreign military personnel to leave the country within seventy-five days.

As a counterweight to Phoumi, Souphanouvong was coaxed out of his grotto headquarters in Sam Neua Province to assume the post of second deputy prime minister. The "Red Prince" arrived in Vientiane amidst great fanfare, attired in the usual drab military tunic favored by modern revolutionaries, his aides toting boxes of photographs for distribution to the press showing Souphanouvong roughing it in his Vieng Sai cave, bent over a crude desk beneath overhanging stalactites, scribbling orders to direct the course of the glorious revolution. So successful was the propaganda that Vientiane newspapers began referring to top leaders of the Pathet Lao as "the cavemen."[40]

To celebrate the new coalition, the government planned a grand parade for August 1962. Military units from the Pathet Lao, Neutralist, and RLA armies were to march together in formation. Phoumi took a personal interest in the event. The parade was to pass before the garish *arc de triomphe* in the traffic circle in front of the National Assembly. Phoumi had erected the monument to immortalize his dictatorship. The memorial was also a testament to corrupt Lao politics. Cement for the monument had been illegally diverted from a runway project funded by the U.S. Agency for International Development.[41]

It occurred to Phoumi that the thousands of potholes pocking the road leading to his monument might detract from the grandeur of the occasion. He ordered his army into action. The day before the parade, trucks rolled into the capital bearing steaming asphalt. When the parade commenced, marching soldiers were greeted with fresh pavement.

The day was hot. The asphalt had not had time to cure. Soldier's boots stamped out deep depressions in the gooey tar. Many boots, buried to the ankles, became stuck. To keep things moving, soldiers loosened their laces and stepped out of their shoes. By parade's end, the route to Phoumi's arch was littered with empty boots, still in marching formation—a more fitting memorial to Phoumi's brief reign than his pretentious arc, and perhaps an apt metaphor for Laotian politics in general.[42]

8

WARLORD

The 1962 Geneva accords obliged America to withdraw all military personnel from Laos. Nearly eight hundred individuals, including military attachés, advisors to the RLA, MAAG staff, and the members of the White Star teams, packed up and left the country.[1] Even the White Star's new logistics center at Sam Thong was abandoned, with supplies still on warehouse shelves and in dispensary cabinets. Hmong quickly swept over the facility and carried everything away.[2]

Washington also ordered the CIA out of the country. The entire Vientiane station moved to Bangkok, but two of Lair's agents, Tony Poe and Vinton Lawrence, illegally remained behind at Long Cheng, along with a PARU team. Lair was too high-profile to stay behind, so he set up a temporary headquarters for his paramilitary operation at Nong Khai, a Thai village across the Mekong from Vientiane. The location kept Lair close to his Hmong, but it lacked security. Local villagers and complete strangers wandered into his facility. Lair finally transferred his headquarters to Udorn Air Base in Thailand. The CIA owned property there, a rundown wooden bungalow just off the huge concrete runway constructed by the US Strategic Air command in the early 1950s. The bungalow was designated with a simple sign as building AB-1.

Lair moved into AB-1 and set up shop, along with Roy Moffit who was in charge of CIA paramilitary operations in southern Laos. For the rest of the war AB-1 would remain the headquarters for all CIA paramilitary operations in Laos, though it would be torn down and rebuilt in 1967. Friendly congressmen on tour continually responded with disbelief when shown the dilapidated bungalow and told it was the nerve center for a major paramilitary operation in Laos. Over Lair's objections (he liked things small and simple), the CIA had AB-1 torn down and replaced with a two-story office building to better fit the image of a high-powered operation.[3]

In the beginning, Lair's work at AB-1 was circumscribed. He was not allowed to ship arms and supplies to the Hmong or sponsor more training. However, Washington did authorize humanitarian aid for the Hmong and this gave Lair plenty to do. He channeled funds into Edgar Buell's refugee relief program and oversaw the logistics of getting supplies into the field. It wasn't the same as fighting a war, but at least it kept the Hmong from starving.

North Vietnam honored the Geneva agreement by infiltrating additional troops into Laos to augment the nearly twenty thousand Pathet Lao already in the field.[4] Vang Pao's intelligence network reported a steady stream of North Vietnamese trucks carrying troops and supplies down Route 6 from Vietnam onto the Plain of Jars. American Voodoo jets, high-flying twin-engine reconnaissance planes, also confirmed the presence of the truck convoys in their aerial photographs.[5] By the fall of 1962, the North Vietnamese had expanded their presence in Laos to ten thousand men.

One reason for the buildup was the failure of the Pathet Lao to bring Kong-Lê into their fold. He took his neutralism seriously and was openly critical of the Pathet Lao's slavish dependence on the North Vietnamese, calling them *kap kap* (the Lao expression for toads) because of their penchant for aping the North Vietnamese obsession with digging trenches.[6] Kong-Lê had forty-five hundred troops under his direct command, distributed over the Plain of Jars, in the Ban Ban Valley, and at Xieng Khouangville. Another fifty-five hundred were scattered throughout central Laos in small garrisons. Once Hanoi realized it could not count on these troops and might very well have to face them in combat, the decision was made to dramatically expand the presence of the NVA.

In March 1963 a sudden escalation in clashes between Neutralists and Pathet Lao forces began to unravel the ten-month-old coalition government. Pathet Lao antiaircraft guns shot down two American transport planes, killing two U.S. pilots attempting to deliver supplies to the Neutralists. This incident caused the Kennedy administration to reconsider the feasibility of a coalition. Even Souvanna Phouma, who had so often championed the coalition idea, began to question its viability, especially after receiving confirmation of a buildup of North Vietnamese forces in his country.[7]

In the end it was the communists who scuttled the coalition by assassinating two of Kong-Lê's top officers. The Neutralists retaliated, gunning down Quinim Pholsena on the front steps of his Vientiane residence. A former librarian and part-time radical, Quinim had jumped on the Pathet Lao bandwagon and wangled the post of foreign minister in the coalition government. Outspoken in his support of the communists, he made an ideal target.

Not wanting the revolution to lose a second hero, and with memories of his year in jail after the collapse of the last coalition government still green, Souphanouvong vacated his post as deputy prime minister and fled to his cave headquarters in Sam Neua. The other communist deputies soon joined him, returning like salmon to their natal stream.

With the coalition government no more, the Pathet Lao stepped up military action, especially against Neutralist forces. For months the communists had been cutting back on the food and military supplies going to Kong-Lê. Now they ceased delivering anything at all. In mid-April, NVA and Pathet Lao units assaulted all Neutralist strongholds on the Plain of Jars. Believing Kong-Lê's army would be destroyed without outside support, Kennedy authorized covert deliveries of supplies to the Neutralists and directed the CIA to do what it could to save them from annihilation.

BACK IN BUSINESS

Bill Lair used the directive as a pretext for reopening the weapons pipeline to his Hmong. With support from the Thai military, he secured a two-story building at Udorn Air Base to warehouse supplies and weapons. The building would become the principal supply headquarters for all U.S. paramilitary operations in Laos for the rest of the war.

With weapons again arriving at Long Cheng, Lair persuaded Vang Pao to conduct a series of diversionary actions on the Plain of Jars to draw the communists away from the Neutralists. Vang Pao went a step further and ordered Hmong to fight alongside the Neutralists garrisoned at Lat Houang and Ban Ban Valley.

The Hmong at Lat Houang came directly from Long Cheng and were battle-tested. The Hmong at Ban Ban were only members of a local ADC. Vang Pao airdropped arms and supplies to the irregulars and sent them a leader, one of his best officers, Major Chong Shoua Yang. Over the next year Chong Shoua hardened the ADC into a formidable guerrilla unit that kept the Pathet Lao out of Ban Ban Valley.

Despite the help, Kong-Lê remained suspicious of Vang Pao and the Americans. To win him over, Washington recalled CIA agent Jack Mathews from Africa. Prior to his Africa assignment, Mathews had worked closely with Kong-Lê, supporting his 2nd battalion in the field. The two men had parted on good terms. Mathews spent three weeks with Kong-Lê on the plain, time enough to secure an agreement from Kong-Lê to establish a permanent network to receive arms and ammunition from the U.S. The logistics support, plus the intercession of Vang Pao's guerrillas, forced a stalemate that saved the Neutralists, at least for the moment. A fly-over by a high altitude U-2 spy plane equipped with high resolution cameras revealed the communists were busily expanding their logistics on the Plain of Jars, preparing for something big.[8]

Over the next ten months fighting was sporadic. Kong-Lê's garrisons held, but three of Vang Pao's momentum sites were overrun and lost.[9] The communists had their own setbacks. Hanoi was using Route 7 to move troops and supplies to NVA garrisons onto the Plain of Jars. Bill Lair decided to close the road down. In August 1963, he sent in PARU demolition specialists to supervise the operation. The Thai organized twelve platoons of elite Hmong troops and deployed them along the road at strategic passes and bridges. Each platoon dug ten holes to receive cratering charges. The charges, plus C-4 explosives, were airdropped to each platoon by Tony Poe.

The demolition job was a huge success. Along one stretch explosions blew the road entirely off the side of a mountain.[10] The flow of troops and supplies to the plain slowed to a trickle. Hanoi rushed NVA labor battalions in to clear away the debris, reconstruct the road, and rebuild bridges.

CAPTURING SAM NEUA CITY

It would take five months for North Vietnamese work crews to finish rebuilding Route 7, giving Vang Pao the breathing space to hit the communists farther north. When Tony Poe first signed on with Momentum, his job was to establish dirt airstrips northeast of the Plain of Jars so STOL aircraft could deliver arms and supplies to Hmong volunteers. Poe was now doing the same thing again, but on a much larger scale. For months he had been expanding the Momentum network, having Hmong clear mountain landing sites throughout northern Laos, many of them behind enemy lines.

Air America pilots flew PARU teams and CIA agents to many of these distant locations to initiate new guerrilla organizations, reinvigorate those that had been allowed to languish, and train volunteers for ADCs. Poe used helicopters from Thailand to ferry Hmong troops to the new airstrips so they could launch surprise assaults against distant Pathet Lao and North Vietnamese posts. The most ambitious of these assaults was an attack on the Pathet Lao stronghold at Sam Neua City.

While crisscrossing the northern highlands searching for potential landing strips, Poe had stumbled on the remnants of former RLA battalions thought to have been destroyed when the Pathet Lao took over Sam Neua Province in late 1960. The soldiers were concealed in highland villages, and survived by raiding Pathet Lao supply stores. To get the soldiers back in uniform and working for him, Vang Pao promoted their commander, Major Khamsao Keovilay, to the post of military subdivision commander for Sam Neua and deputy governor of the province.

Recruitment through promotion was standard procedure in Hmong politics. Touby had used the technique to raise guerrilla units quickly. Loyalty was to clan, and only clan chieftains had the ability to call up hundreds of volunteers for military service almost overnight. The drawback was that clan nabobs were politicians and not warriors. Giving them command over troops risked bungled campaigns due to incompetent leadership.

Khamsao was a trained officer and had survived for nearly three years behind enemy lines, so Vang Pao was not putting a rank amateur in a top leadership slot. The day would come, however, when he would be so desperate for new recruits to fill his depleted ranks that he would give anyone—Hmong, Khmu, or Lao a command position if he could deliver enough warm bodies for duty.

Poe airdropped supplies and ammunition to Khamsao and helped with the training of his troops. Soon Poe had three battalions combat-ready for a surprise assault on the communist bastion at Sam Neua City. Vang Pao contributed two Hmong companies to the force and added a fourth battalion commanded by one of his best officers, and brother-in-law, Major Sao Ly.

The campaign to take Sam Neua City began with a diversionary action. Three of the four battalions overran a Pathet Lao garrison north of the target, then circled east around it. Pathet Lao troops hurried out of the provincial capital to meet the challenge. With the capital only lightly defended, the fourth battalion struck from the west and took possession of the city.

It was a brilliant operation that caught the communists totally off-guard. By contrast, the RLA had nothing to show for itself but a dismal season of military defeats, reason enough to belittle Vang Pao's victory. But since former RLA battalions took part in the campaign, the armchair generals in Vientiane chose to celebrate it as their own. For a brief moment Vang Pao was a national hero. The RLA general staff promoted him to general.

What went unnoticed by the RLA's top brass, but not by Lair and the other CIA case officers on the scene, was that a major factor in the campaign's success was the exemplary performance of Major Sao Ly, who had commanded the only Hmong battalion in the operation. Having followed the major's career with some interest, Lair was convinced Sao Ly had the potential to become another Vang Pao. Lair talked to his PARU teams about grooming Sao Ly to take over for Vang Pao, if he were killed.

Vang Pao was furious when he learned of the plan. A short time later, Sao Ly was murdered by his own troops. According to one of the top PARU officers at Long Cheng, Vang Pao was not "displeased by the turn of events."[11]

ANOTHER COUP

With praise of Vang Pao stinging his ears, Phoumi yearned to score a brilliant victory of his own. In November 1963, he launched a multi-battalion campaign in the upper panhandle. The CIA had advised against it, but Phoumi arrogantly ignored the counsel. The offensive began with a roar and ended in a squeak.

Things went well at first. Phoumi's battalions pushed right to the edge of North Vietnam's border, with Pathet Lao units in the area unexpectedly pulling back, giving ground. Phoumi crowed victory until three NVA battalions suddenly materialized to maul his troops. Phoumi rushed in reinforcements. The North Vietnamese hit them hard and sent them reeling. Pathet Lao troops waiting in the wings reappeared to savage the retreating RLA. For Phoumi it was one more humiliation in an already long list of embarrassments.[12]

Except for Phoumi's botched offensive, the RLA's top generals stayed out of the field. They had other fish to fry. Souvanna Phouma had recently met on the Plain of Jars with representatives from the Neutralists, Rightists, and Pathet Lao to see what could be done to bring an end to the fighting. He thought he had come up with an idea that would be attractive to both the Neutralists and communists: move the seat of government away from Vientiane's nesting ground of Rightist cliques to Luang Prabang and start again from scratch. To his astonishment the Pathet Lao blustered, complained, and generally dug in their heels, revealing they had no interest in a ceasefire under any conditions. The prime minister was stunned, then completely disheartened by their intransigence. He announced his intention to resign.[13]

Sensing a power vacuum forming, the Rightists contemplated a coup. But this time there was dissension in their ranks. Resentment against Phoumi had reached a boiling point. As one Lao politician put it, "none of us with property and servants can be deemed wholly above corruption, but Phoumi . . . has become extremely greedy."[14] Phoumi controlled the narcotics trade in Laos and even ran an opium den in Vientiane, a seedy ramshackle building that handled 150 addicted smokers a day. Narcotics netted him about a million dollars a year. Breaking with the Lao tradition of spreading graft among the ruling elite, he shared very little of the drug profits with the other Rightists. General Ouane Rattikone, who managed Phoumi's sprawling opium administration, received only two hundred dollars a month. And General Kouprasith Abhay, who commanded MR V where most of Phoumi's drug deals were made, was cut out of the drug profits entirely.[15]

In the past, resentment against Phoumi was held in check by the looming figure of Phoumi's cousin, Thai strongman Sarit Thanarat. Sarit commanded the Thai armed forces and had once offered to commit Thai troops to help Phoumi defeat his political enemies. Fear of Sarit had always been Phoumi's trump card, but Sarit had recently died. Phoumi was now on his own.

General Abhay moved quickly to take over the government, elbow Phoumi aside, and co-opt his drug empire. His co-conspirator was General Siho Lamphouthacoul, a man from Abhay's hometown and head of the national police, reorganized in 1961 as a praetorian guard to protect Phoumi from his political enemies. By pirating the best units from the RLA, Siho had shaped the police into a formidable military force, which he advertised by sending his police against Nong Boualo, a Pathet Lao bastion close to the Ho Chi Minh Trail. RLA battalions had assaulted the stronghold many times before and were humiliated on each occasion. Siho's police units routed the communists within a few days.[16]

During the evening of April 18, 1964, on Abhay's orders Siho sent two of his battalions into Vientiane to occupy the airport, radio station, and the national bank. His troops arrested Souvanna Phouma, all pro-Neutralist officials, and numerous French diplomats. For added effect, some of Siho's soldiers looted Kong-Lê's Vientiane residence. With the capital secure, Abhay called for a special convocation of the national assembly to force a settlement that would fill the cabinet with Rightists. Phoumi was never consulted, nor was a place made for him in the new government.[17]

U.S. Ambassador Leonard Unger was out of the country at the time, meeting in Saigon with Secretary of State Dean Rusk. Unger rushed back to Vientiane and, in the company of the French ambassador, sought out the prime minister at his residence. Rightist soldiers in battle fatigues, their rifles slightly raised to appear menacing, stood guard at the house. The soldiers informed the two diplomats that the prime minister was not receiving visitors.

Unger checked to see whether there were guards posted at the sides of the two-story white stucco mansion. There weren't. He had his driver take the car to the side of the house. Unger shouted the prime minister's name. Souvanna Phouma appeared on his French balcony and the two shouted back and forth for several minutes, Unger assuring Souvanna Phouma of America's support, and the prime minister expressing his gratitude. The French ambassador found the exchange quite amusing; "Ah," he exclaimed, "diplomacy à la Romeo and Juliet."[18]

Once Unger confronted him with a threat to cut off all American aid, Abhay agreed to return Souvanna to power, but only on condition that Rightist officers, about eighty in all, be placed in positions of authority. Souvanna accepted the condition and resumed his position as prime minister, with the intention of reasserting his political independence. However, being surrounded daily by newly appointed Rightists had its effect. Only a month after returning to power Souvanna Phouma announced plans to merge the Neutralist and Royal armies.

Conspicuously, Kong-Lê would not receive a position in the merged army's high command. It was an obvious maneuver to end the military independence of the Neutralists and subordinate them to the authority of the Rightists. When Kong-Lê did not protest the proposal, it was understood on all sides that for all practical purposes he had gone over to the Rightists. In protest, several hundred left-leaning Neutralist soldiers bolted to the Pathet Lao.

While the political center had been moribund for some time, there was at least its prostrate body to fight over, giving life, if only flickering, to neutralism and the coalition idea. It kept minds active hatching schemes to manipulate ideas for political advantage. And it kept people talking, even if they were only shouting at each other. Most important, it gave both sides an option besides armed conflict, an incentive to talk as well as to fight.

The communists had allowed Kong-Lê a token presence on the Plain of Jars because neutralism discomfited the Rightists and kept the door ajar for coalition politics. Now with Kong-Lê in the Rightist' camp, he ceased to serve any useful purpose, and posed a military threat. In a joint operation, NVA and Pathet Lao battalions assaulted the Neutralist strongholds at Khang Khay, Phong Savan, Ban Ban Valley, and Xieng Khouangville. To avoid annihilation, Kong-Lê withdrew his forces to the western edge of the plain.

A prime target of the communist offensive was the Hmong ADC militia at Ban Ban Valley, commanded by Chong Shoua Yang. For nearly a year Chong Shoua had frustrated communist efforts to raze the Neutralist garrison at Ban Ban by holding the high ground, principally the mountain villages of Pha Ka and Phou Nong. The Pathet Lao repeatedly tried to dislodge the ADC from the two villages, but on each occasion fell short. During the April 1964 offensive, the communists went after Chong Shoua with four battalions, three of them NVA, unleashing a deadly artillery and mortar barrage that tore the two mountain villages apart.

Chong Shoua retreated, leading his militia and what was left of the villagers south toward nearby mountains. Shells continued to drop from the sky, striking not only Pha Ka and Phou Nong but blasting several other villages nearby. These civilians also fled for their lives. The flood of refugees quickly exceeded fourteen thousand, fleeing in three separate groups. In the past the communists had not bothered to waste bullets on fleeing refugees, but this time they kept up the harassment, driving them on.

One group of six thousand was hounded by a small force, then driven up into the highlands and herded into a bowl-like depression. Waiting for them was a much larger force of four hundred NVA already in position around the edges of the basin. The harassing force pulled back to give the Hmong a false sense of security. The four hundred communists lying in wait watched patiently as the refugees below made camp and tended to their children.

By midnight most of the refugees were asleep. Suddenly, eyes popped open and heads jerked at the whoosh of shells exiting mortar tubes. Dozens of Hmong had already begun to scatter when the missiles exploded, kicking bodies into the air. Bullets from AK-47s tore into the encampment. The refugees ran blindly in the dark from one side of the basin to the other, trying to find an escape route, each time rushing directly into another deadly rifle barrage.

Above, on the rim, an order was barked out in Vietnamese. Soldiers dashed down the hillsides, screaming like banshees, most running at full tilt but a few on the steeper inclines sliding by the seat of their pants over slick limestone to get at the Hmong. When they reached the basin the NVA troops pushed into the confusion of bodies, tossing grenades into clumps of people, shooting until their magazines were empty, then drawing their knives to slash at arms and shoulders and stab at stomachs and backs. A few soldiers picked up small children and swung them like sacks, bashing their heads against rocks.

During the height of the killing, a small group of Hmong discovered an escape route and called out to the others. There was a mass rush to get away. The Vietnamese went after them in the darkness, slitting the throats of some stragglers, disemboweling others, and shooting yet others in the leg so they could be left and finished off at leisure later. Bodies littered the refugees' escape route, life still ebbing from a few who had survived a stabbing or bullet wound, groaning in pain and pleading for someone to help them. By early morning the Vietnamese gave up the chase. Sides heaving, their black pajama uniforms encrusted with blood, they were finally exhausted from their butchery. Nearly thirteen hundred Hmong, including women and children, lay dead, carved up like livestock in a slaughterhouse.[19]

The Vietnamese took two hundred survivors prisoner. The rest of the approximately forty-five hundred Hmong who had escaped the carnage and eluded capture walked forty miles to Muong Meo, a village with an airstrip that had become a magnet for thousands of other Hmong displaced by the communist offensive on the eastern edge of the Plain of Jars. More than twenty thousand refugees were already assembled, waiting to be evacuated. Air America transport planes arrived the next day and ferried refugees nonstop to Vang Pao's SGU training camp at Muong Cha.

For the Hmong the war had taken a nasty turn.

During his retreat Kong-Lê had set up temporary headquarters at Ban Khong on the plain's southwestern rim. He would soon establish permanent headquarters a few miles northwest at Muong Soui, where Neutralists troops were already garrisoned. Moung Soui was next to Route 7 and had an airfield, making it easy to resupply by both land and air. And at this moment supplies were foremost on Kong-Lê's mind.

Lulled into complacency by Hmong victories in Sam Neua Province and the demolition of Route 7, the U.S. had slowed the delivery of provisions to Kong-Lê's forces. The frayed uniforms of his troops were in tatters, their worn-out combat boots splitting at the seams. Some of his units were already out of ammunition. Kong-Lê pleaded for supplies and reinforcements to keep his army intact. While Vientiane air-shuttled a thousand Neutralists garrisoned near the capital to the edge of the plain to fortify Kong-Lê's positions, Washington authorized an emergency airlift to deliver canvas boots and new uniforms recently purchased from Japan, plus four hundred new rifles and a two-month supply of ammunition to provision eight mobile fighting groups.[20]

Much to everyone's surprise, the Soviets donated nine of their own cargo planes to the relief effort. Moscow was just as alarmed as Washington by the massive influx of NVA into Laos. The fear was that the buildup would give the U.S. a pretext for committing its own forces to the conflict, undermining any possibility for détente. The Soviets had voiced these concerns to the North Vietnamese, but they got no response. In a "read my lips" gesture, the Soviets shut down their air transport from Hanoi to Laos, compelling the North Vietnamese to move all supplies overland by truck convoy.

With so much aid going to the Neutralist army, Washington wanted assurances from Kong-Lê that he would not bite the hand feeding him. Jack Mathews was again called back from Africa to meet with Kong-Lê in order to ascertain his intentions. Mathews spent two weeks this time and secured the pledge his superiors wanted. As an added bonus, Mathews arranged a meeting between Kong-Lê and Vang Pao to see what might be done to get them working together. The two montagnard warriors had a grudging respect for each other. Kong-Lê assured Vang Pao that he would continue the fight even if forced off the plain. Vang Pao pledged Kong-Lê sanctuary if that should come to pass, and demonstrated his sincerity by sending Hmong units to the southern edge of the plain as bait to draw the communists away from Neutralist forces.

Vang Pao's attempt at a rapprochement with Kong-Lê was not all bonhomie. He planned to augment Hmong troops with Khmu from Luang Prabang, Sayaboury, and Phong Saly, where there were large concentrations of Khmu tribesmen. As Kong-Lê was the preeminent Khmu military and political figure in Laos, his goodwill was essential to the project.

The chicane was a success. Kong-Lê came to view the Hmong more as potential allies than enemies. He ordered his troops to show greater respect for Hmong villagers, and even executed one of his soldiers for stealing a cow from a Hmong peasant. As a special favor to Vang Pao and his CIA advisors, Kong-Lê delivered into their hands Somboun Chamtavong, a Khmu chieftain from the upper panhandle who had murdered two members of a PARU team and fled to Kong-Lê for protection. Vang Pao had Somboun shot and left to rot next to an airfield.[21]

Turning one of his own tribal leaders over for execution was strong testimony of Kong-Lê's newfound regard for Vang Pao. The message was not lost on Khmu in Sayaboury and Luang Prabang, where PARU teams were beating the bush to recruit Khmu for Vang Pao's army. A month after the recruitment drive Vang Pao was able to add a second SGU battalion to his army; while the officers were all Hmong, over half of the troops were Khmu from Sayaboury and Luang Prabang.[22] In time, Khmu would come to constitute 22 percent of all of Vang Pao's battalion-size units.[23]

THE RLA WINS A BATTLE

True to his pledge, when the communists continued to hammer away at his army, Kong-Lê fought on, holed up in his new headquarters at Muong Soui just west of the plain, kept alive by truck convoys from Vientiane delivering food, fuel, arms, and ammunition. To cut this supply line, the communists overran Sala Phu Khun at the junction of Routes 13 and 7, the link between the highway coming from Vientiane and the road leading to Muong

Soui. The blocking force settled in for a long stay, determined to hold ground until Kong-Lê's army withered on the vine.

In a rare moment, and with considerable pressure from U.S. ambassador Unger, the RLA general staff found some backbone and went after the communists with six regiments, attacking from three different directions. The toughest part was advancing over the thirty-mile stretch between Vang Vieng and Sala Phu Khun. For months the Pathet Lao had been investing the area with troops. The regiments plowed through the communists with relative ease, thanks to a simple scheme devised by an American intelligence officer. Each RLA forward unit carried a large wooden arrow, painted white. Once an advanced unit encountered resistance it laid down the arrow pointing in the direction of the enemy. Forward air controllers flying overhead called in Lao Air Force T-28 bombers to saturate the designated area with heavy ordnance.

In total numbers the six regiments outmanned the Pathet Lao's three battalions at Sala Phu Khun by six to one; the RLA regiments also carried 105-mm and 75-mm howitzers. As the RLA force converged on the town, the Pathet Lao battalions measured their options and withdrew. At the last moment Vang Pao committed one of his SGUs to the campaign, delivering the mobile battalion to Sala Phu Khun by Air America helicopters. Since Sala Phu Khun was deserted, the Hmong were able to liberate the town without firing a shot. The Hmong waited to greet the RLA regiments. The Lao columns arrived the next day. Their commanders, finding only triumphant Hmong grinning from ear to ear, were uncontrollably "livid over the Hmong end run."[24]

The general staff back in Vientiane were elated, however. It was one of the RLA's few authentic victories thus far. Abhay and several other top generals flew to the town to strut and celebrate. As rice whiskey flowed, the euphoria of the moment had the generals boasting that their next move would be to sweep the Pathet Lao and NVA from the Plain of Jars. They were brought back to reality when their troops reverted to form after catching up with the fleeing Pathet Lao battalions near Muong Soui. Meeting stiff resistance, they withdrew south, leaving Kong-Lê's beleaguered soldiers to fend for themselves. Within a few weeks, the Neutralists at Muong Soui were entirely encircled by NVA and a token force of Pathet Lao.[25]

A TASTE OF AMERICAN AIR POWER

The U.S. protested the siege at the United Nations, charging the communists with attempting to eliminate through force the government created by the 1962 Geneva agreement. The diplomatic posturing was little help to Kong-Lê. What he needed was U.S. air strikes to dislodge the communists. Ambassador Unger was of the same mind. He made an urgent request to the Johnson administration to authorize air sorties over Muong Soui.

Shortly after taking office, Lyndon Johnson had confided to Henry Cabot Lodge, "I am not going to be the President who saw Southeast Asia go the way China went."[26] Unlike Kennedy, Johnson welcomed an escalation of the war, convinced that once the North Vietnamese experienced the military might of the U.S. they would negotiate a settlement that would leave them bottled up in the north.[27] Giving them a taste of American air power in Laos seemed a good idea. Unger got his authorization.

To pinpoint enemy positions, twin-engine RF-101 Voodoo jets equipped with an assortment of aerial cameras flew reconnaissance. The communists were ready, having set up antiaircraft cannons at sixteen different sites on the plain. The rapid-firing cannons, capable of 150 rounds per minute, brought down one of the jets. The two Air America helicopters sent to rescue the pilot also came under fire. Shrapnel seriously wounded some of their crew and the rescue was aborted. On the ground, Pathet Lao troops closed in on the downed Voodoo's pilot, Charles Klausmann, and took him prisoner. Another reconnaissance jet went down the next day. This time the pilot was rescued.[28]

In retaliation for the shootdowns, President Johnson ordered an air strike with eight F-100 Super Saber jets, the first use of American offensive air power in Laos. While the Sabers dropped their ordnance on antiaircraft batteries on the plain, the Lao air force launched its tiny armada of World War II vintage T-28s, A-26 light bombers, and hand-me-down Navy A-1 Skyraiders. Carrying bombs recently supplied by the U.S., the propeller-driven planes hammered NVA and Pathet Lao units pressing in on Muong Soui.[29] The communists finally pulled back.

THE AMBASSADOR'S NEW ROLE

The communist offensive on the plain, and downed American aircraft, destroyed whatever was left of America's desire to seek a political settlement in Laos. Washington gave Bill Lair the nod to renew support and training for the Hmong, but now on a much larger scale. The rest of the CIA organization also returned to Laos to resume operations, though under a new set of rules established earlier by President Kennedy.

The Bay of Pigs fiasco had embarrassed Kennedy and revealed the CIA at its most inept.[30] Nevertheless, Kennedy still valued the Agency, partly because he had an "almost obsessive interest in intelligence" and because he was a firm believer in undercover operations, especially counterinsurgency of the Green Beret variety. But the Bay of Pigs convinced him he would have to exercise greater control over the CIA to prevent disasters in the future.[31]

In mid-1961, shortly after the Bay of Pigs, Kennedy had reduced the agency's role in paramilitary operations in Laos, giving more responsibility to the White Star teams for training and support.[32] To guard against renegade operations in the future, Kennedy placed the CIA under the authority of U.S. Ambassador, Leonard Unger. This was part of a larger shake-up in the state department. Kennedy wanted American ambassadors across the globe to take greater responsibility for all U.S. activities on foreign soil, particularly covert operations. On May 29th, 1961, every ambassador received a letter from the President outlining these new responsibilities, which included supervision and control of all U.S. agencies in-country, and even of military forces if an American commander was not on the scene.[33]

Applied to Laos, the new policy was an attempt to prevent diplomatic and covert operations from traveling separate paths, as they had in the months following Kong-Lê's coup. The new policy not only gave Ambassador Unger oversight of all CIA activities, it soon placed him in charge of all U.S. military operations in the country, for after the 1962 Geneva accords there was no longer a U.S. military command in Laos. The military assistance program (MAAG/Laos) had moved to Thailand to become submerged in MAAG/Thailand as DEPCHIEF[35] in order to maintain the pretense of no direct U.S. military action in Laos. The cosmetic move gave Unger, as well as the two ambassadors who would follow him, complete authority over all military and paramilitary operations in the country, making them the equivalent of a Roman proconsul, a combination of state administrator and military field marshal.

To manage this new responsibility, Unger established the Requirements Office (RO). Masquerading as a part of the United States Aid Mission, the RO was where decisions on military operations in Laos were made by Unger in consultation with the CIA section chief and several military attaches. General Reuben Tucker, who commanded DEPCHIEF in Thailand, was never consulted. Left out of policy making, his only role was that of a glorified warrant officer. His job was to insure that the arms, personnel, and supplies requested by Unger reached Laos.[36] To facilitate this task, Tucker supervised a 380-acre munitions storage facility near Udorn air base, plus an Air America facility at Udorn, port facilities in the Gulf of Thailand, and a large warehouse at Bangkok's Don Muang Airport.

While this placed enormous resources at Unger's fingertips, it was only after Washington gave up on neutralism that he had the green light to tap them. By then Unger's tour of duty was nearly over. However, his replacement, William Sullivan, would keep General Tucker busy around-the-clock providing the logistics for Vang Pao's expanding guerrilla army.

PHOUMI'S LAST COUP

1964 was a good year for the communists. They controlled the Plain of Jars, had Kong-Lê bottled up at Muong Soui, and had retaken most of the Sam Neua territory lost to Vang Pao in mid-1963. This should have been cause for concern at RLA headquarters in Vientiane, but the top generals were too busy fighting each other to worry about the enemy.

In August Phoumi attempted a coup. Kouprasith Abhay mobilized his forces and nipped it in the bud. Five months later Phoumi was at it again, this time with the complicity of Colonel Khamkhong Bouddavong, commander of MR II. Abhay requested help from General Siho to suppress the coup attempt, asking that he commit his police battalions to save the capital. Siho sat on his hands and did nothing. It was a bad move.

Abhay raised an entire regiment, secured air support, and went after all three: Phoumi, Khamkhong, and Siho. The national police headquarters outside of Vientiane was soon a burning inferno, blown apart and set ablaze by 155-mm howitzers. Fighter planes bombed and strafed Siho's best battalions billeted twelve miles north of Vientiane. Khamkhong's troops caved in and surrendered, as did Phoumi's. It was Phoumi's last coup. Along with Siho, he fled to Thailand. Khamkhong wound up in jail, leaving MR II without a commander.[37]

WILLIAM SULLIVAN

In January 1965, nearly three years after Phoumi first offered him the position, Vang Pao was again asked to take command of the second military region. This time the offer came from the prime minister, though the decision was probably not Souvanna Phouma's alone. William Sullivan, the new U.S. ambassador, was committed to a clandestine war and believed a guerrilla army could defeat the NVA. Believing Vang Pao to be a military genius in matters of guerrilla warfare, he wanted him in charge of the "real" fighting.

Sullivan had been part of the American delegation at Geneva and helped draft the final document, which prohibited foreign troops from operating on Laotian soil. Since the Geneva agreement carried the imprint of his diplomatic skill, Sullivan had a personal stake in making it work, or at least appear to work. Above all else he wanted to camouflage the true extent of America's illegal involvement in the conflict. A large military mission and arms assistance program like MAAG/Laos was too conspicuous.

Sullivan approved of the earlier decision to move MAAG/Laos out of Laos and hide it inside MAAG/Thailand. He wanted the war in Laos to be invisible to the outside world. He intended to "borrow from the practice of the North Vietnamese and act through a clandestine, deniable system of paramilitary assistance, with any actual fighting being done by indigenous forces . . . drawn from the Hmong tribes." Not only was a guerrilla army easy to conceal, Sullivan was convinced it was the only fighting force capable of thwarting a North Vietnamese victory in Laos.

Two years earlier Sullivan had participated in a controversial war game organized by the Joint Chiefs of Staff to determine the advisability of committing American troops to Vietnam. The generals were divided. Those from the U.S. Air Force believed that superior air power could neutralize communist forces and hamper their supply lines, making it impossible for them to maintain an effective army in the field. Generals from the other services were less confident. To settle the matter, the joint chiefs took part in a war game, with the rules drawn up by the Rand Corporation, a think tank under contract to the defense department.

Sullivan played on the communist team in the role of General Giap. The simulated war covered ten years, with the communists employing traditional guerrilla tactics against the American team's superior weapons and technology. The game ran for a week. At the conclusion, which in game time was the year 1972, communist forces were all over the map of Indochina, covering most of Vietnam and occupying large portions of Laos and Cambodia. American troop strength was at 500,000, with no end to the war in sight. Equally disturbing was the domestic politics component of the game. Ten years of fighting had only increased the solidarity of the North Vietnamese, while American voters were deeply divided; there were antiwar protests on university campuses and Congress was on the brink of revolt against the President.

A few days into the game, still playing the role of Giap, Sullivan launched a guerrilla raid against Bien Hoa Airfield in South Vietnam and, on paper at least, destroyed a large number of American aircraft. The year according to the game's clock was 1964. Sullivan happened to be at Bien Houa in November of 1964 when real communist guerrillas assaulted the airfield. Right on schedule, they blew up fuel storage sites, ammunition dumps, and several planes.

The war game made Sullivan a believer. Guerrilla tactics worked. But it was all theory until the Viet Cong assault on Bien Houa. Suddenly Sullivan understood at gut level that guerrilla action was an effective way to defeat a superior force, something America's military planners had yet to appreciate. Applying this understanding to Laos, Sullivan was convinced that supporting Vang Pao offered a unique opportunity to turn the tables on the North Vietnamese. The Hmong would become America's Viet Cong, an indigenous guerrilla force that harassed and bled a militarily superior enemy, frustrating him at every turn. As ambassador, Sullivan intended to acknowledge Vang Pao's Hmong army as the centerpiece of Laos' response to the invading North Vietnamese. Kennedy's earlier state department policy changes gave him the authority to do so. And Sullivan's standing in Washington gave him the clout to use that authority as he saw fit.

Sullivan had earlier served as chairman of President Johnson's "Vietnam Working Group," a special committee charged with developing strategy for conducting the Vietnam War. The role confirmed Sullivan's reputation as a major player in the Johnson administration and made him a favorite of the president. After Sullivan became ambassador, every six months or so Johnson called him back from Laos to have a look at briefing maps, give Sullivan a pat on the back, and press more money on him to carry out the war in his own way. As Sullivan remembers, "once this was in the form of a snap decision on his part to give me $75 million that neither I nor the Department of State had asked for."[38] Sullivan could run the war any way he wanted.

In retrospect, Sullivan's ambassadorship was the last in a chain of events that made Vang Pao the focus of America's response to communist aggression in Laos. It began with Bill Lair's ambition for a role in Laos for PARU, followed by the CIA's decision to involve PARU teams in Phoumi's assault on Vientiane, placing Lair and his PARU in Laos where they could make contact with Vang Pao. Lair had barely begun to formulate his ideas for a PARU-trained Hmong guerrilla force when Desmond FitzGerald, chief of covert actions for Asia, arrived in Vientiane looking for a new direction for the agency in Laos. Once Lair told FitzGerald about Vang Pao, Operation Momentum was born, then given an unexpected boost by the Geneva accords which forbade an overt U.S. military presence in Laos, making covert operations all the more attractive. With Sullivan as ambassador, the last piece was in place.

VINTON LAWRENCE'S NATION-BUILDING CAMPAIGN

As commander of MR II, Vang Pao had plans to double his army from seven to fifteen thousand troops and to organize the bulk into SGUs: battalion-size units of five hundred soldiers divided into a headquarters unit and three line companies armed with 60-mm mortars, 57-mm recoilless cannons, machine guns, and M-16 rifles.[39] The SGUs were designed to pack a punch and yet remain highly mobile so they could be inserted or extracted at a moment's notice by helicopters or light transport aircraft. Two SGUs were already in operation; four more were in embryonic form. Vang Pao envisaged a dozen SGUs forming the core of his guerrilla army.

The larger units were needed because of the changing nature of the war. Vang Pao's troops had routed the Pathet Lao in nearly every encounter, forcing them by degrees to retire from the serious fighting and allow the North Vietnamese to take their place, turning the war into a contest between Hmong guerrillas and the NVA. At this early stage Vang Pao still imagined that victory was possible, if he could only recruit enough Hmong for the fighting, organize them into air-mobile battalions, and equip his troops with modern weapons.

Recruiting more Hmong was not a simple proposition. Vang Pao may have rejoiced at America's decision to shift support from the regular RLA to his own army, but for ordinary Hmong on the sidelines it was a dubious honor. If the Lao ran away from the Pathet Lao and North Vietnamese, why should the Hmong do their fighting and defend a nation that treated them as inferiors? More than a few Hmong could still recall, prior to Touby's rise to power, how they had had to kowtow to ethnic Lao, crawling on all fours to the desk of a petty Lao bureaucrat to gain an audience. Such memories were not conducive to blind patriotism.

CIA agents working closely with Vang Pao understood the seriousness of the problem. Vinton Lawrence had been in on the start of Momentum and had stayed on at Long Cheng when the rest of the CIA pulled out, as required by the Geneva accords. Only twenty-one, Lawrence was the youngest agent in the field, having signed on with the CIA right after graduating from Princeton. Despite his youth, or perhaps because of his education, Lawrence was prone to reflection.

During his first few months in Laos, Lawrence worked for Lair in Vientiane at "Meo Alley," the compound the CIA had set aside for Lair's headquarters. It was a break-in period, allowing Lawrence time to acclimatize. Lawrence knew nothing about the Hmong and his ignorance troubled him. At nights he went out drinking with the older agents, constantly probing them with questions about the Hmong, wanting to know about their history and culture and how best to deal with them. Lawrence took this same inquisitive spirit into the field, keeping his eyes open to pick up anything and everything that would give him a better understanding of the mysterious mountain people he would soon be advising on matters that could affect their very survival.[40]

After working closely with the Hmong for a year, Lawrence felt he had some grasp of their strengths and weaknesses. He concluded that changing Hmong politics was even more important than training and equipping them to fight a war. The Hmong were hopelessly parochial. The center of their universe was family and village and they felt no call to leave home to fight far away, even to defend fellow Hmong. To fight in distant places for something as abstract as a free Laos made no sense to them at all. The Hmong needed a sense of themselves as one people and a vision of Laos as their motherland.

Lawrence got the CIA to build a house at Long Cheng for the provincial governor, Sai Kham, and persuaded him to move in (which wasn't difficult since the provincial capital was in communist hands) so the Hmong could make contact with a top Lao bureaucrat and identify with him as a leader of both the Hmong and Lao. Even more important to Lawrence's thinking was building a residence for Savang Vatthana, so the king could make periodic visits for the laying-on of hands to consecrate the Hmong war as a national crusade.

The king did show up in late 1963, to red carpets and Hmong children waving Laotian flags; Savang Vatthana affirmed the Hmong were bona fide Laotian citizens and that he was their king and that Laos appreciated the sacrifice they were making for the nation. Lawrence believed the visit had provided Vang Pao "a cachet, that he had been recognized; that his people had been recognized and appreciated." Even Bill Lair, who helped organize the visit, was satisfied that the "Hmong were on their way to being successfully assimilated into the larger Laotian scene."[41]

Lair's enthusiasm persuaded Lawrence to move ahead with his "nation-building" program and establish a radio station at Long Cheng, which he named the Union of Lao Races radio station. Broadcasting daily in Hmong, Lao, and Khmu, the station promoted the idea that the mountain minorities were all Lao citizens who had to unite to defend Laos against communist aggression. Lawrence considered the radio station the crowning achievement of his nation-building campaign.[42]

To help Lawrence's nation-building, USAID took Hmong village leaders to Vientiane and Luang Prabang; the visits were guided tours intended to expose the leaders to the mainstream of Lao society so that it would no longer seem alien. USAID also constructed a road from Route 13 to Long Cheng to integrate Hmong into the national economy and increase the contact between Hmong and Lao. As one USAID official put it: "There was this constant effort to try to tell them that they were part of one country." However, the same official also conceded that "whether they believed it or not or understood it, I make no pretense of even guessing."[43]

Testimony from Hmong interviews suggests that the effort had little effect on the vast majority of ordinary Hmong.[44] They were not even close to being assimilated, nor did they ever develop anything approaching a firm allegiance to the Lao state. The king's visit had done more to legitimize Vang Pao to the Lao elite (though only barely) than to legitimize the Lao state to the Hmong.

Vang Pao knew the Hmong felt little allegiance to Vientiane, that Vinton Lawrence had tried to change Hmong politics and failed. If Hmong politics could not be changed, then it would have to be manipulated to support the war effort. This would not be easy. In the absence of messianic leadership (and Vang Pao did not qualify), cooperation among Hmong on a large scale for any purpose or ideal did not come easily. Divided by narrow allegiances to tribe and clan, Hmong were more prone to dissension than concord.

There were three Hmong tribes in Laos (Green, White, and Striped), each with a unique tribal dress and separate dialect. In the larger villages, families tended to cluster by tribe, spoke to each other in their own dialect, honored tribal dress, and shared religious rituals that set them apart from their neighbors.[45] Though this divided Hmong from each other, it was a far cry from the daggers-drawn diffidence that existed between Hmong tribes in China.[46] Still, there was sufficient tribal bigotry in Laos to poison the wellspring of goodwill, making cooperation, even for mutual benefit, tenuous.

Living in primitive conditions in Sam Neua and Phong Saly in isolated villages on remote mountains, the Striped Hmong were stereotyped by Green and White Hmong as country bumpkins and made the butt of jokes: hardly the sort of thing to inspire ethnic solidarity. Between 1964 and 1966, when NVA units occupied Laos' far north, thousands of Striped Hmong sought sanctuary in Xieng Khouang Province, the hub of the Hmong war effort and White Hmong territory. Despite receiving sanctuary, the refugees refused to contribute soldiers to fight the Vietnamese or gather intelligence on enemy troop movements. Resentment for White Hmong bigotry crowded out the larger issue of race solidarity and the goal of reclaiming their homeland.

Clan loyalty also caused problems. There were eighteen Hmong clans in Laos.[47] Each clan had its own customs associated with birth, marriage, and death that set it apart from the others. More important, obligations for mutual aid were clan-based. A Hmong turned first to his or her immediate family, then to close clan relations, and finally to distant clan cousins for support when in need, for each clan was expected to take care of its own. It was a convention that encouraged Hmong to live in close proximity to fellow clansmen and to trust individuals from their own clan over those from different clans. The effect was to narrow allegiances.[48]

For this reason, except for Pa Chay's messianic movement, Hmong politics in Laos had always been clan-based. To be successful a Hmong politician had to first build a power base within his own clan, then forge alliances with leaders of other clans to establish broad governance which, at least on the surface, purported to represent the Hmong qua Hmong rather than merely the interests of, say, the Ly or Lo clan. Only Touby had pulled this off, and only because he controlled the Hmong opium market that delivered spoils to reward supporters and buy off challengers. If Vang Pao meant to match Touby's achievement, he would have to develop his own source of spoils and on a much larger scale than even Touby had imagined possible.

MACHINE POLITICS HMONG-STYLE

MR II encompassed Xieng Khouang and Sam Neua, two provinces populated mainly by montagnards, primarily Hmong, Khmu, and highland T'ai. One condition Vang Pao attached to accepting command of the military region was that he be granted complete authority over the ethnic minorities.[49] Souvanna Phouma did not object. It transformed Vang Pao into a virtual warlord.

Vang Pao used his new authority to create an independent political administration for Xieng Khouang[50] that would eventually include several hundred nai bans, seventy tassengs, dozens of nai kongs, and five chao muongs, plus hundreds of minor bureaucrats serving as staff for tassengs, nai kongs, and chao muongs.[51] There were also positions on advisory councils attached to chao muongs, groups of clan elders who drew a salary like all the rest. There was a civic administration that included school administrators, public health officials, various advisory boards, and an extensive police force.

Vang Pao did not have the authority to abolish the old Lao provincial bureaucracy. These officials continued to draw salaries from Vientiane, though they no longer exercised real power. In time they would cease maintaining offices and withdraw entirely from the affairs of the province, so completely receding into the background that most Hmong presumed the old bureaucracy had been dismantled and replaced by Vang Pao's vast system of spoils.

To forge alliances with clan chieftains, Vang Pao appointed representatives of the most powerful clans to the top posts in his administration (chao muong, nai kong, tasseng, and nai ban). As the Ly clan was the most powerful, Ly notables received many of the highest offices, which was only good politics. Vang clansmen were also rewarded, and out of proportion to their place in the clan hierarchy. This was bad politics, though by past standards the level of favoritism was not extreme. Only toward the end of the war, when things were going badly in the field and leaders of various clans maneuvered to bring him down, did Vang Pao overload his bureaucracy with Vang.

The higher posts in Vang Pao's administration came with substantial salaries. Eventually, they would grow to become ten times higher than those received by "official" provincial authorities. By the late 1960s chao muongs drew a salary of a hundred thousand kip per month (about four hundred dollars), distributed by Vang Pao at the close of his monthly meeting with all top political appointees. And there were fringe benefits. In 1969 Vang Pao honored five chao muongs drawn from the Ly, Moua, Thao, and Yang clans with brand new jeeps, each vehicle painted white to set it apart from the models used by ordinary soldiers.

Over the years Vang Pao created additional posts, well-paid sinecures with no real duties, to buy off potential rivals and disgruntled political allies. He also used his influence with the CIA and American embassy to wangle positions for Hmong in the national ministries, from low-level bureaucratic posts to top positions in the Ministry of Education, Ministry of Health, Ministry of Agriculture, and Ministry of Justice.

To reach beyond clan leaders to the rank and file, Vang Pao distributed an array of benefits to ordinary Hmong who supported his cause. With the CIA's deep pockets he was able to pay volunteers for full-time military service much higher salaries than that received by regular soldiers in the RLA, eventually ten times more. The highest pay went to Hmong pilots, ordinary Hmong who joined Vang Pao's tiny air force, begun in 1968. Going from rags to riches, some of these pilots earned more than Xieng Khouang's top civil servants, which apart from their derring-do in the skies transformed them into cultural heroes for Hmong peasants secretly resentful of the unearned privileges of clan aristocrats.

For thousands of poor Hmong peasants earning less than lowland rice farmers, soldiering for Vang Pao was a way to abandon a life of grinding poverty for one of relative affluence. During much of the war (before mid-1968) this inducement alone was sufficient to guarantee an adequate supply of recruits, especially as income from military chits came to be treated as appanage. Eldest sons had the right to take the place of wounded or killed fathers to keep the family on the military dole. In time this would extend to the greening buds of the family tree as young teenagers replaced their dead elder brothers, creating platoons of Lilliputian soldiers in baggy uniforms with sleeves rolled up to the elbows to free tiny hands for the operation of man-size weapons.

For Hmong in the ADCs, family dependence on military pay was not a life and death matter. Soldiers were headquartered in their home village, where the family had a farm to fall back on. But the SGUs were at Long Cheng, and Vang Pao encouraged the soldiers in these battalions to relocate their families near the military base. Without a farm to work, military pay was the only thing that kept these families going, which was an additional reason Vang Pao wanted to reorganize his entire army into SGU battalions; it increased his control. As CIA agent Vinton Lawrence put it, "When the families come to Long Cheng, in effect they are hostage to Vang Pao. And Vang Pao knows that. That helps him control the troops."[52]

There were also communal incentives for backing the war effort. Money, rice, and weapons went to every Hmong village that contributed soldiers to the cause. This support was sometimes offered in terms villagers found difficult to refuse: either accept the support and deliver up recruits or be considered pro Pathet Lao, with the implication that the village might be subjected to attack.[53] In 1971 Hmong villagers at Long Pot held fast to their commitment to stay out of the war and refused to support Vang Pao. Long Pot was bombed by T-28s and American jets stationed in Thailand.[54]

Large salaries for soldiers and politicians, bribes to village chieftains, and food and supplies for villages willing to support the war effort required a great deal of money. Vang Pao had the power to tax but never used it. Taxes, largely unofficial, had become burdensome in the last years of Touby's reign. Hmong were paying household taxes, fees for marriage certificates, and sales taxes. Some Hmong officials brazenly appropriated cattle, horses, silver, and opium simply because they had the power to do so. Others solicited bribes to influence legal and administrative decisions. Preoccupied with national politics, Touby did nothing to stop his local appointees from fleecing Hmong communities across the province.

Vang Pao had watched the corruption erode Touby's once impregnable power base and vowed never to make the same mistake. As commander of MR II, he would repeatedly proclaim that he was a soldier and not a politician, and therefore above politics and corruption. It was hyperbole. Over the years Vang Pao would cheat, lie, order assassinations, and fiddle with the public purse. But one thing he did not do was take from the common man. For years this was enough to save him from the taint of corruption, at least in the eyes of ordinary Hmong.

To verify that he was a man of the people, one of Vang Pao's first administrative acts was to abolish all taxes, official and unofficial. It was a popular move, but left him without a source of public revenue. He made up for the loss with funds from other areas—such as soldiers' pay. For much of the war Vang Pao personally delivered soldiers' pay to unit commanders in the field. With each soldier receiving 8,000 kip per month, plus an additional 200 kip per day for combat duty,[55] the total monthly allotment for all of his troops occasionally topped 250 million kip (approximately $1 million). Acting as his own paymaster, it was easy for Vang Pao to skim money, which he did from two ends.

In Thailand Vang Pao's agents converted soldiers' pay, denominated in American dollars, into Thai dollars (baht). In Laos they converted the baht to kip. Thousands of dollars were skimmed during both money exchanges and delivered to Vang Pao, minus what his agents set aside for themselves. Vang Pao's brother-in-law, Pa Chay Thao, was his principal agent for the currency exchanges. By the early 1970s, Pa Chay Thao owned two airplanes, several houses, and extensive property in Thailand.[56]

A transport plane delivered the kip left over from the money exchanges, several tons' worth, to Long Cheng, where Vang Pao took possession and distributed it to troops in the field.[57] The U.S. funded his battalions at full strength, but Vang Pao often kept them staffed far below the required 550, usually by retaining dead soldiers on the pay rosters. A 1970 government audit found that five of his battalions were understaffed by nearly fifteen hundred men. Pay for these dead soldiers netted Vang Pao nearly fifty thousand dollars per month.

And there was money from various businesses. After 1965 the secret war created tens of thousands of refugees yearly, who swarmed into the villages and settlements around Long Cheng for security and to receive aid. The refugees created an expanding consumer market for goods of all kinds. In time there would be more than a hundred thousand Hmong in the area, making Long Cheng the second largest city in Laos. There were also Khmu and Lao refugees, forty thousand of them mixed in with the Hmong. The population growth transformed the once sleepy villages of Ban Some, Sam Thong, Phak Khet, Pha Khao, Muong Cha, and Ban Houakham into bustling centers of commerce fueled by soldiers' pay and a healthy black market in goods distributed to Hmong by USAID.

Vang Pao's airline, Xieng Khouang Air Transport, delivered hundreds of tons of merchandise to villages throughout the region every month. Vang Pao was a major retailer of these goods, employing a staff of Hmong salesmen to peddle items door-to-door in the larger villages.[58] He was also into banking, handling deposits and money exchanges at the Long Cheng Bank, the only Hmong-owned financial institution in Laos.

And then there were narcotics. Vang Pao had mixed feelings about opium. He preached against the evils of addiction, but was pragmatic with addicts; occasionally he airdropped opium to troops in the field so addicted soldiers involved in a prolonged campaign would not suffer withdrawal and impede the effectiveness of their unit.[59] Nor did he have any reservations about trafficking in the drug if it advanced his ends.

Vang Pao first became involved in the opium trade in 1963. Desperate for more soldiers but strapped for the cash to add them to his pay roster, he used military helicopters to collect opium from mountain villages and delivered the narcotics to merchants in central Vietnam where opium fetched top dollar. Most of the money from the sales went for soldiers' salaries, though Tony Poe later claimed Vang Pao grew rich from narcotics trafficking.[60]

Vang Pao greatly expanded his involvement in narcotics once the war heated up after 1965. The intense fighting kept opium merchants out of the highlands. In village after village, opium harvests moldered in sheds instead of reaching the market. Rather than let the fruit of their labor rot in burlap sacks, Hmong farmers in communist-held territory north of the Plain of Jars began selling their harvest to the Pathet Lao and North Vietnamese.[61] Profits from these deals purchased weapons to kill Hmong soldiers. To deny the opium to the communists and to reap the profits for himself, Vang Pao arranged for the CIA to begin transporting opium from the highlands to Vientiane, Saigon, and Bangkok.

To undermine Vang Pao's narcotics operation, Moscow sent Hanoi fifteen tons of silver, plus 3.5 million feet of black, green, and red cloth much prized by the Hmong, to trade for Hmong opium before Vang Pao could get his hands on it. The plan might have worked had the North Vietnamese not botched the operation. To be negotiable, the silver had to be recast into ingots the size of candy bars used by the Hmong in business transactions.

The task seemed beyond Hanoi's ability, and very little of the silver entered the Hmong highlands.[62]

With no serious economic competition from the communists, Vang Pao was able to expand his opium collection network to accommodate nearly all of the Hmong opium grown in Laos, much of it transported by his own private airline, Xieng Khouang Air Transport, launched in 1967 and subsidized with CIA funds.[63] Thousands of Hmong villages in opium growing areas became dependent on him for their cash income, an economic fact of life that made them reluctant to deny his requests for military volunteers to flesh out his growing army.

The money from narcotics, skimmed soldiers' pay, and various business enterprises went mostly to subsidize the political patronage that guaranteed the fidelity of clan leaders. To purchase the loyalty of ordinary Hmong, Vang Pao used refugee relief. At its height, refugee aid funded by the U.S. created jobs, provided services, and distributed food and clothing to more than half of the Hmong in Laos. The principal force behind refugee aid was USAID. With CIA funds the organization established schools, delivered food, clothing, and medicine, and created agricultural projects for Hmong displaced by the war.

Nearly every village of any size supporting the war effort had a school of some kind. In the early 1960s, on his own initiative Edgar Buell had initiated a village school movement with supplies donated by the United States Information Agency and the CIA. Buell would later boast that eighty thousand Hmong children attended his village schools.[64] This was an exaggeration. The real growth in school attendance occurred later, when USAID began to deliver lumber, cement, and tin sheeting to Hmong communities so villagers could erect their own schoolhouses. USAID donated blackboards and chalk, books and school supplies, and trained Hmong to be teachers.

The textbooks for the elementary schools were adapted from those used by the Pathet Lao in their own education programs— books modeled after those used by Hanoi to assimilate ethnic minorities in North Vietnam into the dominant Vietnamese culture and to make them good communists.[65] The Pathet Lao's school books interspersed lessons on useful skills, mainly farming, with short tracts on national history with a Marxist slant, which USAID modified to build rather than tear down allegiance to the Royal Laotian Government.

By the end of 1969, 50 percent of all Hmong school-age children in the sixty-mile refugee corridor south of the Plain of Jars were enrolled in school. An additional three hundred Hmong were at the French high school in Vientiane and thirty-seven were studying abroad. Across Xieng Khouang Province, there were three hundred elementary schools, nine junior high schools, and two high schools.[66] The largest elementary school was at Sam Thong, with seven thousand students. There was also a high school at Sam Thong, teaching grades seven through ten, and a teacher's college. The college was Vang Pao's idea. Too many Hmong were going to Vientiane for teacher training, slipping from his influence and control.

Another service provided by USAID was medical care. Charles Weldon, a physician with USAID, directed a program to establish medical dispensaries in Hmong villages and train Hmong as medics and nurses. Weldon eventually expanded the crude hospital created by Edgar Buell at Sam Thong into a hundred-bed modern facility, staffed by American physicians on contract with USAID. Within a few years there was another modern hospital at Long Cheng staffed by Thai physicians.[67]

All refugees received food, cooking oil, clothing, pots and pans, and medicine (much of it donated by U.S. drug firms because it had passed its expiration date and could no longer be marketed in the U.S.),[68] but only villages solidly behind the war effort became sites for warehouses where these items were stored prior to distribution. Hmong living in these villages had jobs loading and unloading supplies and driving the trucks that delivered goods to refugees. And they could pilfer. This was expected and tolerated, if undertaken in moderation. The pilfering sustained a healthy black market with a reach that extended into the lowlands where food and clothing were not free.

Favored villages got tractors to help with the clearing of land, a welcome gift for swidden farmers like the Hmong who established their plots by clearing virgin forest—back-breaking work felling trees by hand, clearing away bushes with machetes, then gathering it all up into piles for burning so the ashes could be spread to fertilize the soil. It took a month of hard labor to clear and burn just a couple of acres. With a tractor it was finished in a few days. The tractors made Vang Pao a very popular man.[69]

Many of these same villages became sites for USAID agricultural stations. The stations sponsored fish farms, pig farms, poultry farms, and cattle ranches. USAID supplied all the livestock, including the fish (fast-growing Tilapia from Thailand) for the fish farms. The agency delivered truckloads of pigs, cattle, and chickens. USAID volunteers helped Hmong form pig cooperatives and taught them how to run a modern poultry farm, complete with incubators. USAID brought in bulldozers to gouge out swales for fish ponds and delivered building material for chicken coops and pig sheds. Of all these enterprises, cattle ranching was the most prestigious. Vang Pao personally purchased thousands of head of cattle from Thailand for distribution to his political and military cronies to set them up as cattle barons.

Vang Pao's administration was not all graft and patronage. He also tried to tame the clans by schooling them in cooperation, organizing various political councils with members drawn from the different clans. The most prestigious of these bodies was the Hmong Council of Elders, filled with the most respected clan chieftains in the province. All councils were purely advisory, organized to accustom the clans to working together, though Vang Pao also used them to check the pulse of Hmong public opinion and to lend a sense of unanimous support to his own political decisions.

One can only wonder what Vinton Lawrence made of all of this. He left Laos in early 1966, promoted stateside by William Colby. The CIA's Far East Chief wanted the bright young agent back at CIA headquarters at Langley, Virginia as his own special assistant.[70] Sitting in an office at CIA headquarters reflecting on his two tours in Laos, did Lawrence still imagine that Vang Pao was nation-building, rather than simply spawning a political machine to guarantee recruits and generate support for his army?

Certainly Pa Chay would have found all the money laundering, skimmed payrolls, business deals, patronage, bribes, graft, and manipulation of public opinion incomprehensible, but it was the kind of politics that old-fashioned political bosses in America (men like William Tweed of New York's Tammany Hall, Thomas Pendergast of the old Kansas City political machine, and more recently Chicago's Richard J. Daley) would have understood and admired—especially as Vang Pao could do things they could only do in their dreams, such as accumulate wives for political ends and assassinate rivals.

Vang Pao's first marriage was to a strikingly beautiful woman from the Lo clan. She died young, leaving behind three children. Vang Pao married again for love, this time to a woman from the Thao clan. She gave him more children, but favored them over those from his first marriage. Concerned for the children's welfare, Vang Pao married again, this time his first wife's sister, May Lo, knowing she would give them the love they deserved. The rest of his marriages were political, an effort to forge family links to powerful clan leaders or as goodwill gestures to the disaffected.

He married True Ly to create blood ties directly to Touby LyFoung, [71] then wed Chia Moua to gain the allegiance of her father Cher Pao Moua, the warlord of Bouam Long, a strategic stronghold north of the Plain of Jars. Vang Pao took his next wife from Sam Neua to form better relations with the Striped Hmong, [72] and his seventh from Tase, a Moua enclave that had previously shunned his leadership. [73] His eighth wife was a Lao woman, a concession to the ethnic Lao who nearly equaled the number of Hmong in the province. [74] His ninth and last wife was Zong Moua, the daughter of Cher Chou Moua, the chieftain of Long Cheng before Vang Pao made it his headquarters. With refugees spilling into Long Cheng and occupying land reserved for Moua clansmen, relations with Moua villagers became strained. The marriage was intended to cool tempers, as was Vang Pao's decision to elevate Cher Chou Moua to the head of the prestigious Hmong Council that administered Long Cheng's civil affairs and arbitrated inter-clan disputes. [75]

Not only did Vang Pao marry for power, if necessary he assassinated rivals and troublemakers to preserve it. Vang Pao first tried his hand at assassination in 1959, when he ordered an attack on the RLA provincial commander Colonel Khambou Boussarath. Vang Pao was also probably behind the 1963 murder of Major Sao Ly, the Hmong officer being groomed by Bill Lair as Vang Pao's understudy. How many others he ordered killed is impossible to document, though one Hmong in his inner circle believed there may have been dozens; hardly a reign of terror, but substantial nevertheless. Not all of the assassinations went off without a hitch. One had serious repercussions that eroded Vang Pao's power base.

For troops garrisoned in the field, military organization mirrored Vang Pao's political administration. Whenever feasible, Vang Pao gave local clan chieftains command. This disposed nearby villages to gather intelligence and feed soldiers. This also co-opted the chieftains into Vang Pao's network of graft and payoff, for commanders were expected to hold back part of their troops' pay for themselves.

The system had its defects. Clan notables were not always competent military leaders and occasionally reached too far into their troops' pockets, which damaged morale. Besides affecting battle performance, this sometimes resulted in commanders being shot by their own troops. Moderating the level of corruption was an obvious solution, but Vang Pao rejected it. The graft was needed to channel clan loyalties to his regime. Instead, he used spies drawn from the military arm of his secret police, headed by Toupao Ly (the brother of Vang Pao's fourth wife, True Ly), to identify disgruntled soldiers with murder in their hearts so they could be transferred to other units.[76]

Toupao Ly's agents were not unerring, however, and being murdered by one's own troops remained a hazard of command. One episode that occurred at Na Khang required Vang Pao's personal attention. A former French military base, Na Khang had been refurbished and expanded to become Vang Pao's most important northern garrison. As the region was a Vang clan enclave, many of the troops at the garrison and at its forward bases were Vang. A Vang commanded the main garrison, as well as all the forward bases, except one. Vang Pao had given command of this particular forward base to his brother-in-law, Chao Ly.

Chao Ly was not popular. He robbed soldiers of their pay, beat them often, and executed troops for failed missions; also, he was haughty toward civilians, most of whom were Vang clansmen. A delegation of Vang appealed directly to Vang Pao to have Chao Ly removed from command. Vang Pao refused. A few days later Chao Ly was dead, murdered by his own troops.

The ringleader, a junior officer named Tou Vang,[77] fled south to Muong Mok on the edge of Khammouane Province, the fiefdom of Chong Khoua Vue, a Vue chieftain who respected no authority but his own. Chong Khoua had turned a cold shoulder to Touby during his heyday and had attacked Vang Pao's troops when they began operations in Muong Mok without his permission. Vang Pao stayed clear of the area.

Installing a Ly to rule over Vang clansmen was the sort of thing that set Chong Khoua's teeth on edge. Having earlier turned against Touby for meddling with clan autonomy, he jumped at the chance to provide Tou Vang asylum, if for no other reason than to thumb his nose at Vang Pao. It did not faze him that the murder victim was Vang Pao's brother-in-law, as well as the brother of Toupao Ly, the ruthless head of Vang Pao's secret police whose favorite pastime was administering public beatings on the Sam Thong runway to troublemakers and malcontents.

The Ly clan insisted that Vang Pao go after Tou Vang. Vang Pao's own clansmen saw Chao Ly's death as justified homicide and wanted nothing done. It was a no-win situation. If Vang Pao sent troops against Chong Khoua, he would alienate both the Vue and members of his own clan. If he did nothing, he would stir up trouble with the Ly. Things would be simpler if Tou Vang wasn't at Muong Mok.

Vang Pao turned to Sao Hang, a top agent in his secret police who hunted down army deserters and delivered them to Long Cheng for punishment. In addition to being ruthless, Sao had the right family connection: he was Tou Vang's brother-in-law. Sao went to Muong Mok and convinced Tou Vang that if he returned to Na Khang, Vang Pao would take his side in negotiations with the Ly. Full of confidence that all would be made right, Tou Vang climbed aboard the STOL aircraft and headed for Na Khang. During the flight, T-28 fighter planes and helicopters intercepted the STOL and forced it to divert to Long Cheng. Representatives of the Ly clan were assembled and waiting on the runway. They dragged Tou Vang out of the plane and beat him savagely, knocking out his teeth and kicking in his ribs. As he lay near death on the runway, they finished him off with knives.

The Ly were avenged and Sao Hang received a promotion, plus blood money. The whole affair left Chong Khoua Vue in a rage. He vowed to shoot Vang Pao's troops on sight if they ever set foot in Muong Mok. The taunt raised Vang Pao's hackles. Chong Khoua had to go. Vang Pao chose a Vue clansmen for the job, with an offer of advancement to colonel and the position as administrative head of Muong Mok, if he pulled it off.

It took Cher Tong Vue six months to coax Chong Khoua out of Muong Mok to meet with Vang Pao at Long Cheng. Chong Khoua arrived with his son Ger Vue and two bodyguards. Cher Tong was there to greet him, along with a colonel and a squad of soldiers who escorted Chong Khoua to the Long Cheng home of a Moua clansman trusted by both sides. Vang Pao was not at the house when they arrived. It was common knowledge that the general removed himself from the scene when there was to be foul play. Chong Khoua told his son to remain outside. If there was gunfire, he was to kill anyone who came out.

Inside the house the soldiers spread out, backs against the walls. Flanked by his two bodyguards, Chong Khoua faced Cher Tong. He asked after Vang Pao. Cher Tong ignored the question and demanded that Chong Khoua step down as chieftain of Muong Mok or suffer the consequences. Chong Khoua glared at him, his whole body shouting "over my dead body." A moment later Chong Khoua was lying dead on the floor. Cher Tong had shot him with a pistol, point-blank in the face. Then Cher Tong was also down, wounded by one of Chong Khoua's body guards. There were more gunshots. Cher Tong struggled up, blood spurting from his bullet wound, and leaped through a window. He landed outside at Ger Vue's feet. A stray bullet had wounded Ger in the arm, but he could still manage his rifle. He killed Cher Tong before he could rise.

The gunfire in the house suddenly ceased. One of Chong Khoua's bodyguards was dead, but the other one had survived to finish off everyone else, including the colonel. He yelled to Ger that he was coming out and to hold his fire. The Long Cheng police arrived. Ger ignored their shouts to drop his rifle. Cher Tong lay at his feet, obviously dead. Ger coldly pressed the muzzle of his rifle against Cher Tong's head and pulled the trigger.

Vang Pao indemnified Ger for his father's death. Though Ger accepted the money, he did not forgive. For the rest of the war the Vue of Muong Mok denied support of any kind to Vang Pao's troops. On the rare occasion when one of Vang Pao's helicopters or STOL aircraft landed on the village's airfield, the aircraft was searched and the soldiers disarmed. The incident also affected Vang

Pao's relations with Vue clansmen throughout Laos. Many no longer trusted him.[78]

DANGER SIGNALS

Five years would pass before Vang Pao's sprawling political machine began to unravel. Early on there were danger signals that it could not last. Not everything could be manipulated, nor all discontent contained.

Shortly after assuming command of MR II, Vang Pao tried to tame Thao clansmen living south of Long Cheng. They were not run-of-the-mill Thao. For generations they had roamed the dense stretch of forest between Ban Some and the Phu Bia mountains, hunting rather than farming, living off the land and constantly on the move. Thousands of these Hmong hillbillies had left the forest to settle on the outskirts of Phak Khet, Muong Yong, and Ban Houakham, once sleepy villages but now overflowing with refugees receiving handouts from USAID. Money from military payrolls and a hefty black market had energized the local economy. Hmong were working as salesmen, clerks, taxi drivers, day laborers, dentists, and barbers.

The hustle and bustle had attracted Thao huntsmen, drawn not only by the economic opportunity but by the concentrated population that was mostly non-Thao. Exogamous like all Hmong, the forest Thao had difficulty getting brides. Living in the wilderness and forever on the go, they were always weeks away from settlements with maidens from other clans. The population explosion on the western edge of their forest haunts drew them like a magnet.

For more than a decade the forest Thao had been allied with Faydang. Deep in their forests there were Pathet Lao supply posts, bivouacked troops, and an extensive communications network. Thao huntsmen wore the Pathet Lao uniform, so many that they constituted the majority of Hmong fighting under the crimson standard. The top Hmong officer in the Pathet Lao was one of their kinsmen, Saychou Tou Thao.[79]

Alarmed by the migration of so many forest Thao into Vang Pao's orbit, Faydang tried to lure them back with the promise of rapid promotion in the Pathet Lao if they returned to their native

Hmong woman with baby in Moung Soui Refugee Camp, 1970

wilds. Vang Pao wanted them to stay put and called on his old ally Sao Chia, the Thao chieftain who had earlier rallied Hmong on the southern edge of the plain, to prevent a stampede.

Sao Chia visited Phak Khet, Muong Yong, and Ban Houakham, where he linked up with Thao leaders and made tentative offers of positions in Vang Pao's growing provincial administration to gain their loyalty. He also kept an eye out for potential troublemakers. One Thao in particular caught his eye—Shoua Ger, an ambitious young leader with a following at Ban Houakham. Sao Chia arranged a meeting to feel him out. The man was an opportunist and demanded a high post in the district administration for his loyalty. Sao Chia was willing to cut a deal but considered Shoua Ger's demand excessive; he was also annoyed by the young man's imperious attitude. To put him in his place, Sao Chia said he'd get nothing. It was meant only as the opening round in negotiations, but Shoua Ger took it as a final offer.

Several days later Sao Chia was ambushed. The assassins missed their target but succeeded in killing ten of Sao Chia's bodyguards. Before Vang Pao could retaliate, Shoua Ger fled with his supporters (nearly two hundred families) into the forest south of Phu Bia to link up with Faydang and the Pathet Lao. The communists gave him an outlet for his ambition. Shoua Ger assumed command of an all-Hmong unit that went on to achieve distinction in combat against RLA forces.[80] Over the next ten years Shoua Ger would advance throuxgh the ranks to become one of the highest-ranking Hmong officers in the Pathet Lao.

Not all disaffected Hmong bolted to the communists (who had their own share of Hmong defectors).[81] In early 1965, several thousand went over to the Neutralists. The leaders of this mass defection were three of Vang Pao's officers (all clan chieftains) who were unhappy with the slow pace of their advancement through the ranks. All were from Nong Het and had been with Vang Pao from the start. Having recruited large numbers of Hmong for his armée clandestine, they expected to be rewarded with top command positions, but were constantly frustrated by Vang Pao's policy of giving field commands to clan leaders from the theater of operation.

The three officers formed their own units and tried to make a deal with the CIA and RLA to get separate funding for independent operations against the communists. When they were turned away, they approached Kong-Lê. Happy to siphon manpower from Vang Pao's guerrilla army, Kong-Lê offered to integrate them into his own forces, with the promotions they felt they deserved. More than five thousand Hmong arrived at Muong Soui, led by the Ly chieftain Chong Vang Ly and two leaders of the Vue clan, Leng Vue and Xay Toua Vue.

Kong-Lê never fully trusted his new Hmong recruits and reneged on integrating them into his army. Instead, he organized them as a separate force and billeted them at Phu Se, a mountain village near Vang Vieng where they sat out the war, spending their days erecting permanent quarters to accommodate their families who joined them at the camp. In early 1966 the camp was attacked, leaving hundreds killed or wounded. The strike was hit-and-run, so the identity of the attackers was never determined. Some believed the attack was ordered by Kong-Lê; others were convinced it was the work of Vang Pao.

The camp closed in December 1966 when the Neutralist army was absorbed into the RLA, leaving the Phu Se Hmong out in the cold. No longer on the payroll, they were suddenly receptive to

Vang Pao's request that they return to the fold. Chong Vang Ly and Leng Vue, two of the three chieftains who had masterminded the 1965 defection, turned down the reunion offer and stayed clear of Long Cheng. The third chieftain, Xay Toua Vue, returned to Hao Khame, a small village close to Long Cheng. He was murdered shortly after he moved in.[82]

Other clan leaders would also challenge Vang Pao's authority. In 1966, when Vang Pao was away healing from a bullet wound, Ly notables conspired to take over Long Cheng. Others less bold simply distanced themselves from Vang Pao's regime, delivering fewer recruits and dragging their feet in the collection of intelligence. In reaction, Vang Pao began to question the loyalty of many of his top officers and civilian officials.

Moua clansmen were a special concern. Because of their better education, they were used by Vang Pao as interpreters for CIA agents and American special forces. Now it crossed his mind that they might be managing the flow of information to deliberately limit his ability to make sound judgments. The Ly, always too ambitious, were also suspect. And Vang Pao had always been wary of the Lo, whose clan leader, Faydang, was a diehard communist. The Vue weren't to be trusted either. Not only had thousands gone over to the Neutralists in 1965, Vang Pao had Muong Mok to worry about. Except for his own clansmen the only other Hmong Vang Pao completely trusted were Thao clansmen faithful to Sao Chia Thao, the Thao clan chieftain who was a close personal friend and had remained loyal to the last.

Between 1969 and 1972, Vang Pao replaced many Moua, Ly, and Vue with Vang. He sent Vang children to America and France to be educated so they could take the place of Moua interpreters, assume top positions in his army and civil administration, and manage his personal business enterprises.[83] Three of his own sons were in America receiving a modern education. One of the boys, Chong, was at a military academy being groomed for a top military position.

9

A Seasonal War

There are two seasons in Laos: wet and dry. The dry season starts in late December and runs through April. Monsoons arrive in May and drench the land well into November. The weather gave a pattern to the war, which Ambassador Sullivan outlined in his memoirs. According to Sullivan, every dry season the NVA's 316th Division made its move west along Route 7, assaulting Hmong outposts and capturing territory. To avoid casualties, the Hmong withdrew, ambushing the enemy as they retreated, waiting until the 316th's logistics was strung out and its troops isolated into small units and vulnerable to helicopter-borne assaults. Once the rains began and what remained of the 316th started withdrawing along Route 7, helicopters delivered large Hmong blocking forces along the line of march. These forces ambushed the enemy and drew units out into the open, where air attacks could finish them off.[1]

Sullivan's view is roughly accurate, though the NVA 316 Division did not do all the fighting, nor did the communists rely solely on Route 7 or always limit their offenses to the dry season, and large Hmong blocking forces were not used until 1969. Also the pattern Sullivan describes did not emerge all at once; it evolved over a number of years and was dictated as much by Vang Pao's increasing reliance on air power as by the rhythms of nature.

THONG VONGRASSAMY

The NVA's 316th Division kicked off its 1965 dry season offensive in January, using the 174th regiment to spearhead the campaign. Most of the Plain of Jars was still in communist hands, but Vang Pao held isolated positions in northern Sam Neua and along Route 6 above the plain. These northern posts were the off-spring of the mid-1963 capture of Sam Neua City, the stunning victory that earned Vang Pao his general's star and revived the career of Thong Vongrassamy, one of the commanders of the lost RLA battalions discovered by Tony Poe.

Thong was a rarity, a Lao officer who relished combat. Possibly this was because he was not an aristocrat like so many officers in the RLA, and therefore was unaccustomed to having others do the dirty work for him. Thong was born to a peasant family in a small village on the fringes of Vientiane. He left home at nine and survived by hiring out as a paddy laborer. Consumed by a desire to better himself, he squirreled away a portion of his meager income to finance his education at one of the most prestigious schools in Vientiane. He was an excellent student and dreamed of higher education, but on a peasant's wages it was out of his reach. His only chance for professional advancement was in the French-run Lao army. With mediocrity the norm in the army, it was easy for Thong with his intelligence and drive to distinguish himself and wind up in the officer corps.

When the U.S. replaced France, American military advisors instantly saw promise in Thong and sent him to Fort Bragg for advanced training. Three years later he was in Sam Neua commanding his own battalion. When the communists initiated their massive putsch of the province in 1960, Thong was one of the few RLA commanders to hold his ground. His troops were badly mauled; nearly half deserted. He led the survivors into the mountains and lived off the land, conducting occasional raids on Pathet Lao supply posts to keep an edge on his troops' skills and to supplement their meager diet with army rations.

Nearly three years passed before Tony Poe discovered that Thong and his battalion still existed. Poe found Thong dressed in rags, his hair a shaggy mane that draped past his shoulders. After Poe distributed new uniforms and weapons, Thong decided to leave his hair long. A head taller than the average Lao, he was already a striking figure. Now with glistening black hair flaring out beneath his maroon beret, he seemed an Asian version of Che Guevara.

When Thong distinguished himself in the campaign to capture Sam Neua City, Vang Pao promoted him to colonel and gave him a free rein to see what he could do. Thong led his replenished battalion south and established a mountain outpost at Phu Kouk, nineteen miles southwest of Sam Neua City. Then he moved north beyond Sam Neua City and set up a second base at Nong Khang and recruited Hmong troops from the local population for an ADC. Over the next year Thong's two guerrilla units, headquartered forty-one miles apart, harassed the Pathet Lao with night raids and even struck Sam Neua City,[2] which had again fallen to the Pathet Lao shortly after Vang Pao's 1963 blitzkrieg of this Pathet Lao stronghold.

Though Thong's attack on the provincial capital was only a brief mortar barrage, a Pathet Lao envoy in Thailand described it to reporters as a full-scale invasion. This hyperbole was a measure of the impact Thong was having on Pathet Lao morale and why the North Vietnamese singled out Thong's two posts as the first targets of their 1965 dry season offensive. Elements of the 174th regiment overwhelmed Thong's Lao battalion at Phu Kouk, but the North Vietnamese ran into a stone wall at Nong Khang, where Thong's Hmong ADC held on tenaciously to its mountain base. The 174th shifted its attention south to the three Hmong bases overlooking Route 6, positioned to interdict NVA truck convoys.[3]

Normally the truck convoys traveled Route 7, the NVA's main supply line, but the road had been blown apart by American aircraft as part of Operation Barrel Roll. Launched in December 1964, Barrel Roll's principal targets were key junctures along the Ho Chi Minh Trail. There had been no thought of using the planes to help with the war inside Laos. But Barrel Roll violated Laos' air space and therefore required Souvanna Phouma's direct approval. The prime minister gave it, but wanted something in return. The planes would also have to target communist positions around the Plain of Jars.

In late December, F-8 and F-105 jets bombed Route 7 from Nong Pet to Nong Het. In mid-January 1965, C-123 flareships lit up the road for a night attack by F-100 Super Sabres. Several days later sixteen F-105s laid on more bombs and blew up the Ban Ken bridge.[4] The damage from the bombing was even more extensive than that caused by Bill Lair's demolition teams back in August 1963, forcing the communists to switch to Route 6.

To keep traffic moving along Route 6, the communists had to clear out Vang Pao's main harassing posts along the road. The NVA first attacked the Hmong base at Hong Non, perched on a high plateau above an airstrip. Tony Poe was there along with a five-man PARU team, crouched down in trenches with the Hmong, searching the horizon for approaching NVA. The North Vietnamese were a fair distance beyond the airstrip when first sighted. The Hmong shot at them and missed. Forgetting their training, they had failed to adjust their sights to account for the distance. Poe reminded them what to do, then took a rifle to demonstrate. By now the NVA soldiers had closed to two hundred yards. Poe went through several clips of ammunition. A PARU advisor checked with binoculars and counted seventeen bodies.

Believing he had killed everyone in the NVA unit, Poe left his trench to search the bodies. One of the PARU Thai and two Hmong went with him. When they were halfway there, four NVA jumped up from behind bushes and began shooting. A bullet struck Poe in the hip and knocked him to the ground. Poe struggled up and saw NVA soldiers advancing toward him. He lobbed a grenade in their direction, counted to three, and threw another, and then another. There was no more movement. Poe checked behind him and saw that the Thai and two Hmong were dead. Using his rifle as a walking stick, he struggled back to the base.

After a Hmong medic treated his wound, Poe called in a helicopter. Mortar rounds were slamming into the base, their shell fragments tearing large holes in the faces and shoulders of the guerrillas in the trenches. The only safe place for the helicopter to land was about five miles away. Poe directed the chopper there. He ordered the guerrillas to hold the base in his absence, and promised he would return to get them out.

Using his rifle as a cane, Poe hobbled the five miles to the pickup site. When the chopper arrived, Poe ordered the pilot to fly to the base. Poe was deathly white and needed medical attention. The pilot wanted to fly him to a hospital in Thailand. Poe repeated the order to make for the Hmong base. The pilot argued. Filling the helicopter with Hmong would burn out the engine, he explained. He needed to get Poe to a hospital. Poe said he didn't give a damn about the chopper's engine so long as they got the Hmong off the mountain. He'd promised to go back and that was what he was going to do, even if it killed him.[5]

Possibly this was part of Poe's conditioning as a former Marine: never leave your men behind. But Poe also cared about the Hmong as people. A year earlier he had married a woman from the Ly clan. Vang Pao had fancied her himself. The wedding was at Long Cheng. Touby LyFoung showed up. Vang Pao declined to attend.[6]

Poe kept his word and rescued the Hmong, though he didn't die trying. Air America pilots got him to a hospital in time to save his life.

VANG PAO WAVERS

After taking Hong Non, the 174th regiment moved against Houei Sa An and Hua Moung, the other two Hmong bases along Route 6. A SGU battalion was at Houei Sa An. Rather than see it decimated, Vang Pao ordered the battalion to fall back. Hua Moung was also abandoned, but not on Vang Pao's orders.

A full Lao battalion was garrisoned at Hua Moung, commanded by Colonel Khamsao Keovilay, the other forgotten RLA officer uncovered earlier by Poe while meandering across Sam Neua. Vang Pao had used Khamsao as part of the stunning 1963 assault against Sam Neua City, then later appointed him deputy governor of Sam Neua Province to gain his loyalty. But Khamsao's ultimate allegiance was always to Phoumi Nosavan, who made periodic visits to Hua Moung to hand-deliver soldiers' pay. As Phoumi was now in Thailand living in exile, Khamsao no longer wanted anything to do with Vang Pao's war. He deserted the garrison, taking his top officers with him. Leaderless, the Lao troops at Hua Moung fled the moment they spotted NVA forward scouts in the hills, assaying the base's defenses through binoculars.

Vang Pao brought in helicopters to evacuate the SGU retreating from Houei Sa An. He also sent helicopters to Hua Moung to airlift the entire civilian population (about eight thousand people) to the nearby garrison of Na Khang. The mass retreat and the sight of so many refugees momentarily shook Vang Pao's confidence. The NVA had swept over his forces. He could do nothing to stop them. Perhaps if he had air support he might have slowed their advance. Vang Pao had begged Vientiane to send T-28s against the North Vietnamese. He had also asked the CIA to send U.S. Air Force jets based in Thailand. Nothing arrived.[7]

Following the evacuation, Vang Pao called a special meeting at his office in Long Cheng. Vinton Lawrence was there with several of Vang Pao's top aides. Vang Pao talked of all the Hmong commanders who had died, of the civilians killed. He sensed the war was turning into one of attrition, and there were not enough Hmong to fight that kind of war. He questioned whether it made sense to keep on fighting. All he was doing was creating Hmong widows and orphans. He talked of quitting the war and moving everyone to Sayaboury.

Lawrence had never seen Vang Pao in a blacker mood. Neither had Vang Pao's aides. There would be even darker days ahead and bouts of deep depression, but by nature Vang Pao was a man of mercurial emotions and seldom remained depressed for long.[8] By the next day he was his old self, contemplating his next move to defeat the enemy. Tracking the progress of the 174th, Vang Pao concluded Na Khang would be the NVA regiment's next target. He had the thousands of civilians quartered at the garrison moved farther west to Muong Hiem to be airlifted later to Sam Thong and absorbed into Edgar Buell's refugee relief program that was already taking care of nearly 125,000 people. With the civilians out of the way, Vang Pao worked on the garrison's defenses. There was only a single SGU at Na Khang, not enough to hold back a full NVA regiment. He appealed to the RLA for reinforcements. The general staff in Vientiane claimed they had none to spare.

Unexpectedly, reinforcements did arrive, led by Major Douangtha Norasing, a Lao officer and native of Sam Neua, who had earlier served with the recently departed Colonel Khamsao. Douangtha had gathered up part of Khamsao's fleeing troops, formed them into two companies, and marched for Na Khang prepared to fight. Vang Pao positioned the two companies to block an attack from the east and moved his Hmong SGU south to guard Na Khang's southern approach. At the last moment the RLA general staff gave in and contributed two RLA battalions, one from Luang Prabang, the other from Vientiane. Vang Pao placed both of the battalions north of the base. Dug in and ready, he waited for the attack. It never materialized. The NVA's 174th had overextended itself and was too busy regrouping to go after Na Khang.

The NVA's dry season offensive was over. With the rainy season approaching, Vang Pao began to make plans for a summer counteroffensive. Since there were already two thousand troops at Na Khang, Vang Pao transformed the garrison into his military headquarters and logistics center for all northern operations. This decision persuaded the CIA to use the garrison as the launch site for helicopter missions to rescue American pilots shot down over North Vietnam.

One such mission was guided by Colonel Thong, recently appointed by Vang Pao as governor of Sam Neua. The ambitious peasant who had worked his way through school had at last arrived. Only three months after assuming office, Thong learned that two U.S. jet pilots had been shot down close to the border. Since he knew the area, he volunteered to ride in one of the rescue helicopters as a guide. Once the helicopters neared the spot of the shootdown, antiaircraft cannons opened up on them. A round struck the helicopter carrying Thong. A fragment of the shell ripped into his stomach and exited his back. He was flown to a U.S. Air Force hospital in Thailand, underwent emergency surgery, and seemed on his way to recovery when he developed a blood clot. The embolism killed him.[9]

Thong was a symbolic figure. He was a lowland Lao with talent and courage, representing the possibility that there were other ethnic Lao of quality who might rise to the occasion and defend their country. He was also bridge between the Hmong and Lao: a Lao who fought alongside the Hmong and a Lao the Hmong could respect. But Thong was also greatly admired for himself, not only by Vang Pao and his staff but by many CIA agents and USAID officers who had worked with him in the field. Edgar Buell took Thong's death particularly hard and assumed responsibility for the funeral held at Sam Thong. To give the occasion the pomp Buell felt it deserved, he pressured the embassy and top Lao officials in Vientiane to attend the funeral. They all showed up, along with a Vientiane drum and bugle corps. During the ceremonies the buglers marched and played, Buddhist monks prayed and chanted, and Ambassador Sullivan awarded Thong a posthumous medal, a Silver Star, which he presented to Thong's father.[10]

AIR POWER

Vang Pao's top priority for his rainy season campaign was to retake his bases along Route 6, lost to the communists during their dry season offensive, so that he could cut the enemy's supply line. He also aimed at something bigger: liberating Xieng Khouangville, which had been in communist hands for more than a year.

Given the ease with which the communists had brushed aside his units during their offensive, Vang Pao had every reason to expect hard fighting and perhaps another defeat. What he did not know was that for the first time he would receive regular air support and it would change the nature of the war.

In February 1965, President Johnson sent two of his aides, John McNaughton and McGeorge Bundy, to South Vietnam on a fact-finding mission. During the visit the Viet Cong attacked the American air base at Pleiku. On their return to Washington both McNaughton and Bundy advised the President to employ "a regular program of air strikes" to punish North Vietnam for sponsoring such raids and to demonstrate that America had the resolve to stay the course. The result was Operation Rolling Thunder, an air campaign over North Vietnam designed to gradually escalate bombing until Hanoi got the message and agreed to negotiations.

In early March, a task force of 130 planes blew up a storage facility thirty-five miles inside North Vietnam. The intensity of the air raids increased over the next two months, involving more aircraft and more resources. The air campaign was to last only eight weeks, but it continued with brief pauses for three years, with more targets constantly added to the list: roads, bridges, ammunition dumps, oil storage facilities, power plants, factories, and air fields.

To accommodate the needs of Rolling Thunder, additional jet bombers and fighter planes arrived at U.S. air bases in South Vietnam and Thailand, and more aircraft carriers entered the South China Sea. The buildup of air assets meant there was more available for Barrel Roll in Laos, especially during bombing pauses in Rolling Thunder.

A minimum of thirty-two air sorties per day were allocated to support Vang Pao's ground operations, though the hope was that the actual number would be much higher. To accommodate the increased air assets, the CIA selected Vang Pao's northern post at

Na Khang as the site for a communications hub to coordinate all air support for Vang Pao's guerrillas. Technicians set up radar and installed radios. Air communications specialists arrived to direct the air traffic. Two were from the U.S. Air Force. Their job was to select targets and recommend ordnance for American jet fighters and bombers. There were also six forward air controllers from the Royal Thai Air Force (RTAF) to fly unarmed Pilatus Porters (owned by the CIA) and guide "B-Team" attack planes to their targets.[11]

The "B-Team" was an all-Thai air squadron responsible only to the American ambassador. Back in 1964, Lao pilots were just starting their training and weren't very good. American fighter pilots took their place and began flying missions in Royal Laotian Air Force (RLAF) T-28s. It was all quite illegal by Geneva treaty. The American pilots bombed a bridge and blew up NVA trucks traveling Route 7.

In his last year as ambassador, Unger worried that one of the American pilots might be shot down. Dead or alive, the downed pilot would be a major embarrassment, the sort of thing that could ruin a diplomatic career. Unger began to substitute Thai pilots, who were physically indistinguishable from the Lao, for Americans pilots on the more dangerous missions. To distinguish the two pilot teams, the American squad was called the "A-Team" and the Thai pilots the "B-Team." Though the "B-Team" had only a dozen or so planes, it would account for nearly half of the air support going to Vang Pao's guerrillas during his rainy season campaign.

In July 1965 Vang Pao mobilized to retake Hua Muong, the first stage in his rainy season offensive. The NVA's 174th regiment had withdrawn to North Vietnam for rest and replenishment, leaving behind only token forces in various locations. There were only a couple of companies of NVA at Hua Moung, but they had orders to defend the base to the last man. Vang Pao airlifted troops from Na Khang to the site and assessed the situation. The North Vietnamese had dug bunkers into the hillside and were plugged into holes like badgers. A direct infantry assault would result in heavy casualties. Vang Pao had helicopters sling-haul 105-mm howitzers to a nearby hill. A PARU artillery team set up the canons and pounded the enemy bunkers. Then Vang Pao called in air strikes.

Vang Pao had first witnessed what air power could do in mid-1964. Vientiane had sent the "B-Team" to provide air support for Kong-Lê's beleaguered troops being driven off the Plain of Jars. While the T-28 fighter bombers were in the air, Vang Pao persuaded Vientiane to divert three of them against a concentration of enemy troops near his old base at Padong. The T-28s flew in, one after the other, dumping their ordnance. For the communist troops on the ground it was the first experience with air power. They were terrified and scattered. The planes were like magic. They totally demoralized the enemy.

T-28s also assaulted Hua Moung, but in addition to these cast-off trainer aircraft, jury-rigged with bomb racks and side-mounted machine guns, the air attack included high-powered American jets. The jets not only terrified the Vietnamese dug into the hill, they annihilated them. After the T-28s dropped their loads, F-4 and F-105 jets carrying heavy bombs attacked the bunkers. The jets made one pass after another until the area was a moonscape of deep craters.

After the last jet departed there was utter silence. No shots were fired from the bunkers, no Vietnamese emerged to offer to surrender. They were all dead. Vang Pao had lunch on the hill with some of his officers. It was a grisly scene. The ground was covered with human flesh mixed in with dirt. Vang Pao was so pleased with the total destruction of the enemy that he spent the night on the spot and celebrated with airdropped beef and rice.[12]

Two months later Vang Pao went after Houei Sa An, lost to the communists in February. Because he had air support, the base fell quickly into his hands. The retreating NVA left behind fifty-five tons of food and two tons of ammunition.

Vang Pao had plans to move into two other areas, but first he needed more Hmong SGUs to replace the RLA battalions on loan since February and now demanded back. The victories at Hua Muong and Houei Sa An had bolstered his confidence in the effectiveness of his new air mobile battalions. More than five thousand Hmong were already organized as ADC units. Vang Pao's plan was to recast them as SGUs and at the same time launch a recruitment drive to flesh out several more. Previously all SGU training had been in Thailand and at Long Cheng. To speed things up, Vang Pao moved the entire training operation to Muong Cha, a village southeast of Long Cheng at the base of the Phu Bia massif, the tallest mountain in Laos. There were already several ADCs in the area, making it a good place to recruit troops for the new units.

By October, Vang Pao had four battle-ready SGUs. He airlifted two to Na Khang and sent them south for a push into Ban Ban Valley with the intention of taking control of the junction of Routes 6 and 7, a choke point for NVA logistics. The North Vietnamese rushed in troops to halt the advance.

While the Hmong and NVA battled for mastery of Ban Ban Valley, Vang Pao moved his other two SGUs further south to Ban Na Nat. The idea was to have them move up Route 42 and take Xieng Khouangville. The king was scheduled to visit Long Cheng again in January 1966. Vang Pao wanted to present him the liberated provincial capital as a gift.

Divining Vang Pao's purpose, the NVA immediately diverted troops to Route 42 to turn back the assault force. By early December the battle line had stabilized at the road town of Ban Peung, now heavily invested with NVA infantry. Vang Pao brought in howitzers and hammered the village for several days. The communists absorbed the punishment and held their ground.

NVA BUILD-UP

The dry season had arrived—the time for Vang Pao to pull back his forces and prepare for the inevitable NVA onslaught. Yet Vang Pao could not bring himself to break off the campaign to wrest away Xieng Khouangville from the communists. Leaving two SGUs at Ban Peung on Route 42 south of Xieng Khouangville, he moved the other two SGUs at Ban Ban Valley north to strengthen his base at Hua Muong on Route 6, a certain NVA target. He then gathered ADC units in Sam Neua and Xieng Khouang and deployed them in a wide screen north to delay the enemy's advance. The ADCs were not to hold ground, but to effect a slow retreat to minimize Hmong casualties.

Through January and February there was a constant flow of NVA units into MR II, more than ever before. It was all due to misperceptions in Washington about the nature of the war in Vietnam. Earlier, in November 1965, the NVA had engaged U.S. troops in Vietnam in a conventional battle of massed forces for the first time. Previously, American soldiers had faced only guerrilla units, mostly Viet Cong, that employed hit and run tactics. It was a frustrating form of combat, not only for the soldiers but for the generals planning the war.

General William Westmoreland, commander of U.S. armed forces in Vietnam, desperately wanted the opportunity to confront the enemy in a conventional engagement. Not only would it be an opportunity to inflict heavy casualties, Westmoreland was curious to discover how well American forces trained and equipped to fight on the plains of Europe would do against NVA main force units in the tropical terrain of Vietnam.

Westmoreland's NVA counterpart, General Giap, wondered the same thing and decided to find out at Ia Drang Valley where he deployed seven of his battalions to entrap a single American battalion. An avid student of military history, Giap may have thought it propitious, or perhaps ironic, to have chosen this particular American unit to test his troops. It was the 1st battalion of 7th United States Cavalry, the same regiment that had ridden to death and glory with Custer at the Little Big Horn.

On November 14, following reports of large numbers of enemy troops in the central highlands, the 7th Cavalry was airborne in a fleet of helicopters heading for Ia Drang in the early morning darkness. The helicopters delivered their passengers at the landing sight and departed. It wasn't long after the pulsing of the helicopters' rotors had faded away that the battalion was assaulted on all sides.

By late morning, the badly outnumbered Americans were fighting hand-to-hand. A single company in a forward position was cut off from the rest of the battalion and massacred. After the battle a dead American soldier was found in the elephant grass, his hands still clasped around the throat of a dead North Vietnamese. One of the unit's few survivors later remarked that during the fighting he could not help thinking of Custer. History seemed to be repeating itself.[13]

The battalion's commanders were veterans of the Korean War and no strangers to desperate fighting. They kept their heads and called in artillery, directing the fire almost on top of themselves. Shells burst only twenty meters from the 7th Cavalry's perimeter, which was no more than a span of three hundred yards at its widest point. Fighter-bombers arrived to provide constant air support. Later, B-52s pounded the area with five-hundred-pound bombs. By day's end the NVA had withdrawn, leaving behind 634 dead and, by one estimate, carrying away another 600 slain comrades. The 7th Cavalry had 79 dead and 121 wounded.[14]

The battle of Ia Drang was interpreted differently by Westmoreland and Giap. For Westmoreland, it was proof that American forces, even when outnumbered seven to one, could defeat the NVA given adequate artillery and air support. It reinforced his conviction that the search-and-destroy operations he had been conducting throughout South Vietnam could defeat the North Vietnamese and Viet Cong.

Reflecting on Ia Drang, the military scholar Harry Summers later concluded it would have been better if the Americans had lost the battle, just as they had lost the first major battle of the Second World War in the Kasserine passes of North Africa, forcing them to adapt and devise better tactics.[15]

Only the communists drew enlightenment from the engagement. For Giap, the lesson of Ia Drang was simply to avoid engaging the Americans in conventional battles, making it difficult for Westmoreland's search-and-destroy missions to kill large numbers of Viet Cong and NVA.

Not having the benefit of Giap's views, and taking it on faith that Westmoreland had a firm grasp of things, President Johnson concluded that Hanoi had absorbed sufficient punishment from air strikes and military setbacks like Ia Drang to want to come to the bargaining table. As a goodwill gesture to encourage talks, Johnson suspended Rolling Thunder for five weeks.

Instead of entering negotiations, Hanoi took advantage of the bombing pause to move thousands of troops into Laos. The majority were destined for the Ho Chi Minh Trail, but nearly five thousand entered MR II to help the 316th Division establish a secure supply line to the Plain of Jars. Continued air strikes against Route 7 had rendered the road unusable until repairs could be completed.[16] This left Route 6. The NVA still controlled the crucial intersection at Ban Ban, but north of this point Route 6 was in the hands of Vang Pao's guerrillas. Hanoi wanted the road cleared and Vang Pao's Hmong driven entirely out of Sam Neua.

The communists fought on two fronts. NVA battalions moved down Route 42 to reinforce their comrades bottled up at Ban Peung and holding the line against Hmong trying to get to Xieng Khouangville. Within a few days, the entire communist force pushed out of Ban Peung and went full tilt at the SGUs. On Vang Pao's orders, the Hmong retreated.

All of Vang Pao's northern posts in Sam Neua were also under attack. Major Douangtha was at one of the posts, commanding an undermanned Lao battalion. His troops fought well. NVA bodies littered the battlefield. But Douangtha also took casualties. His battalion was down to twenty-six men by the time he decided to withdraw. To avoid more decimated battalions, Vang Pao ordered all of the posts abandoned.

The communists occupied the abandoned posts and sent a battalion from the NVA 168th Regiment against Na Khang. The garrison had become Vang Pao's main supply depot for all northern operations. Almost daily, fully loaded C-123s and Caribous landed at Na Khang to unload arms, ammunition, and supplies. Smaller aircraft (Helio Courier, Pilatus Porters, and helicopters) delivered this cargo to Hmong outposts throughout the region.[17] Even more important to the communists, Na Khang now played a major role in Rolling Thunder. The U.S. Air Force had recently upgraded the garrison's air communications system, enabling U.S. bombers to penetrate even deeper into North Vietnam. Na Khang was also the principal refueling station for helicopter rescue missions for American pilots shot down over North Vietnam. During bombing raids, Jolly Green Giant helicopters remained in a holding pattern at ten thousand feet near the border, waiting for instructions to retrieve downed pilots. Every few hours they returned to Na Khang for refueling and lifted off again, repeating the routine until the bombing run was over and all planes and pilots accounted for.

WOUNDED IN ACTION

The assault on Na Khang caught Vang Pao off guard. He presumed he would have time to reposition troops and reinforce hard-hit posts. He had not expected the enemy to sweep so easily over his northern bases. There was only a skeleton force (two companies) at Na Khang. His other troops were scattered across Sam Neua in full retreat, just trying to survive. From his headquarters at Long Cheng, Vang Pao ordered the entire civilian population at Na Khang evacuated.

Two CIA officers were at the garrison: Mike Lynch and a new agent, Jerry Daniels. A rough-and-tumble sort, Daniels had been recruited out of western Montana, where he worked as a smoke jumper for the Forest Service and in his spare time rode bulls in rodeos. Don Sjostrom, Edgar Buell's assistant for refugee relief, was there too, busy coordinating the evacuation of civilians. Sjostrom didn't leave with the civilians. Neither did Lynch, nor Daniels. All three had worked closely with the Hmong. They insisted on staying behind with Vang Pao's guerrillas: Lynch and Daniels, to fight at their side; Sjostrom, to provide moral support.

Units of the NVA battalion were already probing the perimeter of the base. The CIA agents contacted Ambassador Sullivan to let him know they were trapped at the garrison. They asked Sullivan to call in jets and saturate the entire perimeter with napalm. Only once before had Sullivan authorized the use of napalm. That time it was to ward off enemy troops to save a downed pilot. State Department officials had been furious over the decision. Sullivan was hesitant to use the weapon again, but the idea of CIA agents falling into enemy hands was unthinkable. He agreed to the air strikes.

The jets arrived in the midst of a mass assault. Waves of molten jelly engulfed the North Vietnamese, breaking the back of the attack.[18] As the enemy pulled back to regroup, Vang Pao arrived to personally supervise the defense of the base. He scrounged up more troops and had them airlifted in.

The communists recovered their nerve and began probing for weaknesses. Small battles ignited, then flared out. During one of the lulls, Vang Pao was on the base runway conferring with his officers. Small weapons fire broke out. Bullets plinked into a helicopter that had just landed and kicked up dust on the airfield. One of the rounds hit Vang Pao.[19]

Vang Pao had pushed his luck too far. He was in the field constantly, either in a helicopter giving commands over a radio to troops engaged in battle below or on the ground talking directly with his commanders, often recklessly exposing himself to enemy ground fire. During one battle an errant bomb exploded only twenty yards from where he was standing. The backwash from the explosion sent him flying through the air. For an instant his aides feared he had been killed.

Not only was Vang Pao constantly in the thick of things, he occasionally led troops into battle. Earlier, on one of Ambassador Sullivan's rare visits to Long Cheng, news arrived of a stunning victory against the North Vietnamese. Vang Pao wanted to see it for himself. With Sullivan in tow, Vang Pao boarded a helicopter and flew to the battle scene. The fighting wasn't over. Though the enemy's main force had been routed, a number of Vietnamese were still holed up in a log bunker on the crest of a hill. There were snipers inside. The bodies of Hmong who had tried to assault the bunker were strewn across the hill.

To Sullivan's astonishment, Vang Pao assembled a platoon and handed each man a fragmentation grenade. He led them up the hill, occupied a position with his troops stretched out in a single line, and ordered the first man to rush forward, toss his grenade at the bunker, then roll away and scurry down the hill to take his place at the end of the line. One after another the Hmong rushed the bunker and heaved their grenades. Vang Pao had an entire box full of them at his side and kept handing them out until the box was empty. He led the platoon in a skirmish line up the hill, making them hold their fire until they were within a few yards of the bunker. After they opened up with a volley, they rushed the logs and hauled out the shattered bodies of the Vietnamese.[20]

Spending so much time on the battlefield increased the odds that Vang Pao would be killed or wounded. That he beat the odds so often led others to believe he led a charmed life. Vang Pao half-believed it himself. He was certain his ancestors were always watching over him, warning him when disaster was about to strike. He received such a warning during the 1953 Viet Minh invasion of Laos, while guiding French forces from Muong Hiem to the Plain of Jars. Vang Pao had led the column up into the mountains and, at the insistence of the French commander, established camp in the early evening on a crest. At three in the morning, Vang Pao was awakened by a wild goat that had strayed into the camp. He took it as a warning sign from his ancestors that Viet Minh were nearby. Over the protests of the French commander, who considered talk of signs from ancestors pure nonsense, Vang Pao immediately broke camp and led the column farther up the mountain.[21]

Vang Pao would receive many such warnings over the years. Once, at Long Cheng, he boarded a helicopter and suddenly knew something was wrong and that his ancestors wanted him out of the aircraft. He switched to a different helicopter. The first helicopter took off and exploded in midair. It had been sabotaged with a grenade strapped to its gas tank.[22]

Even with the help of his ancestors, simple probability guaranteed that Vang Pao would eventually be felled in battle. Na Khang was the place it occurred. CIA agent Mike Lynch was next to the helicopter struck by the incoming fire. Lynch ducked down and glanced around. He saw blood on Vang Pao and dragged him to safety behind a hill; then he called in a helicopter. The chopper flew Vang Pao to Muong Hiem where a waiting C-123 transport plane rushed him to the U.S. Air Force hospital at Korat, Thailand.[23]

With Vang Pao injured and gone, morale at Na Khang plummeted. Sullivan ordered all American personnel evacuated immediately. The troops at the base had no desire to fight on alone. The two CIA officers, Lynch and Daniels, decided to get everyone out. Huge Chinook helicopters arrived. The agents crammed Hmong soldiers into the choppers like sardines, two hundred to a Chinook. Shortly after the last helicopter launched into the air, enemy troops streamed down from the hills to claim the base.

The NVA took possession of a death trap. Jet fighters appeared, strafing and bombing North Vietnamese before completely leveling the base. According to intelligence reports, the communists carried away hundreds of bodies. So many had been killed that it would take another month, when reinforcements arrived, before the enemy was able to physically occupy the destroyed garrison.[24]

X-rays revealed that the bullet had sheared off Vang Pao's upper arm bone just short of the shoulder socket. To enable Vang Pao to regain use of his arm, Washington flew him to Hawaii, where he was given an artificial joint and socket for his shoulder at Tripler Army Medical Center in Honolulu. During his hospitalization, rumors spread in Laos that he was near death.[25] Hmong soldiers in the field, and civilians at Long Cheng and Sam Thong, became dispirited and confused. Ly clan aristocrats saw an opportunity to reclaim their clan's leadership over the Hmong. Behind the back of Touby LyFoung, they pressured Colonel Youa Vang Ly, one of their clansmen who commanded an elite battalion, to move on Long Cheng.

Though Youa Vang Ly and Vang Pao had been close friends since their youth, Youa Vang nevertheless agreed to enter into the conspiracy. Envy may have played a role. For years Youa Vang had lived in Vang Pao's shadow. In the early 1950s the two had served together in the Gendarmerie. Youa Vang was a superb soldier, and as much a favorite of French officers as Vang Pao. But having never attended school, he could neither read nor write, which kept him out of the officer corps. While Vang Pao advanced to sergeant, lieutenant, captain, and then major, Youa Vang Ly remained a noncom. It was a decade of disappointment.

Only after the CIA backed Vang Pao did Youa Vang's fortunes improve. After he received special training at PARU headquarters at Hua Hin, Vang Pao promoted him to major and put him in charge of an elite five-hundred-man battalion, the secret army's first SGU. Youa Vang led this same SGU to Long Cheng to carry off a coup and assume control of Vang Pao's army.[26] However, at the last moment his troops lost their nerve and refused to enter the military base.

News of the incident stirred Vang Pao to tape a message in Hmong, Lao, and French from his hospital bed and have it broadcast over the government station in Vientiane, and over Lawrence's Union of Lao Races radio station at Long Cheng. In a steady, strong voice, he assured the Hmong that he was far from dead and would soon be back in harness to direct the war.

BACK IN HARNESS

When Vang Pao returned in May, after just two months convalescence, he immediately recalled the 201st battalion from the field. Everyone presumed Vang Pao had been wounded by a NVA sniper,[27] but Vang Pao was convinced he had been shot by one of his own men, an officer in the 201st.[28] Several weeks before the shooting, the man had questioned his authority; there had been a heated argument.[29] When the 201st assembled at Long Cheng, the suspected officer was absent, having resigned his commission before fleeing to Vientiane.[30] Worried that there were other men in the battalion who also wanted him dead, Vang Pao chose a distinctively Hmong way of dealing with the problem. He had the entire unit swear allegiance to him and drink sacred water to seal the oath.[31] By Hmong belief, anyone drinking the water would be visited by evil spirits and die if the oath was not sincere.

With the rainy season already underway, Vang Pao was anxious to recapture lost territory, especially the garrison at Na Khang. He would not be able to be in the field as much as before, at least for a while. Vang Pao was still recuperating from surgery, his arm was in a sling and he needed daily massage from a medical therapist on loan from the U.S. military to insure that his torn biceps healed properly.

Vang Pao airlifted troops to Muong Hiem, which was to be the staging base for the assault on Na Khang. From there they moved south against the garrison. Before his battalions closed, jet bombers from the U.S. Navy and Air Force pounded the base for two days. The Hmong stormed over Na Khang and drove the enemy back onto the airfield. Out in the open, the North Vietnamese were easy targets for the jets and T-28s circling overhead. When the aircraft initiated their attack, the North Vietnamese sprinted for the tree line. The planes cut most of them down before they reached cover.

Vang Pao's fifth SGU had just completed training at Muong Cha. He brought the battalion to Na Khang by helicopter to remain as a permanent defensive force. His other battalions moved on, probing south and west to gauge the NVA's strength. They met little resistance. Vang Pao suspected the communists were deliberately pulling back, drawing him into a trap where they would envelop his troops, cut them off, and destroy them. He divided his battalions into small units and sent them in different directions to seek contact with the enemy. By late August his guerrillas had pushed northwest as far as Nam Bac, northeast up to Phu Pha

Thi, and as far south as the old Momentum base at San Tiau. There were few NVA anywhere.

Earlier in July, American jets had destroyed several supply depots and ammunition dumps patiently built up by the communists over the previous five months. Without supplies it was impossible for the NVA to maintain a sizable force in the field. Most of the 316 Division had already pulled back to North Vietnam, leaving behind only small units whose main job was to store provisions that would be trucked in along Route 6 in preparation for the next dry season campaign.

THEODORE SHACKLEY

In June 1966, Theodore Shackley replaced Douglas Blaufarb as the CIA's Vientiane station chief. Shackley and Blaufarb were very different men. Blaufarb was a thoughtful, somewhat scholarly individual, with degrees from Harvard and Columbia. When he became station chief back in 1964, the first thing he did was dig up background information about the operation and about the Hmong. He rummaged through classified files and discovered documents describing the use the French had made of the Hmong. It was the first time anyone had bothered to check. Blaufarb appreciated the need to tailor Operation Momentum to the social and political capacities of the Hmong. That had been Lair's approach all along, and Blaufarb saw no reason to change things. He kept out of Lair's way and remained in the background, offering support or counsel only when necessary.

Shackley was a different story. The peculiarities of Hmong culture or Hmong politics were absolutely of no interest to him. Neither was he interested in the welfare of the Hmong, or of the Laotians for that matter. Driven by ambition, his only concern was to accomplish the task assigned to him. The CIA had sent Shackley to Vientiane to help with the war in Vietnam, to use the RLA and Vang Pao's army to drain the NVA's resources and manpower. It was of small importance to Shackley how many Laotians or Hmong perished in the process.

Lair didn't like Shackley. It was not only because Shackley was the first Vientiane station chief to challenge his autonomy. Lair didn't like Shackley because of his blind ambition and because of his utter disregard for the fate of the Hmong. Lair wanted to keep the war in Laos small and manageable, but Shackley insisted that the CIA use the Hmong to mount regimental-size operations against the NVA. Lair knew that the Hmong were not temperamentally suited for that kind of war and lacked the numbers to sustain the huge casualties it would entail. But Shackley was convinced that air power would tip the scales, enabling the numerically smaller Hmong army to best the North Vietnamese. Lair had strong reservations about air power. The Hmong took the offensive only in bad weather, which made air support tricky. It was a mathematical certainty that there would be occasions when air support would be desperately needed but, because of bad weather, would fail to materialize. Hundreds, perhaps thousands, of Hmong would die.[32]

RICHARD SECORD

Shackley was critical not only of Lair's handling of the ground war, but of his management of air assets. The few sorties Lair was getting from Barrel Roll and Rolling Thunder were inadequate. Shackley wanted a man on board who could wring more jets and bombers out of the U.S. Navy and U.S. Air Force. The pentagon sent him Richard Secord, a thirty-four year-old Air Force captain on loan to the CIA.

Secord had volunteered for the job. From 1961 to 1963 he had piloted a T-28 in Vietnam, serving on South Vietnam's equivalent of the "A-Team" flying missions in the place of South Vietnamese pilots. From there he went on to Iran as an advisor to the Iranian air force. Iran was fighting a war at the time against Soviet-sponsored and equipped Kurds. The Iranian air force was a mess. Secord reorganized it and shuffled assets to meet the needs of the moment. He found this was something he was good at. The reforms worked and the Iranians won the war. Secord found that personally satisfying. It was his first experience with a "clear-cut unambiguous victory" in war. It would also be his last.

Secord's commander in Iran was Colonel Harry "Heine" Aderholt. Aderholt had served in Laos, as a "CIA detailee," the nickname for anyone in the military services on temporary loan to the CIA. Aderholt had supervised the construction of the first CIA Lima Sites; and it was Aderholt who organized the first

American bombing missions in Laos. To Secord, Aderholt's account of his tour in Laos sounded "glamorous" and not too dissimilar from what he had been doing in Iran. When Secord learned there was an opening for a "CIA detailee" in Laos, he applied.

Secord arrived in Laos in late 1965. Shackley moved him to AB-1 at Udorn with Lair and Landry, with orders to increase air support for the war. Lair did not hold his bad feelings for Shackley against Secord. After briefing him on the operation he sent Secord on a tour of Laos' five military regions, with stopovers at the major Lima Sites, to get a feel for the complexity of the war. What Secord learned was that the North Vietnamese were tied to the roads. Properly managed, air strikes could destroy their logistics and disrupt their military campaigns.

But first Secord needed more planes. Getting them was a knotty problem. They came from all over the place, from the RLAF and RTAF, from the U.S. Navy and Air Force, and from the CIA's own proprietary air force, Air America. Each organization had its own procedures, its own channels of communication. To gain leverage, Secord networked with every organization and attended the Southeast Asia Coordination (SEACOR) meetings in Saigon, where the different armed services came together to argue, bargain, and divide up the available war assets. Secord's one advantage, in addition to his dogged determination, was that the CIA's communications were plugged directly into all of the channels of the various bureaucracies. He was able to get to the people who made decisions before anyone else.

By early 1966 Secord was delivering more air assets to Vang Pao's guerrillas than ever before. Toward the end of the year Secord finally tried his hand at interdicting NVA truck traffic moving down Route 6. He was confident he could get the airplanes he needed, and he had someone to do the spotting for the strikes, a tall Hmong named Ying Yang (nicknamed "Tallman"), hand-picked by Secord and trained as a forward air controller (FAC). Secord asked Lair for permission to go ahead. Lair gave his approval.

After inserting Tallman along Route 6, Secord wangled modified B-26 bombers, called Nimrods, from the 7th Air Force in Thailand. When fully loaded, the bombers carried napalm, phosphorus bombs, rockets, a dozen fragmentation bombs, and two thousand-pound bombs—in all, ten thousand pounds of ordnance. The NVA moved their trucks at night, so Secord made it a night operation, code-named Night Watch. The Nimrods flew sorties for a week, hitting everything on the road. For thirty days following the bombing there was no more truck traffic on Route 6. Secord had Tallman locate NVA troop concentrations and guide the Nimrods to their locations with devastating results. The bombing was putting a real dent in the NVA's Sam Neua organization.[33] Then Tallman was killed by Hmong troops, forcing Secord to terminate the operation.[34]

KONG-LÊ OUSTED

Shortly before Night Watch was shut down, Kong-Lê quit the war. Earlier in February, when Vang Pao was away receiving medical attention, two NVA battalions had surrounded Muong Soui. For the first time Kong-Lê's soldiers deserted in large numbers. The base was on the verge of being overrun when the U.S. Air Force diverted aircraft from operations over North Vietnam and the Ho Chi Minh Trail to come to the rescue. Averaging thirty-six sorties per day, the bombers broke the siege.

Still, Neutralist morale remained low and there were more desertions. In October, Kong-Lê's top officers mutinied. For some time RLA generals in Vientiane had been wooing them, offering promotions if they would rid themselves of their commander. The insurrection was bloodless. In a conspiracy that apparently included the CIA, Thai military, and Vientiane's generals, Kong-Lê was conveniently called away to Bangkok to meet with CIA agents. Thai officials placed him under house arrest and informed him that he would not be allowed to return to Laos. Kong-Lê had long ago abandoned any hope for real neutralism in Laos, no matter which side won the war. Fed up with RLA scheming, he retired from military life and left for Paris and permanent exile.

As if driven by some irrational urge, the RLA high command continued its reverse Darwinism by forcing out a second "fighting general." He was Thao Ma, former commanding general of the RLAF who had single-handedly fathered the fighter wing of the RLAF. A superb fighter pilot, in late 1963 Thao Ma had volunteered to lead air raids with T-28s against the Ho Chi Minh Trail. The raids began in 1964 with strikes against bridges, roads, and fortifications in the Mu Gia pass, where the Ho Chi Minh Trail first enters Laos. The raids were so successful the U.S. Air Force transferred dozens of T-28s to the RLAF.

Thao Ma's military successes, and his growing influence with American military advisors, made him unpopular with the RLA's armchair generals. It also did not help that he consistently refused to allow RLAF transport planes to be used for drug runs to enrich members of the RLA high command. After bungling an assassination attempt in mid-1965, the generals demoted Thao Ma to Tactical Air Force Commander to take away his authority over the RLAF's transport aircraft.

Thao Ma moved a dozen T-28s and thirty of his best pilots to Luang Prabang and began combat missions in the north. His pilots flew nearly a hundred sorties, tipping the scales in the fighting in upper Luang Prabang. As this only enhanced his influence with the Americans, the Vientiane generals reassigned Thao Ma to a desk in Vientiane. This time Thao Ma did not go quietly.[35] With twelve of his most loyal pilots, he attacked RLA headquarters in Vientiane and blew up the chief of staff's residence.

As part of the coup attempt, an entire regiment (Groupe Mobile 18) was supposed to mobilize and arrest top members of the General Staff. Vang Pao had contributed $31,000 for bribes to insure that the RLA regiment would follow through. It was a risky business for Vang Pao to become entangled in the political infighting in Vientiane, but the risk was worth it if it put Thao Ma in his debt and guaranteed air support for future military operations. Vang Pao's bribe had to change hands a number of times before reaching the Groupe Mobile's commander. Along the way it somehow disappeared. The result was that no one arrested the generals and Thao Ma was left out in the cold. Having burned his bridges, Thao Ma flew to Thailand and exile.[36]

With Thao Ma gone, Vientiane's generals, principally Ouane Rathikone and Kouprasith Abhay, could move their opium in RLAF transport planes at will. And with Kong-Lê out of the picture they were able to put their own hand-picked man, Colonel Sompeth, at the head of the Neutralist army. Sompeth did not hold the position for long. Souvanna Phouma replaced him with his own nephew, Sengsouvanh Souvannarath. Not wanting to miss the endless rounds of dinner parties at the American embassy and at his uncle's villa, Souvannarath transferred Neutralist headquarters from Muong Soui to Vientiane. It set the tone for the future. The Neutralists rapidly became indistinguishable from the regular RLA: ineffective, without backbone, and prone to retreat.[37]

INCREASED AIR POWER

Secord's Night Watch bombing raids along Route 6 were so successful that the communists switched all truck traffic to Route 7. There were reports of an average of thirty trucks a day traveling the road, many of them moving onto the Plain of Jars. Secord wanted to go after the trucks, but needed FACs to accurately guide planes to the targets. His solution was to borrow them from the U.S. Air Force.

A dozen American pilots, all with FAC experience in Vietnam, arrived at Long Cheng in October 1966. Nicknamed the "Ravens," the FACs did their spotting from the air in slow-moving Cessnas and T-28s. In addition to the Ravens, Secord introduced three Thai road watch teams to monitor traffic on Routes 6 and 7. It took Secord several months to get everything coordinated and working smoothly, but once the system was fully functional it proved lethal, not only against road traffic but also against massed troops.

The NVA went after Na Khang in January 1967. After artillery and mortar fire pounded the base, two columns of NVA infantry charged its perimeter. Agents Lynch and Daniels and Buell's assistant Don Sjostrom were at the base, once again in the middle of a raging battle. During the mass assaults an NVA bullet claimed Sjostrom. An urgent request went out for air strikes to save Na Khang. Ravens were soon in the air spotting targets for A-1E Skyraiders. The planes tore up the enemy's columns with their heavy machine guns and cluster bombs. Once the first group of Skyraiders expended their ordnance, a second group arrived to continue the assault. Then F-105 jets arrived, so many that they were stacked in a holding pattern, waiting their turn to shred the enemy's troops. After two days in this meat grinder the communists had so many dead their commanders called off the assault and withdrew.

It would take three more months before the communists could work up the courage for another assault on Na Khang. When they arrived, they discovered a desert in the jungle. Secord had had planes spray defoliants around the base, clearing away all ground cover. The NVA's battalions were out in the open and easy targets for the Hmong, firing from fortified bunkers. Again the communists withdrew.[38]

With a lull in the fighting, Secord went after NVA trucking on both Routes 6 and 7. Thai road watchers located the trucks, Ravens in spotter planes called in the strikes, and Nimrods blew the convoys apart. By June, nearly a hundred trucks were confirmed destroyed. Secord next went after troops. Vang Pao sent his SGUs in three separate directions, drawing out the enemy to make them vulnerable to assaults from the Skyraiders and Nimrods. The communists suffered enormous losses. With their supply lines in tatters and casualties mounting, the main body of the 316 Division retreated to North Vietnam.

The Hmong now faced only small and isolated enemy units. Vang Pao had nine battalions in the field. They swept over Sam Neua, using air support to blast the enemy from their bunkers. Hmong guerrillas also occupied the rice-rich Moung Ngan valley southwest of Xieng Khouangville, depriving the enemy of the area's rice harvest that in the past had filled the bellies of thousands of North Vietnamese soldiers.

Vang Pao's army had never performed so well. Shackley was elated. Secord had delivered the air assets needed and it had made the difference. CIA reports to Washington talked of a permanent shift in power between Vang Pao and the NVA. For Shackley this was confirmation that his general strategy was on the right track. He had achieved what American forces in Vietnam had failed to do, lure battalion and regimental-size NVA units into mass assaults so they could be annihilated by American air power. Only in Laos was war by attrition working in America's favor. In Vietnam American forces had difficulty even locating the enemy, let alone destroying him. For Shackley the next step was to draw the NVA into even larger battles with more troops, exposing them to even more devastating air assaults. Shackley pressured Lair to have Vang

Pao organize his army into regimental units large enough to engage in conventional infantry battles.

Vang Pao was as impressed by air power as Shackley. He believed Secord had "magical powers" and insisted on addressing him as "Colonel Dick," even though Secord had only recently been promoted to major. Believing Colonel Dick would always deliver, Vang Pao formed his first regiment, Groupement Mobile (GM) 21.[39] More GMs would follow, transforming the Hmong army into a force of large units.

Ironically, as Hmong units grew in size, those in the RLA grew smaller. General Kouprasith Abhay wanted to standardize unit size in the RLA at the battalion level, eliminating all regiments. The object had nothing to do with improving fighting efficiency. Abhay's goal was to prevent any officer from having control over a large number of troops, thereby making coups more difficult.[40]

HMONG AIR FORCE

Vang Pao's enthusiasm for air power led him to pressure Lair for a Hmong air force, to be stationed at Long Cheng and under his direct control. Lair wanted the same thing. Secretly, he had been preparing the way. He had begun training Hmong as pilots back in late 1966, just a handful taught by instructors from the Thai Air Force. By the summer of 1967, three groups of Hmong had qualified on Piper Cubs and Cessna 180s. Lair wanted them entered in Waterpump, the flight instruction program established in 1964 at Udorn to train Lao fighter pilots for the RLAF.

At first the RLA high command stonewalled Lair's request, insisting that Waterpump remain an all-Lao operation. But Lair would not take no for an answer. In late 1967, Hmong finally became part of Waterpump, learning to fly T-28s, the mainstay of the RLAF's fighter wing. In January 1968, the first Hmong Waterpump graduates arrived at Long Cheng to take possession of their own fighter planes. Eventually more than a hundred Hmong would graduate from the program, some of them trained by Secord himself, who did it for recreation, a release from the hectic pace of his job at AB-1. At Long Cheng, Vang Pao's tiny air wing continually expanded to accommodate the new graduates, going from a few T-28s in 1968 to over sixty by 1971.

The Hmong pilots had many virtues. They were skilled and they were fearless, but most of all they were always available. Their motto was "fly until you die," adopted from a remark made in a moment of braggadocio by Sue Vang, a swaggering senior pilot who boasted to a CIA official visiting Long Cheng on an inspection tour that he would fly until he died.[41] The motto was not hyperbole. The American Ravens flew six months straight and then were cycled out. Hmong pilots had no set tour of duty. Once they began flying, their tour was for the rest of the war. On the occasions when air assets from the U.S. Air Force or U.S. Navy were withheld because of bad weather or higher priority targets elsewhere, Vang Pao could always count on his "Lord White Buddha" Hmong, the call-sign for Hmong pilots at Long Cheng.

DEBACLE AT NAM BAC

In January 1968, the Royal Laotian Army fought its last big battle of the war. As usual, it was poorly planned and ended in disaster. The battle took place in the far north in Military Region I, at a CIA guerrilla base close to North Vietnam's border.

The CIA had been in MR I since 1960, but it was not until 1964 that the agency began to take a real interest in the region and assign more agents to the area. Tony Poe arrived in the military region in late 1965, sent by Lair to get him out of Long Cheng. Poe and Vang Pao had not been getting along. The two argued over military tactics and the training of troops. After one particularly heated exchange, Poe had cut off all food and military supplies to Long Cheng to let Vang Pao know who was in charge.

Behind the tension was Poe's distaste for Vang Pao's political style. It bothered Poe that Vang Pao skimmed soldiers' pay and gave Hmong from the more powerful clans the best jobs. Poe thought Vang Pao should stick to soldiering and stay out of politics. It did not occur to him that without all the graft and patronage, Hmong support for the war would evaporate overnight.

Lair understood this, which was why Poe had to go. Lair exiled Poe to MR I at a place called Nam Yu as the replacement for an agent who had recently been killed. Nam Yu was far from the mainstream of action. Lair hoped he would never hear from Poe again.

Poe was glad to be away from the corruption at Long Cheng. Off by himself, he could run a clean program. He threw himself into the work, recruiting guerrillas from the local population of Yao, Lu, and Khmu montagnards. By early 1967, Poe had three units under arms and was conducting raids against NVA supply lines.

As an incentive for more aggressive guerrilla patrols, Poe offered a cash bounty of five thousand kip for each set of enemy ears delivered to him personally. He kept the trophies in large plastic bags which kept filling up. Poe congratulated himself on the effectiveness of the program until he came across a kid from a local village without ears and learned the boy's father had cut them off for the money. Poe immediately canceled the incentive program.

Poe had better luck with a brazen plan to liberate Nam Tha, the headquarters of the Pathet Lao 402 battalion. Top officials in the Vientiane government had relatives there and wanted them rescued. Poe's guerrillas held the town for six days, long enough to get everyone out. The operation boosted Poe's standing with the government, but not with Lair, who intended to keep Poe as far on the fringes of the war as possible.[42]

Poe's operation at Nam Yu was small compared to the CIA's other MR I network farther east at Nam Bac. Shackley had seven agents there busy organizing battalion-size units of montagnard guerrillas to engage the NVA—part of Shackley's master plan to increase the size of paramilitary units.

The leader of Nam Bac's CIA team was Eli Popovich, a field agent with experience in paramilitary operations in Burma, Korea, and China. Popovich and his team recruited and trained enough Khmu for several SGUs. Popovich sent one of the battalions to Hua Hin for special training and used it for aggressive raids against NVA supply lines.

The attacks hit the communists too close to home. North Vietnam's border was just north of Nam Bac. An NVA construction battalion arrived to begin work on a road running from the border directly to Popovich's headquarters. NVA infantry battalions followed, bivouacking north and east of Nam Bac, biding their time until the road was finished and they could mount an assault on the CIA guerrilla base.

In July, the NVA battalions unexpectedly shot past Nam Bac to Luang Prabang. Only five months earlier North Vietnamese had mortared the royal capital's airfield, disabling a half-dozen T-28s. The communists went after the airfield again, destroying twelve planes, a third of the RLAF's tiny air command. The U.S. diverted jet bombers from Rolling Thunder and drove the communists back.

Worried that the NVA would return for a third assault, Vientiane's generals made plans to commit a large mobile force north to the Nam Bac Valley and block further NVA activity. The CIA advised against the project, doubting the RLA could manage the logistics of a multi-battalion force positioned so far north. There would be inevitable pilfering. Very few of the supplies would reach front-line soldiers.

The generals ignored the advice. Over the next few months thousands of government troops filled Nam Bac valley, elbowing Popovich's guerrilla operation to the sideline. The NVA matched the buildup, battalion for battalion. By January 1968, nearly the entire NVA 316 Division was on the scene, having arrived along the newly completed road.

In a panic, Vientiane airlifted all available reserves to Nam Bac valley. An urgent request went out to Vang Pao to also commit Hmong troops. In an act of "prudent diplomacy," he sent three thousand of his guerrillas, including one of his best battalions, commanded by Tong Va Lo. The Hmong reinforcements arrived too late. For days enemy artillery had battered Nam Bac without letup. Then NVA units penetrated the garrison's perimeter. The Lao battalions bolted en masse. As the Hmong neared the garrison they encountered wave after wave of retreating soldiers.

Only a single RLA unit stood its ground, the 99th Paratroop Battalion known as the Black Tigers. A last-minute reinforcement, they were just settling in on the edge of Nam Bac when the communists broke through. No one informed the Black Tigers of the pullout. They soon found themselves alone, engulfed in a sea of North Vietnamese. In a rare moment of courage for RLA forces, the Black Tigers engaged the enemy and fought to the last man.

The carnage had only begun. NVA units had already circled around to establish a blocking force to bar the RLA's escape. Additional NVA battalions closed in on the flank in a classic enveloping maneuver. During the encirclement entire RLA battalions were wiped out. Others suffered casualties in excess of 50 percent.

When it was over, an RLA force of nearly twenty thousand had been reduced by one-half. The communists captured 170 heavy weapons, including six 105-mm howitzers and tons of ammunition. And they had three thousand prisoners. The captives were offered a choice: prison camp and forced labor, or enlistment in the Pathet Lao. Six hundred eventually wound up on the Plain of Jars in Pathet Lao uniforms.

The Hmong were also caught in the encirclement, but fought their way through. Three hundred died during the breakout, including seventy of Tong Va Lo's elite troops, all in a lost cause.[43]

With the fall of Nam Bac, and the devastation of the RLA's main army, there was nothing to prevent the North Vietnamese from marching south against Luang Prabang. The sentiment in Vientiane was that it was the start of the communists' final push to take over the country. There was talk in Washington of committing B-52s, but the idea was finally scotched for fear of bad press from escalating the air war. The hysteria was premature. Instead of going south, most of the NVA 316 Division moved east into Sam Neua to join other NVA units mounting a major campaign to capture a strategically important radar installation at a former Momentum site on top of Pha Thi mountain.

THE FALL OF PHA THI

In early 1964, President Johnson had approved the first secret air raids against North Vietnam. He wanted to expand the scale of the air attacks, but needed a pretext to do so. It came in August 1964 when North Vietnamese torpedo boats attacked U.S. Navy destroyers in the Gulf of Tonkin. Only three days after the event Congress passed the "Gulf of Tonkin Resolution" authorizing the President "to take all necessary steps" to defend South Vietnam from armed aggression by the North Vietnamese. Over the next few months Johnson ordered additional air strikes against targets in the north, slowly escalating the air campaign. The air war took a quantum leap in early 1965 with operation Rolling Thunder. By the end of the first year of the bombing campaign, U.S. fighter bombers and B-52s were flying more than twelve thousand sorties a month, mainly over the lower half of North Vietnam.

To provide radar for the air campaign, the U.S. Air Force established tactical air control systems in South Vietnam at Can Tho and atop Monkey Mountain (near Da Nang). As the scale of the air war grew, more advanced tactical navigation was brought on line. Designated as MSQ-77 radar, the new system offered greater accuracy in night bombing and bad weather. Between April 1966 and April 1977, the Air Force set up six of the new radar systems: four spread across the length of South Vietnam (at Bien Hoa, Da Lat, Pleiku, and Dong Ha) and two in Thailand at Nakhon Phanom and at Udorn air base. As the radius of the radar beacons was a hundred miles, the radar network provided a swath of air guidance that encompassed all of South Vietnam, a large chunk of southern Laos, and the bottom third of North Vietnam.

To enable the radar to reach farther north, the Air Force searched for a suitable site in northern Laos for an additional MSQ-77 station that would allow American bombers to strike as far north as Hanoi, at any time day or night and in any weather. The radar complex at Udorn was within walking distance of Lair's headquarters at building AB-1. Air Force strategists paid him a visit to get his opinion. Lair recommended they put the radar on top of Phu Pha Thi, one of the highest mountains in Sam Neua Province. Over a mile high, with sheer sides and a razorback ridge, the mountain's summit was difficult to attack and it was in Hmong country, with Momentum bases in the vicinity. Lair assured the Air Force planners that his people could quickly mount a defense, if necessary.

Helicopters moved 150 tons of equipment from Udorn to Pha Thi's crest. The new radar was called TACAN (Tactical Air Control and Navigation). It was good but not state-of-the-art. By mid-1967 the Air Force wanted to upgrade the TACAN on Pha Thi with the addition of a TSQ-81 system for even greater accuracy. The Air Force invited Lair to the planning session. By now he had second thoughts about Pha Thi. It was only seventeen miles from North Vietnam's border. If the new radar worked out as predicted, the NVA would quickly target it for elimination. The prospect of Hmong guerrillas attempting to hold ground against a regimental-size NVA force was not appealing. Lair considered the whole thing a bad idea. The Air Force generals chose not to listen.[44]

Pha Thi was designated on the CIA's maps as Lima Site 85. The Air Force identified it as AN-MSQ-77 Radar Controlled Directing Central. To the Hmong it was the "Rock," a mountain rising like a giant sentinel above the best opium farming land in Laos. Hmong villages dotted the neighboring hills and crests, providing Vang Pao a readymade information and defense network to protect the radar station from surprise assaults. Unlike Lair, Vang Pao was confident his guerrillas could hold against a concerted attack.

As Lair had feared, once the tonnage of bombs dropped on North Vietnam multiplied, the radar station on Pha Thi moved to the top of Hanoi's hit list. The North Vietnamese scheduled their assault on Pha Thi to coincide with a planned invasion of South Vietnam that would begin on January 31st (later known as the Tet Offensive). If the radar was knocked out and U.S. bombers were forced to fly blind, the U.S. could do little to stem the flow of arms and munitions from North Vietnam to NVA and Viet Cong forces attacking all major cities and military bases in South Vietnam.

NVA engineers began work on a road running directly from Sam Neua to Pha Thi. Secord picked it up while scanning aerial photographs. He understood the danger immediately, not only for America's bombing campaign over North Vietnam (Pha Thi's radar had guided a quarter of the air raids into North Vietnam), but for his own program of air support for Vang Pao's guerrillas. Secord's stunning air offensive during the 1977 rainy season that had stopped all NVA truck traffic on both Routes 6 and 7, and annihilated NVA troop concentrations in Sam Neua, was made possible by Pha Thi's radar.

Secord told Shackley about the road. Shackley ordered Secord to eliminate it. Almost daily Secord requested air strikes from the Air Force but was told there were higher priority targets. All he could get were occasional sorties. The jets destroyed bulldozers and blew chunks out of the road, but the tractors were always replaced and the road continued to take shape, stretching toward Pha Thi at the rate of nearly a kilometer a day.

Two weeks before the Tet offensive, three cloth-covered Soviet biplanes (Antanov AN Colts), piloted by North Vietnamese, crossed the border and swooped out of the clouds to attack Pha Thi's radar. A gift from the Soviets, the ancient aircraft had previously been used only for non-combat purposes. In 1961, it was an Antanov that transported Colonel Lawrence Bailey Jr., the first American POW in Laos (and Indochina), from the Xieng Khouangville airstrip to Pathet Lao Headquarters in Sam Neua City. The attack on Pha Thai was the Colts' first real combat mission.

Once the biplanes were over the radar station, the Antanov's backseaters slipped open their windows and sprayed the installation with machine gun fire. On their second pass the backseaters dropped mortar shells rigged as bombs. The radar station was untouched, but the bullets and bombs killed two women and two Hmong guerrillas.

An American helicopter lifted off to engage the attackers. A crewman leaned out the helicopter's open door and fired an Uzi at a Colt. The biplane went into a spin and crashed. The remaining biplanes lumbered for the border with the helicopter in pursuit. After they had flown eighteen miles a second biplane went down. During a series of evasive turns, the third Colt flew into the side of a mountain.

If the Colts had hit their target, it would have spared the NVA the expense and manpower of massing a major assault. The failed air attack meant there would be no cheap solution. Secord received intelligence that two NVA regiments were already massing for the attack. The regiments had heavy artillery, more than the communists had used at the siege of Dienbienphu.

Sullivan was apprised of the situation but was not overly concerned. In a report to Washington he admitted that "the enemy . . . has the capability of moving artillery or mortar within range of [Pha Thi]" but it "is the consensus here that . . . all reasonable precautions are being taken to safeguard the site." In reality, the radar base's defenses were hopelessly inadequate. Vang Pao had only a few hundred guerrillas on hand, positioned at the base of the mountain and near the top. Shackley persuaded the Thai government to airlift four hundred Thai infantry to beef up troop strength.

Even with the additional troops, Secord believed Pha Thi was no longer defensible. Vang Pao, on the other hand, exuded confidence. He was certain his guerrillas could hold the line. One of his units on the mountain's summit was commanded by Chong Shoua Yang, the Hmong officer who, in 1963, had turned a Hmong ADC into a formidable force and kept the Pathet Lao out of Ban Ban Valley for more than a year. Also, Vang Pao had ordered both of the steep passes leading to the summit heavily mined. He considered them death traps. The communists would never get through. What Vang Pao did not know was that as soon as the mines had been seeded teams of NVA demolition specialists had moved in, working patiently every night to disarm the mines right under the noses of Hmong guerrillas and American technicians. Assuming the mines were still in place, Vang Pao left the passes only lightly defended.

When the two NVA regiments closed within striking distance of Pha Thi, Vang Pao sent out patrols to gather intelligence. One of the patrols ambushed a NVA unit scouting the perimeter of the mountain. Among the effects of a slain NVA officer was a notebook containing a map of the complete battle plan for taking Pha Thi, including the positions of all artillery sites.

Secord had what he needed to eliminate the enemy's firepower. He converted the artillery positions to bombing coordinates and requested air strikes. By now the Tet offensive was underway in South Vietnam. Secord was told all air assets were needed there. As the days passed, the NVA moved in more troops and artillery. Secord made more requests for air strikes and was again turned down. He was dismayed that the Air Force would allow such a valuable asset to fall into communist hands. On March 10, shells from 130-mm cannons began to slam into Pha Thi's summit. A hail of rockets from 122-mm and 107-mm rocket launchers showered the radar base. Three NVA battalions started up the mountain's steep passes, long ago cleared of mines. At the base of Pha Thi, NVA mountaineers began their ascent of the mountain's western cliff.

With shells smashing into the radar base, and enemy soldiers moving toward the summit, Secord was finally able to get the attention of decision-makers high up in the USAF chain of command. Realizing they were about to lose the radar installation, the Air Force began putting together a campaign of massive air support that would be launched the following morning. To hold off the enemy until then, F-4 Phantom jets headed for South Vietnam diverted to Pha Thi. The planes arrived to heavily overcast skies. The pilots had difficulty finding their targets and hit only a few of the NVA's cannons. Meanwhile, NVA artillery continued to pound Pha Thi.

Gathered at Pha Thi's summit were Hmong led by Chong Shoua Yang and a Thai force of two hundred. The Hmong and Thai moved farther down the mountain to position themselves to turn back the advancing NVA battalions. At three in the morning, the Hmong and Thai were still in place, holding the line. However, the twenty NVA mountaineers scaling Pha Thi's western cliff had reached the summit undetected.

On the summit were eighteen Americans, two of them CIA agents and the rest radar technicians. The two CIA agents were in their bunker, some distance away from the radar van where six of the technicians were on duty. The other technicians were attempting to get some sleep before it was time to go back to the van. To get out of the line of fire of NVA artillery, they had slung cargo netting over the edge of the western cliff and climbed down to a ledge to sleep. Though the ledge protected them from artillery fire, it was also a trap. The only way off the ledge was up. Beneath the ledge there was nothing but a sheer droop of fourteen hundred feet.

After the NVA mountaineers killed the technicians in the van, they went after those on the ledges, finishing off five with rifles and grenades. The remaining technicians survived by hiding in small caves. Just above them, near the cliff edge, the mountaineers set up a machine gun nest, oblivious to the Americans crouched in the caves below.

The CIA agents emerged from their bunker at dawn, thankful the Vietnamese had mysteriously ignored them. The agents moved off the summit and down the mountain to the helicopter pad three hundred yards away, crowded with Hmong and Thai waiting to be evacuated. After a brief conference, one of the CIA men decided to return to the summit to check for survivors. Chong Shoua Yang joined him, leading fifteen of his guerrillas. They ran into the mountaineers, exchanged fire and killed one. The group returned to the helicopter pad convinced that none of the technicians had survived.

Suddenly aircraft filled the sky. One observer declared that "it seemed as if every airplane in the world was descending, like a nest of angry hornets." Skyraiders flying low droned around the mountain and over surrounding valleys. F-4 and F-105 jets screamed overhead, moving in every direction. Helicopters appeared, along with Ravens. There were HC-130 tanker planes in high holding patterns waiting to refuel the choppers if needed.

So many fighter and bomber aircraft were in the air there were not enough targets to go around. The NVA road, constructed over a two-and-a-half-month period, was obliterated within the first few minutes of the air assault. The hills and valleys surrounding Pha Thi were ablaze with explosions and with fires ignited by the thousands of bombs, detonating in such rapid succession it sounded as if someone had set of a huge chain of enormous firecrackers.

Two Skyraiders spotted the Vietnamese on the crest, made their passes, and killed them all with their rockets and 20-mm cannons. The American technicians hiding in caves popped a purple smoke canister to let the pilots know they were still alive. A Raven arrived to coordinate the rescue. More Skyraiders attacked to make sure no Vietnamese were left alive on the summit. They dropped their ordnance of conventional bombs, then made another pass with cluster bombs. Thousands of bomblets ripped through the radar facility.

Two helicopters hovered above the cliff while their crews used rescue hoists to reel the technicians in. They had retrieved four of the five Americans when incoming rifle fire drove the choppers off, leaving radar specialist Jack Starling stranded and alone on a ledge.

Another helicopter, a huge HH-53 (a larger version of the ubiquitous Jolly Green Giant), landed at the helipad below the summit to evacuate the Hmong, Thai, and the two CIA agents. The agents jumped on board, then Hmong tumbled in, filling the chopper to capacity. Chong Shoua Yang had seven wounded guerrillas. He yanked healthy Hmong out of the chopper to make room for the injured. More HH-53s landed, loaded the remaining guerrillas, and left for Na Khang.

It was nearly an hour before a helicopter with a rescue hoist returned to search for Jack Starling, the last remaining technician. After he was pulled in and the helicopter had risen to depart, an entire company of NVA emerged onto the summit. A few more minutes and Starling would have been killed or taken prisoner.

At the foot of the mountain Hmong guerrillas were in full retreat. Earlier Vang Pao had airlifted in two battalions as reinforcements. Now that it was clear that the situation was hopeless, he was moving everyone out. He had the supplies and ammunition stored near the airstrip at the base of the mountain destroyed and explosive charges placed in the barrels of his cannons and mortars and detonated. Having removed or demolished everything of any value to the enemy, Vang Pao ordered all troops to pull back to Na Khang.

With Pha Thi in enemy hands, the Air Force wanted the radar at the summit destroyed to prevent the advanced radar technology and its encryption encoding equipment from falling into the hands of the Soviets. A secondary goal was for the bombers to inflict maximum damage on the two NVA regiments before they had a chance to disperse. For a full week American aircraft rained bombs, tearing apart the mountain and surrounding forest. Radio intercepts of NVA communications in the field, all registering panic and terror, indicated the destruction of troops was massive. In one transmission a battalion commander yelled piteously into his radio: "My men are gone. I'm the only one left. Can anybody hear me? Can I come home?"

The air assault transformed the terrain into a ruin of uprooted trees, decapitated hills, and scorched valleys, and a graveyard for thousands of enemy dead. Incredibly, not one bomb made a direct hit on the radar installation. In one last raid, propeller-driven Skyraiders carrying heavy ordnance went after the radar. Every bomb was a direct hit. The Skyraiders literally blew the top off the mountain. [45]

The loss of Pha Thi's radar was a major setback for the air war over North Vietnam. Rolling Thunder had killed over fifty thousand North Vietnamese, destroyed most of the country's oil storage depots, leveled its power plants, knocked out half its bridges, destroyed nearly ten thousand vehicles, and blown up two thousand rail cars. With the radar gone, accurate all-weather air assaults against Hanoi were no longer possible.

President Johnson announced a temporary halt to all bombing north of the 20th parallel. A few months later Rolling Thunder was officially canceled. For the next four years no American bombers would appear over North Vietnam.

Emboldened by their capture of Pha Thi, the North Vietnamese brought in more troops to sweep across Sam Neua and occupy as much territory as possible before the rainy season began. In a change of tactics, NVA units began attacking Hmong communities identified as part of Vang Pao's intelligence network. They drove off villagers and burned their crops to remove any incentive to return, depriving Vang Pao of the eyes and ears for his air mobile operations and surprise attacks behind enemy lines. The scorched earth policy kept Edgar Buell busy locating wandering groups of refugees, dropping supplies, and eventually airlifting ten thousand Hmong to the already overcrowded refugee center at Sam Thong.

Part of the general offensive was a drive against Na Khang, which possessed the last remaining tactical navigation system in northern Laos. By the close of April 1968, five NVA battalions had encircled the garrison. A week later the siege began. Inside were fifteen hundred of Vang Pao's best troops, scanning the skies for air support.

Ironically, with Pha Thi's radar destroyed, Secord was able to provide more air support than before. The bombing halt over North Vietnam freed up air assets for other operations and Secord had made sure that a good deal of it went to MR II. Of course, with the radar on Pha Thi destroyed, Secord could no longer provide all-weather or pinpoint accurate bombing, but he could deliver massive amounts of it, when weather permitted.

For weeks the skies over Na Khang had been overcast, preventing close air support. Suddenly the clouds and haze were gone. Flying out of Long Cheng, Ravens in Cessnas appeared to select targets for the fighter-bombers arriving in droves from Thailand. There were so many in the air at one time that they had to be stacked in holding patterns, as at a civilian airport in bad weather, waiting their turn to attack.

The pilots went at their work with grim determination, hitting everything that moved, motivated as one writer put it by "a vengeance and pent-up frustration" for Pha Thi. The bombing continued for more than a week, sortie after sortie. One NVA battalion was entirely wiped out. Others suffered horrible losses. The communists called off the assault and withdrew.[46]

10

RELIANCE ON AIR POWER

B ack at Long Cheng, Vang Pao faced a minor political crisis. The loss of Pha Thi had undermined confidence in his leadership. Clan elders approached him with the idea of moving some of the refugee population at Sam Thong and Long Cheng to Sayaboury. It would insure their safety, they argued, the clear implication being that Vang Pao could no longer be counted on to keep the North Vietnamese at bay.

Vang Pao was exhausted, both mentally and physically. He had no quick answer, no words to pacify the elders, no strategy to bring them around. He promised to take the matter up with Vientiane. Of course he had no intention of doing so. He was buying time to find some way to restore confidence, perhaps with a major victory, though that didn't seem likely.

The rainy season had arrived, the time when the 316th Division pulled back to North Vietnam for rest and replenishment. As usual there was heavy border traffic, but this time it was in the wrong direction. The 316th Division had not budged. Fresh units from North Vietnam were streaming into Sam Neua to fortify the division.

America had recently initiated peace talks with North Vietnam. Preliminary meetings were already underway in Paris. Back in 1953, the communists had jockeyed for bargaining power with the French by widening the war into Laos. They intended to do the same thing with the U.S. The war in Laos would no longer be seasonal. It would be continuous and accelerated, to dampen U.S. morale and gain leverage at the bargaining table.

To establish a permanent presence in MR II the communists needed improved logistics and, especially, all-weather roads, hard-packed and reinforced to withstand the rain. The task would keep construction crews busy round-the-clock for months at a stretch. Also the roads had to be secure, which meant clearing Hmong guerrillas from strategic choke points. For the next two years, many of the most hard-fought battles would be contests to determine which side controlled the roads.

Vang Pao responded to the NVA buildup with a major recruitment drive. He formed two new regiments and had them trained at Muong Cha. With his troop strength at an all-time high (thirty-nine thousand), he launched his rainy season offensive. Secord had already prepared the way by having a TACAN set up at Na Khang to help guide in air strikes. Vang Pao sent units against major NVA positions in Sam Neua to draw out the enemy so the jets, Skyraiders, Nimrods, and his own Hmong T-28s could go after them. Four hundred air sorties were flown in support of his troops during the campaign. The NVA 316 Division took a terrible pounding.

LAIR DEPARTS

It was now August 1968, and Bill Lair asked the CIA for a transfer. For some time he had been disturbed by the direction the war was taking. Shackley's big unit operations were eventually going to destroy the Hmong. And of course Lair had less control of things. The secret war had developed its own momentum. It had gone high tech. Air power played a central role, and the influence of Air Force strategists was beginning to overshadow that of the paramilitary experts. Lair wanted out.

The CIA offered him a post in South Vietnam working with the Phoenix program, a covert pacification operation directed mainly against the Viet Cong. Shackley was slotted for a promotion that would put him in the thick of things as the Saigon station chief. If Lair went to Vietnam, he would be under Shackley's thumb. He had had enough of Shackley. Lair turned down the Phoenix offer and took an assignment stateside.

Secord was leaving too. His tour of duty was up; it was time to return to regular duty with the Air Force and get on with his career. Secord and Lair left the same day, on the same flight, to the U.S.

Pat Landry, Lair's former assistant, took over Lair's job, answering to Lawrence Devlin, Shackley's replacement as the Vientiane station chief. Landry tried to turn things around, make things small again, a real paramilitary operation rather than the conventional-style war it was becoming. He told Devlin that there were too many Americans involved and that too much money was being spent. It was time to reduce the scale of the program and return it to the natives.

Devlin saw Landry's ideas as a direct challenge to his own authority and dismissed him from his post. Richard Helms, the head of the CIA, intervened to save Landry's job. Even so, Landry was cowed by the experience. He no longer challenged Devlin. Like Shackley, Devlin considered bigger to be better, especially the air support side of the operation. To please Devlin, Landry assumed Secord's old role as manager of air assets. He wasn't as good at it as Secord, but he was adequate.[1]

Aside from Landry's momentary opposition to the direction things were taking, very little had changed.

VANG PAO IN AMERICA

About the same time as Lair and Secord left Laos, Vang Pao departed for America for a brief vacation from the war. He left with one of his wives and Jerry Daniels, the CIA agent from Montana who was now constantly at Vang Pao's side, having become one of his most trusted advisors.

Vang Pao toured the White House and the CIA's headquarters at Langley, where he met with the agency's director, Richard Helms. Vang Pao visited an auto plant in Detroit, then a tractor plant. The huge assembly lines turning out complex machinery dazzled him. Compared to sleepy Laos, still in the Stone Age, America was so advanced it was like an alien world. Then Vang Pao was taken to Williamsburg, Virginia, restored to reflect its colonial past to attract tourists. Vang Pao saw the wood buildings and hand-crafted furniture, hand looms for making cloth, cooking pots for use over open fires, wooden plows, blacksmith forges not unlike those used by Hmong silversmiths in Laos, wagons drawn by horses instead of tractors or trucks. This was how America used to be, like Laos. It was an eye-opener. With education and technology Laos could make the same transition.

It is easy to read too much into this episode, to see it as a moment of epiphany that abruptly transformed Vang Pao's perspective, having him returning to Long Cheng "enthusiastic, wanting his people to become educated, to work hard, and to make that jump themselves into the twentieth century."[2] But there was no epiphany, no sudden transformation. The change that occurred was gradual and was already well underway before Vang Pao's trip to America.

As Touby's protégé, Vang Pao had long ago come to appreciate the importance of education. Like Touby, he wanted more schools for Hmong. In the early 1960s Vang Pao had been influenced by Edgar Buell, who not only championed universal education for the Hmong, but pushed hard for the modernization of Hmong agriculture. It did not take much to win Vang Pao over. He already appreciated the value of education. And almost daily he saw the difference technology could make. From the start, CIA sponsorship made his Hmong the best-equipped guerrilla fighters in the world, delivered to battles in helicopters and supported in the air by fast-flying jet fighters and bombers guided by advanced radar, making them "the world's only guerrilla army with air superiority." Vang Pao was mesmerized by all the military hardware; he could never get enough of it.

Other aspects of Western technology were wonder drugs and the high-tech surgery of the sort that had saved Vang Pao's arm. With Vang Pao's blessing, the CIA brought modern medicine to the Hmong, indirectly challenging the authority of the shamans whose principal function was curing disease. With Buell's encouragement, Vang Pao also broke with tradition by allowing Hmong girls to train as nurses, as he had earlier trampled tradition by opening all schools to girls.

Before his visit to America, Vang Pao had promoted the growth of Hmong commerce and the use of western consumer goods (radios, toothbrushes, motor bikes, jeans, T-shirts, and tennis shoes), not only because he was marketing the goods himself but because he saw such growth as a step toward entering the modern world. He encouraged Hmong to take up western occupations and become dentists, barbers, optometrists, storekeepers, door-to-door salesmen, clerks, butchers, bakers, and radio broadcasters.

The Williamsburg experience only reinforced Vang Pao's commitment to move the Hmong into the twentieth century, though he was clearly more openly vocal about it on his return, announcing that it was time for the Hmong to become more scientific and less superstitious and to accept modern ways, pronouncements that persuaded the Americans working with him at Long Cheng that the trip had changed him dramatically.

ATTEMPT TO RETAKE PHA THI

The NVA began its dry season offensive in October 1968. Strengthened to sixteen battalions, the communists now carried more arms and equipment than any NVA force in South Vietnam. Vang Pao moved out from Na Khang to engage the enemy, striking along Route 6 and moving up the road toward Pha Thi. His troops had air support, including assets from Rolling Thunder, two squadrons of Skyraiders from Thailand, and his own T-28s piloted by Hmong. By late November Vang Pao was within striking distance of Pha Thi. For the next month, using a force of nearly two thousand Hmong, it would become Vang Pao's obsession to pry Pha Thi lose from the North Vietnamese and obtain the victory he imagined was necessary to restore Hmong confidence in his leadership, and to end all talk about falling back to Sayaboury.

The Hmong were met with heavy artillery. Vang Pao pulled back and let Landry put together an air campaign to knock out the cannons and soften up the three NVA battalions holding the mountain. Within two days the planes silenced the artillery. More sorties followed, stretching over a week. F-4 Phantom jets saturated Pha Thi's two slopes with napalm; other fighter-bombers hit the summit. One of the NVA battalions lost half of its men. The other two were also badly depleted.

The Hmong quickly took the airfield at the base of the mountain, but had to fight for every yard going up the slopes. After two weeks of hard fighting one Hmong company reached the edge of the summit, but was driven back by machine gun fire.

By now 50 percent of the Hmong had been killed or wounded, or were missing in action. The offensive was turning into the most costly campaign of the war. Yet Vang Pao kept at it for another two weeks. He had learned from a defector that the NVA on the summit were dispirited and doubted they could hold out much longer.

But the summit's defenders did hold out, long enough for the NVA 148 Regiment to arrive and join the battle. Vang Pao was badly outnumbered. He could not afford more casualties. Reluctantly, he withdrew.

SHONG LUE YANG

Pha Thi was a worm at Hmong morale. To have lost the mountain base was bad enough, but to have sacrificed so many soldiers in a failed attempt to reclaim it seemed utterly senseless. In both battles hundreds of American planes had assaulted the enemy. Vang Pao had claimed that with air support his soldiers were more than a match for the North Vietnamese. Many Hmong had believed him, but now it was shown to be a lie. Too many Hmong were dying in the war. There were too many defeats. The once unshakable faith in Vang Pao's ability to hold back the communists was shattered. A terrible image filled peoples' heads; it was the picture of NVA battalions spilling murderously over the Plain of Jars into the refugee settlements spread out from Sam Thong to Ban Some, settlements that housed almost half of the Hmong in Laos.

Clan elders pleaded with Vang Pao to move civilians someplace far away from the fighting. Messianism was in the air and people were talking of quitting the war altogether and using the Hmong army (with or without Vang Pao) to create an independent kingdom in Sayaboury or in the mountains of northern Thailand.[3]

The inspiration for the messianism was Shong Lue Yang, a Hmong mystic from North Vietnam. To his disciples, Shong Lue Yang was another Pa Chay, an ordinary Hmong peasant transformed by a mystical experience. The metamorphosis occurred in 1959 at Tham Ha, a village in North Vietnam across the border from Nong Het. It was the clearing season, the time when Hmong farmers prepare new land for planting by felling trees, removing brush, and gathering the debris into piles for burning. Day after day Shong Lue Yang labored in his field and each day his wife brought him his lunch in a basket. Then something strange occurred. On her way to deliver his lunch, Shong Lue Yang's wife was swept up by a whirlwind and slammed to the ground and knocked unconscious.

Shong Lue Yang took it as a sign, though of what he was uncertain. The next day, while pondering the matter alone in his hut, he heard a booming voice. He looked around. He was still alone in the hut. Shong Lue Yang feared he was going insane. He received a slap in the face, so hard he saw stars. The voice spoke again: "I am God, your father, who sent you to be born on earth as a human being. You are not crazy, but you must do what I tell you to do."

A few days later while smoking opium, Shong Lue Yang was visited by spirits who taught him the Hmong script and led him to a cache of silver buried in the ground. Shong Lue Yang used the money to build a temple and launch a religious revival. Hundreds of Hmong were caught up in the movement, alarming local officials. A military patrol arrived at Tham Ha to arrest the prophet, but he escaped and went into hiding, continuing his ministry underground.

Rumors of Shong Lue Yang reached Long Cheng, stirring religious emotions. Even Vang Pao was affected. Beneath his embrace of modernity and his tough-minded realism in war and politics, there lingered the old metaphysics that guided the perceptions of ordinary Hmong, a world view that spawned forest genies, dab (evil) spirits, phantasmic manifestations of long-dead ancestors in gusts of wind or the bleating of a wild goat, and a belief in the power of shamans to influence things unseen and unknown.

Once military maps were laid aside and meetings with his military planners concluded, Vang Pao still felt the need to consult a shaman before major battles to discover whether the spirits favored victory. Ya Shao Yang, the most renowned shaman in the province, usually performed this service. It was customary for shamans to use words and scribble incantations from a foreign language (often Chinese) during the performance of magic rites.[4] But Ya Shao wrote strange words only he could decipher, words which many presumed to be fragments of an authentic Hmong script, an accomplishment that added luster to his fame and was a testament to his power.

Still, Ya Shao was no Pa Chay. Only a Hmong who had developed a complete system of writing and could teach it to other Hmong could qualify. Shong Lue Yang had accomplished this feat—proof that he was touched by God. Vang Pao could not help being impressed, even awed, by the achievement. He sent a guerrilla force of four hundred men into North Vietnam to rescue Shong Lue Yang and bring him to Long Cheng.

A number of the prophet's apostles returned with the soldiers, but Shong Lue Yang remained behind, determined to continue his ministry at Tham Ha and to serve as Vang Pao's hired spy, keeping track of communist troop movements near the border and passing the information on to Vang Pao. Because of his espionage, the communists' hunt for Shong Lue Yang intensified. In early 1966, following several brushes with well-armed search parties, Shong Lue Yang abandoned North Vietnam and sought refuge at Long Cheng.[5]

Long Cheng had long ago outgrown its original design as a CIA paramilitary headquarters and evolved into a major population center, rivaling Vientiane. In addition to Hmong soldiers, American and Thai technicians, and CIA operatives, there were tens of thousands of Hmong refugees. An urban sprawl of potpourri dwellings (bungalows, shanties, tarpaper huts) pushed inward to the edges of the base's long air strip and outward into the surrounding hills. There were markets and shops to accommodate the population and taxis to transport Hmong to the other nearby refugee settlements at Ban Some, Phak Khet, Muong Yong, and Sam Thong to do business or visit relatives.

Never had Shong Lue Yang seen so many Hmong concentrated in one place. At Tham Ha he had preached to hundreds. At Long Cheng he could reach out to thousands and spread knowledge of the new script. War refugees, soldiers' families, Hmong from all walks of life flocked to the prophet. Even some of Vang Pao's top officers joined the movement. The groundswell of response did not bode well for Vang Pao.

Shong Lue Yang preached a return to the purity of traditional Hmong culture. He castigated the Hmong at Long Cheng for their blatant materialism and for abandoning their traditional dress. Many women went about in Lao sari instead of traditional pantaloons and embroidered blouses. Men wore jeans and T-shirts or dressed like lowland Lao. Prophesying the imminent coming of a Hmong messiah, Shong Lue Yang warned that the savior would not appear at Long Cheng unless the entire population returned to the old ways in custom, clothing, and belief. Heeding the warning, thousands of Hmong put on traditional clothes and wrapped white and red thread around their sleeves to identify themselves as orthodox Hmong so the messiah would recognize them when he arrived.[6]

Shong Lue Yang's assault on all things modern was a direct challenge to Vang Pao's authority, for it was Vang Pao who had supported new schools and sent Hmong to study abroad. It was Vang Pao who had tolerated modest steps toward women's liberation, allowing Hmong girls to attend the new schools and young women to become nurses. It was he who had transformed Long Cheng, Sam Thong, Pha Khao, and Muong Cha into centers of commerce infected with the consumerism of western societies. It was Vang Pao who had encouraged an ecumenical embrace of Buddhism as a way to foster cultural links between ethnic Lao and Hmong. To a cultural purist like Shong Lue Yang, Vang Pao was more a threat than a savior of his people. He was a warlord, not a messiah, an ordinary politician who had used material interests, rather than high ideals, to cobble together his unwieldy regime.

It was obviously not in Vang Pao's interest to have the Hmong reminded daily that he was no Pa Chay or to be informed by insinuation that he was a corrupting influence, a Hmong Antichrist who malevolently debased Hmong culture and delayed the coming of the messiah. Shong Lue Yang had to go, but to lay hands on a shaman, especially a prophet in possession of a Hmong script, was a serious business fraught with spiritual peril. Ordinarily ruthless and brutal with traitors and enemies, Vang Pao used moderation. In late 1967, he had Shong Lue Yang arrested and imprisoned at Pha Khao.

Shong Lue Yang continued to preach from his jail cell and his disciples multiplied, carrying his ministry to the people and rousing messianic longings that intensified after the fall of Pha Thi. Vang Pao would eventually deal with the prophet and go after his disciples, killing some and forcing others into hiding. But at the moment his own morale was so low he could not summon the energy to reestablish confidence in his authority.

With morale low, troop desertions increased. An even larger number of Hmong soldiers simply retired from the war. It was not difficult to do. For years Vang Pao had recruited soldiers by setting quotas for villages. Village headman selected the necessary number of recruits from the available pool of able-bodied men (and later teenagers) and delivered them to the general's army. Hmong called up for duty did not always serve, however. Like Union draftees during the American Civil War, they could purchase a dispensation. The usual price was a bar of silver tendered to the recruiter, who used it as a draft bonus for anyone willing to take the exempted soldier's place.

This custom was later modified to deal with hardship cases. An eldest son was relieved of duty so he could assume the role of head of the family following his father's death. After losing several sons in battle, a family's last remaining son was allowed to retire from service and return home to insure a continuation of the family line. In such circumstances a silver bar was sufficient to discharge a soldier from active duty, leaving it up to the village recruiter to find a replacement.

Prior to the loss of Pha Thi, such practices did not unduly hamper the war effort unduly. Now they contributed to a hemorrhage of manpower. Village recruiters were inundated with silver bars from families unwilling to squander sons in a lost cause. As in the past, recruiters sported the bullion to attract replacements, but now there were few takers.

Vang Pao needed thousands of new soldiers to replace Hmong recently killed in action. His recruiters were able to round up only three hundred, and 30 percent of these were between the ages of ten and fourteen.[7] Nearly twenty-five thousand Hmong had already died in the war. The significance of this statistic had finally registered. Faith in Vang Pao's leadership was no longer unquestioned. With the failed attempt to retake Pha Thi, many also doubted his military skill.

Vang Pao harbored the same doubts. Edgar Buell was alarmed when he visited the general at his Long Cheng residence. Buell arrived for dinner expecting a large gathering. Vang Pao had a personal expense account of about a thousand dollars per month funded by the CIA, and almost all of it went for the lavish banquets he hosted every evening. Top staff officers and CIA advisors were always in attendance. Sometimes clan chieftains also showed up, or high officials in Vang Pao's civil administration. There was always enough food to feed thirty guests: bamboo baskets full of sticky rice, bowls of steamed vegetables, platters of chicken and beef, bowls of hot sauce, and special Hmong dishes like de-boned chicken wings stuffed with rice and pork, or the Hmong version of egg rolls called *kab yob*.

Buell found the spacious dining room vacant except for Vang Pao, clothed in rumpled and dirty khaki pants and a sport shirt that looked as if it had been worn for several days. Before Buell could get a word out, Vang Pao dropped his head into his hands and began to sob. Buell was more than a little embarrassed. "Where is everybody?" he asked.

"They are afraid to come here. Afraid to be with me," Vang Pao replied. "I have lost face with my people. I have lost face with the whole world."

During World War II Buell had been a supply sergeant in the army, serving stateside at Kansas and Tennessee for the duration. This hardly qualified him as a military expert, but his refugee work had put him in the thick of the war and from what he could see it was far from over. What the Hmong needed most now was military leadership. He urged Vang Pao to get back into harness and plan something.

Vang Pao shook his head. "There is no way we can win."[8]

The facts justified Vang Pao's pessimism. NVA's troop strength in MR II was higher than ever. Large enemy units with armored vehicles had already pushed onto the Plain of Jars. NVA tractors were towing huge 175-mm cannons onto the plain, each with a range of thirty kilometers. It did not take a military genius to realize the communists were planning a major operation. The long-range artillery suggested the North Vietnamese might even be considering an assault on Long Cheng. There had already been probing attacks against outposts ringing the plain. NVA units had even struck Sam Thong. Muong Soui, which had become a forward staging base for the Thai B-Team's T-28 squadron, had also come under attack; only U.S. air strikes had prevented it from falling into enemy hands. It looked like the enemy was preparing for a massive offensive on several fronts.

Whatever the NVA had in mind, it was fortuitously derailed by an observant Raven. Flying over the Plain of Jars, he spotted what appeared to be freshly dug ditches, unwittingly discovering an exposed section of an extensive network of supply trenches containing hundreds of tons of ammunition for the big 175-mm cannons and hundreds of 120-mm rocket launchers. The pilot called in an air strike on the ditch. The astonished Raven watched as the ammunition dump ignited into a prolonged chain reaction of massive explosions. Artillery rounds and rockets continued to cook and explode for an entire day and night at the rate of eighty explosions a minute.[9]

Deprived of their stores of munitions, the NVA 316 Division regrouped, garnered its resources, and went after a single target—Na Khang and its air navigation system that helped guide U.S. planes to communists targets.

Vang Pao suddenly emerged from his depression and got busy organizing the garrison's defense. Perhaps it had been Buell's constant badgering that had goaded the general to stop drowning himself in rice whiskey and re-engage; at least Buell thought so. But it is also true Vang Pao was by nature a man of action. Torpor simply went against his grain. He was bound to come around sooner or later.

Pots of rice again steamed on the huge dining table at Vang Pao's Long Cheng residence. Around the table were Vang Pao's top officers and his Thai and American advisors. It was decided that air power would be the key to saving Na Khang. Without it, the base was doomed.

Na Khang was like a little Dienbienphu, situated in a long valley surrounded by hills. Like Dienbienphu, Na Khang was ringed with barbed wire and its perimeter salted with land mines. Back in 1954, the French had imagined that the Viet Minh would never break through their mines and barbed wire. Vang Pao was not so foolish. He knew that if the North Vietnamese gained a purchase on the hills looming over Na Khang, they would bring in their artillery and blast the base apart, opening the way for a mass assault.

This was precisely how the North Vietnamese carried out the operation. After occupying the hills overlooking the base, they brought in artillery, rocket launchers, and heavy mortars and pounded the post. In the wings, four NVA battalions were assembled, waiting for the signal to attack.

Pat Landry had assembled a formidable air defense. There were so many planes in the air the FACs had trouble managing the air traffic. A-26 Invader bombers went after the NVA artillery, but scored few direct hits. The North Vietnamese had placed the cannons inside caves, making them invisible from the sky and difficult to destroy. Killing enemy soldiers was also difficult. To reduce casualties, NVA battalion commanders had dispersed troops in small units spread out in the surrounding jungle. Tons of bombs excavated the terrain, uprooting trees and cratering hills, but causing few casualties.

Vang Pao tried to draw the NVA away from Na Khang with a diversionary action on the Plain of Jars. Lacking sufficient troops to pull it off alone, he made it a joint operation with the Neutralists at Muong Soui. Hmong would enter the plain from the east, while Neutralist troops from Muong Soui would push onto the plain from the west. Both forces would go after the enemy's logistics. The Thai B-Team would fly air support.

NVA sappers hit Muong Soui the night before the operation was to begin. The Neutralists fled in panic, leaving behind their American advisors and technicians (nearly a hundred individuals) and all of the bombs stored at Muong Soui for the B-Team's T-28s. The sappers planted charges and blew up the bombs. They also killed a number of the Americans before Air America helicopters arrived to fly them to safety.

With the Neutralists out of the picture, Vang Pao called off the operation. It was now up to air power to save Na Khang. Three days later, on February 28, 1969, the four NVA battalions emerged from the hills and descended on Na Khang in waves. A-26 Invaders strafed the enemy's troops with their .50 caliber machine guns. AC-130 gunships raked the soldiers with rapid-firing 7.62-mm Gatling guns and Vulcan cannons. The Invaders and AC-130s killed hundreds before they expended their ammunition and departed. The NVA battalions continued the charge, desperate to swarm over Na Khang before more planes returned.

Once the NVA broke through the base's perimeter, it was all close-in fighting. The Hmong repelled several charges, but took heavy losses. An enemy grenade killed Na Khang's commander in one of the forward trenches. One Hmong battalion lost all of its officers and half of its men. Hmong reinforcements were already in helicopters heading for Na Khang, and in Thailand planes were preparing to launch to provide more air support. The garrison's dwindling number of defenders could not hold until then. They were nearly out of ammunition. The order went out to evacuate. Believing they were surrounded on only three sides, the Hmong retreated into what they took to be an undefended valley. Hundreds of NVA lay in wait. The Hmong were cut down in a relentless crossfire.

The air support finally showed. The warplanes ravaged the enemy's soldiers, but arrived too late to save the base. Hmong survivors were lifted out by helicopter. There were only 286 left out of an original force of 1,800—a casualty rate of 84 percent, higher even than the losses incurred in attempting to retake Pha Thi.[10] Equally devastating was the loss of Na Khang's TACAN radar. It would no longer be possible to hit the enemy from the air with the same accuracy as before.

MORE AIR POWER

The loss of Na Khang and the slaughter of his troops cast Vang Pao into another deep depression. Like his earlier bout, it did not last long. After days of hard drinking and wearing the same rumpled clothes, he put on a clean uniform and announced his intention not only to continue fighting, but to go on the offensive. First he needed more troops. The old system of village recruiters had petered out. Vang Pao needed something new. His solution was a *noblesse de robe*, making it possible for Hmong to purchase rank in his army by delivering troops, the greater the number, the higher the rank. A few ambitious Hmong took him up on the offer, but in the end they were unable to generate the troops needed. Nearly all Hmong men between eighteen and thirty-five were either already serving in Vang Pao's army or dead.

This forced Vang Pao to use young teenagers, often over the objections of their parents. A large number of boys were simply abducted. Ten-wheel transport trucks became a common sight at Hmong schools, especially at the sprawling refugee complex at Sam Thong. The trucks would appear just before school let out. Soldiers lined the boys up and dragged the largest and tallest into the trucks and hauled them away for basic training.

The recruitment drive was only a stopgap measure. There were simply not enough Hmong left to absorb heavy casualties and at the same time continuously field an army at full—strength. Within a year the supply of teenagers would dwindle, leaving Vang Pao no choice but to integrate more non-Hmong into his army. Thousands of Lao serving in the RLA would eventually volunteer for the money. A soldier in Vang Pao's army earned ten times the salary paid to regular RLA troops. There would be Thai volunteers signing up for the pay as well, most of them civilians without previous military training, delivered to Long Cheng by the CIA and organized by Vang Pao into independent battalions.[11] These volunteers would add little to Vang Pao's ability to turn back the NVA. The Lao refused to hold ground. In contrast, the Thai volunteers were tough, but they were amateur soldiers. In mid-1971, two of their regiments would nearly be wiped out in their first engagement with NVA units on the Plain of Jars. Only when Vang Pao began to receive units from the regular Thai army would things begin to turn around. The first trickle of Thai regulars would arrive in late 1969. Discovering that they were excellent and determined fighters, Vang Pao would beg for more and, in time, receive more than twenty thousand. By the end of the war, the Thai regulars, not Hmong, would be the backbone of his army.

But this was in the future. In April 1969 Vang Pao had only his Hmong, and in the midst of trying to recruit more soldiers and rally his forces, he faced a disaster in the making. After losing Na Khang, his fallback position for a northern post was the garrison at Bouam Long. The NVA's 148th regiment now had the post under siege. The commander of Bouam Long was Colonel Cher Pao Moua, the father of Vang Pao's fifth wife. Vang Pao radioed Cher Pao to fight to the last man if necessary.

To draw the communists away from Bouam Long, Vang Pao leapfrogged the garrison and launched an airborne assault against a communist position farther north at Phou Koum. His troops took the post after a hard day's battle. The North Vietnamese broke off their siege of Bouam Long and moved north to retake Phou Koum. Hurling two battalions at the post, they suffered heavy casualties and retreated, leaving behind sixty-seven dead and all of their light artillery. Hmong losses amounted to seven men.[12]

The victory encouraged Vang Pao to launch a major counter-offensive. To pull it off he needed more air power and some easing of the rules of engagement. Referred to as "Romeos" by American pilots, rules of engagement determined what pilots could and could not attack. In Laos, American jets and bombers were restricted to strikes against enemy forces fully engaged with Vang Pao's troops in the field. All civilian targets were off-bounds, as was a ten-mile corridor on the Laos side of the North Vietnam border. The NVA was well aware of these restrictions and used them to their advantage, positioning artillery in populated areas, storing supplies and ammunition in towns and villages, and setting up garrisons and supply depots in the border corridor as a safe harbor for troops and supplies.

The seed from which the rules of engagement sprouted was an early directive from the Kennedy White House prohibiting American pilots from engaging in combat missions unless accompanied by a South Vietnamese crewman. President Johnson, who declared that "no outhouse will be bombed without my approval," was even more concerned than Kennedy to micro-manage the use of American firepower. During Johnson's administration other rules were added to the Romeos and earlier ones modified or scrapped, until the rules of engagement encompassed many pages of detailed operating instructions dictating to Air Force pilots what they could and could not do in combat.

The object of the rules was to control precisely the level of escalation of the air war in Southeast Asia, a strategy that made perfect sense to high level military strategists, but only bewildered and frustrated pilots flying missions. They would risk their lives over the Ho Chi Minh Trail trying to hit communist transport trucks hauling soldiers and weapons to South Vietnam and yet be prohibited from bombing the Mu Gia Pass in North Vietnam, where every day hundreds of the enemy's trucks lined up bumper to bumper waiting for the safety of night to begin their journey down the Trail.

Understandably, there were times when American pilots flying sorties into Laos simply ignored the rules. As one pilot later
admitted, if the Pathet Lao loaded a pagoda up with ammunition
and were stupid and shot at you from inside it, "somehow you just
might slide over the pagoda and—POW—it would cook off and
the ammo inside it would explode for a couple of hours." In 1967
frustrated American pilots lobbed bombs onto the Chinese cultural mission in Xieng Khouangville. "The ammo stored there
cooked off for a week." The incident infuriated Ambassador
Sullivan, as did any others. Sullivan was fanatical about keeping
Romeo violations to a minimum.[13]

Strict compliance with the Romeos was just one of the ways
Sullivan tried to exercise ultimate control over the war, especially
the air power phase. He commanded his own air force, the 56th
Air Commando Wing, and insisted on validating all targets for air
strikes. When Secord was in charge of pulling together air assets
to interdict communist supply lines, bomb enemy troops, and support Vang Pao's forces in the field, he found Sullivan's restrictions
a constant impediment to timely and effective action. He had to
"dogfight with him often on the validation of air targets." Secord
had detested Sullivan, seeing him as a "State Department careerist"
who was dangerous because he was a military incompetent who
micro-managed the entire war. Secord blamed Sullivan more than
anyone else for the loss of Pha Thi.[14]

Vang Pao's request for additional air power and a loosening of
the rules of engagement were propitiously timed. Sullivan was gone,
soon to be replaced by G. McMurtrie Godley. The ambassador's
chair was vacant at the time. This left decisions over air power in
the hands of the embassy's staff in consultation with Air Force
attachés and CIA advisors, who took full advantage of the vacancy
to press for a relaxation of the rules of engagement. The result was
new Romeos. The ten-mile-border corridor was still off-limits,
but any target, even if designated as a town or village on the map,
could be attacked if it fired upon allied aircraft.

The level of air support was also scheduled to increase dramatically. The organization that parceled out air assets to the various
branches of the armed services was SEACOR, a conference hosted
by the 7/13th Air Forces in Saigon. At a recent SEACOR meeting, the total requests were tallied up and found to be far below the

Soldiers at entrance of Tham Kap cave
near Xieng Khouangville, Laos, 1960s

amount of assets available. The Air Force officer in charge asked if
anyone could use the surplus. Colonel Robert Tyrell, a member of
the Vientiane air attaché's office, raised his hand and said he'd take
it all. No one objected. In one stroke, Vang Pao's Hmong received
"one and a half times the number of air sorties allocated to the
whole of Vietnam."[15]

Beginning on March 17, 1969, USAF planes began attacking
all towns occupied by communist forces. They hit Khang Khay,
Phong Savan, and Xieng Khouangville. Over the next three weeks
the planes would fly 730 sorties, blow up hundreds of structures,
and hit NVA troop concentrations on the Plain of Jars and in the
rice-rich Moung Ngan valley wrested away from Vang Pao's guerrillas a year earlier.

On April 7, 1969, Vang Pao witnessed what massive air power
could accomplish under the new liberalized rules of engagement.
Xieng Khouangville had been in communist hands for more than
four years. On and off for two weeks American jets had bombed
the town, yet the communists still held on, refusing to relinquish
possession of the provincial capital. Back at AB-1 in Thailand, Pat

Landry pulled together air assets for another strike. This time he was taking off the gloves.

Vang Pao had airlifted a company of Hmong to the hills overlooking the provincial capital to wait for the American fighter-bombers to mount their final assault. Two of Vang Pao's T-28s flew reconnaissance for the mission. When the planes passed over the town, the sky came alive with antiaircraft fire from 37-mm cannons and rapid-firing 14.5-mm and 12.7-mm antiaircraft guns. The shells hit one of the planes and it went down. The NVA gunners then lowered their cannons and fired directly at Vang Pao's troops in the hills.

Under the old rules of engagement, air strikes against the town would not have been allowed. With the new rules, since the planes had drawn fire, the town was fair game. A Raven began circling a safe distance away to give directions to the F-105 Thunderchiefs (nicknamed "Thuds") breaking out of the clouds to assault the North Vietnamese artillery with 20-mm cannons. The NVA gunners on the ground were fearless. As soon as the Thuds killed one crew, another team of gunners moved in to take its place. At some of the artillery emplacements the bodies of three successive teams lay in piles around the guns. Once the Thuds had silenced the antiaircraft guns they unloaded their bombs on the town. The Ravens called in more strikes, then others.

The "Götterdämmerung of firepower that was the hallmark of the U.S. military in Vietnam" had come to Laos.[16] By the end of the day the town lay in ruins. Huge bomb craters pocked the main street. The few shops and houses still standing were rickety shells on the verge of collapse. Here and there a thick clay wall, cracked and cratered, rose above the surrounding rubble. Sheets of corrugated steel used for roofing lay about in piles, twisted and crumpled like used gum wrappers. Blasts from the bombs had stripped all leaves from the trees, giving them a diseased look. The bombs flattened fifteen hundred buildings and totally annihilated the enemy. Vang Pao's company of Hmong strolled down from the hills and occupied the town without firing a shot.[17]

A Hmong patrol discovered a hospital complex nearby, hidden in a cave. It was the NVA's main medical base for the entire region. Stores of medical supplies were in boxes, stacked against the cave's walls. There were an x-ray machine, an area equipped for major surgery and enough beds to accommodate a thousand patients. CIA agents dumped a transport plane load of land mines, cratering charges, explosives, and several 250-pound bombs into the cave. The detonation collapsed passages and set off an inferno that blazed for hours.

Another patrol found a vast cache of ammunition and supplies and fully operational artillery pieces. Vang Pao had it all hauled back to Long Cheng. One of the cannons wound up in front of his residence as a war trophy.

The easy victory renewed Vang Pao's faith in air power. Assured of air support, he soon had three battalions on the move. Dong Dane fell to his troops after American planes pounded the town into submission. The town was on Route 4 close to the Plain of Jars, giving Vang Pao control over all traffic moving between the plain and Xieng Khouangville.

The next target was the NVA stronghold on Phu Khe, a mountain southeast of the Neutralist headquarters at Muong Soui. USAF planes flew hundreds of sorties, destroying enemy bunkers, trenches, and supply depots. The planes also leveled several nearby towns, killing not only NVA but many innocent civilians.

A third Hmong force of five hundred drove NVA troops off Phu Nok Kok, a mountain overlooking Ban Ban and Route 6. Vang Pao now had troops in position to block all enemy convoys attempting to resupply the NVA on the Plain of Jars.

The communists struck back. An entire regiment closed on Phu Nok Kok with orders to take the mountain at any cost. Will Green, a Black CIA agent code-named "Black Lion," commanded the Hmong on the mountain. After ordering his men to prepare deep foxholes, Green called in air support. For a full week the NVA regiment repeatedly advanced to within twenty to thirty yards of Green's defense perimeter, only to be driven back by the bombs and napalm dropping from the sky. Toward the end, enemy troops were slaughtered by the Gatling guns of C-47 Dragonships circling overhead. What was left of the communist regiment retreated. Again, air support made the difference.[18]

The only setback in Vang Pao's lightening offensive was the loss of Xieng Khouangville. He had left behind only a single company to occupy the town. The communists besieged it with several battalions. Overwhelmed, the Hmong retreated into the hills. The town was becoming increasingly important to the communists. Every rainy season Hmong units attacked trucking along Route 6. The communists had made the decision to switch to Routes 7 and 72 as their major supply lines for all future campaigns to capture the plain. Construction crews were already busy turning the roads into all-weather highways. Holding Xieng Khouangville was crucial to protecting the road improvement already completed on Route 72.[19]

THE DEATH OF LUE LY

It was not only American air power that had made the difference in Vang Pao's lightning offensive that had the communists reeling. His own tiny Hmong air force was constantly in the sky, assaulting the enemy. Of all the Hmong pilots, one stood out— Lue Ly.

Lue Ly had taught high school at Lat Houang before he began flight training in Thailand to become the first fighter pilot in Vang Pao's tiny air force. He was twenty-seven at the time, too old by U.S. Air Force standards to begin training as a combat pilot. Fortunately the air commando school at Udorn was run by different rules, for Lue Ly was a natural pilot. He had superb reflexes, loved flying, and was utterly fearless.[20]

After seeing Lue Ly in action, the American FACs stationed at Long Cheng realized he was not only the best fighter-bomber pilot in Laos but the best they had ever encountered. Long Cheng's Ravens probably logged more flight time than American pilots anywhere else in Southeast Asia. They were in the air nearly every day, sometimes flying from dawn to dusk, but their tours lasted only six months, while Hmong pilots had no set tour of duty. Raven casualties were high, but nothing like the death rate of Hmong pilots. Less than a third survived the war.

Of all the Hmong pilots, Lue Ly seemed immune to fatigue. He was in the air nearly every day, sometimes flying nonstop for up to ten hours, his arms and legs so cramped a flight crew had to pry him out of the plane. His accuracy in bombing was unerring, achieved by daredevil aerobatics—near vertical dives straight onto targets, threading his T-28 through a maze of narrow ravines to strike at an enemy encampment at the base of a cliff and banking sharply only at the last moment to avoid a head-on collision with a sheer rock face. Lue Ly's trademark, however, was his low approach, skimming the ground until he released his ordnance, almost hand-delivering bombs to the enemy. Sometimes when he returned his propeller was covered with the blood of NVA who had failed to duck when he made his pass.

Naturally, the communists wished Lue Ly dead. With his aerial stunts and super low approaches, it was easy for NVA antiaircraft gunners to single him out during an air assault, each one vying for the honor of blowing him to bits. The T-28s he flew returned to base riddled with holes. During the battle to retake Pha Thi, his plane was hit so many times it began to come apart in the air. Lue Ly jumped free only seconds before it crashed. Rescued by an Air America helicopter, he was back in the air the next day.

Lue Ly's longevity was mostly due to his incredible skill, but luck also played a part, and in June 1969 it ran out. As the rainy season was in full swing, Vang Pao expected the North Vietnamese to pull back. Not only did they hold their positions, they brought in seven battalions from the 312th Division. Vang Pao monitored the enemy's supply lines. Because of the bad weather, not much was getting through. He decided to go after the NVA encampment south of Muong Soui.

It was to be a joint operation. The Neutralists were to move out of Muong Soui and attack the enemy from the north while Hmong attacked from the east. The Hmong carried out their side of the operation, but the Neutralists proved to be worthless. After advancing only eight kilometers they ground to a halt. A small NVA unit blocked their advance. To give the Neutralists courage, Vang Pao called in air strikes. The planes dropped thirty-eight tons of bombs in less than two hours. A small number of the enemy survived the battering by crawling into tunnels. The Neutralists still refused to budge. Hmong pilots flying T-28s pounded the NVA tunnel rats. The Neutralists still would not advance. A handful of shell-shocked NVA finally emerged from their tunnels and fired a few unsteady rounds. The Neutralists scampered back to Muong Soui.

Ten days later the North Vietnamese assaulted Muong Soui with a thousand men. Logistically, it was an uneven contest. The Neutralists, supported by a Thai artillery battalion, outnumbered the NVA four to one, yet they were unable to drive the North Vietnamese back. Then the NVA brought in tanks. Though American jets knocked four tanks out of commission, the few that were left terrified the Neutralists, who then pulled back, allowing the communists to capture several Thai artillery batteries.

American advisors on the scene sensed the Lao were about to bolt and decided to evacuate the base before all discipline broke down and the NVA slaughtered everyone. Sixteen helicopters flew around-the-clock, ferrying the Lao and Thai to Long Cheng. Once the evacuation was complete, jets leveled the base to deny the enemy Moung Soui's nineteen 105-mm howitzers, eighty-four trucks, and vast stores of ammunition.[21]

The loss of Muong Soui left the communists in control of Route 7 as it leaves the Plain of Jars. In July, Vang Pao tried in vain to take back the prize. American planes blew up bunkers and ignited an ammunition dump, setting off massive secondary explosions. Hmong pilots strafed the enemy, pinning them down. On the ground, a Hmong force occupied the surrounding hills, waiting for a larger force of a thousand Neutralists to move in. However, the Neutralists abandoned the Hmong, leaving them isolated in the hills. The weather suddenly turned bad, reducing air support to a few sorties per day. With few planes in the air, the North Vietnamese went after the Hmong.

Hmong pilots braved the bad weather to save their comrades. Lue Ly was flying low over the enemy when a 12.7-mm antiaircraft gun zeroed in on his plane, raking it with bullets along one side. The T-28 burst into flames, flew several hundred yards and crashed, exploding into a ball of fire. The NVA gunner jumped up and down in jubilation. NVA soldiers stood tall in their trenches, shouting and clapping with joy. Their artillery had brought down the most famous pilot in Laos.

Vang Pao's American advisors had begged him to force Lue Ly to retire from combat. His value as a symbol and morale booster was too great to be squandered. The wing commander of the Air Commandos suggested Lue Ly be assigned to the flight school at Udorn to pass his skills on to new Hmong pilots and inspire them to greatness. Lue Ly would not hear of retiring from combat, and Vang Pao was too preoccupied with the pressures of war to lose such a valuable military asset. It was only after Lue Ly's plane plummeted to the ground like a fiery meteor that Vang Pao realized the wisdom of the advice he had ignored. His troops were instantly demoralized. Hmong in the refugee camps mourned as if they had lost a king. Vang Pao wept. Lue Ly was only his cousin, but it seemed he had lost a son.

Years after the war, on his mountain ranch in the Bitterroot mountains of Montana, Vang Pao's thoughts would sometimes fix on the dead pilot. Trudging along a mountain crest, rifle in hand, eyes scanning the horizon for elk, he would stop and peer down into a deep gorge. "There," he would say to his hunting companion, "down there." The other Hmong would move to the edge of the crest and peer into the gorge, expecting to see an elk. "Down there by the boulders," Vang Pao would explain. "Lue Ly could hit artillery there in on one pass." Vang Pao would trace an imaginary flight pattern in the air with his index finger. "That's how he'd get out. Like an eagle." His finger would continue to rise. "Right over the top of the mountain." Vang Pao's hand would drop to his side and for a moment he would stare into the sky as if he could actually see Lue Ly's T-28 droning toward Long Cheng.

Vang Pao put aside his military duties to officiate at Lue Ly's three-day funeral. A beautifully carved hardwood casket was on display. A photograph of Lue Ly rested on a pillow on top of the casket. Inside the coffin lay fragments of Lue Ly's helmet and a few pieces of bloody cloth from his flight suit. After hours of searching, it was all of him that could be found.

Top RLA generals attended the funeral. It was the first time most of them had ever seen Long Cheng. They were amazed by the size of the military base. Having followed the war in the newspapers, and through embassy and CIA briefings, it was for some their first realization of the true magnitude of the war being fought by the Hmong in their place.

KOU KIET

After the loss of Muong Soui, enemy traffic picked up on Routes 7 and 72. Vang Pao directed all air assaults against the two roads. Throughout July 1969, U.S. fighter-bombers ripped up sections of highway and blew up transport trucks. Then the weather turned bad and the air sorties fell off. The good news was that heavy rains halted the NVA's logistics.

Battalions from two NVA divisions were spread across the plain, from Muong Soui on the western edge all the way east to Phong Savan. A captured soldier revealed that the battalions had not received supplies for two months. Vang Pao decided to squeeze them harder by completely closing down Routes 7 and 72. In a pincer movement, two of his battalions moved from the north and south on Nong Pet, a town straddling Route 7 as it enters the plain. It was like corking a bottle. Nothing could get through. U.S. bombers resumed their assault on Routes 7 and 72, flying 145 sorties per day, hitting everything that moved. Within two weeks road watchers reported they could detect no traffic of any kind on either road.

By now, NVA on the plain had been without supplies for three months. Vang Pao gathered his forces and went out to engage them. He named the operation Kou Kiet (Redeem Honor). Wherever his soldiers struck, the enemy gave way and retreated. Some NVA units were out of ammunition, while others were too weak from starvation to put up a fight.

Four of the battalions from the NVA 312th Division were full of new recruits, many of them teenagers. Lacking battle experience, they stood in plain few and fired their rifles at American jets passing overhead, exposing themselves to rockets and bombs. Three of the battalions were totally destroyed. The fourth battalion, sensing its impending annihilation, retreated in a panic for its regimental headquarters. Hmong units relentlessly dogged the North Vietnamese, cutting them down from behind. Only three survivors reached the command post.[22]

Ravens from Long Cheng guided U.S. fighter-bombers to every enemy vehicle they could locate on the Plain of Jars. Some were moving away in retreat; others were out of fuel and had been abandoned. The twisted and charred hulks of more than three hundred armored vehicles, tanks, amphibious personnel carriers, and transport trucks lay scattered across the plain.

By early September Vang Pao had established control over half of the plain. He moved his battalions west and drove the North Vietnamese out of Muong Soui. He moved east and retook Xieng Khouangville. The former provincial capital had always had a special symbolic significance for Vang Pao. In his mind the town symbolized legitimate authority. Years earlier he could not imagine a greater gift for King Savang Vatthana than to deliver the town into his hands. Of course the place was now a ruins, but it was still emotionally gratifying to set foot on its soil, especially after discovering that the communists had been using the town as a storage depot for supplies destined for the plain. With all road traffic to the plain interdicted, supplies had piled up. Vang Pao took possession of 3 million rounds of ammunition, 150,000 gallons of gasoline, 12 tanks, 30 trucks, and 13 jeeps.[23]

With the NVA in retreat, Vang Pao wanted to inflict maximum damage. He requested a further relaxation of the rules of engagement, to enable American aircraft to assault the enemy's sanctuaries throughout MR II. The request came at the right time. The Nixon administration wanted the capacity to resume the bombing of North Vietnam. It was therefore necessary to keep pressure on the communists in northeastern Laos to deny them control of strategic areas where new radar might be installed. "What we do in Laos," Nixon proclaimed, "has . . . as its aim to bring about the conditions for progress toward peace in the entire Indochinese peninsula." The threat of renewed bombing was to be a bargaining chip for a peace settlement in Vietnam.[24]

The embassy reduced the protected border corridor from ten to five miles, opening up hundreds of enemy targets previously off-limits. Since communist supply lines had been cut at so many places, the exposed ammunition dumps were full of undelivered ordnance. Single bombs set off massive secondary explosions that lasted hours.

One Raven located what appeared to be a regimental headquarters, nestled in the heart of the previously off-limits corridor. He counted fifty-two buildings in the complex. Within a half-hour Thuds from Thailand were on the scene asking directions for strikes. The first Thud dropped several five-hundred-pound bombs. In the blink of an eye, an area the size of three football fields erupted in a massive chain reaction. The exploding bombs ignited rocket motors that shot off in all directions, creating an awesome fireworks display. The explosions continued sporadically for twenty-four hours.

While American air power ravaged the enemy's supply depots, Vang Pao set a trap for several NVA battalions moving off the plain. He airlifted four 155-mm cannons from Long Cheng and positioned them in the battalions' path. Vang Pao had the artillery shells set to explode sixty feet above the ground. Shrapnel from the shells ripped into the enemy's columns, killing hundreds.[25]

The Hmong continued to take more ground. By the end of the month, Vang Pao commanded all of the Plain of Jars. In many places the plain had become a mass graveyard. The dead were not all soldiers. The unrestricted bombing had killed hundreds, perhaps even thousands, of civilians. Every village and hamlet on the plain had been destroyed. Those who had survived the bombing were destitute. Vang Pao had troops forcibly eject them from the plain and place them in refugee camps. Hmong confiscated the villagers' livestock and looted their battered homes.[26] Modified to spray chemicals, C-123 transport planes crisscrossed the plain dumping defoliants on rice fields to deny the crops to the communists should they ever return. The bombing and spraying transformed the Plain of Jars into a wasteland. For the rest of the war it would remain uninhabited, functioning only as a battlefield.[27]

All that remained to complete Kou Kiet was to clear out isolated pockets of resistance. The cleanup would turn into some of the bloodiest fighting of the campaign.

During the NVA's retreat from Muong Soui, several North Vietnamese units fled south into the rugged grottoes of Phu Khe Mountain. Seng Vue commanded one of the Hmong companies sent in after them. Though he had been in uniform for six years, it was his first real combat experience.

Seng's native village was in Nam Tha Province, far from the war in MR II. Back in 1963, CIA agent William Young had showed up looking for Hmong volunteers for a new guerrilla network. It was mostly Young's idea, undertaken on his own initiative. Young did a lot of things on his own initiative. He had been with Momentum from the start, but didn't get along with one of the other agents at Padong. Before the training base fell to the communists, Young simply walked out of Padong without asking anyone's permission.

Bill Lair didn't discipline the wayward agent. He was too valuable to lose. Instead, he put him on a loose leash, allowing Young to select his own projects. For a while Young scouted out new Momentum sites, then in 1963 he decided to try his hand at organizing an extension of Momentum in Nam Tha. He would be working alone with the montagnards in the area, which was the way he liked it. Young felt at home with the montagnards. His grandfather had been a missionary in Burmese highlands and his father a CIA agent who worked with montagnards in southern China. Living and working with hill tribesmen was a family tradition.[28]

Seng Vue had signed up with Young for the money and for the chance to travel. Young sent Hmong volunteers to Thailand for eight months of training. Seng even spent a few weeks in Vientiane, a place he had only heard about. When Seng returned home, Young assigned him to a guerrilla base in the mountains. Thai PARU, sent by Lair, had joined Young by now. Young wanted things run his way. The Thais had their own ideas. As at Padong, Young just walked away. Lair replaced him with Lewis Ojibway, one of the few Native Americans in the agency.

Seng never saw much of Ojibway or the Thai PARU. His guerrilla base was in an isolated area. Nothing much ever happened. For six years his guerrilla team conducted uneventful patrols, received food and supplies, paid regular visits to their families, and drew their pay. It was an easy job, paid well, and was relatively safe. Then in 1969 a CIA agent showed up to inform Seng's team that the funding for their operation had been cut off and they were on their own.

The guerrilla squad disbanded, but Seng remained at the base with three other team members, hoping the CIA would return and put them all back on the payroll. Late one night NVA attacked the camp. The four Hmong were asleep in their hut on cots arranged side-by-side. The North Vietnamese rolled grenades under their beds. The grenades killed two of the ex-guerrillas, and badly wounded a third. The explosions lifted Seng several feet into the air, but miraculously inflicted only a small flesh wound on his right leg. He examined his cot the next morning. It showed a clear outline of his torso. Shrapnel had shredded every inch beyond the outline, yet somehow missed his body.

There were more NVA raids in the area. The communists were systematically going after all the Hmong communities. The place was no longer safe. Seng and about a hundred Hmong from Young's original network left with their families for Long Cheng. It took a month of hiking to get there. Desperate for troops, Vang Pao immediately formed Seng's band into a company and sent them to root out the NVA in Phu Khe's grottoes.

When Seng's company reached the mountain, they encountered bedraggled groups of Hmong soldiers returning from the grottoes. Their faces were grim. Many were wounded. Seng guided his company into a narrow canyon leading to a series of deep caves. A stream ran down the center of the ravine. Seng moved along the right bank. An hour later one of his men spotted NVA behind rocks, waiting in ambush.

Seng motioned for his men to withdraw. As the Hmong began to pull back, the NVA opened up on them. Within a few minutes half of the men in Seng's company were dead. Seng helped drag out the wounded. Bullets zinged overhead and ricocheted off the rocks. Once they were out of range and under cover, Seng collected the company's grenades and put them into a rucksack. He exchanged his M-16 for the company's only Browning Automatic Rifle (BAR), then ordered his men to carry the wounded down the mountain so they could be medevaced.

It took Seng two hours to scale the side of the canyon and reach the top. Loaded down with thirty pounds of fragmentation grenades and the weight of the sixteen-pound BAR tugging relentlessly at his thin arms, Seng walked the crest to get above the Vietnamese. He spotted the Vietnamese below. There were a dozen of them, hunkered down behind rocks. Two of the NVA manned a machine gun, probably the weapon that had killed so many of Seng's comrades.

Seng searched for a spot to brace his BAR. He took aim. The burst of the Browning had the other Vietnamese crouching down, peering over boulders to locate his position. Seng lobbed grenades onto them. Bullets from an AK-47 slammed into the side of the ravine only five feet from where he was crouched, the pulse of the impacts penetrating the soles of his boots. He angled the Browning to the right and returned fire. Seng saw one Vietnamese go down and then another one splashing up the stream toward the caves. Seng wounded the man in the water, took better aim and finished him off. There was an eerie silence. Seng looked long and hard for movement. After five minutes he tossed more grenades, spacing them out to cover a wide area. The explosions rumbled through the ravine. Still no movement.

Seng worked his way down to the stream, far below the scene of the firefight. He walked up the stream toward the Vietnamese, hoping to find all of them dead. One of the NVA leaped up, firing his AK-47 on automatic. A bullet ripped into Seng's right biceps. His BAR popped into the air. More bullets tore up the ground near Seng's feet. He turned and ran, then stumbled and fell into the stream. Seng struggled to get up and plowed downstream. He managed to get onto the bank. He ran, fell, then got up and ran some more. Several hours later a Hmong patrol discovered him two miles downstream, his body half submerged, unconscious from loss of blood.

While Seng was recuperating at the Ban Some hospital, his dead father visited him in a dream, dressed all in black with a scowl on his face. His father seemed as tall as a tree. "Leave this place," his father's voice boomed. "Or you will be like them." His father's hand pointed to the other patients in the ward. Seng stared in wonder at the wounded soldiers. In his dream tigers were playing with them, batting them around between their paws as though they were rabbits. The next morning Seng thought hard about the dream. When he was released from the hospital, he deserted the army and returned to Nam Tha.[29]

CELEBRATION

Kou Kiet had exceeded everyone's expectations. The Hmong had completely routed two NVA divisions and now controlled all of the Plain of Jars. It was the secret army's greatest victory of the war. America's new ambassador to Laos, McMurtrie Godley, was overjoyed.

Godley had taken over the helm as ambassador in June. His previous post was as ambassador to the Congo (later renamed Zaire and recently changed back to Congo) where he had worked hand-in-glove with the CIA to put down the Simbas, a communist-backed revolutionary group attempting to overthrow the government. Because of Godley's close association with the

CIA, Washington considered him the ideal choice to replace Sullivan. The CIA agreed. Unlike Sullivan, who tried to oversee every aspect of paramilitary operations in Laos, in the Congo Godley had delegated tactical decisions to subordinates and allowed CIA officers to manage things as they saw fit. The hope was that Godley would bring the same management style to Laos. With this in mind, Washington permitted Godley to bring two top individuals (Lawrence Devlin and Charles Mann) in his Congo team to Laos. Devlin became the CIA's Vientiane station chief and Mann assumed the top position in USAID; collectively, the three would come to be known as the Congo Mafia.[30]

The new ambassador did not disappoint the CIA's expectations. Trusting the advice he received from CIA agents in the field, he had put everything into Kou Kiet and it had paid off. Godley organized a media event at Sam Thong where Vang Pao displayed North Vietnamese prisoners to reporters. The ambassador proudly announced to the press that "we believe that the damage to the enemy represents the best results per sortie by tactical air in Southeast Asia,"[31] and that Kou Kiet was the "first major victory in the history of the Royal Government."[32] Godley did not bother to explain that the actual fighting was done by a secret CIA paramilitary force of Hmong guerrillas, rather than by regular troops from the RLA whose officers routinely pocketed an estimated 20 percent of their troops' pay, used RLAF transport planes to traffic drugs, and fought mock battles discharging countless rounds of artillery shells to get the brass casings which they sold on the black market.[33] What Godley knew, but dared not tell the reporters, was that if it were not for the Hmong, the nation would fall to the communists in a fortnight.

11

LONG CHENG
BESIEGED

K ou Kiet was a severe setback for the communists. Vo Nguyen Giap, commanding general of the NVA, suddenly took a personal interest in the war in MR II. He wanted a decisive victory and settled on General Vu Lap to do the job. Vu Lap was an uneducated highland T'ai from the Sip Song who had risen through the ranks by distinguishing himself in battle. Tough and determined, he had nine years experience in organizing operations for MR II. Giap gave Vu Lap the 312th and 316th Divisions, an independent armored regiment, and four battalions of Dac Cong. They were the ingredients for the sort of blitzkrieg used against the Americans during Tet: a combined offensive with armor, infantry, heavy artillery, and Dac Cong.[1]

The entire force plunged across the border in early November 1969, heading for the Plain of Jars. The 316th Division traveled Route 7, while the 312th Division used Route 72. Saturation bombing would have slowed their advance, but not without slaughtering Hmong units near both roads who were occupying territory won during Kou Kiet. Within a week the 316th Division slammed into Nong Pet, the cork in the bottle blocking access to the Plain of Jars. Nong Pet fell, then was retaken with heavy casualties by four Hmong battalions. Farther south on Route 72, a regiment from the 312th Division attacked Xieng Khouangville. The lone Hmong battalion defending the town held out for eight days before retreating. After receiving reinforcements, it charged back to retake the town. Again Hmong casualties were high.

The two NVA divisions continued their drive for the plain. When the weather was good and air support possible, the enemy suffered. Huge bombs, each weighing as much as a small automobile, annihilated Dac Cong assaulting Phu Nok Kok. Will "Black Lion" Green was back on the mountain, commanding Khmu volunteers who had replaced his Hmong. To inflict maximum damage on the enemy, Green directed air strikes almost on top of his own men. Elsewhere, Skyraiders and Phantoms flew as many as five hundred sorties per day, bombing and strafing advancing troops.

Had the skies remained clear, the two NVA divisions might have been decimated, but the weather was erratic. For weeks at a stretch the skies were heavily overcast, reducing or eliminating all air support and forcing the Hmong to hold territory by conventional trench warfare. It was the kind of fighting that favored the NVA. Vang Pao was running out of men and ammunition. Ambassador Godley denied his request for more bullets and ordered him to pull back his troops. Coming on the heels of Godley's glowing tribute to Kou Kiet, the call to retreat left Vang Pao mystified.

Godley was only following orders. The U.S. had begun withdrawing troops from Vietnam. It was the first step in the Nixon administration's "Vietnamization" of the war: turning more of the fighting over to the South Vietnamese and restricting America's role to air support. It was a move calculated to silence war protesters and convince the American public that Washington was serious about ending the war in Southeast Asia. If fighting in Laos were to suddenly heat up and become public, the desired perception that America was at last disengaging would be compromised.

The Senate Committee on Foreign Relations was already holding closed hearings on Laos. The principal witness was William Sullivan, former Ambassador to Laos and now Deputy Assistant Secretary of State. Several senators on the committee were openly critical of Nixon's handling of the Vietnam War. Under their prodding Sullivan revealed the full of extent of American involvement in Laos: the role of the CIA, the secret Hmong army, the massive military base at Long Cheng, and the routine use of American air power to support the Hmong.[2]

The White House feared Sullivan's testimony would be leaked by hostile senators, especially if they believed America was actually widening the war in Indochina. Recent articles in the *New York Times* about Kou Kiet had accurately estimated Vang Pao's Hmong army at about forty thousand and charged that the CIA was its principal sponsor.[3] New reports of major battles on the plain would not serve the administration's interest in giving Laos a low profile.

To set a new tone, Henry Kissinger conceptualized the NVA's MR II offensive as merely an attempt to reestablish the status quo ante, aimed only at preventing Laotian forces from gaining the upper hand. Under this reading, Vang Pao's effort to deny the North Vietnamese reentry onto the plain was unnecessarily provocative.[4]

As Vang Pao was not privy to these considerations, he naturally wondered if the Americans "really wanted to help us win a war against North Vietnam, or if they had something else in their head."[5] Running out of ammunition and under orders to withdraw, he fought in retreat, holding key positions only when they offered a chance to inflict heavy damage on the enemy.[6]

THE SECRET WAR BECOMES BIG NEWS

By mid-February 1970, the NVA occupied most of the Plain of Jars and had established a divisional headquarters on its eastern edge. From the plain the enemy probed south, east, and west, testing Vang Pao's defenses. In a daring night raid, a Dac Cong squad infiltrated Long Cheng and blew up two T-28s and one of the Ravens' Cessnas. Farther east, NVA tanks pushed into Xieng Khouangville and routed the town's garrison, recently invested with new troops, most of them Hmong teenagers with little training and no battle experience. A week later the communists took Muong Soui, giving them control of Route 7 as it leaves the plain. There was nothing to prevent the North Vietnamese from moving on to Vientiane.[7]

Godley made an urgent request to Washington for B-52 strikes against an NVA force of four thousand, moving out of Muong Soui toward the capital. Kissinger decided the North Vietnamese had ungraciously violated what he had earlier described as an "uneasy equilibrium," and advised Nixon to authorize the use of B-52s.

On the evening of February 17th, American Stratofortresses flew thirty-six sorties against the North Vietnamese, dropping 1,078 tons of bombs on troops south of Muong Soui and on the NVA's divisional headquarters on the eastern edge of the plain.[8]

The B-52s flew so high the North Vietnamese were never aware of their presence. To those on the receiving end, the explosions seemed spontaneous, as if the earth had erupted on its own in a thousand places. The night sky was ablaze with secondary explosions. Though the figures were never confirmed, the Air Force estimated that the bombing raids resulted in hundreds of enemy casualties. For several days after the air raid North Vietnamese troops did not venture anywhere on the plain.

A member of the embassy staff leaked information about the air raids to the press. Two days later a report on the use of the B-52s appeared in the *New York Times*, portraying the bombing as a major escalation of the Laotian conflict. The secret war was suddenly big news. More than a hundred war correspondents working in Saigon left for Vientiane to discover the truth for themselves.

In an exercise in damage control, the embassy conducted a guided tour away from the fighting, first herding the reporters south to Pakse and then north to Luang Prabang to take in the local culture. It was not long before the correspondents tired of pagodas and Buddhist shrines and demanded to be taken near the front, especially since Kissinger had recently been quoted saying that the U.S. might consider committing ground forces to Laos if North Vietnamese troops advanced farther south toward the capital.[9] The reporters wanted to see evidence of the NVA offensive, witness the devastation, encounter fleeing Laotian troops, and take a few snapshots of the dead and wounded.

As a compromise, the embassy took the correspondents to Sam Thong so they could at least dateline their dispatches from the Plain of Jars. They were introduced to Edgar Buell, who showed them the refugee camp's hospital and schools and delivered a talk on the enormous scope of the refugee relief program funded by American taxpayers.

Buell gave the same tour to visiting congressmen, who were never allowed to see Long Cheng. The only exception occurred in mid-1967, when Sam Thong's airfield was undergoing repairs. A USAID pilot flew two congressmen to Long Cheng, where CIA operatives in sunglasses put the dignitaries into a helicopter and delivered them to Sam Thong. The congressmen never realized that they had briefly visited the headquarters of the CIA's secret army.[10]

Buell's tour was a huge disappointment. There was no evidence of real fighting anywhere. Three reporters decided to do some exploring on their own, and set out on foot up a road deeply rutted with tire tracks. A footpath ran along the road's edge, worn into a trench from constant use. The reporters were certain the road led someplace important. It would have been a long walk if a Hmong soldier in a jeep hadn't come along and given them a lift to Long Cheng. He presumed they were CIA.

Once the jeep entered the huge military base the reporters had their cameras out, clicking away. They took snapshots of everything: the planes on the runway, lines of military vehicles, the sprawling communications complex, American pilots and military advisors, and thousands of soldiers. A CIA officer discovered the reporters, confiscated their cameras, and informed them that someone from the embassy would be along shortly to fly them to Vientiane.

Vang Pao was furious at the breach of security. He decided the reporters were no better than enemy spies. He suggested putting them in a jeep and blowing it up. The whole thing could be blamed on enemy artillery. Vang Pao's CIA case officer pointed out that should any harm come to the correspondents, who were citizens of three foreign countries (the United States, France, and Britain), the entire press corps would become his enemy. Vang Pao finally gave in and allowed the reporters to go to Vientiane, minus their film and notes.[11]

A few days later, the first of several articles on Long Cheng appeared in the *Bangkok Post*.[12] The stories were picked up by the wire services and appeared in the *New York Times* and *Washington Post*, providing for the first time a glimpse of the true extent of America's involvement in the Laotian war. The articles told of the legions of reconnaissance planes and helicopters stationed at the base, the fighter-bombers taking off and landing every minute, the flight crews in U.S. Air Force uniforms in plain view, the extensive housing for American personnel, easily identifiable by the air conditioners hanging out of windows, and of the CIA's massive communications complex.

The press pressured Nixon for more information about the extent of America's involvement in Laos. Nixon remained evasive until someone leaked portions of William Sullivan's testimony before the Senate Foreign Relations Committee. Bit by bit, reporters began piecing together the full scope of America's involvement in the war. On March 8, 1970, Nixon finally admitted that two hundred Americans had been killed in action in Laos and another two hundred were missing.[13]

SAM THONG FALLS

Had the touring reporters remained at Sam Thong, they would have had their taste of war. Only a month after their visit the NVA 148th regiment attacked the refugee camp. Just a week earlier, the communists had been moving in force off the plain, closing on Long Cheng. It was what Vang Pao had feared most. He had already deployed nearly his entire army just south of the plain, distributed in a wide crescent to block an NVA advance. When the weather permitted, American fighter-bombers, along with AC-47 and AC-130 gunships, attacked NVA troops on the edge of the plain. At night, other aircraft seeded the area with anti-personnel mines. The air support only slowed the advance.[14]

In the second week of March the communists slipped around Vang Pao's forward positions and moved into Tha Tham Bleung, a long valley north of Long Cheng. Then, in a surprise move, instead of attacking Long Cheng the communists went after Sam Thong. As the attack was completely unexpected, the camp was poorly defended. Facing a full NVA regiment were only two hundred soldiers on loan from Long Cheng, plus fifty local militia, all schoolteachers.

Only six miles away, Long Cheng's 105-mm howitzers were manned and ready to fire rounds at the NVA regiment, but no one at Sam Thong had the training to call them in. Of the few shells fired in desperation, one hit the camp and the others missed the enemy. Hmong pilots flying out of Long Cheng encountered the same problem. No one on the ground knew how to direct the T-28s to targets.

By late morning, the non-ambulatory patients at the camp's hospital had already been airlifted south. American aid workers were also gone. Many of Sam Thong's forty-two thousand residents were on the road. The rest soon joined them. By dusk, the camp was empty. The NVA 148 Regiment moved onto the base, looted warehouses containing food, clothing, and medical supplies, and then blew them up. The camp's schools and hospital were the next targets. By evening, homes and shops were ablaze. After occupying the camp for several days and seeing that there would be no immediate attempt by Vang Pao's troops to retake Sam Thong, the 148 Regiment left a token force and pulled back to Tha Tham Bleung.

LONG CHENG EVACUATED

No one doubted the enemy would soon march on Long Cheng. Vang Pao fell into one of his dark moods. There was a confrontation with clan elders. In his depressed states Vang Pao admitted that the war seemed lost. The elders demanded that the entire Hmong refugee population and all military dependents be evacuated to someplace safe, preferably Sayaboury. Elders shouted in Vang Pao's face, an act of defiance unimaginable only a few years earlier.

Sensing his leadership over the Hmong slipping away, Vang Pao suddenly turned paranoid. He imagined that clan chieftains were secretly meeting, planning an exodus on their own, and that top RLA generals in Vientiane were hatching plots to bring him down. He ordered antiaircraft guns readied so he could shoot down the T-28s that he was certain would soon arrive from Wat Tay to finish him off.[15] Of course the planes never arrived.

Vang Pao's paranoia finally lifted, and with a clear head he pondered his options. One thing was obvious; if the communists overran Long Cheng, tens of thousands of Hmong, both soldiers and civilians, could perish. Vang Pao flew to Vientiane to meet with Souvanna Phouma to request that more than one hundred thousand Hmong be moved from MR II to Sayaboury.[16] Souvanna Phouma was dead set against the idea. The prime minister saw the Hmong refugees as a protective buffer against a North Vietnamese move on the capital. Defending their families, Hmong soldiers would likely fight to the last man.

Thousands of Hmong had already moved into Vientiane and Sayaboury provinces on their own initiative.[17] USAID helped them adapt to lowland farming. The Hmong in Sayaboury received the material and equipment for an irrigation system, which transformed the Hmong settlement in the Nam Hia region into a prosperous farming district. By 1970, Sayaboury Hmong were selling their surplus rice, pineapples, and sugarcane to wholesalers from as far away as Luang Prabang.[18]

The American embassy viewed the migration of Hmong to these western provinces with alarm. In a report to the State Department, the embassy warned that if the migration accelerated, it would be "impossible for Vang Pao to prevent his troops from joining their dependents in a mass exodus from MR II."[19] There would then be nothing standing between the NVA and Vientiane.

Despite Souvanna Phouma's opposition, Vang Pao began organizing for a massive airlift of civilians anyway, at least giving the appearance that he had some plan to save his people. Meanwhile he explored other options. In secret he made contact with the Pathet Lao (his older brother commanded a Pathet Lao unit), offering to go over to their side if they allowed him to rule over Xieng Khouang as a semi-autonomous Hmong region. The Pathet Lao were not interested.[20]

Backed into a corner, Vang Pao went ahead with the mass evacuation, emptying Long Cheng of all civilians. They didn't go to Sayaboury, however, but to the Vientiane plain on the southwestern edge of MR II, theoretically still part of the theater of war. It was a stopgap measure to appease clan elders without actually making the fateful decision to evacuate everyone to Sayaboury or Thailand, a move that could trigger mass desertions now that the military situation seemed hopeless.

BATTLE FOR SKYLINE

With the civilians gone, Vang Pao turned his attention to the defense of Long Cheng. There was only a skeleton force at the military base. The majority of his troops were still in forward positions on the edge of the Plain of Jars. Making do with what he had on hand, Vang Pao used raw recruits still in training to establish defensive positions on Skyline Ridge, the name the CIA had given to the continuous line of limestone crests protecting Long Cheng's northern flank (see map "Siege of Long Cheng"). The green troops would never hold back a determined squad of Dac Cong, let alone a mass assault. Fearing the worst, CIA officers hauled boxes of sensitive documents from their office complex and began burning them in empty gas drums.

Vang Pao made a desperate appeal to the RLA general staff for reinforcements from the regular army. As usual, the request fell on deaf ears. The only things offered were more uniforms and boots. Only one RLA commander, General Phasouk Somly Rasphakdi from MR IV, volunteered troops. Phasouk had earlier loaned Vang Pao units for the Kou Kiet offensive (the only RLA general to do so) and at the beginning of the campaign, when no one imagined it had much chance of success. Unlike most RLA generals, Phasouk was an ardent exponent of paramilitary warfare. Between 1963 and 1967, he had run his own guerrilla program, supported by the CIA, in Wapikhanthong Province in the far south. At its inception it had been a lean, efficient operation like Momentum, and had made Phasouk a believer in paramilitary operations. Kou Kiet not only reaffirmed Phasouk's faith in paramilitary campaigns, it briefly placed him in the limelight with Vang Pao.[21]

Phasouk airlifted a full battalion to Long Cheng to help defend the base. Other troops also began to arrive. The CIA had scrounged together six hundred guerrillas from its various paramilitary programs across the country and choppered them in. With direct approval from the White House, Thailand contributed two battalions of mercenaries commanded by officers from its regular army.[22] By March 20, Hmong units were returning from their forward positions. Long Cheng was filling up with soldiers. Vang Pao's depression lifted.

For weeks there had been sightings of enemy units near the base. At the end of the month the first NVA pushed onto Skyline and fired rockets into Long Cheng. As soon as they were driven off, other NVA units took their place. The battle for Skyline dragged on for days. Enemy artillery set up several miles away battered the military base. Sappers infiltrated Long Cheng and set up a mortar. Alert Hmong killed them before they could lob a single shell. Seven women were among the dead, evidence that the North Vietnamese were using desperate measures to fill their ranks.[23]

The Thai "B-Team" flying out of Muong Kassy went after the communists on Skyline. It was the burning season and a thick haze limited visibility. Fighter-bombers from Thailand encountered the same conditions. Few bombs hit the enemy. Suddenly the wind picked up and the skies cleared. Long Cheng's Ravens were immediately in the air, directing air strikes by T-28s from Vientiane and Muong Kassy and fighter-bombers from Thailand. The jets flew 186 sorties, pounding the crests with five-hundred-pound bombs. The main force of NVA finally abandoned the ridge.

To take advantage of the clear skies while they lasted, Vang Pao asked for another air assault, this time against the NVA at Sam Thong. The U.S. Air Force sent a C-130 carrying a single weapon, a giant steel drum packed with highly explosive chemicals. It was the first use of a BLU-82 bomb in Laos. The huge bomb detonated three feet above the ground. The effect was like that of a small nuclear explosion. The blast leveled hills a quarter of a mile away. All NVA within a five-hundred-yard radius of the explosion died instantly.[24]

Hmong farmers set dramatic fires to clear new fields, Laos. 1970.

The North Vietnamese made one last try for Skyline Ridge. A squad of Dac Cong secured a foothold and refused to budge, beating back both Hmong and Thai units. Tony Poe, recently arrived from Nam Yu with a battalion of Yao montagnards, volunteered his guerrillas for the job. The Yao cleared the crest within a few hours. It was a moment of triumph for Poe. Like Bill Lair, he was a proponent of no-frills guerrilla warfare. Poe didn't like the way Vang Pao trained troops or ran operations, which is why he had been transferred to Nam Yu. Now Poe felt vindicated. The troops he trained personally had outperformed Vang Pao's Hmong.

Poe's triumph was short-lived. Vang Pao transferred the Yao to Sam Thong, where they joined Hmong troops charged with the responsibility of keeping the ruined camp out of enemy hands. Thrown together in close quarters, the Yao and Hmong squabbled. The Yao took up arms and drove the Hmong out of Sam Thong. Poe rushed to Sam Thong to put down the mutiny, but the Yao had their blood up and Poe had difficulty getting them under control. Without discipline, they were useless as a fighting force. Poe finally disarmed the entire battalion and returned the Yao to Nam Yu. The episode was a great embarrassment that erased Poe's brief moment of glory on Skyline Ridge.[25]

BOUAM LONG UNDER SIEGE

Having failed to take Skyline, General Vu Lap began consolidating his forces in preparation for his next dry season campaign. Engineers started work on a road from Tha Tham Bleung valley to Sam Thong. Several NVA battalions moved onto nearby mountains (Phu Long Mat, Zebra Ridge, and Phu Phasai) to secure ground for heavy artillery.

The North Vietnamese on the mountains worried Vang Pao the most. Heavy artillery could tear Long Cheng apart. Vang Pao now had three additional battalions on loan from General Phasouk. He sent two of them against the NVA on Phu Phasai and the third, under the command of CIA agent Will Green, against the North Vietnamese on Zebra Ridge. Within a week, the battalions cleared the NVA off Phasai and Zebra. Will Green marched his troops farther north to Phu Long Mat. By the end of the month, it too was cleared of NVA.[26]

Vu Lap did not launch a counteroffensive. The monsoons were only a month away. Remembering Kou Kiet, he worried about becoming overextended. His plan was to withdraw his main force to North Vietnam for rest and refitting, leaving behind several regiments assigned to two limited objectives. One was to maintain a presence at Tha Tham Bleung. The other was to assault Bouam Long, Vang Pao's last remaining post north of the Plain of Jars.

Cher Pao Moua, Vang Pao's father-in-law, commanded the garrison at Bouam Long. The communists had been trying to capture the base for years. It was a formidable undertaking. Bouam Long was a plateau atop a rugged mountain jutting above dozens of smaller mountains. The same forces of nature that had worked Long Cheng into a place of natural beauty had transformed Bouam Long into a grotesque Gothic landscape. There were sheer cliffs riddled with dark caves and twisted and jagged crags that, from a distance, gave the appearance of gargoyles—devilish creatures and wild beasts. Rock spires rose like castle turrets, and along the edge of the plateau were deep moat-like crevasses. To approach Bouam Long, the enemy had to negotiate the rugged mountains ringing the base, then move up the steep rise leading to the plateau. The Hmong laced the crevasses with concertina wire and claymore mines to tear apart NVA who fell in and the CIA sprayed defoliants around the base's perimeter, denying the NVA cover. The North Vietnamese were out in the open when they advanced, and in the rifle sights of Hmong guerrillas hunkered down in the extensive network of concentric rings of trenches girding the plateau.

Cher Pao Moua's guerrillas had already beaten back an assault in February. Now they faced a full regiment. The assaults continued into May, with the North Vietnamese hammering the base with heavy artillery. Bouam Long's defenders went underground, as they had many times before, in deep bunkers constructed over the years. During the artillery barrage the Dac Cong tunneled like gophers into the base's trenchworks, catching the Hmong by surprise and killing dozens in the outermost trenches before being driven off. It was the last time the North Vietnamese would get so close.

Vang Pao sent Cher Pao Moua reinforcements, three battalions choppered in from Long Cheng. There were already six thousand civilians at Bouam Long. The addition of a thousand

troops made for cramped quarters. The smell of decaying Vietnamese, hundreds of them scattered across the rise to the plateau,
only increased the level of discomfort. Toward the end of the month
helicopters delivered yet another battalion, an elite RLA commando
group fresh from special training in Thailand. Vang Pao put the
commandos to the test by having them push out from Bouam Long
to engage the NVA. Supported by T-28s and AC-130 gunships,
the commandos dislodged the North Vietnamese from several
nearby mountains. The aggressive maneuver broke the back of the
NVA's offensive. Exhausted and dispirited, the North Vietnamese
slowly retreated back to their regimental headquarters on the Plain
of Jars.[27]

DEFENSIVE CRESCENT

With a lull in the fighting, Vang Pao concentrated on strength-
ening his positions on the three mountains north of Long Cheng:
Phu Phasai, Zebra Ridge, and Phu Long Mat. Another of Poe's
guerrilla battalions, this one made up of Lu montagnards, arrived
as replacements for Poe's disgraced Yao. Vang Pao put them on
Phu Long Mat. The NVA assaulted the Lu before they had time
to settle in. When their commander was killed in the fighting, the
Lu deserted the mountain and marched to Sam Thong, demanding to be returned to Nam Yu. Vang Pao radioed Poe to come and
get his troops.

For a second time Poe had to disarm guerrillas he had personally trained and return them home.[28] The humiliation was especially
galling because his tour of duty in Laos was near its end (he was
scheduled for transfer to Thailand). Poe had accomplished a great
deal. He had laid the groundwork for dozens of Momentum sites
and personally trained the troops that seized Sam Neua City from
the Pathet Lao in 1963, the campaign that earned Vang Pao his
general's star. And there was Poe's act of heroism in 1965. Critically wounded in the hip, he had forced a helicopter pilot to hold
off flying him to a hospital in order to rescue Hmong at Hong
Nong about to be overrun by NVA. Now all of these things would
likely be crowded out in the memories of those whose respect Poe
desired and replaced by the two mutinies at Sam Thong.

To replace Poe's Lu guerrillas, Vang Pao received five new battalions from Thailand, again all mercenaries. The Thai volunteers fought hard when defending a position but were timid about taking ground from the enemy. Vang Pao positioned them as stationary forces with artillery on Skyline Ridge, Zebra Ridge, Phu Long Mat, and later on Ban Na close to the Plain of Jars. For offensive operations he would still have to depend on his Hmong, and they were in short supply. A recent recruitment drive netted only a few hundred Hmong volunteers, most of them young teenagers, some just twelve. After basic training at Muong Cha, the recruits went to Thailand for advanced training. Their American instructors lined them up, checked their height, and began asking ages. Unwilling to send children into battle, the instructors excused the twelve-year-olds from the program and sent them home.

For the rest of the rainy season Vang Pao probed enemy positions and established blocking forces. Hmong venturing east toward Nong Pet met little opposition, but those moving onto the Plain of Jars encountered large NVA units and were forced to retreat. South of the plain the Hmong retook Ban Na, and to the west wrested Muong Soui away from the enemy. Vang Pao sent a regiment into Tha Tham Bleung Valley, forcing the NVA there to retreat to the plain. Another Hmong regiment set up camp south of Muong Soui to bar the NVA's path to Vientiane, and a third regiment moved into position close to Padong, guarding the eastern approach to Long Cheng. The deployment was a variant of the wide defensive crescent established a year earlier, but with fewer positions and larger units.

1971 NVA OFFENSIVE

Vu Lap began his 1971 dry season offensive in February, attacking Muong Soui, Ban Na, Phu Long Mat, Zebra Ridge, and Tha Tham Bleung Valley. Muong Soui fell, as did Ban Na, but the other positions held. The enemy returned to assault Tha Tham Bleung a second time. As the two forces clashed, Dac Cong slipped through the valley and headed for Long Cheng. On the 11th of February they pushed onto Skyline Ridge. A Dac Cong team on the western edge of the ridge launched rockets into the military base. A second team on the eastern edge set up a recoilless cannon and began its own barrage. NVA heavy artillery positioned a few miles north of Long Cheng opened up, adding their shells to the mix.

As with the NVA assault on Long Cheng the previous year, Vang Pao had made the mistake of deploying nearly all of his forces north as a protective screen, leaving Long Cheng itself undefended. With insufficient troops on hand to dislodge the Dac Cong from Skyline, he requested air strikes by U.S. fighter-bombers. No planes were available. Everything was going to Operation Lam Son.

Years of bombing the Ho Chi Minh Trail had slowed only marfinally the traffic of supplies and soldiers into South Vietnam. From 1965 on, there had been numerous recommendations from various quarters to deploy a large blocking force to enter Laos and park across the trail, cutting it once and for all. Finally, in late 1970, Westmoreland's replacement, Creighton Abrams, presented President Nixon with a plan to use ARVN (Army of the Republic of Vietnam) ground troops, backed by American air power, to push into Laos and cut the Ho Chi Minh Trail. The operation would be called Lam Son, after a famous battle in 917 A.D. in which Vietnamese forces defeated a superior Chinese army. Nixon authorized the operation. The launch date was February 8, 1971.

Several days into the operation, the ARVN force of sixteen thousand ran into thirty-six thousand NVA, including a tank regiment and an artillery regiment. It was a case of bad planning. ARVN was hopelessly outnumbered. Washington rushed to deploy all available air assets (B-52s from the Philippines, fighter-bombers from aircraft carriers, and jets from air bases in Thailand) to prevent the South Vietnamese troops from being completely annihilated.[29] Not a single plane could be spared to help Vang Pao. He was on his own.

On the night of February 14th, Valentine's Day, a Dac Cong unit slipped into Long Cheng with orders to capture a howitzer, depress its muzzle, and fire point blank into the base. The target was a cannon at the foot of the limestone karst known as King's Ridge. The Thai artillery unit manning the 105-mm howitzer fought to the last man. Once they realized they were about to be wiped out, they dropped a thermite grenade down the cannon's barrel. The Dac Cong had brought along a mortar in case they failed to capture the howitzer. After shelling nearby structures, they retreated back to Skyline.

The incident alarmed CIA agent Jerry Daniels. If sappers could move into Long Cheng at will, no one was safe. He asked Vang Pao to leave. Vang Pao balked at the idea until Daniels convinced him he would be of no use to his troops if he were killed or captured. Vang Pao climbed into a T-28 with Daniels and left for Udorn in Thailand.

The Ravens stationed at Long Cheng stayed behind close to their radio, hoping someone would respond to their plea for air support and free up some of the assets going to Lam Son and divert them to Long Cheng. Throughout the night the Ravens scanned the horizon to fix the positions of enemy artillery by watching for muzzle flashes. In the morning they were informed over their radio that two F-4 Phantoms from Udorn were on their way. The Ravens loaded a machine gun with tracer bullets. When the jets arrived, a Raven talked the pilots to their targets, telling them to follow the tracers to the artillery. The pilots misunderstood the order and followed the tracers to their source—the machine gun on the base.

The Ravens watched, horrified, as one of the Phantoms lobbed six cluster bombs onto their position. The bomb pods popped opened and spewed thousands of baseball-sized bomblets, each containing 250 ball bearings. The walls of buildings disintegrated. Entire structures collapsed, as if squashed by a giant foot. The Ravens were face down in the dirt, praying they would survive the maelstrom of searing metal. Incredibly, not one them was injured. The CBUs destroyed the CIA's living quarters, set off an ammunition dump, tore apart a rice storage shed, shredded a mess hall, and collapsed the radio station. The bombs also killed an entire team of sappers who had been closing in on the Ravens when the CBUs were dropped. The pilot's error had saved the Ravens' lives.[30]

With Vang Pao absent and only a few hundred troops on hand to defend the base, Long Cheng was ripe for the taking. Had Vu Lap made his final push, Long Cheng would have been his and the war likely won. But the NVA general held back. His hesitance remains a mystery. During the delay, the U.S. embassy pressured Vientiane to pull together a force of five thousand from the regular army and fly them to Long Cheng. Two weeks later Vu Lap pulled back his forces. Long Cheng was saved a second time.

Over the next month Vang Pao sent units against every NVA position north of Long Cheng, right up to the edge of the Plain of Jars. Two battalions reinforced Phu Long Mat and pushed north to clear NVA from all adjacent hills. Two Hmong regiments swept east from Long Cheng and pacified a fifteen-mile corridor. Recently mobilized ADC units forced a North Vietnamese battalion off of Phu Phasai. The remaining pockets of resistance were quickly neutralized by unrelenting air strikes.

There would be no more sapper attacks against the base, no barrages from heavy artillery, at least not until the next NVA dry season offensive. Vang Pao brought his family back to Long Cheng. Hmong civilians began to return. Within a few months Long Cheng's population was back to twenty thousand, not as large as before but enough to constitute a tentative vote of confidence in Vang Pao's ability to defend the base.

With the rainy season fast approaching, Vu Lap withdrew most of his troops to North Vietnam, leaving behind several regiments to hold the Plain of Jars, and an additional regiment to make another stab at Bouam Long. The siege of the garrison lasted two months. Cher Pao Moua now had radio beacons to guide in AC-47 and AC-130 gunships. The planes' Gatling guns and rapid-firing cannons kept the enemy at bay. Having suffered heavy casualties, at the end of April the NVA regiment abandoned Bouam Long and returned to the Plain of Jars.

NEW NVA ARTILLERY

Long Cheng received more battalions from Thailand, not mercenaries but elements of the regular Thai army, well-trained and as fearless as the Hmong. His confidence revived, Vang Pao was ready to go on the offensive. Four Hmong regiments were already assembled and ready to move. He sent three of them to the edge of the plain to test the waters. When they met with only weak resistance, Vang Pao suddenly had visions of another Kou Kiet. Using helicopter-borne assaults, he leapfrogged enemy positions on the plain and went after their supply lines. Hmong troops captured or destroyed eight hundred tons of war material, including huge stores of bagged rice, enough to feed the communists on the plain for three months.[31] Communist troops were spread across the Plain of Jars, immobilized by the bad weather and low on supplies.

Pat Landry managed to get approval for B-52 strikes. The high-flying bombers flew sorties against NVA base camps and ammunition depots. The bombs killed or wounded thousands, flattened nearly every habitable structure on the plain (there were few left), blew apart armored personnel carriers and Russian-made tanks, and turned supply depots into exploding infernos. By the end of September the plain was a scene of vast devastation.[32]

Even with all the bombing, the NVA still held fast to nearly half the plain. Hmong regiments were exhausted from months of fighting and their morale was low. In September, one of the regiments had retreated before an inferior force. Vang Pao realized it was time to end his rainy season offensive, but he planned to do so in a way that would cost the enemy dearly. Before sounding the retreat, he positioned Thai artillery teams along the plain's southern edge in an interlocking network of firepower. If NVA battalions attacked one firebase, they would be within firing range of the cannons of an adjacent firebase. Hmong regiments began a slow withdrawal from the plain, acting as bait to lure the enemy into the firing radius of the Thai cannons.

The NVA in northern Laos now had a new commander. Giap had replaced Vu Lap with General Le Trong Tan, one of the NVA's most brilliant tacticians. Le Trong was convinced that heavy artillery, long-range 130-mm cannons with the explosive power of the huge bombs carried by B-52s, was the key to taking Long Cheng. His plan was to use the revitalized 312 and 316 regiments, bolstered by seven thousand additional troops, to drive the Hmong off the plain and back to Long Cheng. He would then place the big 130s in hillside bunkers and caves to protect them from air assaults and well beyond the range of Long Cheng's smaller howitzers. After the 130s blew apart Long Cheng, his troops would storm the base and wipe it out.

Le Trong's army moved onto the plain in late November. In mid-December one of his divisions closed on three Hmong regiments. The Hmong were supposed to retreat in an orderly fashion to the firebases, then hold the North Vietnamese in position while

Thai artillery chewed up their ranks. But the NVA division was led by Soviet-made T-34 battle tanks, and the mechanical monsters terrified the Hmong. The regiments fled right past the firebases and off the Plain of Jars, leaving the Thai to fend for themselves. Vang Pao browbeat two battalions into returning to the plain to support the Thai. The Hmong held out against the tanks for only a single day, then ran.

Vang Pao's line collapsed almost overnight. The withering fire from the Thai artillery did not even slow the enemy's advance. The North Vietnamese accepted the casualties and went after the firebases with mass assaults, led by tanks. There were so many NVA around the firebases that it was impossible for resupply planes to land and off-load cargo. The planes began dropping supplies attached to impact chutes from seven thousand feet. Some of it reached the besieged Thai, but a good deal landed among the enemy.

The firebases were in constant radio communication with Long Cheng. One of them reported that NVA had breached their perimeter and were swarming over their bunkers. Then the base went off the air. Other bases reported tanks breaking through their outer concertina wire barricades. One by one the bases fell. A terrified Thai at one 105-mm battery got on the radio and screamed that tanks were inside the base, crushing bunkers filled with men. Suddenly his radio went dead.[33]

Vang Pao sent Hmong units south of the plain to locate Thai survivors and bring them back to Long Cheng. While the Hmong searched, B-52s conducted night raids on the captured firebases. For three days, F-4 Phantom jets from Thailand and Hmong pilots flying T-28s out of Long Cheng hit the area, trying to kill as many NVA as possible. The enemy's new commanding general, Le Trong, had anticipated the air support and placed 12.7 antiaircraft guns across the Plain of Jars. The guns downed one of the Phantoms. For the first time in the war, MIGs appeared over the plain to engage American jets. The MIGs shot down five Phantoms. NVA antiaircraft cannons downed two T-28s.

Meanwhile, reconnaissance photos showed large covered trailers moving along Route 7 toward the Plain of Jars. The trailers carried Le Trong's long-range artillery: sixteen 130-mm cannons, each with an effective range of eighteen miles. As Vang Pao's forces pulled back to Long Cheng, the North Vietnamese hauled the cannons toward the southern edge of the plain, where NVA construction crews were already locating caves and preparing deep bunkers to receive the huge artillery pieces.

THE SHELLS FALL

Vang Pao did not move out to engage the enemy. He had turned sullen. Refusing to talk to the CIA case officers at Long Cheng, he gave no orders and had no plans. Reports of his condition reached Pat Landry at Udorn. Landry and Hugh Tovar, the new Vientiane station chief, flew to Long Cheng to talk with Vang Pao. They discovered he wasn't there. He had gone to Phu Long Mat to stand on the mountain and brood. The two CIA men boarded a helicopter and flew to Phu Long Mat. They found Vang Pao in a hut with a blanket over his shoulders, huddled in front of a fire, nursing a cold. As Tovar recalled, "He wouldn't speak at first, but finally came around and unleashed on myself and Landry about the lack of air support, about his frustrations." Landry and Tovar said nothing, letting Vang Pao get it all out of his system. Finally Vang Pao was ready to talk, to survey the situation and explore his options.[34]

Vang Pao decided to make his stand on Skyline Ridge. Landry had construction crews, bulldozers, and building material airlifted to Long Cheng to create reinforced bunkers on Skyline's crests, and brought in more Thai troops to replace those lost on the plain. An entire RLA regiment arrived from Savannakhet, compliments of General Phasouk. Vang Pao assigned the Thai to the bunkers on Skyline and placed Hmong units at both ends of Long Cheng valley to defend against flanking attacks. Phasouk's regiment occupied Zebra Ridge. Hmong battalions took up positions between Zebra and Long Cheng to harass the North Vietnamese once they marched on Skyline.

Toward the end of the month a Hmong patrol discovered a NVA reconnaissance team hidden in the karst on the east end of Skyline. The Hmong engaged the NVA and killed them. The North Vietnamese were carrying binoculars, firing tables, and plotting boards. They had been mapping Long Cheng for Le Trong's long-range artillery.[35]

The first round from the NVA's 130-mm cannons hit Long Cheng on New Year's Eve, exploding near the Thai headquarters on the east end of the valley. The impact was thunderous. The shock wave from the explosion traveled all the way to the CIA's living quarters several hundred yards away. More rounds followed, ripping great chunks out of King's Ridge. There was a steady bombardment throughout the night, "one monster round after another." Radio operators got on the line to Vientiane, but had difficulty communicating. The sound of the explosions drowned out their voices. A few hours into the bombardment, Long Cheng's 105-mm howitzers began to reply. It was a futile gesture. No one knew the exact location of the 130s. Even if their positions were known, they were well out of range.[36]

In the first week of January 1972, twenty-four NVA battalions pushed through Tha Tham Bleung Valley toward Skyline, flicking aside the Hmong battalions positioned to block their advance. Soon, thousands of NVA were clawing their way up the north slope of Skyline. The Thai in their reinforced bunkers blasted the assault forces with their artillery and, after three days of nonstop fighting, drove them back. The NVA's 130s opened up again. Sappers infiltrated the base and blew up an ammunition dump. Two nights later another group of sappers got into the valley and fired rockets into the CIA headquarters, the radio station, and Vang Pao's residence.

The constant shelling from the 130s was tearing up the base. The twenty thousand Hmong civilians who had moved back to Long Cheng again departed. Most went to Ban Some, which had replaced Sam Thong as the principal center for Hmong war refugees. Vang Pao was desperate for the civilians to return. He needed them on the base as a sign of confidence in his ability to hold back the North Vietnamese. They would never return unless he eliminated the 130s.

Hmong pilots were flying every day, searching for the artillery so they could drop flares and give American jets clear targets for bombing runs. The pilots located only a handful of the cannons and only two of them were destroyed. Vang Pao tried another tactic. He began moving his own artillery emplacements and constantly shifted troop concentrations, forcing the enemy to reposition the 130s repeatedly to put them on target. The ploy slowed the pace of the enemy's artillery barrages.

During the lull, Hugh Tovar made the unprecedented decision to bring reporters to Long Cheng. Tovar wanted them to see that the "enemy around Long [Cheng] was all North Vietnamese." There were journalists from the *New York Times*, *Associated Press*, and *United Press International*, and television crews from the three major networks. The newsmen took a tour of Long Cheng, then boarded helicopters for Skyline Ridge. On the ridge they examined defensive posts, each with a parapet enclosed by a thick semicircular wall and a deep pit with openings to reinforced bunkers under ten feet of earth and rock. They saw craters from artillery rounds and the devastation of numerous battles.

Major Chanh Nosavan, one of Phasouk's officers on loan from Savannakhet, was on the ridge. Reporters approached him and asked for an interview. As Chanh spoke, rounds from heavy artillery began to slam into Skyline. Flying debris struck Chanh in the head. Blood gushed from the wound. While reporters dashed for cover, someone radioed the valley below for a helicopter to medevac Chanh. When it arrived, several terrified newsmen elbowed Chanh aside and leaped on board. Chanh had to wait for a later flight.[37]

Being constantly on the move and going without sleep had finally worn down Vang Pao's iron constitution. Spending every night in a damp bunker, he caught pneumonia. On a brief visit to Padong to check on a recruitment drive for more Hmong soldiers, he suddenly broke down and wept uncontrollably at the sight of war amputees and widows and Hmong boys carrying M-16s. His CIA advisors realized that he was on the verge of a physical and mental breakdown. They rushed him to the base hospital at Udorn and pumped him full of antibiotics. Within a week Vang Pao was back at Long Cheng, revitalized and in command, busy trying to hold things together.

Reports in American newspapers predicted the eminent fall of Long Cheng.[38] The articles reflected the assessment of U.S. military advisors, who urged Vang Pao to abandon the base and establish a defensive position farther south. Vang Pao ignored their advice, but Souvanna Phouma took it to heart. He ordered Vang Pao to pull back his troops to defend the capital. Vang Pao flew to Vientiane to assure the prime minister he could break the siege.

Souvanna disagreed, but was not in a position to dictate terms. The Hmong army was the nation's only effective fighting force. If Vang Pao insisted on remaining at Long Cheng as a condition for continuing the fight, the prime minister had no choice.

The CIA agents at Long Cheng had half-expected, or hoped, Vang Pao would pull out. Air America pilots would no longer land at the base; it was too dangerous. The runway was chewed up and one never knew when or where a big 130 round would hit. Any plane on the ground for a length of time became a certain target. The wreckage of blasted aircraft littered the sides of the airfield. Vang Pao's CIA advisors left the base every night and returned in the morning. Only Jerry Daniels, the roughneck Montanan, stayed behind. But once Vang Pao made it clear he intended to hold the line at Long Cheng, the CIA agents held a meeting and decided to give him their full support. They had hardened bunkers constructed on King's Ridge and moved in.

SKYLINE HOLDS AGAIN

In mid-January 1972, the North Vietnamese stepped up their mass assaults on Skyline and wiped out several Thai bunkers, giving the communists possession of Skyline's eastern crests. Vang Pao expected the enemy to storm the rest of Skyline, but nothing materialized. Several days passed and the enemy had still not undertaken any new offensive action. Suddenly Vang Pao realized the cause of the delay. They were waiting for reinforcements before their final push. He ordered reconnaissance patrols to fan out to locate approaching troops. A full NVA regiment was spotted only a mile south of Long Cheng, proceeding up a valley in close formation, unaware they had been sighted. Vang Pao trained all of the base's artillery onto the valley. The entire regiment was nearly wiped out.

Two days later B-52s droned high above, far out of sight of the engaged forces below, raining bombs on the North Vietnamese holding Skyline's eastern edge. Across the length of Skyline, NVA retreated off the slopes. Hmong in spotter planes tracked their withdrawal. One fleeing column entered a long basin known by local Hmong as the Valley of Bananas, a place densely forested with bamboo and banana trees. The retreating soldiers hacked furiously at the thick bamboo that had them trapped in the valley. Vang Pao sling-hauled artillery to a mountain overlooking the valley and trained the cannons on the NVA column. After the artillery assault, jets arrived from Thailand and bombed the trapped North Vietnamese. Vang Pao boarded a helicopter and flew to the valley to survey the damage. The basin was a wrack of bomb craters, shattered bamboo, and shredded banana trees. Among the wreckage lay the bodies of three thousand NVA soldiers.[39]

With their troop assaults on Skyline stalled, the North Vietnamese switched tactics and brought in tanks. The first tank assault was in daylight. American jets caught the armor out in the open and blew it up. Ten more tanks attacked, but this time at night. Most of the tanks were disabled by mines and rockets fired by Thai soldiers, but three of the tanks made it to the top of Skyline and shot into the valley before withdrawing.

Tanks terrified the Hmong. "With their turret hatches closed and no human drivers in sight, the tanks seemed like metal creatures that clanked and crawled along and spat fire from their snouts."[40] Unlike the Thai regulars who had trained in a conventional army with armor, the Hmong had little experience with armored vehicles and no training in how to deal with them. Usually when they spotted a tank they hid or ran away. There were exceptions.

Earlier, one Hmong had become an instant legend by single-handedly disabling a Soviet-made T-34 assault tank during the tank-led assaults that wiped out Thai firebases on the Plain of Jars. When the T-34 appeared, Cheng Ly's unit was down in a trench. The tank's cannon swiveled toward the Hmong and fired. It was a long round. Bullets from the tank's machine gun raked the trench line. A few Hmong leaped up and ran away while others, paralyzed with fear, lay flat on their face or curled up, knees to chest. The tank lumbered closer, its machine gun still firing.

Cheng Ly was as terrified as the rest and yet he was suddenly standing, a grenade in each hand, facing the tank. He rushed forward. Bullets tore into him. Cheng was hit in both thighs and above his right elbow. One of the bullets had passed through his left cheek and blown away part of his jaw. Cheng staggered forward and fell. The tank made for the trench, passing right by Cheng. He struggled up and lodged both grenades in the tank's steel tracks, then rolled away. When the grenades went off, the tank's left track buckled, then unraveled. Two Hmong rushed out of the trench and carried Cheng away. Cheng survived, permanently disfigured by the facial wound, but a hero—the only Hmong who had killed one of the NVA's metal monsters.[41]

At the end of the month, helicopters delivered eight more Thai battalions to Long Cheng. With the additional troops, Vang Pao began an operation to draw the NVA away from the base. The Thai took the place of the Hmong regiments guarding Long Cheng's eastern flank, freeing the Hmong to march north, while units from Bouam Long marched south, both forces heading for the Plain of Jars, giving the appearance of a campaign to retake the plain. The enemy fell for the deception and diverted eleven battalions from Long Cheng to meet the advance.

The diversion bought only two weeks of relative calm. On March 11, the 130s resumed firing, softening up Skyline in preparation for another major assault. By the end of the month the North Vietnamese had taken the highest point on Skyline and could not be moved. Intercepted NVA radio communications revealed the NVA were confident Long Cheng would soon fall. One Thai battalion after another clambered onto Skyline in an attempt to drive the NVA off the ridge. Hmong soldiers watched from the sidelines, for Vang Pao was now reluctant to commit them to meat-grinder battles. They were his only dependable units for offensive operations, and difficult to replace (nearly all military-age Hmong were either already in service, or dead). CIA agents at Long Cheng were also for conserving Hmong troops. As one of them put it, "I have always believed that the mission of the Vietnamese here is to destroy our Hmong force. Destroy them, and we're left with pretty damn few choices to defend this country. It makes sense to save the Hmong."[42]

The Thai committed to Skyline fought bravely. There were hundreds of battle deaths on both sides, but after two weeks the high ground still belonged to the enemy. Back at AB-1 at Udorn, Pat Landry had been trying to get air support, but nothing was available. Hanoi had committed twelve divisions to a major campaign in South Vietnam. The American military named it the "Easter Offensive." It was so large the only basis of comparison was the massive mobilization of Tet. Giap's aim was to destroy

South Vietnam's armies and capture so much territory that Nixon's Vietnamization policy would be deemed an utter failure, causing Nixon to lose all credibility with American voters and be voted out of office and replaced with a dove. All U.S. air assets were committed to preventing South Vietnamese forces from being annihilated, which they nearly were. Landry kept making his requests, however. Finally he got authorization for some B-52s to deliver heavy ordnance and AC-119 gunships for close support.

The planes arrived on April 10, 1972. To minimize damage to Long Cheng, the B-52s dropped their bombs on the northern face of Skyline. Once the B-52s finished their runs, the gunships moved in, sweeping the crests with their 7.63-mm mini-guns and Vulcan cannons. After the smoke cleared, Hmong commandos moved onto Skyline to root out the remaining North Vietnamese. They met with little resistance. The bombs and gunships had killed all but six of the NVA on the ridges.[43]

While the air sorties nullified the NVA's claim on Skyline, the Easter Offensive ended Le Trong's dry season campaign. Hanoi deprived him of half his troops by ordering the 312 Division to redeploy to Hue in South Vietnam, where ARVN marines were putting up an unexpectedly spirited defense. The 312 arrived too late to turn the tide of battle, but had it been there at the start, along with the 316 Division, things might have turned out differently. Hmong and Thai, plus an assortment of Lao battalions from MR IV, had tied up the two front-line NVA divisions for almost four months. In itself it was a considerable achievement. Given the fact that it may have altered the outcome in South Vietnam, it was a remarkable one.

THE ENEMY PULLS BACK

As Le Trong prepared to withdraw what was left of his army to North Vietnam, he unleashed one last 130 barrage. Since December 1971, Long Cheng had absorbed over eleven thousand artillery rounds, most of them from the 130s. The base's airstrip was scarred with the outlines of filled-in and repaired craters. The slopes of Long Cheng's southern ridges were ragged and gouged from hundreds of long rounds. Homes and shops lay in ruins. Nearly every military installation had been hit. Planes struck by incoming rounds lay among the junk piles of damaged equipment that had grown into hills at the bases of cliffs.

The new barrage was not as intense as others in the past, but it was unrelenting. An American film crew had asked permission to document the siege. Remarkably, the embassy gave its permission. The filmmakers captured the ruined base on film, showing the damage the 130 rounds had wrought. They interviewed Hmong and Thai soldiers and talked to some Ravens. The documentary later aired on American television, giving viewers their first look at the military headquarters of America's *armée clandestine*.[44]

With NVA troop activity winding down, Vang Pao had Hmong with field radios infiltrate enemy lines to locate the 130s and transmit their positions. For two weeks Phantom jets from Thailand went after the cannons, knocking out all but the few that were inside deep grottoes. Finally, laser-guided bombs were added to the jets' arsenal. The "smart bombs" penetrated the grottoes and found their mark.[45]

By now the NVA pullout was in full swing. Le Trong left behind four regiments to guard the plain and secure his two new divisional headquarters, one at Tha Tham Bleung Valley for the 312, the other on Phu Phasai for the 316. The plain, as well as both headquarters, would become targets of Vang Pao's rainy season offensive, but that was still four months away. At the moment Vang Pao had other worries. Long Cheng had survived another dry season offensive, but at enormous cost. Thousands of Hmong soldiers had died; their replacements were youngsters, who now made up 50 percent of Vang Pao's Hmong regiments. Clan elders again demanded a general evacuation to Sayaboury. Vang Pao was noncommittal. He needed to know more about America's plans for Southeast Asia. The Nixon administration was making overtures to Communist China and pulling troops out of Vietnam. Washington might abandon Laos, leaving the Hmong to face the NVA alone.

In secret, Vang Pao flew to the U.S. to meet with Edgar Buell. For the past two years Buell's health had deteriorated. He had a bout with malaria that had kept him bedridden in Vientiane and then he suffered a near-fatal heart attack. Buell had returned to America to recuperate. After a brief reunion, Vang Pao and Buell went to Washington D.C. They talked to politicians, people in the

Pentagon and at the CIA. It became clear that U.S. policymakers were making preparations to get out of Southeast Asia.[46]

Once back in Laos, Vang Pao went through the motions of organizing a rainy season offensive. The CIA rebuilt his military headquarters and Landry delivered thousands of additional Thai soldiers to Long Cheng. Vang Pao's troop strength was up to eleven regiments, but only three were Hmong. The rest were Thai regulars and Lao troops on loan from the RLA. In August, two Hmong regiments pushed onto the Plain of Jars. The regiments were mostly teenagers. Though they enjoyed heavy air support, the regiments buckled and retreated. Landry received reports from his agents assigned to the regiments that the old discipline and aggressiveness that had been the hallmark of Hmong guerrillas was no more. These were just kids and they wanted to go home.

Three months later the Hmong regiments were back on the plain, hugging its southern edge, backed by Thai artillery batteries. In the front line positions, Hmong commanders chose the smallest teenagers in their units for special duty. At night the boys occupied tiny caves, called spider holes, dug into forward slopes. When the enemy tried to sneak up the rises, the boys emerged from their holes and rolled grenades onto them. The kids took the brunt of every assault and were the first killed or wounded. CIA advisors on the scene with front-line units were discomfited by the practice. As one of them confessed, "I was always disconcerted when I saw young boys put into body bags in the early mornings or watched them, so terribly hurt but never crying, as they were put on board Air America helicopters."[47]

As NVA pressure on the regiments mounted, B-52s dropped their huge bombs on the enemy. The NVA pulled back. But when the weather turned bad and air support dropped off, the NVA returned to attack in force. There were Dac Cong and sappers and full battalions in tight formation, blowing whistles and beating drums. Thai artillery teams fired their cannons until the guns became too hot to handle. B-52s returned, but the NVA stayed so close to the Hmong that it was difficult to locate safe targets. Within a week, both Hmong regiments had suffered heavy casualties and were in full retreat.[48]

The NVA emerged from the plain and headed for Long Cheng. Even though they had seen little action, the Lao troops on loan began to desert in large numbers. Only the Thai held their ground. The communists advanced to within six miles of Long Cheng, dug in, and began moving in heavy artillery, preparing for their dry season offensive and another siege of Long Cheng.

The CIA concentrated its efforts on knocking out the artillery and interdicting the NVA's supply lines. Landry ordered up B-52s and fast-moving jets, but the enemy's artillery continued to blast Long Cheng and supplies kept getting through. Finally, Landry added F-111s to his arsenal of air power. The new fighter-bombers carried as much ordnance as an F-4 and F-105 combined (six tons of bombs) and possessed advanced communications that enabled them to fly in any weather and at night. The Air Force set up four radar beacons at Long Cheng to give the F-111s identifiable offset points for radar-guided bomb raids.

The new jets were lethal. One after another the NVA's 130s were hit with pinpoint accuracy. Once the F-111s began flying sorties over Bouam Long, the outpost's commander, Cher Pao Moua, reported back that the new jets were annihilating the enemy. He told Vang Pao he didn't need reinforcements, or any more howitzers, mines, or rockets; "just give Bouam Long the F-111s." The F-111s were extremely quiet, just a faint whoosh passing overhead. The North Vietnamese called them "whispering death," a tribute to their deadly efficiency. CIA agents responsible for battle-damage assessments of the air strikes concluded that if the war had gone on long enough the F-111s would have "destroyed every sizable North Vietnamese unit in MR II."[49]

THE U.S. PREPARES TO LEAVE

But the war did not continue, at least with American backing. While the F-111s were decimating the ranks of NVA in MR II, other planes were raining death on North Vietnam. The NVA's Easter Offensive had convinced Nixon that the Vietnamese would never come to the bargaining table unless compelled by overwhelming force. He told Kissinger, "I intend to stop at nothing to bring the enemy to his knees."[50] After consultations with the Pentagon, Nixon's plan was to block supplies to Hanoi's war machine by mining North Vietnam's principal port, Haiphong harbor, and then punish the North Vietnamese with a withering bombing campaign.

However, before proceeding Nixon wanted to be certain that these actions would not elicit dangerous reactions from China or the Soviet Union. Diplomatic feelers went out and the response was positive. The Soviets were anxious to advance détente and the Chinese desired closer relations with the West. Both communist superpowers promised to hold back and let America work its will.

After mines were dropped in Haiphong, the Soviets obligingly ceased all shipping to North Vietnam and even let Nixon know that he was welcome in Moscow. The Chinese were also accommodating. For three months after the mining of the harbor they refused to ship goods of any kind to North Vietnam and brought an end to all overland delivery of supplies to their communist neighbor. North Vietnam's lifeline was severed. NVA troops operating in South Vietnam were soon low on food and ammunition, forcing them to curtail military operations.[51]

Nixon's next move was to subject Hanoi to two massive bombing campaigns: Linebacker I and Linebacker II. Linebacker I lasted from April through October of 1972, delivering 155,548 tons of bombs that damaged every supply line to the south and destroyed nearly all fixed oil storage facilities and 70 percent of North Vietnam's electric power generating capacity. When Hanoi still showed no signs of interest in a negotiated settlement, Nixon unleashed Linebacker II.

The goal of the first bombing campaign was to wreck North Vietnam's war-making capacity. The object of Linebacker II was to destroy Hanoi's will to fight. It was to be a terror campaign pure and simple, and for the first time the U.S. would be able to monitor closely the reaction of the enemy. The CIA had developed a super-quiet helicopter that was virtually undetectable from the ground when flying at altitudes higher than a hundred feet. On December 6, 1972, eleven days before the launching of Linebacker II, the helicopter flew into North Vietnam and unloaded a team of specialists who put a tap on North Vietnam's major phone lines.[52]

As Linebacker II progressed, bombs tore Hanoi's rail yards apart and blew up storage facilities and anything else of any conceivable worth to the North Vietnamese within a ten-mile radius of Hanoi. American planes knocked the enemy's air force out of the sky. They destroyed all surface-to-air missile sites, leaving Hanoi utterly at the mercy of America's bombers. Because of the phone tap, Henry Kissinger had the upper hand at the ongoing negotiations in Paris. Whatever his North Vietnamese counterparts at the bargaining table may have avowed, Kissinger knew the real reactions to the bombing in Hanoi. And the truth was that the air campaign was wearing them down.

Nixon turned the screw tighter. B-52s attacked Hanoi nonstop in waves, night after night, making it impossible for the residents of the communist capital to sleep. The impact of the bombs shook plaster from the walls of homes miles away; the ground shook as though convulsing in an endless earthquake. Roofs of houses in suburbs caved in. The constant fear, coupled with the lack of sleep, induced a kind of psychosis. Following the air strikes, people wandered around, totally disoriented. American POWs in Hanoi's prison camps saw their guards cower against walls during the bombing, their cheeks ashen in the light of the fiery sky. "By day, interrogators and guards would inquire" about the POW's "needs solicitously."[53]

On December 28th, North Vietnam's leaders caved in. They were ready to go to the bargaining table.

12

A COMMUNIST LAOS

On January 27, 1973, America and North Vietnam signed a ceasefire agreement, bringing an official end to the war and enabling the U.S. to prepare for a complete withdrawal from Southeast Asia. Officials at the American embassy in Vientiane prodded Souvanna Phouma to seek a similar ceasefire agreement with the Pathet Lao and move toward forming a coalition government with the communists.

When Souvanna Phouma resisted the pressure, Henry Kissinger arrived in Vientiane in early February to set him straight. At a dinner party at the Prime Minister's villa, Kissinger listened patiently to Souvanna Phouma's appeal for the U.S. to keep pressure on the North Vietnamese to prevent them from taking over his tiny nation.[1] Despite Kissinger's pledge during his dinner speech that "we have not come all this way in order to betray our friends," he had no intention of reaffirming America's commitment to Laos. "His main purpose, as soon became apparent, was to inform the Laotians that U.S. military support was approaching its end and that unless they soon accepted whatever settlement was being offered by the [communists] in return for a ceasefire, they stood to lose everything."[2]

Kissinger later claimed he experienced "a pang of shame" for abandoning Laos,[3] but the truth is that as early as 1969 the Nixon administration had begun to lay the conceptual groundwork to enable the U.S. to quit Laos with a clear conscience. In closed Senate hearings, William Sullivan spoke for the State Department.

He explained that since the war in Laos was secret, the U.S. had no formal or written obligation either to Laos or the Hmong in Vang Pao's army. Sullivan went on to suggest that the Hmong in particular were owed no moral commitment because they were essentially opportunists: "They have seen lots of white faces, lots of round eyes, and I don't believe that their attitudes in dealing with us are disposed upon matters of sentiment or moral obligations."[4] Sullivan's implication was that the Hmong were mercenaries for hire. We had paid them a fair wage. They had no right to expect anything more.

In the weeks following Kissinger's visit to Vientiane, negotiations between the Royal Laotian Government and the Pathet Lao bogged down. The Pathet Lao were not the main culprits. They bargained hard, but at least they were willing to bargain, for Hanoi had ordered them to reach a political settlement, and quickly. The worry was that with a ceasefire in effect in Vietnam, America might redirect its air power, and perhaps even its ground forces, from Vietnam to Laos. Establishing a coalition government would present Washington with a political solution to the Laotian conflict, making further military intervention unnecessary.[5]

It was the Rightists who were stalling the negotiations. To bring them around, the U.S. delayed food shipments and soldiers' pay. Jeeps and trucks that were promised never arrived.[6] Kissinger's warning of decreasing American aid was finally taken seriously. On February 21, 1973, the Pathet Lao, Neutralists, and Rightists signed the Agreement on the Restoration of Peace and Reconciliation in Laos.

The terms of the agreement were this. There was to be an immediate ceasefire. Vientiane and Luang Prabang were to become neutralized cities, with both communists and noncommunists sharing in their administration. There was to be a new coalition government, the Provisional Government of National Union (PGNU), with executive power invested in the prime minister and legislative power concentrated in a new National Political Consultative Council (NPCC). The bureaucratic details (cabinets, departments, and exact lines of authority) were to be worked out through negotiation. When this work was finished, all foreign troops were to withdraw from Laos within sixty days. Since Hanoi had no intention of removing its soldiers from Laos, the Pathet

Lao were under orders to draw out the discussions over details until all American forces left Vietnam.

Just before the ceasefire went into effect, Washington used the last of its air power in Southeast Asia to hammer the NVA in the Laotian panhandle and MR II. Averaging 350 sorties per day, the planes flew nearly 9,000 missions.[7] The pressure from the air enabled Vang Pao to wrest the crucial junction of Routes 7 and 13 away from the communists, but all of his other targets (Ban Na, Xieng Khouangville, Padong, and Muong Soui) remained in enemy hands.

A month into the ceasefire, the NVA went after the Hmong at Bouam Long. Two weeks later the communists hit RLA troops at Thavieng. Souvanna Phouma moaned to the press, "We have been tricked," and begged the U.S. to intercede.[8] For two days B-52s bombed NVA positions on the Plain of Jars and obliterated the NVA at Thavieng. It was the last air support Laos would receive from America.

In July, 1973, Congress passed legislation that effectively ended all bombing in Vietnam, Cambodia, and Laos. By August, all American Military action in Southeast Asia had ceased. Only fifty U.S. military personnel were left in Vietnam. By the end of the year they were gone, and South Vietnam and Laos were on their own.

On April 3, 1974, Souphanouvong arrived in Vientiane to cheering crowds. For months the communists had stalled negotiations over cabinet posts and the distribution of positions in the NPCC. Suddenly the discussions were concluded within two days. The membership of the NPCC was top-heavy with communists and Neutralists sympathetic to the Pathet Lao. Souvanna Phouma remained as prime minister, but after suffering a heart attack in July, he was too ill to counter his half-brother's machinations. After Souphanouvong dissolved the national assembly, Pathet Lao politicians blocked all efforts to hold elections for new representatives, transforming the NPCC into the nation's de facto legislature. With Souvanna Phouma still recuperating from his heart attack, power shifted to the NPCC, where the communists were firmly in control.

The communists' grand strategy for taking over the country boiled down to what the Pathet Lao called the "three strategic blows." First, their agents would organize popular agitation against the old regime, primarily riots and political demonstrations in the cities; next, Pathet Lao agents would foment mutiny in RLA battalions; and, lastly, communist agents would pressure local authorities, at gunpoint if necessary, to go over to the communist side, severing the link between the national government and the rural population.

Following this blueprint, soon after Souphanouvong arrived in Vientiane, the Pathet Lao recruited eleven thousand students from the nation's secondary schools to demonstrate against the government. The students bullied government employees to go on strike, then set themselves up as negotiators, requiring administrators loyal to the old regime to resign as a precondition for the resumption of work. Protest marchers, mostly students, carried placards demanding that all agencies of foreign governments leave the country.

Rightist mismanagement of government finances paved the way for the "second strategic blow." By June, deficit spending was out of control. Habituated to bribery as a way of life, the Rightists tried to co-opt Pathet Lao politicians by spending $1.4 million to refurbish their houses and provide them with luxury cars. Low on funds, the government had difficulty meeting military payrolls. Soldiers in MR II who hadn't been paid in months were stirred to mutiny by communist agents. The most serious incident occurred at Huoi Sai. Seven battalions of Khmu, formerly attached to Vang Pao's army and only recently integrated into the RLA, rioted and took command of villages in the area.[9]

The communists delivered their "third strategic blow" in early 1975 when Pathet Lao troops entered Pakse, Savannakhet, Thakhek, and several other southern towns to intimidate local bureaucrats, who quickly stepped aside so "people's revolutionary committees" could seize control of local government.[10] Vientiane would eventually topple in the same way.

The only fly in the ointment was Vang Pao, who still continued to fight. He was a less formidable adversary than before. The Thai were gone. So was the CIA and all its money. Hmong soldiers now drew the same wages as ordinary troops in the RLA, a cut in pay of 90 percent. Because of the low wages, a large number retired from service. Out of an original force of forty Hmong battalions, there were now only fourteen.

In October 1974, a combined force of Pathet Lao and NVA had tried to gain control of Sala Phu Khun, the town astride the crucial junction of Routes 7 and 13. Hmong battalions rushed to the town and drove the communists back. The NVA struck again in February 1975 and, again, Vang Pao's battalions repulsed the assault. The communists attacked the town a third time in April 1975. Most of the noncommunist members of the government were in Luang Prabang at the time celebrating Pi Mai, the Lao New Year festival. If the communists controlled the junction, they could ambush the government motorcade when it returned to Vientiane.

Hmong T-28s bombed the enemy's columns, saving the junction and possibly the lives of the government's noncommunist ministers, including Souvanna Phouma. Nevertheless, Souvanna Phouma was furious. Now fully recovered from his heart attack, he was convinced Hanoi intended to grant Laos its independence. That left only the Pathet Lao. Seeing himself as "the acknowledged master of solving national crises through political means," Souvanna was confident that he could cut some kind of deal with the leaders of the Pathet Lao. He was certain that Souphanouvong and other top leaders in the Pathet Lao were still loyal to the king and that they had no intention of replacing the nation's ancient monarchy with a Soviet-style regime.[11] Above all, he wanted no one in the military, and particularly Vang Pao, to antagonize the communists into taking up arms and seizing power by force. It did not cross Souvanna's mind that the life-and-death struggle unfolding in South Vietnam might have momentous consequences for the future of Laos.

Earlier in February, the NVA had crossed the 17th parallel and invaded South Vietnam. Giap had planned a two-year campaign, but since Congress refused to honor Nixon's earlier pledge to provide South Vietnam air support, the campaign turned out to be considerably shorter. The NVA swept everything from its path and reached the central highlands by mid-March. South Vietnam's president, Nguyen Van Thieu, lost his nerve and ordered government troops pulled back from the highlands and consolidated close to Saigon. In early April, government troops finally dug in at Xuan Loc, a mere thirty-five miles north of Saigon. After a twelve-day battle, what was left of South Vietnam's army collapsed. At the end of the month the communists captured Saigon.

Realizing early on that victory would come quickly, Hanoi made the decision to push for a similar lightning campaign in Laos. Saigon and Vientiane might even fall on the same day. The NVA and Pathet Lao assaults on Sala Phu Khun were the opening moves in this campaign. The next move came on May 4th, 1975. Supported by tanks and artillery, Pathet Lao troops assaulted Vang Pao's western positions, forcing a general retreat.

Two days later Vang Pao was in Vientiane in full dress uniform to ask Souvanna Phouma for permission to strike back. The two met in the prime minister's villa. The discussion grew heated. Souvanna reaffirmed his position that Vang Pao must cease military action against the communists and withdraw all troops from the area around Sala Phu Khun. Vang Pao wanted to know his options should the communists pursue his troops to Long Cheng.

Souvanna fiddled uncomfortably with his wire-rimmed glasses. He could not bring himself to give a direct answer. Only later, to the French ambassador, would he speak the truth: "The Hmong have served me well . . . it is a pity that peace may come only at the price of their liquidation."[12] Souvanna offered Vang Pao a deal that would let him off the hook and allow him to save himself. If he relinquished command of MR II, he could have a desk at RLA headquarters in Vientiane. It would make everything simpler. When Vang Pao brusquely turned the offer down, Souvanna suggested he consider leaving the country.[13] Enraged, Vang Pao ripped the three general's stars off his coat and threw them down on the prime minister's desk and in barracks French announced his resignation from the army.

Souvanna Phouma appointed one of his nephews, General Tiao Monivong, as the new commander of MR II. Affecting the manner of French aristocrats, Tiao Monivong smoked cigarettes with a long-stemmed Parisian calumet. He was a comical figure to the Long Cheng Hmong, who nicknamed him General *Yeej Nkab* (General Calumet). Tiao Monivong stayed put in Vientiane. He had no intention of ever showing his face in Long Cheng so long as Vang Pao was there, surrounded by his Hmong.

VANG PAO DEPARTS

At Long Cheng, Vang Pao watched helplessly as NVA units moved onto a nearby mountain to set up artillery. The last of the Thai battalions had returned home a year ago. All he had left were war-weary Hmong veterans and green teenagers. As in the past, when up against the wall, Vang Pao planned something bold. After sending his family to the safety of Thailand, he assembled his top officers and revealed his intention to occupy Vientiane before the North Vietnamese moved on Long Cheng.[14]

As he prepared for the coup, a small liaison plane arrived from Vientiane bearing Yang Dao, the first Hmong to earn a Ph.D. and the author of a study on the Hmong economy. Yang Dao's sister had married into the Vang clan, creating blood ties to Vang Pao who later subsidized Yang Dao's education in France, first at a high school and then at the Sorbonne. The young scholar had come to Long Cheng to honor his debt to the general.

Yang Dao had joined the NPCC in 1973 as a Neutralist. As naive as Souvanna Phouma about the Pathet Lao, he had thrown himself into the effort to generate Hmong support for the new coalition government and to allay fears that the Pathet Lao couldn't be trusted. He had just learned from fellow politicians in Vientiane of the impending assault on Long Cheng. It would not be only NVA attacking the base. Everyone wanted to get into the act: Pathet Lao, Neutralist troops, and even former soldiers of the Royal Laotian Army. The Rightists in particular were anxious to build credibility with the communists. Eight Rightist ministers had resigned and fled to Thailand, along with five RLA generals, making the loyalty of all Rightists suspect. Jumping on the anti-Hmong bandwagon was a means by which the Rightists could prove their allegiance to the new regime and use the Hmong as scapegoats for their own complicity in resisting the communist takeover.

Once Vang Pao learned the facts, his resolve to carry on the struggle dissolved. He was willing to fight the NVA, but not the entire Laotian nation. Several days later he was in a helicopter, heading for Thailand and permanent exile.

For weeks, Vang Pao's CIA contacts in Thailand had been urging him to leave the country and to approve an airlift of his soldiers and their families to Thailand. When Vang Pao finally gave in,

CIA agents rushed to locate pilots for the job. The only C-130 transport pilot still in Southeast Asia was Matt Hoff. Agents found him in the airport in Bangkok, standing in line with his luggage, ready to board a flight home to Houston. On the spot, they offered Hoff five thousand dollars for the job. Hoff was soon joined by three Air America pilots and an off-duty commercial airline captain employed by Continental Air Services, another airline under contract to the CIA.

On the morning of May 14th, a C-130, two C-46s, a helicopter, and a Pilatus Porter landed at Long Cheng to begin loading passengers. The aircraft would made six round trips, transporting several thousand Hmong to Namphong, an abandoned air base fifty miles south of Udorn.[15] Vang Pao's top officers and their families were the first to be flown to Namphong. After they were evacuated, it was unclear who among the thousands crowding the airfield should be allowed to board the planes. Desperate families began offering bribes to flight crews to get on board. One wealthy widow had no difficulty booking passage for her family. She came with three large chests of silver, each so heavy it took several men to hoist them onto the plane. Hundreds of other Hmong with considerable fortunes also received special treatment.

Most of these wealthy Hmong earned their money honestly as tradesmen, cattle ranchers, or professionals. Over the years, refugee relief and soldiers' pay had created a vast market for enterprising Hmong businessmen. It began modestly with coffee stands and noodle vendors setting up booths on the roadsides of the camps and villages overflowing with refugees. The booths became shops, and the shops grew into retail stores hawking a vast assortment of consumer items. In the larger towns, merchants pooled resources and erected small shopping centers—Hmong dime stores where nearly anything could be purchased. There were butcher shops with an abundance of fresh meat provided by Hmong cattle ranchers, some with herds in the hundreds. The ranchers also sold directly to soldiers in the field, slaughtering steers on the spot.

The heavy foot traffic between camps and villages that had worn paths down to knee-deep ditches was eventually relieved by enterprising Hmong, who purchased military vehicles and turned them into taxis, delivering some fares all the way to Luang Prabang or Vientiane.

The major centers of Hmong commerce were Long Cheng, Sam Thong (before its destruction), Pha Khao, and Muong Cha, all crowded with refugees from the war. Vang Pao's Xieng Khouang Air Transport delivered between two hundred and three hundred tons of merchandise from Vientiane to Long Cheng every month. A large portion was sold locally at Long Cheng by six hundred or so Hmong merchants. The rest was carried to Sam Thong (and after its fall to Ban Some), Pha Khao, and Muong Cha via a fleet of Land Rovers, Jeeps, and Toyota cars converted into taxis. From these centers, horse caravans carried goods to the outlying villages in the surrounding mountains. By 1969, Long Cheng enjoyed a brisk wholesale and retail trade. Hmong silver jewelry and brooms were sold in shops alongside Swiss and Japanese radios and toilet paper from America. At Long Cheng there were Hmong tailors and dentists, photographers and cobblers, bakers and radio repairmen. There were a dozen restaurants in town and even an ice factory.[16] There was money to be made, and a good number of Hmong became wealthy.

Not every fortune was honestly acquired, however. In mid-1974, when the CIA stopped all funding for his army, Vang Pao turned to narcotics to get the money to pay his troops. Since the war had devastated most opium growing areas in MR II, he began purchasing Burmese opium in Vientiane to supplement the dwindling supply of Hmong opium, and having it processed into heroin at a small lab in the capital. The heroin had a street value in the millions, but the wholesale price never topped several hundred thousand dollars, which was insufficient to meet the payroll of all his soldiers. To augment narcotics revenues, Vang Pao dipped into funds set aside for refugee relief and agricultural programs, the only U.S. activity that had not been disallowed by the 1973 Agreement on the Restoration of Peace and Reconciliation. When this money ran out he was finally forced to cashier troops.

USAID tried to help out by giving cattle and buffalo, purchased from prosperous Hmong farmers, as demobilization compensation to cashiered officers. For retired enlisted men, the USAID sponsored pig farms and chicken ranches. The result was four large pig farms and three large chicken ranches, hardly enough to absorb more than a fraction of the unemployed.[17] The rest had to shift for themselves, some lashing out in frustration at their former commanders, seven of whom were assassinated within a few weeks.[18] Other disgruntled veterans began to steal military equipment set aside earlier by Vang Pao in secret depots. They drove trucks loaded with green crates of M-16s and rocket launchers and gray boxes of canteens, uniforms, and boots to waiting boats on the Mekong to be ferried across the river to Thailand, where much of it was purchased by the communists to kill Hmong soldiers.

For those without enough money to bribe their way onto the transport planes, it was these nefarious activities that came to mind. All gain was construed as ill-gotten, and the angry crowds pressing in on the planes began to hurl insults at boarding passengers, who vainly protested that their wealth was honestly earned, a few thrusting their hands out through the cargo bay, palms out, as if they expected the labor of a merchant or barber to be etched there as clearly as the calluses of a farmer.

Not all Hmong wanted to leave Laos. Yang Dao believed that with Vang Pao and the bulk of his officer corps in Thailand, the communists might call off their vendetta against the Hmong. Touby was of the same mind, and put Yang Dao in charge of organizing Hmong students in Vientiane to travel to the settlements around Long Cheng to build grassroots support for the new regime and to dissuade Hmong from trying to follow Vang Pao to Thailand.

Touby himself made an appearance at Phak Khet to address several thousand Hmong assembled at the town's airstrip. Also on hand were Yang Dao, Tiao Monivong (Vang Pao's replacement as commander of MR II), and a Pathet Lao general. Yang Dao introduced Tiao Monivong to the crowd, assuring them that the new commander of MR II would guarantee their security. Tiao embraced the Pathet Lao general to demonstrate the atmosphere of fraternity that existed between the communists and members of the old regime. Few in the crowd were swayed by the display.

In time Yang Dao's enthusiasm for Touby's project of reconciliation waned. He began to doubt the communists were really willing to forgive and forget. In late November the government requested all noncommunist members of the NPCC to convene for a special meeting at Luang Prabang. Earlier, in May, all senior RLA officers and staff had assembled at the 5th regimental headquarters, ostensibly for a briefing; all in attendance were flown to prison camps in Sam Neua.[19] Yang Dao suspected a similar trap was being laid for the members of the NPCC. He fled to Thailand.

Yang Dao's suspicions were well-founded. Like the generals earlier, the noncommunist members of the NPCC were taken from Luang Prabang to Vieng Say, the old Pathet Lao stronghold in Sam Neua Province, soon to become a principal site for concentration camps. None of the NPCC members ever returned.[20]

Yang Dao's efforts to persuade Hmong to remain in Laos and cooperate with the communists made him an unpopular figure among Hmong refugees in Thailand. The complaint was that he had cost lives by delaying their departure. There was little evidence that anyone was actually swayed by his appeals, but he was a convenient scapegoat. Hmong at the Namphong camp sent Yang Dao death threats when it was rumored he was to join them.[21] Actually, his destination was the camp at Ban Vinai. Hmong at this second camp also sent Yang Dao a letter informing him he was *persona non grata*. Yang Dao went to Ban Vinai anyway to be processed for resettlement to France. He came to no harm while at the camp.

HIN HEUP

The day after Vang Pao's departure, Colonel Kham Ai led a Pathet Lao battalion into Long Cheng to officially take command of MR II.[22] To avoid bloodshed, he had integrated Pathet Lao Hmong into the battalion. Throughout the war, Hmong on both sides had observed a gentleman's agreement to try to avoid engaging each other in battle. Kham Ai hoped the agreement was still in effect.

Kham Ai and several of his officers rummaged through the offices of Vang Pao's old military headquarters, searching for files containing the names of Hmong who had served in the *armée clandestine*. They found nothing. The files had already been destroyed.[23] While Kham Ai searched, a Hmong platoon left the battalion and headed straight for the Long Cheng Bank.

Vang Pao established the bank in 1967 to develop trust in a paper economy. Before the war, Hmong used silver for nearly all commercial transactions and, by tradition, for the payment of bride price. For a time Vang Pao was forced to bow to this mercantilist mind-set and pay his troops in silver. As the size of his army expanded this proved impractical, and his soldiers had to settle for payment in kip. There was considerable grumbling among the troops, until Vang Pao created the Long Cheng Bank, where kip could be exchanged for silver. While this move created confidence in the kip, currency continued to be exchanged for silver to pay bride prices. To satisfy this demand, the bank maintained a large silver reserve. As the actual size of this stockpile was unknown, it was a popular pastime to ponder the worth of the fortune locked away. Over the years its rumored value inflated to Midas proportions, making it a topic of conversation in Hmong villages throughout the province, even in the Pathet Lao zones.

The Pathet Lao Hmong dashing for the bank hoped it still held a fortune. They were in luck. Because of his hasty departure, Vang Pao had left the silver behind to be transported to Thailand later. Once in the bank, the Hmong hammered furiously on the big German safe with sledges. When this proved ineffective, they strapped grenades to the vault, pulled the pins, and rushed into the street. There were seven blasts in rapid succession. The soldiers rushed back in to find the big safe standing as stolid as ever, its door still shut tight. Ten minutes later someone arrived with plastic explosives. Impressed by the sturdiness of the safe, the Hmong taped four charges to its door. The explosion sent part of the bank's roof into orbit. The vault's door shot through the front of the bank like a cannonball. Shrapnel-sized bits of silver peppered buildings across the street. Inside the bank a cloud of kip confetti billowed up through the yawning hole in the bank's roof. Amazingly, no one was killed. While two of the Hmong used their knives to pry silver nuggets from the wooden storefronts across from the bank, the others carried sliver bars from the bank into the street, creating a mound of silver ingots nearly three feet high. A truck arrived and hauled it all away.[24]

A few hours later the entire Pathet Lao battalion withdrew to a temporary garrison south of the military base. Even with Hmong integrated into his force, Kham Ai had no intention of bivouacking in a sea of former Hmong guerrillas.

The next day two members of the Ly clan arrived from Vientiane to urge cooperation with the Pathet Lao. Ly Tek

Lynhiavu, the younger of the two, did most of the talking. He was handsome, with a broad face and muscular build, and spoke well. Educated abroad, he worked as a civil servant in Vientiane. Strutting like a peacock, he announced that Vang Pao was finished and that the Hmong had to look for new leadership. It was obvious he had himself in mind for the job.

Ly Tek was the son of Pa Ngcha Ly, the tax collector who had alienated so many Hmong on the Plain of Jars during Touby's reign as *roi de Méos*. Pa Ngcha died at Sam Thong in 1965, leaving behind five sons: Ly Tek, Cher Ly, Blong Ly Pa Ngcha, Tou Ly, and Chong Na Ly. All were well-educated, except Chong Na, the eldest. Despite his lack of education, Chong Na seemed to be the only one of the five sons who truly understood the deep hatred for his father, so deep that it extended by association to the rest of the family. Chong Na lived in relative anonymity in Vientiane and stayed clear of Hmong politics, as did Tou Ly, the youngest of the five sons, who was still a teenager. The other three sons, however, yearned for power and authority.

Cher Ly had run for a seat in the national assembly, but received no support. Vang Pao tried to console him with a minor administrative post at Nong Pu, then withdrew the offer when the residents of the town threatened to murder Cher if he ever showed up. Blong Ly Pa Ngcha fared no better. Trained as an engineer in Japan, he pressured Vang Pao for a top job on the Japanese, financed Nam Ngum dam project begun in 1967. When Vang Pao tried to put him in charge of construction, there was such an outcry he was forced to give the job to a Canadian-educated engineer from the Moua clan.

Ly Tek was the most ambitious of Pa Ngcha Ly's sons. He never tired of reminding others that he was a direct descendant of Nhiavu Ly, the first Ly kaitong in Laos. He presumed this gave him the right to flaunt Hmong sexual propriety, which forbade the touching of women sexually in public. On strolls through Long Cheng's open market he would pinch the bottoms of women vendors and occasionally cup a hand over a crotch.[25]

With royal blood coursing through his veins, Ly Tek fancied himself a natural leader. Completely blind to the enormous enmity toward his family, he repeatedly sought to gain a purchase in Hmong politics. Each time he was rebuffed by Hmong unwilling to entrust him with any position of authority. Yet he kept trying, stirring up bad memories and giving Vang Pao headaches.

To get him out of the way, Vang Pao placed Ly Tek on his payroll and assigned him to Vientiane, with no particular duties. In Ly Tek's mind, the assignment was proof that Vang Pao saw him as a political threat and wanted him out of the way. At Vientiane, Ly Tek worked to forge political ties to Touby and to carve out a place for himself in the civil service (he became an official in the Interior Ministry).[26] A complete opportunist, he hedged his bets by establishing friendly contacts with the communists. With Vang Pao's sudden departure, Ly Tek imagined the Hmong at Long Cheng would flock to him as their new savior. What he encountered were frowns and turned backs.

The sudden arrival of Pathet Lao troops caused panic at Long Cheng. The fear was that the troops were the beginning of a mass program that would engulf all of the densely populated Hmong villages and refugee settlements stretching from Muong Cha and Long Cheng to Ban Some. Impressionable schoolchildren, shivering with fear in their seats as their teachers described the butchery to come, carried the gruesome forecasts home and shared them with their parents. By the end of the month, thousands departed for Thailand, streaming out of the resettlement camps and surrounding villages onto the transport road leading to Route 13 and Vientiane. It was a march of the well-to-do: those with money for passage on Mekong ferries, bribes for Thai border guards, and food and housing in Thailand. The very rich, many of whom had tried unsuccessfully to bribe their way onto the CIA transport planes, made the trip by car. The rest walked.

Families had hurriedly liquidated all assets before leaving. Houses, land, motorcycles, radios, tape players, cameras, horses, cattle, pigs, and chickens were sold at bargain prices. Nia Heu Lo, a prosperous farmer in the village of Nam Nhone, made one last tour of his property. There were acres of pineapples, pools full of carp, pens with pigs, flocks of ducks and geese. He doubted he would ever be so well-off again. A Lao merchant had purchased most of his livestock for a few thousand kip. The pineapples would probably rot in the ground. Nia Heu netted some of his carp, butchered chickens and a pig, and invited neighbors for a feast.[27] The same scene was repeated in village after village around Long Cheng, Ban Some, Pha Khao, and Muong Cha.

The departure was so sudden many could find no buyers for their goods. Thousands of farms, hundreds of shops, countless cattle and pigs, and legions of chickens passed into the hands of close relatives. High-level Hmong bureaucrats transferred their seals/relatives of office to favorite, in many instances transforming lowly clerks and farmers into mayors and district supervisors. The massive transfer of titles and property catapulted thousands of ordinary Hmong into the realm of the Hmong middle class, softening the blow of being left behind.

Forty thousand participated in the mass exodus, arranged in a column stretching nearly a mile. Pots and pans strapped to backs clanged in cadence with the marchers' steps. Sacks draped over shoulders, or carried by hand, were bloated with blankets, clothing, packets of rice, and the family fortune: silver ingots, jingling pouches of silver French piasters, and fat wads of Lao kip.

On the evening of the first day, the marchers camped on the side of the road and searched the forest for potable water to cook rice. They cut branches for lean-tos and covered them with banana leaves or black plastic for protection against the night chill and rain. Campfires hissed and sputtered in the drizzle that had begun earlier in the afternoon. Laughter broke out among the knots of men clustered around the fires as someone recalled how Ly Tek had driven up and down the line of marchers in his big Mercedes, dressed in a white tunic like Lao royalty, waving a letter out the window. Ly Tek had distributed copies of the letter earlier, claiming it was from Vang Pao. The letter urged all Hmong to stay put and promised that Vang Pao would return to Laos as soon as things quieted down.[28] It was an obvious forgery.

On the third day, Pathet Lao soldiers appeared in jeeps and Molotova trucks. The chilling sound of bullets sliding from ammunition clips into rifle chambers filled the air as troops emerged from the vehicles and approached the crowd. The marchers feared the soldiers were going to bar their escape and turn them back, but they were only after their wealth. Within a few hours the soldiers had confiscated a fortune in silver.[29] Women wept as they witnessed their family's savings evaporating before their eyes. A few of the men looked on the bright side. The only reason the soldiers were squeezing the last drop out of them was that it was their last chance to do so. The regime was going to let them escape to Thailand.

On the morning of the fourth day, the once-revered Touby LyFoung appeared, slapping road dust from his clothes. A week earlier, at Ban Some, he had climbed onto a roadside vendor's stall to calm fears and urge the Hmong to stay put. Now, standing in his jeep, he asked them to return to their homes. He told them Vang Pao was no longer in Thailand, that he had gone on to America. This was a lie. Vang Pao would not leave Thailand until the end of June, and would go to France before heading for the U.S.

The crowd was not in a mood to listen. Touby had spent too many years away from his people in the capital (first in the national assembly, then on the King's Council, and later as Minister of Health and now as Minister of Telecommunications), rubbing elbows with Lao politicians, American diplomats, and CIA agents.[30] And he had become fat. Short, even for a Hmong, Touby had kept his weight under control when he was younger, maintaining an almost regal bearing despite his diminutive size. Now, at sixty-one, he was extremely fat. The buttons on his coat seemed ready to pop. The old aura of authority, earned when the French ran Laos and traded political favors for a monopoly in Hmong opium, was gone.

"Go home," Touby pleaded, "and make peace with the communists. I will assure your safety." He informed the crowd that he had talked to Faydang and was assured there would be no reprisals. It was difficult to believe Touby's old enemy would lift a finger to help Touby or anyone associated with him. Feet shuffled, people grumbled. Touby promised to return the next morning, precisely at ten, to present written assurances from the government that no harm would come to any Hmong who remained in Laos. He asked for a show of hands from those who planned to stay. Counting only four, he quipped: "Ah well, at least five of us will be left in Laos."[31]

In reality, Touby was as eager as the crowd to quit Laos for Thailand. Anyone with an ounce of political sense knew that the Hmong would not fare well under the new regime. Even Hmong on the Pathet Lao side saw this. Foung Lo, the only communist

Hmong serving on the National Political Consultative Council, harbored deep reservations about the regime's promise of fair treatment for minority groups, especially the Hmong. He had joined the Pathet Lao at its inception and in 1958 ran as a communist candidate against Touby for a seat on the National Assembly. He lost the election but remained involved in communist politics, slowly rising within the Pathet Lao's secret party bureaucracy. During their struggle to capture power, the Pathet Lao had courted the ethnic minorities (Hmong, highland T'ai, Mien, Khmu, and Yao) to provide soldiers for their army. Western apologists cited this as evidence that the Pathet Lao were the only truly representative political force in the nation. The communists' true intentions were revealed only after they seized power. Souphanouvong, Kaysone, and other lowland Lao in the Pathet Lao exercised the real power, while high-ranking Hmong and Khmu such as Faydang and Sithon Kommadan were reduced to mere figureheads and would soon retire from politics.[32]

Once Foung Lo realized that party leaders had no intention of sharing power with the minorities, he made contact with Vang Pao, a close relation by marriage. In the past, Vang Pao had put political differences aside to honor family ties. Though his older brother Ngung Chu was an officer in the Pathet Lao, Vang Pao took in Ngung Chu's son so he could be educated at the new school at Long Cheng. After the boy graduated, Vang Pao delivered him safely to his father in a Pathet Lao zone.[33] Foung hoped for equally sympathetic treatment. Reportedly, Vang Pao gave him five hundred thousand kip, possibly to stake him to a new start in Thailand. Not long after this, Foung began to urge Hmong notables on both sides of the political spectrum to abandon Laos. Unwisely, he failed to take his own advice. In November of 1975, he was arrested and sent to a re-education camp at Phong Savan on the Plain of Jars. A short time later he died of mysterious causes.[34]

Touby had also turned to Vang Pao for help, flying to Namphong in Thailand to seek assurances that his entire family would be provided for, should he decide to escape. Vang Pao pledged his support, even if it meant they would be paupers together, for he claimed his own financial situation was uncertain, referring perhaps to the silver left behind in Long Cheng Bank.[35] Touby interpreted the remark as a polite refusal and as meaning that he was on his own. It was then that Touby decided to seek an accommodation with the communists, trusting that his old ally Souvanna Phouma, brother of the "Red Prince," could protect him.

Touby did not return to address the marchers as promised. He was stuck in Vientiane under house arrest. Within a week he would be in a concentration camp in Sam Neua Province, working the foot pedal on a grinder, sharpening knives. It was a communist joke, a play on an old proverb about unused knives growing dull. The guards poked fingers into Touby's ample belly, evidence that he had gone soft, that he hadn't used his talents to help the Laotian people by joining the communists. Touby sharpened blades for over a month until the guards tired of the jest and put him to work digging ditches and chopping down trees. Touby survived the hard labor on starvation rations for nearly three years until he became too weak and ill to work. He died in the camp infirmary.

When Touby failed to return, the marchers braved the driving rain and moved on toward Vientiane. Ly Tek appeared again, this time issuing warnings that anyone who passed over the Nam Lik River would be shot on his orders. On May 29, the marchers reached the hamlet of Hin Heup, where a bridge spanned the Nam Lik. The sleepy village had enjoyed a moment of notoriety back in 1961. While the big powers were debating Laos' fate at Geneva, Souvanna Phouma, Souphanouvong, and Boun Oum met independently at Hin Heup and agreed to form a coalition government. Back then chauffeured limousines had crowded the lane. Now it was jeeps and military trucks.

Soldiers had set up a rope barricade at the end of the bridge. Behind the rope there were jeeps and trucks parked sideways, blocking the way. As the column of Hmong entered the bridge, the front of the line slowed. Ly Tek was at the rope barricade, flanked by Pathet Lao soldiers, his arms raised, palms out, signaling the marchers to halt. He ordered everyone to turn back. One of the soldiers shouted out, "Go back or we will kill all of you. You will never be allowed to leave."

Xong Thao was near the front of the column. He was only eight and felt a little overwhelmed by the bodies of the adults pressing in on him so tightly he couldn't bend down to pick up the brightly colored stone he had spotted on the bridge. Xong watched an old man at the head of the crowd walk forward and defiantly begin to untie the rope barricade. A soldier rushed forward and struck him with the butt of his rifle, knocking him to the ground. The soldier struck the old man again. As if on signal, the full company of Pathet Lao assembled among the jeeps and trucks began shooting into the crowd. The Hmong on the bridge turned and ran, screaming and shouting. People were knocked down and trampled. Xong Thao tried to keep up with his parents. He was surrounded by pumping legs. Too short to see above the press of bodies, his only clear view was of the bridge beneath his feet. There was blood everywhere, covering the bridge like fresh paint.[36]

The soldiers chased the crowd, shooting and beating Hmong and throwing them off the bridge into the river. Hmong have a terror of deep water, believing evil spirits inhabit lakes and rivers in depths greater than a few feet. Seldom entering water above their waist, few Hmong master as much as a dog paddle. Those thrown into the water thrashed and gasped and then simply disappeared beneath the surface.

One woman with a heavy pack strapped to her back stood leaning against the bridge railing. She had been shot dead. The weight of the pack caused her to tilt slowly. Finally she toppled into the river. Nearby, a baby strapped to his mother's back screamed in pain. The fingers of one of his little hands had been shot away. An old woman carrying a small ax had been knocked down by fleeing Hmong. She struggled up, spurting blood, the ax lodged in her chest.

Neng Vang was also on the bridge, running like everyone else, until he suddenly realized that his wife was no longer at his side. He found her crawling in the middle of the bridge, their youngest child strapped to her back and wailing. He rushed to his wife's side and tried to carry her away. His sister-in-law stumbled toward him and fell. Neng saw that a bullet had shattered her right leg below the knee. The wound gushed blood. AK-47s and M-16s continued to fire. Bullets whizzed around Neng's head. He tried to drag his wife away while holding onto the sack containing all of their possessions: spare sandals, a few pots and pans, blankets and rice. The bridge was littered with dead Hmong. The wounded pleaded for help. Neng heard his aunt call to him. She was holding onto his uncle, who had been shot in the chest. Nearby, one of his brothers was down, clasping a leg. A bullet had severed the femoral artery. Neng realized his brother would be dead within a few minutes. There was nothing he could do to help him.

Pathet Lao surged into the fleeing crowd, stabbing people with bayonets. Neng was certain they would reach him any moment and finish off his wife, and probably kill him too. A soldier yelled at him to drop his wife and leave her behind. He ignored the order and tried to move faster. His other brother suddenly appeared and lent a hand. Then they were off the bridge, merging with the retreating mass of terrified Hmong.[37]

The Pathet Lao herded the column in the direction of Long Cheng, gunning down anyone who tried leave the road and make a break for the jungle. Hundreds of Hmong chanced the dash to safety. Most made it. The bodies of those who didn't were left on the side of the road. The soldiers dogged the column for twelve kilometers to the village of Pong Song. The local police, who had yet to be replaced with loyal communists, were properly alarmed by the butchery. Armed with combat rifles, they confronted the soldiers, who backed down and let the marchers find their own way home.

Once the soldiers were out of sight, several hundred marchers (those with enough money left to rent boats) abandoned the road and headed south for the Nam Ngum river to find boatmen to take them to the Mekong. A Xiong clan elder passed the word to fellow clansmen to head for Muong Kassy, where they would assemble for a dash to the river. A few hundred reached the town, only to find it crawling with Pathet Lao. They returned to Ban Some.[38]

By May 31, rumors of the massacre reached Japanese and Thai journalists in Vientiane. A government spokesman assured the reporters that the incident at Hin Heup was only a minor skirmish. Hmong had assaulted soldiers with knives. Naturally, the soldiers defended themselves. The Hmong involved had returned to their villages. No more trouble was expected.[39]

This confidence was not feigned. Earlier, there had been concern that Vang Pao might cross the border into Laos and launch a counter-revolution with a small army cobbled together from the Hmong airlifted by the CIA to Ubon in Thailand. The communists rushed troops to Pakse, Savannakhet, and Thakhek to counter the expected invasion.[40] It never materialized. With Vang Pao out of the picture, the only worry was the 150,000 leaderless Hmong in the old refugee resettlement areas south of the Plain of Jars. They were still receiving U.S. aid, and as long as it continued they could afford to exercise independent judgment. The Pathet Lao organized demonstrations at the American embassy, demanding that the aid be stopped. On May 28, after protesters had occupied USAID offices for eight days, Christian Chapman, the U.S. Chargé d'Affaires, agreed to suspend all refugee relief to Laos by June 30th.[41] The communists were confident that the Hmong would soon be too busy just trying to survive to foment rebellion. Rigorous in-doctrination and the weeding out of bad elements would guarantee their continued docility.

The cut-off of aid had an unexpected consequence. More than one hundred thousand Hmong in the resettlement areas were ut-terly dependent on the aid for survival.[42] When it ceased, they were left destitute and unable to resume their old lives as swidden farmers. There was no seed to plant corn and rice and the govern-ment denied them permission to move into the highlands to establish homesteads. The Hmong were convinced that the new regime meant to starve them to death. Chancing the fate of those killed at Hin Heup, thousands fled to Thailand, traveling off the beaten path to avoid road patrols. Though many were captured, killed, or turned back, by the end of the year forty thousand had made it across the border.[43]

A few with enough money made the trip safely by purchasing official travel permits from Ly Tek, who auctioned them to the highest bidder. He should have used one himself. His lack of in-fluence over the Hmong made him of little use to the communists. Toward the end of the year he found himself in a concentration camp in Sam Neua. By one account, he was led to the outskirts of the prison compound and summarily executed.[44] In another ver-sion, he mysteriously expired after undergoing minor surgery in the camp's infirmary.[45]

JARRED TO REALITY

The historical record was clear. Everywhere communism degenerated into a totalitarianism of the left. Yet the vast majority of Laotians did not tremble at the thought of communist rule. A year before the Pathet Lao seized power, the newly formed National Political Consultative Council sponsored an eighteen-point program for political reform. As the Council was packed with communists, the program was interpreted by many as a blueprint for future communist rule. The reform package preserved Laos' ancient monarchy and endorsed a variety of democratic freedoms: free speech, free press, freedom of assembly, and freedom of movement. It even recognized the right to private property and the need to guarantee some degree of free enterprise. This led many to imagine that communism in Laos would be communism Lao style: low-key, non-ideological, and unobtrusive. Not really communism at all.

Thousands of lowlanders were jarred to reality in May 1975 when Pathet Lao troops occupied the nation's principal cities. The ranks of these liberation forces were filled with seasoned guerrillas, the majority ethnic minorities (principally Khmu and highland T'ai from the northeastern provinces) recruited by the communists early in the war. For years party cadres had filled their heads with stock propaganda about the lowlanders, depicting them as corrupt lackeys of U.S. imperialism. This indoctrination, coupled with a natural resentment for generations of blatant racial prejudice by lowlanders toward montagnards, did not dispose the guerrillas to embrace the ethnic Lao as fellow comrades. They entered the cities not as saviors but as conquerors, looting homes and businesses, summarily executing hundreds, raping women in the streets, and arbitrarily rounding up terrified civilians for interrogation and torture.

By December, Laos was well on its way to becoming a full-blown communist state. King Savang Vatthana abdicated his throne, Souvanna Phouma stepped down as prime minister, and Souphanouvong became the first president of the Lao People's Democratic Republic (LPDR). The post was mostly window-dressing. Real power was exercised behind the scenes by the Laotian Communist Party's general secretary, Kaysone Phomvihane, and by his Vietnamese advisors, who reported directly to Vo Nguyen Giap in Hanoi.

The Vietnamese standing at Kaysone's shoulder were troubled by reports of continued rough treatment of ordinary citizens by soldiers in the Pathet Lao army, recently renamed and reorganized as the Lao People's Liberation Army (LPLA).[46] The pillaging and violence were hardly the way to win over the masses to communism. As early as June 1975, embittered lowlanders had begun to rebel against the gratuitous brutality. In Champassak Province in southern Laos, loyal supporters of former Prince Boun Oum (now living in exile in Thailand) organized a maquis and ambushed LPLA patrols, driving communist soldiers out of several towns and villages.[47]

To forestall new rebellions, Hanoi suggested the need for greater discipline in Laos' armed forces. Kaysone ordered the LPLA to create a new code of conduct. The code was in place in early 1976, summarized in four don'ts: don't intimidate the people, take property, destroy temples, or take liberties with women. Even with the new code, soldiers continued to brutalize civilians, prompting the LPLA's official newspaper to finally concede that former Pathet Lao guerrillas had become a threat to average citizens. Since Kaysone could not control the soldiers, he ordered them out of all major cities and towns and replaced them with a reorganized national police.[48]

But the damage was already done. Earlier, in August 1975, ethnic Lao from villages along the Nam Ngum River between the Plain of Jars and Vientiane had begun attacking LPLA patrols. Most of the resisters were transplants from the north. Among their number were Pathet Lao deserters who had fled south during the war to find a safe haven from the fighting. There were also war refugees from northeastern provinces who knew what life was like under the Pathet Lao. The communists had commandeered their food and livestock, impressed them into work gangs to build soldiers' barracks and construct roads, and raped their women. The refugees were convinced the same fate awaited all Laotians now that the Pathet Lao controlled the entire country.

Word of the fighting inspired other ethnic Lao from towns and villages along the Mekong River in Vientiane Province to form their own maquis. The new resistance was well armed. The communists had neglected to collect the weapons and munitions that lay in dusty piles in warehouses every few kilometers on the outskirts of the capital, a legacy of the civil defense groups organized by the Rightists when they were in power. The new guerrillas linked up with the Nam Ngum maquis. In joint operations the two groups blew up bridges and ambushed truck convoys.[49]

In January 1976 the first resistance front surfaced, calling itself the "Lao National Revolutionary Front." Its leadership included Vientiane intellectuals and organizers of the earlier Champassak resistance. By February the front was carrying out assaults on LPLA patrols and attacking truck convoys on Route 13 near Paksane. The government rushed troops to the area to guard the Nam Nhiep bridge, used by the Vietnamese to ferry soldiers and supplies to Vientiane. Despite the show of force, the rebels succeeded in blowing up the bridge. Photos of the demolished structure appeared in the *Bangkok Post*. Two weeks later rebels bombed Vientiane's radio station, along with the Soviet and Vietnamese embassies. In April it was the Cuban embassy's turn. The explosion killed one person and wounded five others.

Shortly after the bombings, posters appeared on the walls of public buildings bearing the message: "We Don't Want to be Slaves of the Vietnamese."[50] The slogan was inspired by the thirty to forty thousand Vietnamese troops still in Laos (in another year Vietnamese troop strength would jump to sixty thousand), and for the legions of Vietnamese in advisory positions in the government and the military. There would soon be eight thousand Vietnamese party cadres entrenched in government bureaucracies at the national and provincial levels, infiltrated into the military and operating independently as a secret police.[51]

A fourth resistance group began operations in May 1976. Its leader was Colonel Khambou Phimmasene. During the war he had commanded an RLA airborne battalion, then joined Kong-Lê and the Neutralists. With solid support from local villagers and financial backing from former Kong-Lê supporters in France, Phimmasene organized a maquis of four hundred and assaulted Pathet Lao garrisons near Pha Lan in Savannakhet Province.[52]

In the same month, a fifth maquis sprang up farther south in Sedone and Wapikhanthong provinces near the Cambodian border (the old regime's fourth military region). There had been friction in the area between Vietnamese soldiers and elements of the LPLA. In one incident Vietnamese soldiers fired on LPLA troops when they tried to examine the cargo of a Vietnamese truck convoy, killing twenty Lao.[53] In protest, three LPLA colonels had bolted from the army and formed a guerrilla organization of several hundred, drawn from the RLA Special Guerrilla Unit (SGU) battalions disbanded in May 1975. Unlike most detachments in the RLA, the SGU battalions in the fourth military region had been genuine combat units. "Commanded by the best officers in MR IV," they had kept the region clear of Pathet Lao right up to the end of the war.[54]

In July, refugees in Thailand proclaimed a second resistance front, the "Lao People's Revolutionary Front 21/18." The suffix "21/18" referred to both the February 21, 1973 ceasefire agreement requiring all foreign military forces to leave the country, and to the eighteen-point reform package of May 1974 that outlined the goals of a liberal democracy. It was intended as a rallying cry for all nationalists wanting the Vietnamese out of Laos and the experiment with Soviet-style communism ended. The front quickly launched cross-border military operations against LPLA units garrisoned near the Mekong.[55]

By the end of the year two more rebel organizations were on the scene, one in Sayaboury, the other in Nam Tha Province (see map "Resistance Groups 1975-1985"). The Sayaboury group was composed mostly of ethnic Lao. The Nam Tha rebels were Yao tribesmen, many of them alumni of Tony Poe's late 1960s paramilitary organization headquartered at Nam Yu. The leader of the rebels was Chao La, a Yao chieftain and entrepreneur who owned a lumber mill and trafficked in drugs.[56]

Back in August 1975, Chao La had fled to Thailand with several thousand Yao. There, at the Chiang Khong refugee camp, he organized the Yao into military units and returned to Laos and assaulted LPLA garrisons near the border. His agents infiltrated towns and villages, fomenting insurrection. By early 1977 spontaneous uprisings had occurred in nearly every large town in the province, including the provincial capital. Amidst this turmoil, Chao La's guerrillas moved up Route 3 from Houi Sai and occupied the towns of Man Tha, Ta Pha, Vieng Phu Kha, and Nam Tha.[57]

Vientiane rushed LPLA units to the province to drive the rebels out of the towns, but the government troops were soundly repulsed. Concerned that things could get out of hand, Hanoi sent Vietnamese battalions to the scene to regain control of the province. Rebel forces briefly stiffened against the mass assault, then abruptly collapsed. The Vietnamese took one thousand prisoners and summarily executed all of them.[58]

While the Vietnamese were busy crushing the Yao rebellion, Sayaboury rebels pushed into Luang Prabang Province and captured the town of Muong Nan, located only a few miles south of the King's residence at Luang Prabang. Government forces counterattacked and overwhelmed the rebels. Under torture, captured rebels confessed that the ultimate object of the raid was to enter Luang Prabang and liberate the king. They also revealed that Thai authorities had promised asylum for the deposed sovereign. The rebels planned to use the king as a symbol of Lao nationalism, a live recruiting poster to swell the ranks of resistance forces.[59] By one account, the prisoners also confessed that the CIA had financed and planned the entire operation.[60]

The confessions sealed the fate of the royal family. Alarmed by evidence of CIA backing to whisk the king out of the country, Kaysone ordered King Savang Vatthana, Queen Khamphoui, and Crown Prince Vongsavang arrested and transported to a concentration camp in Sam Neua. In ten months the crown prince was dead. The king followed him three months later. The deaths would go unreported for eleven years.[61]

To head off new uprisings, Kaysone sent additional troops into Luang Prabang, Sayaboury, and Nam Tha. Hanoi added its own troops to the suppression campaign, drawn from the seven Vietnamese divisions that were now bivouacked in Laos.[62] Many of the rebels evaded the Vietnamese by crossing into Thailand. In more than three hundred separate operations, the communists killed only 150 guerrillas and captured just 82.[63]

The increasing numbers of Vietnamese in state and provincial bureaucracies and in the military, coupled with Vietnam's ruthless suppression of Lao insurgents, persuaded hundreds of LPLA officers and high-ranking civil servants to seek asylum in Thailand. The defectors all voiced a common complaint: Laos had become a puppet of Vietnam.[64] Other dissidents who had remained behind met in secret to plot Kaysone's overthrow.

There had already been an attempt on Kaysone's life. In December 1976, assassins ambushed his limousine on the way to the airport. No bullets hit Kaysone, and the would-be assassins, thirty-eight in all, were arrested and executed. Following the incident, Kaysone seldom left his compound on the outskirts of Vientiane. After more than a decade of hiding in Vieng Sai's caves, it was a conditioned response. Originally constructed to house American USAID workers, the compound included an Olympic-size swimming pool, a gymnasium, ranch-style houses with air conditioning, and a heavy detail of elite Vietnamese soldiers serving as Kaysone's personal bodyguards.

The plotters needed Kaysone out in the open. The opportunity presented itself on May 6, 1977, when Kaysone and other party leaders stepped into the limelight to mourn the passing of Sithon Kommadan, one of the party's founders. The assassins had their opportunity, but bungled the job. Twenty-six were arrested and thirteen executed.[65] Two attempts on his life within the span of a few months unnerved Kaysone. Though he was scheduled to greet Lao students returning from study abroad, he could not be coaxed out of his protected compound. His black "limousine drew up to the site of the ceremony, but without Kaysone—a tape of his speech was played instead."[66]

PRISON CAMPS

Kaysone's troubles were of his own making. The Lao communist party had devoted two decades of propaganda to the proposition that the Pathet Lao were the nation's only true patriots, the only ones committed to the welfare of Laotian peasants. Yet Kaysone betrayed Lao nationalism and established economic policies that transformed Laos' manageable poverty into mass destitution.

The revolution had not brought Laos political independence. The Vietnamese effectively ran the country. Hidden in the bowels of the LPDR, inside the Central Office for Lao Affairs, was the Working Committee for the West, code-named CP-38. Staffed entirely by Vietnamese Communist Party cadres, CP-38 exercised oversight over all LPDR policies. There were also Vietnamese advisors in every government ministry, in the military, and in the provincial bureaucracies. In the first year of the regime, Vietnamese soldiers in Laos outnumbered Laotian soldiers two to one. A year later the ratio stood at three to one. Equally ominous, Vietnamese peasants had begun to drift across the border and settle in the eastern provinces. In three years there would be one hundred thousand of them, installed in Vietnamese-style state farms.[67] Hanoi wanted more than merely to rule the nation; the ultimate goal, as described in a secret Vietnamese policy document, was "to regulate and distribute the work force and the population for building grain production bases" for the benefit of Vietnam.[68]

In July 1977, Vietnam's control over Laotian affairs was formalized with the signing of a twenty-five year "Treaty of Friendship and Cooperation" with Vietnam. The treaty ceded territory to Vietnam, gave legal sanction to Vietnamese troops on Laotian soil, and hinted at the eventual union of Vietnam and Laos, with control passing to the Vietnamese Communist Party.[69]

Ordinary Laotians resented Hanoi's dominance of their nation's political life. So did many hard-line Pathet Lao.[70] Though it was never publicized, during the war the NVA came to hold Pathet Lao units in the same contempt the American military and CIA had reserved for the RLA, as incompetent and without backbone. In a crucial battle on the Plain of Jars in 1969, a Pathet Lao artillery battalion fled before Hmong guerrillas and abandoned their precious 37-mm antiaircraft cannons. Following the incident, the NVA began to relegate Pathet Lao units to secondary operations away from the real fighting.

The Pathet Lao had bridled at being treated as inferiors. Toward the end of the war, Pathet Lao bureaucrats complained about the high taxes exacted by North Vietnamese commissars in Pathet Lao-controlled areas. Pathet Lao military officers, including General Phoumma Douangmala who commanded all Pathet Lao forces in southern Laos, were also unhappy over aggressive NVA military actions in densely populated areas loyal to the Pathet Lao, campaigns that killed innocent civilians and alienated the population. In March 1971, a Pathet Lao battalion took their NVA advisor prisoner and defected to the other side. Eight months later General Douangmala died under mysterious circumstances and Pathet

Lao battalions clashed with NVA forces. After being disarmed by the NVA, one of the rebellious battalions made a dash for RLA territory with the idea of defecting to the Rightists. The North Vietnamese pursued the battalion and trapped it at a waterfall. Though the Pathet Lao were unarmed, the North Vietnamese slaughtered them.[71]

The "Treaty of Friendship and Cooperation" stirred up these bitter memories and opened old wounds. The treaty was an admission that Laos was now a virtual puppet of Vietnam, and Laotians second-class citizens. The only consolation was that Laos' cat's-paw government lacked strong centralized control. Because of the country's primitive transportation infrastructure, Hanoi had decided to focus all economic development at the provincial level, with the hope that each province would attain economic self-sufficiency. This required considerable autonomy for provincial bureaucracies, making centralized control difficult.

Difficult but not impossible. The government was able to exercise sufficient authority to dispatch forty thousand Laotians to concentration camps.[72] In this, as in so much else, the LPDR followed Vietnam's lead. Starting in mid-1975, the Socialist Republic of Vietnam (SRV) put several hundred thousand Vietnamese from the Mekong delta into concentration camps. In the first year of their operation, camp authorities executed an estimated sixty thousand prisoners.[73]

In Laos the roundup of "political criminals" began in June 1975, and went into high gear in August with the arrest of former officials and high-ranking officers in the old regime. The communists transported the prisoners, including eight generals and four top government ministers, to Vieng Sai in Sam Neua Province, the site of the regime's first concentration camp.[74] There were as yet no barracks to house them, so prisoners built their own out of rough-hewn logs harvested from the forest, dwelling in caves until the work was finished.

Forcing the prisoners to live in caves as temporary housing may have been a matter of convenience, since Vieng Sai's hills are riddled with caverns. But, vindictiveness may also have influenced the decision. For more than a decade Pathet Lao party bosses, along with support cadres and their families, had lived like rats in the caves (which housed not only people but tool shops, a pharmaceutical factory, a weaving mill, an elementary school, and government offices),[75] while Vientiane's elite made the rounds of lavish dinner parties in Vientiane's French colonial mansions and Mekong villas. Now it was the old elites' turn to experience the cold and gloom of Vieng Sai's limestone grottoes.

Sam Neua would soon have four camps, referenced only by number: camps 3, 4, 5, and 6. Euphemistically labeled by the regime as "R&R" centers (centers for remolding and reconstruction), they were concentration camps pure and simple. Inmates received little food, were worked like slaves, and on occasion were executed. Many perished from disease and few were ever released.[76]

In addition to back-breaking labor, prisoners in the Sam Neua camps underwent unrelenting indoctrination. Divided into small groups, or cells, inmates met to listen to a political commissar bark out the lesson for the day. What the commissars called "debate" followed next, with cell members paraphrasing the drivel that had been force-fed to them during the lecture period. Then came the time for self-criticism. Prisoners revealed errors in their thinking, confessed unregenerate longings for the old capitalist order, and admitted to misgivings about the new communist regime. Since everyone genuinely felt such things, the trick was to make the confession sound contrite rather than unrepentant. Other cell members were obliged to respond to the confession with indignant denunciations. For many it became a game of role-playing, their "only recreation of the day, the only time when they could speak with other inmates."

With the camp administration spending so much time on indoctrination, many inmates believed they would be released once they were deemed fully rehabilitated. But as the years passed, they finally saw the truth. "Then the day came when we understood that no one would ever leave the camp. We were there to die, slowly, cutting wood and clearing away the forest meter by meter in this thick Laotian jungle."[77]

Few prisoners escaped. Two who made it were Hmong. Blong Hao and Nu Ly persuaded camp authorities to allow their families to relocate near their camp. Convinced the two would not escape and leave their families behind to suffer reprisals, camp guards made them trustees. Assigned work with minimum supervision, the two Hmong bolted into the forest several days after their families had quietly slipped away in the night.[78]

In 1976 the regime established six new camps. Two of them, numbered 8 and 979, were in southern Laos; another was in the far north in Phong Saly; two were in Xieng Khouang, and another was in Vientiane Province at the old Sam Khe Prison. There were also camps for smaller fish: low-level civil servants and ordinary foot soldiers of the former regime, plus anyone suspected of counter-revolutionary tendencies. At scores of these "re-education centers," inmates did hard labor on a starvation diet and remained in custody until camp administrators decided they were no longer a threat to the state, which for most meant a prison term of at least three to five years.

To help with local work projects, every province set up make-shift holding centers for Laotians purportedly lacking sufficient enthusiasm for the nation's socialist experiment. It was a badly disguised system of forced labor. Inmates were assigned to labor gangs and invariably released after their work project was completed.

The regime actually arrested some real criminals. Over a thousand of Vientiane's underworld of gamblers, thieves, drug peddlers, and prostitutes were rounded up and placed in the "Re-education Center for Social Evils" near the Nam Ngum Dam.[79] After having their heads shaved, they were put to work finishing construction on the dam. Once the dam was completed in the early 1980s, the majority were released.

Laotians spared the camps had other burdens to bear. Starting in early 1976, communist cadres with notebooks arrived in villages and hamlets throughout the nation, ostensibly to conduct a census ordered by the Ministry of Interior. The census-takers required families to inventory all assets (money, jewelry, even livestock), then liberated anything of value on the list. Understandably, villagers did not always provide an accurate accounting, prompting one top party official to complain that peasants who buried property and gold in the ground in order to hide them from the census authorities displayed an unjustified lack of trust in the government.[80]

Officials from the Ministry of Interior did gather some actual demographic information, for they were keenly interested in the ages of all boys and young men. Villagers knew immediately that the object was to develop draft rosters. Like the state's bureaucracy, the army was constantly expanding. In four year it would grow from 20,000 to 55,000 soldiers.

The population in the concentration camps was also expanding. One function of the national census was to sniff out political criminals. Interspersed with questions about possessions and the ages of sons were inquiries about past military service. Census officials encouraged neighbors to betray neighbors, children their parents. Later, soldiers arrived to haul away individuals fingered as former officers in the RLA or Vang Pao's army.

Understandably, people began to flee the country. Individuals with any standing in the former government were the first to go, along with most professionals and businessmen. Once the concentration camps began to fill, low-level RLG bureaucrats and minor RLA officers also headed for the border. Then Laotian peasants began to leave. To prevent escapes, the regime established stiff travel restrictions. Villagers needed signatures from three government officials to travel from one village to another, and five signatures to cross provincial boundaries.[81] Anyone without proper documents was arrested. To set an example, communist soldiers shot violators and left their bodies on the open road.

Despite the executions, people continued to flee the country. Between mid-1975 and 1977 more than a hundred thousand escaped to Thailand; eventually 340,000 (10 percent of the population) would make it across the Mekong. The mass exodus was not merely a response to oppression. Thousands of ordinary peasants left because of the hard economic times. Throughout 1976, drought plagued much of Laos. Nature overcompensated the following year with massive flooding. The bad weather destroyed crops and caused food shortages. In some provinces people starved.

BACKING INTO CAPITALISM

While the new regime could hardly be blamed for reduced agricultural output due to unseasonably bad weather, it was directly responsible for agricultural policies that turned misfortune into catastrophe. The new programs were an act of desperation to salvage the regime's finances. During the late 1960s and early 1970s, the U.S. delivered approximately $350 million yearly in financial aid to Laos, which was about 75 percent greater than the country's minuscule GNP.[82] The U.S. reduced this amount to $100 million in 1974, then stopped all aid once the communists took over.[83] The cut-off left the new government bankrupt.

Laos' monetary system was also teetering toward collapse. In the last years of the old regime the U.S. propped up the kip by means of the Foreign Exchange Operations Fund (FEOF). Created in 1964, the FEOF was formally housed within the International Monetary Fund (IMF). Though four other nations (France, Britain, Japan, and Australia) contributed money to the fund, the United States bankrolled most of the operation. Each year the FEOF purchased Lao kip, driving up its value. With a stronger currency, Laos was able to purchase foreign goods with fewer kip, reducing its import bill.

In 1974, the FEOF had donated thirty million dollars to this cause. Then Laos fell to the communists. In mid-1975, a confidential World Bank study revealed that closing down the FEOF would do more than merely increase Laos' import costs, it "would cause the collapse of organized administration, and much of urban life."[84] The report brought smiles to the faces of top officials in the United States State Department. The FEOF immediately halted operations and the kip began a free fall, accelerated by the regime's decision to make up for declining purchasing power by printing more money. In the first months of 1976, the kip declined to four thousand per dollar. By June it was down to fourteen thousand per dollar. By year's end Laos' money supply had tripled, making the kip virtually worthless.[85]

Vietnam rushed to Laos' rescue with aid. So did the Soviet Union, outspending Vietnam by nearly three to one.[86] Still, the total was less than half of what Laos formerly received from America, hardly sufficient to support the regime's swelling bureaucracy, which would eventually absorb a full 25 percent of the nation's working population.[87] Desperate for additional revenue, the regime levied a steep tax on farmers and collectivized agriculture, remedies guaranteed to intensify resentment and ruin the economy.

The communists had not risen to power in Laos in the wake of a peasant uprising, sparked by long-standing political and economic injustice. Power was seized by NVA and Pathet Lao soldiers. The regime fantasized that mass indoctrination would rectify this accident of history and win over the peasants. To this purpose, it conducted political seminars throughout the country. Attendance was mandatory. Communist cadres hammered away at the evils of imperialism. They also talked incessantly of exploitation. It was a poor choice of topic. Laos' peasants had been the least exploited in Indochina.

In South Vietnam, before the communist putsch, the peasants were virtually landless: 75 percent of the land in the Mekong delta was held by a mere two thousand families. In Thailand, most of the peasants had been landless for generations, the result of King Chulalongkorn's land reforms in the nineteenth century that enabled aristocrats and state officials to accumulate thousands of square miles of paddy land for commercial farming. Peasants in Cambodia were not much better off. The vast majority had been tenant farmers since the turn of the century. In the midst of this ocean of landless peasants stood Laos, an island of peasant proprietors. Eighty percent of Laos' peasants owned the land they farmed, and paid almost no taxes.

The near absence of taxes was a recent historical aberration. Prior to French rule, Laos' gentry squeezed the peasant class. Peasants with ambition fared the worst, for the slightest sign of material progress, such as larger than normal crops or a new house or the purchase of new cattle, invited ruinous taxation or a forced loan to the gentry, and sometimes the outright expropriation of property. So great was the disincentive to enterprise that "merely getting by" became a way of life, encouraging Westerners to view the ethnic Lao as lazy and indifferent to material progress.

The French continued the tradition of heavy taxation (though light when compared to the taxes the French imposed on the Vietnamese), and superimposed additional taxes that were widely resented. Once Laos gained its independence in 1953, the national assembly immediately abolished one of the most unpopular legacies of French rule, the head tax on peasants. The tax was never reinstated. To make up for the lost revenue the government increased excise taxes and raised fees for trading licenses. The remainder of the revenue shortfall, which by the mid-1960s amounted to approximately 60 percent of the national budget, was covered by American aid.[88]

Having lived virtually tax-free for twenty-three years and sensitized to exploitation by political seminars, Lao peasants were understandably long-faced over the new agricultural tax introduced in September 1976. Even on paper it was extreme. The tax expropriated 30 percent of all rice harvested beyond a one hundred kilogram per person family deduction,[89] eighty grams less than what is required for an adequate diet. In practice, everything over the deductible minimum was usually hauled away to state warehouses, a total of 60 percent of the nation's annual harvest.

None of this surplus was exported to earn capital for economic development. It was consumed by state employees and hungry Vietnamese soldiers, forcing the nation's three million plus citizens to survive on less than half of what went to feed the elite 15 percent of the population.[90] Taxes under the French had never been so onerous—not even in Vietnam, where peasants were forced to endure the highest tax rates in French Indochina.

In addition to high taxes, Laotian peasants had to bear the burden of collectivization. The regime launched its campaign to collectivize agriculture just prior to its introduction of the new agriculture tax. Participation in the collectives was supposed to be voluntary, but peasants who refused to join were subtly forced into submission by frequent visits to reeducation camps until they saw the error of their ways.[91]

By official pronouncement, the transition to collectives was to be phased in gradually, beginning with labor cooperatives where peasants still owned the land but pooled resources and worked under state supervision. Collectivization would then increase by degrees to fully collectivized farms, owned and run by the state. However, a large number of fully collectivized farms were already in operation as early as 1976, many of them in Xieng Khouang Province with Hmong supplying the labor.[92] Whatever the collective's form, farmers were obliged to sell everything harvested to the state at an administered price, which was extremely low so that the state could make a handsome profit.[93]

The collectivization was doomed to failure. Peasants objected to the low prices the state paid for crops. They resented the fact that lazy workers earned the same as those who toiled. And they complained that local party officials who supervised the cooperatives were abusive and corrupt. To reduce the level of discontent, party bosses admonished local officials to adhere to strict guidelines. There was to be no confiscation of private property. Farm managers were to pay peasants rent for land brought into the cooperatives and to allow them private plots for family gardens. Overzealous party cadres and corrupt local authorities flagrantly ignored the guidelines with relative impunity, which was to be expected given the considerable autonomy the regime accorded provincial bureaucracies.[94]

Peasant discontent over the cooperatives resulted in murdered farm managers[95] and inspired a new resistance movement in Pakse, where rebels ambushed government patrols and held meetings to encourage peasants to leave cooperatives.[96] The discontent also contributed to dismal harvests. The impact on the economy might have been even worse had the regime collectivized more than a fraction of the peasantry. By the end of 1978, only 16 percent of the nation's peasants worked in sixteen hundred collective farms, and only a portion of these collectives were honest efforts to reform agriculture along collectivist lines. Many of the collectives had been created for the sole purpose of isolating and monitoring suspect populations. There was a concentration of these "security" collectives in Champassak and Xieng Khouang, two provinces with intense resistance activity.[97]

While the collectives were a drag on the economy, the new agricultural tax, plus unseasonably bad weather, effectively pulled it down. Peasant farmers had no incentive to produce beyond the subsistence level. Everything beyond that was confiscated by the state. The rice harvest in 1977 fell to nearly half of the output for 1976,[98] forcing the government to import 365,000 tons of rice to prevent mass starvation. The harvest was slightly better in 1978, but still far below the level needed for self-sufficiency. More rice had to be imported.

Kaysone tried to put a good face on things, assuring the party faithful that collectivization was "a movement [that] has developed splendidly."[99] Behind the scenes, pressures were building for him to abandon the collectives and roll back taxes. The Soviets, who kept Laos afloat with large subsidies, were convinced that the regime's economic policies were the cause of the mass exodus from the country and, if continued, would provoke more insurrections.

In mid-1979, Soviet Premier Alexsei Kosygin strongly suggested to Kaysone that it was time to drop the collectivization drive and reduce taxes.[100] Though Vietnam also contributed substantial aid to Laos, Hanoi had only ideology and no evidence to recommend staying the course. The SRV had created thirteen thousand collectives in the Mekong delta, monitored their dismal performance, and abandoned all but two thousand.[101] While Kaysone might rely on support from Hanoi to politely ignore Moscow's counsel, he could hardly turn a deaf ear to the quiet, yet compelling, advice of the International Monetary Fund (IMF).

The regime's involvement with the IMF began in 1976. The Soviets had protested,[102] but Kaysone had Hanoi on his side. Vietnam had already secured a $36 million loan from the agency, making it the first communist nation to join the IMF. Like Vietnam, Laos was desperate for funds. Runaway inflation had rendered the kip worthless. With no money to purchase imports, the shelves of stores reserved for state bureaucrats were empty. To keep Vientiane's nomenklatura happy, Kaysone sought and received a $3.2 million loan from the IMF to purchase foreign goods.[103] A second loan followed in 1977, and a third in 1978, with expectations of a fourth loan in 1979. Once Kaysone was hooked, the IMF began to reel him in.

Established in 1945 as a special agency of the United Nations, the IMF evolved from an institution dedicated to maintaining stable exchange rates into the monetary guardian of world capitalism. By the 1960s, the agency had become infamous for its lack of sympathy for non-market approaches to economic development. Poor nations, communist and capitalist alike, caught in its net were invariably forced to slash state expenditures and balance budgets to qualify for more loans. The austerity measures sometimes led to civil disorders, commonly referred to as "IMF riots."

Under IMF prodding, Kaysone moderated the agriculture tax and the state began to pay peasants higher prices for their crops. The IMF wanted more. In late 1979, Kaysone caved into its demands, drastically reducing the agriculture tax and increasing state prices for agricultural products by 500 percent, bringing them close to the free market level. Vientiane reduced subsidies for state en-

terprises, devalued the kip, and encouraged trade between provinces. For the first time since its inception, the regime allowed
private merchants to engage in foreign trade. The last bitter pill
swallowed was an abrupt halt to the campaign to collectivize agriculture.[104] With lower taxes and fewer cooperatives, agriculture
rebounded. By 1981, the country was finally harvesting enough
rice to feed all of its citizens. Over the next decade pressure from
the IMF would induce Kaysone to privatize state firms, permit
free markets for most goods, and open the nation to foreign investment, leaving Laos communist in name only.

DEALINGS WITH THE HMONG

Laos' experiment with Soviet-style communism was relatively
short-lived. Within a few years the agricultural collectives were
gone. By the mid-1980s, free markets had become the rule and
most state enterprises were privatized or allowed to fail. Political
reform proceeded more slowly. Though the state remained authoritarian, political oppression eased over time. Resumption of U.S.
aid, coupled with the need for increased foreign investment, made
the regime increasingly sensitive to criticisms of human rights
abuses. By the mid-1980s Vientiane had closed many of the local
prison camps and begun releasing inmates from the major concentration camps. In some areas, the government permitted
inspectors from the United Nations to monitor the regime's treatment of Hmong.

In retrospect, the prudent course for dissidents would have
been to wait out the storm rather than needlessly sacrifice lives in
an armed insurrection that was bound to fail. But the rebels did
not have the benefit of hindsight. Just as Western analysts working with the best intelligence available failed to anticipate the
precipitous collapse of the Soviet Union,[105] no one in Laos could
have foreseen the rapid demise of the nation's agricultural collectives, the steady drift toward free markets, the closing of
concentration camps, or the gradual decline in political oppression.

More than any group, the Hmong would have gained most
from patience. Despite the expectation that the regime would deal
with them more harshly than with others, Vientiane was relatively

evenhanded in its oppression. Hmong political and military leaders were targeted for elimination, but so were the anti-communist Lao elite. And among the rank and file, ethnic Lao suffered nearly as much as the Hmong.

At least this was true until the Hmong rebelled. Isolated from the general population and unaware that lowland Lao were also suffering under the new regime, many rebels believed the Hmong were the principal target of communist oppression and that a campaign of genocide was underway. By acting from their worst fears, the rebels inadvertently confirmed them. The prospect of a fierce Hmong resistance rising from the ashes of Vang Pao's army stirred Vientiane to mount a campaign of ruthless suppression.

In fairness, it must be said that at the outset the communists did little to allay Hmong apprehensions. Only a few days before Vang Pao's departure from Laos, the official Pathet Lao organ, Khao Xane Pathet Lao, announced it would be "necessary to extirpate, down to the root, the Hmong minority."[106] In the minds of many Hmong, the atrocities committed against unarmed Hmong civilians at the Hin Heup bridge confirmed the worst, as did the occupation of Long Cheng.

Colonel Kham Ai had begun the occupation peacefully. With Hmong units integrated into his battalion, he did no more than make his presence felt before withdrawing without incident to the outskirts of Long Cheng. For two weeks Kham Ai led units back into Long Cheng to conduct interrogations in the hope of identifying former officers in Vang Pao's army. Well-dressed Hmong were of particular interest, for it was presumed former officers would dress the part. Wealthier Hmong put on old clothes, gave up bathing, and rubbed dirt on their faces. Families rich and poor raked their yards looking for shell casings, for interrogations were especially thorough at homes where such telltale signs of military service were discovered.[107]

During the interrogations, LPLA soldiers inventoried all personal property and confiscated items of wealth whenever possible. Only the fear of initiating a riot prevented them from carrying away every silver bar or ceremonial silver necklace. An old matriarch from the Vue clan had hidden chests full of silver bars in her house, each too heavy for one man to lift. Soldiers uncovered the chests during their inventory. On orders the old woman cracked one open, read the intentions of the soldiers from their faces, and began screaming for help. Relatives from nearby houses were soon on the scene. None of the old woman's relatives were armed; nevertheless, their presence rattled the soldiers, who grumbled and then left. The old woman ordered three of her nephews to move the chests to the forest and bury them. When the soldiers returned the next day and found the silver gone they were furious, but could do nothing.

It took a week to complete the interrogations and inventory all property. There was little violence. Soldiers routinely jostled and dispersed residents whenever they gathered in sizable groups, but otherwise left people alone. Only a few Hmong were arrested, mainly those who made frequent visits to outlying villages, arousing suspicions that they were looking for weapons cached in the forest, or meeting with other Hmong to plan an insurrection.

Kham Ai had yet to officially occupy Long Cheng; he withdrew all forces from the former military base at the end of each day. But at the beginning of the third week he made a show of force. Shortly after eight at night his artillery opened up. It was random fire intended to cow the population. The barrage continued throughout the night, each volley preceded by illumination flares to enable spotters to direct the fire. Parents covered their children with their bodies to shield them from the shell fragments that tore through homes. At dawn, the clanking of caterpillar treads replaced the sound of exploding shells as tanks entered Long Cheng, rumbling past shops in the open-air market on their way to Vang Pao's former headquarters. The tanks stayed only a few hours, sweeping their cannons back and forth menacingly to intimidate the population.

After another night of shelling, Kham Ai moved in several battalions and took permanent possession. All Hmong suspected of having served with Vang Pao were arrested. Some Hmong put up a fight and were wounded. These casualties were thrown into the Long Cheng jail with the rest and denied medical treatment, their festering wounds becoming breeding grounds for maggots. Relatives brought the wounded extra food to speed their recovery, but the guards confiscated everything and kept it for themselves.[108]

Every prisoner was questioned about his military service and asked the name of his commander and of the members of his platoon or company. Interrogators required prisoners to estimate the number of Pathet Lao they had killed and to name the villages their units had destroyed during the fighting. By the end of the week, Long Cheng's jail was full and Kham Ai had boxes of dossiers documenting the war crimes of Vang Pao and his officers. The material would never be used in a court of law. A decade would pass before the communists established anything resembling a normal legal system. The purpose of the dossiers was to discover the names of everyone of importance in Vang Pao's military administration and to cull a most-wanted list so that the regime could begin hunting them down.

The arrests continued into the following week. As Long Cheng's jail was already full, trucks arrived daily to haul prisoners away to temporary holding centers on the Plain of Jars. Later they were transferred to Nong Het, the site of the first Hmong prison camp in the province. The camp was not as funereal as the concentration camps at Vieng Sai. No one was worked to death or executed, but prisoners were beaten and women raped by guards, sometimes in full view of male prisoners. There would soon be other camps in the province, some rivaling the brutality of the concentration camps at Vieng Sai.

Following the occupation of Long Cheng, LPLA units swarmed over every major village in the sixty-mile corridor that once sheltered more than a hundred thousand Hmong war refugees. The occupation then expanded east and west. As at Long Cheng, soldiers and government officials interrogated residents, developed dossiers, inventoried and confiscated property, and arrested all Hmong thought to be ex-officers. By the end of the year, LPLA troops were billeted in Hmong communities as far west as Vang Vieng on Highway 13, and as far east as Muong Cha at the base of the Phu Bia massif.[109]

Wherever there were occupied villages there were re-education camps, centrally located to accommodate as many villages as possible. Some of the camps were for adult males only; others were for everyone: old men, young men, teenage boys, elderly matrons, young maidens, and mothers with wide-eyed toddlers hanging onto their skirts. As the Hmong were isolated in the highlands and believed the worst about the regime, they assumed the camps were only for Hmong. The indoctrination centers were everywhere, and lowland Lao as well as Hmong were forced to endure them—with one difference. The regime tailored the seminars in Hmong camps to address Hmong duplicity in the CIA's secret war and to attack what were thought to be retrograde features of Hmong society.

The instructor, usually an ethnic Lao, hammered away at the crimes committed by Vang Pao's "lackey" army. An often-used metaphor was that Vang Pao had planted an evil tree in Laos and the new regime was going to have to use sharp tools to cut it down. Any Hmong who had committed crimes (it was understood that no Hmong was without sin) could obtain absolution only by becoming a good Marxist, which included abandoning polygamy, viewed by the regime as a violation of complete equality between the sexes.

It is entirely conceivable that the communists contemplated ending polygamy in Laos. They had already attacked and destroyed the nation's ancient monarchy. Eventually they would target religion for elimination, though the Buddhism of the ethnic Lao and animism of the montagnards turned out to be so firmly established that they easily withstood the assault. Polygamy would also likely have survived had the regime ever advanced from words to deeds.[110] Yet the verbal assault alone was sufficient to spread alarm throughout Hmong communities.

Before the war, only a minority of Hmong practiced polygamy. It required a good deal of wealth to afford the bride price for additional wives, and a considerable income to support a large polygamous family. The war changed this. The flow of CIA money, and battle deaths that decimated the male population, democratized polygamy. Rising incomes from military chits enabled ordinary Hmong to afford the bride price for several wives. And the tradition of levirate (the duty to care for a dead brother's widow) resulted in many men marrying their sisters-in-law. By the end of the war, polygamous unions had become more the norm than the exception.

Hmong villages hummed with worried deliberation over what to do if the regime outlawed polygamy. Elders advised resignation before a superior force, but some of the younger men were unable to contain their outrage. At the re-education camp at Thane Na Oua, one young man, ignoring the anxious tugs on his sleeve from friends trying to get him to sit down, lashed out at the regime's logic. The state's demand that the Hmong be more productive and also abandon polygamy made no sense, he said. Hmong farmers already worked from dawn until dusk. Unless the communists could make the sun shine longer, Hmong farmers could only increase production by having large families, providing extra hands to do more work.

The next day the young man had vanished. It was not the doing of the communists. His own people drove him away, believing he had placed the entire community at risk by his outburst. Furious at both the communists and his own community, the young man left for Thailand.[111]

Thousands of Hmong were already in Thailand and their numbers were increasing daily, despite the hazards of the trip. Soldiers often shot Hmong traveling on the open road. Military boats cruising the Mekong routinely fired on Hmong spotted in the water. The river crossing was particularly daunting. There was more to fear than bullets from patrol boats. Because of the belief in water spirits—evil genies who inhabit deep ponds, lakes, and rivers and drown all Hmong who come within their reach—every Hmong, child or adult, trembled to enter water above the waist.

A lucky few made it across in hired canoes, but the vast majority used inner tubes, inflated plastic bags, or buoyant bamboo poles. Many lost their grip on the inner tubes and plastic bags in rapids, or had the bamboo poles wrenched away by churning water, and drowned. Yet despite the terrors of the Mekong, Hmong continued to flee to Thailand in large numbers.

Vientiane became obsessed with slowing the exodus and was furious at Thailand for granting the Hmong sanctuary. In July 1975, Lao gunboats assaulted Thai patrol boats on the Mekong. A few weeks later, a Lao artillery unit near Vientiane engaged its Thai counterpart across the Mekong in a duel with artillery and mortars.[112] Less than two months later, Lao cannons lobbed shells over the Mekong onto Ban Nam Lan, a temporary refugee camp for Hmong refugees well inside Thai territory. Reportedly, the attack killed a large number of Hmong in the camp.[113]

The regime stepped up efforts to control the comings and goings of Hmong in the larger communities. Residents of Long Cheng were herded into special zones where they could be more easily monitored. Six months later, the government intensified efforts to regulate Hmong traffic, not only to reduce escapes but to prevent Hmong from making contact with Lao and Yao rebels. Resistance activities by ethnic Lao in Vientiane and Sayaboury provinces, and by Yao montagnards in Nam Tha Province, were gathering momentum. Concerned that the Hmong might be drawn into the insurgency, the regime ordered additional Hmong relocated to areas under tighter military control. Many wound up in the newly created military district that straddled the border of Vientiane and Xieng Khouang provinces. The government moved another thirty thousand close to military garrisons on the Plain of Jars.

13

THE LONG ARM OF PA CHAY

BOUA CHER YANG

Overall, there was little Hmong resistance to the occupations and forced relocations. The only exception was an uprising in villages at the foot of Phu Bia mountain, igniting a messianic revolt that overwhelmed LPLA troops in the area. The organizing force behind the messianism was Boua Cher Yang. She was a disciple of Shong Lue Yang, the Hmong prophet jailed by Vang Pao in 1967 for preaching a cultural purism that impugned his leadership.

Shong Lue Yang escaped from prison in 1970. He was never closely guarded. By one account it was because the guards became converts to the new religion, though it is equally likely that Vang Pao wanted Shong Lue Vang to escape and leave the area, which was preferable to making him a martyr. But Shong Lue Yang obstinately remained in the province, resuming his ministry at Nam Chia at the base of the Phu Bia massif. There he erected a temple on a rise above the village (shaped as a nonagon, as dictated by a vision) and added new converts to the thousands who had already declared their faith, including three thousand who had mastered his Hmong script.

At nine in the morning in mid-February, 1971, five assassins sent by Vang Pao murdered Shong Lue Yang in his home, along with his wife. The assassins had arrived several weeks earlier to get the lay of the land and observe Shong Lue Yang's habits. Somehow Shong Lue Yang guessed their purpose. He entrusted his papers containing the distillation of his thoughts on the new religion and the latest revisions of his Hmong script to one of his followers, then ordered a handful of his most trusted disciples to leave Nam Chia for Houne Kynine.[1]

Boua Cher Yang was among this group. She was a tiny woman, no larger than a boy, but with an independent spirit and boundless energy. Twenty years earlier the untimely death of her husband had left her destitute. Refusing to live off handouts from her husband's clan, she survived by trading shamanist cures for farm labor to keep the family farm afloat. Though now in her mid-sixties, and shrivelled and gray, she still had a sparkle in her eyes and a spring in her step.

At Houne Kynine Boua Cher threw herself into the task of assisting the new leader of the movement, Young Lee Yang, in carrying on the martyred prophet's ministry. Hmong from surrounding villages flocked to the new temple (a replica of the nonagon at Nam Chia) to hear Yong Lee Yang preach, and to be taught the sacred Hmong script. Within a few months the movement had five hundred new converts.[2]

Boua Cher did not remain at Houne Kynine to share in the triumph. Visited by a premonition of impending disaster, she resettled in the remote village of Hayee, on the right bank of the Nam Ngum river. The move probably saved her life. In November 1971, assassins armed with bazookas entered Houne Kynine. They blew up several houses, killed six disciples, including Yong Lee Yang, and wounded sixteen others.

Boua Cher carried on alone at Hayee, spreading the faith, now known as "Chao Fa" (*Cob Fab*), sometimes translated as "Lord of the Sky." She worked underground to avoid assassination, concentrating on a few recruits at a time, organizing them into cells of three individuals, teaching the Hmong script, passing on Shong Lue Yang's message of cultural purism, and distributing cuttings from the blue-green gah (*nkhaj*) plant. Grown in front of a disciple's home, the plant was the only way members from different cells could identify fellow believers.

To get more converts, Boua Cher had her acolytes develop their own network of Chao Fa cells. In time the clandestine religious organization spread eastward from the Nam Ngum River all the way to the base of Phu Bia Mountain. In village after village, gah plants sprouted in front of homes. Despite the secrecy, it was soon common knowledge that the gah plant signified membership in the Chao Fa. Gah sprouted up in nearly every village between the Nam Ngum River and Phu Bia, creating the impression of a vast secret organization. It was whispered that the Chao Fa practiced secret rituals that induced supernatural powers, that the Chao Fa would soon rise up and wrest control of Xieng Khouang Province from the communists.

There was truth behind the rumor. Bou Cher preached revolution to her converts, foretelling the impending arrival of a Hmong king, a giant of a man invested with magical powers who would lead the Chao Fa. Women would fight alongside men, magically diverting the enemy's bullets with a wave of their aprons, and ancestor spirits would appear in the form of tigers to terrorize and devour the enemy.[3] In most essentials, it was the traditional Hmong vision of a messianic rebellion.

Toward the end of 1975, Boua Cher fell desperately ill. Toward the end, feverish and delirious, she murmured through cracked lips that a Chao Fa uprising was near at hand. The presentiment was prophetic. Shortly after her death, Chao Fa assaulted communist units at Muong Cha, Muong Ong, and Pha Lou, three villages clustered at the base of Phu Bia mountain.

TSONG ZUA HER

The concentration of Chao Fa at Phu Bia was due only partly to Boua Cher's religious underground. Even prior to her clandestine evangelism, villagers in the area had been caught up in the movement. The catalyst was Tsong Zua Her.

In 1970 Tsong Zua was serving as a sergeant in Vang Pao's army, stationed at Muong Cha. The town had become the principal training site for Vang Pao's SGUs, a marshaling area for troops preparing for action in the field, and a home base for teams that recruited Hmong for paramilitary service from nearby mountain villages.[4]

For anyone interested in surviving the war, Muong Cha was the place to be. It was a safe haven from the heavy fighting on the Plain of Jars, and far enough from Long Cheng to escape the death and destruction of the NVA's failed 1970 spring campaign to overrun the military base. Other Hmong in Tsong Zua's shoes would have counted their blessings, but he yearned to be in the thick of things, distinguish himself in combat, and earn an officer's rank. It was not all personal ambition. God had commanded him to lead troops into battle.

Well before his posting at Muong Cha, Tsong Zua had fallen under Shong Lue Yang's spell, though he was attracted more to the cultural purist side of the prophet's ministry than to his messianism. This changed shortly after his transfer to Muong Cha. The Hmong Messiah appeared to him in a dream and commanded that he raise an army.

Tsong Zua began to preach the faith, revealing that the Messiah had taught him magical rites to transform believers into an unbeatable army. He assembled a full company of soldiers from his followers and delivered the unit to Vang Pao, taking advantage of the general's offer to barter high rank for new recruits. Promoted to major, Tsong Zua volunteered his company for action against the NVA on the Plain of Jars.

In May 1971, Tsong Zua's unit spearheaded an assault by two regiments of Thai volunteers against NVA infantry on the plain. Before the battle, Tsong Zua distributed green and white stones from Muong Cha caves to his soldiers to make them invincible. As an extra measure of protection, he performed a magic rite. After filling a metal gong with water, then emptying the water into a vessel, he pressed the gong against each soldier's back. If the gong stuck, it meant the soldier would not be killed or wounded. If it fell away, Tsong Zua conducted additional ceremonies to insure that the soldier would survive combat. At the end of the ceremony, everyone drank the gong's sacred water.

The magic did not do much good. Enemy artillery pinned Tsong Zua's company down on the open grassland. Once the Vietnamese emerged from their trenches, they routed the Hmong, then closed with the Thais, decimating their ranks and taking several hundred prisoner.[5]

Vang Pao attributed the poor performance of Tsong Zua's company to the substitution of questionable "magic" for sound military strategy. He retired Tsong Zua from the army with a generous cash bonus and the gift of a small herd of cattle, hoping he would abandon magic and messianism, become a prosperous farmer and stay clear of the war.

Tsong Zua took his severance pay and cattle and moved to a small village close to Phu Ka Mountain, west of the Nam Ngum River. Vang Pao also cashiered Tsong Zua's company, or what was left of it. The man drifted back to Muong Cha, still faithful to Tsong Zua, despite their drubbing on the Plain of Jars. They soon enlisted in Boua Cher Yang's evangelical movement, recruited other Hmong to the cause, and spread the faith.

Government troops had first arrived in the Phu Bia area in August 1975. After occupying the villages of Muong Cha, Muong Ong, and Pha Lou, they impressed villagers into labor gangs to construct a re-education center on the outskirts of Muong Ong. Believing the center was really a concentration camp in disguise, a large number of the villagers fled into the hills.[6] Only a few days after the camp opened, news arrived of Boua Cher Yang's death. It was the spark necessary to ignite an uprising.

Local Chao Fa had already cast aside the security of their clandestine cells to link up with fellow believers. Now they arranged themselves into guerrilla units and went to war, assaulting Muong Cha. The communists had appropriated certain homes in the village to billet their troops. The rebels lobbed mortars onto the dwellings, then cut down LPLA soldiers as they emerged from the collapsed houses. After a half-hearted attempt to return mortar fire of their own,, the communists fled, leaving the town to the Chao Fa. The rebels met with stiffer resistance at Muong Ong and Pha Lou, but it was short-lived.[7] By early afternoon, retreating LPLA troops filled the road that led to Long Cheng and safety.

The ease of the victory, plus the fact that LPLA forces stayed clear of Phu Bia for several months after the raids, greatly enhanced the reputation of the Chao Fa, attracting more converts. Inspired by the Phu Bia insurrection, Hmong rebels south of Long Cheng attacked two Pathet Lao military camps near Pha Khet. During the assault, they killed General Foung Tongsee Yang, commander of all Pathet Lao Hmong since 1963, by placing cases of dynamite under his quarters and blowing it up, killing the Hmong general and fifteen of his soldiers.[8]

Reports of these exploits reached Tsong Zua Her. Having failed at cattle ranching, he had returned to religion. Leading a band of new disciples, he headed for Muong Cha, hoping to secure a place for himself in the rebellion. Despite his earlier failed military career, he was soon acknowledged as the de facto commander of the insurrection.

Still convinced that religion was more important to military success than tactics, Tsong Zua devised rituals and paraphernalia, temples and towers, to make his soldiers invincible. The temples were nonagons like those at Nam Chia and Houne Kynine. The towers, some as tall as sixty feet, were for prayer. It was rumored that Pa Chay had climbed to the top of trees to be closer to heaven when he prayed. Tsong Zua's towers served the same purpose. At the apex of each tower was a flag, emblazoned with symbols representing the moon, the sun, a star, and an elephant head. The moon was honored because it provided light for night raids, the sun because it nourished Hmong crops. The star represented the Hmong people and their burning desire for freedom. The elephant head, like the one on the old Laotian national flag (replaced by the communists with a solid white circle), represented Laos. All Chao Fa were to pray at the towers prior to going into battle, calling on heaven to keep them safe.[9]

Tsong Zua distributed small flags to his guerrillas, to be carried into the battle to protect them from enemy bullets. A virgin was to carry a large flag, staked at the scene of battle for even greater protection.[10] Tsong Zua ordered guerrillas to let their hair grow, promising that if a Chao Fa clamped his tresses in his mouth during battle, he would be immune to communist bullets.[11] And then there were the magic rocks. As in 1971, Tsong Zua gave each guerrilla colored stones from Muong Cha caves to protect them from harm.

This magic was soon put to the test. In March 1976, LPLA troops returned to Phu Bia, occupying five of the villages at the base of the mountain. The communists set up 105-mm howitzers at Muong Cha. The Chao Fa withdrew into the hills, where Tsong Zua readied them for battle. The guerrilla offensive began with attacks on communist troops occupying Pha Lou, Nam Fan, and Tia Neng. Vientiane rushed in reinforcements.

While the fighting raged, other Chao Fa units attacked Muong Ong. The rebels had already sent a message to troops in the village, announcing their intention to fight to the death. The attack began at noon. A Hmong maiden planted a Chao Fa flag in the ground within sight of the communist soldiers. The rebels charged and the communists fled.

As soon as the rebels occupied the town, the howitzers batteries at Muong Cha began raining shells on them. Everyone dashed for the forest. The shelling continued for an hour, then ceased, silenced by a full-scale assault on Muong Cha by another Chao Fa unit. After a brief fight, the communists at Muong Cha also fled, scurrying for the main road, their howitzers in tow. The rebels went after them, hoping to capture the artillery, and ran straight into a full PAVN (People's Army of Vietnam) battalion rushing to Phu Bia to reinforce the retreating LPLA forces.

The PAVN battalion harried the guerrillas all of the way back to Muong Cha. By late evening the Vietnamese had the town surrounded and the Chao Fa guerrillas trapped inside. Throughout the night the Vietnamese dug trenches in preparation for a siege; it began at dawn with heavy mortars and automatic weapons. The Hmong inside Muong Cha were pinned down.

Shortly before noon, two thousand additional Chao Fa emerged from the hills to rescue their comrades. The relief force spread out and ringed the enemy. Caught in a crossfire, the Vietnamese suffered heavy casualties. At six in the evening the Vietnamese began their retreat, leaving behind many dead, including their commander. The Chao Fa dogged the remnants of the PAVN battalion, inflicting more casualties. During the fighting the Hmong captured a field radio. Listening in later, they learned the full extent of enemy losses. Out of a force of approximately one thousand PAVN troops, nearly nine hundred had been killed or wounded. The Chao Fa lost only twelve men.[12]

The fighting wasn't over. Chao Fa were still engaged with LPLA units at Pha Lou, Nam Fan, and Tia Neng. Once these rebels received reinforcements, government troops at all three villages fled in disarray.

The Chao Fa had defeated the best forces the regime could muster and in six engagements had suffered only light casualties. It was proof of the power of their faith. The rebels felt invincible.

SAI SHOUA YANG

This stunning victory was a wake up call for Sai Shoua Yang, the chao muong of Vangxai. At the height of the war, nearly a hundred thousand Hmong lived in the district, most of them war refugees. Youa Tong Yang was then district head, having been rewarded for rallying two hundred Hmong villages to Vang Pao in 1961. In charge of dozens of political appointments, he had been a major player in Vang Pao's civil administration. Sai Shoua was a beneficiary of this power. Youa Tong Yang had made him tasseng of the subdistrict of Muong Pa. It was pure nepotism. Sai Shoua was Youa Tong Yang's second cousin. When Youa Tong Yang fled to Thailand with Vang Pao, Sai Shoua laid claim to the vacated post by hereditary right. The only objection came from Chou Teng Yang. As Youa Tong Yang's first cousin, he felt he had a more legitimate claim to the post. More experienced at politics, Sai Shoua easily elbowed Chou Teng aside.[13]

It was a hollow triumph. The office no longer had any power. Not only had forced relocations drastically reduced the district's population, the occupation of Hmong villages by LPLA troops left little room for self-rule. But that was before the Phu Bia rebellion. Sai Shoua had visions of liberating the entire province from the communists. Though he privately considered the Chao Fa fanatics,[14] he suddenly embraced their cause and raised a rebel army. After promoting himself to general, Sai Shoua established his military headquarters at Pha Khao, close to his former bailiwick at Muong Pa. Able to draw from a larger population, his Chao Fa organization soon dwarfed Tsong Zua Her's guerrilla network.

By early 1977, the two Chao Fa organizations had worked out a modus vivendi. Using the road between Long Cheng and Ban Some as a dividing line, Tsong Zua Her was to confine most of his operations to east of the road, Sai Shoua Yang to the west (see map "Long Cheng and Surrounding Villages"). The division of labor presumed Hmong guerrillas would continue to enjoy easy victories, making joint action unnecessary. The assumption was overly optimistic. Within a year, both groups would be fighting for their lives.

Chao Fa victories had left Kaysone shaken. His fears were only magnified once he received intelligence reports that Hmong were occupying a number of old CIA landing strips in the mountains around the Plain of Jars. Convinced that the Hmong were preparing to receive supplies from the outside, possibly even from the CIA, Kaysone sent government forces to reclaim the landing strips. When Hmong guerrillas roundly repulsed the LPLA units, Kaysone appealed to Vietnam for help. In July 1977, Hanoi committed four regiments to crush the Hmong rebellion. In that same month the Soviet Union delivered ten MIG-21s to Vientiane's Wat Tay Airport to provide air support for the campaign.[15]

Refusing to be intimidated, Hmong rebels launched a series of raids in the far west along Route 13, driving LPLA troops from their garrisons and briefly interdicting road traffic between Vientiane and Luang Prabang.[16] There were also hit-and-run ambushes against LPLA forces throughout Xieng Khouang Province.

The fighting tested the loyalty of Pathet Lao Hmong. During the war, Hmong fighting under the Pathet Lao banner had skirted engagements with Vang Pao's Hmong. Now they were being asked to engage Hmong rebels. Large numbers began to desert. Three thousand of them reached Thailand, many returning to Laos to join the resistance.[17] To the government it seemed that all Hmong were suddenly united.

Unnerved by the rebellion, provincial authorities began permitting thousands of Hmong to leave the agricultural collectives and farm on private plots. Hmong were also allowed to slaughter their livestock, an act previously prohibited by the government to preserve breeding stock and increase the number of chickens, pigs, and cattle in the country.[18] The softening of control, so clearly a result of Chao Fa victories, enhanced the rebels' status in the minds of all Hmong. To many it seemed that the Chao Fa were on the verge of liberating the entire province. There was again talk of an independent Hmong state.

CRUSHING THE CHAO FA

The 1977 dry season arrived in November. With roads again passable and the skies clear, the regime went after the Chao Fa in earnest. Artillery units hauled long-range cannons onto the Plain of Jars and into Long Cheng. Some of the cannons were 130s, the same huge artillery pieces that had almost battered Long Cheng into oblivion five years earlier. For weeks without letup, the artillery teams pounded suspected Chao Fa bases. PAVN forces in platoon- to company-sized units conducted American-style search-and-destroy missions. MIG-21s bombed rebel strongholds. T-28s lobbed napalm on villages. Helicopters equipped with spray-booms spewed Soviet-made nerve agents on rebels and civilian sympathizers.[19]

The offensive was devastating, but lost momentum in March of 1978 when heavy rains bogged down infantry and reduced visibility for bombing. Based on interviews with refugees fleeing the fighting, reporters in Bangkok estimated guerrilla losses to be thirteen hundred killed, eight hundred wounded, and nearly five thousand taken prisoner.[20] The communists would have to wait for the next dry season to inflict further damage.

The nerve agents used against the Chao Fa in the 1978 dry season offensive were later identified by the U.S. State Department as trichothecene mycotoxins and allied nerve gases.[21] A military historian of the Vietnam War, and leading expert on PAVN's military technology, concluded that the chemicals were probably "third-generation chemical warfare agents—biodegradable mycotoxin—being tested by Soviet research-and-development scientists, with the assistance of the PAVN Chemical Force."[22]

Hmong refugees interviewed by reporters in Thailand described the gases as a "yellow rain" and the name stuck, though the neurotoxins sometimes descended from the sky as a red or pink fog. The poison caused people to cough up blood, have severe diarrhea, and suffer skin lesions. Often within a day or two it killed the very young and very old, though Hmong reported people dropping dead on the spot after inhaling a large amount of the poison gas.

In some areas not only people but forest wildlife were affected. After a particularly heavy gas attack, one Hmong traveled several miles into the forest and everywhere found dead birds and rodents.[23] In another location a group of Hmong rebels entered one large scale "chemical killing zone" and found the jungle devoid of life for a five-kilometer radius. "There were no birds, no monkeys or large game at all. And, of course, there were no people. Even the insects seemed to have disappeared."[24]

The poisons had residual effects, collecting and hardening on the leaves of bushes and trees. When the monsoon rains washed over the land, the toxins leached into streams used by Hmong for drinking water, afflicting entire villages with a disabling, painful dysentery.[25]

Though no longer on the scene, Vang Pao informed the American press that the communists had gassed the Hmong as early as August 1975 and that as many as seventeen thousand civilians in the Phu Bia region had been killed by chemical warfare. A defector from the Lao air force, who admitted to firing gas rockets at Hmong rebels, later reported in Thailand that between 1975 and 1978 up to fifty thousand Hmong were killed by yellow rain.[26]

While these numbers were likely a gross exaggeration, it was equally ludicrous to suggest that the gas warfare was a gigantic hoax concocted by the U.S. government and Hmong leaders to undermine Vientiane's legitimacy.[27] The chemical warfare was no hoax. Several hundred technicians from the Soviet's Chemical-Warfare Division were in the country training LPLA personnel. Vientiane maintained four warehouses for chemical and biological agents at Pakse and Seno. Dr. Khamseng Keo Sengsathit, the regime's Director of Public Health, later revealed after his defection to China that his government had indeed used chemical weapons against the Hmong, killing thousands.[28]

As part of the 1977-78 offensive, PAVN troops occupied Muong Ong and Muong Cha, establishing a beachhead at the very hub of Tsong Zua Her's rebel network. Just eighteen months earlier Vietnamese blood had drenched this same soil when an entire PAVN battalion was decimated by Hmong rebels. Understandably, the occupying force was a bit edgy. Hunkered down in their trenches, PAVN troops nervously scanned the hills for Chao Fa high on opium, bearing magic flags, and bent on a fight to the death.

The soldiers need not have worried. Phu Bia's rebels were not the same Chao Fa of 1975. The area had been liberated for nearly two years, creating a false sense of security. Most Chao Fa units had essentially disbanded and returned to full-time farming. Meeting only occasionally for training and field exercises, they now functioned as reserve units rather than liberation forces.

Tsong Zua Her spent most of his time in prayer and religious rituals, ignoring the military side of his duties. No longer maintaining regular contact with local Chao Fa commanders, he had allowed his lines of communication to various units to deteriorate to the point of nonexistence. He seemed unaware that by permitting his troops to stand down he had allowed the momentum to leak out of his holy crusade, a fatal defect for a messianic movement. Earlier Hmong jihads, like the Mad Man's War of 1920 led by Pa Chay, preserved their élan by continuous battles and sufficient victories to persuade Hmong farmers to permanently abandon their fields to pursue territorial conquest and the dream of an independent Hmong kingdom.

Ironically, it was Sai Shoua Yang, the ambitious politician who privately scoffed at Chao Fa ideals, who understood far better than Tsong Zua the importance of building momentum. He had rapidly extended his own guerrilla network northward into the Plain of Jars and west to the edge of the Vientiane plain. During the bad weather months of 1977, his guerrillas ambushed LPLA patrols, blew up bridges, and attacked Vietnamese truck convoys. Though mere pinpricks to the communists, these small victories sustained the myth of Chao Fa invincibility, an illusion that delivered new recruits to Sai Shoua's organization and buoyed up the morale of Chao Fa in the field.

By contrast, Tsong Zua embraced Phu Bia as a sanctuary instead of a home base for launching military operations into enemy-controlled territory. The result was a steady atrophy of his guerrilla organization. His soldiers became weekend warriors, more caught up in the inertia of ordinary living than in pursuing a holy cause. The extent of the organization's deterioration became evident once Tsong Zua bestirred himself to order an attack against the Vietnamese occupying Muong Ong.

The assault, led by Xay Phia Yang, dragged on for two days. Unlike past engagements, Chao Fa casualties were heavy. Xay Phia expected reinforcements. None arrived. In the late afternoon of the second day, he broke off the attack and retreated into the hills. There he waited for orders. They never came.[29]

PAVN patrols fanned out from Muong Ong into the hills to hunt down Xay Phia and his partisans, burning down every Hmong farm they happened upon. Instead of engaging these patrols, Xay

Phia led his guerrillas away. When the communists returned to Muong Ong empty-handed, they vented their frustration with a cannonade of the surrounding hills. Refugees from the shelling wandered the forest, searching for someone to tell them what to do or where to go. Amidst this confusion, Xay Phia disbanded his troops and told them they were on their own. The guerrillas moved down the mountain to search for their families. Some were captured; others were reunited with their wives and children. The rest, having discovered that their families were among the refugees, left to find them.

Tsong Zua had also planned an attack against Muong Cha, to be led by Xeng Xiong, the local Chao Fa commander. For nearly a week Xeng tried to muster troops for the operation. The best he could accomplish was a skeleton force. Though he called off the assault, PAVN units at Muong Cha had received intelligence of the impending raid. Certain there were guerrillas in the woods, the Vietnamese blanketed the hills around the town with artillery fire. The exploding shells sent hill farmers scurrying for cover. They wandered the forest with their families, confused and desperate for leadership.

Xeng ordered his guerrillas to locate the refugees and move them to a grotto farther up the mountain where they would be safe from Muong Cha's artillery. Using the cave as a headquarters, Xeng waited for instructions from Tsong Zua. Low on supplies, he had some of the women return to Muong Cha and surrender. The women snuck back at night and brought food. Xeng remained for a week in the cave awaiting orders that never came.

The feeble Chao Fa resistance encouraged the Vietnamese to occupy more towns in the area. Within a month, Nam Fan, Tia Neng, and Pha Lou came under communist control. PAVN units patrolled the hills. MIG-21s and T-28s bombed outlying settlements. Helicopters sprayed poison gas.

The attacks left the Chao Fa scattered across Phu Bia's forests in complete disarray. Occasionally rebels ambushed Vietnamese units or unleashed rock slides on patrols, but mostly they ran before the enemy. By the middle of the year, some of the rebels and hundreds of the civilians began to surrender. The regime used them as slave labor on rice paddies in controlled areas, keeping them at work in the paddies until the rice harvest in late December. Some of these Hmong were held over after the harvest to work for two additional months in the forest cutting down trees.[30]

Captured Chao Fa received rougher treatment. The Vietnamese routinely handed prisoners over to the LPLA. Lao soldiers blindfolded captives and beat them senseless. They shot off fingers. They grilled captives to get them to reveal the locations of Chao Fa villages, slashing faces and legs, then pouring salt into the wounds to make prisoners talk. Though the torture seldom loosened tongues, it left horrible scars that were carried for a lifetime.[31] In one instance LPLA soldiers skinned a Hmong alive, forcing him to eat strips of flesh cut from his legs, stringing the torture out for four days before the man finally died.[32]

Desperate to regain control of Phu Bia, Tsong Zua Her made contact with Sai Shoua Yang. The two guerrilla chieftains agreed to a joint operation. While Sai Shoua attacked Ban Some, which had become a major holding area for Chao Fa prisoners, Tsong Zua's guerrillas, supported by units contributed by Sai Shoua, would liberate Muong Cha. The coordinated attack occurred toward the end of the year at the close of the rainy season. With most roads still impassable, the communists lacked mobility, and the overcast skies were a shield against attacks from the air.

Despite the bad weather, the communists easily beat back the assault on Ban Some. The rebels made a better accounting at Muong Cha, where LPLA troops had replaced PAVN units. By one rebel's count, the Chao Fa killed over a hundred government soldiers, plus fifty more in a separate engagement nearby.[33] But the rebels also took a beating. One Chao Fa platoon was caught in a crossfire while crossing a bridge and was nearly wiped out.[34] After several days of fighting, the rebels retreated, abandoning all hope of liberating Muong Cha.

In December 1978, with the dry season well under way, a combined force of seven thousand LPLA and PAVN soldiers assailed Chao Fa insurgents throughout Xieng Khouang Province. Sai Shoua had not seen anything like it since the NVA campaign to capture Long Cheng in late 1971.[35] He retreated with his partisans and their families to Phu Bia to join Tsong Zua in the mountains, traditionally the last refuge for Hmong guerrillas battling a vastly superior military force.

The communists attacked Phu Bia from both land and air, using rockets, poison gas, artillery, and napalm to break the back of the resistance. The offensive was timed to coincide with the rice harvest. As the communists moved up the mountain, they burned villages and confiscated rice, reducing the available food supply by half. Hmong dwelling at higher elevations quickly moved rice stores out of their villages and hid them in the forest. Their foresight only delayed the inevitable starvation that would eventually grip everyone on the mountain.

There was no letup in the military offensive. The communists were in a hurry to finish off the Chao Fa before the monsoons returned in May or June. Vientiane measured the progress of the campaign by the altitude of the front line. The plan was to drive the Hmong onto Phu Bia's crests, where there would be no escape. To keep the population moving, PAVN units not only engaged Chao Fa rebels but attacked civilian encampments, usually in night raids with mortars and grenade launchers to scatter people before sweeping over the camp, shooting anything that stirred.

Pa Nhia Vue lost her husband and a son in one of these raids. It was she who had persuaded her husband to move the family from Long Cheng to Phu Bia, the place of her birth. It seemed a good decision until the big communist offensive had her family constantly on the go, moving farther up the mountain to avoid capture. Everyone was asleep when the Vietnamese raided the encampment. Blasts from mortar shells had Pa on her feet scooping up her three-year-old son and leading her four older boys to higher ground. Her husband remained behind to hold off the attackers. A PAVN soldier gunned him down.

Still carrying her three-year-old, Pa guided her other boys up a ridge that led to a cliff, where she hoped to lose the Vietnamese. Her eldest son kept up, but the other boys fell behind. When Pa called to them, soldiers zeroed in on her voice and fired. One of the bullets struck her eldest son. He tumbled off the ridge into a deep ravine. Pa knew he was finished the moment he fell. It was a sheer seventy-foot drop onto jagged rocks.

Pa made a dash for the cliff. Almost there, she suddenly lost her footing. Maybe it was the distraction of her three-year-old squirming wildly in her arms, or the reflexive glance over her shoulder to catch sight of her pursuers. It was only a momentary loss of balance—just a split second. But it was enough to topple her off the ridge and send her sliding and bouncing down the steep incline. Pa instinctively kicked out her legs to break her fall. Her right foot slammed into something solid. A lightening bolt of pain in her knee doubled her up. She pitched forward and tumbled. Unseen branches scratched at her face. Sharp-edged rocks punched her back, sides, and buttocks. Then she slammed into a boulder. The impact knocked the air out of her. As she lay gasping for breath, her bruises throbbing, cuts and gashes stinging, she felt a massive jolt of pain in her right knee. She touched the knee; it was puffed up to the size of a small pumpkin. Pa made a heroic effort to straighten her knee and stand. The pain was so intense she blacked out. When she awoke, still in agony, anxiety for her child momentarily crowded out the pain. He had to be somewhere among the rocks nearby. Pa crawled over rubble, dragging her injured leg like excess baggage, searching for the boy. It seemed like hours before her fingers finally made contact with his tiny body. He spoke to her. She felt him all over, asking if anything hurt. He winced from his bruises, but nothing was broken. She cradled him in her arms and tried to rock him to sleep. Pa was still holding the child when the sun broke over the ridge and she heard people calling to her in Hmong. The voices were from survivors of the raid, out collecting the dead and wounded.

At a new encampment higher up the mountain Pa was reunited with her other three sons. Once she recuperated from her dislocated knee, she was again on the move, trying to stay ahead of the Vietnamese. The pace was never fast enough. There were more night raids. During one, all three of her older boys were killed. Pa had had enough of Phu Bia. She joined a group heading off the mountain. Carrying her three-year-old on her back in a Hmong *nyia* (swaddle), she walked nonstop until Phu Bia was only a silhouette in the distance.[36]

Hmong still on Phu Bia endeavored to avoid PAVN troops by moving farther up the mountain, remaining constantly on the go and living in the open. Sleeping on the ground with only leaves and branches for bedding, nearly everyone became infested with body lice. To keep the lice down, they had to boil their clothes and bathe regularly, a mortifying ritual recalled years later with nearly as much pain as recollections of starvation, disease, and the death of friends and family members.

Few Hmong owned more than a blouse and pair of pants, both patched and tattered. The government had distributed a yard of cloth per family in early 1976, but nothing since. Some families in remote areas had received no cloth at all. It was impossible to make new clothes from so little. For two years Hmong had been recycling their clothing, piecing bits together. Some garments had become so frayed they were almost transparent.

Without a change of clothes, men and women were forced to stand naked in full view while their threadbare shirts and pants boiled in cook pots. Habituated to extreme modesty in public, men and women blushed from head to toe, seldom waiting for their clothes to dry before putting them back on, increasing their chance of illness now that their immune systems were weakened from malnutrition.[37]

Families had been rationing rice from the start to make it last, augmenting their diet with whatever the forest had to offer. At lower elevations banana trees were plentiful. The pulp of the main stalks, made into a stew, fortified with thumb-size green bananas and a sprinkle of rice, helped to stave off hunger and reduce pressure on the rice stores. Banana trees did not grow at the higher elevations, and by then the rice was finished and the only food in abundance was roots. Digging up a sufficient quantity for a single meal took the better part of a day. The roots had to be pounded, shredded, and boiled to break down their cellulose before they could be eaten. Adults feigned gusto for the sour tasting mash to encourage children to clean their bowls. Even with the addition of herbs, if any were available, the roots tasted so sharp and bitter they made youngsters gag.

During the early months of the communist offensive, malnutrition, disease, and frequent enemy raids had persuaded many Hmong to abandon Phu Bia. Some surrendered to soldiers to receive the rice, corn, and clothes that the communists advertised were waiting for all Hmong who submitted.[38] Others were captured trying to escape, though several thousand eluded enemy patrols and got away. As hardships increased, thousands more deserted the mountain, some seeking sanctuary in Hmong villages in the highlands around Phu Bia, others leaving for Thailand.

For those left on Phu Bia, life became incessantly peripatetic, not just to keep ahead of enemy patrols but to find enough to eat. Excavating deep roots consumed more calories than the roots replaced, so whenever the supply of shallow roots gave out, families searched for new supplies farther up the mountain, inadvertently playing into the hands of the communists, whose goal was to box up the Hmong on Phu Bia's crests. Near the mountain's peaks even roots were scarce and people turned to eating fungus and mushrooms moldering under rotten logs. When a batch of poisonous mushrooms killed scores, people switched to eating creeping vines, felling entire stands of trees to get at the high growing tendrils until they, too, played out. Then people ate wood. Gouged out of the spongy boughs of large trees, the wood pulp had to be crushed, carded, and boiled to make it edible. The wood pulp filled stomachs but provided little real nourishment. Children stopped growing and their skin turned chalky white.[39] Some even shrank, loosing an inch or two in height, and remaining stunted for the rest of their lives. Toward the end, hollow-cheeked infants wailed for days before finally slipping into comas and dying.

The elderly also died in large numbers. One emaciated old man, out with a party searching for food, paused briefly to rest against a tree and catch his breath. After one long gasp, he expired on the spot. No one could recall a time when so many had died from disease and starvation.[40] Later estimates would confirm that the mortality rates on Phu Bia exceeded even those of the darkest periods of the secret war.[41] Few infants survived the ordeal; the elderly fared only slightly better.

As the death toll mounted and the suffering from starvation and illness became intolerable, Hmong in large numbers tried to surrender. It was a dangerous business. Many attempting to make contact with the enemy fell into ambushes set up for the last of the diehard Chao Fa guerrillas. A few were bold enough to try to slip through enemy lines and escape. During one of these attempts, a group fell into an ambush and scattered. Ten-year-old Xong Thao became separated from his family, then from the entire group. He crawled through brush until he came on a trail. It led down the mountain into a basin. There he found dead Hmong lying in piles: men, women, children, and infants jumbled together in heaps, all shot in an ambush. Farther down the trail he spied a Hmong woman in a clearing, finely dressed and sitting against a tree. He ran to her, hoping she would lead him to safety. A bag was open at her feet. Faded clothes, thin as tissue paper, were strewn on the ground. The woman was dead. She had put on her funeral clothes, saved in the bag during all these months on the mountain, and swallowed an overdose of opium. Xong sat down next to her and cried.[42]

By March 1979, most of the civilians on Phu Bia had either escaped off the mountain or surrendered. Remnants of the Chao Fa army were bottled up on the crests. The guerrillas made a brief stand, then surrendered in droves. A few units of stubborn hold-outs tried to fight their way out. Chia Xang Yang commanded twenty-eight able-bodied men, all that was left of an original force of three hundred. After three days of hard fighting his platoon-size unit was reduced to a squad. Chia Xang discovered a breach in the enemy's perimeter and broke through, leading his men in a wild dash down the mountain. Miraculously, they all escaped.[43]

Almost to the last, Tsong Zua Her held fast to the belief that the communist offensive could be broken, if only Vang Pao could be persuaded to help. Since early 1978 two of Vang Pao's agents had been on the mountain assessing the situation, hinting that arms, supplies, and men might soon be available to help the beleaguered guerrillas. When nothing was delivered, Tsong Zua concluded that Vang Pao was deliberately dragging his feet. He abducted one of the agents, a former T-28 pilot named Bee Vang, and held him hostage. The other agent, an American Hmong named Pha Vue, bargained and got Bee Vang released. The two agents walked off the mountain and fled to Thailand.[44]

Their departure finally convinced Tsong Zua that he was on his own. Realizing that all was lost, and with his messianic zeal spent, he abandoned Phu Bia in late 1978, leaving behind several thousand diehard followers who fought on for several more months. For the next six years Tsong Zua remained in hiding in the mountain forests south of the Plain of Jars, living off handouts from fellow clansmen, a hunted man whose only goal was to stay alive.

During those six years other Chao Fa survivors fought on, some operating out of secret bases in Thailand. In 1985 Tsong Zua rejoined the movement, leaving Xieng Khouang for a Chao Fa rebel stronghold in Thailand, commanded by his former disciple, Pa Kao Her. No longer a warrior, but still a celebrity, Tsong

Zua gave his full backing to the Ethnics Liberation Organization of Laos (ELOL), the political arm of Pa Kao Her's resistance organization, in an effort to increase its membership. Once support for ELOL increased, Tsong Zua quietly withdrew from the limelight.

Unlike Tsong Zua, Sai Shoua Yang remained on Phu Bia until the very last. With enemy units closing in, he led a column of Chao Fa guerrillas and their families into the forest below. Several times the column drew fire. The guerrillas carried their wounded, but left the dead behind. Once off the mountain Sai Shoua marched the column nonstop to Muong Yong and temporary safety. Within a few months, he was again at work rebuilding the Chao Fa.[45]

CONCENTRATION CAMPS

In October 1980, Quan Doi Nhan Dan, an official organ of the Peoples Army of Vietnam, proudly announced the communist victory over the Chao Fa: "After three years of struggle to crush the Hmong pirates, the soldiers of the Lao Liberation Army have penetrated the last strongholds of the Phu Bia pirates. Fifteen thousand inhabitants of the region have been liberated."[46] Actually, there had been three times that number on Phu Bia. The liberated were those who were captured or had surrendered during the offensive; the rest, perhaps as many as thirty thousand, had escaped.

The so-called liberation consisted of confining thousands to temporary holding centers on the Plain of Jars, where they were grilled about their role in the insurrection.[47] Those identified as guerrillas filled local jails. Noncombatants deemed unrepentant were kept back for additional rehabilitation. The rest went free, though few returned to Phu Bia, a place now associated with intolerable pain and suffering, and instead sought out relatives in nearby villages, hoping they would take them in.

Rehabilitation for the nearly two thousand Hmong still in detention consisted of daily indoctrination sessions to reform their minds, and hard work in corvée gangs to teach them the meaning of self-sacrifice for the greater good. Prisoners constructed quarters for soldiers, repaired roads, chopped down trees, and harvested rice. The rehabilitation was mainly geared to getting pressing work out of the way, for once the rice was in, everyone was let go. The release was not unconditional, however. To keep them on a short tether, Vientiane relocated the majority to a special resettlement camp at Ban Some where they could be closely monitored. A major population center for Hmong during the war, the town was destined to become the largest supervised settlement for Hmong in trouble with the regime.

The Chao Fa in jail were also scheduled for relocation once proper prison camps were built. Most of these facilities were completed by early 1980, the most infamous being the prison camp at Ban Ud on the Plain of Jars. The warden was a Hmong, Naotou Chang, a beneficiary of the regime's affirmative action campaign to fill provincial bureaucracies with montagnards as proof of its commitment to ethnic equality, earlier cast in doubt by the exclusion of hill tribesmen from the communist party's inner councils and ministerial posts in the national government. Oddly, Naotou Chang was the only Hmong on the prison staff. Everyone else, from office clerks to camp guards, was ethnic Lao. It was as if someone did not entirely trust Naotou Chang to do the right thing. Perhaps to prove his loyalty, he turned Ban Ud into a showplace of strict discipline and harsh treatment.

To initiate new prisoners to the brutality of Ban Ud, guards bound them to a plank and left them flat on their backs for a week, with only one meal a day—a ball of boiled rice placed on a prisoner's sternum. With hands pinioned, a prisoner ate by scooting his chin forward and snaking out his tongue to snag grains from the rice ball. The pitiful struggle, and facial contortions from the strain, served as entertainment for the guards, as did the spectacle of bound prisoners struggling to pinch down their pants with their fingertips in a hopeless effort to defecate without fouling themselves. Guards made a great comical show of holding their noses against the stench of soiled pants. Knowing Hmong to be prudish about public nudity, guards also forced prisoners to strip naked at the end of the week-long initiation so they could be hosed down in full view of women from a local village hired to wash inmates' clothes.[48]

Ban Ud's special mission was to break wills with hard and endless labor. Prisoners worked seven days a week, fifty-two weeks a year. The routine was unvarying. At daybreak, inmates ate a meal of meatless rice gruel. Guards then attached logging chains to their ankles. Ten feet long, the chains gouged and bloodied ankles until a protective layer of thick scar tissue formed (a brand shared by all of Ban Ud's alumni). Daily, in groups of three, inmates left for the forest, chains trailing like huge steel snakes. The main work was felling trees, hauled back to the camp on shoulders. The exhausting toil was justified as rehabilitation and for rebuilding Laos' infrastructure, though very little of the harvested timber entered the nation's economy; PAVN lorries carried most of the logs away to Vietnam.

After work, at dusk, prisoners ate their second and final meal of the same meatless rice gruel. Guards then removed the ankle chains, returned the prisoners to their barracks, and locked them in. Constructed of rough-hewn timber, each two-story barracks was ten feet wide and twenty-five feet long. Housing forty men, they provided cramped quarters, not only horizontally but vertically, for the ceilings were only four feet high. Prisoners had no bedding and slept on the floor. Roofing was of rough-hewn logs, so poorly fitted that rain streamed through the gaps, drenching everyone inside.

While a few lucky inmates served terms of less than three years, for the majority the minimum sentence was five years, though even exemplary prisoners had no guarantee of release after serving this minimum. To get released one had to have a sponsor, preferably a close relative, and sponsors were not easy to find. If a released prisoner resumed guerrilla activities, the sponsor went to jail and troops were garrisoned at his village.

As one might expect, a steady stream of letters flowed from the prison to home villages, pleading for sponsorship. Many went unanswered. Others met with polite refusals, which only elicited additional missives full of promises to walk the straight and narrow once released, a back and forth correspondence that sometimes lasted two or three years until a brother or uncle finally gave in.

For those without sponsors, incarceration at Ban Ud was a life sentence. This created an incentive to escape, yet escapes were rare. Tethered to logging chains during the day, locked in their barracks at night, and at the edge of collapse from unrelenting hard labor, few even made the attempt. The handful who tried were easily captured and sent into the field to dig up unexploded bombs, a work detail with few survivors. One Hmong did break out of Ban Ud, but only because he had help from the inside.

Tongkai Yang was interned at Ban Ud until 1984, the year his brother finally agreed to sponsor him. After a year living in his brother's village outside of Nong Het, Tongkai was back in prison, charged with complicity in a rebel uprising near Nong Het. The warden called him into his office to read orders sent down from provincial headquarters. Tongkai was to be held at Ban Ud indefinitely. To Tongkai's surprise, the warden suggested he escape and even offered to help. The warden was married to Tongkai's first cousin. It was blood over politics. When Tongkai bolted at the appointed time, he found his barracks' door unlocked, the sentry away from his post, and provisions cached a few hundred yards down the road. He fled into the mountains, found a guide, and left for Thailand.[49]

Tongkai's escape was the only blot on Ban Ud's otherwise unblemished record. In the other prison camps in the province, where guards were mostly Hmong, escapes were endemic. A guard sympathetic to the plight of a particular prisoner, or related by marriage or clan, sometimes looked the other way during a work detail and allowed him to flee into the forest. Going the extra mile, a guard might even arrange for a prisoner's escape, which, in the case of Wa Nu Lo, was an act that saved his life.

Wa Nu had almost made it to Thailand. Traveling with a group of several hundred, he spent months hiking over mountain trails and pushing through dense lowland jungle seeking safe access to the Mekong. Nearly there, the group was ambushed. Families scattered in all directions. Wa Nu wound up on the outskirts of Vientiane, soliciting boatmen with bribes to ferry his family to Thailand. When a boatman turned him in and authorities learned he was Chao Fa, Wa Nu was in the back of a truck bouncing along Route 4 to a prison camp near Phong Savan.

The prison was top-heavy with Lo clan guards, enabling Wa Nu to smuggle out letters to high-placed Lo clan relatives in the provincial bureaucracy, pleading for sponsorship. Family ties prevailed and Wa Nu got his sponsorship, though the camp director insisted he serve a year before his release. As the months wore on, Wa Nu began to doubt the director would keep his word. A letter to his wife revealing his intention to escape fell into the wrong hands and three more years were tacked onto his sentence.

After Wa Nu turned rebellious, the camp director assigned him heavy labor. When this failed to change Wa Nu's attitude, the director put him to work digging up unexploded bombs. Miraculously still alive after two years of such work, and as rebellious as ever, Wa Nu had become the camp director's personal bête noire. The director scheduled him for "special counseling," a euphemism for execution. In a panic, Wa Nu begged a Lo guard for help. The guard let him slip by his post in the night and directed him to food hidden in bushes beside the road. Next to the backpack crammed with provisions, Wa Nu found a fully loaded rifle.[50]

LIFE ON THE RUN

Nearly thirty thousand Phu Bia Hmong had avoided forced labor and prison by eluding capture. Life on the run was hard. Soldiers routinely arrested Hmong caught traveling the open road and fired on those who fled from their approach. The only way to avoid these dangers was to settle in an established village, but few would take Phu Bia fugitives in. This inhospitableness, so uncharacteristic of Hmong in even the leanest of times, was only partly due to fear of government reprisals. Many Hmong harbored genuine ill-will toward Chao Fa.

During his reign as Chao Fa chieftain, Sai Shoua Yang had aggressively recruited guerrilla fighters across Xieng Khouang Province. Many were eager volunteers, either because they believed in the cause or, like Wang Cheng Vue, were already on the government's most-wanted list and had nothing to lose. As a former official in Vang Pao's administration, Wang Cheng was a hunted man. Having vowed never to be taken alive, he carried a grenade to blow himself up if captured, and take a few of the enemy with him. When the communists caught his scent, he fled west to Na Cha Na Chone and organized a maquis that bloodied LPLA units operating near Bou Nong. When contacted by one of Sai Shoua's agents, Wang Cheng immediately led his guerrillas to Phu Bia to join the fighting.[51]

Unlike Wang Cheng, most Hmong were not hunted men, and once the fighting turned against the Chao Fa, they simply wished to be left alone to cope with the new regime in their own way. Chao Fa recruiters had little sympathy for the war-weary and pressured non-aligned villages to deliver volunteers at gunpoint or under threat of Chao Fa reprisals. The arm-twisting caused resentment. In one village, enraged Hmong went on a rampage and executed all Chao Fa sympathizers, killing entire families.[52]

Sai Shoua's agents also requisitioned supplies, sometimes freely given but just as often confiscated. In those hard times, a sack of rice or corn or a few chickens was a sizable sacrifice for families living on the edge of starvation. The agents also went after the wealthy. One Vang clansman saw his considerable cattle herd, built up over a decade, culled down to a few head by Chao Fa agents. Ironically, he had to relocate to a communist-controlled zone to salvage what was left of the herd.[53]

In addition to the Chao Fa's coercive recruiting practices and confiscation of goods, many Hmong villages bore the brunt of the government's outrage over Chao Fa atrocities. Early in the rebellion it was a common practice for Chao Fa guerrillas to leave their families behind when government troops overran their villages. Wives served as spies and delivered food to their husbands at pre-arranged locations. To frustrate this ploy, the communists began transporting abandoned wives to other areas. Guerrillas raided these convoys to get their women back. They were mostly bloodless operations, for Lao soldiers usually ran away at the first shot. But on occasion the Chao Fa brutalized LPLA soldiers. During one rescue, rebels captured an entire unit, tied grenades to the soldiers' bodies, and blew them to bits. The wanton savagery brought more troops into the area. Soldiers manhandled villagers, tortured people during interrogations, and hauled a number away, presumably to prison camps.

Then there were the inevitable injustices of war. One rebel executed by the Chao Fa as a spy turned out to be guilty of nothing more than trying to save his marriage. Having left his wife behind in occupied Muong Cha to carry on the rebellion in Phu Bia's highlands, he soon accumulated two more wives. To keep his first wife happy, he sneaked back to Muong Cha as often as possible. His frequent visits to the communist-occupied town created the suspicion that he was passing information to the enemy. Without a trial or even a hearing to assess the evidence, his unit commander ordered him executed and his body tossed into a pond on the outskirts of Muong Cha, with instructions that the body not be removed.

For the man's wife and children, the act spawned a deep hatred for the Chao Fa, and a thirst for revenge. Nine years later the man who had ordered the execution arrived at a refugee camp in Thailand. There he encountered the dead man's sons, now young men. With several cousins they organized a hit squad and went after the man. Only the intercession of camp guards saved his life. To prevent his murder, camp authorities transferred him to another camp.[54]

Antipathy toward the Chao Fa only increased after the 1977-1978 communist offensive. With Vietnamese troops swarming over the countryside, many villages wanted nothing to do with the rebels.[55] A few Chao Fa who returned home to visit family were murdered by their own relatives, intent on proving to government authorities that the rest of the family was loyal to the government. Even Chao Fa who retired from the war were unwelcome, since they were magnets for active combatants seeking supplies, couriers, and spies. Villagers dealt with the problem by turning informer and identifying the location of guerrilla bases.

All of this enmity toward the Chao Fa made life difficult for Phu Bia fugitives. Few were able to find sanctuary. Turned away from one village after another, they roamed the highlands, surviving on roots and vines just as they had during their last months on Phu Bia. Gnawing hunger led some to pillage Hmong villages in the dead of night—stealing rice and corn from storehouses, plucking chickens from their roosts by their necks, strangling them so they could not sound an alarm, and killing pigs silently with sledge blows to the head before dragging them away. The thefts further embittered Hmong communities toward Phu Bia fugitives, thousands of whom had already given up hope and fled to Thailand.

FLEEING TO THAILAND

Eight thousand Hmong, many from Phu Bia, had already crossed the Mekong in 1978. Another twenty-four thousand entered Thailand in 1979, followed by an additional fifteen thousand in 1980. Thousands more had set out for Thailand but never made it. The high attrition was inevitable, given the hazards of the trip: disease, starvation, ambushes, and drowning. Things improved once professional guides appeared on the scene, Hmong coyotes who earned substantial incomes by delivering Hmong safely to refugee camps in Thailand.

Prior to the coyotes, groups heading for Thailand had no one to steer them away from communist patrols and had no clear idea of how to reach or cross the Mekong safely. Pathet Lao patrols killed thousands; thousands more died from disease or starvation; others drowned during the river crossing, so many that Lao fishermen began encountering hundreds of bodies, many of them mothers with babies strapped to their backs, "floating lifelessly in the river."[56]

The lucky few who made it to Thailand were near death from disease and malnutrition. Young children were in terrible shape. At one large refugee center the doctor in charge estimated that 50 percent of the camp children were suffering from third-degree malnutrition. A reporter touring the camp wrote of "starved babies, too feeble to cry . . . grotesquely shrunk by months of malnutrition" and resembling "little living corpses." [57]

The most publicized escape without professional guides was that of a group that crossed the Mekong in December 1977. Starting out with slightly more than eight thousand, only twenty-five hundred made it to the refugee camp at Nong Khai. Some gave up along the way and returned to the highlands; others were killed by LPLA patrols; hundreds were captured; others died from disease or exhaustion, or drowned in the Mekong.[58]

Other groups fared even worse, ending up with almost no survivors. Possibly the most ill-fated of these misadventures was that of a Phu Bia group that set out for the Mekong in early 1978. The trip was precipitated by the appearance one clear morning of MIG-21s screaming over the western slopes of Phu Bia. The jets came in so low they cast a shadow. Hmong children stared up slack-jawed, for at close range the eight-ton jets seemed gigantic. After their first pass, the MIGs rose and circled to begin their attack on one of the encampments. Bombs ripped apart crude huts, knocked down trees, and killed dozens of people. The survivors, thirteen families in all, could endure no more. That night they moved down the mountain as a group. Only once did they draw enemy fire and there were no casualties. Their destination was the river town of Paksane nearly a hundred kilometers south, where they planned to cross the Mekong.

During the trip they encountered other refugees, small bands heading in the same direction. The party expanded until it included nearly five hundred people. A few had been to Paksane before, but only by Route 4, the main road. No one was familiar with the hill trails they were following to avoid detection. As it turned out, the trails were closely watched and the column frequently stumbled into ambushes. Even ordinary Lao peasants crept close to the trails to take pot shots.

On a single day, the party was ambushed three times. Crying babies had given them away. Parents began sedating infants with opium. Several babies slipped into comas and died.[59] One mother refused to give any more opium to her infant girl. When the baby wailed steadily for an hour, the mother was told to dope her or leave the group. Once they came to a road she bundled the baby and left her on the side. The woman sobbed uncontrollably, unable to move. Her husband took her by the arm and dragged her away.

As the group neared Paksane they found the trails salted with land mines. Dozens were blown to bits. The group abandoned the trails and pushed through trackless jungle. Already weak from starvation and disease, the effort was too much and they returned to the trails, where the land mines claimed another forty people. They were out of food, starvation and disease competed with the mines to wipe them out. They had been marching nonstop for nearly a month. The group, now down to two hundred, was disease-ridden, bone-tired, and dispirited. It was a bad time to fall into an ambush. Too feeble to run or no longer caring enough eve even to try, they huddled together in resignation—easy targets for the soldiers who had them in a crossfire. The wounded toppled over each other, screaming, moaning, dying. The fusillade continued until there was no more movement in the mounds of bodies littering the jungle floor.

Twelve survived the slaughter by crawling on their bellies into dense underbrush. They regrouped and pushed on, encountering another escape party of eighteen, the remnants of a separate group ambushed earlier, most of them badly wounded and all starving.

Two days later the thirty Hmong stumbled on a storage hut in a jungle clearing and discovered a sack of rice. Lacking a cooking pot, they ate the rice raw, consuming it in small mouthfuls, chewing thoroughly before swallowing, knowing the grains would swell in their stomachs. The discipline of the measured eating proved too much for one man. He scooped handfuls into his mouth, swallowing without chewing. Soon he was doubled up, arms wrapped around his bloated stomach. Within an hour he was dead.

After three more days of slogging through thick bush they could at last smell the river, somewhere ahead but obscured by an impenetrable tangle of jungle. The healthier divided into two search parties of four each. The scouts moving west found a trail to the river and returned for the rest. The other search party was still out. The consensus was to leave without them and cross the river that afternoon. During the crossing a patrol boat spotted them and opened fire. Two made it to the other shore. The rest were killed.

The other search party had become hopelessly lost. They hacked through dense jungle for five days without sighting the river or encountering even a stream or pond. Their canteens were now empty. Two had already passed out from dehydration. The fittest of the four gathered up the canteens and left to find water. He found nothing but a buffalo grazing in a clearing. He shot the animal and drank its blood, heaving up the first mouthfuls but keeping the rest down. Strength returned to his body. He filled the canteens with the buffalo's blood and returned to his comrades. They retched and gagged on the blood, but finished it off. Revitalized, the group resumed their search and found a trail to the river. All four made it across the Mekong safely. Counting the two from the other party, that was six out of five hundred. Everyone else was dead.[60]

Few groups suffered this much or lost so many people, but all had their share of misfortune. Earlier, another group of nearly a thousand had also tried to cross the Mekong close to Paksane, but were driven off by government troops. They retreated to higher ground, moving west over the mountain chain that parallels the Mekong between Paksane and Vientiane. They searched the slopes for a route to the river, found several, followed them down and ran into patrols. After six weeks they reached the outskirts of Vientiane. Finding the hills swarming with patrols, they headed back to

Paksane. By now their food had run out. Mothers with infants lost their milk and their babies died. Older children were so gaunt and exhausted from the constant marching they begged to be left behind so they could rest and die quietly. The elderly coughed and wheezed, ran raging fevers, and died. Close to Paksane, soldiers fired on them, killing dozens. The group, with only three hundred left of the original thousand, retreated back into the hills. Not having the heart for another try at the Mekong, they drifted back toward Phu Bia.[61]

Only a few months later, another group crossed the Mekong near Paksane without incident. The trip was preceded by a sojourn at Phak Khet to hoard food. When the group set out for the Mekong it carried fifty pounds of rice per adult and half that amount for each child. Few escapes were so well-planned. People usually left in a hurry, scrounging together what food they could, which was never enough. Invariably, many died from starvation and disease long before reaching the Mekong. The Phak Khet group stumbled across dozens of these emaciated corpses, so little flesh on their bones that the bodies had not decayed in the normal way and appeared mummified.

Luck was with the escape party. They were never ambushed. No one stepped on a land mine. They crossed the Mekong on makeshift bamboo rafts after midnight to avoid the river patrols. As an extra measure of precaution, they sedated the younger children and infants with opium to keep them quiet. The rafts held together, no one fell overboard, and everyone reached the other side.

In the early morning dark the group moved up the riverbank to a main road. When they reached the highway, they discovered that their luck had finally run out. Some of the children, and all of the infants, showed signs of opium overdose. By dawn, two of the children and all of the infants were dead. Fearing Thai authorities would arrest them for murdering babies, the mothers of the dead waded into a rice paddy. With tears streaming down their faces, they shoved the tiny bodies into the mud, pressing them down with their feet until they were firmly wedged into the paddy's black sediment.[62]

HMONG COYOTES

Starvation, disease, death, and tragedy were a common lot for nearly all groups who tried to flee Laos without the benefit of professional guides. However, with the advent of Hmong coyotes, these hazards were greatly diminished. The coyotes operated out of the refugee camps in Thailand. Most were veterans of the secret war, experienced at operating behind enemy lines and therefore skilled at avoiding enemy patrols.

It was immediately obvious there was a market for such guides when the first surge of Hmong from Phu Bia reached the Thai refugee camps. They told grim stories of hundreds killed, wounded, or captured, of people starving to death along the way, or drowning in the Mekong. These were sad tales, of course, but the coyotes were entrepreneurs with a nose for profit, not humanitarians, and they realized that the refugees would have paid almost any price to have been spared these horrors.

From mid-1978 on, nearly all large escape parties were led by Hmong coyotes. It was a profitable trade. The coyotes, or their relatives, were the ones in the refugee camps with motorcycles, many wives, their own homes, meat on the table, and real estate holdings in Thailand. Refugees complained of the high prices charged by coyotes, but no one denied they provided a valuable service. The groups they led were seldom ambushed, and few starved or drowned. There were still hazards, of course, varying from minor injuries, to a few lost lives, to an occasional catastrophe.

Somewhere near the middle of this spectrum was an escape that occurred in mid-1984 involving 174 people. The coyote was an experienced hand who had led many groups safely to Thailand. The march to the Mekong took twenty-two days and was un-eventful. The coyote knew his business and kept the group away from LPLA patrols. There was even a bit of merriment when a trail crossed a slope of smooth granite and children negotiated the slide by the seat of their pants, squealing with pleasure.

The group crossed the Mekong on bamboo rafts held together by jungle vines. A few of the rafts came apart in the rapids, leaving men, women, and children thrashing wildly in the water. Hmong on rafts still intact were able to rescue a few of the drowning Hmong, but the rest perished in the river.

It was just after midnight when the flotilla reached the other shore. There was a chill in the air, and as everyone was soaked to the skin, the coyote ordered men to gather driftwood and build fires. The entire group clustered around the flames, warming themselves. Some of the Hmong rescued from the river were still coughing up water. One elderly Hmong had just too much of the river in his lungs. Sitting close to a fire, he gasped for breath, then slumped to the ground, his face mottled with purple blotches. Two men rubbed his back to bring him around. The old man's chest rattled one last time and he died.

Someone noticed bodies floating ashore. The coyote organized a party to search the shoreline for others. Twelve were found. That left five still unaccounted for and presumed dead. Men dug graves for the dead on the beach, then joined their families around the fires and dripped off to sleep.

At dawn, Thai soldiers appeared, waving rifles and ordering everyone to get up so they could be counted. The burial mounds were in plain sight. A soldier stomped on a grave, felt the sand sag, and called to the officer in charge. The Thai commander had the bodies dug up and loaded onto a pickup and hauled away. Later, transport trucks arrived to take the Hmong to a holding center for processing.[63]

The loss of eighteen people out of nearly two hundred was high for an escape led by a professional guide. Most groups fared better, but on occasion a few fared much worse.

Toward the end of 1978, Cha Phia, a coyote from the Ly clan, offered to take two thousand Hmong to Thailand. He claimed to have documentation for that number, entitling the possessor to food and housing in a refugee camp. Inner tubes were waiting at the Mekong. There were hired trucks on the other side to transport Hmong to a camp. Thai authorities had been bribed so there would be no trouble with border guards.

The price was a hundred silver bars for the entire group, or about seventy thousand dollars. That was thirty-five dollars per person, and three or four hundred dollars for a sizable family. Over the years the amount charged by coyotes would rise. By the early 1980s the price was a silver bar for four people ($175 per person), a 400 percent increase over Cha Phia's fee. By the mid-1980s the fee was up to a silver bar per person, another jump of 300 percent.[64] Even at thirty-five dollars a head, the price was well beyond the means of most. But coyotes used creative financing. Payment was not demanded on the spot, only a pledge that relatives in the refugee camps, or living in America, would pay later.

There were already nine thousand Hmong in America, and more on the way. By the end of 1979 there would be nearly nineteen thousand, and at the close of 1980 almost fifty thousand. While the majority were on welfare, the average income was still twenty to thirty times that of the richest Lao peasant farmer. Counting only welfare payments, in 1978 the collective income of Hmong refugees in America probably exceeded $10 million.[65] Another fifty thousand Hmong were in refugee camps in Thailand, a substantial proportion beneficiaries of care packages, including money, from relatives in the U.S. Together the two groups had moderately deep pockets, which would become considerably deeper as the number of Hmong in the U.S. continued to increase.

Thus, even as early as 1978 there was a good probability that anyone who wanted to sign on with a coyote had a relative (if only a distant cousin) in the camps or in the U.S. By 1980, this would become almost a certainty. For the few who did not have relatives in the camps or in America, it was always possible to get someone leaving with a coyote to stand surety for their fee in exchange for a service, such as carrying food or baggage.

Cha Phia circulated through villages and encampments in the hills, tallying up the number who wanted to go. In a few days he had fourteen hundred committed to the trip, but insisted on the full two thousand. He traveled farther north and signed six hundred more. Three days later the two groups linked up and Cha Phia led them into the forest, traveling at night to avoid detection. It was the rainy season, so it was slow going. At one point they marched single-file up a steep, slippery mountain slope. The procession began at dusk. Thirteen hours later there were still Hmong at the bottom of the slope waiting to join the line.

For four days the column eluded government patrols; then in a ravine near Muong Hong it was caught in an ambush. Casualties were heaviest at the front of the line. Cha Phia kept the column moving while he gathered a few dozen armed Hmong to counterattack and suppress the enemy's fire. Bodies of the dead and dying clogged the ravine. People stepped over them to get by, trying to ignore the wails of the babies strapped to the backs of dead mothers and the fish-out-of-water gasps of those breathing their last. A few tried vainly to free infants from their slings and carry them off, but the press of the column made it impossible to stop without being knocked down and trampled.

Three days later the column reached the Mekong. After making camp on a hill overlooking the river, Cha Phia went down with twenty armed men to survey the shoreline. Satisfied things were secure, he took ten men to cut bamboo and construct a raft. The work was completed by early evening. Cha Phia was anxious to cross the river to meet his contacts on the Thai side. It would have been safer to wait until after midnight, but Cha Phia had his heart set on dinner in Thailand.

The raft was near the middle of the river when a bullet from a sniper's rifle struck Cha Phia in the stomach, knocking him into the water. An inner tube lashed to his body kept him afloat. There were nine other men on the raft, all with inflated plastic bags strapped to their chests. One of them jumped into the water and dragged Cha Phia to the opposite shore. There was more sniper fire. The other men leaped from the raft. Two made it back to the shore; the other six disappeared in the river.

The main group on the hill was in turmoil. Someone had spotted two men in green berets, standard LPLA issue, moving in the jungle not far away. With Cha Phia gone, decision-making fell to the elders in the group. They selected sixty young men for a reconnaissance patrol to determine the strength and location of the soldiers. Out only a few minutes, the patrol caught sight of LPLA troops in camouflage fatigues just a few hundred yards from the encampment, traveling fast single-file away from the camp. The Hmong set off in pursuit, keeping a safe distance to avoid detection. The soldiers were decoys, leading the Hmong into an ambush with machine guns. The Hmong leading the patrol died instantly. Twelve others were badly wounded. Under the protection of covering fire laid down by their comrades, twenty or so Hmong dragged the wounded back to the camp.

The sight of the wounded spread panic. Soon two thousand Hmong were crashing through the jungle in a hundred different directions. On the other side of the Mekong, Cha Phia's contacts already had him in a car speeding to a hospital. Cha Phia survived his wound and immigrated to the U.S. Those he left behind did not fare as well. Scores were killed by soldiers, while others starved to death in the jungle. A few drowned trying to cross the river on their own. The rest were captured, interrogated, and relocated to the resettlement center at Ban Some,[66] the destination for many Hmong caught trying to escape to Thailand.

BAN SOME

The resettlement center at Ban Some was modest and livable when it first began operation. The government distributed food and clothing to the camp population and allowed families to maintain small gardens. However, once the center became a dumping ground for Hmong "troublemakers," overcrowding set in. There were less than two thousand Hmong in the camp in early 1978. By mid-1980 the number had jumped to between five and six thousand, an increase of more than 200 percent.

The suggestion that six thousand Hmong made Ban Some overcrowded would have seemed ludicrous to Hmong who lived there in the late 1960s. Five to six times that number occupied the town and no one complained of overcrowding. But overcrowding is more than population density. There are more people per square mile in Fremont, a suburb of San Francisco, than in Bangladesh, one of the most densely populated areas of the third world. The residents of Fremont are moderately affluent; those in Bangladesh are desperately poor. Fremont has decent housing and no one starves; famine is a frequent occurrence in Bangladesh and its people live in hovels. This makes Bangladesh overcrowded and Fremont just densely populated.[67] Adequate resources make all the difference.

Before the communists rose to power the fifty thousand plus Hmong living at Ban Some did not feel crowded, because CIA money funneled through USAID maintained them in relative comfort. By contrast, the communists spent next to nothing to maintain Ban Some's resettlement camp. It was not just that the regime was strapped for money. Even had it possessed the CIA's boundless resources, it was not in a mind to reward malefactors with decent treatment.

At first, the strict economizing did not have dramatic ill effects. Camp authorities encouraged new arrivals to establish their own gardens, providing a much needed supplement to the meager food rations distributed to inmates. But once the population expanded, there were simply not enough garden plots to go around. And because so many of the newcomers were "troublemakers," camp authorities confiscated farm tools, fearing hoes, picks, and shovels could conceivably be used as weapons. The only tool permitted was a sharp stick, forcing Hmong to farm with Stone Age technology. The productivity of family plots declined, exacerbating food shortages.

Months of chronic malnutrition took their toll. By early 1980, illnesses of various kinds had spread through the camp population. A few desperate individuals wangled extra food rations for their families, including scarce meat and fish, by signing propaganda leaflets urging Hmong to abandon thoughts of fleeing the country. Perversely, the leaflets highlighted the horrible conditions at Ban Some, by now well known as a depository for captured Hmong escapees, as a reason for laying escape plans aside.

The spread of illness concerned Ban Some's mayor, who saw a plague in the making. After a tour of the resettlement center, he ordered the delivery of more rice and vegetables. Additional food did eventually arrive, but it was not enough. There was more illness, aggravated by inadequate shelter. Earlier, the government had clear-cut the surrounding forest, leaving little timber for housing. Many slept in the open or, if they were lucky, under plastic sheeting to keep out of the rain.

Weakened by hunger and exposed to the elements, Hmong died in increasing numbers. People swelled up and died. They became dehydrated from diarrhea and died. They ran high fevers and died. As wood was scarce, the dead were denied the traditional wood coffin. And as there were no funeral clothes, they went to their graves with what they had on—mostly rags. Even graves were a problem. Denied shovels, burial details dug graves with sticks until the backlog of corpses became so great that guards began lending them their trenching tools.

Toward the end of 1980, two hundred Hmong died in a single month. With so many to bury, it was impossible to conduct traditional three-day funeral rites. Work crews dug a grave, waited a respectful moment to allow relatives to deposit the body, then covered it up and moved on and dug another grave. The death rate continued to climb. By early 1981 the camp director dispatched a worried message to Vientiane, warning that the entire camp population might perish if something wasn't done. Three officials arrived to assess the situation, concurred that matters were serious, but emphatically ruled out additional food rations or improved housing. Instead, they recommended thinning out the population. Those with relatives willing to stand sponsor were the first to go, but as locating a sponsor was time-consuming, the rules were bent to allow anyone with relatives nearby to leave. Within a few months the camp's population was down by half. Disease waned. People stopped dying.[68]

Though Ban Some was no longer a graveyard for Hmong, the image stuck, serving as a deterrent for Hmong contemplating escape to Thailand. More than forty-seven thousand Hmong entered Thailand between 1978 and the end of 1980. This number declined by 71 percent in 1981, then dropped another 58 percent in 1982. How much of this was due to a fear of being captured and winding up at Ban Some is impossible to determine. Anecdotal evidence suggests it played some part. But the main factor was the simple fact that the bulk of the Phu Bia refugees had already reached Thailand by the end of 1980. Never again would Hmong in such large numbers run afoul of the regime and view their only options as death or escape. For the remainder of the decade, the number of Hmong entering Thailand would average only twenty-five hundred per year.

Had all Hmong resistance ceased after the Chao Fa insurrection, it is likely even fewer Hmong would have fled the country. But the resistance continued, sustained by former Phu Bia rebels who refused to give up, and by external support that kept people fighting.

CONTINUED RESISTANCE

Following his escape from Phu Bia, Sai Shoua Yang had struggled to rebuild the Chao Fa. Over the next four years he headed a loose guerrilla organization that operated intermittently from Ban Some to the Plain of Jars, and west to the Nam Ngum River.

Short on men, weapons, and supplies he used squad-sized units to ambush small LPLA patrols, assaults designed to minimize rebel casualties, maximize enemy dead, and result in captured arms and ammunition. At its height, his rebel force totaled no more than a few hundred—hardly a serious threat to the LPLA's standing army of fifty thousand. In 1983, Sai Shoua finally gave up the struggle and fled to Thailand. His departure did not end the resistance. Other Hmong maquis, operating independently of Sai Shoua's organization, continued the struggle.

Pa Kao Her led one of these groups. A former lieutenant in Vang Pao's army and Chao Fa commander, he fled Phu Bia for Thailand in 1978 to seek support from the Thai military for a continued Hmong resistance. There he made contact with former RLA General Boonleurt, living in Thailand and well-connected to the Thai general staff. Boonleurt became a conduit for money, supplies, and arms to sustain a Hmong guerrilla force headquartered on Thailand's border. By early 1979, Pa Kao was already conducting cross-border raids into Laos.[69]

Another Hmong group of LPLA army deserters operated close to the Chinese border. The mass desertion occurred in early 1978, when Vientiane uncovered a conspiracy within the LPLA to keep captured Chao Fa rebels out of internment camps. The leader of the conspiracy was Shoua Ger Thao, a top commander of Hmong troops in the LPLA. Just one step ahead of the authorities, Shoua Ger Thao escaped to Thailand.[70] His entire staff, however, wound up in a concentration camp. At the time, the elite Hmong unit Chao Fa Pachay was on maneuvers in the north. Learning of the crackdown on fellow Hmong in the LPLA, the entire unit defected to China, where it received a warm welcome.[71]

Supporting Hmong rebels was China's way of taking a slap at Vietnam. Since 1975 the two communist nations had quarreled over Cambodia. China supported Pol Pot, Cambodia's virulent anti-Vietnamese prime minister, to frustrate Vietnam's efforts to bring all of Indochina under its heel. As China desired, Pol Pot obstinately refused to become a puppet of Vietnam. But he also went a step further and slaughtered thousands of Cambodia's resident Vietnamese. Holding China partly responsible for these atrocities, Hanoi struck back by hounding Vietnam's Chinese minority, expropriating their property and expelling more than a hundred thousand from the country. China reacted by massing troops on Vietnam's border[72] and declaring its intention to support insurgents trying to topple Vietnam's puppet regime in Laos.

Beijing already had a presence in Laos' far north, where five to ten thousand Chinese workers and soldiers maintained an extensive road system. Constructed over the previous seventeen years, the road network began as an effort to improve communication between China's southwestern provinces of Guizhou and Yunnan, then was expanded to support North Vietnam's military operations in Laos. Once relations between China and Vietnam soured, Beijing constructed additional roads, extending the network all the way to Vietnam's border.[73]

At first the roads worried Hanoi because they gave Chinese soldiers a direct route into Vietnam. But after China's offer of aid to Lao insurgents, the roads became a threat to Hanoi's puppet regime in Laos, being a readymade logistics system for Chinese-trained Lao rebels to launch raids into Laos. Hanoi's worries seemed well-founded. Shortly after China gave sanctuary to the Pathet Lao Hmong, thousands of additional Hmong and Yao insurgents found their way to China to receive arms and training. Delighted by the turnout, Beijing ordered the Red Army to organize the insurgents into a rebel division. By late 1978, the division (about four thousand strong) was already engaging LPLA troops in Phong Saly and Sam Neua provinces.

Kaysone sent reinforcements to the region. The rebels routed them and pushed even farther south. Fearing they planned to liberate Sam Neua's concentration camps and absorb the prisoners into their army, Kaysone had the camps evacuated and the inmates marched to the southern panhandle. Having avoided one catastrophe, Kaysone immediately faced another. China announced that it was opening its doors to the Hmong and Lao in Thailand's refugee camps to flesh out the newly-formed rebel division.[74] To attract volunteers, Beijing named the division "Lanna" after an ancient kingdom on the China/Laos border,[75] creating the impression that China might support the establishment of a new nation as a homeland for Laos' dissidents, carved out of Laos' northern provinces.

China wasn't Kaysone's only worry. Thailand was also openly hostile to his regime, and for good reason. Kaysone had allowed

Vietnam, Thailand's traditional enemy, to billet three of its divisions in Laos and conduct maneuvers close to Thailand's border. Kaysone's administration also gave sanctuary to Thai communist insurgents at war with the Thai military, providing them with home bases in the Laotian panhandle and in Nam Tha Province.[76]

To nettle Kaysone, Thailand began supporting ethnic Lao and Hmong resistance fighters. A special intelligence unit of the Thai military monitored the activities of the various resistance groups and fielded three task forces (TF) numbered 332, 185, and 223 for liaison work. TF 332 kept in constant contact with Hmong loyal to Vang Pao. TF 185 linked up with Pa Kao Her's Chao Fa. And TF 223 organized guerrillas for special clandestine operations inside Laos.[77] The principal form of support, however, was passive—tolerating the use of refugee camps by Hmong insurgents as home bases for cross-border raids into Laos.

The most important of these camps was Ban Vinai. Though originally designed to keep Hmong refugees, many with combat experience, under strict control, once Bangkok realized Hmong freedom fighters could prove useful in a diplomatic tug-of-war with Vientiane, the Hmong at Ban Vinai were permitted greater autonomy. The camp soon had its own guerrilla organization and was launching guerrilla raids into Laos, all with the tacit approval of Thailand's government and military.

Insurgents also received aid from Washington. From 1975 to 1981, the CIA maintained contact with Hmong and Lao resistance forces operating out of Thailand, and occasionally planned and supplied guerrilla actions in Laos. It was a modest undertaking, however, involving few CIA personnel and small sums of money.[78] This changed when Reagan entered the White House. In March 1981, CIA director William Casey wrote a memo outlining a program of covert assistance to anticommunist resistance forces in Afghanistan, Cuba, Grenada, Iran, Libya, Nicaragua, Cambodia, and Laos. The memo became the foundation of what would later come to be known as the "Reagan Doctrine," a program to solicit funds from wealthy individuals, corporations, and foreign powers to underwrite the illegal support of anticommunist forces across the globe.

The conduit for this funding was the President's National Security Council (NSC). Though NSC's staff considered the Laotian resistance fragmented and ineffectual, NSC's director of Asian Affairs, Lt. Colonel Richard Childress, felt the resistance could be of use in locating the gravesites of American MIAs who had fought in the secret war and in ferreting out information about American POWs who might still be alive and held captive in Laos. Working with John LeBoutillier, a former U.S. Congressman turned POW/MIA activist, Childress put the NSC's stamp of approval on LeBoutillier's efforts to solicit funds from Saudis and other foreign nationals to fund a clandestine project, using a nonprofit POW/MIA organization as a front. The money ($578,689) wound up in Bangkok bank in the account of Mushtaq Ahmed Diwan and was later distributed to resistance forces in exchange for help in gathering information about American POWs and MIAs in Laos.[79] How much of the money went to Hmong resistance groups is unknown, but it is likely they received something.

LeBoutillier's fundraising through a front organization would eventually become the model for the NSC's other covert operations to support resistance forces elsewhere, including the Contras in Nicaragua. The more immediate consequence, however, was its effect on the POW/MIA community. Following LeBoutillier's lead, other activists in the movement launched private efforts to search for MIAs in Laos, raising money and hiring members of resistance groups as guides to locate prison camps rumored to hold Americans. Phoumono Nosavan, the son of Phoumi Nosavan, was a frequent middleman for these missions, which for a time became something of a cottage industry. No MIAs were ever located, and judging from the testimony of Americans who participated in these searches, their rebel guides led them on wild goose chases.[80]

Another source of support for the resistance came from the Council for World Freedom, a fundraising front for the Reagan administration's covert operations in Nicaragua, headed up by a veteran of the secret war in Laos, Richard Secord. Retired general John Singlaub worked with Secord on the project. One of Singlaub's jobs was to recruit anticommunist resistance leaders from across the world as guest speakers at highly publicized conferences. The purpose of this was to give the impression that there was a great groundswell of support worldwide for Reagan's anti-communism crusade, diverting attention from the fact that the millions of dollars going to the Council for World Freedom came mainly from foreign nationals and their governments and not from hundreds of thousands of concerned citizens writing small checks.

In 1985 Singlaub latched onto Pa Kao Her as the representative of the Lao resistance and flew him to well-publicized conferences in Angola and Texas to appear as a guest speaker. Singlaub paid Pa Kao Her's plane fare and hotel bills and donated an unspecified amount of money to his guerrilla organization, mainly for the purchase of arms. The exact amount is unknown, but reportedly it was relatively small.[81]

Support from these various external sources (China, Thailand, and the U.S.) began to dry up by the mid to late 1980s. When Laos moved in 1985 to normalize relations with China, Beijing responded by dissolving the Lanna division and closing down the military camps that had once trained up to fifteen hundred rebels per year.[82] Thailand also backed off, in 1989 officially ending all support for Hmong insurgents operating out of the refugee camps. By now Laos was a communist state in name only. Its markets were mainly free and Vientiane welcomed foreign investment, including money from Thailand. Thai entrepreneurs were building factories in Laos and harvesting the nation's forests, all of which encouraged Thailand to seek closer, and warmer, relations with Vientiane. To this end, Thailand's military began cracking down on Hmong involved in cross-border raids.

U.S. support for the rebels also faded away. From the beginning, Washington's principal interest was in acquiring information about American POWs and MIAs. With Vientiane refusing to open its records or allow American teams to search for remains, Washington was forced to rely on clandestine operations with insurgents to locate the graves and crash sites of Americans killed during the secret war. This changed in 1985, when Vientiane unexpectedly offered to cooperate in the search for MIAs. The about-face was partly an effort to get Washington to allow U.S. firms to invest in Laos and to resume government aid, but an additional goal was to persuade Washington to end all support for insurgents and to use its influence to pressure Thailand to do the same. Washington resumed aid to Laos in 1986,[83] and severed all links to the rebels in 1988.

Once foreign support for the resistance began to dry up, Vang Pao suddenly emerged on the scene as a major sponsor of the rebellion. Previously uninvolved in the insurgency, he now embraced it as a holy cause, raised his own maquis and whipped up moral support and financial backing from Hmong immigrants across America.

14

VANG PAO

FROM THAILAND TO MONTANA

In mid-May 1975, the CIA partially fulfilled its pledge to provide defeated Hmong sanctuary by airlifting Vang Pao and five thousand Hmong from Long Cheng to Namphong, an abandoned air base in Thailand. Vang Pao moved his family into the empty commandant's quarters and tried to recreate the atmosphere at Long Cheng by hosting nightly banquets for his top officers and aids. Over the next few weeks thousands of Hmong followed him on foot into Thailand. Daily, scores of these refugees straggled into Namphong. Thousands more were soon scattered along the Thai border in crude encampments, waiting to be processed as legitimate refugees.

Vang Pao frequently left Namphong to inventory these holding centers. The Thai military objected to these jaunts, suspecting correctly that Vang Pao was counting heads for military rosters and making mental notes about the terrain to assess the logistical possibilities. Each time the Thai generals ordered him to stop his wanderings, Vang Pao appealed over their heads to Thailand's Prime Minister Kurkit Pramoj's office, where the staff was more disposed to treat him as a visiting foreign dignitary than a displaced warlord scouting their country's border for potential base camps.

The Thai generals finally ran out of patience and informed the U.S. Embassy that Vang Pao had to go. Once it became clear that the generals were willing to strain U.S.-Thai relations to get their way, the embassy caved in and persuaded Washington to bend immigration laws so Vang Pao could immediately resettle his family in America. There was a brief farewell ceremony at the CIA offices in Bangkok, then Vang Pao was gone (he would not set foot on Thai soil for another seven years), headed first for Paris, then on to America, traveling with only one of his wives (the youngest) because polygamy was illegal in the U.S.; his other wives would join him later, processed by the Immigration and Naturalization Service (INS) as close relatives.[1]

Before leaving Thailand, Vang Pao had prepared the Hmong at Namphong for his departure by passing the torch of leadership to others. The investiture was at a mass meeting, which by one account did not go well for Vang Pao: "[M]any of the tribal elders angrily denounced Vang Pao to his face" and "declared that he had led them to their destruction and that they would never follow him again."[2]Actually, the denunciations were more generic, encompassing anyone of importance (clan elders, former high-ranking officers, and high-placed bureaucrats in Vang Pao's civil administration). The denunciations resulted in an orgy of chest-beating and self-criticism.

For weeks Namphong had been in the grip of religious hysteria. A Hmong in one of the camp barracks claimed to have been visited by Chue Chao. Transformed into a Jeremiah, he demanded that all repent and that leaders confess their sins or have their souls claimed by Chue Chao. When Vang Pao's brother-in-law died suddenly in his sleep, a pall fell over the camp. Clan elders put their heads together and, after a meeting that ran late into the night, announced there would be a day of repentance.

Like little boys before ear-pinching nuns, former majors and colonels took their turn at the confessional, exposing their sins to the entire camp population: pilfered payrolls, personal enemies executed as spies, military supplies sold on the black market. Also in line were once-powerful tassengs and chao muongs, admitting to nepotism and the plundering of food and supplies from USAID warehouses to pad the inventory of the businesses they ran on the side.

Many drank pure water during this jubilee of penance to attest they would sin no more. Only Vang Pao gave a pass to the cup, refusing to admit any wrongdoing. Many expected the camp prophet to press the issue, but Vang Pao had already martyred one prophet for challenging his authority, and the man was no fool.

His only request was that Vang Pao help prepare his people for the time when he would no longer be with them. As if on cue, Vang Pao announced his imminent departure for America and presented the three Hmong who were to be his standard-bearers in his absence. They were: Toupao Ly, the former head of Vang Pao's secret police; Neng Vang, a former colonel; and Youa Tong Yang, the man who had rallied the first recruits for Vang Pao's *armée clandestine*.

Of the three, only Neng Vang would become an acknowledged leader of Hmong refugees, rising to the position of camp leader at Ban Vinai, soon to be the largest Hmong refugee settlement in Thailand. Youa Tong Yang would occupy a less exalted position as chief of one section of Ban Vinai, and then for only two years. Toupao Ly would exercise power in the shadows, as he had at Long Cheng.

Out of public view, Vang Pao selected several other Hmong to monitor things while he was away. One was his father-in-law, Cher Pao Moua, the warlord of Bouam Long. Another was Bee Vang, a former T-28 pilot, nicknamed "Whitey" for his pale complexion. A third was Waseng Vang, a skilled negotiator who had helped Vang Pao resolve clan disputes in the past. All three men would wind up at Ban Vinai, where the steady influx of refugees guaranteed a continuous source of information about events unfolding in Laos, intelligence they would pass on to Vang Pao at his 440-acre ranch at Victor, a ranching community fifty miles south of Missoula, Montana.[3]

Vang Pao's decision to settle near Missoula was influenced by his former CIA case officer, Jerry Daniels. Missoula was Daniels' home town. Earlier Daniels had arranged for three of Vang Pao's sons (Thao, Sisavangvong, and Chong) to attend the city's schools. The boys were still there. There was also the allure of Montana's scenic wilderness. An avid outdoorsman, Daniels had spoken often to Vang Pao of Montana, a sparsely populated mountain wilderness full of wild game and blessed with natural scenery of breathtaking beauty. Missoula was in the midst of this majestic wilderness, nestled in a grassy valley between two rugged mountain ranges, the Bitterroots to the west and the Sapphire Mountains to the east.

Vang Pao had visited Missoula and its forest environs in June of 1972 after traveling with Buell to Washington D.C. to assess America's intentions in Southeast Asia. He took in Missoula's scenery and rode in a car to the timberline to walk in the deep snow. He liked what he saw. Except for the harsh winters, the mountain country around Missoula was much like the Laotian highlands above three thousand feet, where most Hmong lived before the war.

Perhaps, as one writer suggests, Vang Pao made up his mind then and there to retire to Missoula. The Americans working with Vang Pao in Laos saw a change in him after he returned from Montana. "They assumed Vang Pao had arranged for his own private exit from the Laos war, and that if need be he would abandon his people."[4] It is more likely, however, that Vang Pao made the decision at the last moment, once he realized he could no longer remain in Thailand. It was his nature to want to remain at the center of things, even if his cause seemed hopeless. Going to America meant he would be out of the loop. Had he any other choice, he would have taken it.

The CIA helped finance Vang Pao's resettlement. The purchase price of his 440-acre ranch was four hundred thousand dollars.[5] The agency made a substantial down payment to reduce the size of the monthly payments on the remaining contract and provided Vang Pao a life pension of thirty-five thousand dollars a year so he could pay his bills.[6] Vang Pao purchased two other homes in Missoula to accommodate the rest of his family, once they joined him. It is not unreasonable to imagine that CIA money was involved.

TRANSPLANTING HMONG POLITICS TO AMERICA

In 1975, fewer than five hundred Hmong followed Vang Pao to the United States. However, five thousand arrived in 1976. Most were sponsored by church groups and settled close to their sponsors, leaving them far from Vang Pao in Montana. Few spoke any English. All found American society and its culture utterly bewildering. Once they learned how to use a phone, they began calling Vang Pao, collect. Offering advice and moral support over the phone was expensive. Vang Pao's telephone bill averaged twelve hundred dollars a month.[7] There were other expenses. He traveled extensively throughout the U.S., making personal contact with Hmong immigrants. As the bills piled up, Vang Pao realized he needed outside funding.

At the time, one of the largest Hmong communities in the U.S. was in Santa Ana, California. Vang Pao went there in late 1977 to organize Lao Family Community (LFC), an organization to help Hmong refugees adjust to their new life in America by providing them counseling, language training, and job placement. There was funding for refugee self-help groups, both from the federal government and from the state. Shortly after LFC's creation, the state of California awarded the organization a substantial grant. A federal grant soon followed. In time, LFC would prove to be a gold mine.

In late 1975, President Ford had established a task force to review refugee resettlement policy. The group included representatives from the United Nations High Commissioner for Refugees, the State Department, Department of Health Education and Welfare, and international and national voluntary organizations dealing with refugees. Arguing that voluntary organizations are less bureaucratic and truly care about refugees, those on the task force speaking for the nonprofits urged that resettlement services devolve from the state department to voluntary organizations. The task force endorsed the idea, not only on merit but because voluntary agencies have traditionally relied on private donations for funding and have a built-in bias against public assistance. The presumption was that voluntary agencies would work hard to keep resettled refugees off welfare.

The task force's recommendations became federal policy. Under grants that were vague and undemanding, voluntary organizations received a lump sum of five hundred dollars for each refugee they helped resettle. A portion, never clearly specified, went directly to the organization as administrative overhead, and the remainder went to the refugees for food and housing. There was also funding for job training, job placement, and English language training. Money for these services would steadily increase over the years, especially for Hmong refugees. Two new agencies (the Indochinese Mutual Assistance Division of the State Department, and a new branch of the Office of Refugee Resettlement created to administer the Highland Lao Initiative program) channeled nearly all federal funds for these services to voluntary organizations.[8]

With state and federal funds pouring into LFC Santa Ana, Vang Pao set about creating LFC satellites in every Hmong community in the U.S. The LFC satellites attracted more funds and established a network of LFC leaders who took their orders from him. Vang Pao was back in business, though with one drawback. He had not selected LFC directors and their staffs from a list of established Hmong leaders. Instead, he chose them from the younger generation, those literate in English and comfortable with American culture and not at sea with government agencies, local businessmen, and white collar service providers. Inadvertently, he had created a new Hmong elite.

Conflicts between these young Turks and the old guard were inevitable. Because LFC directors were Vang Pao's protégés, the disputes created bitterness toward him, and from Hmong whose support he needed: clan elders, retired officers, and former civil servants who still enjoyed considerable authority within their clans and communities. To calm the waters, Vang Pao was constantly on the road visiting quarreling communities, holding endless meetings. It was time-consuming and frustrating and it did not solve the underlying problem. What Vang Pao needed was a larger organization, with more resources than LFC could generate, to provide leadership positions and patronage for clan patriarchs, cashiered colonels, and retired bureaucrats. And for this he needed a cause for which American Hmong would empty their pockets.

Vang Pao had been working on the problem since 1977, partly out of conviction but mostly from political instinct. News of the Chao Fa rebellion, passed to him by his agents in Thai refugee camps, convinced Vang Pao that he had to jump on the bandwagon or lose face with the Hmong. To give the impression that he was still in the thick of things, he joined the Free Lao National Liberation Movement, a front organization created by Sisouk Na Champassak, a stalwart of the old Rightist regime and former member of Phoumi's CDNI. Along with Kong-Lê, Vang Pao wound up on the front's executive committee.[9]

The front was a charade. No guerrillas were ever organized, no military action undertaken. Vang Pao could have struck out on his own, but chose not to. He had a strong following in the Hmong refugee camps. The camp leader at Ban Vinai, Neng Vang, was his own hand-picked man. A word from Vang Pao and Neng Vang would have raised a guerrilla force and dispatched it to Phu Bia to join the fray. Instead, Vang Pao merely ordered him to send agents to check on the fighting and to promise the rebels that help was on the way.[10]

Bee Vang was one of these agents. Believing Vang Pao was sincere about the offer of aid, he gave Phu Bia rebels his personal assurance that help would soon arrive. When nothing materialized, he felt betrayed. Disillusioned, Bee Vang advised the rebels to abandon the fight and offered to serve as a guide for anyone wishing to follow him back to Thailand. Several thousand took him up on the offer. Repeatedly attacked on the trip, only a fraction of the group crossed the border.[11]

Vang Pao may have had good reasons for not lifting a finger to help the Chao Fa. Far from the scene of battle and preoccupied with helping Hmong adjust to life in the U.S., he lacked both the resources and the time to respond adequately. But perhaps the compelling reason was that he did not command the loyalty of the Chao Fa. He wanted Hmong to liberate Laos, but under his leadership and control. Of course, he publicly cheered the Chao Fa rebellion at Hmong community meetings in St. Paul, Minneapolis, Milwaukee, Spokane, Denver, Seattle, Santa Ana, San Diego, Fresno, Merced, Stockton, and Sacramento. He had no choice. They were the only Hmong doing any fighting. Then came the news of the Chao Fa's crushing defeat. Vang Pao now had a clear field to organize his own insurgency. On his orders, his agents in the camps began their own resistance.

By early 1981 two thousand refugees were enrolled in the new rebel organization, led in the field by Vang Pao's father-in-law, Cher Pao Moua. In that same year Vang Pao participated in the formation of the United Lao National Liberation Front (ULNLF), an umbrella organization encompassing Vang Pao's Hmong, a battalion of Lao guerrillas led by Chokbengbou Thonglith (the last general to command MR V), and a second Lao battalion commanded by the son of Prince Boun Oum, Chao Bouneu Na

Champassak. The ULNLF's executive committee included Kouprasith Abhay and Phoumi Nosavan.[12]

Except for the Chinese-sponsored Lanna Division, the only guerrilla groups doing any real fighting were the two resurrected Chao Fa organizations: Sai Shoua Yang's maquis inside Xieng Khouang Province, and Pa Kao Her's insurgents operating out of Thailand. Both were conspicuously absent from the new front. The ULNLF was a reunion of former players in the old regime, old cronies looking to revive their careers and improve their fortunes. Religious fanatics were not welcome.

ULNLF's first official act was to issue a white paper on Laos. The United Nations had recently hosted an international conference on Cambodia, a nation under Vietnamese occupation since late 1978. It was clear from the comments of the participants, and especially of the representatives from the U.S., that Cambodia instead of Laos was the focus of international attention. There were rumors that Washington intended to offer covert aid to Cambodian guerrillas fighting the Vietnamese. The ULNLF's white paper was a transparent effort to get a share of these funds. Portraying Laos as another occupied nation, the ULNLF argued that "the international community must link the Laotian and Cambodian problems for a global solution."[13]

The rumors of secret aid were true. In 1982 Washington initiated a program of covert assistance to the Cambodian resistance, worth about $15 million a year.[14] A good deal of the aid was channeled through Thailand, where a small fraction was siphoned off to Vang Pao's Hmong and to Pa Kao Her's Chao Fa.

It was not the big response that the ULNLF had hoped for. But unlike Phoumi, Abhay, and Thonglith, Vang Pao could rely on another source of support—American Hmong. While a large proportion were still on welfare, a substantial number were holding down full-time jobs with a median income of a little more than seventeen thousand dollars.[15] Hmong had money, in the aggregate probably in excess of $120 million per year.[16]

Prior to the creation of the ULNLF, Vang Pao visited Hmong communities across America, letting them know he was building his own guerrilla organization (which he called Neo Hom) based in the refugee camps. Everywhere he went he asked for donations for the cause. After the formation of the ULNLF he was again visiting Hmong communities asking for even more money, this time using the liberation front as a selling device. The ULNLF gave the impression that the old war machine was back in operation. Phoumi was involved, along with the former commander of MR V. And there was a bona fide Lao prince. Something big was happening and Neo Hom was part of it.

In 1981, Vang Pao asked every Hmong family in America to donate a hundred dollars to Neo Hom. In 1982 he was back on the stump, asking every Hmong in America—man, woman, and child—to contribute two dollars per month to the resistance. Money poured into Neo Hom's coffers at the rate of $160,000 a month. It went mostly for politics rather than war. Vang Pao used the funds as patronage for Hmong notables (clan leaders and former officers and bureaucrats) excluded from leadership roles in LFC, making them officials of Neo Hom who earned salaries and exercised power. Suddenly, there was less bickering between the old elite and LFC's young Turks. Everyone, young and old, new elite and old guard, was united behind Vang Pao.

Vang Pao had resurrected his old political machine. To complete the resurrection, in late 1983 he formed the Hmong Council, replicating the old council of elders. All eighteen clans in America had representation on the new council. Like the old council of Vang Pao's wartime civil administration, the Hmong Council became a platform for adjudicating disputes between clans and a vehicle for Vang Pao to generate approval, and therefore legitimacy, for his policies.

Vang Pao also sent money to the camps, to be used for patronage and bribes for camp authorities. Soon his agents were in control of the day-to-day administration of the camps, and decisions over housing, food allotment, and work opportunities were in the hands of his men. This did not generate resentment among the refugees. On the contrary, it was taken as evidence that Vang Pao was again in charge and that he would breathe new life into the resistance and bring down the communists. When Vang Pao left Thailand for America in 1975, he had made a great show of predicting that the communists would fall within ten years. The target year of 1985 was not that far away. Many refugees believed they would soon be returning to Laos to pick up the pieces of their lives.

Keeping the wheels of Vang Pao's new political machine properly greased was expensive. Vang Pao's fundraising visits to Hmong communities grew more frequent. When contributions began to lag, he booked a flight to Thailand and from there flew to Yunnan for photo opportunities with guerrillas from the Lanna Division. He persuaded five Chinese Hmong (*Miao*) to join Neo Hom and help train guerrillas (three of them would soon die in guerrilla action in Laos). Then it was back to Thailand for a tour of Ban Vinai and a brief incursion into Sayaboury Province in Laos. Vang Pao's aides videotaped him leading guerrillas in a mock raid, and handing out money to Hmong villagers and dispensing medical supplies. After his return to the U.S., Vang Pao had the videotape played in every Hmong community as proof that he was putting contributions to Neo Hom to good use.

Donations to Neo Hom picked up, but not enough to meet Vang Pao's needs. He came up with a plan for an all-Hmong enterprise, a supermarket in Santa Anna. Hmong contributed roughly $650,000 to the project, with the promise of a five percent return on their investment. The market was actually built. Run by Vang Pao's nephew Lia Vang, it went bankrupt within a year. Hmong investors did not get their money back. Lia Vang became the director of LFC Santa Ana.

Another money-making scheme was selling certificates of appreciation, personally signed by Vang Pao, to Hmong families across America. An 8.5 x 11" certificate sold for five hundred dollars. The 10 x 12" size went for a thousand dollars, and the large 11 x 14" certificate cost fifteen hundred dollars. In home after home, one could find the certificates hanging in fancy frames on living room walls.

Still there was not enough money, mainly because Vang Pao did not bother to keep track of it. During the war there was so much money coming in from various sources that he never had to worry about where it went. This management style now got him into trouble. Top officials in Neo Hom, fundraisers, and agents in the refugee camps were all skimming. Vang Pao's aides drove fancy cars, bought new homes, and took frequent trips to visit relatives in Thai refugee camps. Nearly everything collected was siphoned off in this way, leaving very little to support guerrillas in the field.

Vang Pao never skimmed money for himself. It was a political virtue he had learned in Laos because it was good politics. He never took; he only gave. It placed him above the inevitable corruption of machine politics. To maintain this image, in 1982 he walked away from his Montana ranch and let the bank foreclose on the property.[17] He had been planning to move to southern California anyway. He spent more time in Santa Ana than in Montana, and his wives wanted to move to be closer to relatives. It would have been nice, though, to have kept the ranch as a retreat. Vang Pao loved tramping over the mountains hunting elk. But keeping the ranch would have left the impression he was a wealthy man, and this he wanted to avoid. To preserve the image, when Vang Pao relocated to Santa Ana he rented a modest apartment. He would hold off purchasing a house until 1989, and then it would be an unpretentious ranch-style tract home.

Vang Pao's modest lifestyle enhanced his image, but did nothing to solve his money problems. Run through with corruption, Neo Hom was constantly short of funds. The organization had taken on a life of its own. During the war Vang Pao's political machine served the war effort. Now things were reversed. He had to whip up support for the resistance to attract the funds necessary to keep his political organization afloat.

By now, Vang Pao was spending several months each year visiting Hmong communities asking for donations, collecting about $500,000. His agents in the camps were collecting money, too. Each family was asked to come up with a silver bar per year (about $300). Since few had that amount, they got it from relatives in America. It was a roundabout way of getting American Hmong to donate even more of their income to Neo Hom.

Still it was not enough. In 1987 Vang Pao tried something new. Exuding confidence about Neo Hom's progress in the field, he claimed the communists were close to defeat. It would not be long before thousands of Hmong expatriates in the U.S., France, Australia, Canada and in the refugee camps would be returning to Laos to live under a new regime installed by the resistance. With the communists gone, there would be openings in the government and military. Vang Pao encouraged Hmong to apply for those positions now, rather than wait and let them go to someone else.

The price to be a colonel was fifteen hundred dollars; a promotion to general cost two thousand dollars. By paying a monthly fee of a hundred dollars anyone could become a provincial official. National office cost five hundred dollars per month and a cabinet post a thousand dollars per month. Five hundred Hmong paid the fee to become a colonel. Another two hundred eighty were appointed generals. Nine hundred paid the monthly fee to be appointed a provincial bureaucrat. Another four hundred entered the future national government, and twenty-four Hmong came up with the money to be part of the future cabinet. By the end of 1988, the sale of fictitious offices had earned Neo Hom nearly $9 million. Vang Pao sold the same offices, at much lower prices, to refugees in the camps.[18]

Vang Pao also put Neo Hom into banking. Money loaned to Neo Hom was supposed to go into a special account. The pledge was that only the interest would be siphoned off and the principal left untouched and returned in a couple of years. Hmong loaned Neo Hom between four hundred and five hundred thousand dollars, the largest sum coming from Hmong in Denver who pooled their money and delivered sixty thousand dollars. Within two years, both the principal and interest had vanished.[19]

MAINTAINING THE IMAGE OF A VIABLE INSURGENCY

To keep American Hmong contributing to Neo Hom, Vang Pao had to keep up the pretense that the insurgency was still alive. He ordered occasional raids against isolated LPLA units inside Sayaboury Province, avoiding head-on clashes with the larger and more numerous LPLA forces that roamed the border. Sometimes these guerrillas ran into Pa Kao Her's Chao Fa. The two guerrilla organizations now treated each other more as enemies than allies. Ambushes on both sides were frequent.[20]

Vang Pao also sent reconnaissance teams deep into Xieng Khouang Province. Team leaders carried money (sometimes as much as twenty thousand Thai baht) for distribution to destitute Hmong communities to build good will for Neo Hom. Some money was distributed, but as often as not team leaders pocketed the funds. Many of the volunteers for these patrols were camp refugees seeking a chance to visit relatives left behind in Laos or find new wives. All expected to be paid. The usual fee was six thousand Thai baht per mission. The money went to the team leader to distribute to his men at the end of the mission. It was common for team leaders to hold back part of the money for themselves. Sometimes they kept it all. This led to hard feelings and, occasionally, murdered commanders.[21]

There were also special missions to obtain documentation that Neo Hom was doing its job. These were full-scale ambushes on LPLA patrols and convoys, not hit-and-run raids. The guerrillas had to finish off the enemy and hold their ground long enough to photograph destroyed trucks and dead soldiers. The photos were delivered to America for circulation in Hmong communities.

On the whole, it was not a very aggressive insurgency. But this changed in 1985, the year Vang Pao had prophesied the communist regime in Laos would fall. Since this was not about to happen, Vang Pao needed at least one major victory in the field to reestablish faith in his leadership, especially as he had just circulated a letter on Neo Hom stationary to every Hmong community in the U.S. claiming his guerrillas were heavily engaged with communist forces all across Laos,[22] which they were not.

On Vang Pao's orders, Cher Pao Moua sent a thousand guerrillas deep into Xieng Khouang Province. The force ran into two Vietnamese companies just southeast of Cher Pao Moua's old stronghold at Bouam Long. On May 14, after several days of hard fighting, the guerrillas broke and ran, leaving behind three thousand Hmong, Lao, and Khmu villagers who had been providing them aid. The Vietnamese herded the civilians into a cavern, blocked the entrance with logs, and fired chemical weapons into the cave. A handful of Hmong in the back of the cave survived the gassing, crawled out over the dead bodies, and escaped.[23]

Reports of the defeat, and of the gassing of civilians, reached the refugee camps. To save face, Vang Pao hastily put together a demolition team whose mission was to get into Vientiane and blow up the Vientiane International hotel. One of the members of the team was the son of Cher Pao Moua. The young man had recently arrived from California seeking to enlist in a dangerous mission, the more dangerous the better. For two years he had been running an illegal Thai lottery in California, using counterfeit tickets purchased from Thai mobsters and selling them to Hmong. Having spent the proceeds, he got caught short when someone hit it big. Now he needed a bundle of cash before he could go back home, and hoped to get it from Neo Hom, earned by heroism in the field and a good word from his father. The demolition team got into Vientiane and planted the bomb, but it went off prematurely. One member of the team was killed. It was Cher Pao Moua's son.

The botched bombing was an appropriate ending to the failed campaign. Vang Pao's standing in the refugee camps plummeted. Realizing at last that there was little hope of returning to a non-communist Laos, within a few months nearly ten thousand Hmong refugees signed applications to be considered for resettlement to America.[25] There was also a ripple effect in the U.S. The only challenge to Neo Hom was Pa Khao Her's Ethnics Liberation of Laos (ELOL). Previously, few American Hmong had supported ELOL. Now its membership began to grow.[26]

In late 1989 Vang Pao tried to revive the prestige of Neo Hom by joining with ULNLF in an all-out campaign to bring down Laos' communist regime. The time seemed propitious. The Soviet Union was near collapse, its satellite regimes in eastern Europe were tumbling, and Vietnam had recently downsized its military presence in Laos, withdrawing thirty-five thousand of its forty-five thousand troops. ULNLF believed that its guerrillas would be facing mostly LPLA forces.

On December 6, 1989, ULNLF declared a provisional government for Laos and claimed it was already functioning in the liberated zones of six Laotian provinces.[27] The ULNLF appointed Vang Pao deputy prime minister and co-commander (with former Lao General Thonglith) of all resistance forces. Vang Pao mobilized Neo Hom guerrillas in the refugee camps and sent them into Laos. Their main target was LPLA truck convoys traveling Routes 13 and 7. By early January 1990, Neo Hom guerrillas had destroyed several convoys and completely blocked part of Route 7 as it leaves the Plain of Jars.[28]

Buoyed by these accomplishments, Vang Pao hosted a general meeting of the provisional government to discuss policy, flesh out its cabinet, and appoint individuals to various posts in the ministries that would soon be administering a liberated Laos. The site Vang Pao selected for the conference was inside Thailand close to the Laotian border, safe from LPLA patrols yet close enough to Laos to create a sense that the new government was convening on Laotian soil. Nearly three hundred Lao and Hmong attended, many having just arrived from the U.S. There were also unexpected guests. Thai officials arrived, accompanied by soldiers, to collect all U.S. passports, announcing that Thailand would not tolerate efforts by foreign nationals to overthrow the LPDR. The officials let it be known that anyone wishing to go back to the U.S. immediately would have his passport returned.

The whole affair was a great embarrassment to Vang Pao. For more than five years he had been making regular visits to the Hmong camps without interference. Bribes to Thai officials in the Ministry of Interior (MOI) provided Neo Hom a free hand in conducting raids into Laos from the camps in Thailand. MOI even provided Vang Pao bodyguards. It was now clear that he would no longer receive preferential treatment. American Hmong at the meeting left for Bangkok to reclaim their passports and return home. All were disillusioned. As one of them put it, "Vang Pao had no prestige or power with the Thai government."[29]

There were other setbacks. Shortly after the ULNLF had declared its provisional government, Kaysone announced that he "would continue to drop bombs and seek to destroy" the insurgents "until they were totally wiped out."[30] Kaysone made good on his word. By January 1990, LPLA and PAVN forces were fully engaged with the rebels. Vietnam sent twenty MIG-23 fighter-bombers to help with the campaign. According to one report, the communists were again using chemical warfare.[31] Within a few weeks, nearly every guerrilla stronghold had been destroyed.[32] Everywhere insurgents were on the run. It was a devastating and humiliating defeat.

In America, Hmong support for Neo Hom plummeted. In the early 1980s, nearly 80 percent of Hmong families in America had donated money to the resistance. By 1986, only 50 percent were still giving money. Now less than 20 percent were doing so. With Neo Hom's standing at an all-time low and Vang Pao no longer seeming all-powerful, Hmong in America began complaining to authorities about Neo Hom's fundraising practices.

In June 1990, the Civil Rights Bureau of California's Department of Social Services issued a twenty-one page report charging that LFC offices had forced refugees to contribute money to Neo Hom as a condition of receiving welfare and various social services. Five months later the ax fell on Neo Hom and LFC. The Department of Social Services declared that LFC offices in San Bernadino, Riverside, and Sacramento counties had extorted money from Hmong on behalf of Neo Hom and ordered all social service agencies in the state to cease funding LFC organizations. Kao Thao, a Neo Hom leader and official in LFC, pleaded guilty to two counts of embezzlement and misappropriation of funds and went to prison.[33]

To stay in business, LFC organizations across the country severed all legal and organizational ties to their parent group, LFC Santa Ana, controlled by Vang Pao. The political machine that had taken Vang Pao more than a decade to build was rapidly falling apart. With Neo Hom and the resistance discredited, he needed a new issue to rally support for his leadership. Thailand handed it to him on platter by entering an agreement with Laos and the United Nations High Commissioner for Refugees (UNHCR) to close the refugee camps and repatriate all Hmong to Laos.

THE REFUGEE MESS

From the start, Thailand did not want Laotian, and especially Hmong, refugees on its soil.[34] Thailand had a robust economy while its neighbors to the east were war-torn, destitute, and ruled by oppressive regimes.[35] It was feared that granting Laotian refugees asylum would encourage the poor and oppressed in Vietnam, Laos, and Cambodia to flock to Thailand, creating an economic burden for the government that would discourage foreign investment.[36] The reaction of Vietnam, with its juggernaut army, was also a concern. Since Laos was Vietnam's puppet, providing blanket sanctuary to former RLA government officials and soldiers, and Hmong who had served in Vang Pao's army, could easily worsen already strained relations with Vietnam.[37]

Hmong were also unwelcome for domestic reasons. There were already sixty thousand indigenous Hmong in Thailand, scattered across the highlands of the northern provinces, and they were a constant annoyance. Their slash-and-burn (swidden) farming turned valuable timber into unmarketable ashes. In 1967, government efforts to outlaw the practice resulted in a Hmong rebellion, followed by a brutal suppression by the Thai military.[38] Fearing that the Hmong might rebel again, there was no great enthusiasm over thousands of Laotian Hmong, many of them combat veterans, being added to the mix. [39]

Because of a long history of U.S. aid, and close links between the CIA and Thai military, Thailand did allow the CIA to airlift twenty-four thousand Hmong from Long Cheng to Thailand in May 1975; but no other Hmong were to be granted asylum. On orders from Bangkok, border patrols began to turn back all other Hmong refugees, robbing them of their goods and administering gratuitous beatings. It was hoped that the get-tough policy would send a clear message and persuade the Hmong to remain in Laos.

Thailand's uncharitable stand on Laotian refugees troubled Washington. Feelings ran high that America owed something to its former allies, especially the Hmong. There was talk that during the war the U.S. had promised the Hmong aid and sanctuary if Laos ever fell to the communists. The Office of Refugee Settlement investigated the rumor and concluded there is "no doubt that assurances were made to support the Hmong during the war, and to provide assistance in the event that Laos lost the war."[40]

Pressure from Washington, and a reported grant of three trillion baht (about $150 million) to help defray the cost of Hmong settlement,[41] persuaded Thailand to retreat from its hard-line position on Laotian refugees. Thai Border guards were soon directing Hmong and ethnic Lao to temporary camps, twenty-one in all, set up to receive them. In July 1975 Thailand reluctantly signed an agreement with UNHCR granting the United Nations agency authority to begin coordinating refugee assistance.[42] Part of the agreement was that UNHCR should seek a long-term solution to the refugee problem. Since Bangkok made it clear that the integration of refugees into Thai society was unacceptable,[43] UNHCR looked to resettlement in third countries as a partial solution and repatriation as the principal one.[44]

By the close of 1977, over a hundred thousand Laotians had fled to Thailand. Twenty thousand resettled in third countries, principally America. The rest, slightly more than seventy-nine thousand, were in refugee camps along the Thailand/Laos border. The Thai government, and UNHCR, expressed concern that

America's liberal immigration policy was responsible for the large numbers and an incentive for even more Laotians to seek asylum in Thailand.[45]

To speed up resettlement and reduce camp populations, Washington sent INS case workers to Thailand to screen refugees applying for resettlement to the U.S. To mollify Thai bureaucrats, the INS progressively tightened its criteria. By 1984, only high-risk refugees, those likely to wind up in concentration camps if forced back to Laos, qualified. This included former RLG officials, former officers in the RLA, Lao having been imprisoned by the communist regime, and those who had participated in armed resistance. The only exception to these restrictive criteria were the Hmong. A Hmong simply had to apply to be accepted.[46]

Bangkok did not share Washington's concern for the Hmong. The idea of thousands of battle-seasoned *armée clandestine* veterans swarming into Thailand was unsettling.[47] Although strong pressure from Washington between 1975 and 1977 compelled the Thai to let the Hmong in, the Thai Ministry of Interior tried to isolate them into separate camps, defending the segregation as the only way to prevent violent clashes between lowland Lao and Hmong.

Actually, violence was a problem in only one camp—Nong Khai. Situated directly across the Mekong from Vientiane, the camp's population had swelled to twenty-two thousand by 1977, earning it the nickname "Little Vientiane." Unlike Vientiane, however, the population of Nong Khai was evenly divided between ethnic Lao and Hmong. Fights between Hmong and Lao youths occurred on a regular basis, and in time evolved into organized gang warfare. To reduce the violence, MOI partitioned the camp into two sectors, one Hmong and the other Lao. Yet the violence persisted, usually breaking out after soccer matches between Hmong and Lao teams. In 1978 a Hmong gang lured Lao youths into the forest and beat them to death with clubs. Following the incident, MOI began transferring Hmong to Ban Vinai, eventually moving ten thousand.[48]

The real motive for isolating Hmong in separate camps was to create a separate, high-security camp system to keep Hmong refugees under close supervision so they could not launch raids into Laos or link up with Thailand's Hmong and re-ignite another rebellion. The camps at Ban Vinai, Ban Nam Yao, Sob Tuang, and Chiang Kham were started as exclusively, or predominantly, Hmong camps (see map "Hmong Refugee Camps in Thailand"). The first three opened between 1975 and 1977; Chiang Kham opened in 1982. All were run like prisons; some were brutal.

Amphorn Chai, the camp director of Ban Nam Yao, liberally tortured Hmong inmates. His favorite punishment was to bury a man up to his neck and let his head bake in the sun. When a few inmates protested the practice, Amphorn had them executed. Reporters from the international press unexpectedly paid the camp a visit and photographed Hmong heads, arranged in a neat row like cabbages, roasting in the sun.[49] Once the photos were published, MOI was compelled to dismiss Amphorn from his post.

Banharn Supanich, the commander at Chiang Kham, was almost as brutal and considerably more venal than Amphorn Chai. He confiscated food and clothing donated to the refugees by international organizations and sold it on the black market. He jailed refugees for refusing to bow to him, then had them tortured. He shaved women and children's heads. He raped Hmong women at gunpoint. Five years passed before reports of these abuses finally reached UNHCR officials. Once confronted with the facts, MOI reluctantly ordered Banharn replaced.[50]

MOI's attempt to completely isolate the Hmong in their own camps was perpetually frustrated by the steady influx of additional Laotian and, later, Cambodian asylum-seekers. With not enough camps to go around, new Hmong arrivals sometimes wound up in camps for ethnic Lao. Even after the transfer of ten thousand Hmong from Nong Khai to Ban Vinai, there were still thousands of Hmong intermixed with ethnic Lao in other camps. A thousand Hmong were at Houei Yot, another thousand at Bang Ton, and three thousand at Ubon (the largest camp for ethnic Lao). Soon there would be several hundred more Hmong at a new camp at Ban Napho. It would take seven years for MOI to completely segregate all Hmong into just two camps: Ban Vinai and Chiang Kham.[51] In the interim, Thailand's government stiffened its resolve to slow the refugee flow.

In mid-1977 Thailand signed an agreement with UNHCR to begin screening people at the border to sort out political refugees from economic migrants fleeing Laos' grinding poverty. Concerned for the Hmong, Washington intervened and put the screening on hold. Within a year, fifty-seven thousand new ethnic Lao and Hmong refugees flooded into Thailand. MOI blamed the increase on America's overly generous resettlement policy,[52] ignoring the more obvious causes of the sudden influx of refugees. Massive crop failures had caused famine conditions throughout much of Laos. To elude starvation, thousands of ethnic Lao peasant farmers fled to Thailand. The Hmong refugees were no puzzle either. The LPDR's brutal campaign against the Chao Fa had thousands of Hmong heading for the border.

To stop the flow of refugees, Thailand began pushing back new arrivals (over the protests of Washington), which, by 1979, included Cambodians as well as Laotians. There were already thirty-four thousand Cambodian refugees in Thailand seeking sanctuary from the atrocities of the Pol Pot regime. With Vietnam's invasion of Cambodia in December 1978, Cambodians faced new horrors. Nearly a million swarmed toward Thailand's border. In June 1979 Thai soldiers forced fifty thousand Cambodian refugees back into Cambodia, driving them down cliffs onto mine fields, killing thousands. The outcry from the international press and humanitarian organizations over the incident forced Thailand to publicly recant its push-back policy. Soon another forty-four thousand Laotian refugees entered Thailand, joined by over two hundred thousand Cambodians. To hold back the flood of refugees, in late 1980 Thailand's government quietly initiated a program of "humane deterrence" (it would not become official policy until mid-1981). MOI confined new Cambodian arrivals to border encampments with no chance of resettlement to third countries. The encampments were purposely stark; relief organizations were not let in.[53]

In January 1981 MOI opened an additional camp at Ban Napho to receive new Laotian arrivals. Camp authorities crammed Hmong and ethnic Lao into cement block houses, a hundred to a house, and fed them only "survival-level" rations. Relief organizations were kept out.[54] The austerity of the camps was not just to deter new arrivals; MOI wanted refugees to consider returning to Laos. Thailand had already completed an agreement with Laos for a pilot repatriation program, but it called for voluntary repatriation and UNHCR was looking over Thailand's shoulder. Even at Ban Napho, where conditions were wretched, no Hmong and only a few hundred ethnic Lao could be persuaded to repatriate. Undaunted, MOI continued "humane deterrence," but now as official policy, housing all new refugees in camps designed to make life miserable. MOI also quietly re-instituted the push-back of new arrivals, especially Hmong.

Over the next five years fifty thousand ethnic Lao would get through, but less than thirteen thousand Hmong found their way to camps. The worst year for Hmong asylum-seekers was 1985, when only nine hundred made it across the border.[55] A fact-finding team from the U.S. Committee for Refugees determined that the cause was a deliberate and concerted effort by border police to prevent Hmong from entering Thailand.

Earlier, the U.S. State Department had given tentative support for humane deterrence. Nearly every Hmong who applied for resettlement was accepted, compared to a rate of 50 to 60 percent for ethnic Lao. Even so, few Hmong in the camps bothered to apply. It was imagined that humane deterrence might be a way to nudge them to make the right choice. Push-back was another matter, especially when Hmong were specifically targeted. The U.S. Embassy made it clear to Bangkok that the practice had to stop. To appease Washington, MOI instituted a border screening program to separate economic migrants from political refugees. All political refugees would be granted asylum (ethnic Lao would go to Ban Napho and Hmong to Ban Vinai).

This was for public consumption. Few Hmong were interviewed for screening. The standing policy was to push back all Hmong.[56] Border guards often confiscated everything of value and beat men and raped women before ferrying them back across the Mekong. Border guards maliciously stranded a few groups on islands in the middle of the river; the rest they delivered directly to LPLA on the shore. Most of these Hmong wound up at the re-education camp at Paksane, where frequent inspection tours by UNHCR guaranteed adequate food and minimum brutality. Following several weeks of interrogations and daily indoctrination sessions, most were returned to society, some to their home village, others to new locations. To ease the burden for relocated Hmong, UNHCR donated food and building material for housing. The items did not always go to the intended recipients. One group relocated to the outskirts of Phong Savan received truck-loads of bagged rice (enough for several months), seed for crops, and tons of lumber and metal sheeting for housing. However, once the UNHCR inspector departed, military trucks arrived to haul everything away. In place of the UNHCR rice, the relocated Hmong received bags of unhusked rice from the previous year's harvest, much of it mildewed and unusable.[57]

Hundreds of pushed-back Hmong delivered to LPLA units never made it to Paksane. They were murdered by soldiers who took justice into their own hands. In November 1987, one LPLA unit marched a group of fifty-three returned Hmong deep into the jungle. Stopping near a hill, they ordered everyone to sit down in a line. Mothers with babies strapped to their backs were or-dered to take the babies out and hold them to their chests. Then the soldiers opened up with rifles and rocket launchers. A young girl, wounded in the shoulder and arm, passed out and was left for dead. She remained next to her slain mother for days, diligently picking off the eggs laid by flies swarming over her mother's bloated corpse. Once the smell of decaying flesh became too much, she wandered down to the river. Thai fishermen discovered the girl and rushed her to a hospital in Thailand.[58] Shortly after this inci-dent, another group of sixteen, then a group of one hundred Hmong, were murdered in much the same way.[59] LPLA soldiers drowned other Hmong by placing them in fish nets and tossing them into the Mekong.[60] Once stories of the atrocities surfaced, UNHCR appealed to MOI to moderate its push-back policy. MOI defiantly "declared that it would not reverse its policy to pushback illegal Laotian immigrants."[61]

Though deeply troubled by the atrocities, Washington was unable to convince Thailand's government to change course. To justify its actions, Bangkok complained loudly that if America re-settled more refugees, there would be no need to push anyone back. Actually, the U.S. was resettling every Hmong who applied. It was just that too few were applying, a fact that utterly bewildered a U.N. refugee official who noted that the Hmong were the first refugees he knew of who had been offered resettlement and "in large numbers simply turned it down."[62]

Vang Pao was the principal reason for the low resettlement rate. In the early years the Chao Fa had challenged his hand-picked

Waiting for water in the heat of crowded
Ban Vinai Refugee Camp, ca. 1983

protégés for leadership in the camps, but after the communists crushed the Chao Fa rebellion, interest in the movement all but disappeared.[63] Facing no opposition, by the early 1980s Vang Pao's agents were able to persuade, cajole, and intimidate most refugees into forgoing resettlement and remaining in the camps to insure a critical mass of refugees to provide guerrillas for the Neo Hom resistance, the magnet for financial contributions to Vang Pao's political machine in America. Few Hmong in the camps dared challenge Vang Pao's authority. Those that did paid. In March 1987, Thai soldiers rounded up thirty-eight Hmong at Ban Vinai and forcibly repatriated them to Laos, "the first time the Thais had repatriated Hmong from the sanctuary of a UN refugee camp."[64] All thirty-eight had filed a written complaint to the United Nations High Commissioner for Refugees detailing Neo Hom's practices in the camp, including the extortion of money from refugees to support the resistance. There is little doubt that Vang Pao had arranged for the arrests. Two days before they occurred, he announced at a community meeting in California that a number of troublemakers at Ban Vinai would soon be expelled from the camp.[65]

Neo Hom bullying was not the only reason Hmong remained in the camps. Many had been living as refugees for more than a decade, for some nearly two decades if one factored in the time spent in USAID-sponsored war refugee camps in Laos. It had become a way of life. Going to America meant adapting to a new and bewildering environment. Audio tapes sent by relatives often told of the difficulties of adjusting to American society, which was reason enough to think hard about resettlement, especially when life at Ban Vinai, which housed more than fifty thousand Hmong, was not that hard.

Ban Vinai began as an austere, strictly regimented holding center. Refugees lived in crude bamboo huts and received minimal food and health care (MOI allocated only twenty-five cents a person per day to cover food and medical care). Families maintained small garden plots to grow extra food, though it was never enough. To get extra money for necessities, a few Hmong received permission to work as day laborers for local farmers, though they often failed to receive the pay promised and nearly as often were robbed by Thai thugs on their return to the camp.

Hot boxes under a tropical sun, tin-roofed row houses
at Ban Vinai Refugee Camp, ca. 1983-1985

Life at Ban Vinai soon improved, however. By the end of 1975, the United Nations was already delivering additional food. A year later, MOI permitted fifteen international voluntary agencies to begin operations in the camp. There was new construction for refugee housing: quarters with metal roofs and siding, and later homes made of concrete, adding four thousand rooms to the nearly three thousand bamboo houses already in existence. Over time, camp authorities granted Hmong increasing self-governance, not only for the camp as a whole but more or less complete autonomy over the internal affairs of the camp's various sections (the camp began with three, grew to six, and eventually had nine). Hmong helped with the distribution of food, and shared in decisions over employment opportunities.

By 1986 Ban Vinai had evolved into a sprawling 440-acre settlement with schools for children, job training for adults, and free medical care for everyone. The camp had its own food market. There were shops hawking Hmong handicrafts—traditional Hmong embroidery as well as silver jewelry fabricated in a tiny factory that provided part-time employment for nearly 60 percent of the families in the camp. Hmong-run stores sold western goods to the camp population. There were barbershops and restaurants and outdoor photo studios where Hmong could pose before a backdrop of the Swiss Alps or the Taj Mahal. And there was a robust hidden economy involving Hmong coyotes, narcotics trafficking, and substantial sums of money from Neo Hom that paid the salaries of guerrilla fighters as well as of a sizable body of Neo Hom bureaucrats, giving Ban Vinai "one of the highest living standards of any refugee camp in Southeast Asia."[66]

Oblivious to the power exercised by Neo Hom in the camps, Washington presumed that one possible cause of the low resettlement rate might be the difficulty of the application process. To address this, Washington dispatched teams of volunteers to Ban Vinai and Chiang Kham to conduct interviews and to prepare the necessary documents for anyone interested in immigrating to the U.S. With an eye on INS criteria, volunteers wove the fragmented narratives of the Hmong they interviewed into coherent biographies highlighting events and activities that would convince INS officials that they qualified as legitimate political refugees.[67]

Despite the extra effort, between 1987 and 1988 only eighteen thousand Hmong submitted to interviews. All who had applied were accepted for resettlement, but this still left sixty thousand who gave every sign of intending to stay put, and they were reproducing themselves at an annual rate of 5.5 percent, increasing the size of their population by more than four thousand each year. If unchecked, the number of Hmong in Ban Vinai and Chiang Kham would double by the year 2000. Bangkok was aware of the numbers; the American researcher who worked up the statistics had passed them on to MOI.[68] It was just one more reason Thailand's government wanted all Hmong refugees out of Thailand.

THE REPATRIATION SCARE

MOI saw only two solutions to the Hmong problem, resettlement or repatriation, and by this late date resettlement seemed unlikely. Not only were too few Hmong interested in immigrating to America, Washington was suddenly beginning to waver on the issue of resettlement. Back in 1985 the *New York Times* quoted an unnamed official in the State Department as saying that America "has now paid its moral debt for its involvement on the losing side in Indochina" and is no longer obliged to resettle Indochinese refugees.[69] A few months later America's ambassador to Thailand, Eugene Douglas, sent a letter to the United Nations High Commissioner for Refugees proposing that the Hmong in the camps be resettled in China instead of the U.S.[70] The letter was leaked to the press. Though the White House disavowed the proposal, and nine members of Congress demanded Douglas' resignation (he did resign), it was clear that a shift in attitude was underway.[71]

The primary cause of the change was the mounting pressure from POW and MIA groups for action on locating missing soldiers. The groups were well-organized, persistent, and imbued with moral fervor. Some of these organizations, like the National League of Families, had been in existence for more than two decades, time enough to develop strong allies in Congress. Not only were these groups effective lobbyists, they were morally indignant. Aware that their government had been lying to them for years, they demanded full access to all State Department, CIA, and Pentagon files pertaining to MIAs and POWs. They also wanted a commitment from Washington to send teams into Vietnam and Laos to locate the remains of American soldiers. The incessant lobbying forced the Bush administration to authorize "the most rapid and extensive declassification of public files and documents on a single issue in American history"[72] and to enter into negotiations with Vietnam and Laos to seek cooperation in locating the remains of MIAs.

Laos' cooperation came with strings attached. What sustained the resistance was Lao and Hmong refugees in Thailand. If Washington wanted help on MIAs, it would have to take a stand against the resistance and support the closing of the Thai camps and the repatriation of refugees. The Bush administration immediately severed all official and unofficial contacts with liberation front leaders.[73] In an official announcement (apparently directed at Vang Pao), the State Department warned that any resident supporting the resistance was in violation of U.S. neutrality laws which provided up to three years imprisonment, a three-thousand-dollar fine, or both for anyone who "furnishes money for, or takes part in, any military . . . enterprise to be carried on . . . against any foreign state or people with whom the United States is at peace."[74]

To meet Vientiane's demand for a new refugee policy, out of public view the State Department began brokering an agreement between Thailand, UNHCR, and Laos for the repatriation of all Laotian refugees, including the Hmong. Known as the Luang Prabang Tripartite agreement, the accord was finalized in 1991. To help things along, the Bush administration contributed $15 million to subsidize the cost of closing the camps and transporting Lao and Hmong back to Laos. When Clinton replaced Bush, the White House continued the commitment, donating $3 million between 1993 and 1994 to help defray the costs of repatriation.[75]

The Tripartite Agreement was a tocsin that left Hmong communities throughout America confused and frightened. Nearly every family had relatives at Ban Vinai or Chiang Kham. Many were convinced that Laos' communist regime would brutalize or murder all who were repatriated. Hmong leaders, including Vang Pao, pressured Congress for hearings on repatriation. Vang Pao at last had the issue he needed to revitalize his standing with American Hmong. And he had a villain to pillory—Mai Vue, the Hmong administrative chief of Ban Vinai.

Mai Vue had replaced Neng Vang as camp leader in 1983. Neng Vang did not object. Earlier, in 1980, he had tried to resign. He had relatives in Alabama and wanted to join them. Vang Pao insisted he stay. After receiving death threats, Neng Vang abandoned plans to resettle in the U.S.[76] Then suddenly, in 1983, Vang Pao allowed Neng Vang to leave. By one account it was because camp authorities had discovered that Neng Vang had hired an assassin to eliminate one of Vang Pao's enemies.[77] Whatever the cause, camp administrators relieved Neng Vang of his duties. No longer of use to Vang Pao, he was allowed to immigrate to America. As his replacement, Vang Pao chose Mai Vue.

Until 1989 Mai Vue was an unquestioning supporter of Vang Pao. That was the year of Neo Hom's failed guerrilla offensive, a defeat so complete and humiliating that it was clear that the resistance had no chance of toppling Laos' communist regime. For years UNHCR officials had been preaching repatriation. Now Mai Vue began to listen. With the help of two UNHCR officials (Robert Robinson and Robert Cooper),[78] he composed and sent a letter to UNHCR in March 1991 outlining a repatriation program he believed would be acceptable to all Hmong refugees. Two months later, copies of the "Mai Vue Proposal" were in circulation in Hmong communities in America.

Vang Pao went on the road, speaking to Hmong in Minnesota, Wisconsin, Colorado, and California, portraying Mai Vue as a traitor and urging all Hmong to renounce Mai Vue's plan and demand an immediate end to repatriation. In a countermove, the State Department brought Mai Vue to America to drum up support for repatriation. Mai Vue was not very popular with American Hmong, but as the chief Hmong administrator of Ban Vinai, he had standing with the refugees and could claim with some justification to be their spokesman. To undermine this authority, while Mai Vue was giving speeches in Hmong communities in America, Vang Pao had his agents at Ban Vinai appoint a new camp leader (Xiong Vang). MOI rejected the appointment and insisted that Mai Vue retain his post.

Vang Pao did not intend to let MOI have the last word. Shortly after Mai Vue returned to Ban Vinai, an unidentified Hmong tossed two grenades into his house. Possibly it was meant only as a warning. Mai Vue was away at the time in Bangkok, attending meetings with MOI and UNHCR officials. Thai authorities wanted to take no chances. They kept Mai Vue in Bangkok, guarded by soldiers. He would never set foot in Ban Vinai again. In November 1992, Mai Vue left Bangkok for Vientiane to begin negotiations on repatriation with Laotian officials. Over the next ten months he lobbied tirelessly to wring concessions from the Laotian Ministry of Interior, foremost among them a pledge to relocate repatriated Hmong to areas with good soil so they would have a head start in readjusting to the life of a peasant farmer.

Though he had a personal bodyguard (a Hmong policeman who shadowed him during the day), Mai Vue feared for his life. He constantly received calls at night from unknown individuals requesting a meeting away from his home. Each time he respectfully declined. Then on the evening of September 11, 1993, he left his home for a meeting without his bodyguard and never returned.[80] Neo Hom proclaimed Vientiane the culprit, a view that was widely accepted in Hmong communities in America.[81] Hmong in the refugee camps told another story. When interviewed by priests from the Jesuit Refugee Service, they claimed that Vang Pao's agents had abducted and murdered Mai Vue.[82]

Mai Vue's disappearance did nothing to slow the pace of repatriation. Thailand's Ministry of Interior had already closed Ban Vinai and Chiang Kham, diverting those deemed eligible for resettlement abroad to the processing center at Phanat Nikhom, and transporting the rest to the spartan camp at Ban Napho to await repatriation. Rather than wind up at Ban Napho, thousands of undocumented Hmong at the two camps sought sanctuary at a sprawling Buddhist compound at Tham Krabok.

The Tripartite Agreement mandated that repatriation be voluntary. This required a refugee's signature of assent before he or she could be returned to Laos. MOI made the living conditions at Ban Napho wretched to persuade Hmong to give their written assent. Between 1992 and 1994 fourteen thousand Hmong signed the necessary document and returned to Laos. During the same period twenty-five thousand Hmong resettled in America and thousands more were in the loop, waiting processing before departing. Not counting the nearly fifteen thousand Hmong receiving sanctuary at the Tham Krabok Buddhist monastery, only eight thousand Hmong holdouts remained, all at Ban Napho.

An obvious solution to the problem was for the U.S. to accept everyone at Ban Napho for resettlement (the undocumented Hmong at Tham Krabok had no legal existence and were in legal limbo). But instead of urging American Hmong to support this goal, Vang Pao insisted that the only acceptable solution was an end to repatriation. In a 1992 interview he had attacked the idea of resettling everyone: "Since the camps are the only link with the outside world for our persecuted people in Laos, dismantling the camps would cause panic inside Laos and you would see another 300,000 Hmong fleeing into Thailand, making the refugee problem worse than ever."[83] The truth was that Vang Pao needed Hmong refugees in Thailand to keep the resistance idea alive. Without it, he had no purchase on the allegiance, and pocketbooks, of American Hmong.

Many of the holdouts at Ban Napho refused repatriation out of a genuine fear that they would face reprisals or even death if they returned to Laos. Others refused because they hoped to be accepted for resettlement in the U.S. Then there were those who were part of Vang Pao's Neo Hom, determined to maintain a Hmong presence in Thailand. By spreading rumors of massacres of returnees, and of a renewed genocide campaign against the Hmong, they had the majority at Ban Napho digging in their heels.

Since the LPDR had bloodied its hands in the past, it was easy for Hmong to believe the rumors, despite assurances to the contrary: State Department officials insisted that Vientiane was now behaving itself, and UNHCR claimed it was overseeing the entire repatriation process and that returnees were doing well.[84] UNHCR even had videotapes to back up the claim. In late 1991 UNHCR took three Hmong from Ban Napho on a tour of repatriation sites in Laos. The trip was videotaped and the tapes played at Ban Vinai and Chiang Kham as proof that returnees had nothing to fear.

Of course, UNHCR was hardly an impartial source of information. Independent reports from, say, foreign correspondents on the scene, would have been useful in settling the matter. But as one reporter with a major Asian weekly newspaper complained, "no credible foreign news agency is allowed representation within the country."[85] Only later, in 1995 and 1996, would reputable reports by on-site investigators, one of them a cultural anthropologist, be available for an honest assessment. The reports revealed that returnees did have problems, but not as a result of government persecution. Hundreds of Hmong had been settled on inferior land and were having difficulty farming. Others had good soil but lacked the amenities they enjoyed in the Thai camps, like electricity and easy access to medical care. Some Hmong experienced social discrimination simply because they were Hmong, though others felt that their Lao neighbors had made a genuine effort to be friendly and helpful. A common complaint was that UNHCR did not visit regularly to assess returnees' needs as promised. But nowhere was there evidence of "government-sanctioned persecutions, arrests, tortures, and killings" of the sort advertised by "a strong Laotian resistance lobby in Washington D.C."[86]

Without the benefit of this information, rumors dictated perception. As tales of atrocities committed against returnees circulated through Hmong communities in America, families with relatives at Ban Napho turned frantic, becoming willing to grasp at straws. Hmong leaders at Ban Napho had let it be known that camp officials could be bribed to place Hmong on the resettlement list and divert them to Phanat Nikhom for processing for immigration to America. Nearly a hundred Hmong families begged and borrowed two hundred thousand dollars and sent the money to the camp. As was so often the case with Neo Hom fundraising, nothing was done and the money mysteriously disappeared.[87]

Other anxious families contacted their congressmen for help. House members in states with large Hmong populations (California, Wisconsin, Minnesota, and Colorado) were besieged with letters and phone calls from Hmong pleading that Washington stop the repatriation. To keep the pressure on Congress, Vang Pao organized protest marches in various cities and fed the media anti-repatriation press releases through the Lao Human Rights Council, a Neo Hom-funded organization created earlier by Vang Pao to change his image from failed warlord and machine boss to that of human rights advocate.

Vang Pao already had friends in Congress. They had introduced bills to give veterans' benefits and U.S. citizenship to Hmong veterans of the CIA's secret war. The same congressmen also pressured Washington to give "official" recognition for the Hmong contribution to the war effort, which would finally occur in May

1996 in a ceremony before the Vietnam War Memorial, where three thousand Hmong received Vietnam Veterans National Medals.[88] Since 1992, four Congressmen (Robert Dornan, Duncan Hunter, Ben Gilman, and Randall Cunningham) had been pushing hard for hearings on Hmong repatriation. Other Congressmen now joined the chorus. The hearings were held in April, 1994, by a subcommittee of the House Committee on Foreign Affairs. Hmong community leaders, individual Hmong, and friends of Hmong lined up to give testimony. Even Pa Kao Her showed up, fresh from his jungle headquarters in Sayaboury Province, using the occasion to urge the U.S. and the United Nations to pressure the LPDR to enter direct negotiations with the Chao Fa. Former CIA director William Colby was also on hand to remind Congressmen of the great sacrifices made by the Hmong during the secret war.[89]

Though Vang Pao was largely responsible for the hearings, he did not give testimony. In his native tongue he could hold a Hmong audience spellbound for hours speaking brilliantly and extemporaneously, but his English was halting and thickly accented and he required a prepared text to get through a speech, which invariably sounded plodding and leaden. As this failing was a great embarrassment, he seldom addressed non-Hmong audiences.

The testimony revolved around several themes. There was the past sacrifices of Hmong, the well-known brutality of the LPDR (though no one had hard evidence that this extended to the recently repatriated), and the view that repatriation was forced rather than voluntary, with camp inmates being starved, brutalized, and bullied into giving their written assent to be returned to Laos. Sixteen members of Congress found the testimony sufficiently compelling to send a letter to the King of Thailand, requesting that the repatriation program be abandoned.[90]

The letter worried Bangkok. It was evidence of growing anti-repatriation sentiment in Congress. Presuming (correctly) that Vang Pao was the prime mover in the anti-repatriation drive, Bangkok sent General Sarochma Robbamrung, a senior member of Thailand's National Security Council, to California to meet secretly with Vang Pao to begin negotiations on some kind of settlement. A month later, two more National Security Council members met with Vang Pao in California to continue the talks.[91]

Vang Pao was back in the center of things. Only a few months earlier Thailand's government had announced that it "would not tolerate any attempt by outsiders to use Thailand as a base to engage in hostile acts against neighboring countries," and declared that Vang Pao, who "has made a living by soliciting donations from Hmong residents in the United States," would face immediate arrest if he ever returned to Thailand.[92] Now Vang Pao was negotiating through a backdoor channel with top members of Thailand's government over the fate of Hmong refugees. His standing with American Hmong soared, as did donations to Neo Hom.

There was to be another meeting with Thai officials and members of Congress in Washington in July 1994, but the State Department derailed things by whisking away the Thai delegation to a pro-repatriation meeting in Virginia sponsored by the Hmong National Development Fund, a Hmong organization funded by the State Department. Vang Pao and his congressional allies were left sitting on their hands in a reserved room on Capitol Hill.[93]

It didn't matter. Momentum was gathering in Congress to end repatriation. A congressional fact-finding mission arrived in Thailand in August 1994 to check on conditions at Ban Napho. MOI refused to allow the mission's members inside the camp, forcing them to talk to Hmong through the camp fence. For MOI it was a public relations blunder, compounded by the arrest and imprisonment of six Hmong who talked to the congressional delegation. The inhospitality of MOI, and the imprisonment of camp refugees, stirred Congress to dispatch another mission to Thailand in December. The mission found the six jailed Hmong (headlined in the press as the "Ban Napho Six") still in prison, "suffering deplorably harsh and inhumane conditions . . . with little space, sleep, exercise, food, . . . or medical care." Several months later, Washington announced that the ceiling for Hmong refugee admissions had been raised to include everyone at Ban Napho.[94]

Vang Pao had won. But he had also lost. If everyone were resettled, there would be no Hmong refugees left in Thailand to keep Neo Hom going. Quietly and behind the scenes, Vang Pao pressured Hmong to refuse resettlement to the U.S. It was too late. Few were willing to chance forced repatriation by refusing resettlement. The camp soon emptied, except for a hard-core group of 150 Neo Hom guerrillas and their families who would not budge.

They were not the only Hmong refugees still in Thailand. The Hmong who had avoided internment in Ban Napho by finding sanctuary in the Buddhist temple at Tham Krabok were still there, fifteen thousand of them. And they were doing well. Tham Krabok was not a religious retreat. The monastery's abbot, Pra Chamroon Parnchand, preached a gospel of salvation through good works. Earlier, he had transformed the monastery into a major rehabilitation center for drug addicts. The program was so successful that Parnchand received the Magsaysay award for social service, the Asian equivalent of the Nobel Peace Prize. It made him something of a national hero. He was not the sort of person the government could easily push around.

Parnchand housed the Hmong on a forty-acre plot within the monastery compound. It grew into a bustling self-contained community. Hmong opened shops and sold handicrafts to tourists. Hmong silversmiths and blacksmiths set up forges behind the monastery and went into business. Parnchand found Hmong jobs with local construction crews working on a new road. Other Hmong took jobs in nearby towns and commuted to work daily. It looked as if the Hmong were settling in for good, which was why MOI insisted they had to go. But Parnchand demanded that the police and military leave his Hmong alone. Government ministers fumed and threatened, but in the end did nothing.[95]

VANG PAO MANEUVERS TO RETAIN CONTROL

With only a few holdouts left at Ban Napho, stubbornly refusing repatriation or resettlement in the United States, and the fifteen thousand Hmong at Tham Krabok thriving, interest in the repatriation issue waned and donations to Neo Hom again waned. However, Vang Pao still had another source of income: the Hmong New Year celebration, held in Fresno, California, and sponsored by the Hmong Council. The event netted Vang Pao more than two hundred thousand dollars each year. This income had temporarily slipped away in 1994 when younger Hmong leaders, many of them directors of Lao Family Community organizations in various cities, took over the Hmong Council and the New Year festival.

The 1990 financial scandals exposing links between Neo Hom and Lao Family Community had forced LFC organizations across the country to sever all ties with Vang Pao's LFC Santa Ana. Going it alone, most of these organizations not only survived but prospered, persuading their leaders that it was time for an entirely new political agenda, one less fixated on returning to Laos and more concerned with advancing the interests of Hmong in the U.S., best accomplished by entering the political mainstream. Already, in early 1986, in southern California's Orange county, a young leader in the Moua clan had launched the Hmong American Republican Association. The group provided leadership training and conducted a voter registration drive. Within two years the organization had spread to seven states with large Hmong communities, becoming an effective campaign organization that worked hard for Republican candidates and got out the Hmong vote.[96] By November 1993, Hmong voters in St. Paul, Minnesota, were sufficiently organized to provide the swing vote in the mayoralty race, transforming Republican mayor Norm Coleman into a strong advocate of social programs tailored to the needs of the Hmong community, and attracting the attention of Minnesota state and congressional legislators.[97] Inspired by these political successes, in 1994 a coalition of independent LFC leaders flexed their political muscles and took over the Hmong Council, the Hmong's only national representative body and previously a mouthpiece for Vang Pao. The new leadership turned the Council into a more representative body and used the profits from the New Year festival for social programs to benefit ordinary Hmong, instead of lining the pockets of Neo Hom officials.

Vang Pao parried by creating a new council, the Fresno Council of Hmong International. Run by his son, Cha Vang, the new council proclaimed itself the only official Hmong leadership organization in the country. To get his hands on the profits from the New Year Festival, Vang Pao held his own festival, directly following the traditional celebration. The competing festivals reduced revenues for both sides until 1966, the year Congress reformed welfare.

The Personal Responsibility and Work Opportunity Act of 1996 limited welfare assistance to two years. After this time a recipient had to work at least part-time to continue to receive benefits. Though the majority of Hmong were on welfare, it was not this provision that caused the most concern. The work requirement was two years away and could be satisfied by job training, going to school, or make-work provided by the state—a boon for thousands of Hmong who had been unemployable because of poor English and no job skills. The disturbing part of the new law was section 402 of the act, which denied Supplementary Security Income (SSI) to all legal immigrants. SSI went principally to the blind, disabled, and aged who were unable to work. Close to forty thousand Hmong received SSI income, most of them elderly Hmong who were too infirm to work or were just plain unemployable.

Many of these elderly Hmong lived with their children or grandchildren, families with incomes already below the poverty line. Without SSI, they would become a financial burden. A smaller number of elderly Hmong lived alone, sole survivors of entire families decimated by the war. Without their SSI income, they would be forced to rely on the begrudging charity of distant clan relatives.

For some, the thought of dragging down their family, or relying on handouts from strangers, was too much too bear. The first suicide occurred in rural Wisconsin on April 3, 1997. After receiving a letter informing him that he would soon lose his SSI benefits, Chue Tou Vang walked to a barn near his home, strung a rope over the rafters, and hanged himself.[98] His suicide was only the first of many to follow.

Months before Chue Tou Vang's suicide, Vang Pao had cashed in on the SSI termination scare by announcing that families attending his New Year festival (held in December 1996) would receive his personal attention in a planned campaign to lobby Congress to prevent the cut off of SSI benefits to Hmong immigrants. The ploy was enormously successful. The festival sponsored by the old Hmong Council was poorly attended and lost over twenty thousand dollars. Vang Pao's festival was a sellout, with profits in excess of two hundred thousand dollars.

Vang Pao did keep his promise to lobby Washington. But Congressmen were less moved by his lobbying effort, or Hmong protest marches in Sacramento and St. Paul, then by the sudden rash of Hmong suicides during April 1997. In interviews with the press, Hmong community leaders predicted that hundreds of additional elderly Hmong would kill themselves if the law were not changed. When Clinton signed the welfare reform bill, he had vowed that "the cuts in aid to legal immigrants would be enacted humanely." Press coverage of the suicides, and a public reading by Senator Edward Kennedy of a roster of those who had taken their lives, had Congressmen and the President hurriedly conferring to amend the welfare act and reinstate SSI benefits for all elderly legal immigrants.

A month before Congress reinstated SSI, Vang Pao suffered a stroke. He was sixty-five, had been overweight for years, and was plagued by chronic high blood pressure. It was time for him to retire. With his CIA pension, and the several thousand dollars in donations he receives every month from older Hmong whose faith in him is unshakable, he can live out his remaining days in comfort and bask in the glow of past glory. He was, after all, the RLA's best general, and in his own arena may have even rivaled Souvanna Phouma as a politician. These are notable accomplishments and good reason for Vang Pao to keep his eyes fixed on the past. The Hmong resistance was over, having degenerated into banditry-robbing and killing foreign tourists for profit.[99] American Hmong have outgrown Vang Pao's political style. In the time he has left, he might better serve his people as a symbol of past unity and military glory than as an active politician who is more likely to cause mischief than good.

EPILOGUE

A fter two decades of war and an experiment with Soviet-style
communism, Laos remains in many ways the same Laos of
pre-war years. IMF-mandated reforms forced Vientiane to abandon communist economics for free markets. By 1981 the
agricultural collectives were only a memory. In 1985, Kaysone
opened Laos' doors to foreign investors. Thai timber companies
moved quickly to gain access to the nation's forests. A Japanese
firm started a tin-roofing factory. A Thai company began manufacturing cigarettes. New garment factories started operations in
Vientiane. Soon there was a free market in rice and other food
staples.

The next major reform was in banking. In 1988, Kaysone privatized most of the state's branch banks and allowed Thai banking
companies to open in Vientiane. Two years later, under IMF guidance, Laos created its first central bank, the State Bank of Vientiane.
The new central bank immediately contracted the money supply
and ended all subsidies to provincial banks—the primary source of
funds for state enterprises. Suddenly forced to look at the bottom
line, the provincial banks closed delinquent accounts and refused
to grant new loans to unprofitable state firms. Overnight, provincial irrigation projects, state-run farms, tin mines, and state timber
operations went out of business or sought privatization to survive.

As if to acknowledge Laos' switch to capitalism, the government removed the hammer and sickle from the national flag. Not
long after the flag modification, the government quietly closed
the Revolutionary Museum in Vientiane. Unlike the flag change,
the object was not only to make a point. Few Laotians visited the
museum where the tattered mementos of the communist move-

ment, including faded photographs of revolutionary heroes, were on display.

At the same time that Kaysone liberalized the economy, he struggled hard to consolidate his own political power. It was a formidable task, made even more difficult by the economic reforms forced on Laos by the IMF. When Kaysone first assumed power it was impossible to manage Laos directly from Vientiane. The nation's highways were mainly deeply rutted dirt roads too narrow to permit two-way traffic. By custom, traffic traveled one direction one day, the opposite direction the next, which doubled travel time for long trips since half of the time was spent on the roadside to give oncoming traffic the right-of-way.[1] Provincial roads were even more primitive, and were virtually impassable during the rainy season. The country's tiny airline scheduled only three flights a week to four main towns (Vientiane, Luang Prabang, Savannakhet, and Pakse) and carried passengers just once a week to a few provincial capitals. Even the scheduled flights were irregular. The planes seldom flew in bad weather, and in good weather they were often broken down for several weeks at a stretch.[2]

Not only were the nation's road and communication systems too primitive to permit top-down control, the central government was too poor to undertake economic development on a national scale. This forced the regime to promote economic self-sufficiency in the provinces, a goal that also facilitated the quarantine of rural populations to make it difficult for rebels to organize a nationwide resistance or for peasants to flee to Thailand.

Provincial autonomy steadily devolved power from Vientiane to local party chiefs. From the start, Kaysone had tried to reassert central control by purging local officials who flagrantly strayed from the party line, but these efforts were constantly subverted by Kaysone's economic reforms. In 1977, the IMF had persuaded Kaysone to allow provincial administrations to initiate independent trade ventures with Thailand.[3] Thai firms began logging operations in several northern provinces. As there was little supervision from Vientiane, revenue from the timber deals was not always sent to the central government, allowing provincial officials to prosper at the expense of the state's coffers.[4]

Provincial bureaucrats also grew rich from drug trafficking. In 1976 the government lifted the ban on opium cultivation as an incentive for Hmong to remain in Laos. By the early 1980s, opium production had reached pre-war levels, with the largest harvests in Nam Tha Province. Though the opium was supposed to be sold to the government at a set price, only a fraction reached Vientiane. Provincial authorities collected the opium and sold it to international narcotics traffickers. By the late 1980s, Laos had become the third largest opium producer in the world, harvesting an estimated 375 metric tons of opium annually. With so much money involved, top party leaders in the military edged out local party bosses and took over the drug trade, using the Mountainous Area Development Corporation (MADC) as cover. MADC was a perfect front. Given government funds to underwrite economic development in Hmong areas, MADC used the money to subsidize Hmong opium production and later to establish a pipeline to move Burmese heroin into the international narcotics market[5]

It was difficult for Kaysone to rein in these party mavericks. National policy was made in consultation with the secretariat of the party's central committee and the secretariat had grown accustomed to implementing policy through negotiations with provincial party chiefs. Increasingly, these negotiations led to concessions that allowed provincial authorities to bypass central government policies. The government had banned logging in provinces where clear-cutting caused erosion and flooding, yet the ban was flagrantly ignored. The monitoring of business deals between provincial authorities and foreign investors was so loose as to be nonexistent. And the central government exercised no control over the production and marketing of opium.

One can only surmise that kickbacks from logging and drug profits had to play some part in the secretariat's concessions to local party bosses, for corruption tainted the highest councils of government.[6] Kaysone's own wife, Thongvinh, ran several logging companies that enjoyed huge profits by ignoring the government's temporary ban on logging. And Sisavat Keodounphan, the army's chief of staff and mayor of Vientiane, regularly skimmed money from business deals with Thai timber companies.[7]

In mid-1991, Kaysone maneuvered to acquire greater control of the party and the government. He ejected Sisavat Keodounphan from the politburo, abolished the secretariat, and increased his own powers. Possibly as a concession to party leaders, or simply to appear evenhanded, Kaysone allowed his wife to be dropped from the central committee. Now seventy-one and in poor health, Kaysone had regained some measure of power but lacked the vigor to exercise it. Within several months Sisavat Keodounphan was back in government as minister of agriculture, giving him even greater access to Laos' forests, a decision which one foreign diplomat characterized as "putting Dracula in charge of the bloodbank."[8] Within a year Kaysone was dead and the campaign to consolidate power over.[9]

For a time it seemed that Nouhak Phoumsavan, Kaysone's second in command for more than a decade, would step into the fallen leader's shoes, but prime minister Khamtay Siphandon elbowed him aside to assume leadership of the Lao Communist Party. Under Khamtay's watch, party bosses at the national and provincial levels were permitted to resume their shameless pursuit of profit, made easier by trimming away at the many restrictions on foreign investment until Laos possessed the most liberal investment laws in the region.

As expected, foreign capital poured into the tiny nation. Taiwanese investors established dozens of textile factories near Vientiane, making textiles the second largest producer of export money for the nation. By 1995, Thailand had committed over $2 billion to investment in Laos, and the U.S. $1.5 billion. The investment stimulated growth. Since 1988 the economy has continued to expand at the brisk rate of 7.5 percent annually.[10]

No doubt the economic development will someday benefit ordinary Laotians. The economic potential of Laos is considerable. The country has only recently begun to tap into the enormous hydroelectric power available from the Mekong. Laos is also blessed with abundant natural resources. There are vast deposits of gold, silver, and gemstones, untapped sources of iron ore, tin, gypsum, oil, and natural gas, and endless stands of virgin forest that cover the nation's highlands, which will one day produce billions in timber exports. Laos is also strategically located as the gateway between two booming regions, southern China and Thailand, and is linked by a road network to Vietnam, a nation that began liberalizing its own economy in 1986 and has since enjoyed an annual growth rate of 9.5 percent.[11] Foreign-funded projects are already underway to develop a rail and road infrastructure in Laos to link Thailand

and southern China, which will make Laos a major trade interme-
diary in Thailand's effort to tap into the forty million potential
consumers in China's Yunnan Province.[12]

With all of the investment, Laos' economy should improve
considerably over the next decade.[13] Laotian politics, however, is
likely to remain authoritarian, and corrupt, for some time to come.
This is not to deny that there has been some improvement. To
accommodate foreign investors and a growing tourist trade the
regime has been forced to liberalize politics, up to a point. But the
nation's top leaders have no intention of sharing power with others, let alone deomcratizing politics. Their monopoly on power
has enabled them to cut themselves in on nearly every new business venture launched by foreign investors. Monopoly power has
made them rich and they do not intend to let it slip away. In 1992,
the government jailed five party officials for advocating political
reforms that would permit party competition. These dissidents
joined several hundred political prisoners already in jails and camps
throughout the nation.[14]

Ironically, when the communists rose to power they promised
to sweep away the corruption of the former regime, banish the
prejudice against the ethnic minorities, and rule in the name of all
Laotians. Historian Martin Stuart-Fox recently observed that "[i]f
the Pathet Lao movement had anything positive to offer the country
it was a universal Lao nationalism." [15] The old regime had alter-
nately ignored or repressed the nation's montagnards. Only the
Pathet Lao had bothered to mobilize mountain tribesmen. Highland T'ai, Hmong, Khmu, and Yao tribesmen filled the lower ranks
of the party's bureaucracy. They were the majority of the Pathet
Lao's soldiers. Once the communists seized power, there seemed a
chance that the centuries-old tradition of political dominance by
lowland Lao was at last over. The corruption that infected the
Rightists might also be a thing of the past, since the new rulers
were supposedly motivated by Marxist ideology rather than greed.

Historically, ideologically motivated parties excluded from
politics and organized in opposition to the existing government
have been singularly immune to corruption and steadfast in their
ideals once they acquired power.[16] Had Laos' new rulers continued
to rely on the ethnic minorities as their primary base of support,
they might have conformed to this trend. Instead they relied on

Hanoi and several divisions of Vietnamese soldiers garrisoned in the country to maintain their hold over the population. Having no need to answer to their original constituency, the party's leaders inexorably settled into a style of rule that came naturally to them given their social origins.

Top leaders in the Pathet Lao were disproportionately ethnic Lao. Nearly half came from royalty or were born to wealth; the rest were mainly middle-class. Most were the sons, brothers, nephews, and cousins of the old ruling elite. Despite their communist training, they had not shed the ingrained habits of thought of their class. Like "their RLG predecessors" they were "nurtured in an environment in which the lowland Lao feel a sense of superiority toward the highlanders." Their natural inclination was to exclude the montagnards from the highest circles of power.[17] Vietnamese sponsorship enabled them to indulge this prejudice. T'ai, Khmu, and Hmong leaders in the Pathet Lao were given only ceremonial posts in the new government. The party's powerful Central Committee became a closed club, open only to ethnic Lao.

In addition to racial prejudice, the nation's new leaders inherited the political style of their class. Centuries of corrupt rule (abetted by France's decision to leave the native bureaucracy undisturbed) was ingrained in the consciousness of the ruling elite, communist and noncommunist alike. Having acquired power and no longer answerable to a broad constituency, party leaders were free to follow their political instincts. They used patronage on a massive scale to reward friends and family and to establish a loyal clientele for support in intra-party squabbles. Within a few years thousands of ethnic Lao (nearly 25 percent of the workforce) held posts in the state and provincial bureaucracies. Once foreign investment money began to pour into the country, party leaders cut themselves in on the deals. In the end, the regime had become as corrupt as the one it had replaced and the ideal of "universal Lao nationalism" was no closer to reality than it had been twenty years earlier.

And the Hmong were no better off than before. Indeed, they were worse off. Having fought the communists for nearly twenty years, they were both despised and feared by the new regime, which is why the campaign to crush the Chao Fa was so brutal and why so many Hmong wound up in concentration camps on the Plain of Jars. Ironically, this would not have happened had the Hmong not had such able leaders. Touby LyFoung was the first Hmong politician to fully comprehend that, aside from messianism, only patronage on a massive scale could mute the divisive forces of clan politics and make broad-based politics possible. Vang Pao understood this as well. Both leaders involved Hmong in narcotics and mercenary warfare to generate funds necessary to sustain patronage on a large scale. Vang Pao had more to work with, of course. Besides controlling Hmong narcotics, he was able to pay his soldiers much more than what Touby's guerrillas received; in addition, Vang Pao could count on massive refugee relief, supplied by USAID and subsidized by the CIA. With more money and resources, Vang Pao was able to transform Touby's local power base into a regional political machine that rivaled the politics of Vientiane.

Neither Touby nor Vang Pao sought power as an end in itself. They sought it to improve the lives of ordinary Hmong through greater self-rule at the provincial level, increased representation in national politics, and the integration of Hmong local markets into the national economy. While they held power, both leaders advanced all of these goals. Unfortunately, they made the mistake of linking the fate of their people to the foreign policies of foreign nations. Touby could not imagine that the Viet Minh would eventually defeat the French Expeditionary Corps and that France would abandon Indochina. Vang Pao could not foresee that the U.S. would lose the Vietnam War.

No one can be expected to augur an unlikely future, but the balance sheet must include Vang Pao's leadership after the war. To resurrect his political machine in America, Vang Pao again used patronage on a large scale to transcend the limitations of clan politics. The effort had benefits. For more than a decade the new political organization served as a unifying force for American Hmong immigrants and a protective buffer between them and American society. It also cast up a new generation of Hmong leaders who acquired on-the-job experience in Lao Family Community satellite organizations across the country. On the negative side, the organization unduly delayed Hmong involvement in mainstream society and politics. Also, it became an end in itself. In constant need of money to provide patronage, Vang Pao incessantly beat the war drum, promising that he would bring down the

LPDR and return all expatriate Hmong to Laos. For a time he may have even believed this was possible. But after Neo Hom's humiliating defeat in 1989, it was clear this would never occur. Yet, for nearly another decade, Vang Pao used persuasion, patronage, and intimidation to keep thousands of Hmong in Thai refugee camps in order to keep the resistance idea alive. These people could easily have immigrated to the U.S., but their futures were mortgaged to sustain Vang Pao's political machine in America. For a people already decimated by war, it was an additional burden they should not have had to bear.

NOTES

PREFACE

[1]"Summers, Vietnam War Almanac, p. 196; Shaplen, *Bitter Victory*, p. 157; Robbins, *The Ravens*, p. 352; Hannah, *The Key to Failure: Laos & the Vietnam War*, p. xiii.

[2]Tom Dooley, *The Night They Burned the Mountain*, p. 325; Bailey, *Solitary Survivor*, p. 66; Sheer, "The Vietnam Lobby," pp. 68-81. It is likely that Dooley worked closely with the CIA from the moment he set foot in Laos. During Senate hearings it was disclosed that Dooley was on the CIA payroll. By the late 1950s, CIA agents were making regular visits to his medical stations in the far north, where Dooley's medical staff provided field care for Chinese mercenaries under contract to the CIA.

[3]Boettcher, *Vietnam*, p. 164.

[4]Robbins, *Air America*, p. 189.

[5]Stevenson, *The End of Nowhere*, p. 1; Chagnon and Rumpf, "Decades of Division for the Lao Hmong," p. 12; McCoy, *The Politics of Heroin: CIA Complicity in the Global Drug Trade*, p. 289.

[6]Quoted in Johns, "Let's Not Forget Laos," p. 76.

[7]Johns, "Let's Not Forget Laos," p. 76; Conboy and Morrison, *Shadow War*, p. 249; *War-related Civilian Problems in Indochina*, p. 27; Parker, *Codename Mule*, p. xvii; Lee, "Minority Policies and the Hmong," p. 203. From 1963 on, Hmong battle deaths averaged about 5,000 per year. The Senate subcommittee report estimated that 40 to 50 percent of Hmong men were killed and as many as 25 percent of the women and children perished. One refugee relief worker on the scene claimed that in the early 1960s alone, almost twenty percent of the Hmong died from illness or enemy wounds in their desperate flight from invading North Vietnamese.

CHAPTER 1: SOWING PA CHAY'S WHEAT

[1]Laos is also the least populated nation in Southeast Asia. Of its four neighbors only Cambodia comes close to being so sparsely populated, though there are still more than twice as many people per square

mile in Cambodia as in Laos. Burma's population density is four times greater, and Thailand and Vietnam have higher population densities by a factor of seven and twelve, respectively.

[2]One study (Lebar, *Ethnic Groups of Mainland Southeast Asia*) has identified fifty different ethno-linguistic groups in Laos. The estimate of 300,000 highland T'ai comes from Wekkin, "The Rewards of Revolution," p. 186. The figure of 250,000 Hmong is only a rough estimate. The only detailed census of the Laotian Hmong was collected by Yang Dao in 1968 and published in his *Les Hmong du Laos Face au Developpement*, p. 30 (hereafter cited as *Hmong Poised for Development*). Yang Dao placed the total number for that year at 167,000. Moréchand ("The Many Languages and Cultures of Laos," p. 33) claimed a higher number of 300,000. A decade later Cooper ("The Hmong of Laos," p. 24) estimated there were only 200,000 Hmong in Laos. If accurate, the lower number can be explained by high war casualties and the loss of population due to immigration to Thailand.

[3]This is an anomaly in mainland Southeast Asia, where substantial ethnic minorities are the norm. Thailand is 86 percent ethnic Thai, Vietnam 84 percent ethnic Vietnamese, Cambodia 86 percent Khmer, and Burma 71 percent Burmese. However, it is hardly exceptional worldwide. Less than 50 percent of the world's nations exhibit the ethnic homogeneity of Vietnam or Thailand. Nor is it exceptional in Southeast Asia as a whole. The Malays are barely a majority in Malaysia, and the Javanese are a minority in Indonesia. As in Laos, both ethnic groups dominate the politics and society of their respective nations. See Connor, "A Nation is a Nation, is a State, is an Ethnic Group, is a . . ." pp. 37-39.

[4]Ethnic solidarity has seldom flourished anywhere prior to industrialization. Only after ethnic groups are drawn into a national economy, and homogenized by industrial labor, do divisions of kinship and tribe tend to wither, leaving only language and culture as a source of ethnic identification. No longer divided by clan and tribe, it is easier to close ranks and present a united front. See Fukuyama, *The End of History*, p. 269.

[5]The Hmong rose up as one people between 1918 and 1922 to follow the messianic figure Pa Chay. But once French rifles had destroyed Pa Chay's army, and assassins ended his life, the Hmong lost their unity and resumed their ancient clan rivalries and blood feuds.

The Khmu have not fared much better. At the turn of the century, thousands followed the chieftain Ong Keo in rebellion. Native militia led by French officers savaged the rebels. Ong Keo surrendered and placed himself at the mercy of the French, but the French needed to set an example and marched Ong Keo before a firing squad. The execution did not have the desired effect. Instead of intimidating the Khmu, it reinvigorated the rebellion and cast up a new leader—Kommadan.

Fighting on emotion, the Khmu went from victory to victory. To buy time, the French sued for peace and selected an utterly ruthless individual, Jean Jacques Dauplay, as their representative at the peace talks. Under a flag of truce, Dauplay shot the unarmed Kommadan twice in the chest at close range. To Dauplay's astonishment, the Khmu chieftain did not drop dead at his feet but bolted into the forest and escaped. Kommadan survived his wounds, scored more military victories, and transformed the Bolovens plateau into a Khmu principality. Khmu flocked to the area, not only to be ruled by one of their own—but to avoid French taxes.

It was a dangerous precedent. The French reentered the Bolovens in strength in 1935 with troops gathered from across Indochina. Kommadan mounted a spirited defense but was killed in battle. His political and military organization did not survive his death. As with the Pa Chay rebellion, Khmu solidarity sprang from the charisma of one man. With Kommadan's death the Khmu scattered like leaves in a storm. See McCoy, "French Colonialism in Laos," pp. 88-89; Gunn, *Rebellion in Laos*, pp. 112-126.

[6]Brown and Zasloff, *Apprentice Revolutionaries*, pp. 148-149; Hardy, *Pawns of War*, p. 78.

[7]Stuart-Fox, *Laos: Politics, Economics and Society*, ch. 1.

[8]Virvong, *History of Laos*, pp. 26, 38.

[9]Halpern, *Government, Politics and Social Structure in Laos*, p. 63.

[10]Page, *The Little World of Laos*, p. 78.

[11]Quoted in Champassak, *Storm over Laos*, p. 6. (emphasis added)

[12]The French made the old kingdom of Luang Prabang a protectorate, but directly administered Laos' southern provinces.

[13]Quoted in Duiker, *Sacred War: Nationalism and Revolution in a Divided Vietnam*, p. 11.

[14]Arendt, *Imperialism*, p. 34.

[15]The French were unaware that Laos contained substantial deposits of zinc, potash, gypsum, iron ore, gold, silver, and oil.

[16]McCoy, "French Colonialism in Laos," p 77.

[17]Murray, *The Development of Capitalism in Colonial Indochina*, pp. 167-187, 327-328.

[18]Stuart-Fox, *Laos: Politics, Economics and Society*, pp. 13, 16.

[19]McCoy, "French Colonialism in Laos," p. 67.

[20]On the issue of montagnards, the natives pretty much agreed with the French. "For certain Vietnamese and Chinese, the native montagnards are viewed as less than truly human, and by other ethnics after their own fashion, as extremely inferior." Dassé, *Montagnards Revoltes*, p. 5.

[21]Toye, *Laos*, p. 45.

[22]Stuart-Fox, *Laos: Politics, Economics and Society*, p. 13.

[23]Thompson, *French Indochina*, p. 368.

[24]Quoted in Larteguy, *La Fabuleuse Aventure du Peuple du l'Opium*, p. 95. (Hereafter cited as *Opium People*.)

[25]Bernatzik, *Akha and Miao*, p. 674.

[26]Derived from budget estimates in Gunn, *Rebellion in Laos*, p. 43.

[27]The title is Chinese in origin; loosely translated as "little king", it is likely a Hmong transliteration of the "Tu Kwan" designation assigned by the Ming dynasty to tribal minorities serving as bureaucrats in territorial administrations.

[28]Before the arrival of the Americans, the town was known by both Hmong and ethnic Lao as Xieng Khouang city or Xieng Khouang town. Accustomed to using the suffix "ville" for place names, CIA agents and special forces personnel in Laos began referring to Xieng Khouang city as Xieng Khouangville. The one merit of the vulgarization is that it makes it easier to distinguish the town from the province.

[29]Yang, *Hmong Poised for Development*, p. 55.

[30]It is also possible that the French were sensitive to the fact that no one knew the rugged northeastern mountain regions of Laos better than the Meos. Eleven years earlier, a thousand-man force led by General Roussel de Courcy had pillaged the Vietnamese imperial palace at Hue in an "orgy of killing and looting" that rivaled Britain's infamous sack of the Summer Palace in Beijing in 1860. After slaughtering Vietnamese, de Courcy burned the imperial library to the ground and stripped the palace of its wealth in inlaid gold, silver, and jewels. He even carried away carpets and cutlery. The child emperor Ham Nghi slipped through de Courcy's hands and escaped with his advisors to the highlands of Laos. The French searched for the boy but got

nowhere until Hmong were hired as guides. The French may have reasoned that there might be future occasions when Hmong familiarity with the mountain terrain could prove invaluable (Karnow, *Vietnam: A History*, p. 87).

[31]Yang, *Hmong at the Turning Point*, p. 25.

[32]Yang, *Hmong Poised for Development*, p. 56.

[33]Ibid., p. 45.

[34]Interview with a member of the Vue clan(1985).

[35]Burchett, *Mekong Upstream*, pp. 88-89.

[36]McCoy, "French Colonialism in Laos," p. 83.

[37]Interview with a member of the Ly clan (1985).

[38]Stuart-Fox, *Laos: Politics, Economics and Society*, p. 14.

[39]McCoy, "French Colonialism in Laos," p. 83.

[40]Ruey Yie-Fu, "The Miao: Their Origin and Southward Migration," p. 183.

[41]The Hmong migrated to China from Siberia at a time when Siberia was predominately Caucasian. See Quincy, *Hmong: History of a People*, pp. 18-21, 28-31. Recent discoveries of the mummified remains of Caucasians in northwest China indicate the Hmong were only one of many Caucasian groups who entered northern China prior to 1000 B.C. (Hadingham, "The Mummies of Xinjiang," pp. 68-77). Today, after eons of race mixing, the Hmong appear more Asian than European, though they still have pale complexions and aquiline noses and sometimes lack an epicanthic eyelid fold; occasionally one even finds a Hmong with blue eyes and blond or red hair. Tapp (*Sovereignty and Rebellion*, p. 10) claims that in present-day Thailand such Hmong are sometimes viewed by other Hmong as cursed and not to be trusted. It is not much different in Laos. During French rule the mother of a blond child was often accused of having consorted with a Frenchman. Touby LyFoung, the preeminent leader of the Laotian Hmong during the 1940s and 1950s, fathered a blond child. For years it was whispered behind closed doors that he had persuaded one of his wives to sleep with a high-placed French bureaucrat to advance his own political career (communication from Bliayao Vang, 1995).

[42]Wiens, *China's March Toward the Tropics*, p. 85.

[43]Shrock, *Minority Groups in Thailand*, p. 585; Bernatzik, *Akha and Miao*, pp. 66-67.

[44]Bernatzik, *Akha and Miao*, pp. 66-67.

[45]For one version of the Chue Chao legend current in Hmong communities in Thailand, see Tapp, *Sovereignty and Rebellion*, ch. 7; one apocryphal account (Larteguy, *Opium People*, p. 62) of the last king of the ancient Hmong kingdom places a magic flag in the monarch's hands. He supposedly entrusted it to his virgin daughter, who waved the flag during battles to call up a storm to drive off the Chinese soldiers. The virginity requirement was no easy matter to fulfill. Since Hmong girls (at least in Pa Chay's time) were expected to be sexually active at a young age, and might very well have a lover or two before marriage, remaining chaste was a considerable achievement.

[46]In one version of the lost books story (Shrock, *Minority Groups in Thailand*, pp. 57-89) the Hmong fed the books to their starving horses for fodder during the desperate flight. Occasionally, one hears the claim that Hmong books still exist, hidden away in some secret library. In "Les Ecritures du Hmong," pp. 137-138, Jacques Lemoine reports that at the turn of the century a French officer named d'Ollone traveled extensively throughout Yunnan, Guizhou and Sichuan provinces in China gathering material on the languages and literature of different ethnic minorities. While in Sichuan he was told of the existence of Hmong books containing an entire history of the Hmong people, and shown a dictionary containing 338 characters, some obviously Chinese, others of unknown origin. D'Ollone was led into the mountains to the village where the books were supposedly to be found but came away empty-handed. D'Ollone concluded that the dictionary was pure invention. It would appear that the legend of "lost books" is common among montagnards of southern China and Southeast Asia.

[47]The importance of literacy to the Hmong is highlighted in one legend of a Hmong who took a Chinese to court over a breach of contract. The Hmong plaintiff told the judge his side of the story, but the defendant possessed a signed contract to back up his claim. The Hmong had indeed signed the document, presuming its terms reflected their verbal agreement. His illiteracy made him easy prey for fraud (Graham, *Songs and Stories of the Ch'uan Miao*, p. 139). More generally, written documents were the lifeblood of the Chinese imperial bureaucracy, placing the Hmong at a disadvantage in dealing with Chinese officials who could interpret contracts and treaties as they pleased since the Hmong were incapable of checking documents for verification.

[48]Jenks *(Insurgency and Social Disorder in Guizhou: The "Miao" Rebellion 1854-1873,* pp. 63-64) believes there is evidence that Hmong

messianism during this period was greatly influenced by Chinese folk religion, which contained strong millennialist elements.

[49]Ibid., pp. 164, 148, 89, 92-93, 142, 155, 109, 164.

[50]Tapp (*Sovereignty and Rebellion*, p. 94) suggests Pollard may have spread the 'lost books' rumor himself to gain converts.

[51]Pollard, *The Story of the Miao*, p. 72.

[52]The mission at Stone Gateway remained in operation until 1950, when the communist regime tore it down. Recently (July 1995), state authorities reversed a forty-five year policy of denigrating the work of foreign missionaries in China by officially acknowledging the good work of the mission at Stone Gateway and declaring the ruins of the mission a national monument. Becker, "Homage to Missionary Who Freed the Miao," p. 6.

[53]Tapp (*Sovereignty and Rebellion*, p. 96) also argues for a direct connection between the Methodist relief project and the messianic movement on the Yunnan frontier.

[54]Gunn, *Rebellion in Laos*, pp. 152-153.

[55]Communication from Cher Cha Yang (1986).

[56]Gunn, "Shamans and Rebels: The Batchai (Meo) Rebellion of Northern Laos and Northwest Vietnam," p. 113; Larteguy, *Opium People*, pp. 97, 99.

[57]Gunn, "Shamans and Rebels," p. 114.

[58]Pa Chay's name is sometimes given as Batchay, and his clan has been variously identified as Her, Chao, or Lo, but I follow Yang (*Hmong Poised for Development*, p. 55.), and many Hmong I have interviewed, in placing him in the Vue (or Vu) clan.

[59]According to Nao Yang (interview 1985), Song Tou was actually Pa Chay's uncle.

[60]After Pa Chay's death, his biography entered the realm of legend. Instead of being an ordinary youth, he was invested with remarkable abilities. According to one account (interview with Shue Long Vue, 1985), without going to school, Pa Chay mysteriously acquired the ability to speak and write Chinese, Vietnamese, and Laotian.

[61]By similar athletic feats, fifty years earlier another messianic Hmong named Sioung attracted a large following among the Hmong living near Quan Ba in Tonkin. He piled up benches into a makeshift tower and leaped to the top, where he announced he was the long-awaited king of the Hmong. For an account of Sioung's rebellion, see *Lunet de Lajonquiére, Ethnographie du Tonkin Septentrional*, pp. 297-300.

[62]Pa Chay's transformation unnerved Song Tou Vue. He was certain that Pa Chay's boast about liberating the region from the T'ai and the French would get them all killed. He begged Pa Chay to give it up. The two argued, then struggled. Pa Chay threatened the old man with a hunting spear. The chieftain's wife stepped between the two to stop the fight. With a thrust meant for Song Tou Vue, Pa Chay ran her through. Convinced that Pa Chay was in the grip of evil spirits, or had suddenly gone insane, Song Tou Vue fled to the French garrison at Son La to report the murder and to reveal Pa Chay's plan to mount an insurrection. Not knowing what to make of the old man's story, the post's commander simply jailed him. And there Song Tou Vue remained while Pa Chay made war on the T'ai and the French. A year later, still in the same cell, Song Tou Vue took his own life.

[63]Larteguy, *Opium People*, p. 102.

[64]A French priest who witnessed one of these battles described the girl as "opening her coat to receive our bullets." (Larteguy, *Opium People*, p. 102).

[65]Tapp, *Sovereignty and Rebellion*, p. 130; Larteguy, *Opium People*, pp. 100-101.

[66]Gunn, *Rebellion in Laos*, p. 156.

[67]Ibid., pp. 145-147.

[68]Gunn, "Shamans and Rebels," p. 115.

[69]Alleton, "Les Hmong aux confins de la Chine et du Vietnam: La revolte du 'Fou' (1918-1922)," p. 33; interview with a member of theVue clan (1985).

[70]Interview with a member of the Vue clan (1985); Beauclair, *Tribal Cultures of Southwest China*, p. 68.

[71]Interview with a member of the Vue clan (1985).

[72]Gunn, "Shamans and Rebels," p. 116.

[73]Interview with a member of the Vue clan (1985).

[74]Le Boulanger, *Histoire du Laos Français*, p. 360.

[75]McCoy, "French Colonialism in Laos," p. 92; interview with Shue Long Vue (1985); Larteguy (*Opium People*, p. 103) claims Pa Chay was killed by Khmer tribesmen, but two Hmong, Shue Long Vue and Xia Ying Vue (interviews 1985, 1986), insist it was Hmong who assassinated the messianic leader.

[76]Larteguy, *Opium People*, pp. 103-104.

[77]Gunn, *Rebellion in Laos*, p. 159; within a few years a Hmong would occupy a seat on the Conseil Consultative Indigène, the prestigious

(though essentially powerless) native colonial cabinet; Yang, *Hmong at the Turning Point*, p. 27.

[78]Interview with a member of the Vue clan (1985); communication from a member of the Yang clan (1985); because he held the pig Chue Chao sacred, Shi Yi Xiong refused to eat pork, a mainstay of the Hmong diet.

[79]Interviews with two members of the Vue clan (1985), Xia Ying Vue (1985).

[80]Tapp, *Sovereignty and Rebellion*, p. 130.

[81]Interviews with two members of the Vue clan (1984,1986).

[82]Interview with a member of the Moua clan (1985).

[83]Interviews with two members of the Vu clan (1984,1985).

[84]Interview with a member of the Vu clan(1985).

[85]Interview with a member of the Vue clan (1985). Some Hmong (interview with a member of the Yang clan, 1984) place the rift between the Lo and Ly clans after LoBliayao's death. In this account, May Lo was still alive and so overwhelmed by her father's death that she insisted a lock of her hair be buried with him. Shortly after the burial she fell ill, consulted a shaman, and was told she would die if the lock of hair weren't retrieved. Foung Ly ordered LoBliayao's body exhumed for just that purpose, which infuriated LoBliayao's sons, not only for the sacrilege but because it was believed exhumation causes illness and death to the deceased's relatives.

[86]McCoy, *The Politics of Heroin in Southeast Asia*, p. 118.

[87]Gunn, *Rebellion in Laos*, p. 161.

[88]Roux and Tran, "Some Ethnic Minorities in Northern Tonkin," p. 392; Larteguy, *Opium People*, p. 103.

[89]Actually, Touby's older brother, Page LyFoung, was given the post, but he died after only six months on the job and the position was then given to Touby (interview with a member of the Vu clan, 1984).

[90]The negotiations occurred in late 1945. There were earlier attempts at reconciliation between Touby and Faydang, initiated by leaders of other clans, but they also came to naught.

[91]Interview with a member of the Vu clan (1985).

[92]Viet Minh is an abbreviated form of Viet Nam Doc Lap Dong-Minh (League for the Independence of Vietnam). Organized in 1941 by the Indochinese Communist Party, the league's name was appropriated by both the political apparatus and military units of the Vietnamese communists.

[93]Interview with Bliayao Vang (1995).

CHAPTER 2: JAPANESE OCCUPATION

[1]Lacouture, *Ho Chi Minh*, p. 43.

[2]Halberstam, *Ho*, chs. 2-3.

[3]Toye, *Laos*, p. 102 (note).

[4]Nearly fifty years later, after Laos turned communist, Laotians still had no taste for Marxist ideology. Translations of Lenin distributed to citizens wound up in piles in used-book stalls. A resident of Vientiane confided to a reporter, "You get a headache trying to read that stuff." (*Los Angeles Times*, Dec. 19, 1980.)

[5]Brown and Zasloff, *Apprentice Revolutionaries*, pp. 14-15.

[6]Kolko, *Anatomy of a War*, pp. 16, 28.

[7]Gunn, *Rebellion in Laos*, p. 39; Langer and Zasloff, *North Vietnam and the Pathet Lao*, pp. 24-25.

[8]Thompson, *French Indochina*, p. 376.

[9]According to Langer and Zasloff (*North Vietnam and the Pathet Lao*, p. 17), anti-Vietnamese feelings were only intense among the Lao elite who "fear what they perceive as Vietnamese aggressiveness, as well as organization and drive." Also see Silverman, "Historic National Rivalries and Interstate Conflict in Mainland Southeast Asia," p. 64.

[10]Fall, *The Two Viet-Nams*, pp. 13-15. A less strident judgment comes from Langer and Zasloff (*North Vietnam and the Pathet Lao*, p. 23.): "When in 1893 the French placed Laos under their rule, they probably saved the Lao from being absorbed by their stronger and more vigorous neighbors, the Thai and Vietnamese, who had long been making inroads into Lao territory."

[11]Chanda, *Brother Enemy*, p. 52.

[12]Langer and Zasloff, *North Vietnam and the Pathet Lao*, p. 17.

[13]White and Jacoby, *Thunder Out of China*, p. 49.

[14]Doyle and Lipsman, *The Vietnam Experience: Setting the Stage*, p. 170; Lancaster, *The Emancipation of French Indochina*, pp. 98-99; Marr, "World War II and the Vietnamese Revolution," p. 110.

[15]Decoux's eagerness to cooperate with the Japanese at almost any cost became the model for Colonel Nicholson of the novel *The Bridge*

over the River Kwai, written by Pierre Boulle, a member of Decoux's staff.

[16]Toye, *Laos*, p. 48 (note). According to one study (Whitaker, *Laos: a Country Study*), by 1970 there were eight times more ethnic Lao in Thailand than in Laos.

[17]Brown and Zasloff, *Apprentice Revolutionaries*, pp. 21-23.

[18]McCoy, *The Politics of Heroin in Southeast Asia*, p. 111.

[19]Rice exports increased by 107 percent between 1900 and 1937; from 1915 to 1929 rubber production expanded by 3,359 percent (Murray, *The Development of Capitalism in Colonial Indochina*, pp. 180, 192). Production and export estimates drawn from data in Vu Quoc Thuc, *L'Economie Communaliste du Viet-Nam*, p. 198, and Touzet, *L'Economie Indochinoise et La Grande Crise Universelle*, pp. 69, 76.

[20]Calculated from data in Gunn, *Rebellion in Laos*, p. 45.

[21]McCoy, *The Politics of Heroin in Southeast Asia*, p. 90.

[22]In 1931, nearly two-thirds of the Hmong opium crop was sold to illicit traders (Gunn, *Rebellion in Laos*, p. 163).

[23]McCoy, *The Politics of Heroin in Southeast Asia*, p. 119.

[24]There was precedent for the new policy. In 1896, the French had demanded the Hmong to requite their taxes in opium rather than silver. This, unfortunately, led to a revolt. A more promising precedent occurred in 1933. A year earlier a poor opium harvest, plus an unexpected shortage of cash at the Opium Purchasing Board for purchasing opium, left Hmong farmers too strapped to pay their taxes. After an official report on the matter conceded that the Hmong were "materially incapable" of acquitting their tax obligations, the administration allowed the Hmong to pay their taxes in opium rather than silver (Gunn, *Rebellion in Laos*, p. 164).

[25]Over a three-year period, one Hmong tax collector earned commissions totaling seven hundred bars of silver (interview in 1985, with a Hmong who wishes to remain anonymous).

[26]McCoy, *The Politics of Heroin in Southeast Asia*, p. 95. The Laotian Hmong increased their output of opium by 582 percent (estimate based on figures in Gunn, *Rebellion in Laos*, pp. 44-45).

[27]Gunn, *Rebellion in Laos*, p. 45.

[28]Pietrantoni, "Note Sur les classes de revenues au Laos et au Tonkin avant 1945," p. 190.

[29]Interview with a member of the Yang clan (1992). Touby purchased an automobile a few years later, becoming the second, not the first

Hmong as sometimes reported (Hamilton-Merritt, *Tragic Mountains*, p. 50) to own a motor vehicle.

[30]During the allied push into France following the Normandy invasion, Eisenhower intended to bypass Paris to avoid expected heavy losses to civilians in any attempt to liberate the city from the Germans. However, once French partisans inside the city initiated a liberation on their own, Eisenhower changed his mind. A division of Free French, backed by American troops, closed on Paris on August 19. Six days later Paris fell into Allied hands. De Gaulle was already the head of a provisional French government, formed in 1943. That body now assumed official control of France, with de Gaulle continuing as president.

[31]Wright, *France in Modern Times*, p. 532.

[32]Conboy and Morrison, *Shadow War*, p. 1.

[33]Hamilton-Merritt, *Tragic Mountains*, p. 22.

[34]This may not be entirely true. In mid-1943, a Japanese convoy entering Laos from northern Vietnam along Route 7 was attacked near Nong Het and looted. The Japanese were confident that the assault was a Hmong operation. Under interrogation, Touby denied any Hmong involvement and attributed the attack to Chinese bandits operating along the border between Vietnam and Laos (Larteguy, *Opium People*, pp. 145-146). It is possible Touby lied about the incident, which may have been his first major offensive action against the Japanese in Laos.

[35]Gunn, *Political Struggles in Laos* (1930-1954), p. 108.

[36]It was Leclerc's Second Armored Division, backed by American troops, that had liberated Paris from the Germans.

[37]Hamilton-Merritt, *Tragic Mountains*, pp. 26-28.

[38]Larteguy, *Opium People*, p. 148.

[39]Gunn, *Political Struggles in Laos*, p. 164.

[40]Hamilton-Merritt, *Tragic Mountains*, p. 34; Gunn, *Political Struggles in Laos*, p. 109.

[41]Gunn, *Political Struggles in Laos*, p. 165; Fall, *Anatomy of a Crisis*, p. 33.

[42]Interviews with a member of the Her clan (1987) and a member of the Vue clan (1993). Sa Long Vue was another Hmong who witnessed Japanese brutality toward French prisoners, and overheard one Japanese soldier claim, while tugging so hard on the lead strings to captured French soldier's noses that it caused blood to spurt from their nostrils: "Their noses are too long . . . See this, we are showing you these French who are not humans. They are only ghosts and they

can't control this country." (Quoted in Hamilton-Merritt, *Tragic Mountains*, p. 33.)

[43]According to Hamilton-Merrit (*Tragic Mountains*, pp. 34-35) the Hmong also saved a U.S. Air Force captain named Hughett. Trapped in the Philippines when the Japanese occupied the islands, Hughett stowed away on a ship to escape. Instead of delivering him to freedom, the freighter arrived at Saigon harbor just as the Japanese were launching their coup de main. Hughett was arrested yet managed to escape and headed northwest toward Laos. By the time he reached Ban Ban he was starved, sick, and close to death. A Hmong woman nursed him back to health. Revived, Hughett worked with Hmong guerrillas on intelligence-gathering missions until he was wounded by the Japanese. Having finally had enough of war, he accepted Touby's offer of a Hmong guide to lead him to the safety of China.

CHAPTER 3: THE FRENCH RETURN

[1]Halpern, *Government, Politics, and Social Structure in Laos*, p. 119.

[2]Dommen, *Laos: Keystone of Indochina*, p. 32.

[3]Lee, "Minority Policies and the Hmong," p. 217 (footnote).

[4]White and Jacoby, *Thunder out of China*, p. 280; Olson and Robert, *Where the Domino Fell: America and Vietnam, 1945 to 1995*, p. 26. The Chinese did not pose much of a military threat once they arrived. They entered not as a conquering army but as a ragtag, undisciplined horde. Two hundred thousand of them, barefoot and starving, would make directly for Hanoi, moving through the city like locusts, vandalizing shops and eating everything they could lay their hands on, including bars of soap mistaken for food. Another sixteen thousand equally ravenous Chinese, composing the Kuomintang's 93rd Division, would plunge into Laos and for several months scour the Hmong highlands for opium before working up the courage to head south and enter the nation's major cities to accept the surrender of the handful of Japanese who still remained. The 93rd then entered Burma, where its commander, General Sing Sung Chao, established himself as a warlord and major drug trafficker in heroin for the international narcotics market.

[5]According to Conboy and Morrison (*Shadow War*, p. 2) the king was eager to renounce independence in any case.

[6]Dommen, *Laos: Keystone of Indochina*, p. 35; Langer and Zasloff, *North Vietnam and the Pathet Lao*, p. 230 (note); Burchett, *The Second Indochina War*, p. 105; Lancaster, *The Emancipation of French Indochina*, p. 431; Warner, *The Last Confucian*, p. 198. Arthur Dommen (personal communication, 1998) can find no evidence that Souphanouvong actually joined the ICP. Much more than his turn to communism, Souphanouvong's marriage to a Vietnamese had scandalized the Lao elite. In later years his wife tried to calm the waters by donning traditional Lao clothing; but Souphanouvong's decision to have all of his children educated in Vietnam was evidence enough to many of his true allegiance. See Halpern, *Government, Politics, and Social Structure in Laos*, p. 28.

[7]Dommen, *Conflict in Laos*, p. 21; Dommen, *Laos: Keystone of Indochina*, p. 36.

[8]Toye, *Laos*, p. 79 (footnote); Thee, *Notes of a Witness* (New York: Random House, 1973), p. 87; Conboy and Morrison (*Shadow War*, p. 2) give a much lower figure (250) for the number of resisters killed.

[9]Warner, *The Last Confucian*, pp. 197-198.

[10]Hamilton-Merritt, *Tragic Mountains*, pp. 24-44; Larteeuy, *Opium People*, p. 154.

[11]Gunn, *Political Struggles in Laos*, p. 32; Le Bar and Suddard, *Laos: Its People, Its Society, Its Culture*, p. 273.

[12]By one account (Burchett, *Mekong Upstream*, pp. 263-264), Faydang's wife accompanied him when he ambushed the French, cutting arrows out of bamboo and dipping in them in poison for her husband's crossbow.

[13]Interview with a member of the Moua clan (1985).

[14]Brown and Zasloff, *Apprentice Revolutionaries*, pp. 39-40.

[15]With all of the spying and counterespionage there were bound to be innocent victims. Neng Vue turned seven in 1947. It was a lean year for himself and his two younger brothers, Fu and Ger, and his elder sister, May. That year their father had died, leaving the family destitute. Neng's mother, Bliayang, turned to the Vue clan for aid, but it was whispered she had poisoned her husband and no Vue would raise a hand to help her. She moved the family to the Lo-dominated town of Pak Lak and lived off of Lo charity. But the town's population dwindled once Lo clansmen drifted across the border to join Faydang, leaving little food to share. Huddled in a cold cave, near starvation, and with two children desperately ill, Bliayang went to Xieng Khouangville to seek an audience with her powerful cousin, Touby

LyFoung. Touby gave her enough money to build a proper house and get her and her children through the year. A few months later Touby's soldiers arrived in Pak Lak and arrested twelve Lo clansmen suspected of collaborating with Faydang. The villagers presumed Bliayang was Touby's spy, and threatened to kill her. She left her children and rushed to Xieng Khouangville to ask Touby for protection. While she was gone, Lo clansmen torched her home. Not having the stomach to murder children, at the last moment the arsonists dragged Neng, his sister and two brothers out of the flames (interview with a member of the Vue clan, 1985).

[16]Fall, *Anatomy of a Crisis*, p. 41.

[17]Champassak, *Storm over Laos*, p. 27; Toye, *Laos*, p. 76; Dommen, *Conflict In Laos*, p. 30; Brown and Zasloff, *Apprentice Revolutionaries*, p. 359; Langer and Zasloff, *North Vietnam and the Pathet Lao*, p. 42; Chanda, *Brother Enemy*, p. 57. Originally, the Pathet Lao movement called itself the Neo Lao Issara (Free Laos Front) and reserved the label Pathet Lao for the military arm of the organization. However, the designation Pathet Lao (Lao Nation) was soon commonly used to describe both the Lao communist political party and its military arm.

[18]Dommen, *Laos: Keystone of Indochina*, p. 107; Zasloff, *The Pathet Lao: Leadership and Organization*, p. 105.

[19]Gunn, *Political Struggles in Laos*, p. 228.

[20]Sheehan, *A Bright Shining Lie: John Paul Vann and America in Vietnam*, p. 166.

[21]Between 1947 and 1954 the Vietnamese communists regularly confiscated Hmong opium in northern Vietnam and orchestrated communist uprisings in Laos to coincide with Hmong opium harvests. Six kilos of opium fetched a machine gun and five hundred rounds of ammunition in China. By one estimate, without the money earned from Hmong opium the Viet Minh's war against the French would very early have foundered for lack of funds to purchase arms and food for soldiers. See Feingold, "Opium and Politics in Laos," pp. 335-336, and Wekkin, "The Rewards of Revolution: Pathet Lao Policy Towards the Hill Tribes since 1975," p. 186.

[22]Trinquier, *Les Maquis d'Indochine*, p. 86 (hereafter cited as The Indochinese Maquis).

[23]McCoy, *The Politics of Heroin in Southeast Asia*, pp. 92-108.

[24]Trinquier, *The Indochinese Maquis*, p. 86.

[25]Malo and Servan are two French coastal towns, Saint-Malo and Servan. Both face the islands of Guernsey and Jersey in the English Channel. Saint-Malo was the home town of one of the French instructors.

[26]It was precisely for this reason that twenty-four years later Giap would oppose plans for the famous January 1968 Tet offensive against the Americans and South Vietnamese. He realized from the start that the Tet offensive would play to the strength of the Americans. The plan was to engage U.S. troops in conventional-style warfare where America's superior firepower could easily tip the scales. The main strategy session for the operation occurred in July 1967, five months before the event. Party leaders and top level diplomats, called in from around the world, attended the conference. Ho Chi Minh was very ill at the time, so there was considerable anxiety over achieving victory over the Americans before his death. Due to this concern, Giap's warning that Tet would be a military disaster was ignored. He continued to argue against the offensive for the next two months, causing many who had attended the conference to have second thoughts. A political survivor, he stopped criticizing the plan in September when two hundred party officials, including the head of intelligence, were arrested and jailed for voicing opposition to the offensive. As Giap had predicted, Tet was a military disaster. Of the eighty-four thousand communist troops involved in the battle, over forty thousand were killed. The worst casualties were among the fearless officers and noncoms of the Viet Cong who led the assaults on Saigon and Hue, exposing their troops to American firepower and mass infantry assaults. After Tet, the already depleted troop strength of the Viet Cong was further reduced by mass defections. See Page and Pimlott, *Nam: The Vietnam Experience 1965-1975*, p. 355; Davidson, *Vietnam at War*, p. 450; estimates of battle deaths are from a report by General Earle G. Wheeler, chairman of the Joint Chiefs of Staff, February 27, 1968, reprinted in McMahon, *Major Problems in the History of the Vietnam War: Documents and Essays*, p. 357.

[27]Davidson, *Vietnam at War*, p. 149.

[28]Fall, *Anatomy of a Crisis*, p. 49.

[29]Davidson, *Vietnam at War*, p. 150.

[30]Trinquier, *The Indochinese Maquis*, p. 79.

[31]McCoy, *The Politics of Heroin: CIA Complicity in the Global Drug Trade*, p. 139; Davidson, *Vietnam at War*, p. 152.

[32]Roy, *The Battle of Dienbienphu*, p. 28.

[33]Conboy and Morrison, *Shadow War*, pp. 5-6.

[34]Dommen, *Conflict in Laos*, p. 42; Feingold, "Opium and Politics in Laos," p. 336.

[35]Robbins, *The Ravens*, p. 122.

[36]They were all captured and marched back to Muong Hiem.

[37]Brown and Zasloff, *Apprentice Revolutionaries*, p. 71; Wekkin, "The Rewards of Revolution," p. 182.

[38]Conboy and Morrison, *Shadow War*, pp. 6-8.

[39]Interview with a member of the Vue clan (1987).

[40]Shefter, *Political Parties and the State*, p. 6.

[41]Yang, *Hmong at the Turning Point*, pp. 29-30.

[42]Roffe, "Laos," p. 405.

[43]Touby sent a formal request by post to Bishop Mazoyer requesting Church assistance in establishing a school (Gunn, *Political Struggles in Laos*, p. 229).

[44]Protestant missionaries who succeeded the Catholics, and enjoyed greater success, laid the priests' failure to two causes. Their stand on celibacy was contrary to the Hmong conception of the natural order of things, and they were French, linking the Church to oppressive colonialism (Barney, "Christianity: Innovation in Meo Culture," p. 73). This is not entirely convincing. Chastity occupies an honored place in Hmong messianism. The celibacy of nuns, if not priests, might under a suitable interpretation fit very neatly within the Hmong conception of things. As for "oppressive colonialism," the Hmong of Xieng Khouang were more beneficiaries than victims of French rule.

[45]Davidson, "Hmong Ethnohistory," pp. 93-113.

[46]George Barney took over for the Andrianoffs in 1952. He was even more tolerant of Hmong cultural idiosyncrasies than Mazoyer. He did not censure Hmong polygamy, bride price, pre-marital sexual promiscuity, or even Hmong involvement in the drug trade. His attitude was that "they are problems which can only be solved . . . by the Meo, from within their own society" (Barney, "Christianity: Innovation in Meo Culture," pp. 83-85).

[47]Barney, "Christianity: Innovation in Meo Culture," p. 88.

[48]The original plan had been to create a Hmong script and use it to print Bibles and instructional materials, but Vientiane scotched the idea and insisted that all instruction be in Lao. A romanized script (later known as RPA, Romanized Popular Alphabet) was nevertheless developed by G. Linwood Barney, one of the missionaries at the Xieng Khouang mission, with help from William Smalley and Eves Bertrais,

both missionaries from Luang Prabang with linguistic training; Smalley was a Protestant, Bertrais a Catholic. The script would eventually be widely used by Hmong. For American Hmong it is the preferred script for the Hmong language.

[49]Conboy and Morrison, *Shadow War*, p. 17.

[50]Stevenson, *The End of Nowhere*, p. 44.

[51]Kaufmann, "Nationalism and the Problems of Refugees and the Ethnic Minority Resettlement," pp. 172-173.

[52]Earlier, the two leaders had encouraged intermarriage between the Vang and Ly. By the mid-1950s "there was a regular pattern of exchange of women between the two clans" (Barney, "Meo of Xieng Khouang Province," p. 275).

CHAPTER 4: EXIT FRANCE, ENTER AMERICA

[1]Hauptly, *In Vietnam*, p. 45; Goldstein, *American Policy Toward Laos*, p. 42; Boettcher, *Vietnam: The Valor and the Sorrow*, pp. 31, 43.

[2]De Gaulle, *The War Memoirs of Charles De Gaulle*, p. 242.

[3]Hodgson, *America in Our Time*, p. 29.

[4]Flemming, *The Cold War and Its Origins*, p. 446.

[5]Tucker, *Nation or Empire?: The Debate Over American Foreign Policy*, p. 41; Robertson, *International Politics Since World War II*, pp. 17-18; Divine, *Roosevelt and World War II*, p. 31; Barnet, *Intervention and Revolution: The United States in the Third World*, p. 88.

[6]The theoretician for this view was the Kremlinologist George Kennan, chief of the State Department's policy planning staff. In an influential 1947 article in *Foreign Affairs*, Kennan argued that the Soviets had to be contained by "adroit and vigilant application of counterforce at a series of constantly shifting geographical and political points." Kennan would later back away from this view, saying that he was misunderstood and that counterforce could assume other forms besides military action. He also became a critic of the Vietnam War. See Karnow, *Vietnam*, p. 171.

[7]Marx and Engles, *The Communist Manifesto*, p. 20.

[8]John Adams cited in Arendt, *On Revolution*, p. 15. Christopher Coker (*Reflections on American Foreign Policy* since 1945, pp. 5-9) argues that the idea that America was unique and an example for the rest of

the world was responsible for America's isolationist foreign policy prior to the Second World War; it was feared that too much involvement with European politics would corrupt America; isolationism was a way to keep the "country's virtue intact."

[9]Even at its most fetid, the anticommunist movement never lost its ideological focus. Senator Joe McCarthy, infamous for his "crude, below-the-belt, eye-gouging, bare-knuckled partisan exploitation of anti-Communism," was the first reactionary demagogue in American history to denounce people simply for their political views rather than their race, ethnicity, or religion (Caute, *The Great Fear*, pp. 21, 47).

[10]Arendt, *On Revolution*, p. 49.

[11]Quoted in Caute, *The Great Fear*, p. 47.

[12]Barnet, *The Giants: Russia and America*, pp. 66-67.

[13]The Truman administration saw in Stalin what Hannah Arendt would later describe as the essence of totalitarian politics: a "disregard for immediate consequences," a "neglect of national interests" and a "contempt for utilitarian motives" in order to maintain an "unwavering faith in an ideological fictitious world," a mode of politics that has "introduced into international politics a new and more disturbing factor than mere aggressiveness would have been able to do" (Arendt, *Totalitarianism*, pp. 114-115).

[14]Herken, *The Winning Weapon*, pp. 20, 44-45, 196-197.

[15]Khrushchev, *Khrushchev Remembers*, p. 362.

[16]Sivard, *World Military and Social Expenditures*, p. 15.

[17]The MacArthur quote comes from Summers, *On Strategy*, p. 59; MacArthur's insight was marred by his confusion of military victory with the total destruction of enemy forces. The confusion rightly alarmed congressmen, who dismissed MacArthur's criticism of gradualism as a disguised plea for total war.

[18]Davidson, *Vietnam at War*, p. 359.

[19]Wilson had not always practiced what he preached. He had refused to recognize Mexico's revolutionary government, headed by Victoriano Huerta. Huerta responded by arresting U.S. sailors. Wilson sent U.S. Marines into Veracruz to punish the Mexicans and threaten war. Huerta was subsequently driven from office. Wilson also used American troops in Haiti and Cuba. Both nations became American protectorates during Wilson's presidency.

[20]The ideal of national self-determination was soon conflated with the notion of ethnic self-determination, an idea decidedly at odds with America's own constitutional order which values liberty over ethnicity.

[21]Quoted in Stevenson, *The End of Nowhere*, p. 6.

[22]Caute, *The Great Fear*, p. 310.

[23]Rostow, *The Process of Economic Growth*, p. 317.

[24]Fukuyama, *The End of History*, p. 101.

[25]The economic success of South Korea, Taiwan, Hong Kong, Singapore, Malaysia, and Thailand turned traditional thinking about economic development on its head. Western capitalism was supposed to be the culprit that held back economic growth in the third world. In this view, the economies of the third world have remained backward because Western investment has mainly been for resource extraction rather than true industrialization. But the lesson taught by South Korea, Taiwan, Hong Kong, Singapore, Malaysia, and Thailand was that the only thing keeping poor nations down was their own corrupt and uninspired political leadership.

[26]Halberstam, *The Best and the Brightest*, p. 207.

[27]Kissinger, *White House Years,* pp. 63-64.

[28]Department of State Publication, October 1951. At that time rubber was still thought to be of major strategic value. During World War II the U.S. was denied the rubber produced in Southeast Asia, which crippled war production. To find a replacement, Washington sponsored a program for the development of synthetic rubber on a scale matched only by the effort to develop the atomic bomb. If we are to believe General William Westmoreland, sea power was also a major concern. In his words, the Southeast Asian nations "are astride the water and air routes to the Indian Ocean and thence to the Middle East. If those routes were denied, sea traffic would have to go south of Australia. It was that geographical context which brought forth President Eisenhower's concern for the 'falling of the dominoes'" (quoted in Glasser, *The Secret Vietnam War*, p. xix).

[29]*The Pentagon Papers*, pp. 64-65.

[30]Goldstein, *American Policy toward Laos*, pp. 49, 62; Boettcher, *Vietnam: The Valor and the Sorrow*, p. 63; Fall, *Street Without Joy*, p. 314.

[31]Goldstein, *American Policy Toward Laos*, p. 49.

[32]Fall, *The Two Viet-Nams*, p. 82; Karnow, *Vietnam: A History*, p. 99.

[33]The majority of the Hmong slipped away into the hills once they realized the inevitable outcome of the siege. But a few stayed on to the end.

One of them was Mi Cha Yang. After France recognized North Vietnam as an independent state, the Hmong captured at Dienbienphu (as well as an unknown number of Frenchmen) were not released with the rest of the prisoners, but held in a POW camp near the Chinese border for another twenty-five years. In 1979, following the Chinese invasion of Vietnam, the surviving camp inmates (most had already died), which included Mi Cha Yang, were released to avoid their liberation by the Chinese who, it was feared, would exploit the camp's existence for propaganda purposes (Hamilton-Merritt, *Tragic Mountains*, p. 62).

[34]As early 1953 Navarre's predecessor, General Raoul Salan, had advocated the garrisoning of Dienbienphu "as a means of defending upper Laos" (Davidson, *Vietnam at War*, p. 173).

[35]Fall, *Hell in a Very Small Place*, pp. 34-35.

[36]Doyle, Lipsman, and Weiss, *The Vietnam Experience: Passing the Torch*, p. 62.

[37]Maclear, *The Ten Thousand Day War*, pp. 29, 40-41.

[38]Lancaster, *The Emancipation of French Indochina*, p. 281.

[39]Fall, *The Two Viet-Nams*, p. 117.

[40]Tanham, *Communist Revolutionary Warfare: The Vietminh in Indochina*, p. 71.

[41]The commander of the French garrison, Colonel Christian Castries, was as confident of victory as Giap, boasting that "I'm going to kick General Giap's teeth in, one by one" (Doyle, *The Vietnam Experience: Passing the Torch*, p. 71).

[42]In all, the Viet Minh fired 103,000 artillery rounds into the garrison (Fall, *Hell in a Very Small Place*, p. 451).

[43]Grauwin, *Doctor at Dienbienphu*, p. 89.

[44]Davidson, *Vietnam at War*, pp. 225-226.

[45]Grauwin, *Doctor at Dienbienphu*, pp. 156, 177.

[46]Fall, *Hell in a Very Small Place*, pp. 37-52.

[47]Boettcher, *Vietnam: The Valor and the Sorrow*, p. 99.

[48]Goldstein, *American Policy toward Laos*, p. 50.

[49]Herring, *America's Longest War*, p. 27.

[50]Jah, *Foreign Policy of Thailand*, p. 46; Stevenson, *The End of Nowhere*, p. 33.

[51]Short, *The Origins of the Vietnam War*, p. 213.

[52]Aid agreements similar to the one for Laos were also made with Thailand and South Vietnam. Responding to pressure from Congress, the Truman administration conceived of the aid as a mini-Marshall Plan for Southeast Asia.

[53]Stevenson, *The End of Nowhere*, pp. 27-29; Hall, "The Laos Crisis, 1960-61," p. 38.

[54]Ackland, "No Place for Neutralism: The Eisenhower Administration and Laos," p. 143. Article six of the 1954 Geneva Agreement banned foreign military aid to Laos. Though the U.S. did not feel bound by the treaty, the Eisenhower administration worried about world opinion and considered it imprudent to flaunt the treaty's provisions.

[55]There was also a Commodity Imports Program for South Vietnam; as in Laos, it enriched the members of the country's political elite.

[56]Goldstein, *American Policy toward Laos*, p. 301.

[57]Inflation rate calculated from commodity prices listed in Dommen, *Conflict in Laos*, p. 106.

[58]Warner, *The Last Confucian*, p. 203. Washington finally placed restrictions on the program in July 1962 by announcing it would no longer pump more dollars into the Lao government's secret account to prevent inflation caused by the unauthorized printing of kip (Stevenson, *The End of Nowhere*, p. 178).

[59]*Wall Street Journal*, 9 April 1958.

[60]Halpern, *Economy and Society of Laos*, p. 126.

[61]Goldstein, *American Policy Toward Laos*, pp. 181-193; Stevenson, *The End of Nowhere*, p. 55.

[62]Myrdal, *Asian Drama*, vol. 2, p. 948.

[63]Halpern, *Economy and Society of Laos*, p. 132.

[64]Dommen, *Conflict in Laos*, pp. 106-107.

[65]Warner, *The Last Confucian*, p. 204.

[66]MacMullen, *Corruption and the Decline of Rome*, p. 174.

[67]The number of legionnaires in Algeria would eventually exceed 760,000. The French were determined not to repeat the same mistakes in Algeria that they had made in Vietnam. One of the lessons they learned in Vietnam was the need to maintain an 11-to-1 ratio of troops to guerrillas, and to set no deadline for victory. The French fought for eight years and reduced the Algerian forces from 65,000 to 7,000 men. They won militarily, but at a heavy political cost. France became the symbol of colonial oppression in the international community, and the war destabilized French domestic politics and

led, in 1958, to the overthrow of the government in a bloodless coup (Fall, "Theory and Practice of Insurgency and Counterinsurgency," p. 221).

[68] Seven former legionnaires pulled off Vientiane's first bank robbery in late 1966. Their target was the city's largest bank, the Banque de Indochine. Like clockwork, twice each week the bank dispatched several suitcases of hard currency in a Citroën to Wat Tay Airport for delivery to Hong Kong. The ex-legionnaires intercepted the Citroën, liberated the suitcases, and made their getaway in a stolen car, a brand-new Land Rover, owned by Father Loosdregt, the Bishop of Vientiane.

[69] Simpson, *Inside the Green Berets*, p. 86.

[70] Fall, *Anatomy of a Crisis*, p. 173.

[71] *The Pentagon Papers*, vol. 2, p. 647.

[72] Sananikone, *The Royal Lao Army and U.S. Army Advice and Support*, p. 50.

[73] Conboy and Morrison, *Shadow War*, pp. 67, 72.

[74] Quoted in Boettcher, *Vietnam: The Valor and the Sorrow*, p. 165. One Lao battalion even mutinied and imprisoned its White Star advisors. The leader of the mutiny was a company officer angry at the battalion commander, who kept sending him out on patrols so he could cheat with his wife. A White Star officer, Patrick Marr, flew out to the base camp. On his order, helicopters carrying armed soldiers with rifles clearly visible through the open doors circled overhead while he confronted the mutinous officer. After Marr promised to fire the battalion commander, the Lao officer allowed him to depart with the White Star team (Conboy and Morrison, *Shadow War*, p. 70).

[75] Simpson, *Inside the Green Berets*, pp. 89-90.

CHAPTER 5: BACKING THE WRONG MAN

[1] Dommen, *Conflict in Laos*, p. 21; Thee, *Notes of a Witness*, p. 72; Larteguy, *Opium People*, p. 233.

[2] Stevenson, *The End of Nowhere*, p. 48.

[3] Nearly twenty years later Foung Lo would again emerge on the political scene when the communists put him forward as a member of the

National Political Consultative Council, an advisory body created in mid-1974 as part of the new coalition government.

[4]Stevenson, *The End of Nowhere*, p. 41.

[5]Eisenhower, *Peace with Justice*, p. 97.

[6]Nixon's remarks appear in Department of State Bulletin, July 16, 1956, p. 94.

[7]Dulles' speech is reported in Department of State Bulletin, July 23, 1956, p. 147.

[8]Stieglitz, *In a Little Kingdom*, p. 33.

[9]Used to infiltrate troops into South Vietnam, the trail's main route would eventually stretch 625 miles and feed 12,500 miles of arterial roads. By the late 1960s, 3,000 miles of pipeline had been laid along the trail to keep trucks and tanks supplied with fuel. In 1985 Hanoi published a booklet on the trail, boasting that over the course of the war "two million people used the trail" and "forty-five million tonnes of material were transported along its length." (Summers, *Vietnam War Almanac*, p. 196; Shaplen, *Bitter Victory*, p. 157; Robbins, *The Ravens*, p. 352; Hannah, *The Key to Failure: Laos & the Vietnam War*, p. xiii).

[10]Dommen, *Conflict in Laos*, p. 117.

[11]In 1963 Vang Pao's guerrillas would kill Saychou in an ambush.

[12]Larteguy, *Opium People*, pp. 212-213. The Pathet Lao had a different story, which they told to Wilfred Burchett (*The Second Indochina War*, p. 129). The communists claimed that the 2nd battalion "made an epic fighting march for almost one month from the Plain of Jars straight back to their former base in Sam Neua Province, where they were received with open arms by the population." Just how they accomplished this while at the same time engaging Vang Pao's 10th Battalion near the Vietnamese border in Xieng Khouang Province was never made clear.

[13]This was the estimate made by the Laotian foreign minister and reported in the *Times* (London), on August 5, 1959.

[14]Dommen, *Conflict in Laos*, pp. 120-121.

[15]Fall, *Street Without Joy*, pp. 302-303.

[16]Goldstein, *American Policy Toward Laos*, pp. 152-153.

[17]Ibid., p. 174.

[18]Gibson, *The Perfect War*, p. 385; Sananikone, *The Royal Lao Army and U.S. Army Advice and Support*, p. 60; Dommen, *Conflict in Laos*, pp. 62-63, 134.

[19]Fall, *Anatomy of a Crisis*, p. 181.

[20]Burchett, "Pawns and Patriots," pp. 290-291; Langer and Zasloff, *North Vietnam and the Pathet Lao*, pp. 67, 236 (note); Thee, *Notes of a Witness*, pp. 97-98; Burchett, *The Second Indochina War*, p. 132.

[21]Champassak, *Storm over Laos*, p. 155; Conboy and Morrison, *Shadow War*, pp. 21, 28 (note).

[22]Fall, *Anatomy of a Crisis*, p. 187.

[23]Champassak, *Storm over Laos*, p. 158.

[24]Beech, "How Uncle Sam Fumbled in Laos," p. 89.

[25]Menger, *In the Valley of the Mekong*, p. 111.

[26]Dommen, *Conflict in Laos*, p. 145; Kong-Lê speech cited in Halpern, *Government, Politics and Social Structure in Laos*, p. 40; Champassak, *Storm over Laos*, p. 158.

[27]Warner, *Back Fire*, p. 24.

[28]*New York Times*, 20 September 1960.

[29]The PEO officers were Col. Albert Brownfield, Lt. Col. Jack Wood, Maj. Eleaser Parmly, and Maj. Robert McKnight (Conboy and Morrison, *Shadow War*, p. 34).

[30]Conboy and Morrison, *Shadow War*, pp. 34-35; Stevenson, *The End of Nowhere*, p. 96; Ray Bowers, *The United States Air Force in Southeast Asia*, p. 441.

[31]Sananikone, *The Royal Lao Army and U.S. Army Advice and Support*, p. 60.

[32]Menger, *In the Valley of the Mekong*, p. 114.

[33]Stieglitz, *In a Little Kingdom*, p. 34.

[34]Bailey, *Solitary Survivor*, p. 61.

[35]Dommen, *Conflict in Laos*, p. 77.

[36]Stieglitz, *In a Little Kingdom*, p. 10.

[37]Stevenson, *The End of Nowhere*, p. 119.

[38]Dommen, *Conflict in Laos*, p. 178.

[39]Ibid., p. 185.

[40]Sananikone, *The Royal Lao Army and U.S. Army Advice and Support*, p. 75.

[41]Warner, *The Last Confucian*, p. 213.

[42]In 1964 the U.S. Ambassador to Laos, Leonard Unger, summed up America's experience with the RLA: "MAAG and White Star teams

did a highly commendable job under difficult circumstances, but their experience demonstrated that it is almost impossible to put any real spine into [the RLA]" (quoted in Castle, "At War in the Shadow of Vietnam: United States Military Aid to the Royal Lao Government", p. 178).

[43]Dommen, *Conflict In Laos*, p. 183.

[44]Senate, *Hearings, United States Security Agreements and Commitments Abroad, Kingdom of Laos*, pp. 412-413.

[45]The men who went down with the plane were: Ralph Magee (pilot), Oscar Weston (copilot), Glenn Matteson (navigator), Alfons Bankowski (engineer), Fredrick Garside (assistant engineer), Leslie Sampson (radio operator), and Edgar Weitkamp who was just hitching a ride to Saigon, like Bailey. All seven died in the crash.

[46]Bailey was not the first American MIA in Laos. According to Defense Intelligence Agency (DIA) records, the first MIA in Laos was Charles Duffy, an embassy employee. In January 1961, Duffy went on a hunting trip in the jungles outside Vientiane and never returned.

[47]Tilford, *Search and Rescue in Southeast Asia*, pp. 34-5.

[48]Sananikone, *The Royal Lao Army and U.S. Army Advice and Support*, p. 73.

[49]Bailey, *Solitary Survivor*, pp. 152, 155, 161; Conboy and Morrison, *Shadow War*, p. 56 (note); Schanche, *Mr. Pop*, p. 94; Stanton, *Green Berets at War*, p. 40. Moon escaped twice from the aid station but the communists recaptured him each time. He received a head wound during his first escape that left him confused and debilitated. In his weakened condition it was relatively easy for the guards to run him down when he tried it again. One of the guards knocked Moon to the ground. As he lay there face down, the guard shot him several times in the back, then used the butt of his M-1 rifle to cave in Moon's skull. After Moon's death the Pathet Lao transferred Ballenger to a prison camp at Nong Het. Ballenger found other Americans at the prison. There was Grant Wolfkill, an NBC cameraman. Wolfkill was covering the war in May 1961 when his helicopter developed engine trouble and went down in communist-held territory in Xieng Khouang Province. The helicopter's crewmen, Edward Shore Jr. and John McMorrow, both CIA employees, were also at the prison. At night the Pathet Lao kept Ballenger and the others in small windowless cells. In the daytime, for twelve hours at a stretch, the prisoners were pinioned in stocks "like Salem witches." In early 1962 a special Hmong unit stormed the camp to rescue the Americans, but Ballenger and the other prisoners suspected a trap and refused to

leave. In August 1962 the Pathet Lao released Ballenger and the others in a prisoner exchange.

[50]Langer and Zasloff, *North Vietnam and the Pathet Lao*, pp. 72-73; Sananikone, *The Royal Lao Army and U.S. Army Advice and Support*, pp. 72-76.

[51]Conboy and Morrison, *Shadow War*, p. 26.

CHAPTER 6: COLONEL BILLY DISCOVERS VANG PAO

[1]There were five military regions in Laos. MR I was in the northwest, MR II in the northeast, MR III the northern panhandle, MR IV the southern panhandle, and MR V encompassed Vientiane Province.

[2]Warner, *Back Fire*, p. 91.

[3]Kuhn, Oral history interview, p. 35.

[4]The taboo is still strictly observed by American Hmong. After nearly two decades in America, there have been very few incidents of violations of this incest taboo in Hmong refugee communities. When it has occurred, ostracism has been immediate and unforgiving.

[5]In later years, when Vang Pao's power was at its apogee, he moved to erase this blemish on his reputation. Calling together the heads of his clan, he let it be known that all future violations of the incest taboo by Vang clansmen would be punished by execution.

[6]Interviews with a member of the Yang clan (1992) and a member of the Vue clan (1992).

[7]Interview with a member of the Yang clan (1992).

[8]Because of Faydang Lo's ties to the communists, only Lo clansmen in the region felt secure with so many communist troops nearby.

[9]Larteguy, *Opium People*, pp. 215-216. Ya Shao was from the Yang clan, and a very odd duck. The wizened old shaman did not look much like a Hmong, being as tall as a Frenchman and possessing milk-white skin. Despite his fame he dressed like an impoverished peasant, including the traditional buffalo dung hat—a swirled cloth cap which, from a distance, looks remarkably like cow flop. And he talked to ghosts—not just while in a trance (when shamans normally communicate with the spirit world), but at any time, whether working in his garden or on a leisurely stroll. Hmong overlooked these eccentricities because of Ya Shao's remarkable powers. After falling

into a trance he was able to visualize the location of a lost article or fix the identity of a thief. There were many eyewitness accounts of Ya Shao plucking a bullet from a wound with his bare hands. And it was widely believed that he had the power to combat black magic, imagined by many Hmong to be the cause of a lingering illness.

See Vue was a member of the famous shaman's household as a young boy, and later remained in close contact. The shaman died in 1973.

[10]A decade later, in an interview, Touby offered a different account, claiming Souvanna Phouma sent him to Xieng Khouangville to persuade Vang Pao to give up the plan to organize a Hmong maquis. At the time of the interview Touby was still in the government, riding Souvanna Phouma's coattails. It was not in his best political interests to reveal that he had once conspired with Vang Pao behind Souvanna Phouma's back to bring down his government. The gist of the interview is in McCoy, *The Politics of Heroin: CIA Complicity in the Global Drug Trade*, p. 311.

[11]Barney, "Meo of Xieng Khouang Province," p. 275 (note); Fall, *Anatomy of a Crisis*, p. 189.

[12]Conboy and Morrison, *Shadow War*, p. 66 (note). Later, when the CIA became interested in the Hmong, Phoumi tried, unsuccessfully, to get all logistic support for the Hmong channeled through the RLA so it would be under his control. While part of the motivation was to have access to the supplies for plunder, the larger reason was to keep the Hmong under control.

[13]The rank of colonel was standard, but there were exceptions. MR II's first commander was Sang Kittirath; at the time he was only a major.

[14]Larteguy, *Opium People*, pp. 216-217.

[15]Warner, *Back Fire*, pp. 89, 270.

[16]Robbins, *The Ravens*, p. 155.

[17]Interview (1994) with a former Hmong soldier who wishes to remain anonymous. Boussarath not only survived the assassination attempt but survived the war. He now lives in Texas.

[18]McCoy, *The Politics of Heroin in Southeast Asia*, pp. 268-269.

[19]Larteguy, *Opium People*, pp. 217-220; Conboy and Morrison, *Shadow War*, p. 61.

[20]Conboy and Morrison, *Shadow War*, p. 60.

[21]Kerdphol, *The Struggle for Thailand: Counter-insurgency 1965-1985*, pp. 76-80; Conboy and Morrison, *Shadow War*, p. 58.

²²Conboy and Morrison, *Shadow War*, p. 58.

²³Ibid., p. 61.

²⁴Parker, *Codename Mule*, p. xi.

²⁵Warner, *Back Fire*, p. 48.

²⁶Hamilton-Merritt, *Tragic Mountains*, p. 92.

²⁷Warner, *Back Fire*, pp. 31, 44-47.

²⁸Hamilton-Merritt, *Tragic Mountains*, p. 92.

²⁹Xiong, letter to President William Clinton.

³⁰Tim Pfaff interview with Chia Koua Xiong, in Pfaff, *Hmong in America*, p. 38.

³¹Stevenson, *The End of Nowhere*, p. 124.

³²Dassé, *Montagnard Revolts*, p. 181.

³³Dyer, *War*, pp. 24-25.

³⁴At the time, the Russians were far behind the U.S. in the ICBM race. To acquire some degree of parity in destructive capacity, the Soviets placed inexpensive short range nuclear missiles in Cuba only ninety miles from America's coast. When aerial photographs revealed the existence of the missiles, President Kennedy ordered a naval blockade of Cuba. By international law this was an act of war against Cuba, inviting a confrontation with Soviet naval vessels already steaming for the island nation. Because of the Bay of Pigs humiliation, Kennedy was not entirely clearheaded on the matter of Cuba. If Khrushchev had not backed down and promised to remove the missiles, Kennedy was prepared to authorize air strikes against the missile bases, followed by a full-scale invasion of Cuba. Soviet soldiers and technicians would certainly have been killed, initiating the outbreak of hostilities between the armed forces of the world's two nuclear superpowers, bringing the world to the brink of nuclear war. See Miroff, *Pragmatic Illusions: The Presidential Politics of John F. Kennedy*, pp. 97-98.

³⁵According to the revised Field Service Manual: "Victory alone as an aim of war cannot be justified, since in itself victory does not always assure realization of national objectives." Cited in Summers, *On Strategy*, pp. 61-62.

³⁶Osgood, *Limited War Revisited*, p. 10.

³⁷Davidson, *Vietnam at War*, p. 339.

³⁸Lomperis, *The War Everyone Lost-and Won*, p. 9.

³⁹The Vietnam War was not the first war in which American citizens questioned the wisdom of their government's policies. America's

occupation of the Philippines in 1898 met with armed resistance from Filipino freedom fighters, who objected to American colonialism as intensely as they had Spain's. Reports of American soldiers committing atrocities against the guerrillas and Philippine citizens reached the press. There were calls for a congressional investigation. In 1902, the Senate opened hearings on the matter. General Robert Hughes, commander of Manila, admitted openly in testimony that the atrocities had indeed occurred, but made no apology for them. As a result of the hearings, for the first time Americans in significant numbers began to question their nation's military policy. One voice raised was that of Mark Twain, who wrote: "[W]e have crushed a deceived and confiding people; . . . we have robbed a trusting friend of his land and his liberty; we have invited our clean young men to shoulder a discredited musket and do bandits' work under a flag which bandits have been accustomed to fear, not to follow; we have debauched America's honor and blackened her face before the world." Quoted in Severo and Milford, *The Wages of War*, pp. 226-7.

[40]Grinter and Head, *Looking Back on the Vietnam War*, p. 79; Sevy, *The American Experience in Vietnam*, p. 10.

[41]Kissinger, *American Foreign Policy*, p. 129.

[42]Mao's kind of war is actually more difficult to win. When the enemy is an indigenous force rather than a foreign occupation army, it cannot simply cut its losses and go home. Defeat is a life and death matter, which explains why guerrilla armies fighting indigenous forces have seldom emerged victorious. The exceptions are Mao's victory in China in 1949, Castro's ascension to power in Cuba in 1959, and the victory of the Sandinistas in Nicaragua in 1979. By contrast, the natural antipathy of the population toward occupation forces provides guerrillas popular support and a pool of willing recruits, all of which is denied to the enemy.

[43]Sheehan, *After the War Was Over: Hanoi and Saigon*, p. 59.

[44]Fall, *The Two Viet-Nams*, p. 113.

[45]Millet, *A Short History of the Vietnam War*, p. 33.

[46]Simpson, *The Undeclared War*, p. 226.

[47]Kissinger, *White House Years*, p. 298.

[48]Conboy and Morrison, *Shadow War*, p. 248. Ho Chi Minh also counted heads for the war in South Vietnam, estimating that the rural areas in the south and north of Vietnam could provide between 250,000 and 300,000 new recruits every year, indefinitely (Olson and Roberts, *Where the Domino Fell*, p. 144).

[51]Chanda, *Brother Enemy*, p. 298.

[52]Livo and Cha, *Folk Stories of the Hmong: Peoples of Laos, Thailand, and Vietnam*, pp. 67-68.

[53]Warner, *Back Fire*, p. 52.

[54]Conboy and Morrison, *Shadow War*, p. 62.

[55]Larteguy, *Opium People*, pp. 217-220.

[56]Conboy and Morrison, *Shadow War*, p. 62; Warner, *Back Fire*, pp. 52-53.

[57]Landry soon left the field to join Lair in Vientiane as his deputy.

[58]Conboy and Morrison, *Shadow War*, pp. 62-63; Warner, *Back Fire*, p. 52.

[59]Larteguy, *Opium People*, p. 221.

[60]In these early years the CIA called the landing strips "Victor Sites." Later they were called Lima Sites (LS). Only a dozen of the landing stripes were in place by the end of 1961. Three years later there would be more than a hundred. By 1970 the number had grown to more than four hundred (Parker, *Codename Mule*, p. xiii).

[61]Warner, *Back Fire*, p. 72.

[62]Schanche, *Mr. Pop*, pp. 65, 84.

[63]In addition to the C-47s, the USAID later used C-46s, Pilatus Porters and Helio Courier to deliver rice to refugees. A fully loaded C-46 could carry nearly five tons of rice; a Pilatus carried more than ton, and a Helio could transport up to six hundred pounds (Kuhn, Oral history interview, pp. 23-24).

CHAPTER 7: WHILE SEEKING A POLITICAL SOLUTION

[1]Eisenhower had left office with the Laos in turmoil, a testament to America's failed policy in the country. Thinking of the new administration, he could only regret that he had left a "legacy of strife and confusion in Laos" (Eisenhower, *The White House Years: Waging Peace*, p. 612). Things were a mess. For the first two months of his administration, Kennedy "spent more time on Laos than on anything else" (Schlesinger, *A Thousand Days: John F. Kennedy in the White House*, p. 163).

[2]Halberstam, *The Best and the Brightest*, p. 113; Goldstein, *American Policy Toward Laos*, p. 234.

[3]Gibbons, *The U.S. Government and the Vietnam War*, p. 24.

[4]Rostow, *The Diffusion of Power*, p. 266.

[5]Dommen, *Conflict in Laos*, p. 201.

[6]Stevenson, *The End of Nowhere*, p. 140; Goldstein, *American Policy Toward Laos*, pp. 235, 239.

[7]Castle, "At War in the Shadow of Vietnam," pp. 92-93.

[8]On reflection, Kennedy realized that the Bay of Pigs had been a blessing in disguise. As he commented to his White House aides, "Thank God the Bay of Pigs happened when it did, otherwise we'd be in Laos by now and that would be a hundred times worse" (Sorenson, *Kennedy*, p. 644).

[9]Halberstam, *The Best and the Brightest*, p. 116.

[10]Langer and Zasloff, *North Vietnam and the Pathet Lao*, p. 79.

[11]Goldstein, *American Policy Toward Laos*, p. 260.

[12]Hillsman, *To Move a Nation*, p. 136.

[13]Conboy and Morrison, *Shadow War*, p. 64.

[14]According to a captured North Vietnamese officer who served in Laos, it was always easy to spot NVA officers during a battle "as they attack with the headquarters element. The headquarters element consists of the CO, XO, radioman, and runner. The officers don't wear pistols or insignia of rank during the battle and are dressed the same as each soldier" (Garland, *A Distant Challenge*, p. 173).

[15]Warner, *Back Fire*, p. 67.

[16]Larteguy, *Opium People*, p. 223.

[17]Dommen, *Laos: Keystone of Indochina*, p. 70.

[18]Dommen, *Conflict in Laos*, p. 207.

[19]Conboy and Morrison, *Shadow War*, p. 65.

[20]Jane Hamilton-Merritt sets the figure (including soldiers and civilians) much higher at 10,000 (*Tragic Mountains*, p. 96).

[21]Schanche, *Mr. Pop*, pp. 88-90.

[22]Ibid., p. 100.

[23]Seventeen-year-old Nao Ying Yang had joined a volunteer unit because his schoolteacher was the commander. The unit went out on patrols to gather intelligence. His teacher carried the only weapon, a knife; there were no rifles, not even an old Hmong flintlock. Each time

they encountered the enemy, they had to run for their lives. The humiliation ate away at Nao Ying. There was talk that cases of modern rifles had been airdropped to Hmong partisans at Phong Savan. Nao Ying walked the thirty miles to claim one of the rifles for himself.

Nao Ying discovered that the Hmong volunteers at Phong Savan were as poorly equipped as his own group back home, and under more pressure. Neutralist patrols hounded them daily. Nao Ying fled with the guerrillas, thirty in all, and hid in the forest. It was three months before the group finally received weapons, along with a field radio. Their orders were to gather intelligence on enemy troop movements and relay the information by radio to Pha Khao. They used the radio only twice; each time they were attacked. Someone who understood Hmong, probably one of Faydang's men, had to be listening in. The radio was equipped to send Morse code, but no one had been taught it. Nao Ying was eventually sent to Vientiane to learn Morse code, after he'd been in the field for nearly a year, lugging a radio he never used (interview with a member of the Yang clan, 1984).

[24]Warner, *Back Fire*, p. 88.

[25]Ibid., p. 72.

[26]Parker, *Codename Mule*, p. xiii.

[27]Castle, "At War in the Shadow of Vietnam," p. 106; Conboy and Morrison (*Shadow War*, p. 88) list the authorized increase at 12,000 men.

[28]Conboy and Morrison, *Shadow War*, p. 98.

[29]Colby, *Honorable Men*, p. 193.

[30]Schanche, *Mr. Pop*, pp. 148-151.

[31]Robbins, *The Ravens*, p. 456 (note).

[32]Yang (*Hmong Poised for Development*, p. 37) claims the king and queen visited Long Cheng annually after 1964.

[33]Gibson, *The Perfect War*, p. 388.

[34]"Will Reds Take Southeast Asia?" p. 44.

[35]Apart from secret funds from the CIA, the Laotian government was receiving $3 million a month from the U.S. in "official" aid; the government had little revenue of its own.

[36]Conboy and Morrison, *Shadow War*, p. 105.

[37]Sananikone, *The Royal Lao Army and U.S. Army Advice and Support*, p. 106.

[38]Conboy and Morrison, *Shadow War*, pp. 70-73.

[39]*New York Times*, 12 May 1962.

[40]Brown and Zasloff, *Apprentice Revolutionaries*, p. 143.

[41]Robbins, *The Ravens*, p. 38.

[42]Stieglitz, *In a Little Kingdom*, p. 64.

CHAPTER 8: WARLORD

[1]Huston, "Air Operations Over Northern Laos," p. 121.

[2]Conboy and Morrison, *Shadow War*, p. 93 (note).

[3]Warner, *Back Fire*, pp. 86, 198.

[4]Conboy and Morrison, *Shadow War*, p. 95.

[5]Dommen, *Conflict in Laos*, p. 238.

[6]Ibid., p. 258.

[7]The U.S. Ambassador to Laos, Leonard Unger, showed Souvanna Phouma aerial photographs of North Vietnamese truck convoys moving daily into Laos (Unger, "The United States and Laos, 1962-5," p. 278).

[8]Conboy and Morrison, *Shadow War*, p. 109.

[9]Ibid., p. 125.

[10]Warner, *Back Fire*, p. 111.

[11]Conboy and Morrison, *Shadow War*, pp. 100, 104 (note).

[12]Ibid., p. 101.

[13]Brown and Zasloff, *Apprentice Revolutionaries*, p. 186.

[14]Stieglitz, *In a Little Kingdom*, p. 79.

[15]McCoy, *The Politics of Heroin in Southeast Asia*, p. 261. Back in 1960 Abhay had prepared the way for Phoumi's coup with diversionary attacks against Kong-Lê's forces inside Vientiane, enabling Phoumi's forward units to parachute onto the edge of the capital undetected and unopposed. Abhay's reward had been a promotion to general and command of the fifth military region, making him a major player not only in the military but in capital politics.

[16]Conboy and Morrison, *Shadow War*, p. 106.

[17]Ibid., pp. 105-106.

[18]Unger, "The United States and Laos, 1962-65," p. 180.

[19]Interview a member of the Vue clan, 1984; Schanche, *Mr. Pop*, pp. 196-198, 229; Robert Shaplen, *Time Out of Hand*, p. 349; Hamilton-Merritt (*Tragic Mountains*, p. 121) gives the date of the massacre as August 1962, nearly two years too early. Father Lucien Buchard, a Catholic priest working near Phou Nong, later claimed the number of Hmong killed was much smaller than the 1,200-to-1,300 figure reported. According to Buchard, at most only a couple of hundred were killed. Cited in Conboy and Morrison (*Shadow War*, p. 137, note). Buchard based his estimates on a census of refugees at Phou Nong, but the assault occurred farther south, and included refugees from other towns.

[20]Conboy and Morrison, *Shadow War*, pp. 107-108; Sananikone, *The Royal Lao Army and U.S. Army Advice and Support*, p. 121.

[21]Conboy and Morrison, *Shadow War*, p. 92 (note).

[22]Ibid., pp. 108, 126.

[23]The figure is based on Vang Pao's own records (Larteguy, *Opium People*, p. 226).

[24]Conboy and Morrison, *Shadow War*, p. 112.

[25]Ibid., pp. 110-112.

[26]Boettcher, *Vietnam: The Valor and the Sorrow*, p. 198.

[27]After leaving office, Johnson claimed that early on he realized that a continuation of the war would be a political disaster. "I knew from the start that I was bound to be crucified either way I moved. If I left the woman I really loved—the Great Society—in order to get involved with that bitch of a war on the other side of the world, then I would lose everything at home. . . . But if I left that war and let the Communists take over South Vietnam, then I would be seen as a coward . . ." Quoted in Karnow, *Vietnam: A History*, p. 320.

[28]Tilford, *Search and Rescue in Southeast Asia*, p. 49.

[29]Huston, "Air Operations Over Northern Laos," p. 122.

[30]The Bay of Pigs invasion was the brainchild of Jake Engler, the agency's station chief in Venezuela. Engler gathered together operatives who earlier had organized the overthrow of the Guatemalan government in 1954. The Guatemalan operation had required only 150 exiles and a handful of World War Two P-47 fighter planes. Engler imagined toppling Castro's regime would be just as easy. Intelligence-gathering for the Cuba operation was slipshod. No one was informed that there were coral reefs in the Bay of Pigs, which made a successful amphibious landing impossible. Secrecy fell apart. Castro knew there

would be an invasion and suspected the Bay of Pigs as the landing site (Wyden, *Bay of Pigs*, pp. 20-34).

[31]Fairlie, *The Kennedy Promise*, pp. 193-194.

[32]Conboy and Morrison, *Shadow War*, p. 88. The CIA objected to the assault on the agency's autonomy in Laos. In an August 1961 memorandum to the Defense Department, Richard Bissell, the CIA's Deputy Chief for covert actions, noted that few U.S. military personnel were involved in the program and that the CIA was doing nearly all of the training and supplying of the Hmong. Bissell argued that as long as the program remained covert, the CIA's paramilitary experts should continue to run things in the field (Bissell memorandum).

[33]The letter reads: "You are in charge of the entire U.S. Diplomatic Mission, and I expect you to supervise all of its operations. The Mission includes not only the personnel of the Department of State and the Foreign Service, but also representatives of all other United States agencies. . . . As you know, the United States Diplomatic Mission . . . does not . . . include United States military forces operating in the field where such forces are under the command of a United States area military commander" (Castle, "At War in the Shadow of Vietnam," pp. 141-142).

[34]While the State Department had labored to bring Phoumi into Souvanna Phouma's coalition government, the CIA had maneuvered behind the scenes to keep Phoumi out of the coalition and supplied him with arms to topple the new regime.

[35]Deputy Chief, Joint United States Military Advisory Group, Thailand.

[36]Castle, "At War in the Shadow of Vietnam," pp. 139-140.

[37]Conboy and Morrison, *Shadow War*, pp. 123-125.

[38]Sullivan, *Obbligato*, pp. 213, 210, 179-180, 220.

[39]Larteguy, *Opium People*, p. 225.

[40]Warner, *Back Fire*, p. 76.

[41]Ibid., pp. 116-118.

[42]Ibid., p. 178.

[43]Kuhn, Oral history interview, p. 43.

[44]Among the Hmong I interviewed the prevailing view was that the Lao state and its political apparatus was fundamentally corrupt and hostile to the interests of the Hmong as a people.

[45]Cooper, *The Hmong*, p. 25.

[46]Jenks, *Insurgency and Social Disorder in Guizhou*, p. 36.

[47]The eighteen clans are: Yang, Vang, Vue, Xiong, Lo, Ly, Her, Moua, Hang, Kue, Khang, Fa, Chang, Thao, Chue, Cheng, Kong, and Pha. Hmong clans are probably as old as those of the Chinese. Some scholars claim there were originally only twelve Hmong clans; others limit the number to eight (Mottin, *Elements de Grammaire Hmong Blanc*, p. 157; Yang, "Why Did the Hmong Leave Laos?," p. 3). Save for the Vue clan, which contains only White Hmong, both Blue and White Hmong are represented in the eight larger clans. The lesser clans (Hang, Kue, Khang, Fa, Chang, Thao, Chue, Cheng, Kong, and Pha) are mostly Blue Hmong.

[48]Two institutions, exogamy and bride price, served as a counterweight to expand loyalties beyond clan. Marriages were always between clans, never within them, making marriage a natural leaven for the enlargement of attachments. Married women were quiet though effective spokespersons for their natal clan; and family gatherings with in-laws forged affective links that cut across clans. The bride price, paid by the groom's family to the bride's relatives, also diluted clan parochialism. Though the exact sum was set by custom and circumstance, unsettled disputes between clans could always affect the size of the final settlement. A wronged clan might demand a higher than normal bride price as remedy for perceived damages, drawing out the negotiations. Complaints would be heard, excuses or regrets offered in defense. To reach an accommodation, both sides were compelled to present arguments that transcended selfish clan interests and addressed obligations acknowledged as legitimate by all Hmong, regardless of clan or tribe. See Betrais, *The Traditional Marriage among the White Hmong of Thailand and Laos*, pp. 267-269.

[49]Larteguy, *Opium People*, p. 224.

[50]Vang Pao also established a bureaucracy for Sam Neua, but the province was so often under enemy control that it remained mostly a paper government.

[51]According to Tou Yer Moua the new chao muongs were: Neng Thong Ly, Xiong Ly, Xa Chia Thao, Youa Tong Yang, and Geu Moua Noutoua Moua (Moua, "Hmong Values and Political Leadership as Perceived by the U.S. Hmongs," p. 38); once refugees swelled the population of Long Cheng to nearly fifty thousand souls, Vang Pao reorganized the town's civil administration to provide the different clans their fair share of office holders.

[52]Warner, *Back Fire*, p. 121.

[53]McCoy, *The Politics of Heroin in Southeast Asia*, p. 274.

[54]Evans, *The Yellow Rainmakers*, p. 19.

[55]Sananikone, *The Royal Lao Army and U.S. Army Advice and Support*, p. 138.

[56]In 1988, Laos' communist regime persuaded the Thai government to confiscate Pa Chay Thao's holdings and transfer the assets to the Laotian government. Pa Chay Thao died penniless in a Thai refugee camp in 1991.

[57]Unit commanders also padded rosters to increase their own incomes. This abuse increased over the years as the salaries of chao muongs and tassengs outpaced those of top military officers. Vang Pao generally tolerated the corruption if a commander continued to win battles with fewer men; the delivery of military pay for the regular RLA was more direct. Top commanders showed up at the Green House (CIA headquarters in Vientiane), where Marine guards unloaded bundles of kip from a warehouse onto the waiting trucks. Top RLA officers in charge of distributing the kip no doubt skimmed as much, and likely more, than did Vang Pao.

[58]Interview with a member of the Vue clan (1993).

[59]Westermeyer, *Poppies, Pipes, and People*, p. 278.

[60]It was common knowledge that Vang Pao owned two homes in Vientiane to house his many wives and children. But Poe alleged that Vang Pao also owned a Mercedes Benz, apartments, and hotels. See McCoy, *The Politics of Heroin: CIA Complicity in the Global Drug Trade*, pp. 318, 558 (note).

[61]Schanche, *Mr. Pop*, pp. 240-244.

[62]Thee, *Notes of a Witness*, p. 112.

[63]Robbins, *Air America*, p. 128.

[64]Schanche, *Mr. Pop*, p. 92.

[65]The Pathet Lao texts are mentioned in Warner, *Back Fire*, p. 217.

[66]Yang, *Hmong at the Turning Point*, p. 98.

[67]Warner, *Back Fire*, pp. 104, 110; Westermeyer, *Poppies, Pipes, and People*, p. 10.

[68]Kuhn, Oral history interview, p. 24.

[69]The anthropologist Jan Ovesen found it took on average three days for a Hmong to clear a third of an acre of wilderness that was not heavily forested. If there were large trees, the time required was much longer (Ovesen, *A Minority Enters the Nation State*, p. 53).

[70]Warner, *Back Fire*, p. 177.

[71]Tor the same purpose, Vang Pao later arranged marriages between Touby's children and his own.

[72]For generations, relations between Hmong from Sam Neua and Xieng Khouang had been strained. The Sam Neua Hmong resented being caricatured as artless rustics. The marriage was Vang Pao's attempt to break down this barrier of distrust and gain cooperation for his expanded guerrilla operations in the province. As it turned out, his new bride was overwhelmed by life in Long Cheng, which was slowly evolving into the most densely populated Hmong settlement in Laos. She begged to be returned to her mountain village. By custom, returning a bride to her family was a breach of contract. The prescribed remedy was a fine. Vang Pao had already paid a substantial bride price for the woman. As a goodwill gesture, he offered an even larger amount to indemnify the girl's parents for the loss of face and to maintain good relations.

[73]Vang Pao had earlier tried to draw these Moua clansmen into his guerrilla network, but they wanted nothing to do with the war and permitted the Pathet Lao to operate freely in their district. To win them over, he hosted a large and lavish party in the town, a feast that lasted several days. During the festivities, a lovely Moua girl caught his eye and became his seventh wife. As with his Sam Neua wife, the swarming population of Long Cheng proved too much for the new bride and she had to be returned home. Vang Pao paid another large fine, sufficiently generous to soothe feelings and dispose the villagers of Tase to join the war effort.

[74]Though she would not be his last wife, Hmong fell into the habit of referring to her as "Maelot," the Laotian word for "last one."

[75]Zong was a nurse at the field hospital at Vang Vieng. Only fifteen, she caught Vang Pao's eye while he was visiting wounded soldiers. The two entered into a love affair even though Zong was already married to man from the Lo clan, Ma Lo. Zong's youthful blush may have animated Vang Pao's passion, but it was her family connections that prompted the marriage.

[76]Interview (1988) with a Hmong who wishes to remain anonymous.

[77]This is a pseudonym.

[78]Communication with Ger Vue (1992).

[79]Lee, "Minority Policies and the Hmong," p. 219 (note).

[80]Interview with a member of the Vang clan (1992).

[81]As the war progressed, disaffection spread among Hmong units in the Pathet Lao. In addition to many desertions, some units actually

planned to surrender to Vang Pao's forces, but as they were seldom allowed to engage Royalist Hmong units, they never had the opportunity (interview with Xia Vang Vue, 1993).

[82]Interviews with a member of the Ly clan (1993) and a member of the Yang clan (1992); Leng Vue survived the war and immigrated to the United States. Still fearing a reprisal for joining the Neutralists, he changed his name (1993 interview with a member of the Vue clan who wishes to remain anonymous).

[83]Toufu Vang was one of the few Vang who had already been educated abroad. He was quickly promoted through the ranks of the army and then relieved of duty to spend full time cultivating Vang Pao's business concerns. He developed a distribution network for the sale of western goods, a sales region that eventually encompassed Long Cheng, Ban Some, Pha Khao, and Muong Cha.

CHAPTER 9: A SEASONAL WAR

[1]Sullivan, *Obbligato*, pp. 211-212.

[2]Schanche, *Mr. Pop*, pp. 222-225; Warner, *Back Fire*, pp. 140-141.

[3]Conboy and Morrison, *Shadow War*, p. 127.

[4]Van Staaveren, *Interdiction in Southern Laos*, pp. 45-48.

[5]Warner, *Back Fire*, pp. 144-146.

[6]Ibid., *Back Fire*, pp. 146-149.

[7]Conboy and Morrison, *Shadow War*, pp. 127-128.

[8]Warner, *Back Fire*, p. 153.

[9]Conboy and Morrison, *Shadow War*, p. 128; *Back Fire*, p. 170.

[10]Warner, *Back Fire*, p. 171.

[11]Clodfelter, *The Limits of Air Power*, p. 57; Glasser, *The Secret Vietnam War*, pp. 43-44.

[12]Warner, *Back Fire*, p. 135; Conboy and Morrison, *Shadow War*, p. 129.

[13]Sheehan, *A Bright Shinning Lie*, p. 579.

[14]Davidson, *Vietnam at War*, p. 362.

[15]Shaplen, *Bitter Victory*, pp. 178-9.

[16]*New York Times*, 19 April 1965.

[17]Kuhn, Oral history interview, p. 12.

[18]Huston, "Air Operations over Northern Laos," p. 123; Hamilton-Merritt, *Tragic Mountains*, pp. 144-145; Conboy and Morrison, *Shadow War*, p. 113.

[19]According to one account (Kuhn, Oral history interview, p. 20), Vang Pao was hit by sniper fire just as a Vietnamese soldier penetrated the base. A hand grenade blew the Vietnamese apart, severing his head from his body. The head whizzed past Vang Pao. When the head came a stop, Vang Pao left a protected position to examine it. It was then he was struck by bullets, one shattering his arm, another grazing his neck.

[20]Sullivan, *Obbligato*, p. 214.

[21]Larteguy, *Opium People*, p. 207.

[22]Robbins, *The Ravens*, p. 232.

[23]Conboy and Morrison, *Shadow War*, p. 152. Sullivan (*Obbligato*, p. 215) tells a different story: "Vang Pao had gone, along with some of our American relief workers, to a village which had reported a Vietnamese raid that had destroyed all its food supplies. . . . When they landed, Vang Pao opened the hatch to be, as usual, the first man on the ground. As he poised to jump, he was hit in the shoulder by a rifle bullet and knocked back onto the deck. A young American welfare volunteer, who was a conscientious objector, caught Vang Pao's M-16 as it fell, saw the North Vietnamese ambusher rising to fire again, and drilled him through the head. The helicopter took off in a hail of bullets, but with no other casualties."

[24]Conboy and Morrison, *Shadow War*, p. 152.

[25]While it was presumed Pathet Lao were the source of the rumors, it is equally likely that they were started by Hmong seeking to undermine Vang Pao's hold over the Hmong at Long Cheng.

[26]Conboy and Morrison, *Shadow War*, pp. 60, 63, 98; Hamilton-Merritt (*Tragic Mountains*, p. 146) claims Touby LyFoung was behind the coup attempt. We can find no evidence to support this conclusion. One of Touby's daughters was married to Vang Pao's son, François Vang, and one of Vang Pao's daughters was married to one of Touby's sons. Given these close family ties, it is unlikely that Touby would have directly supported plans to bring Vang Pao down. The coup attempt did not end Youa Vang's military career. Shortly after the incident Vang Pao gave him command of a newly formed regiment. Vang Pao knew Ly patriarchs had planned the coup (Youa Vang refused to reveal their identities), and preferred to believe Youa Vang was an unwilling pawn in their grab for power. He saw Youa Vang as a simple man with simple vices: he drank too much and was constantly

in debt from gambling. He was in over his head in politics, but otherwise an excellent soldier.

[27]Sullivan, *Obbligato*, pp. 215-216.

[28]Kuhn, Oral history interview, p. 20.

[29]Report of a coversation with Vang Pao (1980) from a Hmong who wishes to remain anonymous.

[30]The suspect remained in Vientiane until the fall of Laos in 1975. Today he lives in the United States and maintains he did not participate in, or have any knowledge of, the assassination attempt.

[31]Castle, "At War in the Shadow of Vietnam," p. 201.

[32]Warner, *Back Fire*, pp. 182-193.

[33]Secord, *Honored and Betrayed*, pp. 29-53.

[34]Warner (*Back Fire*, p. 193) claims that Vang Pao had the suspects publicly beaten on the runway at Sam Thong. But Kuhn (Oral history interview, p. 30) states that the suspects were beaten by a crowd that descended on them as they were hauled off an airplane at Sam Thong. If Vang Pao had ordered a public beating, it would have been carried out by Toupao Ly, the head of Vang Pao's secret police. Toupao often conducted public beatings to punish malcontents, slackers, and troublemakers and to intimidate the general population. Kuhn claims that the suspects were imprisoned and released after a few years. But it is more likely that they were executed.

[35]Just two weeks earlier Thao Ma had been hospitalized for fatigue, and was still highly agitated; by one account, he was close to a nervous breakdown, which might also explain his precipitous decision to attack Vientiane (Kuhn, Oral history interview, pp. 28-29).

[36]Van Staaveren, *Interdiction in Southern Laos*, p. 165; Conboy and Morrison, *Shadow War*, pp. 156-158.

[37]Hardy, *The Pawns of War*, p. 80.; Sananikone, *The Royal Lao Army and U.S. Army Advice and Support*, p. 125; McCoy, *The Politics of Heroin in Southeast Asia*, p. 295.

[38]Conboy and Morrison, *Shadow War*, pp. 159, 168; Warner, *Back Fire*, p. 196.

[39]Command of the regiment went to Youa Vang Ly, the Ly clansmen who had earlier conspired to take over Long Cheng in Vang Pao's absence.

[40]Conboy and Morrison, *Shadow War*, p. 199.

[41]Parker, *Codename Mule*, p. 103.

[42]Warner, *Back Fire*, pp. 124-126, 174; Conboy and Morrison, *Shadow War*, p. 165.

[43]Conboy and Morrison, *Shadow War*, p. 184-187; Schanche, *Mr. Pop*, p. 295; Huston, "Air Operations over Northern Laos," p. 131.

[44]Warner, *Back Fire*, p. 205.

[45]Huston, "Air Operations over Northern Laos," p. 126; Vallentiny, "The Fall of Site 85," pp. 14, 30; Larteguy, *Opium People*, pp. 227-228; Secord, *Honored and Betrayed*, pp. 86, 88; Conboy and Morrison, *Shadow War*, pp. 196-197; Clodfelter, *The Limits of Air Power*, p. 134; Van Staaveren, "The Air War against North Vietnam," p. 88; according to Glasser (*The Secret Vietnam War*, p. 142, note) the loss of Pha Thi "severely hampered the U.S. military's ability to accurately bomb much of North Vietnam, and no doubt had some role in the President's March 31 announcement to restrict bombing."

[46]Warner, *Back Fire*, pp. 237, 240.

CHAPTER 10: RELIANCE ON AIR POWER

[1]Warner, *Back Fire*, pp. 247-249.

[2]Conboy and Morrison, *Shadow War*, p. 249; Warner, *Back Fire*, p. 262.

[3]Castle, "At War in the Shadow of Vietnam," p. 204. Garrett ("The Hmong of Laos: No Place to Run," p. 101), claims Vang Pao also pushed the idea of an independent state during this period. But it was not until 1971 that Vang Pao considered it prudent to move Hmong refugees into the western provinces, not for the purpose of creating a Hmong state but to isolate refugees from the ravages of the war so that his soldiers, anxious over the safety of their families, would remain focused on the defense of Long Cheng.

[4]Mottin, *Allons Faire Le Tour Du Ciel et de La Terre*, p. 13.

[5]Smalley, *Mother of Writing*, p. 20.

[6]Lemoine, "Les Ecritures du Hmong," pp. 142-144.

[7]Shaplen, *Time Out of Hand*, p. 346.

[8]Schanche, *Mr. Pop*, p. 306.

[9]Robbins, *The Ravens*, pp. 173-174.

[10]Huston, "Air Operations over Northern Laos," p. 127; Robbins, *The Ravens*, pp. 176-179, 187; Larteguy, *Opium People*, p. 229; Conboy and Morrison, *Shadow War*, p. 209.

[11]Hardy, *The Pawns of War*, p. 103; Sananikone, *The Royal Lao Army and U.S. Army Advice and Support*, pp. 135-136.

[12]Larteguy, *Opium People*, p. 229.

[13]Berger, *The United States Air Force in Southeast Asia*, p. 13; Santoli, *To Bear Any Burden*, p. 142.

[14]Secord, *Honored and Betrayed*, pp. 76, 88-89.

[15]Robbins, *The Ravens*, p. 189.

[16]Prisor, *The End of the Line: The Siege of Khe Sanh*, p. 17.

[17]Robbins, *The Ravens*, pp. 191-192.

[18]Ibid., pp. 198-200.

[19]Conboy and Morrison, *Shadow War*, p. 213.

[20]One of Lue Ly's instructors could not praise him enough: "He was a splendid pilot, excellent—so vastly exceptional to all the Lao pilots who came before him there was no comparison. He was very bold, very reckless, extremely courageous . . . He would go anywhere against all odds." Robbins, *The Ravens*, p. 83.

[21]Huston, "Air Operations over Northern Laos," p. 130.

[22]Robbins, *The Ravens*, p. 239.

[23]Huston, "Air Operations over Northern Laos," p. 130.

[24]Scott, "Laos: The Story Nixon Won't Tell," p. 40. Henry Kissinger later maintained that the Nixon administration's military object in Laos was twofold: to defend a noncommunist government that permitted U.S. air strikes against the Ho Chi Minh Trail, and to prevent the NVA in northern Laos from pushing all the way west to the Mekong, cowing the Thai into denying the U.S. the use of Thai airbases, which Kissinger claimed was "essential for our B-52 and tactical air operations in Vietnam" (*White House Years*, p. 451.)

[25]Larteguy, *Opium People*, p. 231.

[26]Warner, *Back Fire*, p. 271.

[27]Conboy and Morrison, *Shadow War*, p. 215.

[28]Robbins, *Air America*, pp. 124-125.

[29]Interview with a member of the Vue clan (1985).

[30]Kuhn, Oral history interview, p. 32.

[31]Conboy and Morrison, *Shadow War*, p. 217.

[32]Huston, "Air Operations over Northern Laos," p. 130.

[33]Conboy and Morrison, *Shadow War*, p. 365.

CHAPTER 11: LONG CHENG BESIEGED

[1]Conboy and Morrison, *Shadow War*, p. 248, 251.

[2]*Hearings, United States Security Agreements and Commitments Abroad, Kingdom of Laos.*

[3]*New York Times,* 27 & 28 October 1969.

[4]Kissinger, *White House Years*, p. 451.

[5]Larteguy, *Opium People*, p. 233.

[6]At one forward post in the path of NVA armor, Hmong dug in and waited. As Dac Cong probed the base's outer defenses, three C-147 gunships circled overhead, their Gatling guns ripping into the attackers, leaving seventy-six dead draped over the base's outer wires. Four NVA PT-76 tanks moved up for their attack and fell into a trap. CIA personnel had planted anti-tank mines around the base's perimeter. All four tanks were blown up. Having exhausted their tactical advantage, the Hmong withdrew (Conboy and Morrison, *Shadow War*, p. 252).

[7]Huston, "Air Operations over Northern Laos," p. 131.

[8]Kissinger, *White House Years*, p. 452-453; Huston, "Air Operations over Northern Laos," p. 131.

[9]*New York Times,* 18 March 1970.

[10]Warner, *Back Fire*, p. 209.

[11]Robbins, *The Ravens*, p. 293.

[12]Allman, "Long Cheng Yields Its Secrets."

[13]Robbins, *The Ravens*, p. 280. Two more decades would pass before Washington would deliver accurate statistics on the number of Americans lost in Laos, listing nearly six hundred Americans killed or missing. In the spring of 1992, a representative of the Lao Peoples Democratic Republic admitted that 522 missing Americans had been killed by Lao villagers ("Villagers Killed Airmen in War").

[14]Huston, "Air Operations over Northern Laos," p. 131.

[15]Warner, *Back Fire*, p. 293.

[16]*New York Times,* 12 March 1970.

[17]In 1968 the National Statistics Bureau of Laos listed fifteen thousand Hmong living in Vientiane Province, and another 30,000 in Sayaboury.

[18]Chan, *Hmong Means Free*, p. 68.

[19]Cited in Lofgren and Sexton, "Air War in Northern Laos," p. 86.

[20]Conboy and Morrison, *Shadow War*, p. 254.

[21]Ibid., p. 141.

[22]Kissinger, *White House Years*, p. 457.

[23]By the late 1960s there were few men left between the ages of 17 and 35 in the villages and hamlets of North Vietnam. A captured North Vietnamese officer from Ninh Binh Province related that in his home village "there were only three or four men of the 17 to 35 age group left and they were not in good health. They were either sick, deformed or paralyzed" (Garland, *A Distant Challenge*, p. 170).

[24]Conboy and Morrison, *Shadow War*, p. 256.

[25]Warner, *Back Fire*, p. 288.

[26]Conboy and Morrison, *Shadow War*, p. 257.

[27]Ibid., pp. 261-262

[28]Ibid., p. 262.

[29]Glasser, *The Secret Vietnam War*, pp. 164-165.

[30]Robbins, *The Ravens*, pp. 327-331.

[31]Lofgren and Sexton, "Air War in Northern Laos," p. 73.

[32]Hardy, *The Pawns of War*, p. 100. In the early 1920s, an American journalist named Harry Franck rented a car in Vietnam and drove up Colonial Route 7 over the Annamite mountain chain into Laos, searching for something exotic to write about. The car was an ancient and temperamental Fiat that sputtered, twisted, and groaned over the rutted highway, until it broke down for good at the border. Franck hitched a ride with a French general in a sturdy Citröen and continued on into Laos. Two days later, early in the morning, the Citröen emerged onto the Plain of Jars. The plain was shrouded in dense fog, but as they drove on it began to lift. Little by little Franck realized the immensity of the high plateau. It took his breath away: "About us lay vast rolling meadows of great beauty, as virgin as a world in which animal life had not yet been created." There were wildflowers of stunning bright colors everywhere, some the size of dinner plates. The plain seemed endless and untouched. Had there been no road and had he walked onto the plain, Franck believed he could have been deluded into thinking he had discovered a new world beyond

civilization (Franck, *East of Siam*, p. 276). Fifty years later, John Wisniewski encountered a different scene. Wisniewski was one of Long Cheng's new Ravens, just beginning his six-month tour of duty as a forward air controller. He was in the back seat of an 0-1, a small single-engine spotter plane, headed for his first look at the Plain of Jars. As the 0-1 began descending out of the clouds, Wisniewski prepared himself for a visual feast. He had heard stories about the plain's beauty and expected music from the heavens to sound when he finally broke through the overcast and caught his first glimpse of the heart-shaped plateau. Instead Wisniewski was stunned. "Everything was bombed out. Everything was worked over with bombs. I couldn't believe it! Anyplace you would go on the [Plain of Jars] would be pockmarked with bomb craters. There were burnt-out C-47's, abandoned tanks, destroyed trucks . . . just left lying around." (Robbins, *The Ravens*, p. 340).

[33]Parker, *Codename Mule*, pp. 48-49.

[34]Conboy and Morrison, *Shadow War*, p. 327.

[35]Parker, *Codename Mule*, p. 65.

[36]Ibid.

[37]Conboy and Morrison, *Shadow War*, p. 331.

[38]*New York Times*, 6, 7, 8, 9, & 10 January 1972.

[39]Larteguy, *Opium People*, p. 234.

[40]*Back Fire*, p. 316.

[41]Interview with a member of the Xiong clan (1985).

[42]Parker, *Codename Mule*, p. 72.

[43]Conboy and Morrison, *Shadow War*, p. 339.

[44]Robbins, *The Ravens*, p. 344.

[45]Huston, "Air Operations over Northern Laos," p. 134.

[46]Warner, *Back Fire*, p. 318.

[47]Parker, *Codename Mule*, p. 110.

[48]Ibid., p. 112.

[49]Ibid., p. 167.

[50]Nixon, *RN*, p. 63.

[51]Gelb, *The Irony of Vietnam*, p. 356.

[52]Conboy and Morrison, *Shadow War*, p. 385.

[53]Clodfelter, *The Limits of Air Power*, pp. 157, 184-190, 195.

CHAPTER 12: A COMMUNIST LAOS

[1]Kissinger, *Years of Upheaval*, p. 22.

[2]Dommen, *Laos: Keystone of Indochina*, pp. 93-94;

[3]Kissinger, *Years of Upheaval*, p. 23.

[4]Quoted in Hamilton-Merritt, *Tragic Mountains*, p. 227.

[5]Brown and Zasloff, *Apprentice Revolutionaries*, p. 103.

[6]Sananikone, *The Royal Lao Army and U.S. Army Advice and Support*, p. 150.

[7]Robbins, *The Ravens*, p. 390.

[8]Hardy, *Pawns of War*, p. 106.

[9]Brown and Zasloff, *Apprentice Revolutionaries*, p. 118.

[10]Dommen, *Laos: Keystone of Indochina*, p. pp.

[11]Stieglitze, *In a Little Kingdom*, p. 205.

[12]Larteguy, *Opium People*, p. 238.

[13]Brown and Zasloff, *Apprentice Revolutionaries*, p. 117.

[14]Jane Hamilton-Merritt (*Tragic Mountains*, p. 334) claims that Vang Pao intended to take command of the Lao Air Force only to beef up air support for his troops.

[15]Thailand's Office for Human Development maintains that the U.S. evacuated additional Hmong on May 21, bringing the total number of Hmong flown to Namphong during May to 24,600. See *The Indochinese Refugees*, p. 15.

[16]Yang, *Hmong Poised for Development*, pp. 129-131.

[17]Yang, *Hmong at the Turning Point*, p. 150.

[18]Cazaux, "Vang Pao of Laos and the Politicking of a Warlord."

[19]Sananikone, *The Royal Lao Army and U.S. Army Advice and Support*, p. 175.

[20]Santoli, *To Bear Any Burden*, pp. 262-263.

[21]Hamilton-Merritt, *Tragic Mountains*, p. 356.

[22]Vang Pao's earlier replacement, RLA general Tiao Monivong, had been relieved of command.

[23]Roger Warner (*Back Fire*, p. 349) asserts that Pathet Lao intelligence operatives found the file cabinets at Vang Pao's headquarters full of records "dating back to the beginning of the war" listing "the company commanders, the spies, and all kinds of other information the Pathet Lao and Vietnamese could use to hunt down and persecute Hmong who stayed under a communist regime." However, two Hmong officers on the scene, Colonel Teng Lee and Major Kaneng Yang, recall vividly the destruction of the files (interviews 1985, 1987). Certainly had such records existed, the Pathet Lao would not have needed to spend weeks interviewing Long Cheng's residents, asking details about their military service and the identity of their unit commanders.

Gayle Morrison conducted extensive interviews with Hmong and CIA agents on the fall of Long Cheng and the CIA's rushed air evacuation of Hmong to Thailand (see her *Sky is Falling: An Oral History of the CIA's Evacuation of the Hmong from Laos*). In a letter to Arthur Dommen, Morrison stated that she could find no corroboration in her Hmong interviews that the files were ever destroyed (communication from Dommen). On this, she joins with Warner. My only answer is that the Hmong I interviewd tell a different story.

[24]Interview with Pa Nhia Vue (1992).

[25]Interview with Ly Lo (1989).

[26]"End of Laos War Has Brought No Peace to Thousands in Meo Clans," p. 2.

[27]Larteguy, *Opium People*, p. 243.

[28]Interview with a member of Yang clan (1992).

[29]The regime would continue to confiscate Hmong silver over the next five years. Many of the silver bars eventually wound up in shops in Vientiane, earmarked for sale to tourists to attract hard currency.

[30]Lee, "Minority Politics and the Hmong," p. 204.

[31]Larteguy, *Opium People*, p. 246.

[32]Brown and Zasloff, *Apprentice Revolutionaries*, p. 148. Kommadan died in 1977. Faydang returned to Nong Het in the early 1980s, where he ended his days (he died in 1986) under close guard by Pathet Lao soldiers (Lee, "Ethnic Minorities and National Building in Laos," p. 4).

[33]Chagnon and Rumpf, "Decades of Division for Lao Hmong," p. 10.

[34]Lee, "Minority Policies and the Hmong," p. 208.

[35]Communication with Vang Pao (1984). Vang Pao may have had other funds. In a 1986 affidavit filed in federal court, the Christic Institute (a public policy and public interest law firm) alleged that CIA agents had "transferred large quantities of Vang Pao drug money to a secret account in Australia." Affidavit of Daniel P. Sheehan, p. 2.

[36]Interview with a member of the Thao clan (1992).

[37]Larteguy, Opium People, pp. 248-249.

[38]Interview with a member of the Xiong clan (1992).

[39]The Bangkok Post (May 31) reported only five Hmong killed and thirty wounded.

[40]Stuart-Fox, "National Defence and Internal Security in Laos," p. 223.

[41]Hardy, The Pawns of War, p. 134.

[42]Garrett, "The Hmong of Laos: No Place to Run," p. 111.

[43]This was not just the Hmong view. Courtland Robinson ("Laotian Refugees in Thailand," p. 218) claims that the Hmong most certainly faced "large-scale famine."

[44]Interview with a member of the Lo clan (1991).

[45]Lee, "Minority Policies and the Hmong," p. 206.

[46]The name change had actually occurred much earlier, in 1965. To attract Neutralist opponents of the Royal Laotian Government to their cause, Pathet Lao party leaders concluded it was prudent to drop the Pathet Lao label for its military arm and give it a more non-partisan designation. The name change fooled no one. Prior to their victory, communist forces continued to be referred to as Pathet Lao.

[47]Stuart-Fox, "National Defence and Internal Security in Laos," p. 223.

[48]Stuart-Fox, "The Lao Revolution: Errors and Achievements," p. 9; Stuart-Fox, "National Defence and Internal Security in Laos," p. 227.

[49]Hamel, Resistance en Indochine, pp. 84, 127, 130, 131.

[50]Ibid., pp. 127, 130, 131.

[51]Van de Kroef, "Laos: Paradoxes and Dilemmas of Survival," p. 162.

[52]Stone, "Nationalism and the Lao Resistance," p. 271.

[53]Shaplen, A Turning Wheel, p. 74.

[54]Vongsavanh, RLG Military Operations and Activities in the Laotian Panhandle, pp. 35, 41, 44, 71, 96.

[55]Stuart-Fox, "The Lao Revolution: Errors and Achievements," pp. 7, 12-13.

[56]Warner, *Back Fire*, pp. 252-253.

[57]Cartmail, *Exodus Indochina*, p. 84; Stone, "Nationalism and the Lao Resistance," p. 273.

[58]Stone "Resistance: Beyond Equilibrium," p. 56.

[59]Stuart-Fox, "National Defence and Internal Security in Laos," p. 233.

[60]Shaplen, *A Turning Wheel*, p. 77.

[61]*Economist,* 7 December 1991, p. 37.

[62]Dommen, *Laos: Keystone of Indochina*, p. 116.

[63]Stuart-Fox, "National Defence and Internal Security in Laos," p. 235.

[64]Vanes-Beck, "Refugees from Laos," p. 327.

[65]Brown and Zasloff, *Apprentice Revolutionaries*, pp. 144-145.

[66]Shaplen, *A Turning Wheel,* p. 75.

[67]Brown and Zasloff, *Apprentice Revolutionaries*, pp. 159-161; Dommen, *Laos: Keystone of Indochina*, p. 125; Van de Kroef, "Laos: Paradoxes and Dilemmas of Survival," p. 162.

[68]The quote is from an early 1980 report by Che Viet Tan, a senior Vietnamese planning official, cited in Chanda, *Brother Enemy*, p. 123. For a more benign interpretation of Vietnam's intentions in Laos see Evans and Rowley, "Laos: The Eclipse of 'Neutralist' Communism."

[69]Dommen, *Laos: Keystone of Indochina*, p. 124.

[70]Nagorski, "Who's Really in Charge Here?"

[71]Conboy and Morrison, *Shadow War*, pp. 248, 286-287.

[72]The total number of camps has been estimated at 35, though it is likely there were many more. See Van de Kroef, "Laos: Paradoxes and Dilemmas of Survival," p. 163.

[73]Shaplen, *Bitter Victory*, p. 20.

[74]As reported by Kham Ouane Douangphrachanh, a lieutenant colonel in the RLA who was released from the Vieng Sai camp in 1981, the eight generals interned were Boun Phone, Phasouk, Ly Ratanbanlang, Chao Sinh Saysana, Thong Phanh Kanockay, Sourith, Kane Insixiengmay, and Nou Pheth. The four government ministers were Phen Phongsavanh, Soukanh, Phayatou Ly Fung, and Pravongviengkham (Barnes, *Bohica*, appendix 37-B).

[75]Hiebert, "Soft-Sell Socialism in Northeast Laos," p. 1.

[76]In 1985, Amnesty International estimated that between 1979 and 1981 approximately two thousand prisoners were released from the numbered camps (*Background Paper on the Democratic People's Republic of Laos (DPRL) Describing Current Amnesty International Concerns*, p. 4).

[77]Interview with an RLA lieutenant who escaped from the camp at Oudom-Say, quoted in Willem, *Les Naufragés de La Liberté*, pp. 190-191.

[78]Interview with a member of the Lo clan (1993).

[79]U.S. Committee for Refugees, *Refugees from Laos: In Harm's Way*, p. 4; Brown and Zasloff, *Apprentice Revolutionaries*, p. 177.

[80]Cited in Evans, *Agrarian Change in Communist Laos*, p. 14.

[81]Brown and Zasloff, *Apprentice Revolutionaries*, p. 173.

[82]Stevenson, *The End of Nowhere*, p. 4.

[83]Congressional action prohibited any further aid to Laos. This ban was lifted at President Reagan's request in 1986 to gain leverage with the LPDR in searching for American MIAs.

[84]Hiebert and Hiebert, "Laos Recovers from America's War," p. 20.

[85]Chanda, "Economic Changes in Laos, 1975-1980," p. 119.

[86]Stuart-Fox, "Foreign Policy of the Lao People's Democratic Republic," p. 197.

[87]"Welcome to the 20th Century," p. 33.

[88]Evans, *Lao Peasants Under Socialism*, p. 34.

[89]Evans, *Agrarian Change in Communist Laos*, p. 12.

[90]Stone, "Nationalism and the Lao Resistance," p. 257; Stone, "Resistance: Beyond Equilibrium," pp. 48-50.

[91]Evans, *Agrarian Change in Communist Laos*, p. 41. As one peasant observed: "They say that joining a co-operative is voluntary, but if you don't become a member, you must be educated. They will come and explain to you endlessly." Another peasant cautioned that: "Once a member, if you are unhappy and want to withdraw, they will take you to a seminar . . ."

[92]Chanda, "Economic Changes in Laos, 1975-1980," p. 121.

[93]In this, Laos followed communist tradition. Marx had envisaged communism rising from advanced capitalism when productive capacity had reached its historical zenith. Control of this great economic engine would then pass to communists, who would redistribute wealth and husband the economy, insuring a continuously

high level of output and perpetual affluence. This was the plan, but history took a different turn. Communism did not take root in the industrialized West, but in pre-capitalist Russia and the Third World. Marx did not consider this possibility because it made no sense. What would be the point? Since pre-capitalist economies have no productive capacity, there is nothing to redistribute.

Since Marx offered no theoretical guidance, the rulers of the new communist states improvised, touting centralized planning, which Marx considered appropriate only after capitalism had maximized productivity, as economically more efficient than free markets. The belief was that under state guidance, crude peasant economies could deliver modern factories, dams, and highways rivaling anything in the capitalist West. All that was needed was startup capital to get things going. Capitalist nations had plenty, but were unwilling to share. This meant the communists had to pull themselves up by their own bootstraps by squeezing the needed funds from the only resource in abundance, the labor of peasants. This was not a fact communist regimes wanted publicized, especially as they were supposed to end exploitation rather than sponsor it.

As in other communist states, Laos' new rulers turned to collectivization so they could work peasants hard, pay them little, and pocket the difference. This surplus could then be used to fund economic development. Rather than admit the facts, the LPDR defended the move to collectivism as a way to increase the nation's agricultural output (Evans, *Lao Peasants Under Socialism*, p. 49). Given the dismal track record of collectivized farming, this was unlikely. As one expert on the Soviet economy put the matter, "collective farm agriculture is unreliable, irrational, wasteful, unprogressive—almost any pejorative adjective one can call to mind would be appropriate here." (Campell, *Soviet Economic Power*, p. 96.) By the 1970s the Soviet Union had collectivized 96 percent of all arable land, yet collective farms were responsible for only 75 percent of total crop output. The other 25 percent was produced on private plots occupying only 4 percent of the nation's farmland. (Goldman, *USSR in Crisis*, p. 83.)

Collective farms fared no better in China. To their credit, the Chinese tried to ease into collectivization to discover what worked best. But under all forms collectivization proved a failure. By 1960, malnutrition was widespread, millions were starving, and the communists had to swallow their pride and import millions of tons of grain (Snow, *Red China Today*, p. 591). While this did not persuade the government to abandon collectivism, it did convince Beijing to stop collecting statistics on agricultural output (Fairbank, *The United States and China*, p. 374).

Unlike China, Vietnam rushed headlong into collectivization, partly out of pique. Nixon had secretly promised North Vietnam nearly $5 billion in aid as an incentive for signing the 1973 Paris Peace Accord. After the fall of Saigon, the communists moved quickly to normalize relations with the U.S., collect the promised money, and begin economic reconstruction, which was to include foreign investment and trade with the West. It was a pragmatic move that placed national interest above ideological purity. President Carter wanted to make good on Nixon's pledge of aid, but Congress refused to allocate the funds or to support the normalization of relations with Vietnam (Chanda, *Brother Enemy*, pp. 143, 149, 157). When Hanoi learned of the decision, Vietnam turned its back on capitalism and the West and embraced collectivization. Within four years Vietnam was home to more than ten thousand collective farms, nearly all economic failures.

[94]Stuart-Fox, "Socialist Construction and National Security in Laos," p. 69.

[95]Evans, *Lao Peasants Under Socialism*, p. 163.

[96]Stuart-Fox, "Socialist Construction and National Security in Laos," p. 66.

[97]Evans, *Agrarian Change in Communist Laos*, p. 38.

[98]Van de Kroef, "Laos: Paradoxes and Dilemmas of Survival," pp. 161, 166.

[99]Quoted in Evans, *Lao Peasants Under Socialism*, p. 58.

[100]Van de Kroef, "Laos: Paradoxes and Dilemmas of Survival," p. 166.

[101]Shaplen, *Bitter Victory*, pp. 85-86.

[102]Hiebert and Hiebert, "Laos Recovers from America's War," p. 4.

[103]Chanda, "Economic Changes in Laos, 1975-1980," p. 119.

[104]Ibid., pp. 120-124.

[105]During the 1980s, CIA estimates of the health of the Soviet economy were consistently in error. The intelligence agency calculated the growth rate of the Soviet economy to be close to that of the U.S., while in reality it was contracting in most years. This left the false impression that the Soviet economy was healthy and the government stable. See Moynihan, "The Peace Dividend," p. 3.

[106]Larteguy, *Opium People*, p. 243.

[107] According to Jane Hamilton-Merritt (*Tragic Mountains*, p. 365), Pathet Lao soldiers sometimes planted weapons near homes to provide an excuse for arresting Hmong suspected of serving under Vang Pao.

[108] Interview with a member of the Vue clan (1992).

[109] At some villages, Pathet Lao Hmong were employed to smooth the way prior to full occupation by government troops. Intelligence reports from party cadres at Vieng Fa had identified the nearby Hmong village of Ban Houakasy as a potential trouble spot. The village had contributed recruits to a band of Hmong insurgents operating on the northwest edge of the Plain of Jars. Also Yee Leng Vang, the village shaman, had stirred up people with a prophetic vision of American transport planes landing on a vast airfield, returning Vang Pao and thousands of Hmong soldiers to Laos. The shaman ordered everyone to prepare for the general's second coming. Chue Vang, the village headman, organized a work crew and cleared an airstrip on the edge of town. Daily, villagers scanned the sky for signs of aircraft, some carrying weapons retrieved from hiding places in the forest.

During this time of excitement a squad of Pathet Lao Hmong arrived in rundown boots and hand-me-down uniforms, sent by the regime as goodwill ambassadors. These soldiers had long harbored reservations about the communists and would have defected to Vang Pao during the war if the opportunity had arisen. They informed villagers that Lao officers in the LPLA treated Hmong soldiers like second-class citizens. Revealing their intention to escape to Thailand, they urged everyone at Ban Houakasy to do the same before regular troops arrived, bearing gifts for village children to get them to reveal who had weapons hidden away or had served with Vang Pao, disclosures that could land villagers in a concentration camp.

The Hmong soldiers stayed only a week, long enough to convince nearly everyone to take up arms and fight. Yee Leng Vang was again seeing omens, interpreting the fact that no aircraft had landed on the airstrip as a sign that the Hmong had to provide their own leadership and conduct a guerrilla war against the communists. Before the villagers could act, LPLA soldiers attacked in the dead of night. They killed scores of Hmong, set rice fields on fire, and put Ban Houakasy to the torch (interview with a member of the Vue clan, 1991).

[110] The regime would eventually take an official stand against polygamy but without any serious effort to enforce it. The practice of bride price, however, was outlawed and enforced. Remarkably, the Hmong appear to have made little fuss over the abolishment of this central feature of their culture.

[111]Interview with a member of the Vue clan (1994).

[112]Hamel, *Resistance en Indochine*, p. 84.

[113]Wekkin, "The Rewards of Revolution," p. 192.

CHAPTER 13: THE LONG ARM OF PA CHAY

[1]Smalley, *The Mother of Writing*, pp. 35, 38, 133.

[2]Ibid., p. 38.

[3]Interview with a member of the Vang clan (1994). He was a disciple of Boua Cher Yang and was with her during her last days.

[4]Conboy and Morrison, *Shadow War*, p. 279 (note).

[5]Sananikone, *The Royal Lao Army and U.S. Army Advice and Support*, p. 135.

[6]Interview with a member of the Lo clan (1993).

[7]Interview with a member of the Vang clan (1994).

[8]Yang, *Through the Spirit's Door*, p. 60; Chagnon and Rumpf, "Decades of Division for the Lao Hmong," p. 14.

[9]Interview with a member of the Vang clan (1993).

[10]Interview with a member of the Xiong clan (1986).

[11]Interview with a member of the Vang clan (1993)

[12]Katoua Xiong (1986), Wa Nu Lo (1993), Nhia Yeng Xiong (1993), and Tongkai Yang (1993).

[13]In 1978, Sai Shoua Yang permanently removed Chou Teng Yang from politics by having him executed.

[14]Sai Shoua (interview, 1995) claims he eventually became a sincere convert to the new religion.

[15]Stuart-Fox, "National Defence and Internal Security in Laos," pp. 234-235.

[16]Lee, "Minority Policies and the Hmong," p. 212.

[17]Stuart-Fox, "National Defence and Internal Security in Laos," p. 235.

[18]Interview with a member of the Lo clan (1993).

[19]Kreiger, "Still Waging the Vietnam War," pp. 48-49.

[20]Hamel, *Resistances en Indochine*, p. 231.

[21]*Chemical Warfare in Southeast Asia and Afghanistan*, p. 6.

[22]Pike, *PAVN*, p. 259.

[23]Interview with a member of the Vue clue (1991).

[24]Yang, *Through the Spirit's Door*, p. 219.

[25]Yang, "Why Did the Hmong Leave Laos?" p. 17.

[26]Hamilton-Merritt, "Gas Warfare in Laos," p. 83.

[27]Grant Evans is the major proponent of the hoax theory, claiming that, because of Hmong susceptibility to mystical or magical explanations of natural phenomena, the U.S. easily duped them with propaganda charging communist duplicity in chemical warfare (Evans, *The Yellow Rainmakers*, chs. 6 & 8).

[28]Hamilton-Merritt, *Tragic Mountains*, pp. 417, 446.

[29]Interviews with a member of the Lo clan (1993).

[30]Interview with a member of the Vu clan (1992).

[31]Interviews with a member of the Xiong clan (1992) and a member of the Vue clan (1992).

[32]Hamilton-Merritt, *Tragic Mountains*, p. 406.

[33]Interview with a member of the Yang clan(1993).

[34]Hamilton-Merritt, *Tragic Mountains*, p. 397.

[35]Interview with a member of the Yang clan (1995).

[36]Interview with a member of the Vue clan (1994).

[37]Interviews with a member of the Xiong (1993) and a member of the Vang clan (1993).

[38]Interview with a member of the Xiong clan (1993).

[39]Interview with a member of the Vue clan (1994).

[40]Interviews with a member of the Thao clan (1993), a member of the Yang clan(1992), and a member of the Vue clan (1992).

[41]Lee, "Minority Policies and the Hmong," p. 211.

[42]Interview with a member of the Thao clan (1993).

[43]Larteguy, *Opium People*, pp. 253-254.

[44]Interview with a member of the Vue clan (1993).

[45]Interview with a member of the Vu clan (1993).

[46]Cited in Hamel, *Resistance en Indochine*, p. 232 (note).

[47]Lee, "Refugees From Laos: Historical Background and Causes," p. 11.

[48]Interviews with a member of the Chang clan (1993) and a member of the Lo clan (1994).

[49]Interview with a member of the Yang clan (1991).

[50]Interviews with a member of the Lo clan (1993, 1994).

[51]Interview with a member of the Vue clan (1993).

[52]Interview with a member of the Xiong clan (1993).

[53]Interview with a member of the Yang clan (1994).

[54]Interview with a member of the Yang clan(1993).

[55]David Stone ("Nationalism and the Lao Resistance," pp. 271-272) learned from informants that "villagers increasingly beg the guerrillas not to provoke the government locally," and that "the guerrillas usually honored these requests in return for food and intelligence."

[56]Lawyers Committee For Human Rights, *Forced Back and Forgotten*, pp. 8-9.

[57]Ibid., p. 9.

[58]*Asiaweek,* 1 October 1978, p. 38.

[59]This preoccupation with silence was an obsession with many escape parties, religiously observed by doping infants and by limiting communication between adults to occasional whispers. If the trip took months (a few took more than a year), toddlers who would normally be babbling their first words arrived in Thailand totally mute and wide-eyed over their first exposure to human speech.

[60]Interview with a member of the Vue clan (1994).

[61]Interview with a member of the Yang clan (1993).

[62]Interview with a member of the Xiong clan (1993).

[63]Interview with a member of the Vue clan (1993).

[64]Interview with a member of the Vang clan (1994) and a member of the Vue clan (1993).

[65]The figure for welfare income is estimated from average federal AFDC payments per recipient plus average AFDC contributions from state and local governments cited in *Statistical Abstract of the United States* (1979), pp. 352-354.

[66]Interview with a member of the Lo clan (1993).

[67]O'Rourke, *All the Trouble in the World,* pp. 50-58.

[68]Interview with a member of the Lo clan (1993).

[69]Interview with a member of the Xiong clan (1993).

[70]Interview (1994) with a Hmong who wishes to remain anonymous.

[71]Wekkin, "The Rewards of Revolution," p. 194.

[72]In February 1979, China invaded Vietnam with an army of a quarter of a million men. Ten thousand Vietnamese soldiers died in combat. Before withdrawing, the Chinese leveled every Vietnamese provincial capital along the border.

[73]Godley and St. Goar, "The Chinese Road in Northwest Laos 1961-1973," pp. 285-295, 310.

[74]Stuart-Fox, "National Defense and Internal Security in Laos," pp. 237-238. Only 2,500 refugees left the camps for China (Brown, "Inside Indochina").

[75]Brown, "Easing the Burden of Socialist Struggle in Laos," p. 154.

[76]However much Thailand bristled over these things, the presence of the PAVN divisions ruled out direct armed confrontation, for it risked war with Vietnam. Only once did Thailand violate this principle. In November 1987, Thai troops engaged LPLA forces in a pitched battle at the border village of Ban Rom Klao in Sayaboury Province. Thai loggers were clear-cutting near the village. Laotian authorities disputed their right to log the area and called in troops to force the loggers out. An entire LPLA division rushed to the area. When Thai military units arrived to protect the loggers, fighting broke out. The battle raged for days. The Lao shot down a Thai fighter-bomber. Thai forces killed 340 Lao and wounded 257 others. Thai losses were 103 dead and 606 wounded.

[77]Conboy and Morrison, *Shadow War*, pp. 422, 423 (note).

[78]Interview (1994) with former Hmong resistance fighter who wishes to remain anonymous.

[79]According to Scott Barnes (*Bohica*, pp. 115-130), in 1981 the CIA funded an operation involving Hmong guerrillas to locate a suspected POW camp in Laotian panhandle. Barnes claims to have been part of the team and that he photographed two Americans at the camp.

[80]Ross, "Probe Links 'Reagan Doctrine' to Covert Aid to Laos Rebels"; Select Committee on POW/MIA Affairs, pp. 440, 474-480.

[81]Interview (1994) with a Hmong who wishes to remain anonymous.

[82]China's object had never been to topple Laos' communists regime, but only to pressure Vientiane to distance itself from Hanoi. Lanna was only a paper tiger. Beijing made sure that Lanna guerrillas carried only light weapons and were organized into small units (squads and platoons) so they could not engage in large-scale military action. Kaysone did not know this, of course, and overreacted, launching a conscription campaign for all Laotian males between the ages of fifteen and forty-five to beef up the LPLA. His determination to

confront Lanna with military force was not shared by other party leaders fearful of a military conflict that might escalate and involve the Chinese directly. Some were for seeking a rapprochement with China and had, on their own, established unauthorized contacts with Chinese diplomats. Though Kaysone purged these renegades from the party, he moved too late. The dissidents had already changed attitudes and Kaysone lost party support for a hard line on China. Reluctantly, Kaysone softened his stand and moved to normalize relations with Beijing. See Van de Kroef, "Laos: Paradoxes and Dilemmas of Survival," pp. 166-167, 171; Stone, "Resistance: Beyond Equilibrium," p. 57.

[83]Brown, "Easing the Burden of Socialist Strugge in Laos," p. 154).

CHAPTER 14: VANG PAO

[1]This ploy was soon in wide use by other Hmong polygamists, who usually declared second and third wives as sisters-in-law or close cousins.

[2]Warner, *Back Fire*, p. 350.

[3]Interview (1995) with a former Namphong camp refugee who wishes to remain anonymous.

[4]Warner, *Back Fire*, p. 319.

[5]According to McCoy (*The Politics of Heroin: CIA Complicity in the Global Drug Trade*, p. 331), Vang Pao's ranch cost more than a half-million dollars. I tried to obtain a copy of the transaction from the county clerk at Victor, Montana. I was informed it was not available. A written request to the state capitol for a copy of the record remains unanswered.

[6]The existence of the pension became common knowledge not only to American Hmong, but to Hmong refugees in Thailand. Some Hmong notables in the camps hoped they could get a similar deal once they immigrated to the U.S. One of them, a former tasseng, visited my home in Spokane, Washington to see what could be arranged. It was a great disappointment to the man, and certainly diminished the stature of the author in his eyes, to learn that he had no influence with the CIA.

[7]Vang Pao, "Keynote Address."

[8]McInnis, *The Hmong in America*, p. 4; Olney, "We Must Be Organized," pp. 67-70.

[9]Stuart-Fox, "National Defense and Internal Security in Laos," p. 235.

[10]The other agent was an American Hmong named Pha Vue.

[11]Interview with a member of the Yang clan (1991).

[12]Cooper, "Laos 1982," p. 200; Moua, "Hmong Values and Political Leadership as Perceived by the U.S. Hmongs," p. 48.

[13]ULNLF, "White Paper on the Situation of Laos," p. 17.

[14]Chanda, *Brother Enemy*, p. 402.

[15]Hacker, *Money: Who Has How Much and Why*, p. 161.

[16]Calculated from data in the Statistical Abstract of the United States 1991, p. 372.

[17]Interview (1997) with former Hmong interpreter for the CIA who wishes to remain anonymous.

[18]In tabular form the revenue from selling offices was:

Position	Price	Number	Per Month Fee	Annual Total
Colonel	$1,500	500	—	$750,000
General	$2,000	280	—	$560,000
Local Government		900	$100	$1,080,000
National Office		400	$500	$2,400,000
Cabinet Minister		24	$1,000	$288,000
			1 year total	$5,078,000
			2 year total	$8,846,000

[19]Interview (1996) with a Neo Hom fund raiser who wishes to remain anonymous; Mydans, "California Says Laos Refugee Group has Been Extorted by Its Leadership"; Hammond, "Sad Suspicions of a Refugee Ripoff." Earlier in 1983, Ruth Hammond had written a series of articles critical of Vang Pao for the *Twin Cities Reader*. After the first article was published, Hammond and the paper's editor received repeated calls from Hmong threatening that they would be killed if more articles critical of Vang Pao were published.

[20]Interview with a member of the Yang clan (1993).

[21]Interviews with a member of the Yang clan (1993) and a member of the Thao clan (1993).

[22]Hammond, "Sad Suspicions of a Refugee Ripoff."

[23]Hamilton-Merritt, *Tragic Mountains*, p. 488.

[24]Interview (1994) with former Neo Hom guerrilla who wishes to remain anonymous. Deatiled information on the underground Thai lottery was graciously supplied by William Stevens (communication, 1996).

[25]Ranard, "The Last Bus," p. 28.

[26]Moua, "Hmong Values and Political Leadership as Perceived by the U.S. Hmongs," p. 50.

[27]Rosett, "A Lonely Lao Fight For Freedom." The provinces declared by UNLF to be fully liberated were: Xieng Khouang, Luang Prabang, Sayaboury, Oudomsay (a new name for Nam Tha), Vang Vieng (which is not a province but part of Vientiane Province), and Borkihane. See de Silva, "Flight of the Princes."

[28]Richburg, "Insurgency in Laos Seeking to Emerge From Anonymity."

[29]Interview (1994) with a former Neo Hom guerrilla who wishes to remain anonymous.

[30]Hamilton-Merritt, *Tragic Mountains*, p. 499.

[31]Rosett, "Yellow Rain in Laos: New Reports."

[32]Hamilton-Merritt, *Tragic Mountains*, pp. 499-500.

[33]Mydans, "California Says Laos Refugee Group Has Been Extorted by its Leadership"; Hoge, "Laotian Aid Unit Facing Funds Cutoff"; Bell, "Laotian-Aid Group, State Near Accord on Funding"; Hoge, "State Probes Laotian Refugee Aid Group"; Johnson, "Extortion Probe Botched, Refugees' Complaints were Ignored, State Says."

[34]Thomson, "Refugees in Thailand: Relief, Development and Integration," p. 125.

[35]Between 1961 and 1966, the nation's GNP increased a hefty 45 percent and averaged a 9 percent annual growth for the entire decade. By 1975, industry had become a major, and rapidly growing, sector of Thailand's economy. Foreign investment was brisk.

[36]Long, *Ban Vinai*, p. 37.

[37]Thailand also had a legal pretext for denying refugees sanctuary. The country was not a signatory to the 1967 Geneva protocols on refugees, and its own legal code defined refugees as displaced persons who could be imprisoned, fined, or expelled from the country. See Robinson, "Laotian Refugees in Thailand: The Thai and US Response, 1975 to 1988," pp. 218-220.

[38]To persuade Hmong to abandon swidden farming, the government offered free acreage in the lowlands, plus economic development programs, to help Hmong become successful wet rice farmers. Only a handful of Hmong took up the government's offer. Few of the

promised economic development programs were ever enacted and most of the money for the projects was pocketed by corrupt bureaucrats. Also, the quality of the land set aside for the Hmong was extremely poor. Even had it been prime paddy fields, there was little incentive to move to the lowlands; opium thrives only in the mountains and opium was the principal source of Hmong income. Subsequent efforts to reduce swidden farming only further embittered the Hmong toward the government.

After the 1967 Hmong rebellion, the government established development projects for the Hmong in their highlands (enabling them to continue to grow opium). The projects offered high-quality land for farming, irrigation systems to encourage the cultivation of rice, and ready access to markets for harvested crops. There was also a major effort to assimilate Hmong into Thai culture by increasing their literacy in the Thai language and exposing them to Buddhism. The economic side of the program was sufficiently successful to cause the insurrection to fade. But the assimilation campaign foundered, creating apprehensions that there might be more problems with the Hmong in the future. See Dassé, *Montagnard Revolts*, pp. 76-80.

[39]Dassé, *Montagnard Revolts*, pp. 76-80; Vanes-Beck, "Refugees from Laos, 1975-1979," p. 329.

[40]Robinson, "Laotian Refugees in Thailand: The Thai and US Response, 1975 to 1988," p. 220.

[41]"How Much Did the U.S. Give For Meos?"

[42]Robinson, "Laotian Refugees in Thailand: The Thai and US Response, 1975 to 1988," p. 218.

[43]In 1984, with a subsidy of forty thousand dollars from voluntary agencies, several hundred Hmong from Nam Yao camp were permitted to establish permanent residence at Ban Sob Kok. They would be the only Hmong "officially" permitted to settle in Thailand.

[44]Creating camps to provide refugees long-term asylum was not an option considered. UNHCR had once championed this idea, but that was before 1971 when the war between Pakistan and Bangladesh created ten million refugees, all seeking asylum in India. Providing housing and food for so many drained UNHCR's coffers and persuaded the refugee agency to suddenly jettison its policy on asylum and embrace resettlement and repatriation as the preferred remedies.

[45]The U.S. had only recently revised its immigration policy. Previously, immigration quotas were small and excluded Asians, Africans, and Hispanics. The 1965 Immigration and Nationality Act reversed this trend. Inspired by John Kennedy's book, *A Nation of Immigrants*, which

condemned America's immigration policy as racist, the act increased quotas and placed Asians, Africans, and Hispanics on a par with western Europeans. It was meant only as a symbolic gesture against racism. No one expected it would lead to a flood of Asian immigrants, for the act's architects could not foresee the eventual magnitude of the Vietnam War, nor imagine that the communists would win. Just before the fall of Saigon, the U.S. evacuated nearly fifty thousand Vietnamese, all of whom were granted asylum in America. Another eighty thousand would enter the U.S. before the end of 1975. More Vietnamese would follow, as would Laotians and later Cambodians, totaling almost a million Indochinese by 1988.

Few of these refugees were processed as ordinary immigrants. Not only would doing so have been cumbersome, the Immigration and Nationality Act limited refugee admissions to less than twenty thousand per year. The remedy was section 212 of the act, which gave the President power (parole authority) to grant refugees temporary entry into the country in emergency cases. By means of this loophole, 210,000 Indochinese refugees, most of them Vietnamese, were allowed to immigrate to the U.S. between 1975 and 1980.

It was not a large number, considering the estimated 7.5 million immigrants (legal and illegal) who entered the U.S. during the same period. Yet, because immigration levels were so high, accounting for 25 percent of America's population growth, Indochinese refugees became a scapegoat for the growing public discontent over the nation's liberal immigration policy.

In 1980 Congress revoked parole, requiring the president to consult with Congress to admit additional refugees. When Reagan assumed office in 1981, he promised to clean up "the immigration mess." Yet at the end of his two terms an additional half-million Indochinese refugees were in America, beneficiaries of Reagan's crusade against the "evil empire" of world communism that involved increased military spending, an invasion of the tiny island of Grenada, support for Afghan rebels and Nicaraguan Contras, and a face-lift for the Vietnam War. Instead of a humiliating defeat, the Vietnam War became a "noble effort" whose hapless victims were the refugees from Laos, Cambodia, and Vietnam. Ensnared by Reagan's rhetoric, Congress offered only feeble resistance to the President's annual request for the mass admission of additional Indochinese refugees.

[46]Robinson, "Laotian Refugees in Thailand: The Thai and US Response, 1975 to 1988," pp. 227, 233.

[47]Vanes-Beck, "Refugees from Laos, 1975-1979," p. 329.

[48]Ibid., p. 331.

[49]Ban Nam Yao was also dangerous. Plopped down in Thailand's northeastern jungle wilderness, MOI was unaware that the new camp was only a short distance away from a secret Thai communist field headquarters, hidden deep in the jungle. In late 1976 Pathet Lao agents crossed the border and joined the field headquarters as advisors. In 1977 and 1980 they organized raids on Ban Nam Yao. During one of the attacks, the entire camp was set ablaze, leaving eight thousand homeless. In the second raid, rockets fired into the camp school killed several Hmong children and wounded dozens of others. The Thai soldiers guarding the camp were worse than useless. Instead of engaging the attackers, they remained behind cover and fired indiscriminately, killing several Hmong without wounding a single rebel. See Willem, *Les Naufragés de la Liberté*, pp. 5, 9, 31-32.

[50]*Forced Back and Forgotten*, pp. 33-35.

[51]From 1979 to 1987 MOI shuffled Hmong from one camp to another. The first move was from Nong Khai to Ban Vinai. This was followed by a transfer of Hmong from Chiang Kham to three camps: Ubon, Chiang Khong, and Ban Nam Yao. MOI next moved Hmong from Sob Tuang to Ban Vinai, and from Ubon to both Ban Vinai and Chiang Kham. Later Hmong were reshuffled from Nam Yao to Ban Vinai and Chiang Kham. Finally, by 1987 MOI had sorted things out: all Hmong were in two camps, Ban Vinai and Chiang Kham.

[52]The Carter administration paroled eight thousand Laotian refugees in 1977. While this may have been an incentive for some Laotians to flee to Thailand in 1978, the desire to avoid starvation appears to have been the stronger motivator.

[53]*The CCSDPT Handbook*, pp. 1-3.

[54]Fifty-two voluntary organizations (volags) were in Thailand administering to the needs of refugees. They provided a host of services, from food supplementation, literacy training, opium detoxification, family planning, adult education, vocational training, hospital aid, prosthesis training, recreation services, and public health, to the building of sanitation infrastructure. Some of the most active volags (listed alphabetically) working in the Thai camps were: Christian and Missionary Alliance Church (CAMA), The Church of Christ in Thailand (CCT), Catholic Office for Emergency Relief and Refugees (COERR), Ecoles Sans Frontieres (ESF), Food for the Hungry International (FHI), Interaid International (ICA), International Rescue Committee (IRC), Japan Sotoshu Relief Committee (JSRC), Operation Handicap International (OHI),

Southeast Asian Outreach (SAO), Thai-Chinese Refugee Service (TCRS), Zuid-Osst-Azie (ZOA).

[55] Robinson, "Laotian Refugees in Thailand," p. 228.

[56] Some got through, though, smuggled past border guards by coyotes who delivered them to Ban Vinai, joining the already large number of undocumented Hmong at the camp. Camp officials estimated the number of illegals to be three thousand; Hmong section leaders knew the real number to be closer to ten thousand.

A documented refugee was one with a numbered Ban Vinai card, or BV number. Anyone with a BV number received food allotments from HCR and was counted a documented refugee. Those without BV numbers had to fend for themselves. There was a healthy black market in BV numbers. The cards were from Hmong who resettled, or returned to Laos without notifying camp authorities, or were killed in the resistance. These cards were sold by relatives to card brokers (often camp leaders) who auctioned them off to newly arrived illegals. Since several thousand illegals held cards, the official estimate of undocumented Hmong in the camp was invariably too low.

[57] A government bureaucrat arrived with the trucks, chauffeured in a jeep. Husky and square-jawed, he was no stranger to the Hmong, at least by name. He was Faydang's brother, Nhia Vue Lo. He had risen higher than any other Hmong in the Pathet Lao hierarchy, having served briefly on the party's secretive Central Committee. Nhia Vue lectured the Hmong on communism. He vilified Vang Pao. Finally, he got to the business at hand. With a jabbing finger and baleful glare, he warned the assembled Hmong that if any of them revealed that the supplies had been confiscated, they would be "cut into little pieces." (Interview with a member of the Vue clan, 1993).

[58] *Forced Back and Forgotten*, pp. 16-17.

[59] "Laotians May Have Killed 16 More."

[60] *Forced Back and Forgotten,* pp. 17-18.

[61] Ibid., p. 18.

[62] Quoted in Fadiman, *The Spirit Catches You and You Fall Down*, pp. 167-168.

[63] Between 1975 and 1978, Chia Koua Vang and Gnia Yee Yang, two of Shong Lue Yang's disciples, controlled an entire division of Ban Vinai. There were a temple and schools and Chao Fa priests who preached the faith and made new converts. However, after 1978, when Chia Koua and Gnia Yee left for America, the movement languished. By

the early 1980s, interest in the Chao Fa had all but disappeared. The temple was a ruins and its grounds had become a soccer field.

[64]Ranard, "The Last Bus," p. 32.

[65]Hammond, "Sad Suspicions of a Refugee Ripoff."

[66]Robinson, "Laotian Refugees in Thailand," p. 226.

[67]Long, *Ban Vinai*, pp. 156-158.

[68]Renard, "The Last Bus," p. 28.

[69]*New York Times,* 3 March 1985.

[70]*Sacramento Bee,* 18 December 1986.

[71]For a detailed account of the shift in attitude, see Sutter, *The Indochinese Refugee Dilemma*, ch. 5.

[72]Select Committee on POW/MIA Affairs, p. 9

[73]Reuters Electric Mail, Sept. 9, 1992.

[74]Statement by office of Assistant Secretary, U.S. Department of State, Oct. 19, 1992.

[75]"Report to the Congress of the United States: Fact-Finding Mission to Thailand Regarding the Status of Hmong/Lao Refugees and Asylum Seekers. Dec. 28, 1994 - Jan. 2, 1995." p. 4; interview with Tim Bartl (1995).

[76]Hail, "Dilemma for the Hmongs," p. 21.

[77]Interview (1994) with a former Ban Vinai camp inmate who wishes to remain anonymous.

[78]Hamilton-Merritt, *Tragic Mountains*, p. 511.

[79]Interview (1994) with a former Ban Vinai camp inmate who wishes to remain anonymous.

[80]Vue, "Hmong Repatriation to Laos," pp. 4-5.

[81]Recently (1998) Joseph Davy (Davy, "Repatriation: How Safe Is It?", p. 2) claimed to have special information revealing that Mai Vue was "secretly arrested by the Lao government," reviving the view that Vientiane was responsible for Mai Vue's disappearance.

[82]"JRS Mission Report," Part 1, p. 5.

[83]Tyson, "The Hmong of Laos—America's Former Allies—Continue to Suffer."

[84]Bonner, "Hmong Cite Hidden Cases of Genocide."

[85]Gluckman, "Land in Slow Motion," p. 36.

[86]Ovesen, *A Minority Enters the Nation State*, pp. 15-16; "JRS Mission Report," Part 2, pp. 1-4. Testimony from Hmong in Laos, via tape cassettes set to relatives in America, suggests that some repression still exists, though on a modest scale. The reports are unverified and probably unverifiable. Here is one example.

In late 1995, provincial authorities in Xieng Khouang arrested three Hmong for attempted murder. While hunting in the hills around the village of Kong Kai, and finding no game, the three Hmong had come across a Lao farmer's cow and led it away. When the farmer suddenly appeared, the Hmong subdued the man, tied him up and took him with them. Held prisoner for a day and a night, the Lao farmer untied himself and tried to escape. The Hmong shot him and left him for dead. The farmer survived the injury and reported the incident to authorities.

To shift the blame to others, during interrogation the three Hmong claimed that they had shot the Lao farmer on orders from Chao Fa rebels. The fabrication ignited a heated search for Chao Fa in the area. Several months into the search, authorities arrested two Hmong who, after interrogation, admitted they were Chao Fa. In exchange for lenient treatment they turned in their leader, Tong Kai Yang. A former Chao Fa commander, Tong Kai Yang had kept up the resistance since the Chao Fa was crushed in 1978. In February 1996, LPLA soldiers arrived in his village near Muong Soui and cut him down, along with most of his family.

Believing the area to be a hotbed of Chao Fa rebels and their sympathizers, Vientiane ordered two Hmong villages (about one hundred people in all) near Muong Soui relocated to Sayaboury province. (Interview with a member of the Yang clan, 1998).

[87]Magagnini, "Scam Devastates Families Who Paid to Free Kin from Thai Camps"; letter describing the fraud from Wendy Sherman, Assistant Secretary for Legislative Affairs, Department of State, to Representative Lee Hamilton, Chairman, Committee on Foreign Affairs, House of Representatives, April 25, 1994.

[88]Fadiman, "Heroes' Welcome," p. 60.

[89]Moskal, "Hmong Say Relatives Being Forced Back to Laos."

[90]The congressmen who signed the letter were: Duncan Hunter, James Oberstar, Bill McCollum, Pat Schroeder, Ben Gilman, Tom Lantos, Toby Roth, Gary Conduit, Wally Herger, Randy Cunningham, Bob Dornan, Dan Schaefer, Steve Gunderson, Jim Moran, Porter Goss, and Jay Kim.

[91]"Report to the Congress of the United States: Fact-Finding Mission to Thailand Regarding the Status of Hmong/Lao Refugees and Asylum Seekers. Dec. 28, 1994 - Jan. 2, 1995," p. 5.

[92]"Wat Tham Krabok, Thailand."

[93]"Report to the Congress of the United States: Fact-Finding Mission to Thailand Regarding the Status of Hmong/Lao Refugees and Asylum Seekers. Dec. 28, 1994 - Jan. 2, 1995," p. 5.

[94]Ibid., p. 8.

[95]"Wat Tham Krabok, Thailand"; Tansubhapol, "Prachuab in Quick Visit to Hmong."

[96]Moua, "Hmong Values and Political Leadership as Perceived by the U.S. Hmongs," pp. 49-54.

[97]Ragsdale, "No Longer Refugees, Hmong are at Crossroads," p. 1.

[98]Nichols, "The Grim Toll of Welare Reform: Suicides."

[99]Lintner, "Road of Death," p. 32.

EPILOGUE

[1]Menger, *In the Valley of the Mekong*, p. 69.

[2]Cooper, "Laos 1982: A Good Year All Round," p. 191.

[3]Chanda, "Economic Changes in Laos, 1975-1980," p. 122.

[4]Nearly two decades later provinces were still withholding revenue from Vientiane.

[5]Senate testimony of Melvyn Levitsky; Wallace, "Golden Triangle's Blooming Threat"; Hiebert, "A Kinder, Gentler Laos," p. 26. The Vietnamese communists were also making money off of drugs. High officials in Vietnam's Interior Ministry (the agency charged with policing narcotics in the country) regularly marketed large amounts of heroin to international narcotics traffickers in Hong Kong ("Vietnam Drugs Bust Traced to High Command").

[6]Even Souphanouvong was infected by the rising tide of avidity. As Souvanna Phouma lay dying in seclusion and under guard, Souphanouvong rewrote his brother's will, which had left everything to the grandchildren—all of his properties and investments in Laos and France, worth many millions of dollars. The new will cut the grandchildren out and left everything to Souphanouvong, making

him Laos' first communist millionaire (Stieglitz, *In a Little Kingdom*, p. 214).

[7]*Economist,* December 1991, p. 38.

[8]Quoted in "The Lost World of Laos," p. 38.

[9]"Laotian Leader Gains with New Constitution," *New York Times*, 6 August 1991.

[10]Gluckman, "Land in Slow Motion," pp. 37-39. By cutting themselves in on the investment dollars, party leaders became rich, substantiating the IMF's claim that much of the "debt of the most heavily indebted nations of the world is in private accounts in tax havens." (Report by The Marek Enterprise).

[11]Nguyen, "Assessment of VN Economy," part 5, p. 4.

[12]"Road Link to Laos, China to Open in 2 Years."

[13]The one drawback is that Laos' labor force is small and most of it is located in the hinterlands, placing a limit on the number of new manufacturing enterprises that can be sustained in the nation. See Witter, "Laos Reaches for Share of Asia's Prosperity."

[14]Department of State, "Laos Human Rights Practices, 1995," (March 1996). In August 1996, pressure from foreign governments resulted in a grant of amnesty for 137 political prisoners and reduced sentences for another two hundred (Denny, "Grants of Amnesty in Laos").

[15]Stuart-Fox, "On the Writing of Lao History: Continuities and Discontinuities."

[16]Shefter, *Political Parties and the State*, p. 32.

[17]Brown and Zasloff, *Apprentice Revolutionaries*, p. 149.

SOURCES

BOOKS & STUDIES

Amnesty International USA. *Background Paper on the Democratic People's Republic of Laos (DPRL) Describing Current Amnesty International Concerns.* New York: Amnesty International USA, 1985.

Arendt, Hannah. *Imperialism.* New York: Harcourt, Brace & World, Inc., 1951.

_____. *On Revolution.* New York: The Viking Press, 1963.

_____. *Totalitarianism.* New York: Harcourt, Brace & World, Inc., 1951.

Bailey, Col. Lawrence R., with Ron Martz, Jr. *Solitary Survivor: The First American POW in Southeast Asia.* Washington D.C.: Brassey's, 1995.

Barnes, Scott. *Bohica.* Canton, Ohio: Bohica Corp., 1987.

Barnet, Richard. *Intervention and Revolution: The United States in the Third World.* New York: Meridian Books, 1968.

_____. *The Giants: Russia and America.* New York: Simon and Schuster, 1977.

Bernatzik, Hugo. *Akha and Miao.* Translated from the German by Alois Nagler. New Haven, Conn: Human Relations Area Files, 1970.

Betrais, Yves. *The Traditional Marriage among the White Hmong of Thailand and Laos.* Chiengmai, Thailand: Hmong Center, 1978.

Boettcher, Thomas D. *Vietnam: The Valor and the Sorrow.* Boston: Little, Brown and Company, 1985.

Bowers, Ray. *The United States Air Force in Southeast Asia Tactical Airlift.* Washington, D.C.: Center for Air Force History, 1983.

Branfman, Fred. *Voices from the Plain of Jars.* New York: Harper & Row, 1972.

Brewster, Lawrence, and Michael Brown. *The Public Agenda.* New York: St. Martin's Press, 1994.

Brimelow, Peter. *Alien Nation.* New York: Random House, 1995.

Brown, MacAlister, and Joseph Zasloff. *Apprentice Revolutionaries: The Communist Movement in Laos, 1930-1985.* Stanford, CA: Hoover Institution Press, 1986.

Burchett, Wilfred. *Mekong Upstream.* Berlin: Seven Seas Publishers, 1959.

————. *The Second Indochina War*. New York: International Publishers, 1970.

Campell, Robert. *Soviet Economic Power*. 2nd ed. Boston: Houghton Mifflin, 1966.

Cartmail, Keith. *Exodus Indochina*. Auckland, New Zealand: Heinemann, 1983.

Castle, Timothy. *At War in the Shadow of Vietnam: U.S. Military Aid to the Royal Lao Government 1955-1975*. New York: Columbia University Press, 1993.

Caute, David. *The Great Fear: The Anti-Communist Purge under Truman and Eisenhower*. New York: Simon and Schuster, 1978.

Champassak, Sisouk Na. *Storm over Laos*. New York: Frederick A. Praeger, 1961.

Chan, Sucheng, ed. *Hmong Means Free: Live in Laos and America*. Philadelphia: Temple University Press, 1994.

Chanda, Nayan. *Brother Enemy: A History of Indochina Since the Fall of Saigon*. New York: Collier Books, 1986.

Chantavanich, Supang, et al. *The Lao Returnees in the Voluntary Repatriation Programme from Thailand*. Bangkok, Thailand: Institute of Asian Studies, 1992.

Chard, Chester. *Man in Prehistory*. 2nd ed. New York: McGraw-Hill Book Co., 1975.

Chomsky, Noam. *For Reasons of State*. New York: Vintage Books, 1973.

Clodfelter, Mark. *The Limits of Air Power: The American Bombing of North Vietnam*. New York: The Free Press, 1989.

Coker, Christopher. *Reflections on American Foreign Policy since 1945*. New York: St. Martin's Press, 1989.

Colby, William. *Honorable Men*. New York: Simon and Schuster, 1978.

Conboy, Kenneth, and James Morrison. *Shadow War: The CIA's Secret War in Laos*. Boulder, CO.: Paladin Press, 1995.

Coon, Carleton. *The Living Races of Man*. New York: Alfred A. Knopf, 1965.

Cooper, Robert; Nicholas Tap; Gary Lee; and Gretel Schwoer-Kohl. *The Hmong*. Bangkok: Artasia Press, 1991.

Dassé, Martial. *Montagnards Revoltes et Guerres Revolutionnaires en Asie du Sud-Est Continentale*. Bangkok: D. K. Book House, 1976.

Davidson, Phillip. *Vietnam at War*. Novato, CA: Presidio Press, 1988.

De Gaulle, Charles. *The War Memoirs of Charles De Gaulle*. Vol. 3. New York: Simon and Schuster, 1960.

Divine, Robert. *Roosevelt and World War II*. Baltimore: Johns Hopkins Press, 1969.

Dommen, Arthur. *Conflict in Laos*. New York: Frederick A. Praeger, 1965.

Dommen, Arthur. *Laos: Keystone of Indochina*. Boulder, Colorado: Westview Press, 1985.

Dooley, Tom. *The Night They Burned the Mountain*, in *Dr. Tom Dooley's Three Great Books*. New York: Farrar, Straus & Company, 1960.

Doyle, Edward, and Samuel Lipsman. *The Vietnam Experience: Setting the Stage*. Boston: Boston Publishing Company, 1981.

Doyle, Edward; Samuel Lipsman; and Stephen Weiss, eds. *The Vietnam Experience: Passing the Torch*. Boston: Boston Publishing Company, 1981.

Drury, Richard. *My Secret War*. New York: St Martin's Press, 1979.

Duiker, William J. *Sacred War: Nationalism and Revolution in a Divided Vietnam*. New York: McGraw-Hill, 1995.

Dyer, Gwynne. *War.* New York: Crown Publishers, Inc., 1985.

Eisenhower, Dwight D. *Peace with Justice: Selected Addresses of Dwight D. Eisenhower*. New York: Columbia University Press, 1961.

Eisenhower, Dwight D. *The White House Years: Waging Peace*. Garden City, New York: Doubleday, 1965.

Elegant, Robert. *Pacific Destiny: Inside Asia Today*. New York: Crown Publishers, 1990.

Emerson, Gloria. *Winners & Losers: Battles, Retreats, Gains, Losses, and Ruins from the Vietnam War*. New York: W.W. Norton & Company, 1985.

Evans, Grant. *Agrarian Change in Communist Laos*. Singapore: Institute of Southeast Asian Studies, 1988.

_____. *Lao Peasants Under Socialism*. New Haven: Yale University Press, 1990.

_____. *The Yellow Rainmakers*. London: Verso Editions, 1983.

Fadiman, Anne. *The Spirit Catches You and You Fall Down*. New York: Farrar, Strauss and Giroux, 1997.

Fall, Bernard. *Anatomy of a Crisis: The Laotian Crisis of 1960-1961*. New York: Doubleday & Company, 1969.

_____. *Hell in a Very Small Place*. Philadelphia: Lippincott, 1967.

_____. *Last Reflections on a War*. New York: Doubleday & Company, 1967.

_____. *Street Without Joy*. New York: Shocken Books, 1972.

_____. *The Two Viet-Nams: A Political and Military Analysis*. Rev. ed. New York: Frederick A. Praeger, 1964.

Fairbank, John King. *The United States and China*. 3rd ed. Cambridge, MA: Harvard University Press, 1972.

Fairlie, Henry. *The Kennedy Promise*. New York: Doubleday & Company, 1973.

Flemming, D. F. *The Cold War and Its Origins*. Vol. 1. New York: Doubleday & Company, 1961.

Franck, Harry. *East of Siam: Rambling in the Five Divisions of French Indo-China*. New York: The Century Co., 1926.

Freeman, John. *An Oriental Land of the Free*. Philadelphia: The Westminster Press, 1910.

Fukuyama, Francis. *The End of History and the Last Man*. New York: The Free Press, 1992.

Garland, Albert, ed. *A Distant Challenge*. New York: Jove Press, 1985.

Gelb, Leslie, with Richard Betts, *The Irony of Vietnam: The System Worked*. Washington, D.C.: The Brookings Institution, 1979.

Gibbons, William C. *The U.S. Government and the Vietnam War: Executive and Legislative Roles and Relationships, Part II: 1961-1964*. Princeton, New Jersey: Princeton University Press, 1986.

Gibney, Frank. *Pacific Century: America and Asia in a Changing World*. New York: Charles Scribner's Sons, 1992.

Gibson, James William. *The Perfect War*. New York: Vintage Books, 1986.

Glasser, Jeffrey D. *The Secret Vietnam War*. Jefferson, N.C.: McFarland & Company, Inc., 1995.

Goldfarb, Mace. *Fighters, Refugees, Immigrants: A Story of the Hmong*. Minneapolis: Carolrhoda Books, 1982.

Goldman, Marshall. *USSR in Crisis: The Failure of an Economic System*. New York: W.W. Norton & Co., 1983.

Goldstein, Martin. *American Policy Toward Laos*. Cranbury, New Jersey: Associated University Presses, Inc., 1973.

Graham, David Crockett. *Songs and Stories of the Ch'uan Miao*. Washington, D.C.: Smithsonian Institution, 1954.

Grauwin, Paul. *Doctor at Dienbienphu.* New York: The John Day Company, 1955.

Grinter, Lawrence, and William Head. *Looking Back on the Vietnam War.* New York: Greenwood Press, 1993.

Gunn, Geoffrey. *Rebellion in Laos: Peasant Politics in a Colonial Backwater.* Boulder, Colorado: Westview Press, 1990.

_____. *Political Struggles in Laos (1930-1954).* Bangkok: Editions Duang Kamol, 1988.

Hacker, Andrew. *Money: Who Has How Much and Why.* New York: Scribner, 1997.

Halberstam, David. *Ho.* New York: Vintage Books, 1971.

_____. *The Best and the Brightest.* New York: Fawcett Publications, 1969.

_____. *The Reckoning.* New York: William Morrow and Company, 1986.

Halpern, Joel. *Economy and Society of Laos.* New Haven: Yale University Southeast Asia Studies, 1964.

_____. *Government, Politics, and Social Structure in Laos.* New Haven, Conn.: Yale University Southeast Asia Studies, 1964.

Hamel, Bernard. *Resistances en Indochine, 1975-1980.* Paris: IREP, 1981.

Hamilton-Merritt, Jane. *Tragic Mountains: The Hmong, the Americans, and the Secret Wars for Laos, 1942-1992.* Bloomington, Indiana: Indiana University Press, 1993.

Hannah, Norman B. *The Key to Failure: Laos & the Vietnam War.* New York: Madison Books, 1987.

Hardy, Gordon; Arnold Isaacs; and MacAlister Brown. *Pawns of War.* Boston: Boston Publishing Company, 1987.

Hauptly, Denis. *In Vietnam.* New York: Atheneum, 1985.

Herken, Gregg. *The Winning Weapon: The Atomic Bomb in the Cold War.* New York: Vintage Books, 1982.

Herring, George C. *America's Longest War.* New York: Wiley & Sons, 1979.

Hillsman, Roger. *To Move a Nation: The Politics of Foreign Policy in the Administration of JFK.* Garden City: Doubleday, 1967.

Hodgson, Godfrey. *America in Our Time.* New York: Doubleday & Company, 1976.

Horie, Shigeo. *The International Monetary Fund.* New York: St. Martin's Press, 1964.

Hudspeth, Will H. *Stone-Gateway and the Flowery Miao.* London: The Cargate Press, 1937.

Jah, Ganganath. *Foreign Policy of Thailand.* New Delhi: Radiant, 1979.

Jenks, Robert D. *Insurgency and Social Disorder in Guizhou: The "Miao" Rebellion 1854-1873.* Honolulu: University of Hawaii Press, 1994.

Jones, Maldwyn. *American Immigration.* Chicago: Chicago University Press, 1992.

Karnow, Stanley. *Vietnam: A History.* New York: The Viking Press, 1983.

Kennedy, John F. *A Nation of Immigrants.* New York: Harper & Row, 1964.

Kerdphol, Saiyud. *The Struggle for Thailand: Counter-insurgency 1965-1985.* Bangkok: S. Research Center Co., 1986.

Khrushchev, Nikita. *Khrushchev Remembers.* Translated by Strobe Talbott. Boston: Little, Brown and Company, 1970.

Kissinger, Henry. *American Foreign Policy.* New York: W.W. Norton & Company, 1974.

_____. *White House Years.* Boston: Little, Brown And Company, 1979.

_____. *Years of Upheaval.* Boston: Little, Brown and Company, 1982.

Kolko, Gabriel. *Anatomy of a War.* New York: W. W. Norton & Company, 1985.

Lacouture, Jean. *Ho Chi Minh.* Translated from the French by Peter Wiles. New York: Vintage Books, 1968.

Lancaster, Donald. *The Emancipation of French Indochina.* London: Oxford University Press, 1970.

Langer, Paul, and Zasloff, Joseph. *North Vietnam and the Pathet Lao.* Cambridge, Mass: Harvard University Press, 1970.

Larteguy, Jean. *La Fabuleuse Aventure du Peuple du l'Opium.* Paris: Presses de la Cite, 1979.

Lawyers Committee for Human Rights. *Forced Back and Forgotten: The Human Rights of Laotian Asylum Seekers in Thailand.* New York: Lawyers Committee for Human Rights, 1989.

Le Boulanger, Paul. *Histoire du Laos Français.* Paris: Librairie Plon, 1931.

LeBar, Frank, et al. *Ethnic Groups of Mainland Southeast Asia.* New Haven: Human Resource Area Files, 1964.

Le Bar, Frank, and Adrienne Suddard, eds. *Laos: Its People, Its Society, Its Culture*. New Haven, Conn.: Human Relations Area Files Press, 1960.

Lemoine, Jacques. *Un Village Hmong Vert du Haut Laos*. Paris: Editions du Centre Nationale de la Recherche Scientifique, 1972.

Levitan, Sar. *Programs in Aid of the Poor*. 6th ed. Baltimore: Johns Hopkins Press, 1990.

Lewis, Judy. *Minority Cultures of Laos: Kammu, Lua', Lahu, Hmong, and Mien*. Rancho Cordova, California: Southeast Asia Community Resource Center, 1992.

Lewis, Paul, and Elaine Lewis. *People of the Golden Triangle: Six Tribes in Thailand*. New York: Hudson Inc., 1984.

Livo, Norma J., and Dia Cha. *Folk Stories of the Hmong: Peoples of Laos, Thailand, and Vietnam*. Englewood, CO.: Libraries Unlimited, 1991.

Lomperis, Timothy. *The War Everyone Lost-and Won*. Baton Rouge: Louisiana State University Press, 1984.

Long, Lynellyn D. *Ban Vinai*. New York: Columbia University Press, 1993.

Lunet de Lajonquiére, Etienne. *Ethnographie du Tonkin Septentrional*. Paris: Ernest Leroux, 1906.

Maclear, Michael. *The Ten Thousand Day War, Vietnam: 1945-1975*. New York: St. Martin's Press, 1981.

MacMullen, Ramsay. *Corruption and the Decline of Rome*. New Haven: Yale University Press, 1988.

Marx, Karl, and Frederick Engles. *The Communist Manifesto*. New York: International Publishers, 1962.

McCoy, Alfred. *The Politics of Heroin in Southeast Asia*. New York: Harper & Row, 1972.

_____. *The Politics of Heroin: CIA Complicity in the Global Drug Trade*. New York: Lawrence Hill Books, 1991.

McInnis, Kathleen M., et al *The Hmong in America: Providing Ethnic-Sensitive Health, Education, and Human Services*. Dubuque, Iowa: Kendal/Hunt Publishing Company, 1990.

Menger, Matt J. *In the Valley of the Mekong: An American in Laos*. Paterson, N.J.: St Anthony Guild Press, 1970.

Millet, Allan R. *A Short History of the Vietnam War*. Bloomington: Indiana University Press, 1975.

Miroff, Bruce. *Pragmatic Illusions: The Presidential Politics of John F. Kennedy*. New York: David McKay Company, 1976.

Morrison, Gayle. *Sky is Falling: An Oral History of the CIA's Evacuation of the Hmong from Laos.* London: McFarland & Company, 2000.

Mottin, Jean. *Elements de Grammaire Hmong Blanc.* Khek Noy: Don Bosco Press, 1978.

_____. *Allons Faire Le Tour Du Ciel et de La Terre: Le Chamanisme des Hmong Vu Dans Les Textes.* Sap Samothot, Thailand: n.p., 1981.

Mowry, George E. *The Era of Theodore Roosevelt, 1900-1912.* New York: Harper & Row, 1958.

Murray, Martin J. *The Development of Capitalism in Colonial Indochina: 1870-1940.* Berkeley: University of California Press, 1980.

Myrdal, Gunnar. *Asian Drama: An Inquiry into the Poverty of Nations.* 3 vols. New York: Pantheon, 1968.

Nixon, Richard. *RN: The Memoirs of Richard Nixon.* Vol. 2. New York: Warner Books, 1978.

O'Rourke, P. J. *All the Trouble in the World.* New York: The Atlantic Monthly Press. 994.

Office for Human Development. *The Indochinese Refugees.* Bangkok: Office for Human Development, 1980.

Olson, James, and Randy Roberts. *Where the Domino Fell: America and Vietnam, 1945 to 1995.* 2nd ed. New York: St. Martin's Press, 1996.

Osgood, Robert. *Limited War Revisited.* Boulder, CO. Westview Press, 1979.

Ovesen, Jan. *A Minority Enters the Nation State.* Uppsala Research Reports in Cultural Anthropology. No. 14. 1995.

Page, Homer. *The Little World of Laos.* New York: Charles Scribner's Sons, 1959.

Page, Tim, and Pimlott, John, eds., *Nam: The Vietnam Experience 1965-1975.* New York: Barnes & Noble, 1995.

Parker, James E. Jr. *Codename Mule: Fighting the Secret War in Laos for the CIA.* Annapolis: Naval Institute Press, 1995.

Pfaff, Tim. *Hmong in America: Journey from a Secret War.* Eau Claire, WI: Chippewa Valley Museum Press, 1995.

Phillips, Kevin. *The Politics of Rich and Poor.* New York: Random House, 1990.

Pike, Douglas. *PAVN: People's Army of Vietnam.* Novato, CA: Presidio Press, 1986.

Pollard, Samuel. *The Story of the Miao.* London: Henry Hooks, 1919.

Prisor, Robert. *The End of the Line: The Siege of Khe Sanh.* New York: W.W. Norton, 1982.

Quincy, Keith. *Hmong: History of a People.* 2nd. rev. ed. Cheney, WA: EWU Press, 1995.

Remers, Howard. *Still the Golden Door.* New York: Columbia University Press, 1985.

Robbins, Christopher. *Air America.* New York: Avon Books, 1979.

_____. *The Ravens: The Men Who Flew in America's Secret War in Laos.* New York: Pocket Books, 1987.

Robertson, Charles. *International Politics Since World War II.* New York: John Wiley & Sons, 1966.

Rostow, Walt. *The Diffusion of Power: An Essay in Recent History.* New York: Macmillan, 1972.

Rostow, Walt. *The Process of Economic Growth.* 2nd edition. New York: W.W. Norton & Company, 1962.

Roy, Jules. *The Battle of Dienbienphu.* Translated by Robert Baldick. New York: Harper & Row, 1965.

Sananikone, Oudone. *The Royal Lao Army and U.S. Army Advice and Support.* Christiansburg, VA: Indochina Monographs, 1984.

Santoli, Al. *To Bear Any Burden.* New York: Ballantine Books, 1985.

Schanche, Don. *Mr. Pop.* New York: David McKay Co., 1970.

Schlesinger, Arthur. *A Thousand Days: John F. Kennedy in the White House.* Boston: Houghton Mifflin, 1965.

Secord, Richard. *Honored and Betrayed.* New York: John Wiley & Sons, 1992.

Severo, Richard, and Lewis Milford. *The Wages of War.* New York: Simon and Schuster, 1989.

Sevy, Grace. *The American Experience in Vietnam.* Norman, Oklahoma: University of Oklahoma Press, 1989.

Shaplen, Robert. *Time Out of Hand: Revolution and Reaction in Southeast Asia.* New York: Harper & Row, 1969.

_____. *A Turning Wheel.* New York: Random House, 1979.

_____. *Bitter Victory.* New York: Harper & Row, 1986.

Sheehan, Neil. *A Bright Shining Lie: John Paul Vann and America in Vietnam.* New York: Random House, 1988.

_____. *After the War Was Over: Hanoi and Saigon.* New York: Vintage Books, 1992.

Shefter, Martin. *Political Parties and the State*. Princeton: Princeton University Press, 1994.

Short, Anthony. *The Origins of the Vietnam War*. New York: Longman, 1989.

Shrock, Joanne, et al. *Minority Groups in Thailand*. Washington, D.C.: Department of the Army, 1970.

Simpson, Ben. *The Undeclared War*. New York: Random House, 1989.

Simpson, Charles. *Inside the Green Berets: A History of the U.S. Army Special Forces*. Novato, CA: Presidio Press, 1983.

Sivard, Ruther. *World Military and Social Expenditures*. Leesburg, VA: World Priorities, 1985.

Smalley, William; Chia Koua Vang; and Gnia Yang. *Mother of Writing: The Origin and Development of a Hmong Messianic Script*. Chicago: University of Chicago Press, 1990.

Snow, Edgar. *Red China Today*. New York: Vintage Books, 1970.

Sorenson, Theodore. *Kennedy*. New York: Harper & Row, 1965.

Stanton, Shelby. *Green Berets at War*. New York: Dell, 1985.

Stevenson, Charles. *The End of Nowhere*. Boston: Beacon Press, 1972.

Stieglitz, Perry. *In a Little Kingdom*. Armonk, N.Y.: M.E. Sharpe, Inc., 1990.

Strobel, Frederick. *Upward Dreams, Downward Mobility*. Boston: Rowman & Littlefield, 1993.

Stuart-Fox, Martin. *Laos: Politics, Economics and Society*. London: Frances Pinter, 1986.

Sullivan, William. *Obbligato: Notes on a Foreign Service Career*. New York: W.W. Norton & Company, 1984.

Summers, Harry G. Jr. *Vietnam War Almanac*. New York: Facts On File Publications, 1985.

Summers, Harry. *On Strategy: A Critical Analysis of the Vietnam War*. Novato, CA: Presidio Press, 1982.

Sutter, Valerie O'Conner. *The Indochinese Refugee Dilemma*. Baton Rouge: Louisiana State University Press, 1990.

Tanham, George. *Communist Revolutionary Warfare: The Vietminh in Indochina*. New York: Frederick A. Praeger, 1961.

Tapp, Nicholas. *Sovereignty and Rebellion: The White Hmong of Northern Thailand*. Oxford: Oxford University Press, 1989.

The Pentagon Papers: The Defense Department History of United States Decisionmaking on Vietnam. The Senator Gravel Edition, Vol. 1. Boston: Beacon Press, 1973.

Thee, Marek. *Notes of a Witness*. New York: Random House, 1973.

Thompson, Virginia. *French Indochina*. New York, Macmillan Co., 1937.

Tilford, Earl. *Search and Rescue in Southeast Asia, 1961-1975*. Washington, D.C.: Office of Air Force History, 1980.

Touzet, Andre. *L'Economie Indochinoise et La Grande Crise Universelle*. Paris: Marcel Girard, 1934.

Trinquier, Roger. *Les Maquis d'Indochine*. Paris: Albatros, n.d.

Tucker, Robert. *Nation or Empire?: The Debate Over American Foreign Policy*. Baltimore: The Johns Hopkins Press, 1968.

Unger, Sanford J. *Fresh Blood: The New American Immigrants*. New York: Simon & Schuster, 1995.

Valeriano, Napolean D. and Charles T. R. Bohannan. *Counterguerrilla Operations*. New York: Frederick A. Praeger, 1962.

Van Staaveren, Jacob. *Interdiction in Southern Laos 1960-1968*. Washington, D.C.: Center for Air Force History, 1993.

Virvong, Maha Sila. *History of Laos*. Translated by U.S. Joint Publications Research Service. New York: Paragon Book Reprint Corp., 1964.

Vongsavanh, Soutchay. *RLG Military Operations and Activities in the Laotian Panhandle*. Washington, D.C.: U.S. Army Center of Military History, 1981.

Vu, Quoc Thuc. *L'Economie Communaliste du Viet-Nam*. Hanoi: Presses Universitaires du Viet-Nam, 1951.

Warner, Denis. *The Last Confucian*. New York: The MacMillan Company, 1963.

Westermeyer, Joseph. *Poppies, Pipes, and People: Opium and Its Use in Laos*. Berkeley: University of California Press, 1982.

Whitaker, Donald, et al. *Laos: A Country Study*. 2nd ed. Washington, D.C.: Government Printing Office, 1979.

White, Theodore, and Annalee Jacoby. *Thunder Out of China*. New York: William Sloane Associates, Inc., 1961.

Wiens, Herold. *China's March Toward the Tropics*. Hamden, Conn: The Shoe String Press, 1954.

Willem, Jean-Pierre. *Les Naufragé s de la Liberté : Le Denier Exode de Méos*. Paris: Editions S.O.S., 1980.

Wongboonsin, Patcharawlai, ed. *Current Indochinese Economies*. Bangkok: Institute of Asian Studies, 1992.

Wright, Gordon. *France in Modern Times*. Chicago: Rand McNally & Company, 1966.

Wyden, Peter. *Bay of Pigs: The Untold Story*. New York: Simon and Schuster, 1979.

Yang, Dao. *Les Hmong du Laos Face au Developpement*. Vientiane, Laos: Edition Siaosavath, 1975.

_____. *The Hmong: Enduring Traditions*. Minneapolis, Minnesota: Worldbridge, Inc., 1992.

_____. *Hmong at the Turning Point*. Edited by Jeannie Blake. Minneapolis: Worldbridge Associates, 1993.

Yang, Hueson. *Through the Spirit's Door: A True Story of the Hmong People at War (1975-1980)*. Arlington, TX: HYCO International, 1993.

Zasloff, Joseph. *The Pathet Lao: Leadership and Organization*. Lexington, MA: Lexington Books, 1973.

ARTICLES

Ackland, Len. "No Place for Neutralism: The Eisenhower Administration and Laos." In Nina Adams and Alfred McCoy, *Laos: War and Revolution*. New York: Harper & Row, 1971.

Adams, Willi Paul. "A Dubious Host." *Wilson Quarterly*. vol. 7. no. 1. 1983.

Alleton, I. "Les Hmong aux confins de la Chine et du Vietnam: La revolte du 'Fou' (1918-1922)." In Pierre Brocheux, ed. *Histoire de l'Asie du Sudest: Révoltes, Réformes, Révolutions*. Lille: Presses Universitaires de Lille, 1981.

Arndt, Dorthea. "Foreign Assistance and Economic Policies in Laos: 1976-86." *Contemporary Southeast Asia*. Sept. 1992.

Barney, Linwood. "Meo of Xieng Khouang Province." In Peter Kunstadter, ed. *Southeast Asian Tribes, Minorities, and Nations*. Vol. 1. Princeton, New Jersey: Princeton University Press, 1967.

Becker, Jasper. "Homage to Missionary Who Freed the Miao." *South China Morning Post International Weekly*. December 2, 1995.

Beech, Keyes. "How Uncle Sam Fumbled in Laos." *Saturday Evening Post*. April 22, 1961.

Branfman, Fred. "The President's Secret Army: A Case Study - The CIA in Laos, 1962-1972." In Robert Borosage and John Marks., eds. *The CIA File*. New York: Grossman Publishers, 1976.

Brown, MacAlister. "Easing the Burden of Socialist Struggle in Laos." *Current History*. April 1987.

Burchett, Wilfred. "Pawns and Patriots: The U.S. Fight for Laos." In Nina Adams and Alfred McCoy, *Laos: War and Revolution*. New York: Harper & Row, 1971.

Chagnon, Jacqui, and Roger Rumpf. "Decades of Division for the Lao Hmong." *Southeast Asia Chronicle*. Oct. 1983.

Chanda, Nayan. "Economic Changes in Laos, 1975-1980." In Martin Stuart-Fox., ed. *Contemporary Laos*. New York: St. Martin's Press, 1982.

Connor, Walker. "A Nation is a Nation, is a State, is an Ethnic Group, is a . . ." In John Hutchinson and Anthony Smith, eds. *Nationalism*. Oxford: Oxford University Press, 1994.

Cooper, Robert. "Laos 1982: A Good Year All Round," Southeast Asian Affairs 1983. Singapore: *Institute of Southeast Asian Studies*, 1983.

Cooper, Robert. "The Hmong of Laos: Economic Factors in the Refugee Exodus and Return." In Glen Hendricks, Bruce Downing, and Amos Dienard, eds. *The Hmong in Transition*. New York: Center for Migration Studies, 1986.

Cumming-Bruce, Nick. "Lao Communists do an About-Face." *U.S. News & World Report*. July 3, 1989.

Davy, Joseph. "Repatriation: How Safe Is It?" *Hmong Studies Journal*. vol. 2. no. 2. Spring 1998.

De Silva, Errol. "Flight of the Princes." Focus. Sept. 1981.

Dia, Cha, and Cathy Small. "Policy Lessons From Lao and Hmong Women in Thai Refugee Camps." *World Development*. vol. 22. no. 7. July 1994.

Dommen, Arthur. "Laos in 1993: The Revolution on Hold." *Asian Survey*. vol. 34. no. 1. Jan. 1994.

Doty, Roland, and Doris Krudener. "Control of Strike and Defense Forces." In Carl Berger, ed. *The United States Air Force in Southeast Asia*. Washington D.C.: Office of Air Force History, 1977.

Dunnigan, Timothy. "Segmentary Kinship in an Urban Society: The Hmong of St. Paul-Minneapolis." *Anthropological Quarterly*. vol. 55. July 1982.

Evans, Grant and Kelvin Rowley. "Laos: The Eclipse of 'Neutralist' Communism." In Grant Evans and Kelvin Rowley, *Red Brotherhood at War: Vietnam, Cambodia, and Laos Since 1975*. London: Verso, 1990.

Fadiman, Anne. "Heroes' Welcome." *Civilization*. vol. 4, no. 4 (Aug./ Sept. 1997).

Feingold, David. "Opium and Politics in Laos." In Adams and McCoy, *Laos: War and Revolution*. New York: Harper & Row, 1971.

Garrett, W. E. "The Hmong of Laos: No Place to Run." *National Geographic*. Jan. 1974.

Gluckman, Ron. "Land In Slow Motion." *Asiaweek*. January 26, 1996.

Godley, G. McMurtrie, and Jinny St. Goar. "The Chinese Road in Northwest Laos 1961-1973: An American Perspective." In Joseph Zasloff and Leonard Unger, eds. *Laos: Beyond the Revolution*. New York: St. Martin's Press, 1991.

Gunn, Geoffrey. "Shamans and Rebels: The Batchai (Meo) Rebellion of Northern Laos and Northwest Vietnam." *Journal of Siam Society*. vol. 74. 1986.

Gurtov, Melvin. "Security by Proxy: The Nixon Doctrine and Southeast Asia." In Mark W. Zacher and Stephen Milne, eds. *Conflict and Stability in Southeast Asia*. New York: Anchor Books, 1974.

Hadingham, Evan. "The Mummies of Xinjiang." *Discover*. April 1994.

Hail, John. "Dilemma for the Hmongs." *Focus*. Dec. 1980.

Hall, David K. "The Laos Crisis, 1960-61." In Alexander L. George, David K. Hall, and William F. Simons, eds. *The Limits of Coercive Diplomacy: Laos, Cuba, Vietnam*. Boston: Little, Brown and Company, 1971.

Hamilton-Merritt, Jane. "Gas Warfare in Laos: Communism's Drive to Annihilate a People." *The Reader's Digest*. Oct. 1980.

Hemastol, Sumitr. "The Secret Army at Nam Phong." *Bangkok World*. May 22, 1975.

Hiebert, Linda, and Murray Hiebert. "Laos Recovers from America's War." *Southeast Asia Chronicle*. vol. 61. March-April 1978.

Hiebert, Murray. "A Kinder, Gentler Laos." *Far Eastern Economic Review*. vol. 29. March 1990.

Hiebert, Murray. "Laos: Flexible Policies Spark Tenuous Recovery." *Indochina Issues*. no. 37. May 1983.

———. "Soft-Sell Socialism in Northeast Laos." *Indochina Issues*. Sept. 1984.

_____. "The Lao Dilemma: Division or Dependence." *Indochina Issues*. no. 27. August, 1982.

Huston, John W., et al. "Air Operations over Northern Laos." In Carl Berger ed. *The United States Air Force in Southeast Asia*. Washington D.C.: Office of Air Force History, 1977.

Johns, Michael. "Let's Not Forget Laos." *Current Issues*. Sept. 1995.

Johnson, Stephen T. "Laos in 1992: Succession and Consolidation." *Asian Survey*. vol. 33. no. 1. Jan. 1993.

Karnow, Stanley. "Free No More: The Allies America Forgot." *Geo*. vol. 2. 1980.

Kaufmann, H. K. "Nationalism and the Problems of Refugees and the Ethnic Minority Resettlement." *Proceeding of the Ninth Pacific Science Congress*. vol. 3. 1957.

Knott, David. "Laotian Style Privatization." *The Oil and Gas Journal*. vol. 90. no. 48. Nov. 30, 1992.

Kreiger, John. "Still Waging the Vietnam War." *U.S. News & World Report*. Sept. 14, 1992.

Lee, Gary Y. "Minority Policies and the Hmong." In Martin Stuart-Fox, ed. *Contemporary Laos*. New York: St. Martin's Press, 1982.

Leibowitz, Arnold. "The Refugee Act of 1980: Problems and Congressional Concerns." *Annals of the American Academy of Political and Social Science*. May 1983.

Lemoine, Jacques. "Les Ecritures du Hmong." *Bulletin des Amis du Royaume Lao*. nos. 7 & 8. 1972.

Lewallen, John. "The Reluctant Counterinsurgents: International Voluntary Services in Laos." In Nina Adams and Alfred McCoy, *Laos: War and Revolution*. New York: Harper & Row, 1971.

Lintner, Bertil. "Road of Death." *Far Eastern Economic Review*. Nov. 28, 1996.

Lofgren, William, and Richard Sexton. "Air War in Northern Laos, 1 April - 30 November 1971." *Office of Air Force History*, Bolling Air Force Base, Washington D.C., Project CHECO Report.

Mahajani, Ushah. "U.S. Intervention in Laos and Its Impact on Laotian Relations with Thailand and Vietnam." In Mark W. Zacher and J.R. Stephen Milne, eds. *Conflict and Stability in Southeast Asia*. New York: Anchor Books, 1974.

Marr, David. "World War II and the Vietnamese Revolution." In Alfred McCoy, ed. *Southeast Asia Under Japanese Occupation*. New Haven: Yale University Southeast Asia Studies, 1985.

McCoy, Alfred. "French Colonialism in Laos, 1893-1945." In Adams and McCoy, *Laos: War and Revolution*. New York: Harper & Row, 1971.

Mirsky, Jonathan, and Stephen Stonefield. "The Nam Tha Crisis: Kennedy and the New Frontier on the Brink." In Adams, Nina and Alfred McCoy, *Laos: War and Revolution*. New York: Harper & Row, 1971.

Moréchand, Guy. "The Many Languages and Cultures of Laos." In Nina Adams and Alfred McCoy, *Laos: War and Revolution*. New York: Harper & Row, 1971.

Moynihan, Daniel Patrick. "The Peace Dividend." *New York Review of Books*. June 28, 1990.

"Mutiny." *Asiaweek*. Sept. 1, 1995.

Nagorski, Andrew. "Who's Really in Charge Here?" *Newsweek*. May 19, 1980.

Ngô, Vinh Hai, "Postwar Vietnam: Political Economy." In Douglas Allan and Ngo Vin Long, eds. *Coming to Terms: Indochina, The United States, and the War*. Boulder, CO.: Westview Press, 1991.

Pietrantoni, Eric. "Note Sur les classes de revenues au Laos et au Tonkin avant 1945." *Bulletin de la Societé des Etudes Indochinoises*. vol. 43. 1968.

Radetzki, Marcus. "From Communism to Capitalism in Laos." *Asian Survey*. vol. 34. no. 9. Sept. 1994.

Ranard, Donald. "The Last Bus." *The Atlantic*. Oct. 1987.

Reiners, David. "Recent Immigration Policy-An Analysis." In Harry Chiswick, ed. *The Gateway: U.S. Immigration Issues and Policies*. Washington, D.C.: American Enterprise Institute, 1982.

"Report by General Earle G. Wheeler, chairman of the Joint Chiefs of Staff, February 27, 1968." In Robert J. McMahon, ed. *Major Problems in the History of the Vietnam War: Documents and Essays*. Lexington, Mass: D.C. Heath and Company, 1990.

"Report by The Marek Enterprise." Jan. 23, 1996.

Robinson, W. Courtland. "Laotian Refugees in Thailand: The Thai and US Response, 1975 to 1988." In Joseph Zasloff and Leonard Unger, eds. *Laos: Beyond the Revolution*. New York: St. Martin's Press, 1991.

Roffe, Edward G. "Laos," in Don Hoke (ed.), in *The Church in Asia*. Chicago: Moody Bible Institute, 1975.

Roux, Henri and Chu Van Tran, "Some Ethnic Minorities in Northern Tonkin," *France-Asie*, nos. 92 & 93. Jan.-Feb. 1954.

Scott, Peter. "Laos: The Story Nixon Won't Tell." *New York Review of Books*. April 9, 1970.

Sheer, Robert. "The Vietnam Lobby." In Walter Capps. *The Vietnam Reader*. New York: Routledge, 1991.

Shreeve, Gavin. "Welcome to the 20th Century." *The Banker*. December 1991.

Silverman, Jerry. "Historic National Rivalries and Interstate Conflict in Mainland Southeast Asia." in Mark W. Zacher and Stephen Milne. eds. *Conflict and Stability in Southeast Asia*. New York: Anchor Books, 1974.

St. Goar, Jinny and Houa Phan. "Poppy Diplomacy." *Far Eastern Economic Review*. May 24, 1990.

Stauffer, Kent. "Fundamental Economic Changes in Laos Usher in a New Period for U.S. Business." *Business America*. Feb. 27, 1989.

Stone, David. "Beyond an Equilibrium?" *Focus*. Feb/Mar, 1981.

Stone, David. "Nationalism and the Lao Resistance: A Personal View." *Contemporary Southeast Asia*. vol. 2. Dec. 1980.

Stuart-Fox, Martin. "Foreign Policy of the Lao People's Democratic Republic." In Zasloff, Joseph and Leonard Unger, eds. *Laos: Beyond the Revolution*. New York: St. Martin's Press, 1991.

Stuart-Fox, Martin. "National Defence and Internal Security in Laos." In Martin Stuart-Fox, ed. *Contemporary Laos*. New York: St. Martin's Press, 1982.

Stuart-Fox, Martin. "On the Writing of Lao History: Continuities and Discontinuities." *Journal of Southeast Asian Studies*. vol. 24. no. 1. March 1993.

Stuart-Fox, Martin. "Reflections on the Lao Revolution." *Contemporary Southeast Asia*. June 1981.

Stuart-Fox, Martin. "Socialist Construction and National Security in Laos." *Bulletin of Concerned Asian Scholars*. vol. 13, no. 1. 1981.

Stuart-Fox, Martin. "The Lao Revolution: Errors and Achievements." *World Review*. vol. 16. 1977.

Suhrke, Astri. "A New Look at America's Refugee Policy." *Indochina Issues*. no. 10. September, 1980.

Tapp, Nicholas. "Squatters or Refugees: Development and the Hmong." in Gehan Wijeyewardene. ed. *Ethnic Groups Across National Boundaries in Mainland Southeast Asia*. Singapore: Institute of Southeast Asian Studies, 1990.

Tasker, Rodney. "Neighborly Gestures." *Far Eastern Economic Review.* April 25, 1993.

Thomson, Suteera. "Refugees in Thailand: Relief, Development and Integration." In Elliot Tepper, ed. *Southeast Asian Exodus: From Tradition to Resettlement: Understanding Refugees from Laos, Kampuchea, and Vietnam in Canada.* Ottawa: Canadian Asian Studies Association, 1980.

Tyson, James. "The Hmong of Laos—America's Former Allies—Continue to Suffer." *Human Events.* Jan. 4, 1992.

Unger, Leonard. "The United States and Laos, 1962-5." In Joseph Zasloff and Leonard Unger, eds. *Laos: Beyond the Revolution.* New York: St. Martin's Press, 1991.

Van de Kroef, Justus. "Laos: Paradoxes and Dilemmas of Survival." *Asian Thought and Society.* vol. 5. no. 14. September 1980.

Van Staaveren, Jacob. "The Air War against North Vietnam." In Carl Berger, ed. *The United States Air Force in Southeast Asia.* Washington D.C.: Office of Air Force History, 1977.

Vanes-Beck, Bernard. "Refugees from Laos, 1975-1979." In Martin Stuart-Fox, ed. *Contemporary Laos.* New York: St. Martin's Press, 1982.

Vang, Pao. "Against All Odds: The Laotian Freedom Fighters." Heritage Foundation. 1987.

Waters, Tony. "The Parameters of Refugeeism and Flight: The Case of Laos." *Disasters.* Sept. 1990.

Wekkin, Gary. "The Rewards of Revolution: Pathet Lao Policy Towards the Hill Tribes since 1975." In Martin Stuart-Fox, ed. Contemporary Laos. New York: St. Martin's Press, 1982.

"Welcome to the 20th Century." *The Banker.* Dec. 1991.

White, Peter. "Laos." *National Geographic.* no. 171. 1987.

"Will Reds Take Southeast Asia?" *U.S. News & World Report.* May 28, 1962.

Yang, Dao. "Why Did the Hmong Leave Laos?" Translated by Sylvianne Downing. In Bruce T. Downing and Douglas P. Olney, eds. *The Hmong in the West: Observations and Reports.* Minneapolis, St. Paul: University of Minnesota Press, 1982.

Yie-Fu, Ruey. "The Miao: Their Origin and Southward Migration." Proceedings: International Association of Historians of Asia. October 1962.

Zasloff, Joseph. "Political Constraints on Development in Laos," In Joseph Zasloff and Leonard Unger, eds. *Laos: Beyond the Revolution.* New

York: St. Martin's Press, 1991.

NEWSPAPERS

"1,000 Yao Flee Laos." *Bangkok Post.* April 5, 1975.

"15,000 Laotian Refugees Find Haven at Thai Temple." *Baltimore Sun.* April 9, 1995.

"20,000 Being Evacuated From Periled Laos Area. *New York Times.* Feb. 12, 1971.

Allman, T. D. "Long Cheng Yields Its Secrets." *Bangkok Post.* Feb. 25, 1970.

"Barred by Thais, Laotians Being Killed." *Chicago Tribune.* March 3, 1989.

"Battered Laotian Tribes Afraid US Will Abandon Them." *New York Times.* Oct. 11, 1972.

Bell, Ted. "Laotian-Aid Group, State Near Accord on Funding." *Sacramento Bee.* Oct. 20, 1990.

Bender, Marc. "US Team Beefs Up Operation to Demine Lao Countryside." *Bangkok Post.* June 14, 1966.

Bender, Marc. "US Team to Demine UXOs." *Bangkok Post.* June 14, 1966.

Bonner, Brian and Yee Chang. "Holding Out for a Homeland." *St. Paul Pioneer Press.* April 16, 1995.

Bonner, Brian. "Hmong Cite Hidden Cases of Genocide; Planned Testimony Attracts Concern." *St. Paul Pioneer Press.* April 25, 1994.

Brown, Tiffany. "Inside Indochina." *Bangkok Post.* January 22, 1996.

"California Says Laos Refugee Group Is a Victim of Leadership's Extortion." *New York Times.* Nov. 7, 1990.

Castaneda, Carol. "Misuse of Funds Alleged." *USA Today.* Jan. 14, 1993.

Cazaux, Jean-Jacques. "Vang Pao of Laos and the Politicking of a Warlord." *Voice of the Nation* (Bangkok). Feb. 27, 1975.

"CIA Aided Laos Base Hit Hard." *New York Times.* Jan. 20, 1972.

"CIA Aides Reported Leading Commando Raids in N. Laos." *New York Times.* July 8, 1971.

"CIA Role in Laos: Advising an Army." *New York Times.* March 12, 1971.

"Clandestine Laotian Army Turned Tide in Vital Region." *New York Times.* Oct. 28, 1969.

"Communist Units in Laos Reported Gaining Ground." *New York Times.* Oct. 29, 1972.

De Silva, Errol. "Guerrilla Groups Plan Anti-Regime Strategy." *Bangkok Focus.* Sept. 1980.

_____. "Rebels' New Game Plan." *Bangkok Focus.* Sept. 1981.

"End of Laos War Has Brought No Peace to Thousands in Meo Clans." *New York Times.* July 13, 1975.

"Enemy Drive Poses Major Threat to Laos." *New York Times.* Jan. 9, 1972.

"Evacuation Started at Key Laotian Base." *New York Times.* March 18, 1960.

"Ex-General Raising Cash to Liberate Laos; Report Says Refugees Pressured to Pay." *San Jose Mercury News.* July 23, 1989.

"General Reported in Thailand." *New York Times.* May 13, 1975.

Gray, Denis D. "Laos Stalked by 'Black Beast' as it Opens Doors to Outsiders." *Bangkok Post.* June 12, 1996.

Hail, John. "Laotians Ponder Their Future After 20 Years Isolation." *United Press International.* April 1, 1996.

Hammond, Ruth. "Sad Suspicions of a Refugee Ripoff." *Washington Post.* April 16, 1989.

"Hanoi Buildup in Laos Reported." *New York Times.* Jan. 24, 1970.

Hawkins, William R. "U.S. Must Stop Sending Hmong Back to be Persecuted in Laos." *St. Paul Pioneer Press.* May 13, 1994.

"Hmong Leader Vang Slowed." *St. Paul Pioneer Press.* March 7, 1997.

"Hmong Refugee Repatriation to Laos May be Delayed a Year: UNHCR." *Agence France Presse.* June 28, 1994.

"Hmong." *Sacramento Bee.* Dec. 18, 1986.

"Hmong—By Any Name Homeless." *New York Times.* March 30, 1980.

Hoge, Patrick. "Laotian Aid Unit Facing Funds Cutoff." *Sacramento Bee.* June 26, 1991.

_____. "State Probes Laotian Refugee Aid Group." *Sacramento Bee.* Oct. 17, 1990.

"How Much Did the U.S. Give for Meos?" *Bangkok World.* July 16, 1975.

"Immigrants Rally Against Welfare Cuts." *Los Angeles Times.* March 19, 1997.

Johnson, Steve. "Extortion Probe Botched, Refugees' Complaints Were Ignored, State Says." *San Jose Mercury News.* Nov. 4, 1990.

Kamm, Henry. "End of Laos War Has Brought No Peace to Thousands in Meo Clans." *New York Times.* July 13, 1975.

Kamnodonae, Yuthapong. "Lotto Operators Resort to Hi-Tech to Evade Police." *Bangkok Post*. March 13, 1966.

Kaufman, Marc. "Hmong Expulsion Charges Prompt Hearing." *St. Paul Pioneer Press*. April 10, 1994.

King, Peter. "Transplanted Hmong: Adjustment in Fresno." *Los Angeles Times*. April 7, 1985.

Landsbaum, Mark. "Two Garden Grove Men Feared Held by Thais." *Los Angeles Times*. Oct. 16, 1992.

"Laos Regime Slows Collectivization." *Los Angeles Times*. Dec. 19, 1980.

"Laos, Tiny Nation of 3 Million, Ravaged by Decades of War." *New York Times*. Feb. 22, 1973.

"Laotian General Concedes Prisoners Tortured." *New York Times*. Oct. 20, 1969.

"Laotian General Said to Ask For Reinforcements." *New York Times*. Feb. 11, 1971.

"Laotian Leader Gains with New Constitution." *New York Times*. Aug. 6, 1991.

"Laotian Military Reshuffle Reported." *New York Times*. Aug. 7, 1971.

"Laotian Said to Ask Massive Evacuation." *New York Times*. March 12, 1970.

"Laotians Lose Base for Actions Against Enemy's Supply Trail." *New York Times*. March 11, 1971.

"Laotians May Have Killed 16 More." *Bangkok Post*. Nov. 21, 1987.

"Laotians Repairing War's Damage." *Los Angeles Times*. Dec. 18, 1980.

"Laotians Start Offensive." *New York Times*. Sept. 12, 1970.

"Laotians to Fight Delaying Action." *New York Times*. Feb. 10, 1970.

Leung, James. "Laotian Aid Group Under Fire." *San Francisco Chronicle*. Nov. 8, 1990.

"Long Tieng a Ghost Town." *New York Times*. Jan. 7, 1972.

"Long Tieng Reported Encircled." *New York Times*. Jan. 15, 1972.

"Loss of Key Base in Laos Feared." *New York Times*. Jan. 6, 1972.

Magagnini, Stephen. "Scam Devastates Families Who Paid to Free Kin from Thai Camps." *Sacramento Bee*. Dec. 4, 1993.

Marukatat, Saritdet. "Freeing-up of Economy Hinges on Ruling Party Changes." *Bangkok Post*. Feb. 13, 1996.

"Meo General Leads Tribesmen in War With Communists in Laos." *New York Times*. Oct. 27, 1969.

"Meo Said to Retreat." *New York Times*. Nov. 16, 1972.

"Meo Tribesmen Face Death in Thailand." *New York Times*. August 15, 1975.

Moskal, Jerry. "Hmong Say Relatives Being Forced Back to Laos." *Gannett News Service*. April 26, 1994.

Mydans, Seth. "California Says Laos Refugee Group has Been Extorted by Its Leadership." *New York Times*. Nov. 7, 1990.

Naylor, Kate, and Lisa Upton. "Land-Locked and Shell Shocked." *Bangkok Post*. July 8, 1996.

Nichols, John. "The Grim Toll of Welfare Reform: Suicides." *The Capital Times*. April 17, 1997.

Orwall, Bruce. "Thai Camps' Closings Stir Hmong Fears." *St. Paul Pioneer Press*. March 8, 1993.

Ragsdale, Jim. "Hmong Refugees Told There's No Real Danger If They Return to Laos." *St. Paul Pioneer Press*. March 24, 1993.

_____. "No Longer Refugees, Hmong are at Crossroads." *St. Paul Pioneer Press*. Feb. 19, 1994.

"Reds in Laos Seize Key Base Operated by US Near Plain." *New York Times*. March 18, 1970.

"Report Says Reagan Aide Sent POW Funds to Rebels." *Washington Post*. Jan. 14, 1993.

Richburg, Keith. "Insurgency in Laos Seeking to Emerge from Anonymity." *Washington Post*. Feb. 11, 1990.

"Rights Group Blasts Thailand Refugees Forced Back into Laos to be Killed, Report Claims." *Sacramento Bee*. March 3, 1989.

"Road Link to Laos, China to Open in 2 Years." *Bangkok Post*. Jan. 21, 1996.

Rosett, Claudia. "A Lonely Lao Fight For Freedom." *Wall Street Journal*. June 13, 1990.

_____. "Yellow Rain in Laos: New Reports." *Wall Street Journal*. June 14, 1990.

Ross, Michael. "Covert CIA Search in 1981 Found No POWs in Laos, Documents Disclose." *Los Angeles Times*. Aug. 6, 1992.

_____. "Probe Links 'Reagan Doctrine' to Covert Aid to Laos Rebels." *Los Angeles Times*. Jan. 23, 1993.

"Silent Sacrifice: Hmong and Lao Veterans are Finally Honored." *St. Paul Pioneer Press*. May 15, 1997.

Spigarelli, Asunta. "Bomb Removal Project in Laos." *California Hmong Times*. March 1, 1995.

"Supplies Flown to Base Ringed by Enemy." *New York Times*. Jan. 2, 1972.

Sweeney, Mike. "Hmong Still Waiting for Vet Benefits." *St. Paul Pioneer Press*. April 3, 1994.

Tansubhapol, Bhanravee. "Prachuab in Quick Visit to Hmong." *Bangkok Post*. Jan. 11, 1997.

"Thai Chief Says VP Will Leave for Exile." *New York Times*. June 10, 1975.

"Three Vietnamese Die Fleeing Captor." *New York Times*. Sept. 14, 1970.

"Tribesmen Flee From Laos Reds." *The Voice of the Nation*. March 8, 1975.

"Tribesmen's Offensive in Laos Slows and Fears for Base Rise." *New York Times*. Oct. 1, 1972.

Trouillaud, Pascale. "'Bombies' Continue to Take Deadly Toll in Rural Laos." *Bangkok Post*. May 14, 1966.

"US Runs a Secret Laotian Army." *New York Times*. Oct. 26, 1969.

"Vang Pao Goes to Paris." *Bangkok World*. June 18, 1975.

"Vang Pao Leaves Asia." *New York Times*. June 18, 1975.

"Villagers Killed Airmen in War." *Washington Digest*. April 25, 1992.

Vitale, Bob. "Hmong Seek End to Repatriation." *Post-Crescent*. July 28,1995.

Waas, Murray. "Reagan Aides Ran a Covert Bid to Aid Rebels in Laos, Records Show." *Boston Globe*. Jan. 13, 1993.

Wallace, Charles. "Golden Triangle's Blooming Threat." *Los Angeles Times*. July 24, 1990.

"War in Laos Imperils the Survival of Meo Tribes." *New York Times*. March 16, 1971.

Wittaya, Prasong. "A Sticky Situation." *Bangkok World*. June 17, 1975.

_____. "Vang Pao Goes to Paris." *Bangkok World*. June 18, 1975.

Witter, Willis. "Laos Reaches for Share of Asia's Prosperity." *Bangkok World*. July 30, 1995.

"You get a headache trying to read that stuff." *Los Angeles Times*. Dec. 19, 1980.

GOVERNMENT AND ORGANIZATION
DOCUMENTS

"Chemical Warfare in Southeast Asia and Afghanistan." Report to the Congress from Secretary of State, Alexander M. Haig, Jr.. March 22, 1982.

"Country Report on Human Rights Practices for 1996." U.S. Department of State. Jan. 1997.

Department of State Bulletin. July 16, 1956.

Department of State Bulletin. July 23, 1956.

Department of State Dispatch. "Participation in Resistance Activities in Thailand and Laos." Oct. 19, 1992.

Department of State Publication 4381. Far Eastern Series 50, October 1951.

Jesuit Refugee Service-Asia/Pacific. "JRS Laos Mission Report. Jan. 1996." Parts 1 and 2.

"Laos Human Rights Practices, 1993." United States Department of State Dispatch. Feb. 1994.

"Laos Human Rights Practices, 1995." United States Department of State Dispatch. March 1996.

"Narcotics Control Efforts in Southeast Asia." Staff Report to the Committee on Foreign Affairs, US-House of Representatives. Feb. 1991. 101st Congress, 2d session.

"Report to the Congress of the United States: Fact-Finding Mission to Thailand Regarding the Status of Hmong/Lao Refugees and Asylum Seekers. Dec. 28, 1994 - Jan. 2, 1995." *Statistical Abstract of the United States* 1991. 11th Edition. Washington D.C.: Bureau of the Census, 1991.

Testimony by Melvyn Levitsky, Assistant Secretary of State, before the Select Committee on Narcotics Abuse and Control in U.S. Congress, House, Select Committee on Narcotics Abuse and Control. *Heroin Trafficking and Abuse: A Growing Crisis*, Hearing before the Select Committee. July 19, 1991. 101st Cong., 2nd sess.

Thailand Office for Human Development. *Indochinese Refugees*. Bangkok: Office for Human Development, 1980.

The CCSDPT Handbook. Bangkok: CCSDPT *U.S Committee for Refugees, Refguees From Laos: In Harm's Way*. Washington, D.C.: U.S. Committee for Refugees, 1986.

U.S. Congress, House of Representatives, Committee on Foreign Affairs, Subcommittee on International Operations. *The Refugee Dilemma in Europe and Asia and the United States' Response*, Hearings. 101st Cong., 2nd sess., 1990.

U.S. Congress, Senate, Committee of the Judiciary. *Refugee and Civilian War Casualty Problems in Indochina*. 91st Cong, 2nd sess. Washington, D.C.: U.S. Government Printing Office, 1970.

U.S. Congress, Senate, Committee on Foreign Relations, Subcommittee on United States Security Agreements and Commitments Abroad. *Hearings, United States Security Agreements and Commitments Abroad, Kingdom of Laos*, 91st Cong., 1st sess., 1969.

U.S. Congress, Senate, Committee on the Judiciary. *War-related Civilian Problems in Indochina: Problems Connected with Refugees and Escapees.* Part I, 92nd Cong., 1st sess., 1971.

U.S. Department of Health and Human Services, Office of Refugee Resettlement. *The Hmong Resettlement Study.* vol 2, 1988.

United Lao National Liberation Front (ULNLF). "White Paper on the Situation of Laos," Sept. 7, 1981.

Vallentiny, Edward. "The Fall of Site 85." Project CHECO Report, Project CHECO 7th Air Force, DOAC. August 9, 1968.

Vang, Pobzeb. "White Paper on Genocide in Laos." Lao Human Rights Council Report. Aug. 1996.

INTERNET DOCUMENTS

Ackerman, Gary L. "Hmong Repatriation to Laos." Testimony April 26, 1994 House Foreign Affairs/Asian and Pacific Affairs. In Hmong Electronic Resources Project. [tc.umn.edu/nlhome/g450/vueb0001/HER].

Ashworth, Tomas. "The Continuing Hmong Betrayal." Candian POW/MIA Information Center. June 13, 1996. [ipsystems.com/powmia/documents.html].

Cha, Dia. "Hmong Repatriation to Laos." Testimony April 26, 1994 House Foreign Affairs/Asian and Pacific Affairs. Hmong Electronic Resources Project. [tc.umn. edu/nlhome/g450/ vueb0001 /HER].

"Final Report of the Select Committee on POW/MIA Affairs." Senate Report 103-1. 1993. POW/MIA Information Center. [ipsystems.com/powmia/documents].

Her, Pa Kao. "Hmong Repatriation to Laos." Testimony April 26, 1994 House Foreign Affairs/Asian and Pacific Affairs. Hmong Electronic Resources Project. [tc. umn.edu/nlhome/g450/vueb0001/ HER].

Herr, Paul Pao. "Hmong Repatriation to Laos." Testimony April 26, 1994 House Foreign Affairs/Asian and Pacific Affairs. Hmong Electronic Resources Project. [tc. umn.edu/nlhome/g450/ vueb0001 /HER].

Hmong Americans for a Peaceful Future. "Hmong Repatriation to Laos." Testimony April 26, 1994 House Foreign Affairs/Asian and Pacific Affairs. [tc.umn.edu /nlhome/g450/vueb0001/HER].

Lee, Gary. "Ethnic Minorities and National Building in Laos: The Hmong in the Lao State." [stolaf.edu/people/cdr/hmong/hmong-au/ hmonglao]

Mennonite Central Committee. "Making Life in Laos a Little Less Risky." Nov. 3, 1995. [SEASIA-L@msu.edu].

Mennonite Central Committee. "MCC's 'Step of Faith' Results in Worldwide Attention to Problem of Unexploded Ordnance in Laos." June 23, 1996. [SEASIA-L@msu.edu].

Nguyen, Kim. "Assessment of VN Economy." [SEASIA-L@msu.edu], Feb. 12, 1997.

Nguyen, Kim. "Interview with Bui Tin." [SEASIA-L@msu.edu], May 22, 1996.

Ruiz, Hiram A. "Hmong Repatriation to Laos." Testimony April 26, 1994 House Foreign Affairs/Asian and Pacific Affairs. Hmong Electronic Resources Project. [tc.umn.edu/nlhome/g450/vueb0001/ HER].

Sheehan, Daniel P. Affidavit filed on behalf of the Christic Institute. District of Columbia. December 1986. [dcia.com/sheehan].

Sloan, Cliff. "Heroin in Burma." April 13, 1995. [SEASIA-L@msu.edu].

Vue, Wa. "Hmong Repatriation to Laos." Testimony April 26, 1994 House Foreign Affairs/Asian and Pacific Affairs. Hmong Electronic Resources Project. [umn.edu /nlhome/g450/vueb0001/HER].

U N P U B L I S H E D   D O C U M E N T S

Barney, Linwood. "Christianity: Innovation in Meo Culture: A Case Study in Missionization." M.A. thesis. University of Minnesota, 1957.

Bissell, Richard, Jr. "Memorandum for Director of Central Intelligence." August 10, 1961.

Castle, Timothy. "At War in the Shadow of Vietnam: United States Military Aid to the Royal Lao Government." Unpublished Ph.D. dissertation, University of Hawaii, 1991.

Davidson, Jack. "Hmong Ethnohistory: An Historical Study of Hmong Culture and Its Implications for Ministry." Ph.D. dissertation. Fuller Theological Seminary, 1993.

Kuhn, Ernest C. Oral history interview, Foreign Affairs Oral History Collection. Georgetown University Library, December 1988.

Lao Human Rights Council. Letter to Congressman Duncan Hunter of California. March 7, 1994.

Moua, Tou Yer. "Hmong Values and Political Leadership as Perceived by the U.S. Hmongs." Unpublished Ph.D. dissertation. United States International University, 1994.

Olney, Douglas Philip. "We Must Be Organized: Dual Organizations in an American Hmong Community." Unpublished Ph.D. dissertation. University of Minnesota, 1993.

Scott, George M. "Migrants without Mountains: The Politics of Sociocultural Adjustment, among the Lao Hmong Refugees in San Diego." Unpublished Ph.D. dissertation. University of California, San Diego, 1986.

Vang, Pao. "Keynote Address." National Conference on Hmong Resettlement in the United States. St. Paul, Minnesota. June 18, 1981.

Xiong, Nhia Koua. Letter to President Bill Clinton. March 7, 1997.

INTERVIEWS

(anonymous) Ban Vinai refugee. (1994)

(anonymous) Ban Vinai refugee. (1994)

(anonymous) Ban Vinai refugee. (1995)

(anonymous) Former CIA agent (1997).

(anonymous) Former Hmong tax collector. (1985).

(anonymous) Hmong fund raiser, (1995)

(anonymous) Hmong soldier. (1994)

(anonymous) Member of the Vue clan. (1993)

(anonymous) Namphong camp refugee. (1995)

(anonymous) Neo Hom member. (1993)

(anonymous) Neo Hom member. (1994)

(anonymous) Neo Hom member. (1994)

(anonymous) Neo Hom member. (1994)

(anonymous) Pa Kao Her guerrilla. (1995)

Bartl, Tim. Assistant to Representative Steve Gunderson (R-Wisconsin). (1995)

Member of the Chang clan (1993)

Member of the Her clan (1987)

Member of the Ly clan (1985)

Member of the Ly clan (1993,1995)

Member of the Ly clan (1993, 1994)

Member of the Ly clan (1987)

Member of the Lo clan (1993, 1994)

Member of the Lo clan (1993)

Member of the Lo clan (1991, 1993)

Member of the Moua clan (1985)

Lao wife of Hmong soldier (1993)

Stevens, William. communication (1996)

Member of the Thao clan (1992, 1993)

Member of the Vang clan (1995)

Member of the Vang clan (1992, 1993)

Vang, Pao. (1980)

Member of the Vang clan (1993)

Member of the Vue clan (1984, 1985)

Member of the Vue clan(1985, 1987)

Member of the Vue clan (1984, 1985)

Member of the Vue clan (1992, 1993)

Member of the Vue clan (1992)

Member of the Vue clan (1991, 1993)

Vue, Mai. (deceased) (1991)

Member of the Vue clan (1985)

Member of the Vue clan (1985, 1987)

Member of the Vue clan (1992, 1993)

Member of the Vue clan (1993)

Member of the Vue clan (1985)

Member of the Vue clan (1985)

Member of the Vue clan (1985, 1986, 1992, 1993)

Member of the Vue clan (1993)

Member of the Vue clan (1993)

Member of the Vue clan (1985, 1986)

Member of the Xiong clan (1993)

Member of the Xiong clan(1986)

Member of the Xiong clan (1992, 1993)

Member of the Xiong clan (1993)

Member of the Yang clan (1993)

Member of the Yang clan. communication (1985, 1986)

Member of the Yang clan(1985)

Member of the Yang clan (1993)

Member of the Yang clan (1984, 1992)

Member of the Yang clan (1985)

Member of the Yang clan (1993, 1994)

Member of the Yang clan (1992, 1993)

Member of the Yang clan (1998)

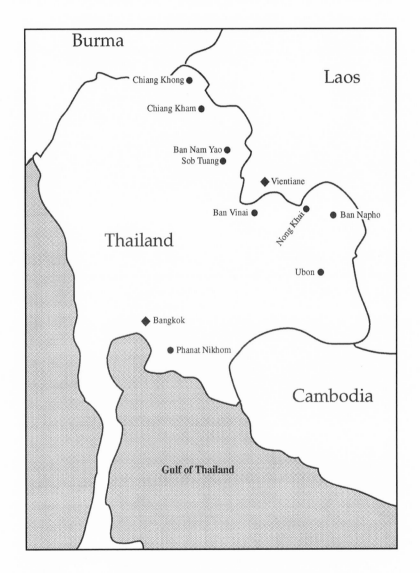

Hmong Refugee Camps in Thailand

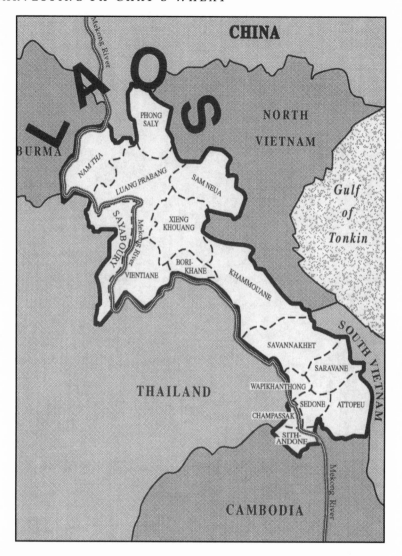

Laos

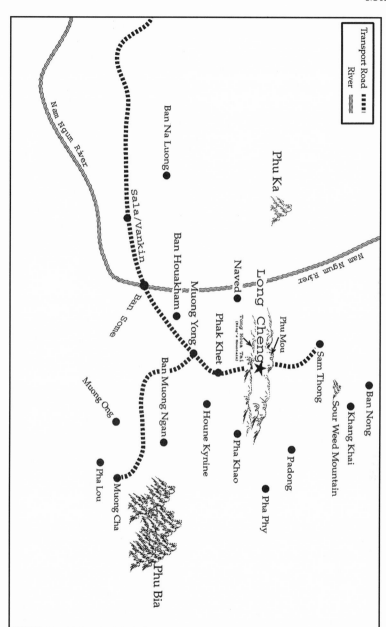

Long Cheng and Surrounding Villages

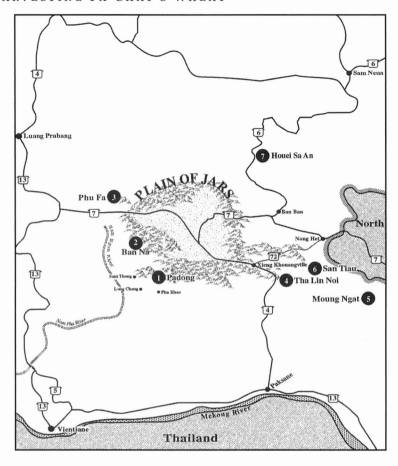

Momentum Sites

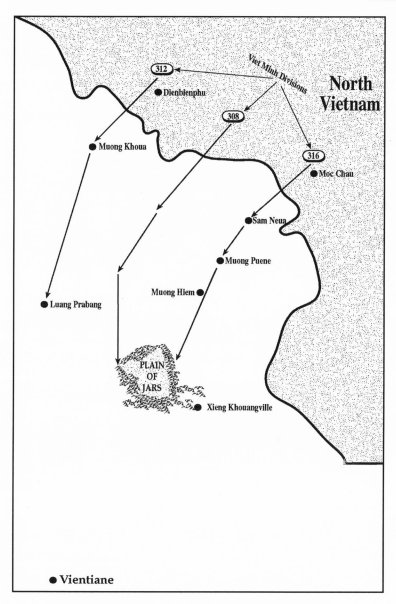

North Vietnamese Invasion of Laos (April 1953)

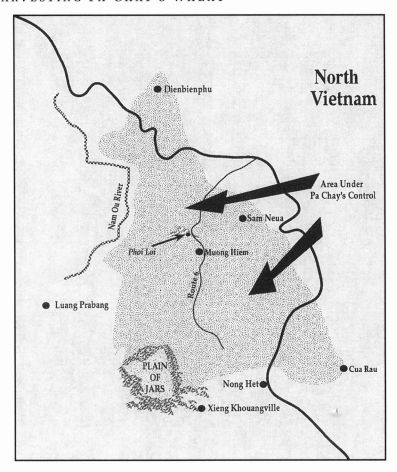

Pa Chay Campaign

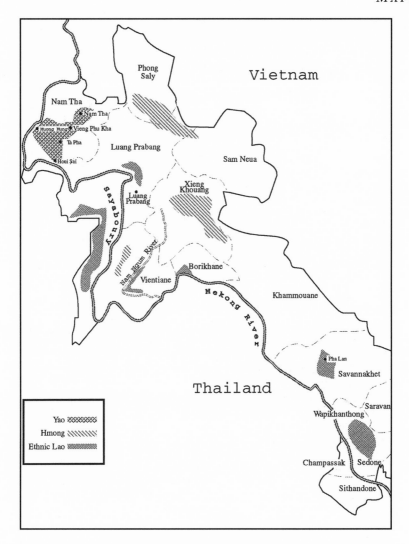

Resistance Grougps (1975-1985)

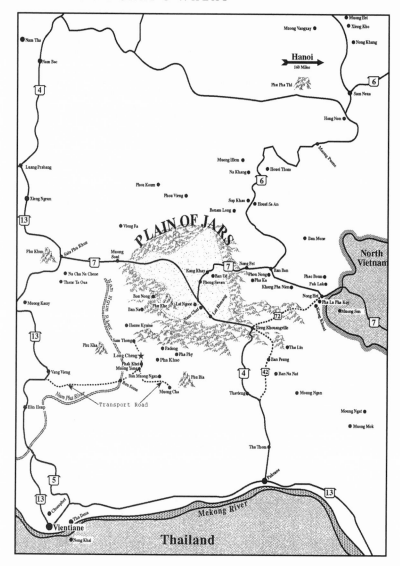

Plain of Jars

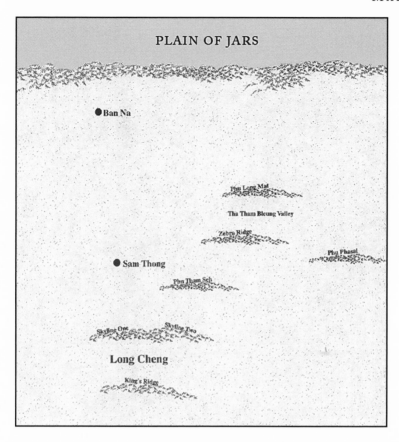

Seige of Long Cheng

M

MAAG/Laos (Military Assistance Advisor's Group/Laos) 157, 190, 200-201, 211, 214, 229, 231

MAAG/Thailand (Military Assistance Advisor's Group/Thailand) 229, 231

MAAG/Vietnam (Military Assistance Advisor's Group/Vietnam) 127

MacArthur, Douglas Gen. 114

MADC (Mountainous Area Development Corporation) 482

Madman's War 41, See also La Guerre du Fou

Magsaysay award for social service 476

Mai Vue 469-471

Mai Vue Proposal 470

Maleplatte (colonel) 90

Malo maquis 88-89, 91, 94-95, 139, 160-161, 165, 167, 172, 175

Man Tha 380

Mann, Charles 324

Mao Zedong 73, 115-116, 184-185, 197

Marshall Plan 108, 112, 120

Marx, Karl 118

Marxism 112

Marxist-Leninism 51, 53

Mathews, Jack 217, 225

May Lo (LoBliayao's daughter) 46

May Lo (one of Vang Pao's wives) 246

Mayer (French officer) 68-69

Mazoyer, Jean-Henri 67-68, 98-101

McNaughton, John 261

Mein Kampf 112

Mekong River 9, 14, 16-17, 55, 72-73, 76, 81, 83, 86-87, 130-131, 148, 158, 179, 214, 365, 369, 375, 378, 380, 384-385, 387, 389, 392, 398, 422, 425-431, 433, 460, 463-464, 483

Meo 21

Meo Alley 234

Merced 449

Mesnier, Max 95, 160-161

Methodist missionaries (China) 26-28

Miao 5, 24, 452

MIAs (U.S. soldiers missing in action) 440-441, 468-469

Mien (ethnic minority) 372

Milwaukee 449

Minneapolis 449

Minnesota 470, 473, 477

MIRV (multiple, independently targetable re-entry vehicles) 114

Mission d'Organization de la Gendarmerie 132

Missoula (Montana) 445-446

Moc Chao 88

Moc Chau 186

Moffit, Roy 214

N

ACKNOWLEDGMENTS

Research for this book was funded by a grant from the North west Institute for Advanced Studies and funds from the E.W.U. Research and Scholarship Committee and the E.W.U. Foundation.

Various individuals contributed in major ways to the writing of this book. In addition to offering generous encouragement, Arthur Dommen saved me from several embarrassing errors of fact and identified valuable sources of information of which I was unaware. Robin Vue-Benson took time away from his important work at the *Hmong Studies Journal* to give the entire manuscript a careful reading and offer suggestions for improvement. Following her advise greatly improved the finished product. Anna Quincy read numerous early drafts of the book and offered unflagging encouragement while holding me to my pledge to write a book intelligible to the general reader. Another champion of the general reader was Dale Forbes Bormann, who read hundreds of pages of the manuscript in various stages of development, monitoring narrative and style to make the book accessible to the non-specialist.

Dr. David Bell and Dr. Ernest Gohlert of the E.W.U. Department of Government offered useful advise on research and shared their insights on Southeast Asian politics in general. While away on their own research projects in Thailand and Asia, Dr. Bell and Dr. Gohlert kept an eye out for material on the Hmong. It was through Dr. Bell that I acquired stacks of documents from Thailand's Ministry of Interior full of information about Hmong refugee camps in Thailand. I should add that twice Dr. Bell graciously adjusted department teaching schedules to smooth the way for sabbatical leaves. Another colleague, Dr. Kenneth Finegold, directed me to Martin Shefter's Political Parties and the State, which gave me a conceptual framework for understanding the Pathet Lao's transformation from an ideologically-based mass movement into a traditional Lao party, dominated by ethnic Lao and fueled by patronage.

Several members of the E.W.U. administration deserve mention. President Mark Drummond was an enthusiastic supporter of the book, as was Vice-Provost Robert Herold. And Dr. Ron Dalla,

Director of Graduate Studies, was instrumental in processing a last-minute request for sabbatical leave.

The idea for the book was James McAuley's. It was during his tour as director of E.W.U. Press that I completed the revised edition of my *Hmong: History of a People*. James had a definite vision of what the book should be and when it was finished he insisted that a second should follow, and perhaps a third.

Having an eye for good editors, James selected Julie Mayeda to edit the manuscript for this book. For me, the choice was a piece of good luck. Genuinely interested in the topic, Julie rummaged through libraries for books on the CIA, Southeast Asian history, and the Hmong, checking that I had covered everything important. She mastered the subject sufficiently to ask insightful questions about the direction of my arguments. She checked facts, cross-checked geographical references in the text against the book's maps, worried over the spelling of names, reorganized chapters, and agonized over particular sentences or phrases until I re-worked them to her satisfaction. Julie also worked up the nucleus of the book's index. It is a much better book because of her.

ABOUT THE AUTHOR

Keith Quincy is chairman of the Department of Government at Eastern Washington University, where he teaches political science and philosophy. Before coming to EWU, he was a fellow at the Institute of Higher Education at Claremont University, taught philosophy at California Polytechnic Institute and at University of California (Riverside), and was a political consultant for California congressional and state campaigns. He is the author of numerous articles and five books, including *Hmong: History of a People*. In his spare time he raises and trains horses on a ranch on Marshall Creek near Spokane, Washington.